W9-ATY-179

BEADWORK®

Creates

Bracelets

edited by **Jean Campbell**

INTERWEAVE PRESS

Interweave Press
201 East Fourth Street
Loveland, Colorado 80537 USA
www.interweave.com

Printed and bound in China through Asia Pacific Offset

Library of Congress Cataloging-in-Publication Data

Campbell, Jean, 1964-
  Beadwork creates bracelets / Jean Campbell.
    p. cm.
  ISBN 1-931499-20-9
  1. Beadwork. 2. Bracelets. I. Beadwork
          (Loveland, Colo,) II. Title.
  TT860 .C357 2002
  745.58'2--dc21

                    2002005717

10 9 8 7 6 5 4 3 2

• Project editor: Jean Campbell
• Technical editor: Dustin Wedekind
• Illustrations: Ann Swanson
• Photography: Joe Coca
• Book design and production:
  Paulette Livers
• Proofreader: Nancy Arndt

Dear Reader,

Bracelets are hot! They're beautiful, they're easy to wear, and they work up quicker than many other beadwork projects.

As editor of *Beadwork®* magazine, I get to see beautiful beadwork designs from all over the globe. *Beadwork Creates Bracelets* is a collection of thirty of my favorite bracelet designs—all original pieces created by innovative beadwork artists. The projects include wirework, peyote and brick stitch, netting, stringing, loomwork, and even macramé.

I've included a Tips section at the back of the book (page 90) that you should be sure to read; it will help you as you start each project. There is also a Stitches section (page 92) that clearly defines each stitch used in this book; it's a useful tool for those who need to learn new stitches or are just feeling a little rusty.

So sit down and cozy up with your beads. You've got some great bracelets to make!

—Jean Campbell
Editor, *Beadwork®*
magazine and books

On the cover, Diamond Back, page 49; on page 1, Jump Back, page 62; on page 2, Dimensional Kisses, page 40.

tents

6

Simple as Pie

Jean Campbell

Materials
Assortment of beads
Soft Flex .019" beading wire
4 crimp beads
Clasp

Notions
Wire cutter
Flat-nose or crimping pliers

This basic bracelet can be made in under half an hour. Experiment with color, bead size, and placement to make your own special statement.

Step 1: Measure your wrist. Add 5". Take this measurement and cut that length of wire.

Step 2: String 2 crimp beads on the wire. Pass the wire through one side of the clasp and back through the two crimp beads leaving a 2" tail (Figure 1). Crimp the beads.

Step 3: String an assortment of beads, making sure you cover the double tail at the beginning of the wire. When you reach about 2½" from the end string 2 crimp beads.

Step 4: Pass through the other side of the clasp and then back through the crimp beads you just strung. Continue to pass back through as many beads as possible on the strand. Pull the wire tight, taking up any slack. Crimp the beads. Trim the tail close to the work.

Figure 1

Simply Vines

Barbara Grainger

Materials

Size 11° green seed beads (vines)
Size 11° purple seed beads (leaves)
Size 15° seed beads in same color
    as size 11° green beads
Size B Nymo or Silamide beading thread
1 toggle clasp set
2 large jump rings

Notions

Size 12 beading or sharps needle
Beeswax or Thread Heaven
Scissors
Needle-nose pliers

This branched vine delicately encircles your wrist like a fairy-tale forest. These instructions make a 7" bracelet. Adjust bead counts as necessary to change size.

VINE

Make three.

Step 1: Using two yards of waxed thread, string a tension bead and leave a 6" tail. Counting 1 size 11° and 1 size 15° as a set, string 96 sets of vine-colored beads.

Step 2: String 8 more size 11° vine beads. Pass through all 8 beads two more times to form a secure circle.

Step 3: Working back up the vine, pass through 6 size 11° seed beads, skipping the size 15° beads. Pull tightly so the vine kinks (Figure 1).

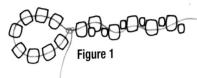

Figure 1

LEAF

Step 4: Note: The thread path in this technique deviates from normal flat peyote because it's worked in an oval-circular pattern instead of back and forth.

Rows 1 and 2: String 2 size 11° vine beads and 7 leaf beads and pass back through the fifth bead of the leaves (Figure 2).

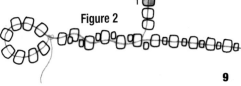

Figure 2

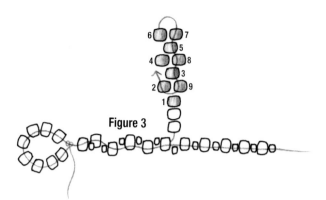

Figure 3

Row 3: Work regular peyote for the eighth bead. String the ninth bead but DO NOT pass back through the first bead as you normally would. Instead, pass the needle back up through the second bead (Figure 3).

Row 4: Work regular peyote for the tenth and eleventh beads.

Row 5: String the twelfth bead and pass back down through the seventh bead. Work regular peyote for the thirteenth and fourteenth beads. Pass down through the first bead, the two branch beads, and six of the vine beads. Pull tight to kink the vine (Figure 4).

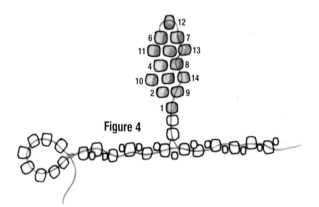

Figure 4

Continue making leaves until you reach the end of the vine, then make another 8-bead loop, passing through it several times. Pass back through the vine and secure the thread in one of the leaves. Remove the tension bead from the original thread tail and pass through the loop. Secure the thread in a different leaf.

Step 5: To finish, use a needle-nose pliers to attach a jump ring to the clasp. Thread the vines onto the ring. Close the ring and repeat for the other end of the clasp.

Barbara Grainger is an internationally recognized beadwork author, instructor, and designer who specializes in innovative beadwork techniques.

Lucy's Purple

Lucy Elle

Materials
1 tube or hank of 8° beads
3 strands of 11° beads in 2 colors
3mm round beads
1 clasp bead
Six 14° beads
Beading thread in color to complement beads

Notions
Size 12 beading needle
Scissors

This pretty bracelet resembles delicate ribbon from afar, but what a surprise when you learn it's made of glass!

BASE
Rows 1 and 2: Using a yard of thread and leaving a 10" tail, string a tension bead and ten 8° beads.

Row 3: Work two-drop peyote by passing through the fifth and sixth bead from the last of the 10 just added. String 2 beads and pass through the third and fourth beads from the last 2 beads worked.

Row 4: String 2 beads. Pass through the last 2 beads of Row 3. Repeat the steps for Rows 3 and 4 until you have the desired length of your bracelet. Weave your thread through the beads so that you exit toward the center of the bracelet from the last two-bead set added.

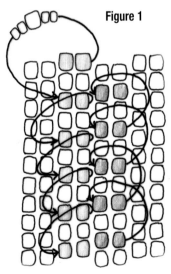

Figure 1

CHEVRON
Half A: *String two 11°s, one 3mm, and two 11°s. Pass through the two-bead set 2 rows down as indicated in the diagram (Figure 1). Repeat from * for the length of the bracelet. Weave your thread through the beads so that you exit toward the center of the bracelet from the second two-bead set added.

Half B: *String two 11°s, one 3mm, and two 11°s. Pass through the two-bead set 2 rows up, as indicated in the diagram. Repeat from * for the length of the bracelet. Exit from the center of the bracelet.

CLASP

String enough 11° beads to equal ¼ of the circumference of the clasp bead, plus five and then three 14° beads. Pass back through the last 11° bead and pull tight. String the clasp bead.

String one 11° bead and three 14° beads. Pass back through the 11° bead just added. String enough beads to equal ¼ of the clasp bead circumference.

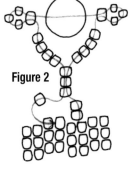

Figure 2

Pass through the first 3 beads of the extra 5. Pull tight. String one 11° bead. Pass back through all until the thread is tight in the holes (Figure 2).

LOOP

Begin a new thread at the other side of the bracelet and exit from the center bead. String enough beads to go around the clasp bead. Pass through the center beads of the last row of the bracelet. Pass through all of the beads of the loop until the thread is tight. To tighten the loop, exit from the first bead of the loop. String 2 beads. Work your thread in a figure eight around the 3 beads at the base of the loop.

EDGING

Figure 3

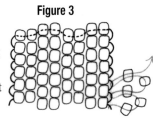

With your thread coming out of the last bead of the last row, string 3 beads. Pass under the first loop of thread at the side of the bracelet and back up though the last bead of the 3 just added.

*String 2 beads. Pass under the next loop of thread and back up through the second bead just added (Figure 3). Repeat from * to the opposite end of the bracelet. Pass through the last row and begin again.

Lucy Elle is fifty years old and has just returned to beading over the past five years. She lives in the south end of Seattle, Washington, with her rabbits, chickens, cats, crow, miniature hamsters, and one VERY supportive husband.

Elizabethan Cuff

Dona Anderson-Swiderek

Materials
Size 1 Japanese bugle beads
174 crystals or pearls
5 gr. charlottes
5 gr. Delicas
1 three-hole clasp
Power Pro, Silamide, or Size D Nymo beading thread

Notions
Size 12 beading needle
Scissors (or cutters for the Power Pro)

After I suffered a mind block about right-angle weave, my good friend Kim Rueth of Knot Just Beads, pulled me free by explaining the stitch with bugle beads. I expanded on her example by creating this gem-encrusted three-dimensional cuff.

Step 1: Measure the length of your clasp and write down the measurement. Using 2 yards of thread, tie 4 bugles in a tight ring using 2 knots. Do not weave around this ring again. Pass through the adjacent bugle.

Step 2: Make a right-angle weave ladder as long as needed to fit around your wrist, less the length of the clasp plus ½".

Step 3: Build 5 rows off of the ladder. The two outside rows are the two outside walls of the three-dimensional base of your bracelet.

Make the first and last rows of the right-angle weave stand up. With these outside walls standing up and the ends completed, now build interior walls down the two rows of horizontal bugles. You will find these rows by pushing up the outer 2 walls. Make interior walls by stringing 3 bugles and working right-angle weave with the base bugles. Only add 3 bugles when you start a row. Thereafter only 2 bugles are needed to complete a block of the inside wall. You will have a band three squares wide to embellish.

Figure 1

Figure 1a

Step 4: Attach the clasp by sewing several times through the loops of the clasp and back into the horizontal bugles at the ends of the bracelet. Do this on each end of the bracelet.

Step 5: Close the top by adding bugles vertically to the tops of the horizontal interior and exterior walls (Figure 1).

Step 6: Once the base structure is complete, begin a new thread in the corner of an intersection at the bottom of the bracelet. Pass through a bugle, string a charlotte or Delica, and pass through the adjoining bugle. This will make the weaves square and give them extra strength. Pull the thread gently but tight to snap the beads into all the intersections.

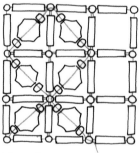

Figure 2

Step 7: Add crystals and pearls, using the inter-section seed beads to weave in a diagonal on the top and sides of the bracelet. Use doubled thread with the crystals and add a charlotte on either side to protect the thread (Figure 2). Do not embellish the inside of the bracelet that touches the wrist.

A regular contributor to Beadwork®, *Dona Anderson-Swiderek is the author of the self-published books* Beading Heart Designs: Amulet Purses *and* Let's Face It. *Find Dona's teaching schedule on her website,*
http://members.tripod.com/~beadingheart.

Woven Wave

Mindi Hawman

Materials

Size 11° mauve seed beads (A)
Size 11° pale lavender seed beads (B)
Size 11° silver-lined transparent seed beads (C)
Size 11° pale purple seed beads (D)
Size 11° orange seed beads (E)
Size 8° matte purple hex beads (F)
Size 14° shiny mauve seed beads (G)
Size 6° silver-lined lavender seed beads (H)
Focal bead for closure
Nymo D or Silamide beading thread in color to
   complement beads

Notions

Size 11 or 12 beading needle
Beeswax
Scissors

This bracelet is designed with wide-holed beads at the center
and a set of nets working its way across the whole bracelet.
Play with the look of the bracelet by making the nets pointy,
wavy, spiky, woven, or layered—it's up to you.

Step 1: Using 1½ yards of doubled thread and leaving a 6"
tail, loosely attach a tension bead. Make a base strand by
repeating this pattern—F, A, A, B, A, A—until it is 3" less than
the desired length. End the strand with an F bead.

Step 2: Make a closure by stringing D, B, D, F, D, B, D, F, D, D,
D, F, D, B, D, F, H, focal bead, H, F, D, B, D, F, D, D, D. Pass
through the second F and continue around
the circle to exit the focal bead. String 4 D
and pass back through the focal bead to create a picot. String 4 D and pass through the
focal bead to create a second picot. Note:
The picots act as stoppers for the closure to
make it more secure. Continue around the
circle and exit from the second F (Figure 1).

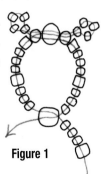

Figure 1

Step 3: String D, B, D, F, D, B, D. Pass
through the last F of the chain.

Step 4: Make a netting through the hex beads on the main strand by *stringing 5 C, 1 D, and 5 C. Pass through the next F on the chain. Repeat from * to the end of the strand. Remove the tension bead and tie the working thread to the tail.

Step 5: Make a beaded loop by stringing enough size 11° seed beads to accommodate the closure. Pass back through the last F.

Step 6: Manipulate the nets so that they oppose each other (one on one side of the center strand, the next on the other). Pass up through the first 3 Cs in your net. *String 3 D. Pass down through the third bead on the other side of this net. String 7 D. Pass up through the third bead of the first side of the next net. String 3 D. Pass down through the third bead on the other side of the net (Figure 2). Repeat from * across until you reach the focal bead. Pass through the figure-eight closure, skipping the picots, to give the closure extra strength.

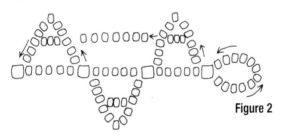

Figure 2

Step 7: Repeat Step 6 for the other side of the bracelet. Finish the step by weaving around the closure loop for extra strength.

Step 8: *String 11 G and pass the beads over the top rung created in Step 6. Pass through the B (or middle) bead of the 5 beads on the base strand. String 11 G and pass the beads under the bottom rung created in Step 6. Repeat across the length of the bracelet, always over and through, under and through, to create a new netting pattern. Exit from the fifth bead of the first set of 6-bead patterns on the base strand.

Step 9: String 5 E. Pass through the third, fourth, and fifth bead of the 6-bead pattern on the base strand (Figure 3). Continue across to the end.

Figure 3

Mindi Hawman has retired from teaching and nursing but continues to bead and be a mom. The beads provide the sparkle and light that is sometimes lacking in her home state of Alaska.

Wagon Wheels

Sharon Bateman

Materials
Size 11° seed beads in an assortment of colors
Button clasp
Beading thread in color to match the beads
White glue

Notions
Size 12 needle
Scissors

These wheels roll across your wrist like wagons on the trail.

WHOLE WHEEL
Make 1.

Round 1:
Step1: String 8 beads and tie a knot to make a circle. Trim the tail and secure the end with glue.

Step 2: String 10 beads. Pass through the next bead of the circle and up through the last 3 beads of the 10 just added (Figure 1).

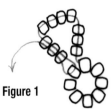

Figure 1

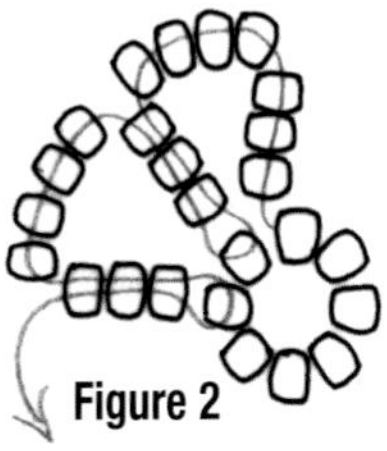

Figure 2

Step 3: *String 7 beads. Pass through the next bead of the circle and up through the last 3 beads of the 7 just added (Figure 2). Repeat from * all around the circle five times to make a total of 7 rungs.

Step 4: String 4 beads. Pass down through the first 3-bead rung of the round. Pass through the first bead of the circle and back up through the first rung of the row (Figure 3).

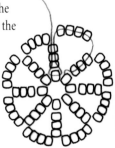

Figure 3

Round 2:
Step1: String 2 beads. Pass through the first 2 beads of the closest rung and back through the 2 beads just added to make a

square stitch. String 3 beads. Pass through the next 2 beads of the last round and back through the last 2 beads of the 3 just added (Figure 4).

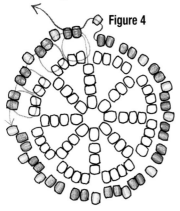

Figure 4

Step 2: String 3 beads. Pass back through the next 2 beads of the last round and through the last 2 beads of the 3 just added. String 2 beads and pass back through the next 2 beads of the last round and the 2 just added.

Step 3: Repeat Step 2 all around.

Step 4: String 1 bead. Pass through the first 2 beads added in this round.

Round 3:

Step 1: String 2 beads. Square-stitch these 2 beads onto the next 2 beads of the previous round. String 3 beads. Pass through the next 2 beads of the last round and back through the last 2 of the 3 just added. Repeat this step all around until you have only 4 beads left on the last round.

Step 2: Square-stitch 2 beads to the 2 beads below on the previous round twice.

Step 3: String 1 bead. Pass through the first set of 2 beads in this round to close it.

HALF WHEELS

Make nine consecutive half wheels for a small bracelet.

Round 1: String 5 beads. Pass into the last wheel 3 beads away from where the thread exited and then through 6 beads to the left (Figure 5).

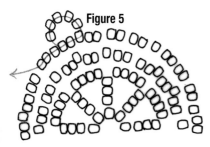

Figure 5

Round 2:

Step 1: String 5 beads. Pass through the first bead of Round 1 and back up through the last 3 beads just added. Pull tight.

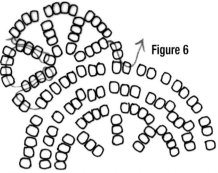

Figure 6

Step 2: String 7 beads. Pass through the next bead of Round 1 and back up through the last 3 beads just added (Figure 6). Pull tight.

Step 3: Repeat Step 2 three more times, working on consecutive beads of Round 1.

Step 4: String 2 beads. Pass through the fourth bead from the end of Round 1.

Round 3:

Step 1: String 3 beads. Square-stitch the last 2 beads added onto the first 2 beads of the last round.

Step 2: Repeat Step 1 around to the opposite side. Exit from the second bead up from Round 1 on the last wheel.

Round 4:

Step 1: String 3 beads. Square-stitch the last 2 of the 3 beads just added onto the first 2 beads of the last round. Stitch 2 beads onto the 2 beads below on the previous round for 2 more sets.

Step 2: Repeat Step 1 to the opposite side.

Step 3: String 1 bead. Pass through the second bead on the last wheel, up from Round 3. Pass through 20 beads to the top of the wheel.

CLASP

String on enough seed beads to slip around the button clasp. Pass back into the beads of the last row of the wheel and weave through several beads to strengthen. Tie a knot between beads, pass through several more beads to hide the knot, and trim the thread close to the work.

Sew the clasp bead or button down to the center of the whole wheel at the start of the bracelet.

Sharon Bateman lives in North Idaho, and has been beading professionally since the early nineties. She can be reached for questions or comments at www.sharonbateman.com.

Crochet Chips

Dustin Wedekind

Materials
Stone chips
26-gauge wire in a color to match the chips
Magnetic clasp

Notions
2mm steel crochet hook
Wire cutters or old scissors
Needle-nose pliers

Wire crochet is not rocket science. Using wire instead of yarn means that the beads slide easily and the loops stay open so you know where the hook is going.

Step 1: String approximately 7" of chips onto the wire. Do not cut the wire from the spool.

Figure 1

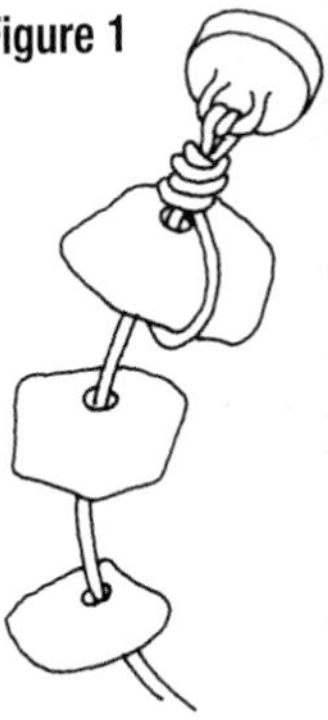

Step 2: Pass the loose end of the wire twice through one half of the clasp and pull tightly, leaving a 2" tail. Slide 1 chip down over the tail. Wrap the tail over the chip and then around the wire several times, tucking the end under the wraps (Figure 1).

Step 3: Begin to crochet by making a loop around the hook near the first chip. *Slide 1 chip down the wire. Bend the wire slightly to grab it with the hook and pull it through the loop. Keep the hook inside the newly formed loop. Repeat from * to the desired length (Figure 2). The clasp will take up ½" of the length.

Figure 2

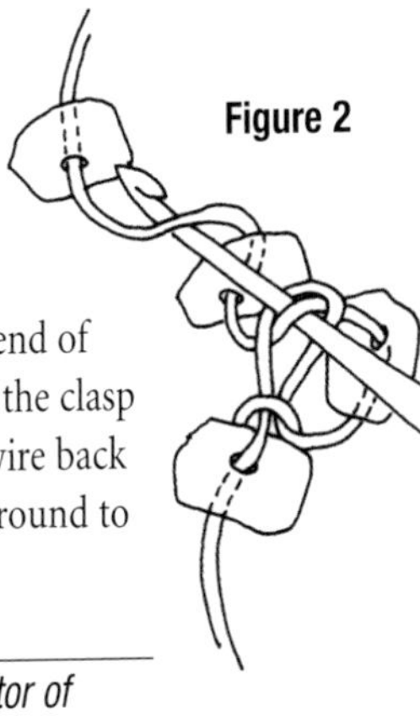

Step 4: Cut the wire 2" beyond the end of the bracelet. String the other half of the clasp and pass through it twice. Pass the wire back through the last chip, then up and around to finish as in Step 2.

Dustin Wedekind is the managing editor of Beadwork®.

Peekaboo Bracelet

Jane Tyson

Materials

10 gr. large Delicas
10 gr. size 8° hex beads
12mm fold-over clasp with 7 holes
Nymo O beading thread in color to complement the Delicas

Notions

Size 12 beading or sharps needle
Scissors

A combination of square and odd-count peyote stitches, this bracelet resembles chain link.

Step 1: Using 1 yard of thread and leaving a 12" tail, string a tension bead. String 1 Delica, 1 hex, 1 Delica, 1 hex, 1 Delica, 1 hex, and 2 Delicas.

Step 2: Work peyote stitch by passing back through the last hex strung. String 1 Delica and pass through the next hex. String 1 Delica and pass through the next hex. String 1 Delica and pass through the Delica of the row below, exiting your thread toward the center of the beadwork (Figure 1).

Figure 1

Step 3: Peyote stitch 1 hex between each Delica. Weave your thread up into the next Delica, exiting your thread toward the center of the beadwork (Figure 2).

Step 4: String 1 Delica and square-stitch it to the Delica on the row below, passing through 1 hex and 1 Delica. Repeat from * three times so that there are four columns of three Delicas in the bracelet. Turn and pass through the last bead, exiting toward the center of the beadwork (Figure 3).

Figure 2

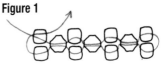

Figure 3

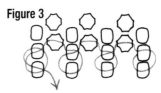

Figure 4

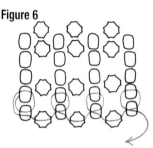

Step 5: Peyote stitch 1 hex between each Delica of this row to add a total of 3 hex beads (Figure 4).

Figure 5

Step 6: Peyote stitch 1 Delica between each hex. Square stitch the last Delica (Figure 5).

Step 7: String 1 Delica and square stitch it to the previous row. String 1 hex and 1 Delica and square stitch to the next Delica of the previous row. Repeat to the end of the row (Figure 6).

Figure 6

Step 8: Repeat Steps 6 and 7 until the bracelet is the required length. End with a row that looks like Step 7 and finish by inserting three hex beads to match the start of the bracelet. Remember to allow an extra measurement for the clasp. Sew the bracelet neatly to the clasp, checking that the bracelet is the right way up on the clasp before you sew. Remove the tension bead and use the tail to sew this end to the other end of the clasp.

Gold bracelet by Donna Zaidenberg

Jane Tyson is a Tasmanian beadwork teacher and bead seller. She can be contacted at jrtyson@netspace.net.au.

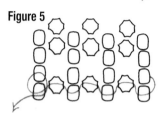

Green bracelet by Dorothy House

Loomworked Duo

Suzanne Golden

LITTLE DUTCH FOLKS
TAXI! TAXI!

Materials

Dutch Folks:

Size 11° seed beads in black, yellow, white, red, light green, dark green, light blue, dark blue, and pink
32 heart beads
1 clasp bead
Beading thread

Taxis:

Size 11° beads in black, yellow, white, and red
27 size 6° or 8° beads
1 or more clasp beads
Beading thread

Notions

Loom
Size 12 beading needle
Scissors

Loomwork is an easy and fun way to make patterns with beadwork. Try these cute charted bracelets to get your beadworking juices flowing.

Step 1: Warp your loom according to loom instructions.

Step 2: Weave your beads following the charts provided. Work the strip and then work the points as indicated for each.

Step 3: Remove your work from the loom and weave in all of the warp threads except the center warp thread.

Step 4: Use your center warp thread to make your bead and loop clasp.

Step 5: Use a new thread to sew on your fringe at the edges.

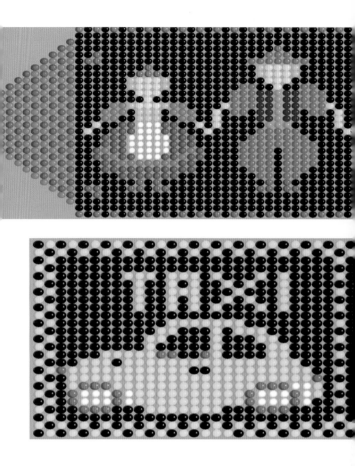

END POINTS

Use the center warp thread to create a loop on one end of the bracelet. Attach your clasp bead on the other end. Weave the tails into the beads and tie off.

Another way to finish is to brick-stitch along the end of your beadwork. Pass through the end beads as you add each bead. Work up to an even row, making a blunt tip.

Add a bead/loop clasp onto the brick-stitch points. Pass back through the edge beads into the loomwork.

FRINGE

Add fringe as desired along the edge of your loomwork.

Suzanne Golden finds many aspects of beading that she enjoys, from forming the idea and finding the right colors to working with her hands and delighting in the finished work. And never underestimate the anticipation when looking at trays and trays of beads, glorious beads.

Befitting Bracelets

Jean Campbell

Materials
Clear vinyl ½" tubing
⅜" brass barb hose fitting
1 large tube of size 11° seed beads or other beads
    less than ⅜"

Notions
Scissors

These are the quickest bracelets to make in the universe! Plus, they look très chic. Take a trip to your local hardware store to get most of the materials.

Step 1: Cut the tubing into a 9" length. Push one side of the tubing onto one side of the barb fitting until the tubing meets the center of the fitting (Figure 1).

Step 2: With one finger over the open end of the fitting, pour the beads into the other end of the tube until they reach 1" from the end.

Step 3: Push the open end of the tube onto the open end of the barb fitting until the tube meets the center of the fitting where it closes.

Figure 1

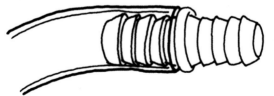

Ellen's Flower Garden

Ellen Sadler

Materials

Size 8° and 11° green seed beads for the base
Size 11° seed beads for the flower bodies
Size 8° seed beads for the flower centers
Drop beads for the centers
Beading thread in color to complement beads

Notions

Size 12 beading or sharps needle
Scissors

Year-round springtime flowers adorn you as you wear this bracelet.

BASE

Use right-angle weave to make a cuff that is 5 sets wide and 24 rows long. Each set will have 4 groups of 3 beads (11°, 8°, 11°). Add more rows as necessary for length.

CLASPS

Step 1: Brick-stitch a square that is 6 beads wide by 6 rows tall. Sew the edges together by running thread through the edge beads to create a tube. Pull tight. Make 2.

Step 2: Brick-stitch 2 leaf shapes that are 6 beads wide (Figure 1). Sew the leaves onto the brick-stitched tubes.

Step 3: Reinforce the end of the bracelet by adding size 8's between the size 11's at one end (Figure 2). Exit from the 8°

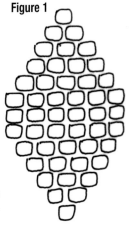

Figure 1

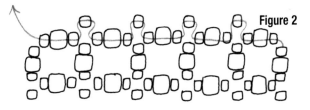

Figure 2

closest to one edge of the cuff. String 4 size 11's. Pass through the beads of the cylinder. String 4 size 11's. Pass through the three-bead group that the thread is exiting from. Pass through all again to strengthen. Work the thread through the right-angle weave to exit the opposite corner and attach the second clasp (Figure 2).

Step 4: Reinforce the other end of the bracelet as you did in Step 3.

Step 5: Exiting at a corner bead at the other end of the cuff, string 21 size 11's or enough to fit around the leaf at the other end. Skip two three-bead groups and pass through the fourth three-bead group. Make another loop and pass back through the last size 11° of this row of the cuff (Figure 3). Pass through all the beads again and part of the cuff to strengthen.

Figure 3

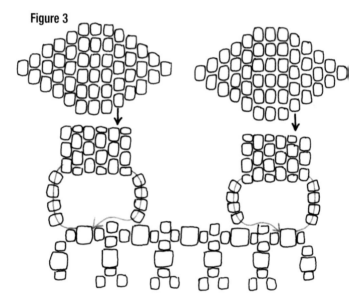

FLOWERS

Make 27.

Step 1: Work a ladder stitch 12 size 11's or fewer wide. Connect the first and last beads added with a stitch. The threads that connect each bead will be called bridges.

Step 2: Work brick stitch off of the ladder to form a tube. Keep the bridges an even number.

Step 3: Note: In the sample bracelet, every flower is worked differently. These instructions are for the basic techniques, not for each flower.

Divide the number of bridges by the number of desired petals. This will let you know how many beads to work on each bridge in the first row of each petal. For example, if you have 12 bridges and want 4 petals you will work the first row over 3 bridges.

Step 4: Work the rest of the rows for the petal of this first row, increasing or decreasing as needed (Figure 4). Once the point is worked, weave down through the rows to the cup and begin the next petal.

Figure 4

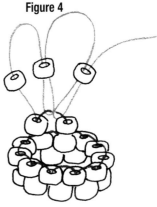

You can work each flower differently by
• Changing the number of beads in the circle base. This will change the number of petals you can add, or the width of the base row of each petal.
• Altering the height of the circle base by adding more layers.
• Varying the width, length, and points of the petals to produce different effects. You can even alternate variations of the petals on the same flower.
• Changing the color(s) and the pattern in which you use the colors can alter the effect of the flower.

FINISHING

Use the flowers' tails to sew them randomly to the bracelet base. Start at one corner of the bracelet and work your way across. Do so by passing through one of the beads on the bracelet base and then passing back up through the circle base of the flower. Add extra seed or drop beads in the center of each to finish each flower. Alternate sewing through the bracelet base and the flower base until each flower is secure. Tie off and trim the thread.

Ellen Sadler is thrilled to have found the perfect creative outlet sized for New York City apartments. She maybe reached at ellensadler@juno.com

Charmed, I'm Sure

Jean Campbell

Materials
12–20 charms
Chunky chain in color to match the charms
Lobster clasp in color to match chain
22 or so jump rings in color to match clasp

Notions
Wire cutter
Needle-nose pliers

Charms are all the rage lately and can be had at just about any bead shop or craft store. Make an identity bracelet for yourself by including charms that speak about who you are.

Step 1: Cut a length of chain to fit your wrist.

Step 2: Attach one jump ring to each end of the chain, always opening the jump ring laterally (Figure 1).

Step 3: Attach the lobster clasp to one of the jump rings.

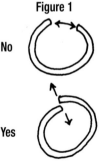

Figure 1

No

Yes

Step 4: Lay out your chain and approximate where you would like each charm to go by lining them up on your work surface. Vary placement according to the length and width of each charm.

Step 5: Attach the first charm to the chain with a jump ring. Lay the chain down and check where the next charm will go according to your design in Step 4. Continue across the chain, always setting it down to check the design after attaching a charm (from time to time your original arrangement may need revising).

Step 6: Attach the other half of the clasp to the other end of the chain with another jump ring.

Dimensional Kisses Bracelet

Sharon Rawson

Materials

Size 11° Japanese seed beads in a main color (MC)
Size 11° Czech seed bead in an accent color (A)
70 faceted or round 3mm beads
One 4mm bead
Beading thread in color to complement MC beads
Fish hook clasp

Notions

Size 12 beading or sharps needle
Scissors

Line up your kisser for this sweet series of Xs.

Instructions are for a 7" bracelet. For every ¼" that you wish to add or subtract, raise or reduce the number of 3mm beads by four.

Step 1: Using 4 yards of doubled thread and loose tension, string 12 MC, tie into a circle, and pass back through the first seven just strung.

Step 2: String 13 MC. Pass through the bead you last exited in Step 1 and through the first seven of this new loop.

Step 3: String 11 MC. Pass through the bead you last exited in the previous step. Pass through the first six of the new loop (Figure 1).

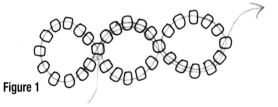

Figure 1

Step 4: Repeat Step 3.

Step 5: String 3 MC, 5 A, and 3 MC. Pass through the bead you last exited in the previous step. Pass through the first six of the new loop.

Step 6: String 2 A, 7 MC, and 2 A. Pass through the bead you last exited in the previous step. Pass through the first six of the new loop.

Repeat Steps 5 and 6 for the length of your bracelet, minus 1" for the clasp.

Step 7: String 5 MC, the hook, and 6 MC. Pass through the bead you last exited in the previous step. Pass through the first six of the new loop.

Step 8: String 11 MC. Pass through the bead you last exited in the previous step. Pass through the first six of the new loop.

Step 9: String 3 MC, the 4mm bead, and 1 MC. Pass back through the 4mm. String 3 MC and pass through the bead you last exited in the previous step.

Step 10: Weave through the beads so that you exit from the middle bead on one side of the hook loop. String one 3mm bead. Pass through the middle bead of the next loop (Figure 2) and pull tight. Continue until you have added the 3mm between the fourth and fifth loops. Make sure the tension is tight. Weave through the first three loops for reinforcement.

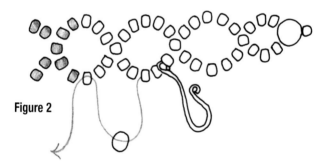

Figure 2

Step 11: Add the 3mm beads on the other side of the bracelet. Make a knot between beads and pass through several beads to secure. Trim thread close to work.

Step 12: Pop up the A beads with the toothpick to make the Xs dimensional.

A florist by trade, Sharon Rawson began beading a long time ago—before books, bead stores, or magazines. Since then she's taken all the beading classes should could find and read all the magazines and books available. She has begun teaching now and especially enjoys teaching bracelets.

Piano Notes

Judi Wood

Materials

10–15 gr. of ivory opaque shiny Toho triangle beads
5 gr. black opaque shiny Toho triangle beads
5 gr. metallic opaque Toho triangle beads
Size B Nymo beading thread or 10-lb test PowerPro string
Designer Findings Snap-Lock clasp with ends
Two 4mm jump rings in color to match clasp or button
Glue
½" lampworked button with metal loop

Notions

Size 12 beading needle
Sharp scissors for thread or wire cutter for PowerPro

The perfect bracelet for music lovers! The triangle beads give the keyboard a mosaic feel and the notes look like they've been written in italic.

Step 1: Using a yard of either Nymo or PowerPro, string a tension bead and 12 white beads for the first row. String 2 white and begin to square stitch the second row. After two to three rows of white, work 5 black at the start of the next row. This starts your keyboard. After a row or two of the black, begin the notes. I find that placing them randomly on the keyboard gives the cuff an informal look, as if a musician had placed them there.

Step 2: Continue to work in square stitch following the chart. Check to see when your bracelet fits comfortably around your wrist, making sure to compensate for the length that your clasp finding or a button and loop closure will take up.

Step 3: For the clasp finding, work the tail threads into the bracelet. Run a thin bead of glue along the edge of the beads and carefully bend the metal bar over them.

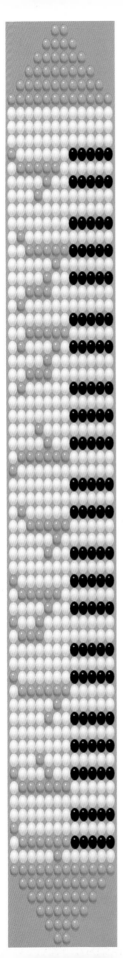

If you are using a button, work decreasing square stitch on each end of the bracelet. Attach the button on one side, passing through it several times and working the tail into the work. Make a peyote or square stitch loop on the other end to fit around the button, and work the tail into the work.

Award winning artist Judi Wood is a frequent contributor to Beadwork®. Her work and show information can be seen at her website www.JudiWood.com.

by Sharon Bateman

by Theresa Grout

Serendipity Bangles

Theresa Grout

Materials

Size 6° beads in the primary color
Size 4° beads in a contrasting or complementary color
Assortment of smaller beads (14° or 11° and/or cylinder)
8mm or larger decorative beads (a minimum of 64)
12 to 24mm clasp bead
Heavy bead thread in color to complement beads

Notions

Size 10 or Big Eye needle
Scissors

Make these fun bangles as simple or as fringed as you like. Add fringe legs, fringe loops, or fringe ruffles for a variety of effects.

Step 1: Use a 6° bead to create a tension bead. String 63 beads, alternating between first a 4° and then a 6°, for a total of 64 beads.

Step 2: Work five rows of peyote stitch using 6° beads. Work one row using the 4° beads. Your bracelet should have a total of eight rows. Tie a knot to secure.

Step 3: Sew the edges, pulling the beads together like a zipper to make a tube. Double-stitch the last bead and tie a knot on the bridge of thread between the beads. Work your thread between the first and last rows of peyote.

Step 4: Add a clasp by stringing three size 6° beads and your clasp bead to one end of the bracelet. String 1 size 6° and pass back through the clasp bead and the first 3 size 6° beads strung. Pass through all several times to secure.

Begin a thread at the other end of the bracelet and make a loop using enough size 6° beads so that it is just large enough to slip over your clasp bead. Pass through all beads several times to secure.

Figure 1

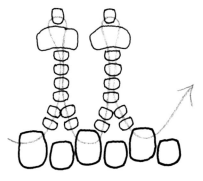

FRINGE

Step 5: Use a new thread to add fringe between each of the 4°
beads along the seam. Pass through a 4° bead, string 6 to 10
smaller beads, 1 decorative bead, and 1 smaller bead. Skipping
the last bead strung, pass back through all but the first 2 beads
strung. String 2 smaller beads and pass through the next 4°
bead along the seam (Figure 1). Make a full fringe by working
between each of these 4° beads as well as on them. (Note:
Making a full fringe will increase your decorative beads to 96.)

*Theresa Grout has been a jewelry designer since 1992, and
a glass bead maker since 1993. She has had a lifelong
passion for seed beads and loves to incorporate them into
her jewelry along with her own handmade glass beads. She
currently lives and works in Western Montana where she has
plans to open a retail bead store. She can be reached through
her web site www.rebeads.com.*

Diamond Back

Jan Wasser

Materials
42 round or faceted 3 or 4mm beads
20 bicone 4mm crystals
Size 11° seed beads
Size 13° or 14° seed beads
Size B or D Nymo beading thread
Toggle clasp
Hypo glue

Notions
Size 12 beading needle
Thread Heaven
Scissors

This crisscrossing beauty can be made in an evening.

Step 1: String 9 size 11°s and one half of the toggle clasp. Pass through all 2 times and tie a knot.

Step 2: String 9 size 11°s. Pass through the fifth bead strung in the previous step. Pass through the first 5 beads strung in this step.

Step 3: String 11 size 11°s. Pass through the fifth bead strung in the previous step and the first 6 beads strung in this step (Figure 1).

Figure 1

Step 4: String 11 size 11°s. Pass through the sixth bead strung in the previous step and the first 6 beads strung in this step.

Step 5: Repeat this 11-bead loop enough times to reach your desired length. For a small bracelet using 4mm crystals along the edge, make 22 loops; if you use 3mm crystals, make 24 loops. For a large bracelet using 4mm crystals along the edge, make 24 loops; if you use 3mm crystals, make 26 loops.

Step 6: String 9 size 11's. Pass back through the sixth bead of the last loop in the previous step and the first 5 beads strung in this step.

Step 7: String 9 size 11's and the second half of the toggle clasp. Pass back through all a few times to reinforce the clasp.

Step 8: Weave through the beads to exit from the sixth bead of the first 11-bead loop. *String 1 size 13° or 14°, 1 crystal, and 1 size 13° or 14°. Pass through the crossover bead of the next loop (Figure 2). Repeat from * until you reach the last set of size 11's. Note: Pull the thread snug, but not too tight. Too much tension and the bracelet will stiffen up and not lie right. Pass through the crossover beads in opposite directions, zigzagging down the bracelet.

Figure 2

Step 9: Pass back through the crystal sets to the opposite end of the bracelet. Pull the thread snug, but not too tight. This pass will straighten the bicone crystals.

Step 10: Pass through the ninth bead of the last 11-bead loop so that you exit from the top bead of the loop. *String 1 size 13° or 14°, one 3 or 4mm, and 1 size 13° or 14°. Pass through the top bead of the next loop (Figure 3).

Figure 3

Repeat from * along the side of the bracelet. When you reach the opposite end, weave around the last loop and repeat from * to the other end.

Step 11: Tie a few half-hitch knots in between the beads of the loops, near the clasp. Glue the thread and allow it to dry. Trim the tail of the thread close.

Jan Wasser lives in Spokane, Washington. She started her love for glass beads and stones in late 1997. Needless to say she became a "beadaholic." She's a freelance designer and commissions some of her one-of-a-kind work.

Netted
Garden

Margo C. Field
Buttons from Ashes to Beauty Adornments

Materials

Size 11° seed beads in background (B)
    and contrasting (C) colors
Size 11° seed beads in five colors for the garden
Assortment of 3mm fire polished beads
3mm druks, glass pearls, or freshwater pearls
4mm square beads
Accent beads
Button for clasp
Nymo B beading thread in color to complement beads

Notions

Size 12 beading or sharps needle
Beeswax
Scissors

After you create the netted base, decorate it with other colors
of seed beads and the accent beads. The author likes to call
this "planting the garden."

NETTED BASE

Step 1: Using 2 yards of single waxed thread and leaving a 2'
tail, string a tension bead. String 22 B and pass back through
the seventeenth bead strung.

Step 2: Work netting across the beads strung in Step 1. String
3 B and pass back through the thirteenth bead strung in Step
1. String 3 B and pass back through the ninth bead strung.
String 3 B and pass back through the fifth bead strung. String
3 B and pass back through the first bead strung (Figure 1).
Tighten so work is snug.

Figure 1

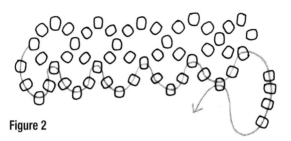

Figure 2

Step 3: Work netting to the other side. Start by stringing 4 B and passing through the second bead of the last three-bead group added in Step 2. *String 3 B and pass through the second bead of the next three-bead group added in Step 2. Repeat from * across the work. The last stitch passes through the second bead of the four-bead loop (Figure 2).

Step 4: Repeat Step 3 for the length of the bracelet, minus the length of the clasp.

EDGING

Step 5: Using 2 yards of thread and exiting from the first shared bead on the bracelet, string 3 C and pass through the next shared bead in the same direction. Your thread should exit the same way it did on the first shared bead to make the beads create a slant (Figure 3). Repeat for the length of the bracelet, and then weave over and do the other side.

Figure 3

PLANTING THE GARDEN

Step 6: After the edging is complete, plant the garden. You can continue to use the thread that you used for the edging or you can weave in a new thread. As you plant the garden it is a good idea to anchor and reinforce the plantings by making a couple of half-hitch knots on the back.

Exiting from one of the shared beads at one corner of the bracelet, string 3 C and pass through the next shared bead of that row.

Step 7: Make a nine-bead leaf using one of the garden-colored size 11's on each side of the shared bead. To make a leaf, string 6 beads, pass back through the fifth bead, string 3 beads, and pass back through the first bead (Figure 4). After adding the two

Figure 4

nine-bead leaves, add three vine-colored beads and advance to the next shared bead.

ALTERNATIVE CULTIVATING TECHNIQUES

• Make the vine curvy by passing through a common bead of an adjoining row. You may have to add more than three beads to cover the space.

• In place of nine-bead leaves, plant a bead flower using the size 11° seed beads and one of the druks, fire polished, square, or other accent beads.

• Make some common beads have three sprouts instead of the usual two.

• End the vine at any point and start it somewhere else.

• Put a little sprout in a empty space all by itself

Margo C. Field "discovered" beads in 1990. After retiring from a career in Hospital Pharmacy, she opened Poppy Field Bead Company in Albuquerque, New Mexico. She teaches classes at her store and workshops across the United States.

Pearls and Twists

Lilli Brennan

Materials
20-gauge gold-filled or brass non-tarnish wire
22-gauge gold-filled or brass non-tarnish wire
4mm pearls
6mm gold colored magnetic clasp
Gold-filled or brass non-tarnish jump rings

Notions
Hand drill
Cup hook bit
Cotton pads
Wire cutter
Nylon jaw pliers
WigJig Cyclops

This bracelet is a clever working of wire and pearls. It encircles your wrist like a golden guard!

Figure 1

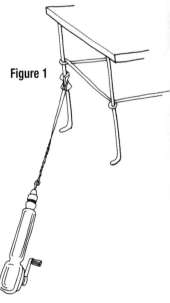

Step 1: Cut a 6' length of 22-gauge wire and double it around a table leg. Protect the leg with cotton pads. Place the cup hook in the drill and secure the wire to the cup hook. While holding the wire tight, slowly turn the drill handle (Figure 1). Twist the wire on the drill until you get a consistent and tight twist. It should resemble a rope. Clip the wire from the hook and the table leg. Gently straighten, if necessary, using nylon jaw pliers.

Step 2: Make a starting loop on one end and put it on the upper left peg of the jig (Figure 2). Bring the wire tail to the far right peg and form a loop around that peg to make a link. Remove from the jig and clip the wire tail (Figure 3). Repeat to form 19 links.

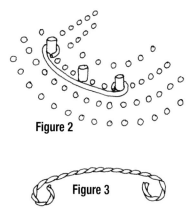

Figure 2

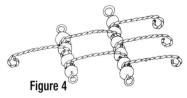

Figure 3

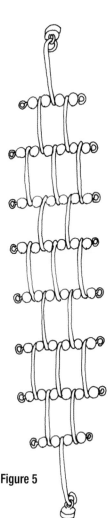

Figure 4

Step 3: Make a loop in one end of a short length of 20-gauge wire. Thread the links interspersed with pearls in the pattern shown (Figure 4) to form the first section of the bracelet. Close with a second loop and trim the wire. Repeat, following Figure 5 to form the entire bracelet.

Step 4: Use a jump ring to attach one side of the magnetic clasp to the single link at one end of the bracelet. Repeat for the other side.

Lilli Brennan, a resident of East Stroudsburg, Pennsylvania, has been designing wire and bead jewelry in conjunction with WigJig for the past several years. A passionate jewelry lover all her life and a crafter in many media, she finds the most satisfaction in producing beautiful, delicate pieces.

Figure 5

Chunky Decadence

Judi Mullins

Materials

47 bicone 8mm crystals or 65 bicone 6mm crystals
Optional crystal for dangle
2 yards of Soft Touch wire
Two-strand clasp
4 crimp tubes in color to match clasp

Notions

Wire cutters
Flat-nose or crimping pliers
Pin
Foam

Create this beautifully sparkling bracelet using two-needle right-angle weave without the needles!

Step 1: Cut the wire into two equal pieces. Attach one end of each length to the two jump rings on one side of the clasp. Leave a short tail of wire to tuck into the first beads.

Step 2: String two crystals with one wire and one crystal with the other wire. Pull all the crystals tight to the clasp and thread the tails left on the wires into the first crystal on either side. Cut any excess off. Pass the wire that has only one crystal on it through the last crystal on the other wire starting from the opposite side. You should now have a wire coming out of either side of that crystal (Figure 1).

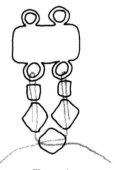

Figure 1

Step 3: Continue adding crystals in this fashion, until the bracelet is the length you desire (Figure 2). It is essential that you keep a very tight tension on the wires, because the tension will tend to loosen as you go. It is often helpful to pin the bracelet to a foam board to minimize the movement of the bracelet.

Step 4: Attach the wires to the other side of the clasp the same way as in Step 1. End the bracelet with one crystal on each wire. String a

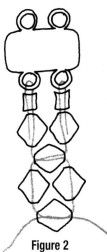

Figure 2

crimp tube, pass through a jump ring and back through the crimp tube and crystal. Tighten well before crimping by pulling on the ends of the wires coming out of the last beads. Crimp and cut off any excess wire.

Judi Mullins has been doing beadwork off and on for most of her adult life. She has been published in several magazines and has taught around the Northwest area. She is now teaching classes and doing beadwork designs out of her home in Tigard, Oregon. You can contact her at bead.garden@verizon.net.

Jump Back!

Jean Campbell

Materials
Assorted beads
Memory wire

Notions
Round- or needle-nose pliers

Memory wire is just what its name implies—it doesn't forget its shape no matter what you do to it. Have fun playing with bead sizes, colors, and types to make your bracelet your own.

Step 1: Use the pliers to bend back one end of the wire to act as a stopper (Figure 1).

Figure 1

Step 2: String beads as desired. Make sure that the bracelet is long enough to stay coiled around your wrist.

Step 3: When you've reach your desired length, snap the end of the wire about ½" from the last bead by bending the wire back and forth several times until it breaks. DO NOT use a wire cutter to snip this wire or you'll damage the cutter.

Step 4: Rep Step 1, ensuring the beads are snug.

Fences and Flowers

Jeri Herrera

Materials

4mm bicone Swarovski crystals
Size 11° Japanese seed beads
Size D Nymo beading thread
3-loop clasp

Notions

Size 12 beading or sharps needle
Scissors

This seemingly complicated pattern is a snap! Just follow the instructions and illustrations, and use the crystal placement as your guide.

Step 1: String 4 crystals and tie a knot to make a circle. Pass back through the crystals again to strengthen.

Step 2: String 6 seed beads, 1 crystal, and 6 seed beads. Pass through the third crystal strung in Step 1. Pass through the first 6 seed beads and the crystal strung in this step.

Step 3: String three crystals and pass back through the single crystal strung in the previous step and the first two just strung (Figure 1).

Repeat until the bracelet is your desired length, compensating for the clasp width.

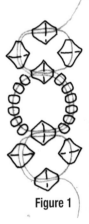

Figure 1

Step 4: String 6 seed beads, pass through the center loop of the three-loop clasp and string another 6 beads. Pass back through the crystal and seed beads several times to strengthen. Weave your thread to the next crystal (Figure 2).

Step 5: String 3 seed beads, 1 crystal, 6 seed beads, 1 crystal, 3 seed beads, and pass through the crystal you last exited in Step 4.

Step 6: Pass through the first 3 seed beads, 1 crystal, 6 seed beads and 1 crystal you strung in the previous step.

Figure 2

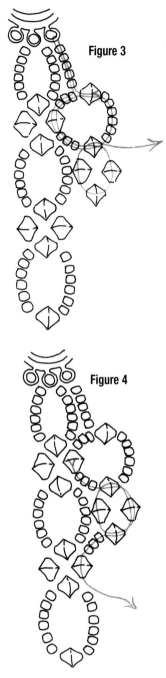

Figure 3

Figure 4

Step 7: String 5 seed beads and pass through the loop in the clasp. Pass back through the seed beads and around the loop. Repeat to strengthen. Exit from the crystal farthest from the clasp. Add 3 crystals and form a loop (Figure 3). Exit from the second crystal of the last 3 you added.

Step 8: String 3 seed beads and pass through the crystal on the next circle (Figure 4).

Step 9: String 3 seed beads, 1 crystal, 6 seed beads, and pass through the crystal from the previous loop in Step 7.

Step 10: Pass through 3 seed beads, a crystal from the main bracelet, 3 seed beads, and a crystal. String 6 seed beads, a crystal, and 3 seed beads. Pass back through a crystal on the main bracelet. Repeat these steps down the entire length of the bracelet.

Step 11: Once you reach the end, complete the last loop and weave through the very first crystal of the bracelet. String 6 seed beads and pass through the middle loop of the clasp. String 6 more seed beads and repeat to strengthen.

Step 12: Pass back through the last crystal in the last loop of the second row. String 5 seed beads and pass through the next loop in the clasp. Pass back through the 5 seed beads and around the loop. Repeat to strengthen. Weave your thread through the beads to exit from the first outside crystal on the other side of the bracelet.

Step 13: String 3 seed beads, 1 crystal, 6 seed beads, 1 crystal, and 3 seed beads. Pass through the crystal on the main bracelet and the beads and last crystal just added (Figure 5).

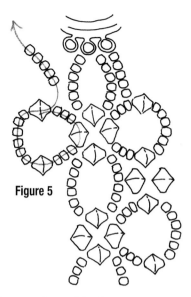

Figure 5

Step 14: String 5 seed beads. Pass through the third loop in the clasp. Repeat to strengthen. Work down the other side of the bracelet as you did for the first side. String 5 seed beads to the last open loop of the clasp.

Finish by tying a knot between beads and weaving thread through several beads to secure. Trim tail close to work.

Jeri Herrera has been beading for the last nine years and begun teaching last year in her local community. Jeri can be reached at jeri@dbeadmama.com or www.dbeadmama.com.

Slither Chain

Jane Tyson

Materials
3–4 gr. size 11° triangle beads
6 gr. size 8° seed beads in two colors
Size B Nymo beading thread in color to
    complement beads
Clasp
1.4mm gimp (French wire) to match clasp

Notions
Size 10 or 12 beading needle
Beeswax or Thread Heaven
Scissors

This really versatile bracelet is a natural
for any attire. Alternating matte and
shiny beads of the same color makes a
very effective look.

Step 1: Using 1 yard of conditioned
thread, string 1 seed bead and a triangle bead leaving a 6" tail. Pass through
the seed bead again so that the triangle bead sits next to the seed bead
(Figure 1).

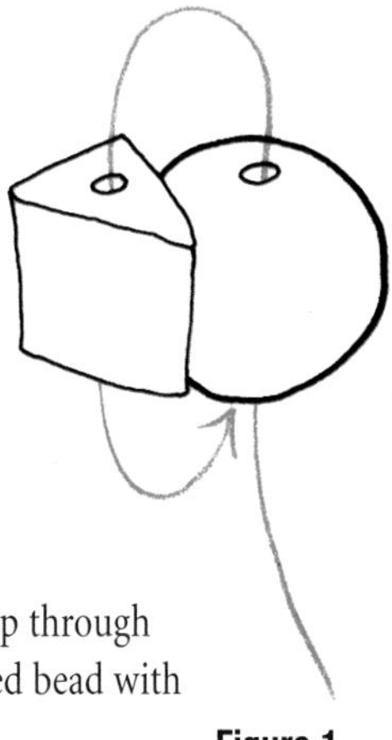

Step 2: String 1 triangle bead and pass up through
the seed bead. You should now have a seed bead with
a triangle bead on either side (Figure 2).

Figure 1

Step 3: String 1 seed bead and
a triangle bead. Pass down
through the right triangle and
up through the two center seed
beads (Figure 3). String 1 triangle bead and pass down
through the left triangle and up
through the two center seed
beads.

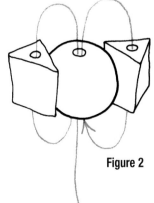

Figure 2

Figure 3

Step 4: Repeat Step 3 until the bracelet reaches your desired length. Remember to compensate for the clasp width.

Step 5: String 1 cm of gimp and weave the gimp through the clasp connection. Weave through the gimp again for strength. Weave down through the line of seed beads, working the thread into the bracelet to make the clasp secure. Trim any excess thread.

Step 6: Repeat Step 5 at the other end of the bracelet to attach the other side of the clasp.

Tips

• Cull your beads for this project. Many triangle beads are off shape. Try to use only the triangles with straight ends. Make sure they are about the same height vertically as the seed beads. If anything, the triangles should be a little shorter than the seed beads.
• Watch your tension. Do not pull your beads too close together.
• Check that you have passed through the center beads without piercing the thread within. Once pierced, the thread is almost impossible to work through.

Jane Tyson is a Tasmanian beadwork teacher and bead seller. She can be contacted at jrtyson@netspace.net.au.

Lazy Square Stitch Cuff

Barbara Grainger

Materials

Size 11° seed beads in main and
   contrasting colors (MC and CC)
1 small decorative button
Size B Nymo or Silamide beading thread

Notions

Size 12 beading or sharps needles
 Beeswax

Figure 1

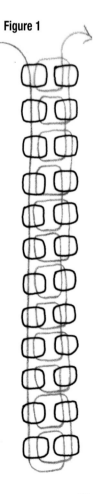

This beautiful leaf-like cuff is made
with a square-stitch pattern that's easy
to do.

Rows 1 and 2: Using two yards of
single-strand waxed thread, string a
tension bead leaving an 8" tail. String
13 CC seed beads. Bring the thirteenth
bead beside the twelfth bead and pass
down through the twelfth bead and
back up through the thirteenth bead.
Continue working square stitch for the
rest of the row (Figure 1).

Rows 3–5: Using CC beads, work
square stitch for the first two beads.
*String 3 MC beads and 1 CC bead.
Skip three beads on the previous row
and work square stitch with the CC
bead only in the fourth bead. Work
one more CC bead square stitch.
Repeat from * to finish the row (Figure
2.) The strung beads may not lie flat
but create a random texture.

Figure 2

Rows 6–8: Work square stitch using CC for the first two beads. * String 4 MC beads and 1 CC bead. Skipping the strung section of the previous row, work square stitch with the CC bead only in the CC bead of the previous row. Work one more CC bead square stitch. Repeat from * to finish the row (Figure 3).

Rows 9–24: Continue increasing one MC bead in each strung section every fourth row. For example: Rows 9–11 have 5 beads in each strung section. Rows 12–14 have 6 beads in each strung section, etc. You should have 10 strung beads between the square stitch sections by the time you finish Row 24.

Rows 25–72: Work the same as Row 22 without increasing the strung beads.

Rows 73–75: Work the same as the previous rows, except decrease the number of MC beads to 9 in each strung section.

Figure 3

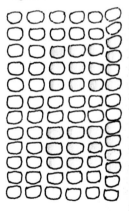

Rows 76–93: Continue to decrease MC beads by one bead in each strung section every fourth row. For example: Rows 76–78 have 8 strung beads in each section. Rows 79–81 have 7 strung beads in each section, etc.

Rows 94 and 95: Using CC, work square stitch in every bead. Do not finish off the thread.

Finish the bracelet by adding a button/loop clasp.

Barbara Grainger is an internationally recognized beadwork author, instructor, and designer who specializes in innovative beadwork techniques.

Knotty

Dustin Wedekind

Materials

9" Soft Flex .019" beading wire
Assorted beads
Assorted fancy ribbons
Clasp
2 crimp beads

Notions

Crimping pliers
Tapestry needle

Step 1: String a crimp bead and one half of the clasp onto the wire. Pass 1" of wire back through the crimp bead and crimp it. Cut 16" of ribbon and pass half of it through the clasp.

Step 2: Cut approximately 60" of ribbon and tie a square knot over the crimped bead and the ribbon, with 30" ribbon on each side (Figure 1). Continue tying square knots, over the wire and ribbon core, for approximately 1".

Step 3: String 1 bead on the wire. Hold the wire up out of the ribbon and tie a series of knots the length of the bead. Return the wire to the core and tie more knots.

Step 4: Add beads and knots for the length of the bracelet, minus 1".

Step 5: String the other crimp bead and half of the clasp. Pass the wire back through the bead and crimp. Lay the tail of the wire with the ribbon core and tie more knots over it. When you reach the clasp, pass through it with the ribbon and use the tapestry needle to thread the ends of the ribbon into the bracelet.

Dustin Wedekind is the managing editor of Beadwork®.

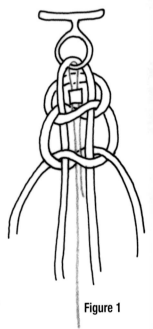

Figure 1

Twist and Shout

Jean Campbell

Materials
Assortment of beads in the same palette
Soft Flex .019" beading wire
12 crimp beads
2 jump rings
Magnetic clasp

Notions
Wire cutter
Flat-nose or crimping pliers

This bracelet is very simple to make. It's just three simple bracelets twisted together.

Step 1: Open one jump ring and attach it to one end of the clasp. Do the same for the other end.

Step 2: Measure your wrist. Add 4". Take this measurement and cut that length of wire.

Step 3: String 2 crimp beads on the wire. Pass the wire through one of the jump rings and back through the two crimp beads leaving a 2" tail. Crimp the beads.

Step 4: String an assortment of beads, making sure you cover the double tail at the beginning of the wire. When you reach about 2" from the end string 2 crimp beads.

Step 5: Pass through the other jump ring and then back through the crimp beads you just strung. Continue to pass back through as many beads as possible on the strand. Pull the wire tight, taking up any slack. Crimp the beads. Trim the tail close to the work.

Step 6: Repeat Steps 3–5 to add another strand.

Step 7: Repeat Steps 3–5 to add a third strand, but make this one longer than the others—long enough so that it can wrap around the other two. Do this wrapping right before attaching it to the other jump ring.

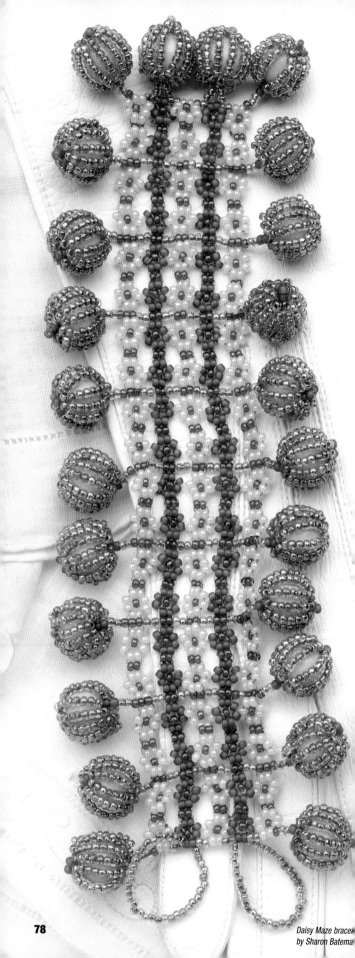

*Daisy Maze bracelet
by Sharon Batema*

Daisy Maze

Suzanne Golden

Materials
Size 11° seed beads in two colors, A and B
4mm or larger round beads
Size B Nymo or Silamide beading thread

Notions
Size 12 beading or sharps needle
Scissors

This cheerful bracelet is made up of lines of daisy chains, cleverly connected and finished off with beaded beads. Your needle will go in several different directions while making the chains, so be sure to note the difference between "pass through" and "pass back through."

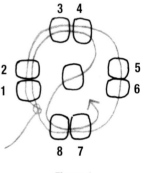

Step 1: Using a yard of thread, string 8 A and tie into a circle. Pass through the first 4 beads just strung.

Step 2: String 1 B. Pass back through the eighth and seventh beads strung in Step 1 (Figure 1).

Figure 1

Step 3: Pass back through the bead strung in Step 2. Pass through the fifth and sixth beads strung in Step 1.

Step 4: String 2 B. Pass through the fifth and sixth beads strung in Step 1 and the beads just strung.

Step 5: String 2 A and repeat Step 4.

Step 6: String 6 beads and repeat Step 1, using the 2 A strung in Step 5 as the first and second beads of your circle (Figure 2).

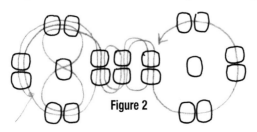

Figure 2

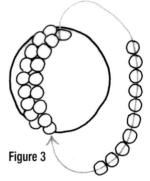

Figure 3

Step 7: Make 5 daisy chains your desired bracelet length. Allow some room for the clasp. Make two chains with the main color A, and 3 with the main color B.

Step 8: Using 1½' of thread and leaving an 8" tail, string a 4mm round bead. String enough size 11° beads to reach from the top hole to the bottom hole. Pass through the hole again, pulling tight (Figure 3). Continue adding beads and passing through the hole until you've covered the round bead with size 11°s. When you've finished wrapping, string 3 size 11°s and pass back though the round bead. Tie a square knot with the tail to secure the thread. Make enough of these beaded beads to embellish the edge of your bracelet plus two for the clasp.

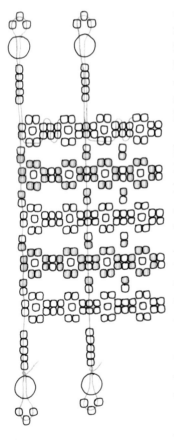

Step 9: Follow the illustration (Figure 4) to assemble the bracelet, using the long tails of the beaded beads to connect the chains. String 5 size 11°s and pass through 2 beads of a chain, string 2 size 11°s and pass through two beads of the next chain. Repeat and tie off each as you go.

Step 10: Add loop and bead clasps along the ends.

Suzanne Golden finds many aspects of beading that she enjoys. From forming the idea and finding the right colors to working with her hands and delighting in the finished work. And never underestimate the anticipation when looking at trays and trays of beads, glorious beads.

Figure 4

Simply Sparkly

Bill Monaghan

Materials
Twenty-five 4mm crystals
70 round 3mm beads
Size 11° seed beads
Silamide beading thread
Clasp

Notions
Size 12 beading needle
Scissors

Simply crystals and sparkle—and oh, so easy to make.

Step 1: String one 3mm, 1 size 11°, one 3mm, 1 size 11°, one 3mm, 1 size 11°, one 3mm, 1 size 11°. Pass through all again and tie a knot. Trim the tail thread and pass through the nearest 3mm and size 11°.

Step 2: *String one 3mm, 1 size 11°, one 3mm, 1 size 11°, and one 3mm. Pass through the size 11°, 3mm, and size 11° you exited in the last step and the next 4 beads of the 5 just added (Figure 1). Repeat from * working in a figure-eight pattern to reach the desired length of the bracelet less the width of the clasp.

Step 3: String 5 size 11°s, 1 crystal, 7 size 11°s, one side of the clasp, and 5 size 11°s. Pass back through the first two beads added after the crystal and the crystal. String 5 size 11°s and pass through the last three-bead set added on the last set made in the previous step.

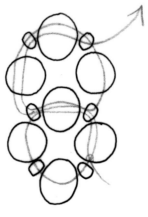

Figure 1

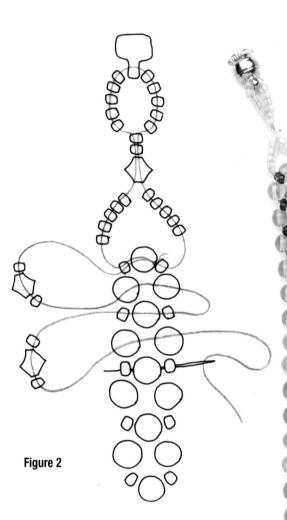

Figure 2

Step 4: *String 1 size 11°, 1 crystal, 1 size 11° and pass through the next three-bead set of the bracelet (Figure 2). Repeat from * for the length of the bracelet.

Step 5: Repeat Step 3 for the second side of the clasp.

Bill Monaghan is the bead gnome forever stuck in the back room filling tubes, but when his boss/wife isn't looking, he occasionally gets to play with the beads.

Cuffed

Jean Campbell

Materials

14-gauge silver wire
18-gauge silver wire
Assorted beads including pressed glass, pearls,
    and liquid silver
8½" wide paper

Notions

Scissors
Pencil
Wire cutter
Needle-nose pliers

Create this fanciful wire cuff in an evening. Let the beads be
your design guide.

Step 1: Cut the bottom of the paper the width you'd like your
final bracelet to be. The bracelet shown is 2" wide. Place the
paper around your wrist and mark the length you'd like your
bracelet to be. The result should be a long thin piece of paper.

Step 2: Beginning at the upper left corner of the paper's rec-
tangular shape, lay the 14-gauge wire across the length of the
paper. When you reach the first corner, use the needle-nose
pliers to bend a 90-degree angle. Continue around the perime-
ter of the rectangle, making bends at the corners. When you
finish the last corner, leave enough wire to run across the
length of the rectangle and cut the wire.

Step 3: Take the wires that lie across the top of the rectangle
and make two twists at the center (Figure 1). Bend them back
and coil them on themselves (Figure 2).

Figure 1

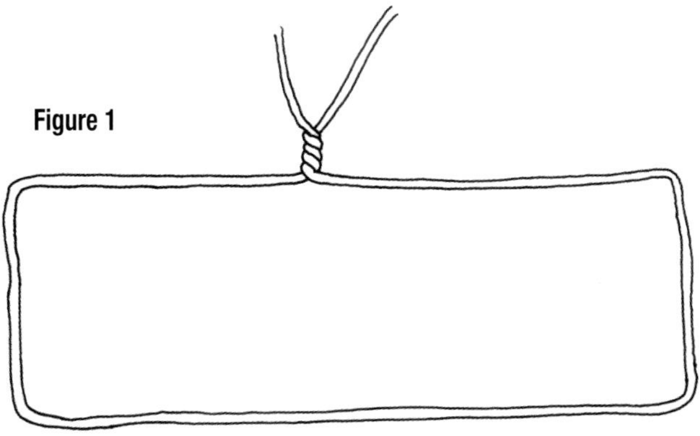

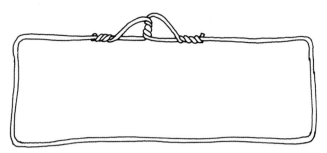

Figure 2

Step 4: Cut an 8" length of 18-gauge wire and begin a coil at one edge of the wire rectangle (Figure 3). Slide on enough beads to reach the other edge of the wire rectangle. Attach the beads by coiling the 18-gauge wire around the 14-gauge wire. Continue adding beads and weaving back and forth on the rectangle. Also weave from one 18-gauge length to another. If you find you need more wire for weaving, simply end the

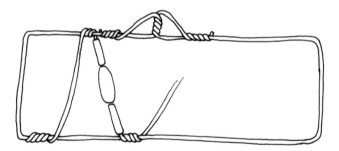

Figure 3

old one by coiling it off and trimming it close to the wire. Start a new one by repeating Step 3.

Three Step Bracelet

Margo C. Field

Materials
Delica beads
Size 15° seed beads
Size 11° seed beads
Button for clasp
Size B Nymo or Silamide beading thread

Notions
Size 10 and 12 beading needles
Scissors

This bracelet is made by creating a band of flat peyote three Delicas wide, which is then embellished with size 15° seed beads. The result is a delicate but sophisticated-looking chain.

PEYOTE WORK

Step 1: Using 2 yards of waxed single thread and leaving a 2' tail, string 2 Delicas. Pass through the first bead just strung.

Step 2: String 3 Delicas. Pass through the second bead just strung.

Step 3: Reinforce the beads by passing back through the fifth, third, second, and first beads to make the beads look like a capital I (Figure 1).

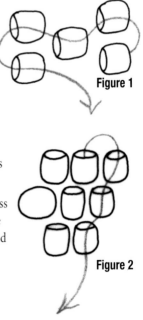

Figure 1

Step 4: String 1 size 11° and pass through the fourth and fifth beads.

Step 5: String 1 Delica and pass through the second bead.

Step 6: String 1 Delica and pass through the bead strung in the previous step and the edge bead on the diagonal (Figure 2).

Figure 2

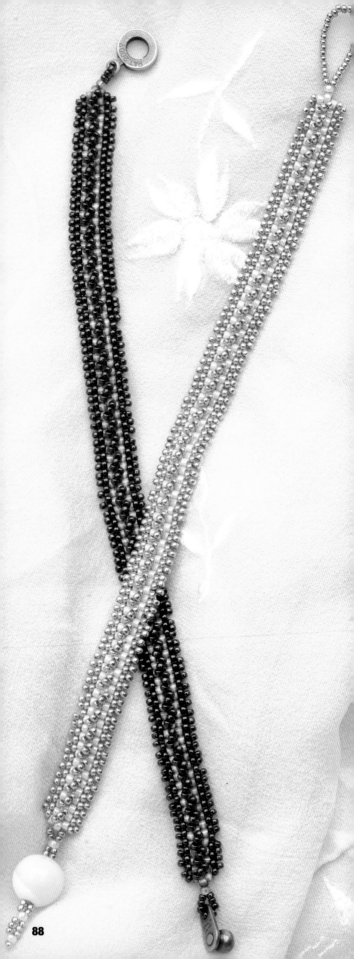

Figure 3

Step 7: String 1 Delica and pass through the center bead and the edge bead on the diagonal (Figure 3).

Step 8: Pass through the next edge bead. String 1 Delica and pass through the edge bead on the other side.

Step 9: Repeat Steps 6–8 until you reach the desired length and be sure that the center bead total is an odd number. Allow a space for your clasp. Finish with the last bead added being a size 11° as in Step 4.

APPLIQUÉ

Exiting from the center end size 11°, string 3 size 15°s. Skip the next center bead and pass through the second center bead in the same direction so that the thread exits from the same side of the bead as it did before. This will make the three beads lie diagonally. Continue to the other end. Note: You will be using all the odd-count center beads and will end up in the size 11° at the beginning end.

EDGING

Step1: Weave through the beads so that the thread exits from the first edge bead of the three-bead peyote strip. String 3 size 15°s. Pass under the first exposed thread loop at the edge and pass back through the third bead.

Figure 4

Step 2: String 2 size 15°s. Pass under the next exposed thread loop and pass back through the second bead. Repeat the two-bead step to the end (Figure 4).

Repeat the same steps on the other side.

Use the tail thread to attach a basic button and loop clasp.

Margo C. Field "discovered" beads in 1990. After retiring from a career in Hospital Pharmacy, she opened Poppy Field Bead Company in Albuquerque, New Mexico. She teaches classes at her store and workshops across the United States.

Tips

BUTTON/BEAD AND LOOP CLASP

Here's how to make a good-looking clasp with the beads you're already using on your bracelet.

Materials
Size 11° seed beads
Button or bead that measures 12mm or so
Beading thread

Notions
Size 12 beading needle
Scissors

Step 1: Sew a button or bead at one end of your bracelet.
Step 2: Start a thread at the other end of your bracelet and exit from one of the center beads.
Step 3: String a loop of seed beads just long enough to allow the button or bead at the other end to fit in snugly.
Step 4: Sew back into the bead you exited in Step 2.
Step 5: Pass through all the beads two more times to strengthen.
Step 6: Secure and trim thread.

STARTING A NEW THREAD

There's no doubt that you'll run out of thread as you work on your bracelets. It's easy to begin a new thread. There are a couple of solutions. I prefer the first way because it's stronger.

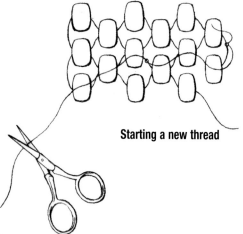

Starting a new thread

Solution 1: Tie off your old thread when it's about 4" long by making a simple knot between beads. Pass through a few beads and pull tight to hide the knot. Weave through a few more beads and trim the thread close to the work. Start the new thread by tying a knot between beads and weaving through a few beads. Pull tight to hide the knot. Weave through several beads until you reach the place to begin again.

Solution 2: Here's how to end your old thread without tying a knot. Weave the thread in and out, around and around, through several beads and then trim it close to the work. Begin a new thread the same way, weaving the end of the thread in and out, around and around, and through several beads until you reach the place to begin again.

PASSING THROUGH VS. PASSING BACK THROUGH

Passing through means that you are moving your needle in the same direction as the beads have been strung. Passing back through means that you are moving your needle opposite to the direction the beads have been strung.

TENSION BEAD

A tension bead (or stopper bead) holds your work in place. To make one, string a bead larger than those you are working with, then pass through the bead again, making sure not to split your thread. The bead will be able to slide along, but will still provide tension to work against.

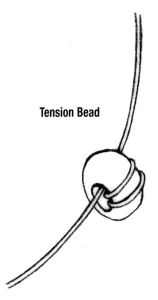

Tension Bead

Stitches

Brick stitch

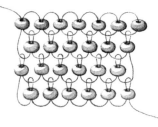

Begin by creating a foundation row in ladder stitch (see below). String one bead and pass through the closest exposed loop of the foundation row. Pass back through the same bead and continue, adding one bead at a time.

Ladder

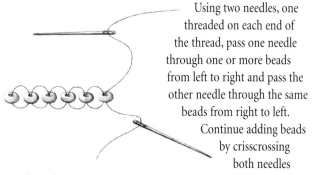

Using two needles, one threaded on each end of the thread, pass one needle through one or more beads from left to right and pass the other needle through the same beads from right to left. Continue adding beads by crisscrossing both needles through one bead at a time. Use this stitch to make strings of beads or as the foundation for brick stitch.

Loomwork

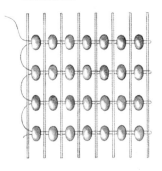

After warping your loom, use a separate thread ("weft") to string the number of beads needed for the first row. Bring the weft thread under the warp threads and push the beads up with your finger so there is one bead between each of two warp threads. Hold the beads in place, bring the weft thread over the warp threads, and pull back through all the beads. Repeat these steps for each row.

Netting

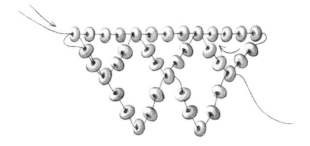

Begin by stringing a base row of 13 beads. String 5 beads and go back through the fifth bead from the end of the base row. String another 5 beads, skip 3 beads of the base row, and go back through the next. Rep to end of row. PT the fifth, fourth, and third beads of those just strung, exiting from the third. Turn the work over and go back across the same way.

Peyote stitch

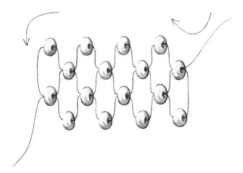

This stitch can also be referred to as gourd stitch.

One-drop peyote begins by stringing an even number of beads to create the first two rows. Begin the third row by stringing one bead and passing through the second-to-last bead of the previous rows. String another bead and pass through the fourth-to-last bead of the previous rows. Continue adding one bead at a time, passing over every other bead of the previous rows.

Two-drop peyote is worked the same as above, but with two beads at a time instead of one.

Right angle weave

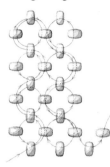

The illustration refers to bead positions, not bead numbers.

Row 1: String four base beads. Pass through beads in positions 1, 2, and 3. The bead in position 3 will become the bead in position 1 in the next group. String 3 beads. Pass through bead in position 3 of last group (now position 1 of this group), bead in position 2 and bead in position 3 (now position 1 of next group). String 3 beads. Continue working in this pattern until the row is to a desired length. In the last group, pass through beads in positions 1, 2, 3, and 4.

Row 2: String 3 beads. Pass through bead in position 4 of previous group and bead in position 1 of this group. String 2 beads. Pass through bead in position 2 of Row 1, bead in position 1 of previous group, and the beads just added. Pass through bead in position 4 of Row 1. String 2 beads. Pass through bead in position 2 of previous group and bead in position 4 of Row 1. Pass through first bead just added. String 2 beads. Pass through bead in position 2 of Row 1, bead in position 1 of previous group, and the first bead just added.

Row 3: Repeat Row 2.

Square stitch

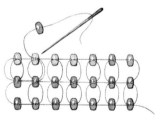

Square stitch

Begin by stringing a row of beads. For the second row, string 2 beads, pass through the second-to-last bead of the first row, and back through the second bead of those just strung. Continue by stringing 1 bead, passing through the third-to-last bead of the first row, and back through the bead just strung. Repeat this looping technique across to the end of the row.

To make a decrease, weave thread through the previous row and exit from the bead adjacent to the place you want to decrease. Continue working in square stitch.

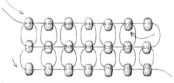

Square stitch decrease

Also available

THE
MAMMOTH BOOK OF

BEST NEW
HORROR

VOLUME FIFTEEN

Edited and with an Introduction by
STEPHEN JONES

CARROLL & GRAF PUBLISHERS
New York

Carroll & Graf Publishers
An imprint of Avalon Publishing Group, Inc.
245 W. 17th Street
New York
NY 10011_5300
www.carrollandgraf.com

AVALON
publishing group incorporated

First Carroll & Graf edition 2004
Reprinted 2006
First published in the UK by Robinson,
an imprint of Constable & Robinson Ltd 2004

ISBN 0–7867–1426–3
ISBN 978–0–78671–426–1

Printed and bound in the EU

CONTENTS

ACKNOWLEDGMENTS

I would like to thank David Barraclough, Kim Newman, Hugh Lamb, Nick Austin, Pete Duncan, Ellen Datlow, Gordon Van Gelder, Barbara Roden, Rodger Turner and Wayne MacLaurin (sfsite.com), David J. Schow, Dennis Etchison, Mandy Slater, Brian Mooney, Ray Russell, Ramsey Campbell, Richard Dalby, Sara and Randy Broecker, Robert T. Garcia, Andrew I. Porter, Kelly Link, Peter Coleborn, Douglas E. Winter, Basil Copper, Sue and Lou Irmo, Harris M. Lentz III, Andy Cox, Robert Morgan and David Pringle for all their help and support. Special thanks are also due to *Locus, Interzone, Classic Images, Variety* and all the other sources that were used for reference in the Introduction and the Necrology.

In memory of
Hugh B. Cave
(1910–2004)
Goodbye old friend.

INTRODUCTION

Horror in 2003

IN JANUARY 2003, AOL Time Warner posted the biggest loss in corporate history. The multi-media giant lost more than $100 billion (£60 billion), a figure larger than the gross domestic product of Egypt. The losses resulted in the resignations of both Chairman Steve Case and Vice-Chairman Ted Turner. When the combined company was formed just two years earlier, it was estimated to be worth £212 billion, since then shares have fallen seventy per cent. It was also announced that the company would phase out the "AOL" from its name by the end of the year.

Also in January, Chairman and CEO Peter Olson announced that he was merging the Random House Trade Group and Ballantine Books into one new company – Random House Ballantine Publishing Group, headed by President and Publisher Gina Centrello. Centrello took over from Ann Godoff, Editor-in-Chief of Random House since 1997, who was dismissed and her position eliminated.

According to the *New York Times*, Godoff had teamed with Centrello's Ballantine imprint to buy the rights to *Black House*, Stephen King and Peter Straub's sequel to *The Talisman*, for a reported advance of "well more than $10 million". *Black House* was released on 17 September 2001, shortly after the terrorist attacks on New York City and Washington. Book sales in general slumped following the tragedy, with horror particularly unpopular. Much of the book's publicity campaign was cancelled or reduced, and hardcover sales were described as "dismal", resulting in a multimillion-dollar loss for the Random House Trade

Group, which had consistently fallen short of its annual profit-ability targets.

In Britain, Pan Macmillan launched the Tor UK genre imprint in March with books by Neal Asher, Andy Secombe and New Zealand writer Juliet Marillier. Four months later, Simon & Schuster announced that it was terminating its UK genre imprint Earthlight by the end of the year and laying off seventy-five staff worldwide (the majority in the US). One of those to lose his job was Senior Editor Darren Nash, who took over the Earthlight line in August 2002 after the departure of founding editor John Jarrold.

In August, co-founder of Carroll & Graf and Vice-President of Avalon Publishing Group Herman Graf stepped down to become an editor-at-large. He was succeeded by former Senior Editor of Editorial, Will Balliet.

The following month, Arnaud Nourry, President and Director-General of Hachette Livre and Chairman of the Orion Publishing Group, announced that Anthony Cheetham was stepping down as Chief Executive of the Orion Publishing Group in the UK. Cheetham was one of the founders of Orion in 1991, along with Peter Roche, who replaced Cheetham as Chief Executive. Malcolm Edwards (who joined the company in 1998) took on the newly created role of Deputy Chief Executive and Publisher.

Towards the end of the year, the editorial department of NAL's Roc imprint was merged with that of Berkley/Ace following the resignation of Executive Editor Laura Anne Gilman, who left in November to pursue her writing career full-time.

According to the BBC, J.K. Rowling became the highest-paid author in history, doubling her annual income for the third year running and earning an estimated £125 million in 2003 or the equivalent of £388.00 for each word in *Harry Potter and the Order of the Phoenix*, which sold more than 230 million copies worldwide.

At 255,000 words and running to nearly 800 pages, Rowling's fifth book in the incredibly popular series was a third longer than the previous volume. For the first time, American publisher Scholastic printed a library edition with a reinforced spine, and fans could also buy one of 350,000 copies of a $60.00 deluxe edition that came with gold embossing, a slip cover, printed end-sheets and "special deckled edges".

The initial print run in America was 6.8 million for the launch date of 21 June, with a further 1.7 million available two weeks later. A synchronized worldwide campaign meant that it was the biggest book launch of all time, with pre-orders outselling any new book in US publishing history. However, that didn't prevent Scholastic from making a four per cent cut in its global workforce in May.

British publisher Bloomsbury subsequently acknowledged that the record-breaking success of *Harry Potter and the Order of the Phoenix* during the first few days of release would set the template for forthcoming books in the series. The company's sales leaped twenty-two per cent to £83.1 million in 2003, with more than £12.5 million generated by Rowling's hardcover.

Although Stephen King praised the author as "bursting with crazily vivid ideas and having the time of her life", prizewinning author A.S. Byatt was accused of professional jealousy when she dismissed the book in the *New York Times* as being "written for people whose imaginative lives are confined to TV cartoons and the exaggerated – more exciting, less threatening – mirror world of soaps, reality TV and celebrity gossip."

In February, the Vatican gave its official blessing to the adventures of Harry Potter, saying that Roman Catholics could enjoy them with a clear conscience. "They are not bad or a banner for anti-Christian ideology," said a spokesman. "They help children understand the difference between good and evil." Two months later, an Arkansas judge ruled that the *Potter* novels did not promote witchcraft and ordered the Little Rock school board to put the books back on library shelves.

However, even though *God, the Devil and Harry Potter* was a defence of the series written by Christian minister John Killinger, it was announced that the *Harry Potter* series once again topped 2002's "Most Challenged Books" list, issued by the American Library Association for Banned Books Week in September. According to a spokesperson, detractors continued to claim that the books "glamorize the occult and will attract (readers) to Satanism."

Meanwhile, according to Rowling's agent Christopher Little, the five books in the *Potter* series had collectively sold more than a quarter of a billion copies and had been translated into sixty languages. Yet when Rowling's estranged father attempted to sell seven first-edition presentation copies of the *Potter* books at auction in December, the volumes made just £50,000 after three failed to sell. Sotheby's was reportedly expecting the sale to reach £120,000.

As a real sign of her success, the normally reserved Rowling voiced a cartoon version of herself in an episode of the Fox Network's *The Simpsons*, in which the dysfunctional family visited England.

Stephen King's first "Dark Tower" novel, *The Gunslinger*, was reissued in June in a greatly revised and expanded edition with changes to almost every page, including deletions and an extra three new scenes totalling nearly 9,000 words. There was a new Introduction to the series by the author that also appeared in reprint editions of the three sequels.

The fifth volume in the sequence, *The Dark Tower V: Wolves of the Calla*, appeared in November. The novel included a surprise reappearance of a major character from King's earlier *'Salem's Lot*.

The book was initially published by Donald M. Grant in a limited "Artist Edition" of 3,500 copies signed by illustrator Bernie Wrightson, and a 1,300 copy deluxe boxed edition signed by both King and Wrightson for $175.00. The Scribner trade hardcover of *Wolves of the Calla* was co-published with Grant and went into a third edition in its first week, with 735,000 copies in print.

Stephen King's The Dark Tower: A Concordance Vol.1 by the author's research assistant, Robin Furth, covered the first four books in the series and included a Foreword by King.

On 19 November, King was presented with the National Book Foundation's Medal for Distinguished Contribution to American Letters in a controversial move designed to expand the NBA's definition of "American Letters". The author received a standing ovation from the 900-plus audience. Previous recipients include John Updike, Arthur Miller, Philip Roth and Ray Bradbury.

King had previously responded to the award with the observation: "This is probably the most exciting thing to happen to me in my career as a writer since the sale of my first book in 1973." He decided to return the $10,000 cash award, but kept the medal which he would ". . . treasure for the rest of my life."

However, Harold Bloom, a Yale professor and critic, lashed out at the decision, comparing King with Charles Dickens: "He is a man who writes what used to be called penny dreadfuls. That they could believe that there is any literary value there or any aesthetic accomplishment or signs of an inventive human intelligence is simply a testimony to their own idiocy."

Neil Gaiman subsequently stepped into the fray with his pithy observation: "Harold Bloom is a twerp."

On 23 November King was admitted to hospital suffering from pneumonia. He had surgery to remove scar tissue and fluid from his right lung, apparently connected to the accident in 1999 that almost killed him, and was released in December after twenty-five days of treatment.

Meanwhile, "The Stephen King Horror Library" offered hardcover book club editions of *The Haunting of Hill House* by Shirley Jackson, *Rosemary's Baby* by Ira Levin and *Ghost Story* by Peter Straub, all with reprint Introductions by King. King also had a new story, "Rest Stop", in the December issue of *Esquire* magazine.

Anne Rice announced that her twenty-fifth book, *Blood Canticle*, which was a sequel to *Blackwood Farm* and a crossover with the "Mayfair Witches" series, would be the last of her "Vampire Chronicles". The initial print run of 300,000 copies was quickly supplemented with a second printing of a further 16,000 copies.

lost boy lost girl was Peter Straub's first (albeit short) horror novel since 1999 and concerned a long-abandoned house with an evil history and a serial killer terrorizing a Wisconsin town. It reintroduced two characters from the author's previous works.

James Herbert's *Nobody True* involved a man who returned from an out-of-body experience only to discover that he had been brutally murdered. His spirit then watched over his family as they were stalked by a disfigured serial killer. A three-hour audio version was also available, and film rights were optioned for a high six-figure sum.

A short-order cook discovered that he could communicate with the dead in Dean Koontz's *Odd Thomas*, while *The Blind Mirror* by bestselling YA author Christopher Pike was an adult horror-thriller about an aspiring book-cover artist accused of ritually murdering his mysterious girlfriend.

Come Fygures, Come Shadowes was a previously unpublished opening section of an abandoned novel by veteran Richard Matheson, published as a slim hardcover by Gauntlet Press in a signed edition of just 500 copies. It involved a young girl being groomed to become a professional medium by her spiritualist mother in 1930s New York.

From Subterranean Press, *Off Beat: Uncollected Stories* contained eleven tales (four original) by Matheson along with a personal Introduction and checklist of first editions by William F. Nolan. It was available in a signed, limited edition of 750 copies, and a fifty-two-copy lettered and traycased edition with an extra story for $200.00.

Let's All Kill Constance was Ray Bradbury's sequel-of-sorts to *Death is a Lonely Business*, about a 1960s novelist tracking down an old film star and unravelling her Books of the Dead.

Bradbury Stories: 100 of His Most Celebrated Tales was exactly what it claimed on the dust jacket, along with an Introduction by the author. The final publication from Stealth Press was *They Have Seen the Stars: The Collected Poetry of Ray Bradbury* which gathered 167 poems and another new Foreword by Bradbury.

Bradbury also told the *New York Daily News* that he was never a science fiction writer, claiming that he really wrote science-based fantasy.

Into the Woods and *Hidden Leaves* were the fourth and fifth volumes in the "De Beers" series credited to V.C. Andrews® (Andrew Niederman). The latter book also included *Dark Seed*, only previously available as an e-book. *Broken Wings* and *Midnight Flight* comprised a new two-part Gothic series by the prolific, long-dead author.

David J. Schow's *Bullets of Rain*, which was billed as "a novel of suspense" by the HarperCollins imprint Dark Alley, was about a reclusive widower who began to lose touch with reality. Schow's other new novel of the year was *Rock Breaks Scissors Cut*, which involved an experimental sleep-research project that awakened hidden memories within its subjects. Illustrated by Caniglia, the book was published in a signed, limited edition of 750 numbered copies and twenty-six lettered copies by Subterranean Press.

A sequel-of-sorts to *Threshold*, and featuring some of the same characters, Caitlín R. Kiernan's *Low Red Moon* was a serial-killer novel set in an alternate world where the events of the earlier book never happened.

In *The Restless Dead*, a fun paperback original by veteran pulp author Hugh B. Cave, a university professor investigated a decaying old mansion and its reclusive family lingering under a voodoo curse. A female lawyer returned to Tananarive Due's *The Good House* to learn the secrets of another voodoo curse, an apparently homeless girl and a mysterious clearing in the woods.

From Five Star, *Eternal City* by Nancy Kilpatrick and Michael Kilpatrick was a novel about sinister happenings in the Canadian woods surrounding a mysterious gated community, and an eccentric billionaire and his guests spent the night in a building with an evil history in Dale Bailey's *House of Bones*,

Published posthumously with an anecdotal Introduction by Dean Koontz, Richard Laymon's *Amara* was about the eponymous living mummy of a 4,000-year-old princess of Egypt.

Originally published as a print-on-demand title, Sara Stamey's *Islands* was reissued in a substantially revised edition. It concerned an archaeologist's visit to a Caribbean island to discover how her brother drowned, and the various ancient mysteries she uncovered.

In *Tropic of Night* by Michael Gruber, an anthropologist hiding under an assumed identity in Miami teamed up with a Cuban-American police detective when she was pursued by her ex-husband, a serial-killing African shaman.

Charlee Jacob's *Haunter* involved Cambodian demons released in west Texas, and *Fire & Flesh* by Evan Kingsbury (Robert W. Walker) was about a series of bizarre incendiary deaths that were linked by a detective and a medical examiner to a legendary serpent god.

Wither's Rain by John ("J.G.") Passarella was a sequel to the author's earlier *Wither*, and Karen Michalson's *Hecate's Glory* was a sequel to *Enemy Glory* and once agin featured evil cleric Llewelyn.

The Lamp of the Wicked was the fifth volume in Phil Rickman's series about parish exorcist the Reverend Merrily Watkins who, with the help of musician Lol Robinson, investigated the connection between a confessed serial killer and a small English village dealing with alleged angelic visitations.

A crashed government satellite affected the adult inhabitants of a small Northern California town in John Shirley's *Crawlers*. J.D. Landis's *The Taking* was set in a small town that was about to be flooded, while the quirky inhabitants of a small Appalachian mountain town were menaced by a creeping alien virus in Scott Nicholson's *The Harvest*.

A supernatural evil haunted a small Mississippi town in *Dark Corner* by Brandon Massey, a 300-year-old evil invaded a New England town in *Don't Close Your Eyes* by Robert Ross, and yet another evil force threatened a California town in Darrin Wilson's *Pine Shallow: The Serpent Prophecies*.

Still Life with Crows by Douglas Preston and Lincoln Child was about a string of strange murders in another small town. A bio-engineered creature stalked the city's sewers in *The Unnatural* by Alan Nayes, and David Bergantino's *Bard's Blood: Midsummer Night's Scream* featured a sinister carnival coming to town in the second volume in a series.

A young orphan discovered a world of lost children behind her wallpaper in Graham Masterton's *Hidden World*, while a female police detective investigated a series of ritual murders in the same author's *A Terrible Beauty*. Masterton's 1998 thriller *Genius* (originally published under the pseudonym "Alan Blackwood") was reissued in hardcover.

In T.M. Wright's *Laughing Man*, unpredictable New York City detective Jack Erthmun investigated a series of grisly murders committed by an apparently inhuman killer. From the same author came *The House on Orchard Street*.

A detective continued to pursue a body-hopping demon in W.G. Griffiths's *Takedown*, a sequel to *Driven*, while in *Bed of Nails*, Michael Slade's Special X Mountie, Inspector Zinc Chandler, pitted his wits against an old nemesis with the World Horror Convention as a backdrop.

A musician returned for a Hallowe'en concert in Salem in Shannon Drake's *The Awakening*, and a singer confronted the supernatural in *Echo and Narcissus* by Mark Siegal.

The Fury and the Power was the third in "The Fury" series by John Farris, featuring a girl with the power to create her own doppelgänger.

Something very deadly was kept cryogenically frozen beneath the Pentagon in *Sleeper* by Steve Harriman (Steven Spruill). A military experiment involving psychic powers went wrong in *Shadow Game* by Christine Feehan, and a psychic woman travelled back in time to 1968 while looking for her kidnapped daughter in T.J. MacGregor's *Black Water*.

Jim Brown's *Black Valley* featured an immortal time-travelling serial killer. A mysterious stranger came into a family's life in *The Deceiver* by Melanie Tem, and a series of paedophile child murders were at the core of Shaun Hutson's *Hell to Pay*.

Bentley Little's *The Policy* concerned a protection racket from Hell, and a scriptwriter encountered his long-dead parents in *Strangers*, translated by Wayne P. Lammers from Taichi Yamada's 1987 Japanese novel *Ijin-tachi to no Natsu*.

A suicidal ghost-hunter fell in love with a woman dead for eighty years in *Second Glance* by Jodi Picoult, and a woman thought she might have been possessed in *Come Closer* by Sara Gran.

Irish writer John Connolly's *Bad Men* involved policeman Melancholy Joe Dupree, a sufferer from genetic gigantism, protecting a woman and her son from escaped serial killer Moloch on the mysterious Maine island of Sanctuary. The novel even included a brief cameo by Connolly's usual protagonist, offbeat detective Charlie "Bird" Parker.

Psychic detective Cree Black investigated a reputedly haunted house in New Orleans in Daniel Hecht's *City of Masks*, while down-at-heel private investigator John Taylor searched for a runaway in an otherworldly area of London where it was always 3:00 a.m. in Simon R. Green's *Something from the Nightside*, the first in a new hard-boiled mystery series.

Edo van Belkom's *Scream Queen* was about a competition to become a horror-film star in a real haunted house, and a family's country house was haunted by a woman searching for her past in *The Awakening* by Donna Boyd.

A Stir of Bones by Nina Kiriki Hoffman was also about a haunted house and was a prequel to the author's *A Red Heart of Memories*, while Susie Moloney's *The Dwelling* was a haunted-house novel that concentrated on the building's various residents and their realtor. It was originally published in the UK under the title *362 Belisle St.*

The Sorority was the overall title of Tamara Thorne's trilogy about a secret society of witches. In Christine Feehan's *The Twilight Before Christmas*, a novelist and her witchy sisters confronted an ancient evil threatening a small town, and a witch was asked by a ghost to solve a murder in Yasmine Galenorn's mystery *Ghost of a Chance*.

Don Festge's *Night of the Witches* series kicked off with *The Beginnings* and *The Bocor*, and was about a 17th-century woman using voodoo to revenge herself on those who raped her.

The Witches of Chiswick was another comedy novel by Robert Rankin, in which a cabal of Victorian witches rewrote 19th-century history with the help of super-computers.

David Bergantino's *Hamlet II: Ophelia's Revenge* involved a haunted Danish castle, while Ray Gordon's *Dark Desires* was an erotic horror story set inside yet another haunted house.

Anita Blake, Vampire Hunter, was forced by a magic spell to have sex twice a day in *Cerulean Sins*, the eleventh volume in the popular series by Laurell K. Hamilton. The book had a first hardcover printing of 100,000 copies and quickly went back to press three times for an additional 33,000 copies.

Midnight Harvest was the sixteenth novel in Chelsea Quinn Yarbro's Chronicles of Saint-Germain, set during the 1930s Great Depression, where vampire Ferenc Rogoczy once again encountered one of the great loves of his life, Rowena Saxon, while being tracked by a ruthless assassin.

Cold Streets was the latest volume in P.N. Elrod's *The Vampire Files* series and involved vampire detective Jack Fleming in a gang war in 1938 Chicago. Elrod's earlier novels in the series, *Bloodlist*, *Lifeblood* and *Bloodcircle*, were collected in the omnibus *The Vampire Files: Volume One*.

Death Masks by Jim Butcher was the fifth volume in the "Dresden Files", in which Chicago wizard Harry Dresden searched for the stolen Shroud of Turin while preparing to battle a vampire to the death.

Simon Clark returned to the desolate North Yorkshire moors for another tale of the undead in *Vampyrrhic Rites*, and Christopher Golden continued his "Shadow Saga" about former-vampire-turned-mage Peter Octavian with the fourth volume, *The Gathering Dark*.

James M. Thompson's *Immortal Blood* was the third volume in the series that began with *Night Blood*, while *The Destructor* and *The Syndicate* were the third and fourth books to feature Jon F. Merz's vampire "fixer" Lawson.

Robin McKinley's *Sunshine* was about the eponymous heroine's encounter with a handsome vampire who needed her help, and a New Zealand investigator stumbled upon a community of Gallic vampires while on vacation in Elizabeth Knox's *Daylight*.

Barb and J.C. Hendee's *Dhampir* featured bogus vampire-hunter Magiere and her half-elf partner Leesil who discovered they were suddenly being pursued by real vampires. It went through six printings in a year from Roc.

Club Dead was the third volume in Charlaine Harris's series of lightweight "Southern Vampire" mysteries. This time, accompanied by a handsome werewolf and an undead Elvis, telepathic waitress Sookie Stackhouse went looking for her kidnapped vampire boyfriend Bill. All three books were collected in the Science Fiction Book Club omnibus *Dead in Dixie*.

Wm. Mark Simmons's *Dead on My Feet* was a humorous sequel to *One Foot in the Grave*, about a man who accidentally received an undead blood transfusion, and Andrew Fox's comedic debut novel *Fat White Vampire Blues* was set in New Orleans and featured an overweight bloodsucker who found himself in a conflict with black vampire activists.

Craven Moon concluded Billie Sue Mosiman's "Vampire Nation" trilogy, and *Crimson Shadows* was the final volume in Trisha Baker's trilogy about twin children, one human and the other vampire.

From the author of *I, Vampire*, Michael Romkey's *The Vampire's Violin* featured the undead Dylan Glyndwr in search of a legendary musical instrument.

Nocturne was the latest volume in Elaine Bergstrom's "Austra Family" series, and a singer battled vampires threatening her record company in *Minion*, the first in the "Vampire Huntress Legends" series by L.A. Banks (Leslie Esdale-Banks a.k.a. "Leslie E. Banks"). It was followed by *The Awakening*.

Area 51: Nosferatu, the most recent volume in the series by Robert Doherty (Bob Mayer), was a simultaneous paperback and e-book release. *Way of the Wolf* by E.E. Knight (Eric E. Frisch) was the first volume of "The Vampire Earth", in which an invasion by soul-sucking aliens was opposed by a resistence group known as the Wolves. It was originally published as an e-book.

Karen Harbaugh's romantic *Night Fires* was about reluctant vampire Simone de la Fer, roaming the French countryside, who couldn't resist a human spy. *Dark Enchantment* was a sequel, in which notorious French swordswoman Catherine de la Fer and English mercenary Jack Marstone teamed up in a daring act of rescue.

Night Embrace was the second volume in the "Dark-Hunters" vampire romance series by Sherrilyn Kenyon (a.k.a. "Kinley MacGregor"), set during the New Orleans Mardi Gras. It was followed by *Dance With the Devil*, which also included a short story.

Christine Feehan's *Dark Symphony* was the latest volume in the "Dark" series of romantic vampire novels about an ancient race called the Carpathians, and there were more romantic vampires in Susan Sizemore's *I Burn for You*. *Laws of the Blood: Heroes* was the fifth in Sizemore's series about vampire "Enforcers".

His Immortal Embrace collected four vampire romances by Hannah Howell, Lynsay Sands, Sara Blayne and Kate Huntington.

Vampire Thrall was Michael Schiefelbein's sequel to the equally gay *Vampire Vow*, and *Masters of Midnight: Erotic Tales of the Vampire* was an omnibus of four gay vampire novellas by William J. Mann, Michael Thomas Ford, Sean Wolfe and Jeff Mann.

An undead Marquis de Sade moved in with a suburban family of bloodsuckers in Mary Ann Mitchell's *Tainted Blood*, while Morven Westfield's *Darksome Thirst* was a first novel.

Kelley Armstrong's novel *Stolen* was about a female werewolf and was a sequel to the author's *Bitten*.

Set in 19th-century Boston, Matthew Pearl's debut novel *The Dante Club* featured a number of real historical figures on the trail of a serial killer inspired by images from Dante Alighieri's seminal work.

Kunma was the novel debut of 79-year-old New York stage director Frank Corsaro and involved the eponymous Buddhist demon. *Jinn* was a first novel by Matthew B.J. Delaney, about a supernatural killer plaguing Boston, and a woman suspected that her new boyfriend was really Satan in *Devil May Care* by Sheri McInnis.

A pair of siblings attempted to escape from their evil father in Tim Vargo's *Unbound*, published by Willowgate Press. A dead Los Angeles teenager regretted his early death in Michael Scott

Moore's first book, *Too Much of Nothing*, while a man destroyed most of the world's population in *Noble Savage* by Liz Moore.

Australian writer K.J. Bishop made her debut with the baroque dark fantasy *The Etched City*, published by Prime Books.

Published as a mainstream title, *Full Dark House* was the first "Bryant & May" mystery by Christopher Fowler, in which the solution to a case involving London's longest-serving detectives dated back to the Blitz. The characters previously appeared in Fowler's novels *Rune* and *Darkest Day*.

The Lamplighter by Anthony O'Neill involved a series of horrific murders in 19th-century Edinburgh and a troubled young woman who claimed to have dreamed of the crimes.

The Mistressclass was a literary ghost novel by Michèle Roberts, as was *The Night Country* by Stewart O'Nan, narrated by a number of teenagers on the eve of the anniversary of their death.

In Louis Baynard's *Mr Timothy*, the adult Tiny Tim was haunted by his father's death in a dark-fantasy sequel to Charles Dickens's *A Christmas Carol*, and a woman's father used Egyptian magic to force his unfaithful wife to return in Rikki Ducornet's *Gazelle*.

In Jasper Fforde's *The Well of Lost Plots*, the third adventure of Thursday Next, the Literary Detective was hiding out in an unpublished novel when the much-awaited upgrade to the centuries-old book system resulted in multiple murders.

According to online bookseller Amazon, when *The Lord of the Rings* won the much-hyped BBC-TV show *The Big Read* with fewer than half a million votes cast during the 13 December final, sales of DVDs and videos of the top titles increased far more than the sale of books.

Inspired by the idiosyncratic list of 100 favourite books announced during *The Big Read* campaign, UK bookstore chain W.H. Smith launched a paperback series of "Little Reads", reprinting the first chapter of selected books as a £1.00 "sampler". Titles included *The Lord of the Rings*, *The Hobbit*, *Alice in Wonderland*, *The Lion, The Witch and The Wardrobe* and *Lord of the Flies*.

The "Penguin Classics" series continued with new editions of *Dracula* by Bram Stoker and *The Fall of the House of Usher and Other Writings* by Edgar Allan Poe, with updated appendices and other material.

Published as part of Pocket Books's "Enriched Classics" series, a new paperback edition of Stoker's *Dracula* included quotes from reviews and critical works (1897–2002), plus notes and an Introduction by editor Joseph Valente. *Great Tales and Poems of Edgar Allan Poe*, also published by Pocket, collected twenty-one stories and thirty-four poems, along with excerpts from twenty critical writings on Poe and a suggested further reading list.

Barnes & Noble's "Collector's Library" of mini-hardcovers published Poe's *Tales of Mystery and Imagination*, collecting twenty-two stories and a new Afterword by Ponty Claypole. New editions of Bram Stoker's *Dracula* and Oscar Wilde's *The Picture of Dorian Gray* were also available in the same format, with Afterwords by Claypole and Peter Harness, respectively.

Paul Féval's 1875 vampire novel *Le Chevalier Ténèbre* appeared as *Knightshade* from Black Coat Press, translated with a lengthy Introduction and Afterword by Brian Stableford. The same imprint also issued Féval's novels *Vampire City* and *The Vampire Countess*, also translated by Stableford.

From Stark House, *The Lost Valley and Other Stories* was a reprint of Algernon Blackwood's 1910 collection of ten stories with a new Introduction by Simon Clark, while *Pan's Garden* reprinted Blackwood's 1912 collection of fifteen nature stories with an Introduction by Mike Ashley.

Casting the Runes and Other Ghost Stories was a reprint of the 1987 collection by M.R. James edited by Michael Cox, with a new Introduction by Michael Chabon.

Featuring such stories as "The Lurking Fear", "Cool Air" and "Herbert West – Reanimator", *Wake Up Screaming* was another re-packaged and retitled compendium of thirteen stories by H.P. Lovecraft from Del Rey. Published by Gateways Retro Science Fiction imprint, *None But Lucifer* was a welcome reissue of the classic deal-with-the-Devil tale by Horace L. Gold and L. Sprague de Camp, originally serialized in *Unknown* in 1939.

Supernatural Tales: Excursions into Fantasy was a reprint of the 1955 Peter Owen collection of six stories by Vernon Lee (Violet Paget), with an Introduction by Irene Cooper Willis.

Seen as a response to the *Harry Potter* phenomenon, America's HarperCollins Children's Books launched an Eos young-adult

line in January. The adult and children's lines were run and
marketed separately but remained closely linked.

Del Rey's trade paperback young-adult line Imagine made its
debut in the Spring and included reissues of Del Rey titles deemed
suitable for young teenagers, which sometimes resulted in minor
editing. Prospective titles were evaluated by Random House
School & Library to ensure suitability.

Following the Starscape imprint, Tor Teen was a second YA
mass-market line from Tor Books, launched in July for ages twelve
and upwards. Once again, the list included reprints of adult titles
considered suitable for teenagers, along with original books.

Predictably hyped as "hotter than Potter" by the British tabloid
press, *Shadowmancer* was initially self-published in 2002 by the
Reverend Graham Taylor under the byline "G.P. Taylor" before
the title was picked up by Faber and Faber in the UK. Although the
book involved an evil 18th-century clergyman and sorcerer, three
years earlier the author had complained that "The problem with
the Harry Potter books is that at the core of the subject is the occult,
nicely dressed up and sanitized and made all chummy". *Shadowmancer* subsequently sold to Penguin in the US for $500,000.

In settlement of a 1997 legal dispute, Scholastic Corp. agreed to
pay Parachute Press $9.65 million for the "Goosebumps" trade-
mark and the right to publish and develop all existing and future
titles in the R.L. Stine series.

Meanwhile, in Stine's *The Sitter*, a nanny suspected that her
young charge had been possessed, and a pair of twins appeared to
be turning into vampires in the author's *Dangerous Girls*.

Killers of the Dawn and *The Lake of Souls* were the ninth and
tenth volumes, respectively, in *The Saga of Darren Shan*, credited
to the book's young protagonist (actually Darren O'Shaugh-
nessy). The first three books in the series were collected in the
omnibus *Vampire Blood Trilogy*.

A teenage Goth suspected that the new family in town were
bloodsuckers in *Vampire Kisses* by Ellen Schreiber, while *Piggies*
by Nick Gifford (Keith Brooke) was set in an alternate world
populated by vampires.

Patrick Jennings's *The Wolving Time* was about a family of
werewolves in 16th-century France, and a boy's parents may have
been killed at sea by a legendary New Jersey devil in Carol Plum-
Ucci's *The She*.

The Whistle, The Grave and The Ghost by Brad Strickland was the latest adventure in the "Lewis Barnavelt" series created by the late John Bellairs. *Haunted: A Tale of the Mediator* was the fifth volume in the series about a girl who speaks to the dead by Meg Cabot (a.k.a. "Jenny Carroll"), and a young girl was worried about her sister's attempts to contact the dead in *Starry Nights* by Judith Clarke.

In Martin Chatterton's *Michigan Moorcroft R.I.P.*, a teenager woke up dead and discovered that things were not much different, while a teen athlete's dead brother watched over him in Rich Wallace's *Restless*.

A girl mourning the death of her best friend encountered a ghost in *The Presence* by Eve Bunting, *Dark Secrets: The Deep End of Fear* was the fourth in the series by Elizabeth Chandler (Mary Claire Helldorfer), and *Lily's Ghosts* was a humorous first novel by Laura Ruby.

The Haunting of Swain's Fancy by Brenda Seabrooke involved Civil War ghosts, and more phantoms turned up near a plague island in Tom Pow's *Scabbit Isle*. Catherine MacPhail's *Dark Waters* was a ghost story set in Scotland.

New titles from Scholastic UK included *The Unseen* by Richie Tankersley Cusick, *Demon* by Samantha Lee and *X-Isle* by Peter Lerangis, while a phantom carnival featured in Neal Shusterman's *Full Tilt*.

Wicked: Curse, *Legacy* and *Spellbound* were the latest volumes in the series about a family of witches by Nancy Holder and Debbie Viguié. *Kindred Spirits* and *The Witch Hunters* were the seventh and eighth volumes of the *T*witches* series by H.B. Gilmour and Randi Reisfeld, about teenage twin sisters with magical powers. The ninth volume, *Split Decision*, was a "Special Edition" that included a separate Almanac.

Susan Davis's *Delilah and the Dark Stuff*, a sequel to *The Henry Game*, was about a witch who used her powers for romance, and *The Wild West Witches* by Michael Molloy was the third book in the trilogy that began with *The Witch Trade*.

Sorcerers of the Nightwing: Demon Witch was the second volume in the "Ravenscliff" series by Geoffrey Huntingdon (William J. Mann), in which Devon March confronted a 16th-century sorceress in a New England mansion built over a hellhole.

In Terry Pratchett's *The Wee Free Men*, a "Discworld" novel for young adults illustrated by Paul Kidby, a young girl wanted to become a witch so that she could rescue her baby brother from the Fairy Queen.

In the UK, Bloomsbury reprinted Neil Gaiman's *Coraline* in paperback and finally included the interior artwork (along with a new cover) by Dave McKean.

Comic-book writer Steven T. Seagle and Nickelodeon Films animator Marco Cinello teamed up for IDW Publishing's all-colour children's hardcover *Frankie Stein!*, while Daniel Pinkwater's *The Picture of Morty and Ray* was a spoof of *The Picture of Dorian Gray*, illustrated by Jack E. Davis.

Robert D. San Souci's *Dare to Scare: Thirteen Stories to Chill and Thrill* was published by Cricket Books, and *Every Day's a Holiday: Amusing Rhymes for Happy Times* collected sixty-four poems by Dean Koontz celebrating both real and imagined holidays, illustrated by Phil Parks.

Edited by Edo van Belkom, *Be Very Afraid!: More Tales of Horror* featured fourteen young adult stories by Robert J. Sawyer, Tom Piccirilli and Tanya Huff, amongst others.

Glen Hirshberg's first collection, *The Two Sams: Ghost Stories*, contained five superb novellas (one original), along with a brief Introduction by Ramsey Campbell.

Demonized was the latest collection from Christopher Fowler, containing seventeen clever and disturbing stories (four reprints) by one of Britain's best and most innovative writers of short horror fiction. The book concluded with Fowler's hundredth published story.

Harry Keogh Necroscope and Other Weird Heroes! was a new collection by Brian Lumley containing three reprint stories featuring Titus Crow, two reprint stories about Hero and Eldin, and three original tales (including a short novel) of Harry Keogh: Necroscope.

Duel: Terror Stories by Richard Matheson collected eighteen classic tales along with a 1988 appreciation of the author by Ray Bradbury.

Phyllis Eisenstein's *Night Lives: Nine Stories of the Dark Fantastic* was a welcome reprint collection from Five Star that included three collaborations by the author with her husband Alex and a new Introduction.

From the same imprint, *Rough Beasts and Other Mutations* contained nineteen reprint stories and a one-act play by Thomas F. Monteleone, along with a personal Introduction by John DeChancie. *Uncanny Tales* contained sixteen stories by Robert Sheckley, and *Apprehensions and Other Delusions* collected thirteen horror stories (one original) by Chelsea Quinn Yarbro, with notes by the author and an Introduction by editor Patrick LoBrutto.

Also from Five Star, Nina Kiriki Hoffman's *Time Travellers, Ghosts and Other Visitors* contained nine stories (one original) from the past thirteen years with an Introduction by Kelly Link.

The best horror anthology of the year was without doubt *The Dark: New Ghost Stories* edited by Ellen Datlow. It contained sixteen superior supernatural tales by a stellar line-up of authors, including Tanith Lee, Mike O'Driscoll, Gahan Wilson, Stephen Gallagher, Ramsey Campbell, Sharyn McCrumb, Charles L. Grant, Kathe Koja, Lucius Shepard, Kelly Link and Glen Hirshberg. In their afterwords, the authors described their favourite ghost stories.

As a three-continent collaboration between veteran editors Jack Dann, Ramsey Campbell and Dennis Etchison, more was expected of *Gathering the Bones: Thirty-Four Original Stories from the World's Masters of Horror*. There were certainly enough gems among the thirty-four new stories, but with a line-up of contributors that included Terry Dowling, Kim Newman, George Clayton Johnson, Lisa Tuttle, Tony Richards, Thomas Tessier, Gahan Wilson, Ray Bradbury, Michael Marshall Smith, Steve Rasnic Tem, Peter Crowther, the late Cherry Wilder, Joel Lane, Melanie Tem and Graham Joyce, it was the fiction from the newer names that impressed the most. The original Australian edition was apparently re-edited for the American market by Tor, with Dann and Etchison's billing reversed on the dustjacket.

Originally published in slightly different form as the Winter 2002–03 issue of *McSweeny's Quarterly*, available only to subscribers, *McSweeny's Mammoth Treasury of Thrilling Tales* was a pastiche of pulp magazines, illustrated by Howard Chaykin and featuring twenty original stories by Stephen King (a new "Roland" tale), Michael Crichton, Michael Moorcock, Harlan Ellison, Neil Gaiman, Carol Emshwiller, Kelly Link, Karen Joy

Fowler, Elmore Leonard, Nick Hornby and others. Guest editor
Michael Chabon contributed a story along with an Introduction
confirming that he was totally ignorant about genre anthologies.

Hot Blood XI: Fatal Attractions marked the return of editors
Jeff Gelb and Michael Garrett's erotic horror anthology series,
now published as a classy-looking trade paperback by Kensing-
ton Books. The stronger-than-usual line-up of eighteen stories
(including two uncredited reprints) featured work by Christa
Faust, Sephra Giron, Stanley Wiater, Yvonne Navarro, Graham
Masterton, Nancy Holder, David J. Schow, Mick Garris, Brian
Hodge and editor Gelb.

Shadows Over Baker Street may have been one of the dumbest
ideas ever for an anthology, but it also had the strong commercial
potential of combining Sherlock Holmes with H.P. Lovercraft's
Cthulhu Mythos. Under editors Michael Reaves and John Pelan the
results were not as bad as they might have been, and the book's
eighteen stories included contributions from Neil Gaiman, Brian
Stableford, Poppy Z. Brite, Caitlín R. Kiernan, Richard A. Lupoff
and one of the editors. As a personal caveat, I should add that it was
a shame that the publisher used a title that made the book appear to
be part of a pre-existing Lovecraftian anthology series.

Mojo: Conjure Stories edited by Nalo Hopkinson featured
nineteen stories (one reprint) about "personal magic" by Neil
Gaiman, Tananarive Due, Gregory Frost, Andy Duncan, Barbara
Hambly, Steven Barnes and others.

Edited by Sheree R. Thomas, *Dark Matter: Reading the Bones*
contained twenty-four stories (seventeen original), two essays and
a panel transcript by such African-American writers of speculative fiction as Samuel R. Delany, Nalo Hopkinson, Walter
Mosley, Charles R. Saunders, Tananarive Due, Pam Noles and
Kevin Brockenbrough.

From editors Steven H. Silver and Martin H. Greenberg,
Horrible Beginnings was a clever idea that collected together
seventeen "first" stories by Robert Bloch, Henry Kuttner, Ramsey
Campbell, Tanith Lee, F. Paul Wilson, Neil Gaiman, Kim Newman, Poppy Z. Brite, Kathe Koja and others, with introductions
by the living authors and others. *Magical Beginnings* was a
companion volume devoted to fantasy writers.

Co-edited by Brian Thomsen and Greenberg, *The Repentant*
featured thirteen original stories about reformed vampires, were-

wolves and witches, etc. with contributions from Edo van Belkom, Nina Kiriki Hoffman, Tanya Huff (a new "Henry Fitzroy" story), P.N. Elrod (a new "Jack Fleming" mystery) and Chelsea Quinn Yarbro (a new "Saint-Germain" tale).

From editors Greenberg and Brittiany A. Koren, *Pharaoh Fantastic* contained thirteen original stories involving Ancient Egypt by Tanya Huff, Nina Kiriki Hoffman, Mickey Zucker Reichert, Alan Dean Foster and others.

The Best of Dreams of Decadence edited by Angela Kessler collected twenty-one stories and twenty-two poems from the small-press vampire magazine. Contributors included Tanith Lee, Charlee Jacob, Sarah A. Hoyt, Lawrence Watt-Evans and Brian Stableford.

When Darkness Falls contained three romantic dark fantasy novellas by Susan Krinard, Tanith Lee and Evelyn Vaughn.

Edited by Charles A. Coulombe, *Classic Horror Stories* contained sixteen out-of-copyright tales by Charles Dickens, Robert W. Chambers, Washington Irving and others.

The Year's Best Fantasy & Horror: Sixteenth Annual Collection edited by Ellen Datlow and Terri Windling contained forty stories, eight poems, and an essay by Elizabeth Hand, along with detailed end-of-the-year summations by the editors, Edward Bryant, Charles Vess, Joan D. Vinge and James Frenkel. Windling announced that she would be stepping down as co-editor after this volume and her duties would be taken over by Kelly Link and Gavin Grant.

The Mammoth Book of Best New Horror Volume Fourteen edited by Stephen Jones (who also designed the cover with Michael Marshall Smith) contained twenty stories and novellas, along with an extensive overview of the year by the editor, a detailed necrology by Jones and Kim Newman, and a listing of useful addresses.

Both "Year's Best" books overlapped by eleven authors and a record number of stories from Brian Hodge, Stephen Gallagher, Graham Joyce, China Miéville, Kim Newman, Nicholas Royle, Jay Russell and Don Tumasonis.

BarnesandNoble.com announced in September that it had stopped selling e-books because "Sales did not take off as we and many others expected." It was estimated that retail sales for e-books in 2003 would reach somewhere around $10 million.

Kim Newman's 1998 "interactive" novel *Life's Lottery* was reissued by Crow Street Press and Scorpius Digital Publishing as the first electronic choose-your-own adventure for adults. At 190,000 words long and with 300 hyperlinked chapters, it allowed readers to follow many possible lives (and deaths).

Gary A. Braunbeck's collection *Sorties, Cathexes, and Personal Effects*, issued by Lone Wolf Publications on multimedia CD, contained more than forty stories and the novels *The Indifference of Heaven* and *Keepers*, with the author's personal introductions, discussions and readings in mp3 digital audio.

In April, the BBC launched a five-part animated horror series on its website entitled *Ghosts of Albion*. Each twelve-minute episode, created and written by actress Amber Benson (Tara on TV's *Buffy The Vampire Slayer*) and author Christopher Golden, followed a brother and sister with magical powers who became the mystical guardians of early-19th-century England.

Before changing its title to *Metropole*, the downloadable electronic magazine *The Spook* featured fiction by Stephen Mark Rainey and an illustrated interview with artist Gahan Wilson. The serialization of a Robert McCammon novel was suddenly cancelled when the book's print publisher complained it would harm sales.

In February, Judi Rohrig became the new editor and publisher of the weekly e-zine *Hellnotes*. It was also announced that Kathryn Ptacek would serve as senior editor, while Hank Wagner was named as the new reviews editor. Mark Lancaster and Donald Koish joined the staff as associate editors. To mark the changes, there were subscription deals and special prizes offered.

Having taken over from founding editor John B. Ford, Hertzan Chimera (Mike Philbin) relaunched *Terror Tales* as an e-zine. The look and the content of the title were substantially changed, with issues more focused towards quarterly themes. The first issue looked at "Body Horror" and included an exclusive interview with actor Bruce Campbell, articles on body mutation, embalming and Horror Metal, and fiction and poetry from Edward Lee, Charlee Jacob, Michael Arnzen and others.

New editors Nanci Kalanta and Ron Dickie took over Andy Fairclough's *Horror World* website. They updated message boards and set up a group of new boards for Independent Press writers.

The webzine *Chiaroscuro* featured fiction and poetry by James S. Dorr, Charlee Jacob, Bruce Boston and others, and authors appearing on *Gothic.Net* included F. Paul Wilson and Michael Marano.

Ellen Datlow's monthly on-line site *Sci Fiction* included stories by Maureen F. McHugh ("Frankenstein's Daughter"), Glen Hirshberg, Nathan Ballingrud, David Prill, Lucius Shepard, Terry Bisson, Paul McAuley, Paul Di Filippo and Howard Waldrop, plus reprint fiction from Frank Belknap Long, Chelsea Quinn Yarbro, Charles L. Grant, Anthony Boucher and many others.

Created in 2000, British print-on-demand publisher Big Engine ran out of capital and owner Ben Jeapes decided not to re-invest. This resulted in SF magazine *3SF* being "suspended" after just three issues. John Betancourt's Wildside Press withdrew an offer to purchase the assets of Big Engine in July after reportedly receiving no response from the company's liquidator.

Published in hardcover as a collaboration between Wildside and W. Paul Ganley: Publisher, *A Witch's Dozen* collected thirteen stories (one original) by Janet Fox, with a cover and frontispiece by Stephen E. Fabian.

Also from Wildside Press, *Fangs and Angel Wings* collected fifteen stories (ten reprints) and two poems by Karen E. Taylor, with an Introduction by Mike Resnick and and Afterword by William Sanders.

From the Wildside Fantasy Classics line, *At Chrighton Abbey and Other Horror Stories* collected five classic stories by Mary Elizabeth Braddon (1835–1915) with a historical Introduction by John Gregory Betancourt.

The Book of Wonder, *Time and the Gods* and *Plays of Gods and Men* were three reprint collections by Lord Dunsany featuring Introductions by Lin Carter and John Gregory Betancourt.

The Double Shadow and Other Fantasies was a reprint of Clark Ashton Smith's scarce 1933 collection of short stories, while *Graveyard Rats and Others* collected six macabre detective stories by Robert E. Howard with an Introduction by Don Herron. Introduced by Ben J.S. Szumskyj and with an Afterword by the ubiquitous S.T. Joshi, *Fritz Leiber and H.P. Lovecraft: Writers of the Dark* collected stories, poems, essays and letters by Leiber that had some connection with HPL.

Edited by Andy W. Robertson, *William Hope Hodgson's Night Lands Volume One: Eternal Love* contained thirteen stories set in Hodgson's Night Land, with a Preface by John C. Wright whose own on-line novella "Awake the Night" was also included.

J.F. Gonzalez's werewolf novel *Shapeshifter* had previously appeared as an e-book.

With the first volume published in 1971 by Arkham House, it took quite some time for *Songs & Sonnets Atlantean: The Second Series* to appear. Despite what the cover copy claimed, this was a completely new collection of forty poems by Californian Romanticist and protégé of Clark Ashton Smith, Donald Sidney-Fryer, also from Wildside Press.

Published as a print-on-demand title by Prime Books, *Kissing Carrion* was the first collection from Canadian writer Gemma Files, containing seventeen stories (one original) with an Introduction by Caitlín R. Kiernan. *Weirdmonger: The Nemonicon: Synchronized Shards of Random Truth & Fiction* was a long-overdue collection of sixty-seven(!) stories by D.F. Lewis, which were originally published from 1987 to 1999.

Jeffrey Thomas's quasi-Lovecraftian *noir* novel *Monstrocity* was set in a run-down city on a distant planet.

Strange Pleasures 2, edited and introduced by John Grant and Dave Hutchinson, contained twelve supposedly erotic "strange" stories by N. Lee Wood, David V. Barrett, Keith Brooke, Paul Kincaid and others, including a previously unpublished novella by the late John Brunner.

Also from Prime, *Darkness Rising 2003* was the latest volume in the annual anthology series edited by L.H. Maynard and M.P.N. Sims. It contained twenty original stories by Paul Finch, William P. Simmons, Phil Locascio, James Burr and others.

Edited by the redoubtable Philip Harbottle, *The Best of Sydney J. Bounds* was published in two volumes, 1: *Strange Portrait and Other Stories* and 2: *The Wayward Ship and Other Stories*, by on-demand imprint Cosmos. Together, the books collected twenty-six reprint stories (including two novels published for the first time in English) and a speech by the unjustly overlooked British author, along with fascinating historical Introductions by the editor.

Cosmos also continued Harbottle's series of *Fantasy Adventures* pulp paperback anthologies with three new editions featuring original science fiction, fantasy and supernatural tales by such veterans as Sydney J. Bounds, E.C. Tubb, John Glasby, Brian Ball, "B.J. Empson", A.J. Merak, Philip E. High, Tony Glynn, Peter Oldale and "David Somers". Each volume also included a complete short novel by John Russell Fearn that had never been published before in the US, and all the covers were by the late Ron Turner.

Published by Wheatland Press, *Greetings from Lake Wu* was a collection of thirteen stories and novellas (six original) by Jay Lake with illustrations by Frank Wu. There were also Introductions to the author and artist, respectively, by Andy Duncan and Lori Ann White.

From the same imprint, *Polyphony: Volume 2* and *Volume 3*, both edited by Deborah Layne and Jay Lake, featured "slipstream" stories by Lucius Shepard, Jack Dann, Bruce Holland Rogers, Michael Bishop, Carol Emshwiller, Don Webb, Barry Malzberg, Nina Kiriki Hoffman, Jeffrey Ford, Ray Vukcevich and many others.

T.M. Wright's *Cold House* was a print-on-demand haunted-house novel with an Introduction by Jack Ketchum, while *This Cape is Red Because I've Been Bleeding* was a collection of sixty poems by Tom Piccirilli, both from Catalyst Press.

California's on-demand imprint Medium Rare Books Publishing debuted *Teratologist* by Edward Lee and Wrath James White, *Appalachian Galapagos* by Weston Ochse and David "shy" Whitman, and *Oogie Boogie Central* by M. Stephen Lukac at the 2003 World Horror Convention in Kansas City. From the same imprint, Michelle Scalise's *Intervals of Horrible Sanity* collected fourteen stories and sixteen poems, while Adam Pepper's *Memoria* was about a scientist's attempts to discover the soul.

Ray Emerson's novel *The Riddle of Cthulhu* claimed to be inspired by Jules Verne, H.G. Wells, H. Rider Haggard and H.P. Lovecraft and was published by Florida's Llumia Press. A would-be pianist was obsessed with *Rachmaninoff's Ghost* in M.F. Korn's novel from Silver Lake Publishing.

Brett Blumfield's *The Outer Realm* from Trafford Publishing involved a supernatural mystery in the town of Silver Oak. From Invisible College Press, Shaun Jeffrey's novel *Evilution* exposed a village's dark secrets, and evil powers tried to destroy a woman and her daughter in *From the Dark Places* by Margaret Carter, from Amber Quill Press.

Giant ants invaded Florida in *Mandibles* by Jeff Strand, published by Mundania Press and previously available as an e-book. Also originally published electronically, R.S. Hill's serial-killer novel *Under the House* appeared as an on-demand paperback from 1st Books Library.

From Writers Club Press, Joseph Armstead's *Darkness Fears: A Tale of the Moon-Chosen & Le Grymmeuere* featured scientifically created vampires.

William Meikle's *Watchers: The Coming of the King* and *Watchers: The Battle for the Throne* were the first two volumes in a historical vampire series set in the 18th century, published by KHP Industries/Black Death Books. From the same imprints, Karen Koehler's *Slayer: Stigmata* featured vampire hunter Alek Knight, while Timothy Whitfield's *Witchblood* was a first novel and the beginning of a new series.

The Blackest Death Volume I was an anthology of twenty-six horror stories from KHP/Black Death Books, featuring work by Lavie Tidhar and William P. Simmons.

From Pocket Star Books, *Wither's Rain* by John Passarella was a sequel to *Wither*, in which small-town witch Wendy Ward confronted a demonic entity, and Justin Gustainis's *The Hades Project*, published by Brighid's Fire Books, involved a Federal agent investigating the demonic killing of a group of scientists.

Available from PublishAmerica, Wade Hunter's (Aaron Buterbaugh) second novel, *Judgment*, involved three disparate people battling a monstrosity with unimaginable powers, while L. Marie Wood's *Crescendo* was a first novel about a man haunted by a family curse. *Feast of Faust* from the same imprint collected forty-five stories (seventeen reprints) and an Afterword by T.M. Grey.

Published by Flesh & Blood Press, *Under Cover of Night* was a collection of seven stories (three original) by Mary SanGiovanni with a Foreword by John R. Platt and an Introduction by Shikhar Dixit.

Edited by Kevin L. Donihe, the on-demand anthology *Bare Bone #4* collected stories and poetry (two reprints) by forty-four authors, including Mark McLaughlin, Scott H. Urban, Derek M. Fox, Kurt Newton, Jeffrey Thomas, Gerard Daniel Houarner, John B. Rosenman, Phil Locasio, Amy Grech, Rhys Hughes, Wendy Rathbone, Denise Dumars, Michael Arnzen, Steve Rasnic Tem, Charlee Jacob and many others.

*   *   *

With a string of awards and even more nominations to its name, Peter Crowther's British small-press imprint PS Publishing became a major genre player in 2003.

Told by the Dead was Ramsey Cambell's first short-story collection in five years and contained twenty-three reprint stories along with an Introduction by Poppy Z. Brite and an entertaining Afterword by the author. Illustrated by Richard Lamb, it was published in a slipcased edition of 200 hardcover copies signed by Campbell and Brite, and a 500-copy numbered edition signed only by Campbell.

Also from PS, *Bibliomancy: Four Novellas* was a welcome reprint collection by Elizabeth Hand with an Introduction by Lucius Shepard. Again, it was limited to 200 slipcased copies signed by both contributors and a 500-copy numbered edition signed only by Hand.

Paul Di Filippo's *Fuzzy Dice* was a comedic fantasy novel about a reality-hopping bookstore clerk. With an Introduction by Rudy Rucker, it was published in an edition of 500 numbered copies and a 200-copy signed and slipcased edition with stunning dust-jacket art by Todd Schorr.

With an Introduction by M. John Harrison, *The Tain* was a new novella by China Miéville, set in a post-apocalyptic London overrun by vampiric "imagos". Introduced by Joe R. Lansdale, Stephen Gallagher's short novel *White Bizango* featured resurrected Louisiana detective John Lafcadio on the trail of a powerful voodoo priest, while Lucius Shepard's *Floater* was introduced by Jeffrey Ford and also involved voodoo revenge as a New York detective found his sight progressively occluded by something in his eye. All three titles appeared in signed and numbered editions of 400 hardcovers and 500 paperback copies.

Shepard also contributed the Introduction to Robert Freeman Wexler's *In Springdale Town,* a novella set in an impossibly tranquil New England village. *Righteous Blood* contained two novellas by Canadian author Cliff Burns with an Introduction by Tim Lebbon and cover art by Richard Powers. Both books were limited to 500 signed and numbered paperback copies and 300 hardcover copies.

By Moonlight Only was the second volume in editor Stephen Jones's revived "Not at Night" series from PS Publishing. It contained ten stories (two original) by David Case, Hugh B.

Cave, Harlan Ellison, Christopher Fowler, Marc Laidlaw, Terry Lamsley, Joe R. Lansdale, Tanith Lee, Peter Straub and Lisa Tuttle, illustrated by Randy Broecker.

Jones also supplied the Introduction to *More Tomorrow & Other Stories*, a major retrospective of Michael Marshall Smith's work from Earthling Publications, available in a hardcover edition of 1,000 numbered copies plus twenty-six traycased copies, signed by all the contributors, for $250.00. Collecting thirty stories (four originals, plus one only available with the lettered edition), this attractive volume also featured a colourful wraparound dust jacket by John Picacio.

From the same imprint, *Exorcising Angels* was a slim hardcover limited to 750 numbered copies and twenty-six traycased lettered copies that featured two individual Arthur Machen-inspired stories by Simon Clark and Tim Lebbon, along with the collaborative novella of the title. The wraparound dust-jacket art was the work of Edward Miller (Les Edwards).

Also from Earthling, *Graveyard People: The Collected Cedar Hill Stories* was the first of several proposed volumes collecting all Gary A. Braunbeck's tales set in his fictional town. It was published in a signed hardcover edition of 750 copies, illustrated by Deena Holland Warner.

From its superb Brom cover to its useful lists of Bram Stoker Award and International Horror Guild Award winners, *13 Horrors: A Devil's Dozen Stories Celebrating 13 Years of the World Horror Convention* was one of the strongest anthologies of the year. Edited by Brian A. Hopkins with an Introduction by Joe R. Lansdale, the book featured original fiction from Graham Masterton, Ramsey Campbell, Chelsea Quinn Yarbro, Gene Wolfe, Steve Rasnic Tem, Charles L. Grant and others. Launched at the 2003 World Horror Convention by the Kansas City Science Fiction & Fantasy Society, it was available as a 650-copy trade paperback and a signed and numbered hardcover limited to just 150 copies.

Caitlín R. Kiernan's long unpublished "first" novel, *The Five of Cups*, finally appeared from Subterranean Press in a hardcover edition of 1,000 numbered copies and fifty-two lettered copies. A vampire story involving the Holy Grail, the book also included a revealing Preface by the author and a 1996 Introduction by Poppy Z. Brite.

Brite's own *The Devil You Know* collected thirteen stories (one original) and had a new Introduction by the author. It was published by Subterranean in a de luxe hardcover edition. From the same writer and imprint, *The Value of X* was a short associational novel about two friends growing up gay in New Orleans.

The Book of Days by Steve Rasnic Tem was a piecemeal compendium of oddities that added up to a novel-of-sorts, published in a signed edition of 600 copies and a lettered edition, costing $125.00, of twenty-six copies.

The Devils in the Details collected a new ghostly story each by James P. Blaylock and Tim Powers, plus a collaboration between the two authors. It was available in a signed edition of 1,250 copies and a fifty-two-copy lettered edition. Blaylock's *In for a Penny* contained five previously uncollected stories and novellas set in an imaginary California. It was limited to 1,000 signed and numbered copies.

Peaceable Kingdom contained thirty-two stories (three original) by Jack Ketchum, and David Prill's *Dating Secrets of the Dead* collected three stories (one reprint) in a signed edition of 500 copies and a twenty-six-copy lettered and slipcased edition priced at $100.00.

Graham Joyce's *Partial Eclipse* was the author's first collection of short fiction, available from Subterranean Press in an edition of 1,250 signed and numbered copies.

Edited with an Introduction by David J. Schow, *The Lost Bloch Volume III: Crimes and Punishments* collected four obscure stories from the 1940s and 1950s by the late Robert Bloch, along with a short novel and an article on the inspiration for *Psycho*. The book also featured a second Introduction by Gahan Wilson, an interview with Bloch by Douglas E. Winter and a brief Afterword by the author's widow, Eleanor Bloch.

Schow's own new collection of stories from Subterranean Press, *Zombie Jam*, contained a quartet of previously uncollected living-dead tales (some originally published under the byline "Chan McConnell") linked by four vignettes, along with a detailed Introduction and Afterword by the author.

Night Shade Books had a busy year, starting off with Tim Lebbon's latest collection *White and Other Tales of Ruin*. The book featured six stories and novellas (two original), along with a chatty Introduction by Jack Ketchum and story notes by the author. It was available in both trade and limited hardcover editions. Jack Cady's *Ghosts of Yesterday* collected two essays, one poem and ten stories (four reprints), although some were no more than vignettes. A signed, limited edition was also available with a bonus chapbook.

Graham Joyce's 1998 novel *The Stormwatcher* received its first US publication from Night Shade, which also produced *Things That Never Happen*, a welcome retrospective collection of twenty-four reprint stories by M. John Harrison with a somewhat impenetrable Introduction by China Miéville and a much more accessible Foreword by the author. The 150-copy signed edition included an extra chapbook.

Tom Piccirilli's novel *A Choir of Ill Children* was an accomplished slice of Southern Gothic set in the decidedly weird backwater town of Kingdom Come, while *Bubba Ho-Tep* not only collected Joe R. Lansdale's original short story, but also Don Coscarelli's screenplay for his 2002 movie, along with new Introductions by both writers.

Midnight Sun: The Complete Stories of Kane collected all Karl Edward Wagner's stories and poetry about his flame-haired Mystic Swordsman, with an Introduction by Stephen Jones. It was available in both a trade hardcover and a slipcased edition signed by artist Ken Kelly, which sold out prior to publication.

Night Shade finally completed its five-book series *The Selected Stories of Manly Wade Wellman* with the final two volumes, *Sin's Doorway and Other Ominous Entrances* and *Owls Hoot in the Daytime and Other Omens*, the latter collecting all the John the Balladeer stories. David Drake contributed an Introduction to the former, while the final volume featured a reprint Introduction by the late Karl Edward Wagner and an Afterword by Gerald W. Page.

The first volume in *The Collected Fiction of William Hope Hodgson*, *The Boats of the "Glen Carrig" and Other Nautical Adventures*, included the title novel and twenty-two stories with an Introduction and notes on the text by Jeremy Lassen.

Edited by Scott Connors and Ronald Hilger (who also supplied the Introduction), *Red World of Polaris: The Adventures of Captain Volmar* collected four early stories by Clark Ashton Smith with an Afterword by Donald Sydney-Fryer.

Night Shade also published a signed limited edition of Jeff VanderMeer's quirky SF novel, *Veniss Underground*, set on a far-future Earth where a mad scientist was engineering a new sentient species. The 750-copy limited edition included an exclusive After-word/story, and illustrations by Myrtle Vondamitz, III. Edited by "Doctors" VanderMeer and Mark Roberts, *The Thackery T. Lambshead Pocket Guide to Eccentric & Discredited Diseases* was designed by John Coulthart and included sixty-five bizarre and outlandish contributions from Michael Bishop, Richard Calder, Neil Gaiman, Jeffrey Ford, David Langford, Tim Lebbon, China Miéville, Michael Moorcock, Alan Moore, Brian Stable-ford, Steve Rasnic Tem, Gahan Wilson and others. The first printing quickly sold out, and a limited edition of 650 copies signed by all the contributors was also available.

In January, Jeff VanderMeer's Ministry of Whimsy Press became an imprint of Night Shade Books. VanderMeer retained creative control, with editor Forrest Aguirre running the imprint's day-to-day operations.

Album Zutique was the first Ministry of Whimsy/Night Shade Books release. The small, square-sized anthology contained fif-teen decadent and surreal stories from Stepan Chapman, Jeffrey Ford, Steve Rasnic Tem, Jay Lake and others, including two stories each from Rhys Hughes and D.F. Lewis, plus a novel excerpt by Elizabeth Hand. It was followed by *In & Oz* by Steve Tomasula, a short novel about five people seeking a better life.

From Arkham House, *Selected Letters of Clark Ashton Smith* collected 276 letters by Smith to such correspondents as H.P. Lovecraft, August Derleth, Frank Belknap Long and Donald Wandrei, edited, annotated and with an Introduction by David E. Schultz and Scott Connors. The book also included twelve pages of black and white photographs. *A Rendezvous in Aver-oigne* was a reprint of the 1988 Arkham collection of Smith's fiction, with the Introduction by Ray Bradbury and illustrations from J.K. Potter. It added the first publication of "The City of the Singing Flame", as taken from the manuscript in the John Hay Library at Brown University.

A plaque honouring Clark Ashton Smith in his home town of Auburn, California, was unveiled on 11 January in a public ceremony.

Following a couple of years of inactivity, Fedogan & Bremer was back with the long-awaited collection *The Eerie Mr Murphy: The Collected Fantasy Tales of Howard Wandrei, Volume II,* edited with introductory notes by D.H. Olsen and containing twenty-nine stories (thirteen previously unpublished) along with a gallery of Wandrei's black and white art. The book was limited to a 1,500-copy trade edition and a 100-copy slipcased edition with an additional chapbook of correspondence and diary entries.

Just in time for Hallowe'en, Cemetery Dance Publications launched a new anthology series, *Trick or Treat*, with five novellas by Al Sarrantonio, Gary A. Braunbeck, Nancy A. Collins, Rick Hautala and Thomas Tessier, edited by Richard Chizmar. The book was available in a trade edition, a signed slipcased edition limited to 400 copies, and a fifty-two copy de luxe traycased lettered edition for $250.00.

Launched at the HorrorFind convention in Maryland, Chizmar also edited *Shivers II*, a trade paperback anthology from CD featuring twenty-four new stories from Douglas Clegg, Rick Hautala, Brian Keene, Kelly Laymon, Edward Lee, Bentley Little, Graham Masterton, Thomas F. Monteleone, Tom Piccirilli, Al Sarrantonio, Thomas Tessier, F. Paul Wilson and others.

Edited by Tom Piccirilli, *The Devil's Wine* was an anthology of 200 poems published by Cemetery Dance. Contributors included Ray Bradbury, Peter Straub, Graham Masterton, Brian Hodge, Michael Bishop, Elizabeth Massie, Peter Crowther and many others, along with several contributions written during his college years by Stephen King.

A revised version of Jack Ketchum's (Dallas Mayr) supernatural novel *She Wakes*, with a completely rewritten ending, received its first hardcover publication from Cemetery Dance in a 1,000-copy signed edition, while *The Crossings* by Ketchum was a weird Western novella, published in a 1,500-copy edition. Both books were also available in fifty-two copy traycased lettered editions.

Other CD novellas included *Cold River* by Rick Hautala, about an insomniac who saw strange things at night in a Maine town; David Niall Wilson's *Roll Them Bones*, in which four friends returned to face a childhood horror at Hallowe'en, and Edward Lee's *Infernal Angel*, which was a sequel to the author's *City Infernal* and was once again set in Mephistopolis, Lucifer's city of the damned. All were published in signed editions of 750 copies and traycased lettered editions of twenty-six copies each.

From the same publisher, *The Machinery of Night* was a massive retrospective collection of Douglas Clegg's short fiction, limited to 1,500 signed copies and a twenty-six-copy traycased lettered edition, bound in leather with additional full-colour artwork. Cemetery Dance also issued Clegg's novella *The Necromancer*, which explored the story of Justin Gravesend's youth and was a prequel-of-sorts to the author's *Nightmare House* and other novels. It was available in a signed edition of 1,500 copies and a fifty-two-copy signed and lettered traycased edition with added colour art for $125.00.

Published by The Alchemy Press and introduced and edited by Joel Lane, *Beneath the Ground* was a trade-paperback anthology of thirteen superior subterranean stories (three reprints) by Ramsey Campbell, Pauline E. Dungate, David Sutton, Tim Lebbon, D.F. Lewis, Nicholas Royle, Simon Bestwick and others.

Edited by Michael Penncavage, *Tales from a Darker Side: Stories of Terror and Suspense from The Garden State Horror Writers* collected seventeen original stories, plus a Foreword by Douglas Clegg and an Afterword by Jack Ketchum.

Published by Chaosium, *Disciples of Cthulhu II: Blasphemous Tales of the Followers* edited by Edward P. Berglund collected thirteen Mythos stories (two reprints) by Scott Aniolowski, A.A. Attanasio, Donald Burleson, C.J. Henderson, Brad Linaweaver, Gary Myers, Will Murray, Robert M. Price, Fred Olen Ray, Brad Strickland, Robert Weinberg and others. From the same imprint, *The White People and Other Tales* collected twenty-one stories and was the second volume in "The Best Weird Tales of Arthur Machen" series edited with an Introduction by S.T. Joshi.

Daniel Harms's *Encyclopedia Cthulhuiana: A Guide to Lovecraftian Horror* was an expanded and revised second edition from Chaosium with illustrations by Dave Carson.

Edited by Kevin L. O'Brien and published by Lindsfarne Press, *Strange Shadows & Alien Shadows: The Dark Fiction of Ann K. Schwader* collected nineteen stories (including nine Cthulhu Mythos tales), with an Introduction by Robert M. Price.

Edited by rising star Kelly Link for Small Beer Press, *Trampoline: An Anthology* contained twenty cross-genre stories (one reprint) by Glen Hirshberg, Jeffrey Ford, Carol Emshwiller, Christopher Barzak, Karen Joy Fowler and others.

Introduced by Robert E. Howard scholar Patrice Louinet, *Conan of Cimmeria Volume 1 (1932–1933)* was the long-awaited first volume in a proposed series of three from Wandering Star. It included a previously unpublished version of Howard's debut Conan tale, "The Phoenix on the Sword", in the original draft initially submitted to *Weird Tales*. Along with twelve other classic stories, the book also contained contextual notes, synopses, plot outlines, initial drafts and original ideas, plus five full colour paintings and numerous interior illustrations by Mark Schultz.

From 3F Publications, Kealan-Patrick Burke's *Ravenous Ghosts* contained sixteen stories (six reprints) along with an Introduction by Jack Cady, an Afterword by Gary A. Braunbeck and story notes by the author.

Marking the launch of David Kerekes's Headpress fiction imprint, Diagonal, *Creatures of Clay and Other Stories of the Macabre* contained thirty short-short stories (eighteen original) and a poem by Stephen Sennitt, with illustrations by Sean Madden.

John F. Conn's *The Society* was set in a refuge for serial killers and was published by Meisha Merlin, as was *Serenity Falls* by James Moore, set in the eponymous town and featuring supernatural investigator Jonathan Crowley from *Under the Overtree*.

Yvonne Navarro's 1993 vampire novel *AfterAge* was reissued in hardcover by The Overlook Connection Press along with the story upon which the book was based, a prologue from a sequel-in-progress, an Introduction by Brian Hodge and an Afterword by the author. It was available in three different states, the most expensive costing $350.00.

Sci-Fi Womanthology, compiled and edited by Forrest J Ackerman and Pam Keesey, was a feminist-themed anthology from Sense of Wonder Press that included new and classic SF and fantasy stories by Andre Norton, C.L. Moore, Mary E. Counselman and others.

After nine years, editors Elizabeth E. Monteleone and Thomas F. Monteleone revived their anthology series *Borderlands* with a fifth volume under the imprint of the same name. Despite an inappropriately science-fictional dust-wrapper illustration, the book contained twenty-five original stories by Stephen King, John Farris, Whitley Strieber, Bentley Little, David J. Schow, Tom Piccirilli and others. It was available as both a trade edition and as a signed and numbered limited edition but, due to a printer's error, the final sentences from three stories were missing and an errata sheet had to be included.

Also from the recently revived Borderlands Press, John

Maclay's *A Little Red Book of Vampire Stories*, Tom Piccirilli's *A Little Black Book of Noir Stories*, Joe R. Lansdale's *A Little Green Book of Monster Stories* and Gary A. Braunbeck's *A Little Orange Book of Odd Stories* were small-format collections available in signed and numbered editions limited to 500 hardcover copies each.

The Mothers and Fathers Italian Association was a collection of Thomas F. Monteleone's opinionated columns from *Cemetery Dance Magazine* and elsewhere, limited to 1,000 signed and numbered copies and a lettered edition.

The Keep was the first volume in a series of reprints by F. Paul Wilson that made up "The Adversary Cycle", limited to 1,000 signed and numbered copies. Each volume had spine art by Caniglia that when placed side by side would create a complete picture. The same numbered ($60.00) or lettered ($250.00) edition could be reserved for the entire series from Borderlands.

F. Paul Wilson's latest "Repairman Jack" novel from Gauntlet Press, *Gateways*, featured the author's anti-hero in the Florida Everglades investigating an accident at the eponymous retirement community that left his father in a coma.

Limited to 750 signed hardcovers, the tenth-anniversary edition of Poppy Z. Brite's vampire novel *Lost Souls* included correspondence, a "lost" chapter and an associational story.

Gauntlet also published the first of three volumes reprinting the 1989 Dream/Press volume *The Collected Stories of Richard Matheson*, edited by Stanley Wiater and with a new Introduction and story notes by the author. There were also tributes from admirers such as Stephen King, Ray Bradbury, Robert Bloch, William F. Nolan and others.

The debut title from Maryland's Endeavor Press was Tom Piccirilli's *Fuckin' Lie Down Already*, illustrated by Caniglia. It was published in a 200-copy signed and numbered edition, and a $100.00 traycased lettered edition of just twenty-six copies that also included an audio CD. *The House of the Temple* by Brian Lumley was the second volume in Endeavor's Novelette Series. The slim volume, limited to 300 signed and fifty-two lettered copies, contained the 1980 Cthulhu Mythos novella and a whimsical reprint story, along with new Introductions by the author. The hardcover featured ugly dust-jacket art by Alan Clark and six interior illustrations by Allen K (Koszowski).

From Marietta Publishing in hardcover and trade paperback, *New Mythos Legends* edited by Bruce Gehweiler collected sixteen new Cthulhu Mythos stories by Hugh B. Cave, Tom Piccirilli, Jeffrey Thomas, Stephen Mark Rainey, W.H. Pugmire, Norman Partridge, Don D'Ammassa, James Dorr and others, including the editor.

Cody Goodfellow's *Radiant Dawn* and its sequel *Ravenous Dusk* were both modern-day Mythos novels, from Perilous Press.

Hastur Pussycat, Kill! Kill! was an irreverent anthology of fifteen Cthulhu Mythos stories from Vox 13 Publishing. Contributors included Tim Curran, John Urbancik, Joseph Nassise and Mark McLaughlin.

Edited by Steve Lines and John B. Ford, *The Derelict of Death & Other Stories* from Rainfall Books contained twelve tales by Simon Clark, Mark Samuels, Joe S. Pulver, Sr., Michael Pendragon, Paul Finch and others, including two each by the editors.

Also edited by Ford for Rainfall, Mark Samuels's *Black Altars* contained six stories and an Introduction by Quentin S. Crisp, with artwork by the author. Peter James contributed the Introduction to *Ghost Far from Subtle*, the second dark fiction collection from Joe Rattigan, while Mark West's *Strange Tales* collected eleven stories. *Spare Parts* contained six tales of love and death by Stuart Young with an Introduction by Tim Lebbon.

Inspired by the works of H.P. Lovecraft and Robert W. Chambers, *Nightmares from Infinity* collected the poetry/lyrics from musician Steve Lines's numerous albums. Edited by Jim Xavier and John B. Ford, it also included Introductions by Randolph Evans, Lewis Carter and Lucy Francis.

Published in trade paperback from Rainfall and edited by John B. Ford and Paul Kane, *Terror Tales #1* contained stories by Christopher Fowler, Mark Samuels, Neal Asher, Steve Harris, Michael Pendragon, Simon Clark, Stanley C. Sargent and others, along with a "Dark Debate" between Simon Clark, Paul Finch, Stephen Gallagher and Tim Lebbon on dark fantasy/horror publishing and reviews.

Tom Piccirilli's *Mean Sheep* from Delirium Books collected sixteen short horror stories (twelve reprints) and fifteen poems. It was available in a signed, limited edition of 400 copies.

Under the same imprint, Brian Keene's *No Rest At All* was a revised collection of nineteen stories (one original), containing the author's preferred text. *The Rising* was a zombie debut novel from the same author, while David B. Silva's *All the Lonely People* was about a mysterious box that had the power to change lives and included an Introduction by Dean Koontz. Both were published in signed 300-copy editions and as twenty-six de luxe leather-bound copies.

In Greg F. Gifune's *The Bleeding Season*, a group of friends realized that one of their number might not be quite who they thought, and *Settling in Nazareth* by Sandy Deluca was about a woman who experienced psychic visions.

Also published by Delirium, *Sesqua Valley and Other Haunts* contained eighteen Lovecraft-inspired stories and a sonnet cycle by W.H. Pugmire, limited to just 250 signed hardcover copies.

Lucius Shepard's *Louisiana Breakdown*, from Golden Gryphon Press, was a Southern Gothic set in the small Louisiana town of Grail and involving its dark tradition of crowning a Midsummer Queen every twenty years. The novella was illustrated by J.K. Potter (who also contributed an Afterword) and featured a Foreword by Poppy Z. Brite.

Howard Waldrop's typically quirky novella *A Better World's in Birth!* was set in 1876 Dresden and involved an investigation into the apparent ghosts of Karl Marx, Friedrich Engels and Richard Wagner.

Mockymen was a new novel by Ian Watson from Golden Gryphon that combined Nazis, drugs, black magic, enigmatic aliens and Norwegians, while Dale Bailey's *The Resurrection Man's Legacy and Other Stories* collected eleven stories with notes by the author, plus an enthusiastic Introduction by Barry N. Malzberg.

From the same imprint came the first paperback edition of the 2000 collection *High Cotton: Selected Stories of Joe R. Lansdale*, containing twenty-one stories.

The Silver Gryphon, edited by Gary Turner and Marty Halpern, was the twenty-fifth book published by the small-press imprint founded by the late James Turner, with twenty contributions from Michael Bishop, Andy Duncan, Jeffrey Ford, Geoffrey A. Landis, Joe R. Lansdale, Richard A. Lupoff, Lucius Shepard, Howard Waldrop, Ian Watson, George Zebrowski and other writers previously published by Golden Gryphon.

Telos Publishing's horror and dark fantasy list included Alistair

Langston's debut serial-killer novella, *Aspects of a Psychopath*, written in diary form and originally published online in 2001, while *King of All the Dead* by Steve Lockley and Paul Lewis was about a couple who discovered that they could not cheat the Grim Reaper.

From the same publisher came a revised and updated edition of Stephen Laws's 1986 novel *Spectre*, published in both paperback and a signed and numbered hardcover edition. Also from Telos, Paul McAuley's *Doctor Who: Eye of the Tyger* included a Foreword by Neil Gaiman and the de luxe edition featured an additional frontispiece illustration by Jim Burns.

Probably one of the most important debut collections by a writer of ghost stories since Terry Lamsley and Thomas Ligotti burst onto the scene more than a decade ago, *The White Hands and Other Weird Tales* contained nine strange stories (two reprints) by Mark Samuels and was limited to just 350 copies from Tartarus Press.

Echoes and Shadows collected twelve atmospheric stories of unease (two reprints) and an Epilogue by Welsh-born writer Jon Manchip White, while *Masques and Citadels: More Tales of the Connoisseur* was the second collection featuring Mark Valentine's occult investigator, containing ten stories (one reprint), two of which were written in collaboration with John Howard. Both books were limited to 300 copies each.

From Tartarus and limited to 500 copies, *Tarnhelm: The Best Supernatural Stories of Hugh Walpole* contained twenty-five tales, including two previously uncollected stories, with an Introduction by George Gorniak. The four stories collected for the first time in *Three Miles Up* represented the sum of Elizabeth Jane Howard's short supernatural fiction. The book also featured an Introduction by Glen Cavaliero.

Strange Tales was the first anthology from Tartarus for eight years. The beautifully designed volume contained fourteen original stories by Quentin S. Crisp, Rhys Hughes, Mark Valentine and John Howard, Tina Rath, Len Maynard and Mick Sims, and Don Tumasonis, amongst others. With a Foreword by Rosalie Parker, it was limited to only 300 copies.

An updated edition of the *Tartarus Press Guide to First Edition Prices 2004/5* by R.B. Russell provided a useful checklist to the value of more than 33,000 collectable books from over 600 authors and artists.

Originally published in 1904 in an edition of just three copies, *The House of the Hidden Light* was an occult text by Order of the Golden Dawn members Arthur Machen and A.E. Waite. Co-produced by Tartarus Press and Ferret Fantasy, the new edition was edited with an Introduction by R.A. Gilbert.

Crampton & The Unholy City from Durtro contained a screenplay-novel by Thomas Ligotti and a music CD featuring six poems read by the author. It was limited to just 510 copies.

From Sarob Publishing, *The House of the Wolf* was a reprint of Basil Copper's 1983 Arkham House werewolf novel, published for the first time in Britain with a new Introduction by the author, an Afterword and interior illustrations by Stephen Jones, and a wraparound dustjacket by Randy Broecker. It appeared as a de luxe signed and lettered edition of fifty-two copies, a 150-copy limited hardcover edition, and in trade paperback format.

Also published as a signed slipcased hardcover and in a paper-back edition, *Mirror of the Night* collected ten reprint super-natural stories by E.C. Tubb dating from the mid-1950s to the late 1990s, with a historical Introduction by Philip Harbottle.

The Seminar was a novel by L.H. Maynard and M.P.N. Sims about a centuries-old witch who used a writing conference for teenagers as a cover for her nefarious needs. It was published by Sarob as a small-size paperback with artwork by Richard Lamb.

The sixth volume in Richard Dalby's "Mistresses of the Ma-cabre" series from Sarob, *The Relations and What They Related & Other Weird Tales*, was a revised and expanded edition of the 1902 volume by G.M. Robins (Mrs Baillie Reynolds). Limited to just 225 copies, and with a historical Introduction by editor Dalby, the book contained twelve stories and a 1916 article about the author.

The Substance of a Shade collected sixteen original ghost stories by British veteran John Glasby, with a Foreword by Dalby. A de luxe edition of just thirty-five slipcased copies was sold out before publication. Limited to only 200 copies, *Small Deaths* was a slim volume from Sarob collecting sixteen short-short horror stories (nine reprints) by Alison L.R. Davies, with an Introduction by Graham Joyce.

Limited to 500 copies from Ash-Tree Press, *Yesterday Knocks* by clergyman Noel Boston (1910–66) was a reprint of the scarce 1953 privately printed volume of five ghost stories, together with six previously uncollected stories and an Introduction by Patricia and Lionel Fanthorpe.

Edited by Jack Adrian and limited to 600 copies, *The Face* was the fourth volume in the "Collected Spook Stories" of E.F. Benson and covered the period between 1923–27.

The Experiences of Flaxman Low by Kate and Hesketh Prichard was the latest volume in "The Ash-Tree Press Occult Detectives Library" also edited by Adrian and limited to 500 copies. The book collected twelve stories by the mother-and-son team, which were first published under the pen name "E. and H. Heron" in 1898–99.

Limited to 600 copies, Margery Lawrence's *The Casebook of Miles Pennoyer Volume 1* collected the first six stories featuring "psychic sleuth" Miles Pennoyer, who resided at Number Seven, Queer Street. It had an Introduction by Richard Dalby.

Also limited to 600 copies, *Night Creatures*, edited with an Introduction by Peter Ruber and Joseph Wrzos, collected eleven *Weird Tales* stories by Seabury Quinn, including one featuring his occult detective Jules de Grandin.

Edited with an Introduction by Jessica Amanda Salmonson, *The Empire of Death and Other Stories* contained twenty-six tales by New England writer Alice Brown (1857–1948). Salmonson's own collection, *The Deep Museum: Ghost Stories of a Melancholic*, brought together the majority of the author's supernatural tales and poems. Both books were limited to 500 copies each.

A reprint of William Hope Hodgson's 1909 novel *The Ghost Pirates* included an Introduction by A.F. Kidd and an Afterword by Douglas A. Anderson, while Matt Cardin's *Divinations of the Deep* was a collection of spiritual horror stories.

The Haunted Baronet and Others: Ghost Stories 1861–1870 collected seven stories by J. Sheridan Le Fanu, edited with an Introduction by Jim Rockhill and limited to 650 copies.

Edited as usual by Jack Adrian, *The Ash-Tree Press Annual Macabre 2003: Ghosts at "The Cornhill" 1931–1939* was the second of two volumes, reprinting fifteen stories from the British magazine (1860–1975) and available in an edition of 500 copies.

Edited by John Pelan, *What Shadows We Pursue: Ghost Stories Volume Two* was the second of two collections containing twelve tales by Russell Kirk, with a cover illustration by the author. Pelan and Christopher Roden edited *The Basilisk and Other*

Tales of Dread, which brought together for the first time all of the known weird stories of R. (Robert) Murray Gilchrist (1868–1917), including his two vampire tales, "The Crimson Weaver" and "The Lover's Ordeal". Both books were published in 500-copy editions by Ash-Tree Press.

From John Pelan's Midnight House, *The Garden at 19* was a reprint of the scarce 1910 novel of modern paganism by Edgar Jepson, with a historical Introduction by Pelan. Companion imprint Darkside Press offered *No Place Like Earth*, the first volume in the "John Wyndham Collection". It contained sixteen stories (one previously unpublished), along with an Introduction by Pelan and story notes by Philip Stephensen-Payne and was limited to 510 copies.

Edited by Stefan Dziemianowicz and Jim Rockhill, who supplied the Introduction and Afterword respectively, *The Idol of the Flies and Other Stories* collected all twenty-two horror and weird fiction stories (one original) by the late Jane Rice and was also limited to 510 numbered copies from Midnight House.

From the Ghost Story Press, *They Might Be Ghosts: Ghost Stories of an Artisan* collected twenty-eight tales by David G. Rowlands, limited to only 250 signed copies. Originally reprinted by Ghost Story Press in 1994, David Tibet and GSP also reissued L. (Leslie) A. (Allin) Lewis's 1934 collection *Tales of the Grotesque: A Collection of Uneasy Tales* in a new edition of 300 copies, with the addition of an extra story and a revised Introduction by Richard Dalby.

Although marred by poor design and irritating typographical errors, *The Dreams of Cardinal Vittorini & Other Strange Stories* contained fifteen tales (two reprints) by actor, playwright, artist and biographer Reggie Oliver. It appeared in a hardcover edition of 300 copies (fifty signed by the author), marking the debut of Christopher Barker's The Haunted River imprint.

From Ireland's The Lilliput Press, John Gaskin's *The Dark Companion: Ghost Stories* collected eleven supernatural tales.

Published by Imagination Forum, Peter Valentine Timlett's *A Singing in the Wilderness* was a collection of twenty-seven stories (fifteen original), each introduced by the author.

Sex Crimes was an anthology of explicit fiction and art from Chanting Monks Press with contributions by David J. Schow,

Bernie Wrightson, Stephen Bissette, Christa Faust, Wayne Allen Sallee, Victor Heck and others.

Published by Bedlam Press/Necro Publications, Jeffrey Thomas's *Letters from Hades* featured its suicidal narrator's travelogue of Hell. The 1992 story that inspired the novel was also included.

Edited and introduced by David E. Schultz and S.T. Joshi from Hippocampus Press, *From the Pest Zone: Stories from New York* contained five annotated stories by H.P. Lovecraft plus a preface by Frank Belknap Long, Jr. to "The Shunned House". Joshi and Schultz also edited *Letters to Alfred Galpin*, a youthful prodigy who was one of Lovecraft's most ardent correspondents.

Just in case there was not already enough marginal material out there, *Primal Sources: Essays on H.P. Lovecraft* collected a number of articles written by Joshi himself.

Published as part of the "Lovecraft's Library Series" by Hippocampus, Herbert Gorman's 1927 novel *A Place Called Dagon* reflected many of HPL's own fictional themes. It was introduced by Larry Creasy with an Afterword by the inexhaustible S.T. Joshi.

For the same imprint, Joshi also edited and introduced the last major work written by Lord Dunsany, *The Pleasures of a Futuroscope*, dating from 1955 and previously unpublished, as well as *The Thirst of Satan: Poems of Fantasy and Terror*, the first selection of George Sterling's verse in more than thirty years.

Michael Moorcock supplied the Introduction to *Martian Quest: The Early Brackett*, a collection of twenty classic stories by Leigh Brackett from Haffner Press. From the same publisher, *Spider Island: The Collected Stories of Jack Williamson Volume 4* contained ten tales from the pulps with an Introduction by Edward R. Bryant.

Produced by IFD Publishing and featuring an Introduction by F. Paul Wilson, *Pain & Other Petty Plots to Keep You in Stitches* was a large-sized softcover that contained four stories (two original) by Alan M. Clark, Randy Fox, Mark Edwards, Troy Guinn and Jeremy Robert Johnson, based around nearly thirty illustrations by Clark.

The self-published trade paperback *Even Odder: More Stories to Chill the Heart* collected fifteen original young-adult stories by former pastor Steve Burt, self-proclaimed "Storyteller of the

Heart", with illustrations by Jessica Hagerman. Also self-published, under the Visibility Unlimited Publications imprint, *Grey Areas* was a slim volume of six "tales of the bizarre" (three reprints) by T.A. Freeman.

Edited by Victor Heck, *Asylum 3: The Quiet Ward* made its debut at the HorrorFind weekend in August. The anthology included stories by Edo van Belkom, Kealan Patrick Burke, Sephera Giron, Don D'Ammassa and others.

Publisher Joe Stefko revived his Charnel House imprint to publish *The Book of Counted Sorrows*, a collection of poetry by Dean Koontz. It was available in an edition of 1,250 numbered copies at $100.00 and a $2,000.00 twenty-six-copy lettered and traycased edition, each signed by the author. From the same imprint came two further books by Koontz: the first edition of *The Face*, about a Hollywood star who received a series of horrific packages, and *Odd Thomas*, which featured a man who could see the dead. The latter volume was designed to resemble a bowling alley. Both were available in 500-copy signed and numbered de luxe editions for $150.00 and as twenty-six-copy lettered and slipcased editions.

The third volume of *Nemonymous: A Megazanthus for Short Fiction* contained twenty-one uncredited stories. Contributors to part two were revealed to be Rhys Hughes, Joel Lane and Robert Morrish, among others.

Published by Sandglass Enterprises, *Southern Blood: New Australian Tales of the Supernatural*, edited with an Introduction by Bill Congreve, contained sixteen stories (three reprints) by Terry Dowling, Robert Hood, Sean Williams, Rick Kennett, Stephen Dedman, Lucy Sussex and others, including the editor. The stories were illustrated by various artists, including Cat Sparks, who edited her own anthology, *Agog! Terrific Tales: New Australian Speculative Fiction*. The second volume in an annual series, it collected twenty-one stories (two reprints) by Kyla Ward, Lucy Sussex, Robert Hood, Leigh Blackmore, Janeen Webb, Sean Williams, Scott Westerfield, Jack Dann and others. Simon Brown's story "Waiting at Golgotha" appeared in both volumes.

From Canada's Double Dragon Publishing, *Femmes de la Brume (Women of the Mist)* was edited by Nicole Thomas and featured eighteen stories by Amy Grech, Monica J. O'Rourke and others, along with an Introduction by Tamara Thorne.

Open Space: New Canadian Fantastic Fiction was edited by Claude Lalumière with an Introduction by Cory Doctorow and an Afterword by John Rose. Published by Red Deer Press, the original anthology featured twenty-one stories by new and up-and-coming writers. Also edited and introduced by Lalumière, *Island Dreams: Montreal Writers of the Fantastic* was published by Véhicule Press and contained twelve original stories by more new Canadian writers.

The Stars As Seen from This Particular Angle of Night was an anthology of speculative verse edited by Sandra Kasturi and published by Canada's The Bakka Collection/Red Deer Press. The book contained forty-two poems by such writers as Gemma Files, Charlee Jacob, Mark McLaughlin, Peter Crowther, Bruce Boston, Tom Piccirilli and others, along with a Foreword by John Rose, an Introduction from Phyllis Gotlieb and an Afterword by James Morrow.

A spoof of *Martha Stewart's Living*, Michael Arnzen's *Dying* from Tachyon Publications collected some decidedly offbeat household tips in poetic form.

Visions & Voyages was a welcome new chapbook collection of four original stories (two featuring turn-of-the-century sea captain Luís da Silva) by Chico Kidd with an Introduction by the author.

From Paul Miller's Earthling Publications, *The Rise and Fall of Babylon* contained a pair of back-to-back stories by Brian Keene and John Urbanick, published in an edition of 400 signed copies and fifteen lettered hardcovers signed by the authors and artist Deena Holland Warner.

Brian Evenson's *The Brotherhood of Mutilation* was about a crippled detective investigating a secret amputation cult, while Jeffrey Thomas's *Godhead Dying Downwards* had an Introduction by Brian Keene and was set in Victorian England. It involved a priest's quest to confront the evil that destroyed his church. Each chapbook appeared from Earthling in a signed edition of 300 numbered softcovers and as a fifteen-copy lettered and traycased hardcover.

The Earthling Sampler Volume 1, published for Hallowe'en, collected eight short stories by Brian A. Hopkins, Jeffrey Thomas, Michael Marshall Smith, Peter Crowther, Gary A. Braunbeck, Tim Lebbon, Simon Clark and Brian Evenson.

Caitlín R. Kiernan's recurring character Dancy Flammarion returned in the dark fairy tale *Waycross*, a nicely produced chapbook published by Subterranean Press in a signed edition of just 250 numbered copies and twenty-six lettered copies, illustrated by Ted Naifeh.

From the same imprint and author, *Trilobite: The Writing of Threshold* was a fascinating look, through unused excerpts and a short story, at the conception of Kiernan's second novel. *Embrace the Mutation: Limited Edition Chapbook* contained a short story each by artist J.K. Potter and Kiernan.

The Feast of St Rosalie contained another story about the Stubbs family (from *The Value of X* and *Liquor*) by Poppy Z. Brite, published by Subterranean as a de luxe two-colour chapbook.

Sideshow and Other Stories contained five stories by Thomas Ligotti with notes for a sixth. It was published in a signed edition limited to 350 copies and was out of print upon publication.

In Graham Masterton's *Sepsis*, the disappearance of a pet cat led two obsessive lovers into a realm of indescribable greed. It was limited to 500 chapbooks and a hardcover printing of only 200 copies.

Also from Subterranean, *Duck-Footed* was a previously unpublished "lost" story by Joe R. Lansdale with an Introduction by William Schafer.

Illustrated by Alan M. Clark, Norman Partridge's *The House Inside* was about a group of toys that came to life. It appeared in a signed and numbered edition of 250 copies and twenty-six lettered copies, also from Subterranean.

Published to celebrate The Dracula Society's 30th Anniversary Convention in October, *Conventional Vampires* edited by Tina Rath contained nine decidedly offbeat tales about the undead from Michael Chislett, Berni Stevens, Katherine Haynes and others, along with two poems by the editor. The handsomely produced chapbook also sported a stunning two-colour cover by artist Ken Barr.

Produced by the obscure Sidecar Preservation Society, the first English-language edition of *With Marlowe in LA* was a guide to Raymond Chandler's city by William F. Nolan, while David Drake's *Codex* was a previously unpublished horror story from 1967. Both booklets were limited to 175 copies, a number of which were bound in hardcovers.

Bittersweet Creek and Other Stories contained five beautifully written stories (one original) by Christopher Rowe, published in an edition of 500 copies by Small Beer Press.

Produced in an edition of only 150 signed and numbered copies by W. Paul Ganley: Publisher, *Episode of Pulptime & One Other* contained a further brief adventure featuring H.P. Lovecraft, Sherlock Holmes and Frank Belknap Long by P.H. Cannon, along with a previously unpublished vampire story. A number of copies were also bound in hardcovers.

From Maryland's The Dream People Publications, *Unknown Pleasures: Dark Erotica* contained two stories by Mark Howard Jones and another by Jeffrey Thomas.

Tiny Torments collected eight short-short horror stories (three reprints) by Gary McMahon, self-published under the ZedHead Press imprint. In his Introduction, the author admitted that he had put the booklet together in an effort to have his work read by a wider audience.

Published by California's Bloodletting Press in a signed edition of 300 softcovers and fifty-two hardbound lettered editions, *Ever Nat* was a chapbook by Edward Lee with cover art by Caniglia.

Dead Cat . . . Bigger Than Jesus was available in a signed, limited edition of 400 chapbooks and 100 hardcovers from Necro Publications/Bedlam Press. It included two stories by Gerard Houarner and one by illustrator GAK. The dead cat supplied the Introduction.

From Yard Dog Press, *More Stories That Won't Make Your Parents Hurl* was edited by Selina Rosen and featured twenty young-adult tales.

Filet of Sohl: The Classic Scripts and Stories of Jerry Sohl from BearManor Media was edited by Christopher Conlon and collected ten stories (one original) plus two unproduced *Twilight Zone* scripts and a story treatment by the late author. Along with an Introduction by Sohl initially written for an unpublished 1959 collection, this also included a Foreword by William F. Nolan, an Afterword by Allan Sohl, plus appreciations by Richard Matheson, George Clayton Johnson, Marc Scott Zicree and Jennifer Sohl. From the same imprint, *Have You Seen the Wind?: Selected Stories and Poems* by William F. Nolan contained six stories (one original) plus verse on topics ranging from Bradbury to Hemingway.

Mark McLaughlin's *Professor LaGungo's Exotic Artefacts & Assorted Mystic Collectables* from Flesh & Blood Press contained twenty-four poems about a selection of bizarre curios. McLaughlin's *The Spiderweb Tree* was part of the Yellow Bat Press's Pocket-Sized Chapbooks of Poetry, containing eleven linked poems. Other volumes in the series included *Letting in the Dark* by Denise Dumars, *Dancing in the Haunted Woodlands* by Wendy Rathbone and *The Body's Last Days* by John Grey.

Gary William Crawford's *Robert Aickman: An Introduction* was a critical biography and bibliography, published by Gothic Press.

Available in a 100-copy edition from The Haunted River, the self-published *Plagiarism & Pederasty: Skeletons in the Jamesian Closet* was a controversial essay by Christopher Barker about M.R. James's sexual predilections, along with the Reverend A.D. Crake's six-page story "The Three Black Cats", which Barker claims was the template for James's "The Ash-tree".

Wormhole Books's holiday cards included a signed Independence Day story by Edward Bryant and a signed Christmas story by Steve Rasnic Tem. They were limited to 500 and 450 copies respectively.

John Betancourt's print-on-demand imprint Wildside Press bought a forty-nine per cent share in *Weird Tales* and became co-publisher with Warren Lapine's DNA Publications, with plans for the periodical to eventually become bi-monthly. *WT* celebrated its eightieth anniversary in 2003 with five new issues featuring fiction by Nina Kiriki Hoffman, Sarah Hoyt, James Van Pelt, Thomas Ligotti, Tanith Lee, Gene Wolfe, David J. Schow and Robert Sheckley. Unfortunately, the overall standard of the magazine appeared to drop again, and only the excellent interior art and an evocative reprint cover by Les Edwards exhibited the quality this revered title deserved.

Back issues of *Weird Tales* #305–320 (1992–2000) were reprinted by Wildside Press over five print-on-demand trade paperback volumes.

Wildside also revived another 1930s pulp magazine, under the editorship of Robert M. Price. The "eighth" issue of *Strange Tales* featured new stories by Richard Lupoff, Adrian Cole, Gary Myers, Darrell Schweitzer, Stanley C. Sargent, John Gregory

Betancourt and others. The square-bound format was a definite improvement over the look of *Weird Tales*, but the rebirth was let down by a lack of interior artwork and inappropriate cover art by Jason Van Hollander.

H.P. Lovecraft's Magazine of Horror was launched by Wildside with Marvin Kaye as editor. Although dated Spring 2004, a "Special Collector's Issue" of the first edition appeared in 2003 printed on superior paper. Basically an advertisement forum for the numerous print-on-demand titles published by Wildside, the debut issue also featured fiction from Darrell Schweitzer, the late Jean Paiva, Brian Lumley (a short-short), Tanith Lee and Lovecraft himself (a minor piece from 1920), along with an interview with Ramsey Campbell, book reviews by Craig Shaw Gardner and a spoof letters column.

Wildside Press also acquired the remaining publishing assets of Borgo Press, which went out of business in 1998. These included the imprints Starmont House, FAX Collector's Editions and Brownstone Books.

David Pringle's venerable *Interzone* ran into scheduling problems in 2003. After publishing a number of double issues during the year, the editor finally conceded the move from monthly to official bi-monthly publication with the November/December issue. The magazine continued to run fiction from Paul Di Filippo, Mat Coward, Michael Bishop, Eric Brown, Darrell Schweitzer, Geoff Ryman, John Shirley, Jay Caselberg, Sarah Ash, Tanith Lee, Ian Watson and the interminable Zoran Živković, among others, alongside interviews with Octavia Butler, Judith Clute, Jack McDevitt and Stan Nicholls. There were the usual columns by David Langford, Nick Lowe, the controversial Evelyn Lewes, Bruce Gillespie and various book reviews, plus a guest editorial by Paul Brazier and an opinion piece by Ian R. MacLeod. Ramsey Campbell and Lisa Tuttle were among those who responded to Gary Westfahl's provocative article, "Who *Didn't* Kill Horror?", published in the April issue.

Richard T. Chizmar and Robert Morrish's *Cemetery Dance Magazine* celebrated fifteen years of publishing with six issues containing the usual mix of fiction, articles and columns with stories by Tom Piccirilli, Thomas Tessier, Stanley Wiater, Tim Waggoner, Tony Richards, Hugh B. Cave, Gary Raisor, Jay Bonansinga, Michael Reaves, Tim Lebbon, F. Paul Wilson,

P.D. Cacek, Elizabeth Engstrom, Jeffrey Thomas, Ian McDowell, Donald Burleson, Al Sarrantonio, David J. Schow, T.M. Wright, Edo van Belkom and Gary A. Braunbeck; interviews with Piccirilli, Wilson, Schow, van Belkom, Nancy A. Collins, Michael Garrett and Jeff Gelb, Ramsey Campbell, Graham Joyce, Jack Ketchum, Caitlín R. Kiernan, Richard Christian Matheson and Joe Bob Briggs, plus reviews and opinion pieces from Bev Vincent, Paula Guran, Michael Marano, Thomas F. Monteleone and John Pelan. After thirty-two instalments, Charles L. Grant decided to end his long-running "Ramblings from the Dark" column and was replaced by Ed Gorman. *Cemetery Dance* #46 marked the first "All-Fiction Special" since the fourth issue back in 1990.

Gordon Van Gelder's *The Magazine of Fantasy & Science Fiction* entered its fifty-fifth year of publication with fiction by John Varley, Ursula K. Le Guin, Charles Coleman Finlay, Arthur Porges, Dale Bailey, Joyce Carol Oates, Robert Sheckley, Ron Goulart, Adam-Troy Castro, Carol Emshwiller, Pat Murphy, Scott Bradfield, Esther M. Friesner (a vampire comedy), Terry Bisson, Fred Chappell, Gene Wolfe and Michael Reaves, among others. The June edition was a "Special Barry Malzberg Issue" with contributions from Jack Cady, John Kessel, Bill Pronzini and others, including a fascinating article by Malzberg about his time working at the Scott Meredith Literary Agency, and the October/November issue was the usual double anniversary issue. Contributors to the "Curiosities" column included Peter Atkins, Graham Andrews, Stephen Jones, Jack Williamson, F. Gwynplaine MacIntyre, Bill Sheehan, Paul Di Filippo and Henry Wessells, and there were the usual thoughtful book and film reviews by Charles de Lint, Elizabeth Hand, Michell West, Lucius Shepard and Kathy Maio, along with an insightful and entertaining opinion piece by Robert K.J. Killheffer about print-on-demand books.

F&SF expanded its foreign editions to include an Israeli reprint to add to editions already produced in Russia, Japan and Sweden. Audible.com began publishing audio versions of the magazine, with readers including Harlan Ellison, and a new message board was established on the Night Shade Books website.

After a four-year hiatus, publisher and editorial director James A. Owen relaunched the second issue of *Coppervale's Interna-*

tional Studio in a stunningly produced oversized format. Inspired by the arts magazine of the early twentieth century, it included full-colour profiles of such illustrators as James Christensen, the late Eyvind Earle, Tony Harris and John Picacio.

Owen also complained publicly that Coppervale's beautifully slipcased revival of the oldest fiction magazine, *Argosy*, launched at the World Fantasy Convention under the editorship of Lou Anders and himself, was being boycotted by such national book-selling chains as Barnes & Noble, Borders and Books-A-Million, because retailers did not know what to do with the two-volume format. Even the inclusion of an additional flysheet containing the barcode that could be removed and scanned did not help. As a consequence, the second quarterly issue was delayed.

The four issues of Andy Cox's always striking *The 3rd Alternative* included "slipstream" fiction from Brian Hodge, Mary Soon Lee, Brian Aldiss, Lynda E. Rucker, Eric Brown, Mike O'Driscoll, Jay Lake, Ian Watson and Lucius Shepard, regular columns by Christopher Fowler (on European horror films) and Allen Ashley, interviews with Graham Joyce, John Connolly and Trevor Hoyle, and guest editorials by M. John Harrison, Muriel Grey, China Miéville (in support of Harrison's irrelevant "New Weird" movement) and Justina Robson.

From the same publisher, the two issues of *The Fix* contained numerous reviews of small press magazines with short features by James Van Pelt and Peter Tennant. Also from TTA Press, *Crimewave 7: The Last Sunset* contained thirteen dark stories and two novel extracts from Christopher Fowler, Muriel Grey, Gary Couzens, Mat Coward, Stephen Volk, John Grant and others.

Shawna McCarthy's *Realms of Fantasy* included an unusual werewolf story by Tanith Lee, along with Gahan Wilson's always entertaining book reviews.

The first issue of *Lighthouse Magazine* edited by Paul Calvin Wilson was a "Special Brian Lumley Horror Issue" that included interviews with Lumley, Robert Weinberg, Stanley Wiater, artists Dave Carson and Bob Eggleton, and sculptor Paul Brown. There was also an interview with Jack L. Chalker, some terrible fan fiction and poetry (several by the editor), and numerous competitions. The second issue was even more eccentric, featuring more bad fiction, poetry by Brian Lumley, plus interviews with Alan Dean Foster, Eric Van Lustbader, Kim Newman, Ted V. Mikels, fantasy artist Jael, plus Joan Collins, singer Pete Burns and *Dallas* actor Steve Kanaly!

A companion title from Wilson was *Media One*, a digest magazine designed to fill the gaps between appearances of *Lighthouse*. The first issue included very short interviews with Ridley Pearson, Ann Rule, Pete Burns, Graham Joyce and several other writers, along with a brief piece about Brian Lumley's KeoghCon and more fiction by the editor.

From editor Christopher M. Cevasco, the first two issues of *Paradox: The Magazine of Historical and Speculative Fiction* contained stories and poetry by Brian Stableford, James Van Pelt and others.

The third (and apparently final) issue of Big Engine's *3SF* included stories by Ian Watson, Colin Greenland, Liz Williams and others, along with interviews with S.M. Stirling and Tim Powers.

Edited by Shar (Sharon) O'Brien, *NFG* billed itself as "Writing with Attitude" and featured fiction, poetry, and interviews with Michael Marshall Smith and Nancy Kress.

Rod Gudino's bi-monthly multi-media Canadian magazine *Rue Morgue* celebrated its "6th Anniversary Halloween Issue" with interviews with Richard Matheson, Bruce Campbell, Don Coscarelli and Joe R. Lansdale, along with numerous reviews and colourful advertisements.

Tim and Donna Lucus stuck to their monthly schedule with *Video Watchdog* and also celebrated their 100th issue. After starting the year with an "all-review" edition, other issues covered the new wave of Japanese horror, a comparison between the two versions of *Night of the Demon*, the Filipino *Blood* series, our fascination with the lost *London After Midnight* and *The Outer Limits* Season 2 on DVD, along with interviews with Richard Kiel and director Gordon Hessler. Alas, yet another year went by without any sign of their long-promised book on Mario Bava.

Michael Stein's always-interesting *Filmfax* also celebrated its 100th edition with a giant-sized issue that included interviews with Peter Fonda, William Peter Blatty, Ellen Burstyn and Curtis Harrington.

From editors Kevin Clement and Ted A. Bohus, the glossy *Chiller Theatre* continued to concentrate on older movies with the second part of John O'Dowd's shocking chronicle of the fall from grace of actress Barbara Payton, a guide to Edgar Allan Poe's Baltimore, and Tom Weaver's terrific interview with the late Herman Cohen.

Scott Edelman's slick bi-monthly *Scifi: The Official Magazine of the Sci Fi Channel* contained the usual puff pieces on all the latest movie blockbusters and hit TV shows. Michael J. Weldon's *Psychotronic* included interviews with actors Malcolm McDowell and Don Stroud, while *Alternative Cinema: The Magazine of Independent and Underground Filmmaking* featured an interview with maverick director Brett Piper.

Stephen King joined *Entertainment Weekly* in August as a regular columnist with "The Pop of King", a light-hearted look at pop culture by the King of Horror.

Britain's monthly *Book and Magazine Collector* included M.J. Simpson's informative article on different editions of *King Kong* and an interview with veteran editor Peter Haining by R.M. Healey.

Peter Straub was spotlighted in an "Innovators Series" column in the October *Publishers Weekly*, in which the author and others talked about the marketing of *lost boy lost girl*.

The September issue of DNA Publications's *Chronicle: SF, Fantasy, & Horror's Monthly Trade Journal* featured an extensive interview with *New York Times* bestselling author Laurell K. Hamilton.

Locus: The Magazine of the Science Fiction & Fantasy Field included interviews with Garth Nix, Michael Moorcock, Charles de Lint, Gardner Dozois, Robert Sheckley, Paul Di Filippo, Jonathan Carroll, Terri Windling, Ian R. MacLeod, Howard Waldrop and M. John Harrison. The April *Locus* featured a special horror-themed section, guest-edited by regular columnist Edward Bryant, that included an in-depth interview with Ramsey Campbell and commentary by Ellen Datlow, Tim Lebbon, David J. Schow, David J. Skal, Peter Straub, Steve Rasnic Tem and Douglas E. Winter, among others. Artist Charles Vess guest-edited the July issue devoted to graphic novels. Along with an interview with the normally reticent Alan Moore, it featured contributions from Neil Gaiman, Harlan Ellison, Bryan Talbot, Charles de Lint and Richard Pini.

China Miéville made yet another attempt to legitimise his and M. John Harrison's "New Weird" banner with a reprint of his article from *The 3rd Alternative* in the December *Locus*. Anyone else remember the "splatterpunks"?

Always ably edited by Barbara Roden and Christopher Roden, the three issues of The Ghost Story Society's journal *All Hallows* included fiction by James Doig, Phil Locascio, Susan Davis, Stephen Volk, Robert Morrish, Simon Beswick and others, along with articles on Stella Gibbons, Phil Rickman's Reverend Merrily Watkins, Robert Aickman's *The Wine-Dark Sea*, and the movies *Diary of a Madman*, *Shock Waves* and *Corridor of Mirrors*. Ramsey Campbell joined the regular line-up with a welcome return of his "Ramsey Campbell, Probably" opinion column, alongside the usual features by Roger Dobson and Richard Dalby and a lively letters section. Artwork was supplied by Paul Lowe, Douglas Walters, Alan Hunter, Jason C. Eckhardt, Dallas Goffin and Allen Koszowski.

Editor David Longhorn not only decided to continue publishing *Supernatural Tales*, but expanded the size and format of the small-press magazine with his second issue of the year. Steve Duffy, Reggie Oliver, Adam Golaski, Michael Chislett, Katherine Haynes and Chico Kidd (a new da Silva story) were among those who contributed fiction, and there was an article on vampires by Tina Rath, plus various book reviews.

Having apparently moved to a twice-yearly schedule, Patrick and Honna Swenson's perfect-bound *Talebones: A Magazine of Science Fiction & Dark Fantasy* included fiction and poetry by James Van Pelt, Jack Cady, Michael A. Arnzen, Nina Kiriki Hoffman and Don Webb, interviews with Joe Haldeman and Kevin J. Anderson, reviews by Edward Bryant, plus the usual excellent interior artwork by Tom Simonton, Frank Wu and other artists.

Flesh & Blood: Tales of Dark Fantasy and Horror edited by Jack Fisher was revamped with its thirteenth issue, featuring fiction by Tom Piccirilli, D.F. Lewis and Mark McLaughlin, an interview with Leisure Books editor Don D'Auria, and a publisher's spotlight on Night Shade Books.

Gordon Linzer's *Space and Time* included fiction and poetry by Mary Soon Lee, Jill Bauman, A.R. Morlan and Jeffrey Goddin, plus a brief interview with Thomas Ligotti. The two issues of Pitch Black's *Horror Garage* featured stories by Norman Partridge (a chapbook reprint), Mark McLaughlin and others, plus interviews with Joe R. Lansdale and Sephra Giron.

Edited by Dave Lindschmidt, *City Slab* was a new quarterly small-press magazine that included fiction by Poppy Z. Brite and Brian Hodge, alongside interviews with actress Ingrid Pitt and Elizabeth Massie.

The debut issue of Gary Fry's *Fusing Horizons*, subtitled "Dark Fiction for Imaginative Readers", featured stories from Joel Lane, Ramsey Campbell (a reprint), Andrew Hook, Charles Gramlich and others, including the editor, along with a very short interview with Michael Marshall Smith.

From Small Beer Press and editors Gavin J. Grant and Kelly Link, *Lady Churchill's Rosebud Wristlet* published stories, poems and articles by many new and upcoming authors.

Edited by William Smith, the first issue of *Trunk Stories* contained five new tales, a poem and reviews, while the third issue of Christopher Rowe, Gwenda Bond and Alan DeNiro's *Say . . . Aren't You Dead?* included fourteen stories and poems by Justina Robson, Scott Westerfield, Mark Rich and others, along with a two-page comic strip.

Edited by Heather Shaw and Tim Pratt, *Flytrap* #1 was a twice-yearly magazine of "slipstream" fiction and poetry featuring, amongst others, Jay Lake and Michael J. Jasper. Jasper's own publication, *Intracities*, included all of the above, along with Jay Caselberg, Jeffrey Turner, Mark Siegel and Peter Hagelslag.

From Edgewood Press, *Alchemy* #1 edited by Steve Pasechnick published six stories by Alex Irvine, R.A. Lafferty, Carol Emshwiller and others.

Mythos Collector #5 edited by Brian Lingard featured Cthulhu Mythos fiction and poetry by Paul Pinn, W. Paul Ganley and others, plus interviews with Graham Masterton and C.J. Henderson and an article on "Mythos Collecting in the UK". Edited by C. Brut, *Dreaming in R'Lyeh* #1 included Lovecraftian fiction by Stanley C. Sargent and Jeffery Thomas, plus a special Robert E. Howard section.

Lovecraft's Weird Mysteries #6 from Pentagram Productions presented an interview with Hugh B. Cave, along with articles, fiction and poetry. Oliver Baer's *Cthulhu Sex: Blood, Sex and Tentacles* published four issues that would probably have had HPL spinning in his grave.

Cathy Heath's Romances with Attitude was a ring-bound publication that was subtitled "New Weird and Spicy Pulp Fiction". The eighth issue included the short novel "Beauty and the Werewolf" by Reginald Watson and a report on the 2003 Windy City Pulp & Paperback Convention in Chicago. That event produced its own perfect-bound booklet: *Windy City Pulp Stories* featured fiction and articles by Hugh B. Cave, Will Murray, Frank M. Robinson and others, with art by Rich Larson.

The second issue of James R. Cain's Australian quarterly *Dark Animus* included a short story by Graham Masterton.

Published by Seele Brent Publications, *Studies in Modern Horror 1: A Scholarly Journal for the Study of Contemporary Weird Fiction* was a special issue devoted to Jack Ketchum (Dallas William Mayr), and included a selected bibliography.

Florida Atlantic University's quarterly academic publication *Journal of the Fantastic in the Arts*, included an article on modernity in three H.P. Lovecraft stories.

Published by The London Vampyre Group and billing itself as "The UK's Leading Vampyre Magazine", editor Becky Probert's nicely produced *The Chronicles* featured articles on a wide range of subjects, including Aleister Crowley, vampires in science fiction, and *Doctor Who*, along with media reviews and convention and trip reports.

The February issue of *The New York Review of Science Fiction* included an article on corporate horror in the work of Thomas Ligotti.

The Bulletin of the Science Fiction and Fantasy Writers of America looked at cover art by Amy Sterling Casil, with notes by Bob Eggleton, and featured some suggestions by Brenda W. Clough about how to behave at Worldcons. It included the very sensible advice that "comfortable shoes are a must"! There was also an article on publicity by Milton Kahn, a discussion about professionalism between Mike Resnick and Barry Malzberg, and all the usual columns and market reports.

With a publishing schedule split between print and on-line editions, Kathryn Ptacek's *The Official Newsletter of the Horror Writers Association* included the usual columns by HWA president Joe Nassise, Charles L. Grant, Stephen Dedman and Sephera Giron; articles by Edo van Belkom about self-promotion and the death of Edgar Allan Poe, plus market reports by the editor. The monthly *HWA Internet Mailer* also kept members up to date with news and signings.

After some initial scheduling problems, The British Fantasy Society published four editions of *Prism* in 2003. Boasting some impressive colour cover art by David Bezzina, Dominic Harman and Les Edwards, the perfect-bound magazine featured interviews with Neil Gaiman, Elastic Press publisher Andrew Hook, Graham Joyce, Gary Couzens, Stephanie Bedwell-Grime, Juliet Marillier, Joe R. Lansdale, Stephen Gallagher, J.M. Morris (Mark Morris), Marion Arnott and Jonathan Aycliffe; articles by China Miéville, Tony Richards and the prolific Jeff Gardiner; a regular opinion column from Chaz Brenchley, plus the usual copious reviews. New editor Marie O'Regan took over with the May issue and put the magazine back on a firm quarterly schedule.

The BFS also managed to turn out two editions of *Dark Horizons* under the editorship of Debbie Bennett. Also sporting full-colour covers, these perfect-bound issues included fiction and poetry by Allen Ashley, Marion Pitman, Tina Rath and David J. Howe, among others.

From The Overlook Connection Press, *Horror Plum'd: An International Stephen King Bibliography and Guide 1960–2000* by Michael R. Collings was yet another in-depth guide to King's massive body of work.

James Herbert: Devil in the Dark by Craig Cabell was an authorized biography from Metro Publishing, written with the full co-operation of its subject and based on a series of exclusive interviews. The book also included an Introduction by Ingrid Pitt, a restored chapter from *Sepulchre* and a short story.

Shirley Jackson's American Gothic was a critical examination of the author's work by Darryl Hattenhauer, published by State University of New York Press.

The late Douglas Adams was the subject of two biographies published in 2003. *Wish You Were Here* was billed as "The Official Biography" of the author of *The Hitchhiker's Guide to the Galaxy*, written by Adams's editor and friend Nick Webb, while M.J. Simpson's *Hitchhiker: A Biography of Douglas Adams* was described as "the definitive biography" and featured a Foreword by BBC producer John Lloyd. The American edition was updated and added a new Foreword by Neil Gaiman. Gaiman's own 1988 book *Don't Panic: Douglas Adams & The Hitchhiker's Guide to the Galaxy* was reissued by Titan Books with the additional chapters from the 1993 edition by David K. Dickson and the 2002 edition by M.J. Simpson, and another new Foreword by Gaiman.

Published by Mythos Books LLC, *Robert E. Howard: The Power of the Writing* was edited with an Introduction and Afterword by Ben Szumsky and included contributions from Howard (including some previously unpublished fiction), Joe Patrice Louinet, Rusty Burke and others, along with an interview with Glenn Lord by Joe Marek. The oversized trade paperback was illustrated by Gary Gianni, Rick Cortes, Mark Schultz, Rick McCollum and David Burton.

From print-on-demand publisher Wildside Press, *The Thomas Ligotti Reader: Essays and Explorations* edited by Darrell Schweitzer contained twelve articles (seven original) and two interviews with the author by Robert M. Price, Stefan R. Dziemianowicz, Ben P. Indick, S.T. Joshi and others, plus a Ligotti Bibliography compiled by Douglas A. Anderson and an Index.

Gary Braunbeck's *Fear in a Handful of Dust: Horror as a Way of Life* was a semi-autobiographical look at horror writing, featuring samples of the author's own fiction, from Wildside/Betancourt.

Also from Wildside, *Giants of the Genre: Interviews with Science Fiction, Fantasy, and Horror's Greatest Talents Conducted by Michael McCarty* contained twenty-one very short interviews (many of them previously published) with Peter Straub, Poppy Z. Brite, Neil Gaiman, Graham Masterton, Forrest J Ackerman, Dan Curtis, J.N. Williamson, William F. Nolan, Ray Bradbury, Dean Koontz and others, along with an Introduction by Mark McLaughlin.

Going some way to make up for the late, lamented, *Necrofile* (did anybody ever have their subscriptions refunded by the publisher?), the first paperback volume of *Wormwood* edited by Mark Valentine for Tartarus Press contained articles on Gustav Meyrink, E.R. Eddison, Ernest Bramah and Thomas Ligotti, along with an extremely brief interview with Dame Muriel Spark and various book reviews.

The Essential Guide to Werewolf Literature by Brian J. Frost was published by the University of Wisconsin/Popular Press and attempted to summarize every werewolf story published.

The Gothic Vision: Three Centuries of Horror, Terror and Fear was an overview of Gothic literature by Dani Cavallaro from Continuum, while Peter K. Garett's *Gothic Reflections: Narrative Force in Nineteenth-Century Fiction* from Cornell University Press included separate chapters on *Frankenstein, Dracula, The Strange Case of Dr Jekyll and Mr Hyde* and Edgar Allan Poe.

Published by Greenwood Press/Libraries Unlimited, Michael Burgess (a.k.a. "Robert Reginald") and Lisa R. Bartle's *Reference Guide to Science Fiction, Fantasy and Horror: Second Edition* was aimed at librarians and listed more than 700 titles, including 160 new listings and numerous revisions. From the same imprints, Anthony J. Fonseca and June Michele Pulliam's *Hooked on Horror: A Guide to Reading Interests in Horror Fiction: Second Edition* was aimed at a similar market, and heavily revised from its initial 1999 first edition.

Carol A. Senf's *Science and Social Science in Bram Stoker's Fiction* was a critical examination of the themes in the work of the author of *Dracula*, also published by Greenwood.

Vampire Legends in Contemporary American Culture was a critical examination of the current popularity of the undead by William Patrick Day, published by the University Press of Kentucky.

Written by Constantine Gregory and annotated by "vampire expert" Craig Glenday, *The Vampire Watcher's Handbook: A Guide for Slayers* was described as a "must-have guide to hunting down vampires" and, despite the title, had absolutely nothing to do with *Buffy*.

Suman Gupta's *Re-reading Harry Potter* looked at the social implications of the publishing phenomenon, while Edmund M. Kern's *The Wisdom of Harry Potter: What Our Favorite Hero Teaches Us About Moral Choices* was aimed at parents who wanted to discuss Rowling's series with their children.

Ultimate Unofficial Guide to the Mysteries of Harry Potter by Galadriel Waters and Astre Mithrandir examined the first four books for possible clues to future plot developments, and *J.K. Rowling* by Charles Lovett was a guide to the first three books and was #6 in "The Library of Great Authors" from Barnes & Noble/SparkNotes.

With an Introduction by Michael Moorcock, *A Tea Dance at*

Savoy from Manchester's Savoy Books contained seven illu-strated essays by *New Worlds* contributor Robert Meadley cover-ing such diverse and controversial topics as the novels of David Britton, Princess Diana's funeral, the Holocaust and 9/11.

Games Workshop combined its Black Flame and Black Library imprints under publishing subsidiary BL Publishing to create tie-in books based on movie and game concepts. The company also entered into agreements with New Line Cinema and computer games developer Rebellion (which owns *2000 AD* comics).

Ring (*Ringu*), Koji Suzuki's 1991 novel about a cursed video-tape, was translated from the original Japanese by Robert B. Rohmer and Glynne Walley for a film tie-in edition.

The year's other Big Movie tie-ins included *The Core* by Dean Wesley Smith, *Bulletproof Monk* by J.M. Dillard, *Daredevil* and *Underworld* by Greg Cox, *X-Men 2* by comics writer Chris Claremont, *Hulk* by Peter David, *The League of Extraordinary Gentlemen* by K. (Kevin) J. Anderson, *Terminator 3: Rise of the Machines* by David Hagberg, *Lara Croft: Tomb Raider: The Cradle of Life* by Dave Stern, *Freddy vs. Jason* by Stephen Hand and *The Butterfly Effect* by James Swallow. Stephen King's *Dreamcatcher* was also reissued with a new movie tie-in cover.

Terminator 3: Terminator Dreams by Aaron Allston was an original novel set in the same world as the movie, while Mike Resnick's *Lara Croft: Tomb Raider: The Amulet of Power* was based on the video-game adventures.

Buffy the Vampire Slayer: Chosen was an anonymous nove-lization of the entire seventh (and final) season of the cult TV series. It was originally announced as being written by Nancy Holder, but she reportedly left the project for undisclosed rea-sons.

Holder did write the *Buffy* novelization *Blood and Fog*, and other titles in the popular series included *Chaos Bleeds* by James A. Moore and *Mortal Fear* by Scott Ciencin and Denise Ciencin.

Buffy the Vampire Slayer: Tales of the Slayer Volume 2 and *Volume 3* collected further stories and novellas about Slayers down the ages. An omnibus of both volumes was published by the Science Fiction Book Club.

Monster Island by Christopher Golden and Thomas E. Snie-goski was the first *Buffy/Angel* hardcover crossover novel. It was followed by *Seven Crows* by John Vornholt and *Cursed* by Mel Odom.

Other novels in the *Angel* series included *Impressions* and *Fearless* by Doranna Durgin, and *Sanctuary* and *Solitary Man* by Jeff Mariotte.

The Charmed series of tie-ins remained as popular as the TV show, with *Shadow of the Sphinx* by Carla Jablonski, *Something Wiccan This Way Comes* by Emma Harrison, *Mist and Stone* by Diana G. Gallagher, *Mirror Image* by Jeff Mariotee, *Between Worlds* by J.G. Bobbi Weis and Jacklyn Wilson, and *Truth and Consequences* by Cameron Dokey. *Charmed: Seasons of the Witch Volume 1* was a young-adult anthology of three stories.

Even more successful were the tie-ins to *Smallville*, the WB's contemporary re-imagining of Superboy. These included Nancy Holder's *Hauntings* and *Silence*, *Animal Rage* by David and Bobbi Weiss, *Whodunnit* by Dean Wesley Smith, *Speed* and *Greed* by Cherie Bennett and Jeff Gottesfeld, *Buried Secrets* and *Runaway* by Suzan Colón, *Shadows* by Diana G. Gallagher and *Curse* by Alan Grant.

Although the show was cancelled, *Witchblade: Demons* was the latest volume in the tie-in series by Mike Baron, and *Dark Angel: Skin Game* and *Dark Angel: After the Dark*, both by Max Allan Collins, were also based on another now-defunct series.

Sabrina the Teenage Witch may also have finally come to the end of its TV run, but the novelizations continued past fifty volumes with *Where in the World is Sabrina Spellman?* and *Ten Little Witches* (a special Hallowe'en volume) by Paul Ruditis, *Witch Glitch* by Leslie Goldman, *What a Doll!* and *Christmas Crisis* by Nancy Krulik, and *Now and Again* by David Cody Weiss and Bobbi J.G. Weiss.

Published by ibooks, *The Twilight Zone Book 1: Shades of Night, Falling* by John J. Miller was the first of a trilogy of original novels inspired by Rod Serling's classic CBS-TV series. Subsequent volumes in the series were written by Russell Davis and John Helfers. From the same imprint also came *The Outer Limits: Always Darkest*, a novelization by Stan Timmons packaged by Byron Preiss Visual Publications.

Published by Gauntlet Press and edited by Mark Dawidziak, *The Kolchak Scripts* contained Richard Matheson's teleplays for the first two TV films *The Night Stalker* and *The Night Strangler*, plus his unproduced screenplay for a third "Kolchak" film, *The Night Killers*, written by Matheson and William F. Nolan. The book also included interviews with Matheson, Nolan, Jeff Rice and Dan Curtis.

Edited by Stanley Wiater, *Richard Matheson's The Twilight Zone Scripts Volume Two* contained six scripts and was published by Gauntlet/Edge Books. From Cumberland House, *The Twilight Zone Scripts of Earl Hammer* collected eight scripts from the original TV series along with an Introduction by the writer, plus an interview with Hammer and commentary on each episode by Tony Albarella.

Based on the DC Comics graphic series created by Neil Gaiman and John Bolton, *The Books of Magic: The Invitation*, *Bindings* and *The Children's Crusade* were the first three volumes by Carla Jablonski aimed at young adult readers, with series introductions by Gaiman.

Vampire: The Madness of Priests and *Vampire: The Wounded King* by Philippe Boulle were the second and third volumes in the "Victorian Age Trilogy", based on the White Wolf *World of Darkness*® role-playing game. *Dark Ages: Setite* by Kathleen Ryan, *Lasombra* by David Niall Wilson, *Ravnos* by Sarah Roarl, *Malkavian* by Ellen Porter Kiley and *Brujah* by Myranda Kalis were the latest titles in the thirteen-part vampiric "Dark Ages Clan" series, while *Vampire: Slave Ring* and *Vampire: The Overseer* were the first two books in the "Clan Brujah Trilogy" by Tim Dedopulus.

The first of four trade paperback omnibus volumes, *The Fall of Atlanta: The Clan Novel Saga Volume One* reorganized the chapters from all thirteen "Clan" novels (1999–2000) in strict chronological order with additional new material. *Orpheus: Haunting the Dead* edited by Philippe Boulle was an original anthology of four novellas.

Ashes and Angel Wings, *The Seven Deadlies* and *The Wreckage of Paradise* by Greg Stolze comprised the "Trilogy of the Fallen" series, based on the White Wolf role-playing game *Demon: The Fallen*.

Edo van Belkom's "lost" zombie gaming novel *Army of the Dead* finally saw publication from Prime Books/SFR after five years in limbo. Based on the *Dragon Dice* battle game, the book was originally written for TSR, which was subsequently acquired by rival gaming company Wizards of the Coast, who cancelled the contract.

Once again edited by James Lowder, *The Book of Final Flesh* was an anthology of twenty-four zombie stories, the third in the series based on the Eden Studios role-playing games *All Flesh Must Be Eaten*.

To tie in with Eden's *Buffy The Vampire Slayer Roleplaying Game*, *The Magic Box* was a full-colour illustrated supplement that included new character-creation ideas. From the same publisher came the *Angel Roleplaying Game Corebook*.

Hollywood's Stephen King by college English professor Tony Magistrale looked at the films based on King's work, along with an interview with the author.

Denis Meikle's *Vincent Price: The Art of Fear* was about the career of the late horror-film star and featured more than 120 stills.

In All Sincerity . . . Peter Cushing by Chris Gullo featured tributes to the late actor by Christopher Lee, Val Guest, Forrest J Ackerman, John Carpenter, Caroline Munro and the late Sir Nigel Hawthorne, among others.

From the University Press of Kentucky, Arthur Lennig's *The Immortal Count: The Life and Films of Bela Lugosi* was a revised and expanded edition of the author's 1974 volume *The Count*.

Christopher Lee updated his 1977 autobiography for the second time under the new title *Lord of Misrule*. This third edition featured a new Introduction by New Zealand director Peter Jackson, although the actor might have preferred someone else after their very public falling-out when Jackson cut Lee's performance from the third *Lord of the Rings* film.

Ray Harryhausen: An Animated Life was a new book about the special-effects wizard, written by Harryhausen with Tony Dalton and featuring hundreds of previously unpublished photos.

The Cinema of George A. Romero: Knight of the Living Dead by Tony Williams was billed as the first in-depth English-language study of the maverick director.

From FAB Press, *Fear Without Frontiers: Horror Cinema Across the Globe* was edited by Steven Jay Schneider and looked at horror films from other countries in essays and interviews from Kim Newman, Pete Tombs, Pam Keesey, Ken Hanke and others.

Creeping Flesh: The Horror Fantasy Film Book edited by David Kerekes also looked at obscure films from around the world, and *Spooky Encounters* by Daniel O'Brien was a welcome overview of Hong Kong ghost films.

Fangoria's 101 Best Horror Movies You've Never Seen by Adam Lukeman and Fangoria Magazine failed to come up with many rarities, while Joe Bob Briggs's *Profoundly Disturbing: Shocking Movies That Changed History!* examined such controversial titles as *The Exorcist, Reservoir Dogs, Blood Feast, The Wild Bunch* and *Deep Throat.*

Peter Hutchings's *Dracula: A British Film Guide* looked in detail at Hammer's ground-breaking 1958 film version, and veteran Hammer scriptwriter Jimmy Sangster set forth his advice in *Screenwriting: Techniques for Success.*

David Hughes's *Tales from Development Hell: Hollywood Film-Making the Hard Way* from Titan Books chronicled the genesis of such troubled or unproduced projects as the *Planet of the Apes* remake, *The Lord of the Rings, Total Recall, Indiana Jones IV,* Neil Gaiman's *The Sandman, Outbreak, Tomb Raider* and other movie-making disasters.

The Texas Chainsaw Massacre Companion by former *Shock Xpress* editor Stefan Jaworzyn was an in-depth look behind the scenes at Tobe Hooper's influential slice of Southern Gothic cinema and its increasingly bizarre sequels. It included interviews with key cast and crew members, previously unpublished photos, and a Foreword by the original "Leatherface", Gunnar Hansen.

Xena: Warrior Princess: The Complete Illustrated Companion by K. Stoddard Hayes not only covered all six seasons of the popular TV series (1995–2001), but also profiled the major characters, investigated the fans, took a look behind the scenes, and featured an A-Z of Greek mythology.

Also from Titan, *The Worldwide Guide to Movie Locations Presents London* by Tony Reeves revealed where such films as *An American Werewolf in London, A Clockwork Orange, Dracula A.D. 1972, Frenzy, Gorgo, I Don't Want to Be Born, Konga, The Omen, Peeping Tom, The Quatermass Experiment, The Satanic Rites of Dracula, A Study in Terror, Theatre of Blood* and the *Harry Potter* films, to name only a few, were actually shot.

The Art of X2, designed and edited by Timothy Shaner, was a handsome hardcover look behind the scenes of the blockbuster sequel, along with the (almost) complete script by Michael Dougherty and Dan Harris.

Robert Cettl's *Serial-Killer Cinema: An Analytical Filmography* appeared from McFarland & Company, as did *Horror at the Drive-In: Essays in Popular Americana*, edited by Gary D. Rhodes.

Eye on Science Fiction: 20 Interviews with Classic SF and Horror Filmmakers by the apparently indefatigable Tom Weaver was available from the same publisher.

The Pocket Essentials Roger Corman by Mark Whitehead was a short guide (in the "Pocket Essentials Film" series) to the career of the influential producer/director.

Candace Havens's *Joss Whedon: The Genius Behind Buffy* and *Slayer Slang: A Buffy the Vampire Slayer Lexicon* by Professor Michael Adams took very different critical approaches to the popular TV series.

Seven Seasons of Buffy: Science Fiction and Fantasy Writers Discuss Their Favorite Television Show edited by Glenn Yeffeth for BenBella Books included contributions from such writers as David Brin, Scott Westerfield, Chelsea Quinn Yarbro, Nancy Kilpatrick, Laura Resnick, Michelle Sagara West, Jean Lorrrah, Lawrence Watt-Evans and Nancy Holder, with a Foreword by Drew Goddard.

Small Town, Strange World was an unofficial and unauthorized episode guide to the *Smallville* TV show written by Mark Clapham.

Published by Dinoship, *Monster Kid Memories* was a wonderful reminiscence by veteran film-memorabilia collector Bob Burns as told to Tom Weaver. The book, covering Burns's friendships with such legendary movie personalities as George Pal, Glenn Strange, William Castle, Jack Pierce and many others, included more than 300 rare photos and featured a Foreword by Leonard Maltin and an Introduction by Joe Dante.

Tomart's Price Guide to Horror Movie Collectables was an overpriced but still fascinating full-colour guide to obscure action figures, model kits and tie-ins. For people who will collect anything, Jimbo Matison's *So Crazy Japanese Toys* was an illustrated guide to all those weird and wonderful monsters from Japanese TV shows and movies.

*   *   *

Spectrum 10: The Best in Contemporary Fantastic Art was edited by Cathy Fenner and Arnie Fenner and contained more than 300 colour images chosen by a jury from over 200 artists, including Brom, John Jude Palencar, Michael Whelan, Bob Eggleton, James Gurney, Garry Gianni, Jim Burns, Rick Berry, Donato Giancola and numerous others. The book also included a review of the year by Arnie Fenner and a profile of 2003 Grand Master recipient Michael Kaluta.

Compiled by John Grant (Paul Barnett) and Elizabeth Humphrey with Pamela D. Scoville, *The Chesley Awards for Science Fiction & Fantasy Art – A Retrospective* was a long-winded title for an attractive collection celebrating the past two decades of the annual award named after renowned SF illustrator Chesley Bonestell. The square-sized volume contained more than 300 pieces of art, most of it in full colour, by such illustrators as Rick Berry, Brom, Thomas Canty, Alan M. Clark, Bob Eggleton, Frank Frazetta, Frank Kelly Freas, Brian Froud, Stephen Hickman, Tom Kidd, Alan Lee, Don Maitz, Ian Miller, John Jude Palencar, Alex Schomburg, Michael Whelan and many others.

John Grant subsequently resigned his editorial position with Paper Tiger to concentrate more time on his own books.

Primal Darkness: The Gothic & Horror Art of Bob Eggleton by Shinichi Noda collected a selection of the multiple-award-winning artist's darker work between hardcovers for Steve Jackson Games/Cartouche Press. It included commentary by the artist and an Introduction by Brian Lumley.

Gahan Wilson's Monster Party was a book of ghoulish cartoons published by ibooks, and *The Wolves in the Walls* by Neil Gaiman with art from Dave McKean was a large-sized children's picture book about Lucy, a little girl whose family did not believe that wolves lived in the walls of their house.

From artist Gary Gianni and publisher Wandering Star, *Robert E. Howard's Conan of Cimmeria* was an attractive chapbook of preliminary drawings and sketches with commentary by the illustrator.

Published by Pantheon Books and designed by Chip Kidd, *Mythology: The DC Art of Alex Ross* was a huge hardcover compendium of Ross's superb superhero paintings with comentary from the artist. Ross also contributed a striking cover to an updated edition of Les Daniels's DC Comics: A Celebration of the World's Favorite Comic Book Heroes.

Five years after entering bankruptcy protection and posting a loss of $8 million (£5 million) in 2002, Marvel Enterprises reported a $42.2 million profit during the first three months of 2003, with revenues rising fifty-three per cent to $87.4 million. The rise was due to the success of the movie adaptations of Marvel properties. Although comic sales grew only four per cent during the same period, licensing revenue jumped 500 per cent. Following a leap in second-quarter profits of 400 per cent, with net income soaring from $8.38 million to $32.8 million, a full-year forecast had the company set to make $100 million.

The result of two year's work, Neil Gaiman returned to the universe he created with the hardcover graphic novel The Sandman: Endless Nights from DC Comics/Vertigo. The book collected seven stories involving each of the "Endless" – Death, Destiny, Destruction, Delirium, Desire, Despair and Dream – illustrated by P. Craig Russell, Milo Manara, Bill Sienkiewicz, Miguelanxo Prado, Barron Storey, Glenn Fabry and Frank Quitely, with a cover by Dave McKean.

The Sandman: King of Dreams was a hardcover look at the whole Sandman phenomenon by former Vertigo editor and writer Alisa Kwitney. The book included previously unpublished artwork and an Introduction by Gaiman.

Again written by Alan Moore and illustrated by Kevin O'Neill, The League of Extraordinary Gentlemen Volume II collected another six-part adventure in which the group of Victorian champions resisted an invasion of Martian war machines. The hardcover compilation from America's Best Comics also featured a bizarre novella, "The New Traveller's Almanac" (taking in everything from Arkham to the Black Lagoon!), plus various games and diversions.

Heroes & Monsters: The Unofficial Companion to The League of Extraordinary Gentlemen by Jess Nevins featured critical essays and panel-by-panel annotations of the original comic book miniseries, with commentary by co-creator and illustrator Kevin O'Neill and an interview with Alan Moore, who also supplied the Introduction.

Published by Burlyman Entertainment, The Matrix Comics was a compilation of twelve stories originally published on The

Matrix.com website. Edited by Spencer Lamm and based on the concepts created by Larry and Andy Wachowski, the book included contributions from Bill Sienkiewicz, Ted McKeever, Dave Gibbons and others, including a short story by Neil Gaiman.

iBooks Graphic Novels was launched in March with a monthly list that included the continuing adventures of "A Boy and His Dog", *Vic and Blood* by Harlan Ellison (who added an ® symbol to his name in 2003 and is now a registered trademark) and Richard Corben. From the same publisher, *The Best of Ray Bradbury: The Graphic Novel* was a reprint collection of twelve graphic adaptations from 1992–96, illustrated by Corben, P. Craig Russell, Mike Mignola, Dave Gibbons, Dave McKean, Moebius, Mike Kaluta, Kent Williams, Wayne Barlow and others, with an Introduction by Bradbury himself.

Published by Dark Horse Comics, *The Dark Horse Book of Hauntings* was an attractive hardcover edited by Scott Allie collecting seven full-colour comic strips by Mike Mignola (a new "Hellboy" story), P. Craig Russell, Evan Dorkin and others, including a reprinting of the short story "Thurnley Abbey" by Perceval Landon, illustrated by cover artist Gary Gianni. Also from Dark Horse, *Isolation and Illusion: Collected Short Stories 1977–1997* compiled artist P. Craig Russell's adaptations of work by H.P. Lovecraft, O. Henry and Cyrano De Bergerac, among others.

Joss Whedon's eight-issue run of *Fray*, about a vampire slayer from the future, was also released as a paperback by Dark Horse. The same company began reprinting Marvel's entire 1970s *Conan the Barbarian* series with the graphic-novel collections *The Chronicles of Conan Volume 1: Tower of the Elephant and Other Stories*, *2: Rogues in the House and Other Stories* and *3: The Monster of the Monoliths and Other Stories*. Written by Roy Thomas with digitally recoloured art by Barry Windsor-Smith, Gil Kane and others, each book contained a fascinating Afterword by Thomas talking about the history of the original series.

Vampire Legends from Black Swan Press was illustrated by Mike Hoffman, Jeff Gan, Norm Watson and others.

Devil in the Details was the fifth in Moonstone Books' *Kolchak* series, scripted by Stefan Petrucha with art by Trevor Von Eeden. From CGE and written by William O'Neill, the bi-monthly *John Carpenter's Snake Plissken Chronicles* debuted in June with three different covers by Travis Smith, Tone Rodriguez or John Van Fleet.

Launched at the Halloween 25th Anniversary Convention, *Halloween: One Good Scare* was independently published as a limited-edition comic book scripted by Stefan Hutchinson with art by Peter Fielding.

In an attempt to pare down its cast, Top Cow's *Witchblade* series culminated in the deaths of two main characters, voted for by the readers. From writer J. Michael Straczynski and artist Gary Frank, Top Cow's *Midnight Nation* involved an LAPD homicide detective who was guided by an enigmatic young woman on a quest through a parallel world to recover his soul.

Written by Fiona Avery and Tippi Blevins with artwork from Romano Molenarr, *Cursed* was a four-issue miniseries from Top Cow about Egyptian curses, bizarre murders, mystical amulets and Queen Cleopatra in modern times.

Cyberosia Publishing relaunched Ray Fawkes's independent zombie-spy comic *Spookshow* as a graphic novel.

From IDW Publishing, Steve Niles and Ben Templesmith took the idea from a story in EC's *Tales from the Crypt* #26 (also reworked as a 1986 *Twilight Zone* episode by Michael Cassutt) and created *30 Days of Night*, set in an Alaskan town where a month of darkness attracted a band of bloodthirsty vampires. Niles and Elman Brown also adapted Richard Matheson's classic vampire novel *I Am Legend* for the same company.

Featuring a team of vampire spies, described as "a unique cross between James Bond and Dracula", Jeff Mariotte's *CVO: Artifact* was a three-issue miniseries with art by Gabriel Hernandez. Also from IDW, *Grumpy Old Monsters* was a four-issue miniseries for children featuring the classic creatures, written by Kevin J. Anderson and Rebecca Moesta with art by Paco Cavero and Guillermo Mendoza.

From Vanguard Productions, *Neal Adams' Monsters* was the first English-language hardcover reprint of the artist's graphic novel featuring The Frankenstein Monster, Vlad Dracula and The Werewolf, digitally recoloured. The hardcover was also available in a signed de luxe edition featuring a sixteen-page bonus portfolio section.

Published by Digital Webbing and Fiction Factory for Hallowe'en, C.G. Kirby's *Freakshow* was a one-shot anthology of four stories inspired by such classic horror comics as *Creepy* and *Eerie*.

Eureka Productions's *Graphic Classics: Edgar Allan Poe* featured twelve stories and poems by Poe, plus a sequel to a Poe story by Clive Barker and an Introduction by Joe R. Lansdale. In *Graphic Classics: H.P. Lovecraft*, artists such as Richard Corben, Tom Sutton, Stephen Hickman and Chris Pelletiere adapted nine stories and the poem "Fungi from Yuggoth". There was also an Introduction by Gahan Wilson and a cartoon biography of Lovecraft by George Kucher. *Graphic Classics: Bram Stoker* featured an Introduction by Mort Castle and comic-strip adaptations of *Lair of the White Worm*, *The Jewel of Seven Stars*, *Dracula* and five other Stoker tales from artists Rico Schacherl, J.B. Bonivert, Glenn Barr, Hunt Emerson and others. Other volumes in the series were devoted to Arthur Conan Doyle, H.G. Wells, Jack London and Ambrose Bierce.

From Checker Book Publishing, the two reprint volumes of *Clive Barker's Hellraiser: Collected Best* contained contributions from Neil Gaiman, Larry Wachowski, John Bolton, Alex Ross and, of course, Barker himself.

Introduced by Neil Gaiman, Batton Lash's *Sonovawitch! and Other Tales of Supernatural Law* collected more strange cases handled by attorneys Wolff & Byrd, including a man accused of "hexual harassment".

Thomas Edison's first film version of Mary Shelley's classic became the basis of *Edison's Frankenstein 1910: A Graphic Interpretation of a Lost American Classic* by Chris Yambar and Robb Bihun. The black and white illustrated adaptation also included a section on the film (of which only one print is known to exist) by historian Frederick C. Wiebel, Jr. and was also available in a signed and numbered edition.

The Hulk became the first comic-book character to be honoured on official United States coinage. A limited edition 2003 Kennedy half-dollar struck by the US Mint depicted the Marvel hero in full colour and was not released into circulation to the general public.

With genre films representing nine out of the top ten titles of 2003, the summer box office was awash with sequels. The previous year's hit, *The Lord of the Rings: The Two Towers*, continued to add to its overall total, with a North American gross in excess of $300 million. However, the Wachowski Brothers's *The Matrix Reloaded*, the much-anticipated sequel to their 1999 cult box-office smash, had the second-best opening weekend in movie history, taking more than $93 million before passing $200 million in its second week. The film also broke records on the other side of the Atlantic, grossing £12 million in the fourth-biggest opening weekend in the UK.

With more impressive special effects and a less pretentious script than the original film, the first *Matrix* sequel was one of the biggest hits of the year. Unfortunately *The Matrix Revolutions*, released just a few months later, was a disappointing return to the inanity of the original and consequently only managed to gross half the takings of its predecessor.

In an attempt to make some sense of it all, nine short animated films set in the same universe were released on video and DVD under the title *The Animatrix*.

Bryan Singer's superior *X-Men* sequel, simply titled *X2*, gave *The Matrix* films a run for their money with a first-week gross of almost $86 million. The movie opened on the same day in ninety-five countries worldwide and was the fourth-biggest combined opening of all time, following *Spider-Man* and the first two *Harry Potter* films.

Terminator 3: Rise of the Machines was also an improvement over its predecessor, but even with the impressive stunts and a surprise dystopian ending the film was a disappointment at the box-office, possibly because audiences were sequeled out by the time it reached the screen.

Despite opening at #1 and breaking the $100 million barrier, *Spy Kids 3-D* was the least successful of writer-director Robert Rodriguez's sci-spy series for children, perhaps because of the headache-inducing virtual-reality effects and a terrible performance by Sylvester Stallone as the evil Toymaker.

David Zucker's lowbrow horror-spoof *Scary Movie 3* had the best October debut for a film ever, taking nearly $50 million in its first weekend. However, it only barely managed to gross a $100 million total, despite a PG-13 rating and a cast that included Charlie Sheen, Pamela Anderson, Peter Boyle, George Carlin, William Forsythe, Macy Grey, Leslie Nielsen, Jenny McCarthy, Jeremy Piven, Denise Richards and *American Idol*'s Simon Cowell.

A demonic Freddy Krueger (Robert Englund) used a zombified Jason Voorhees (Ken Kirzinger) from the *Friday the 13th* series to force the dumb teenagers of Springwood to remember him in Ronny Yu's gore-filled showdown, *Freddy vs. Jason*.

The producers blamed the new computer game for the poor box-office results of *Lara Croft: Tomb Raider: The Cradle of Life*, in which Angelina Jolie's archaeologist (complete with odd British accent) was hired to recover Pandora's Box from Africa. They should have blamed Jan De Bont's lacklustre direction and the forgettable script instead.

The Grim Reaper was hunting down more teenagers who had managed to elude him in *Final Destination 2*, and the scarecrow-like Creeper attacked a bus full of high-school football jocks and their cheerleaders in the equally unsuccessful *Jeepers Creepers II*.

After a hectic summer, it was announced that Hollywood was looking for new ideas after evidence that sequels were faltering at the box-office. Even so, the year ended as it had begun, with the third instalment of Peter Jackson's epic fantasy adaptation, *The Lord of the Rings: The Return of the King*, raking in almost $300 million at the American box-office and breaking records for the largest Wednesday opening and the largest single day's takings in December.

With #1 openings in both America and Britain, Gore Verbinski's *Pirates of the Caribbean: The Curse of the Black Pearl* was also one of the year's most successful films. Based on the classic Walt Disney theme-park attraction, Johnny Depp's marvellously eccentric pirate set out to rescue a governor's feisty daughter from a mutinous Geoffrey Rush's band of skeleton cut-throats. Also based on a Disneyland theme ride and starring a less irritating than usual Eddie Murphy, *The Haunted Mansion* didn't perform quite so well, despite Terence Stamp's fun turn as a sepulchral butler.

Following the huge success of the *X-Men* films and *Spider-Man*, two more Marvel Comics heroes reached the big screen in 2003. But whereas Ang Lee was unable to convince audiences that scientist Eric Bana could turn into a green CGI monster in the overblown *Hulk*, Mark Steven Johnson's darker *Daredevil* failed to find the audience it deserved, even with an uncomfortable-looking Ben Affleck in the red leather suit.

Affleck also starred as an unlikely action-adventure computer engineer who had his mind wiped in John Woo's dumb thriller *Paycheck*, based on a short story by Philip K. Dick. Following a Third World War, Christian Bale's cleric was ordered to seek out and eradicate emotion in the totalitarian future of Kurt Wimmer's *Equilibrium*, filmed in Germany. In Vencenzo Natali's *Cypher*, Jeremy Northan and Lucy Liu manipulated a plot by rival companies to brainwash industrial spies, while Michael Winterbottom's *Code 46* starred Tim Robbins and Samantha Morton and was set in another dystopian near-future where everyone needed permission to travel.

Thanks to an intensive promotional campaign, the low-budget British zombie film *28 Days Later* finally opened in America and took a very respectable $40 million. Based on the video game, Artisan promoted its zombie thriller *House of the Dead* with a miniature comic-book adaptation. It didn't help the poor box-office results of the American-German-Canadian co-production.

Given a minimal showcase theatrical release, Don Coscarelli's award-winning *Bubba Ho-Tep* was based on a short story by Joe R. Lansdale and pitted a seventy-year-old Elvis Presley (a brilliant performance by Bruce Campbell) and a black John F. Kennedy (Ossie Davis) against a soul-sucking Egyptian mummy.

Campbell was also the producer of Michael Kallio's grim serial-killer thriller *Hatred of a Minute*. Paul F. Ryan's *Home Room* was another independent chiller, starring Busy Philipps and Erika Christensen, while Angela Bettis was the eponymous obsessed teen in Lucky McKee's low-budget *May*.

An evil Tooth Fairy (the film's original title) returned to the town of *Darkness Falls* after 150 years and threatened Chaney Kley's childhood sweetheart (*Buffy*'s Emma Caulfield) and her younger brother.

The Texas Chainsaw Massacre was a nasty and pointless remake of the 1974 original from music-video director Marcus Nispel, while Glen Morgan's remake of *Willard* didn't stand a rat's chance at the box-office, despite the usual eccentric performance from Crispin Glover.

Although it starred George Clooney and had James Cameron as a producer, Steven Soderbergh's remake of *Solaris*, based on the book by Stanislaw Lem, proved to be just as tedious as the 1972 Russian original.

Adapted from a silly alien-invasion novel by Stephen King, *Dreamcatcher* was a mess. It died at the box office, despite a script co-written by director Lawrence Kasdan and the legendary William Goldman.

Scientists Aaron Eckhart, Hilary Swank and Stanley Tucci discovered that the Earth's magnetic centre had stopped spinning in John Amiel's big-budget disaster movie *The Core*, which sat on the shelf for a year.

Tibetan mystic Chow Yun-Fat teamed up with New York thief Seann William Scott to protect an ancient scroll and foil an aged Nazi's bid for world domination in *Bulletproof Monk*, and Hong Kong police officer Jackie Chan was raised from the dead by *The Medallion* to battle villain Julian Sands in an unfunny comedy credited to five scriptwriters.

James Mangold's *Identity* was a modern version of the old darkhouse mystery starring John Cusack and Ray Liotta. A clever and intelligent thriller set in a run-down motel, it was only let down by a twist ending that was a little too contrived for its own good.

A crazed Sigourney Weaver and Jon Voight forced delinquent teenagers at a desert camp in Texas to dig *Holes*, a surprise box-office hit for Disney based on the bestselling young-adult novel by Louis Sachar.

Disney-Pixar's *Finding Nemo* broke box-office records for a cartoon, taking more than $70 million on its opening weekend. After nine weeks in the charts it became the most successful cartoon of all time, surpassing the studio's 1994 blockbuster *The Lion King*.

A voice cast that included Brad Pitt, Catherine Zeta-Jones, Michelle Pfeiffer and Joseph Fiennes failed to entice similar audiences into DreamWorks's animated *Sinbad Legend of the Seven Seas*.

Eliza Dushku was among a group of campers trapped and hunted in the West Virginia wilderness by cannibalistic mountain men in Rob Schmidt's by-the-numbers slasher *Wrong Turn*, and Ray Wise took his family on an ill-advised short cut through the woods in *Dead End*, written and directed by Jean-Baptiste Andrea and Fabrice Canepa.

There were more backwoods horrors in Eli Roth's highly derivative *Cabin Fever*, when five vacationing college kids became infected with a deadly flesh-eating disease, and the year's best slice of unrelenting Southern Gothic was Rob Zombie's long-delayed directorial debut, *House of 1000 Corpses*, starring Karen Black, Michael J. Pollard and the great Sid Haig among the redneck psychos and mad doctors.

Penelope Cruz's cameo as an apparently crazy inmate of a haunted asylum was the only interesting thing about Matthieu Kassovitz's *Gothika*, another dud from Dark Castle Entertainment. The actress also portrayed a demon from Hell battling for a man's soul against a Heaven-sent Victoria Abril in the French/Spanish co-production *No News of God*.

The award-winning *Fausto 5.0* was a modern reworking of the traditional deal-with-the-Devil story, set in a nightmarish version of Spain.

Loosely based on the graphic novel by Alan Moore and Kevin O'Neill, *The League of Extraordinary Gentlemen* was not quite the romp it should have been, despite having Sean Connery's Allan Quartermain, a half-vampiric Mina Harker, and a host of other literary heroes teaming up to prevent the masked "Fantom" from starting a world war.

Kate Beckinsale's sexy vampire assassin made the mistake of falling in love with one of her shape-shifting enemies in Len Wiseman's directorial debut, *Underworld*. However, White Wolf and author Nancy A. Collins filed suit in September against Sony Pictures, Screen Gems and Lakeshore Entertainment for copyright violation/infringement. The case alleged that *Underworld* deliberately infringed on White Wolf's role-playing games *Vampire: The Masquerade* and *Werewolf: Apocalypse* in general, plus a 1994 short story Collins wrote set in the same "World of Darkness"®.

Renegade Catholic priests Heath Ledger and Mark Addy pursued a mythical immortal through the streets of Rome in Brian Helgeland's muddled *The Sin Eater* (a.k.a. *The Order*). The film's release was reportedly delayed four times after the laughable special effects sequences of departing souls had to be reshot following test screenings.

New York yuppies Dennis Quaid and Sharon Stone moved into an isolated mansion and discovered that former owner Stephen Dorff was a crazy psycho in Mike Figgis's predictable *Cold Creek Manor*.

A group of archaeologists travelled back in time to 14th-century France to rescue their professor (an unlikely Billy Connolly) in Richard Donner's dumb *Timeline*, based on a 1999 novel by Michael Crichton.

The best thing about *Looney Tunes Back in Action*, Joe

Dante's slapstick blend of live action and animation, was a sequence featuring Robby the Robot, the Metaluna Mutant, The Man from Planet X, Robot Monster, a Triffid, the Daleks, a Fiend Without a Face and a monochrome Kevin McCarthy still clutching a body-snatching pod! Other cameos included Dick Miller, Roger Corman, Peter Graves, Mary Woronov, Batman, and Scooby-Doo and Shaggy.

Jason Isaacs portrayed both the black-hearted Captain Hook and the nervous Mr Darling in P.J. Hogan's faithful live-action version of *Peter Pan*, which should have done better than it did with Christmas audiences.

Tim Burton's *Big Fish* was a bizarre American fable about a story-teller (played by both Ewan McGregor and Albert Finney) whose tall tales turned out to be true, including the one about Danny DeVito's lycanthropic ring-master.

From Italy, Ivan Zuccon's shot-on-video *The Shunned House* combined incomprehensible adaptations of the title story, "The Music of Eric (sic) Zann" and "The Dreams in the Witch-House", all of which would have had H.P. Lovecraft spinning in his grave.

The former inhabitants of a family guest house emerged from their graves as singing and dancing zombies in Takashi Miike's bizarre black comedy *The Happiness of the Katakuris*. *A Tale of Two Sisters* was a box-office smash in its native Korea and concerned a pair of twins living in a haunted house with a ghost and their psychotic stepmother.

The original *Alien* was released in a "Director's Cut", and Fritz Lang's 1927 classic *Metropolis* was reissued in a restored and re-edited print before both went to DVD.

Held at Hollywood's famed Egyptian Theatre, The World 3-D Film Expo showed thirty-three features and twenty-one shorts over ten days in September. Amongst those titles revived in all their 3-D glory were *House of Wax*, *It Came from Outer Space*, *Robot Monster* and, of course, *Creature from the Black Lagoon*.

The Lord of the Rings: The Two Towers collected three awards at Britain's BAFTA awards ceremony, held in London in February. These were for Best Costume Design, Best Special Effects and Film of the Year.

The seventy-fifth Academy Awards ceremony was held in Los Angeles on 23 March. Because of the war in Iraq, there was no red carpet and a number of celebrities, including *The*

Two Towers director Peter Jackson, did not attend. The latter film picked up Oscars for Visual Effects and Sound Editing, but lost out on the major prizes. The Japanese fantasy *Spirited Away* won for achievement in Animated Film, and Eric Armstrong's SF-themed *The Chubbchubbs*! was voted Best Animated Short.

For the first time, it looked as if Britain might soon become the biggest film market in Europe. In 2003, an estimated 180 million cinema tickets were sold, compared to 175 million in France (down almost seven per cent on the previous year) and 165 million in Germany.

For vampire fans, one of the most exciting DVD releases of 2003 was a previously unrecorded version of Bram Stoker's novel from Pakistan. Made in 1967, and thought lost for many years until Mondo Macabro rediscovered the only surviving negative, *Zinda Laash* (*The Living Corpse*) was an almost shot-for-shot recreation of Hammer's 1958 *Dracula*. The Mondo Macabro label also issued Michel Lemoine's 1974 French obscurity *Seven Women for Satan* (*Les Weekends Malefiques du Comte Zaroff*). Both discs included interviews with cast and crew members.

Presented by Wes Craven, *Dracula II Ascension* was a direct-to-DVD sequel to *Dracula 2000* and starred Craig Sheffer as the leader of a group of New Orleans medical students who revived a blond Dracula (Stephen Billington) in a bath of blood. Roy Scheider also turned up in little more than a cameo.

Warner Home Video issued both the 1932 and 1941 versions of *Dr Jekyll and Mr Hyde* on a single DVD, as well as pairing up the 1933 *Mystery of the Wax Museum* with its 1953 remake, *House of Wax*.

The 1933 British film *The Ghoul*, starring Boris Karloff and Ernest Thesiger, was finally issued in a beautifully restored version on DVD by MGM Home Entertainment. The MGM release of Roger Corman's *The Tomb of Ligeia* also included the 1972 ABC-TV special *An Evening with Edgar Allan Poe*, in which Vincent Price recited four of Poe's classic stories.

The DVD for *The League of Extraordinary Gentlemen* was very noticeably lacking any involvement from credited director Stephen Norrington and included twelve deleted scenes, while the "Special Collector's Edition" DVD of *Attack of the Killer*

Tomatoes featured more than four hours of extras, including audio commentaries, deleted scenes and the original 8mm student film.

The Alien Quadrilogy (sic) was a nine-disc set containing theatrical and alternate versions of all four *Alien* films along with numerous extras, totalling an exhausting sixty-two hours of material.

Firefly: The Complete Series collected all fourteen episodes of Joss Whedon's failed 2002 TV series set 500 years in the future, including three shows that never aired in America.

Poor old Richard Lynch's career hit rock bottom when he turned up in the soft-core lesbian antics of Donald F. Glut's *The Mummy's Kiss* from Seduction Cinema, with special make-up effects by John Carl Buechler.

At least Tony Marsiglia's *Dr Jekyll & Mistress Hyde* and *The Witches of Sappho Salon* tried to do something serious with their minuscule budgets. Seduction was also not slow to cash in on the previous year's blockbusters with an uncut collector's edition of *Lord of the G-Strings: The Femaleship of the String* and a two-disc presentation of *SpiderBabe*, both starring Mundae and Darian Caine.

The two actresses (to use the term loosely) also turned up in the Shock-O-Rama double feature DVD *Satan's School for Lust*, which included *Blood for the Muse*, featuring Tina Krause as a dubious bonus. On the same label, Brett Piper's *Screaming Dead* starred the ubiquitous Mundae and was set in the supernatural dungeon of an abandoned insane asylum.

The survivors of a plane crash defended a desert farmhouse against giant stop-motion spiders in Piper's other low-budget release of the year, *Arachnia*, from MTI Home Video.

Despite the original 2001 movie being considered a box-office flop, Disney released the animated *Atlantis: Milo's Return* directly to DVD in May, and in *Scooby-Doo and The Legend of the Vampire*, Scooby and the gang found themselves investigating a remote Australian castle and a vampire who was turning rock music acts into fanged creatures like himself.

For fans of the old-time horror stars, Image Entertainment's double-disc set *Heroes of Horror* not only contained the superb Biography Channel documentaries about Boris Karloff, Lon Chaney Jr., Bela Lugosi, Peter Lorre and Vincent Price, but also a wealth of fascinating extras, including numerous trailers and rare featurettes.

Issued by Warner Home Video/TCM Archives, the *Lon Chaney Collection* was a two-disc set that collected three rare titles featuring the great silent-film star – *The Ace of Hearts* (1921), *Laugh Clown Laugh* (1928) and *The Unknown* (1927) – along with Kevin Brownlow's terrific documentary *Lon Chaney: A Thousand Faces*, and Rick Schmidlin's stills "reconstruction" of *London After Midnight*. The package also included stills and memorabilia galleries, plus optional audio commentaries by Chaney, Sr. biographer Michael F. Blake.

In July, a "video nasty" banned for almost thirty years was finally given a certificate by the British Board of Film Classification. *Snuff*, originally shot in 1971 under the title *Slaughter* by Michael and Roberta Findlay, was deemed unreleasable until producer Allen Shackleton added extra scenes supposedly showing a crew member being tortured and killed.

The Diary of Ellen Rimbauer was a prequel to the 2002 miniseries *Stephen King's Rose Red*. Starring Steven Brand and Lisa Brenner, the ABC-TV movie explored the haunted history of the Seattle mansion.

Candice Bergen played a murder-mystery author terrorized in her isolated beach house in John Badham's CBS-TV movie *Footsteps*, based on an unproduced play by Ira Levin, while Kirstie Alley and Gloria Reuben starred in CBS's *Salem Witch Trials*, which also featured special appearances by Peter Ustinov and Shirley MacLaine.

The CBS movie *Back to the Batcave: The Misadventures of Adam and Burt* was a surreal blend of fact and fiction as actors Adam West and a rotund Burt Ward, playing themselves, followed a series of clues to recover the stolen Batmobile while recalling the history of the 1960s *Batman* TV series. Former guest villians Lee Meriwether, Frank Gorshin and Julie Newmar also turned up to add to the confusion.

A police officer (Thomas Gibson) learned that a college professor planned to bring the serial-killer murderer of his wife back to life in the TBS Superstation original movie *Evil Never Dies*. Also on TBS, *Red Water* was an anaemic *Jaws* knock-off starring Lou Diamond Phillips, Kirsty Swanson and Coolio.

On the SciFi Channel, Chicago power worker Richard Grieco had problems destroying a race of spider-people from a parallel universe in David Wu's pulp SF adventure *Webs*.

A trio of 1950s movie monsters were accidentally released into the real world in Hallmark Entertainment's Hallowe'en film for children, *Monster Makers*, starring Adam Baldwin, George Kennedy and Linda Blair.

Twentieth Century-Fox's series of 1930s and 1940s *Charlie Chan* films were pulled from the Fox Movie Channel's cable schedule during the summer as a result of complaints from individuals and a Washington-based civil rights advocacy group called the Organization of Chinese Americans, Inc. Most of the complaints to the network concerned the stereotyping of the Charlie Chan character and the fact that he was played in the films by non-Asian actors.

Reformed vampire-slayer Faith (Eliza Dushku) returned to both *Angel* and *Buffy the Vampire Slayer* for its final season. The latter concluded in May with an apocalyptic showdown between Buffy's rag-tag band of Slayers and The First, resulting in the death of a major character and the apparent demise of another.

After his SF Western *Firefly* was abruptly cancelled by the Fox Network, *Buffy* creator Joss Whedon remained loyal to his stars, casting Nathan Fillion as serial-killer priest Caleb in UPN's *Buffy* and Gina Torres as Cordelia's demon offspring Jasmine in the WB's *Angel*.

At the end of the fourth series, The Beast was defeated, Angelus turned back into Angel (David Boreanaz), and Conner (Vincent Kartheiser) settled with a new family after a change in reality. The new season of *Angel* opened with the vampire and his gang (including new series regular Spike, played by James Marsters) now running the evil law firm of Wolfram & Hart.

Sarah Thompson joined the cast as Eve, a conduit to Wolfram & Hart's mysterious "Senior Partners", while Mercedes McNab returned as airhead vampire Harmony and Juliet Landau reprised her role as Drusilla. Veteran British actor Roy Dotrice guest-starred as Wesley's critical father in a story involving cyborg assassins, and the show's 100th episode marked the return of Christina Carpenter as Cordelia Chase, in a poignant coda to that character's storyline.

Unfortunately, The WB kept shifting the day and time period

for *Angel*, making it difficult for even the most diehard fans to keep track of it in the schedules.

After *Buffy* ended, Eliza Dushku got her own series with the Fox Network's *Tru Calling*, about medical student and morgue worker Tru Davies who could talk with the newly dead and relive a day in order to change fate. Meanwhile, CBS-TV's *Joan of Arcadia* starred Joe Mantegna, Mary Steenburgen, and Amber Tamblyn as teenager Joan Girardi who received unexpected visits from God in various guises.

After celebrating its 200th episode and nine seasons, Monica (Roma Downey) faced a celestial review board in the two-part series finale of CBS-TV's *Touched by an Angel*.

The WB's turgid update of *Tarzan* starred male model Travis Fimmel as a well-groomed King of the Jungle, transposed to the Big City where he accidentally caused the death of policewoman Jane's (Sarah Wayne Callies) detective boyfriend. Lucy Lawless and Mitch Pileggi were also around as the Ape Man's relatives.

After guest appearances by Richard Lynch and Cheryl Ladd as emissaries of evil, and the birth of Piper's magical baby, the fifth season of The WB's *Charmed* finished with a two-hour story in which the three witchy Halliwell sisters were turned into Greek goddesses. Meanwhile, "White Lighter" Leo (Brian Krause) became an Elder and found himself replaced by Chris (Drew Fuller), a mysterious young guardian from the future.

Following a guest appearance by the 1970s Man of Steel himself, Christopher Reeve, Lana (Kristin Kreuk) encountered the apparent ghost of a childhood friend and the wonderful Michael McKean turned up as an alcoholic Perry White in The WB's increasingly downbeat *Smallville*, which moved to a new day and a new time. Rutger Hauer and Patrick Bergin also both made appearances as crime boss Morgan Edge.

ABC-TV's *Veritas: The Quest* involved teenager Nikko Zond (Ryan Merriman), who teamed up with his archaeologist father (Alex Carter) to solve the mysteries of history and civilization. In April, ABC predictably pulled the plug on its new supernatural drama *Miracles*, in which disillusioned priest Skeet Urich investigated unexplained phenomena after his own near-death experience and joined Angus MacFadyen's paranormal investigator and Marisa Ramirez's former police officer in a group who believed that the end of the world was approaching.

Other shows that were cancelled included the long-running *Sabrina the Teenage Witch* and UPN's revived-again *Twilight Zone*. Hosted by Forrest Whitaker, the latter included such episodes as "It's Still a Good Life", in which Cloris Leachman and Bill(y) Mumy reprised their roles from the original 1961 show, and "Monsters on Maple Street", which starred veteran Andrew McCarthy in a remake of a classic 1960 episode.

After ratings plummeted by thirty-two per cent during the second season, UPN's *Star Trek* series *Enterprise* was revamped for its third year, with Scott Bakula's dull Captain Jonathan Archer and crew exploring the uncharted Delphic Expanse, seeking revenge on the alien Xindi who had killed millions of people on Earth in the previous season's finale.

Christopher Gorham played a teenage super-secret agent working for the National Security Agency whose body was invaded by nano-technology in UPN's struggling *Jake 2.0*. The best episode featured guest star Lee Majors (*The Six Million Dollar Man*) as a secret agent lured out of retirement.

HBO's new supernatural miniseries *Carnivále* was possibly the best genre show of 2003. It followed a bizarre travelling carnival around the Depression-era Dust Bowl of the 1930s. The twelve-episode season set up parallel stories featuring Ben Hawkins (Nick Stahl), a mysterious fugitive with hidden psychic abilities who was taken in by the carnival, and demonic priest Brother Justin Crowe (Clancy Brown), who used his powers of persuasion for evil. This beautifully produced series also starred Michael J. Anderson, Adrienne Barbeau, Patrick Bauchau and John Fleck. A second season of the modestly rated show was scheduled for early 2005.

A close runner-up was Showtime's equally quirky *Dead Like Me*, which was the network's highest-rated series during the summer. When dysfunctional nineteen-year-old slacker Georgia "George" Lass (Ellen Munth) was killed by a toilet seat from space, she found herself reincarnated as an undead "Reaper", who was sent by her boss Rube (Mandy Patinkin) to collect the souls of the about-to-be-departed. Co-star Rebecca Gayheart left the show midway through the season and was replaced by Laura Harris.

Another equally oddball series was the Fox Network's retro sitcom *The Pitts*, about the eponymous suburban family who were cursed with bad luck. After having to contend with a psychotic babysitter, a haunted VW car, turning into werewolves, and being evicted from their home by an evil ventriloquist dummy, their bad luck continued and the show quickly disappeared from the schedules.

Following a break after losing even more viewers during the February sweeps, USA's *The Dead Zone* returned in July for a seven-episode "extension". In the second-season finale, Johnny Smith (Anthony Michael Hall) encountered a visionary from the future (Fran Whaley) who offered to stop Armageddon for a price.

Based on the likeable movie series, the SciFi Channel's *Tremors* retained the same offbeat humour as the inhabitants of Perfection Valley, Nevada, co-existed with giant Graboid worm El Blanco, Shriekers, AssBlasters and other bizarre creatures, the results of secret government experiments. Michael Gross returned as paranoid survivalist Burt Gummer, and Christopher Lloyd was a semi-regular along with various guest stars from other SF and fantasy TV shows.

Scraping the bottom of the reality barrel, *Scare Tactics* lamely tried to frighten people with obvious genre-inspired stunts filmed by "hidden" cameras. It was presided over by a grumpy-looking Shannen Doherty (who probably wished she'd never left *Charmed*).

The BBC all but ignored the fortieth anniversary of *Doctor Who*, failing to deliver any worthwhile tribute but opting instead to release a bunch of "collectable" tat in time for the Christmas toy and entertainment market.

At least the Corporation managed to give us *Strange*, a fun six-part series created by Andrew Marshall about de-ordained occult investigator John Strange (Richard Coyle), local nurse Jude Atkins (Samantha Janus) and the enigmatic Canon Black (the wonderful Ian Richardson). Guest stars included Anna Massey, Imelda Staunton, Ian McNeice, Tom Baker and Jim Carter.

Maxwell Atoms's *The Grim Adventures of Billy and Mandy* returned to The Cartoon Network as a full half-hour series in June. In the second-season premiere, the Grim Reaper got his two young friends into Toadblatt's Summer School of Sorcery. In NBC-TV's animated *Tutenstein*, based on the comic books by Jay Stephens, a ten-year-old mummified Pharaoh was struck by a bolt of lightning and brought back to life 3,000 years later in a large metropolitan museum, where he was befriended by Cleo and her talking cat Luxor.

As if the new school term wasn't bad enough, in Wham!'s comedy cartoon *Seriously Weird* a teenager was cursed with being a magnet "for all that is weird". Jerry Lewis played the reanimated corpse of Professor Frink's father in the "Frinkenstein" segment of the annual Hallowe'en episode of *The Simpsons*, *Treehouse of Horror XIV*. In "Reaper Madness", Homer was forced to take Death's place, and Bart and Millhouse found themselves trapped in a world frozen in time in "Stop the World I Want to Goof Off". Other guest voices in this episode included boxer Oscar de la Hoya and Jennifer Garner.

Matt Groenig's equally inventive *Futurama* ended its erratic five-year run on Fox with an episode in which Fry struck a musical bargain with the Robot Devil to finally woo Leela.

In May, ABC's eccentric daytime soap opera *Port Charles* added veteran Hollywood star Anne Jeffreys to the cast as a wealthy socialite who signed over her fortune to vampire Joshua Temple (Ian Buchanan). The low-rated show finally ended its six-year run in October with vampire lovers Caleb and Livvie getting married. However, the storyline hinting that Alison was carrying Caleb's demon baby was left unresolved.

Meanwhile, former *Rowan & Martin's Laugh-In* comedian Ruth Buzzi joined the cast of NBC-TV's *Passions* as a nosy nurse. The equally nutty soap featured its usual mix of witches, angels, more demonic babies and even an appearance by Death amongst the *Bewitched* in-jokes. On the syndicated show *Beyond with James Van Praagh*, the celebrity psychic medium apparently put Juliet Mills in touch with her deceased *Passions* co-star, Josh Ryan Evans, as well as family friend Sir Laurence Olivier.

Marti Nixon, Maitland McDonagh and Lisa Bernhard were among those interviewed in The Women's Entertainment Channel documentary *Night Bites: Women and Their Vampires* in May, while in September, AMC's *Fang vs. Fiction: The Real Underworld of Vampires and Werewolves* was a documentary that also managed to tie in with the recent movie starring Kate Beckinsale.

Professor Robert Winston introduced and narrated the BBC dramatized documentary *Frankenstein: Birth of a Monster*, about Mary Shelley's early life.

In October, Britain's Channel Four broadcast *The 100 Great-*

est Scary Moments. Introduced by irritating stand-up comedian Jimmy Carr, this four-hour show, shown over two consecutive nights and voted for by the public, included often lengthy and well-chosen clips and trailers from movies, TV shows, commercials, public service announcements and music videos, with commentary by Patrick Allen, Jane Asher, Rick Baker, Doug Bradley, Bruce Campbell, John Carpenter, Chris Carter, Alice Cooper, Wes Craven, Sean Cunningham, Shelley Duvall, Robert Englund, Fenella Fielding, William Friedkin, Mark Gatiss, Jerry Goldsmith, Muriel Grey, Gunnar Hansen, Dennis Hopper, Sara Karloff, Mark Kermode, John Landis, Christopher Lee, Janet Leigh, Kevin McCarthy, Kyle McLachlan, Michael Madsen, Nigel Kneale, Kim Newman, Dave Prowse, Ed Sanchez, David Skal, Stephen Spielberg, Stephen Volk, Sigourney Weaver and Joss Whedon, among many others.

That same month, cable and digital channel BBC Four showed <<*Time Shift*>>: *The Kneale Tapes*, a forty-minute look at the career of Nigel Kneale that included a contemporary interview with the author and his wife Judith Kerr, commentary from such admirers as Jeremy Dyson, Mark Gatiss and Kim Newman, and rare clips from *The Quatermass Experiment, Nineteen Eighty-Four, Quatermass II, Quatermass and the Pit, The Year of the Sex Olympics, The Stone Tape* and *Quatermass*.

For Hallowe'en, Bravo's three-part *Creature Features: Greatest Movie Monsters* looked at "The Machines", "The Beasts" and "The Dead".

In early June, BBC Radio 4 broadcast producer Lawrence Jackson's forty-five minute adaptation of J. Sheridan Le Fanu's classic vampire tale *Carmilla*, featuring David Warner, Kenneth Cranham, Celia Imrie, Jacqueline Pearce, and Brana Bajic as the undead seductress.

Radio 4 also broadcast a two-part dramatization of John Wyndham's (John Beynon Harris) classic *The Midwich Cuckoos*, set in 1950s Britain and starring Bill Nighy. The centenary of Wyndham's birth was celebrated in London on 10 July.

Starting at the end of November, and broadcast in ten fifteen-minute episodes, Radio 4's *Book at Bedtime* presented an abridged version of Bram Stoker's *Dracula* read in the original diary format by four different people.

The Dark House was an interactive play about a local radio reporter sent to investigate a haunted house. The BBC Radio 4 drama switched between three characters depending upon which one the listening public voted for by telephone or text.

The BBC World Service *Masterpiece* programme broadcast *Monsters* in September, a half-hour show in which Nick Rankin explored the monsters that populate our cultural life. A tie-in episode of *Music Review* on the same channel looked at H.K. Gruber's orchestra movement *Frankenstein!!*

In October, British digital radio station Oneword broadcast an adaptation of Neil Gaiman's spooky novella *Corline* in daily episodes read by comedy actress Dawn French.

Over Christmas, BBC Radio 2 broadcast *Edgar Allan Poe's Gothic Tales*, three fifteen-minute adaptations of "The Tell-Tale Heart", "The Cask of Amontillado" and "The Pit and the Pendulum", read by Christopher Lee.

Produced by DreamHaven Books on CD, *Telling Tales* featured Neil Gaiman reading his original short stories accompanied by percussionist Robin "Adnan" Anders.

Joe R. Lansdale read his stories "Steppin' Out Summer '68" and "By Biazrre Hands" on a signed and limited audio CD from Lone Wolf Publications.

Presented by Nyarlathotep the Crawling Chaos, the music CD *Our Thoughts Make Spirals in the World* was inspired by the works of Caitlín R. Kiernan.

The H.P. Lovecraft Historical Society Carol Songbook: A Very Scary Solstice featured a chapbook with an Introduction by S.T. Joshi and a CD featuring twenty-five seasonal songs rewritten for the Chthulhu Mythos. The same musical group also issued *A Shoggoth on the Roof: A Cthulhu Mythos Musical Inspired by the Works of H.P. Lovecraft*.

Staged at Los Angeles's Theatre West in June, *The October Country* consisted of three one-act plays by Ray Bradbury, "Banshee", "The Jar" and "Cistern", directed by Charles Rome Smith.

A summer revival of Joseph Kesselring's wonderful 1940s play *Arsenic and Old Lace* in London's West End failed to pull in the audiences, perhaps because Stephen Tompkinson was no Cary Grant and Michael Richards wasn't a patch on Boris Karloff.

Meanwhile, Andrew Lloyd Webber's musical stage show of *The Phantom of the Opera* celebrated its 7,000th performance in London in August. The production, which opened in 1986, has grossed more than £1.6 billion around the world.

An all-female version of Anthony Burgess's *A Clockwork Orange* was staged by the Snap Theatre Group in London, while *Dragula* was described as "London's newest 1980s retro musical".

Aimed at children aged eight and up, Green Ginger's puppet show *Frank Einstein* saw the mad doctor and his hunchbacked assistant Ivor attempt to create the "Power of Life".

In December, London's Royal Opera House revived Stephen Sondheim's 1979 musical *Sweeney Todd* as a co-production with the Lyric Opera of Chicago. Thomas Allen portrayed the cut-throat barber in the critically acclaimed production, with Felicity Palmer as his accomplice Mrs Lovett.

When Nintendo's GameCube missed its sales targets, profits fell by thirty-seven per cent to £350 million in the year to March. Just under ten million units were sold, compared to more than fifty-one million of Sony's rival PlayStation, leading to speculation that the GameCube was in danger of being discontinued.

Written and directed by The Wachowski Brothers for PlayStation 2, Xbox, Nintendo GameCube and PC, Atari's *Enter the Matrix* included specially shot footage of the film actors alongside the interactive graphics. The game sold more than one million copies worldwide in its launch week. According to some sources, *Enter the Matrix* cost around $70 million to buy, develop and market, and it needed to sell four million copies just to break even.

Lara Croft Tomb Raider: The Angel of Darkness featured an older version of the buxom heroine (made up of ten times as many polygons as before) in a murder mystery set in Paris and involving her former mentor. The London Symphony Orchestra supplied the music score.

Resident Evil Zero on the GameCube was a prequel to the hit zombie game set in Racoon City, and there were more apocalyptic predictions on a Biblical scale in *Devil May Cry 2* from Capcom on PlayStation 2.

Fox Interactive's latest *Buffy the Vampire Slayer* game, *Chaos*

Bleeds, was intended to be a "lost" episode from the show's fifth season. Written by Christopher Golden and Tom Sneigoski, with voices recorded by the cast members themselves, Buffy, Xander, Willow, Spike, Faith and Sid the Dummy had to prevent The First from casting the world into permanent darkness.

Adapted from an original script by veteran James Bond screenwriter Bruce Feirstein, Electronic Art's multi-platform game *Everything or Nothing* featured the voice of Pierce Brosnan as Bond, along with John Cleese as Q, Dame Judi Dench as M, Richard Kiel as Jaws, Willem Dafoe as villain Nikolai Diavolo, Shannon Elizabeth as Bond girl Serena St Germaine, and Heidi Klum as the malevolent Katya Nadanova.

Also from EA Games, *Harry Potter: Quidditch World Cup* was the big computer game for Christmas. Released on the same day as the *Lord of the Rings* game, *Return of the King*, it was the third official *Potter* game.

From Wacky Wobblers came hand puppets of Universal's Frankenstein Monster and Creature from the Black Lagoon. The same company also issued wobblers of Herman and Lily Munster from the cult 1960s TV show. Other new bobble heads included Flash Gordon, an *Army of Darkness* Stretched Ash, and various Living Dead Dolls.

Mezco issued a new Living Dead Doll of Jack the Ripper, limited to 4,000 pieces. From the same company, the *Army of Darkness* three-pack included miniature block figures of Ash, Evil Ash and the Bog Witch.

An eight-inch bust of Ash from Diamond Select Toys was sculpted by Andy Bergholtz and limited to 7,500 items, each of which came with an individually hand-numbered certificate of authenticity. The twelve-inch-tall *Army of Darkness 10th Anniversary Ash Poster Statue* was sculpted directly from the 1993 movie poster by Gabriel Marquez, limited to 1,993 pieces at $250.00 each.

The Kucharek Brothers' "Creatures of the Night" collectable resin busts featured *The Werewolf* and *Dracula*, limited to 1,000 fully painted pieces each, from JohnsToys.

Moore Creations' limited-edition Faith statue from *Buffy the Vampire Slayer* was 1/12th scale.

Sculpted by Sam Greenwell and designed by Ed Repka, the

Friday the 13th Snow Globe and *A Nightmare on Elm Street Snow Globe* featured Jason and Freddy respectively, each menacing a female victim.

For those with a bit more money to spend, the Dracula's Castle Lighted Façade was a hand-painted porcelain recreation of the Count's castle with an accessory figure sculpted to look like Bela Lugosi.

To tie in with the release of the movie *Underworld*, a series of action figures featured such characters as Selene, Viktor, Lucian (vampire form), Raze and Michael (werewolf form) on a diorama display base.

Reel Toys released seven-inch fully poseable action figures of Clive Barker's demonic Cenobites Pinhead, Chatterer, CD, Chatter Beast, Wire Twin and Stitch from the *Hellraiser* films. A second series released later in the year featured another version of Pinhead, along with Butterball, Surgeon, Barbie, Julia and Angelique. You had to collect all six to build your own nine-inch Pillar of Souls.

Anybody could call up the Cenobites with a mahogany and brass replica of the Lament Configuration Box, limited to 2,000 pieces and based on the actual film prop. The Box was also available as an Engraved Acrylic Paperweight with Pinhead in the centre.

From Film Freaks/Majestic Studios came twelve-inch collectable figures from *Return of the Fly* and *Jeepers Creepers*.

Jeepers Creepers II merchandising from Factory X included a seventeen-inch-high Creeper Statue limited to 1,000 numbered pieces, a Beatngu Water Globe, a Scarecrow Water Globe and replicas of The Creeper's Bone Throwing Stars cast from the original movie props and limited to 1,000 pieces.

The first series of poseable *Gremlins* scale action figures featured Gizmo, Stripe, Brain and Poker Player. Meanwhile, Barbie, Ken and Skipper dolls were turned into the Scooby-Doo gang.

From Japan came four-inch resin statues of Godzilla, 1955 and 1985 versions, Anguirus, and King Ghidorah. A twelve-inch resin statue of the 1956 version of Rodan came with a detailed base featuring a hatchling and Meganuron larvae. A Daimajin vinyl action figure and a flying Gamera 1999 figure were also available, along with the giant turtle's foes Iris, Gyaos 1995 and the Legion Soldier.

The three-inch Godzilla Mini-Bobbers included Godzilla, King Ghidorah, Rodan and Mech Godzilla. The *Godzilla Realistic Plush* doll was described as the "most complex and authentic Godzilla plush ever made," while the *King Ghidorah Realistic Plush* was "over a year in the making".

Sculpted by *Gamera* special-effects artist Fuyuki Shinada, the *Reptilicus* and *Rat-Bat-Spider* (from *Angry Red Planet*) vinyl figures were limited to 1,000 and 2,000 pieces respectively.

Also from Japan came various zombie and biker figures from George A. Romero's *Dawn of the Dead*, and the four-piece *Edward Scissorhands* Kubrick Set featured Edward Scissorhands, Kim, Tree and Ice Angel.

Fans of artist Bernie Wrightson were spoiled for choice with limited edition T-shirts from Chanting Monks Press featuring his "Bursting from the Grave", "Zombie in a Graveyard", "Hanging Lady" and "Frankenstein Cover" illustrations.

The Cthulhu plush hand puppet featured a hidden ring that resulted in the Elder God giving the finger when it was pulled! There were also large Santa Cthulhu and Shoggoth plushes, while Innsmouth fans could get a Deep One plush designed by Ron Spencer and limited to 1,500 pieces.

The 13th World Horror Convention was held over 17–20 April in Kansas City. The fairly nebulous theme was "Monsters in Time", and Brian A. Hopkins was a last-minute replacement for Writer Guest of Honour Graham Masterton when the latter was unable to attend because of his wife's illness. Other Guests of Honour included Toastmistress Laurell K. Hamilton, Publisher Don D'Auria and Artist Nick Smith. Forrest J Ackerman, still recovering from a serious operation, was Special GoH; Mort Castle conducted a writer's workshop, and Chelsea Quinn Yarbro was named Grand Master.

Edward W. Bryant announced at World Horror that author and editor Charles L. Grant had been chosen by The International Horror Guild as the recipient of its Living Legend Award, presented to an individual who has made meritorious and notable contributions and/or has substantially influenced the field of horror and dark fantasy.

With no live presentation, the remaining International Horror Guild Awards were announced on 23 May. Recognizing outstanding achievements in the field of horror and dark fantasy from the year 2002, IHG judges Edward Bryant, Stefan R. Dziemianowicz, Bill Sheehan and Hank Wagner gave the Novel award to *A Winter Haunting* by Dan Simmons, and presented the First Novel award to *A Scattering of Jades* by Alexander Irvine. Thomas Ligotti's "My Work is Not Yet Done" won in the Long Form category; there was a tie for Intermediate Form between "Death and Suffrage" by Dale Bailey (from *The Magazine of Fantasy & Science Fiction*, February 2002) and "Pavane for a Prince of the Air" by Elizabeth Hand (from *Embrace the Mutation*), and the Short Form award went to "The Prospect Cards" by Don Tumasonis (from *Dark Terrors 6*). Chet Williamson's *Figures in Rain* from Ash-Tree Press won for Collection, and the Anthology award went to *Dark Terrors 6: The Gollancz Book of Horror* edited by Stephen Jones and David Sutton. *Ramsey Campbell, Probably* by Ramsey Campbell collected the award for Non-fiction, and Clive Barker's *Abarat* won for Graphic Narrative. *The Magazine of Fantasy & Science Fiction* came top in the Periodical category and Jason Van Hollander won for Art. *Frailty* picked up the Film award, and the HBO series *Six Feet Under* was the surprise winner in the Television category. Nominations were derived from recommendations made by the public and the judges' knowledge of the field.

The Horror Writers Association presented the annual Bram Stoker Awards for superior achievement on 7 June at its Annual Conference, held at the Park Central Hotel in New York City. The Novel award went to *The Night Class* by Tom Piccirilli, while *The Lovely Bones* by Alice Sebold won First Novel. There was a tie for Long Fiction between *El Dia De Los Muertos* by Brian A. Hopkins and *My Work is Not Yet Done: Three Tales of Corporate Horror* by Thomas Ligotti. Piccirilli also picked up the Short Fiction award for "The Misfit Child Grows Fat on Despair" (from *The Darker Side*); *One More for the Road* by Ray Bradbury won the Fiction Collection award and the Anthology award went to *The Darker Side* edited by John Pelan. *Ramsey Campbell, Probably* by Ramsey Campbell won for Non-fiction, Marvel's *Nightside* #1–4 by Robert Weinberg was awarded the prize for Illustrated Narrative, and the Screenplay prize went to *Frailty* by Brent Hanley. *Coraline* by Neil Gaiman won in the Work for Young Readers category, *The Gossamer Eye* by Mark

McLaughlin, Rain Graves and David Niall Wilson won the Poetry Collection award, and Lone Wolf's multimedia CD *Imagination Box* by Steve and Melanie Tem won the Alternative Forms prize. Lifetime Achievement Awards went to Stephen King, who sent a videotaped speech, and J.N. Williamson, who was the only winner present.

Held over 17–20 July in Rhode Island, the relaxing Necon 23 featured Richard Christian Matheson and Elizabeth Hand as Guests of Honour, Richard Chizmar as Editor Guest of Honour and Omar Rayyan as Artist Guest of Honour. Toastmaster was James Moore, while Gahan Wilson was simply billed as "Legend".

The third HorrorFind Weekend was held over 15–17 August in Hunt Valley, Maryland. Along with Guest of Honour Alice Cooper and movie celebrities Tony Todd, Bill Moseley and Doug Bradley, horror authors present included Jack Ketchum, F. Paul Wilson, Thomas F. Monteleone, Edward Lee, Nancy Kilpatrick, Tom Piccirilli, Karen Taylor, Mark McLaughlin and Brian Keene.

The 29th Annual World Fantasy Convention was held in Washington DC over 30 October to 2 November. With a theme of "Dark Fantasy: Honorable Traditions", the poorly edited souvenir book included new fiction by Writer Guest of Honour Brian Lumley and Toastmaster Douglas Winter, along with contributions by and about other Guests – Allen Koszowski, W. Paul Ganley and an absent Jack Williamson.

Winners of the 2003 World Fantasy Awards were as usual announced after the Banquet on Sunday. The Novel award was a tie between *The Facts of Life* by Graham Joyce and *Ombria in Shadow* by Patricia A. McKillip. Zoran Živković's "The Library" (from *Leviathan 3*) won in the Novella category and Jeffrey Ford's "Creation" (from *The Magazine of Fantasy & Science Fiction*, May 2002) picked up the prize for Short Fiction. The award for best Anthology was another tie, this time between *The Green Man: Tales from the Mythic Forest* edited by Ellen Datlow and Terri Windling, and *Leviathan 3* edited by Forrest Aguirre and Jeff VanderMeer. Jeffrey Ford won again when *The Fantasy Writer's Assistant and Other Stories* received the award for best Collection. Tom Kidd collected the Artist award. The Special Award, Professional, went to Gordon Van Gelder for *The Magazine of Fantasy & Science Fiction*, and Jason Williams, Jeremy

Lassen and Benjamin Cossel were presented with the Special Award, Non-Professional, for Night Shade Books. Life Achievement awards were announced for Donald M. Grant and Lloyd Alexander.

In a break from tradition, The British Fantasy Convention followed The World Fantasy Convention. FantasyCon 2003 was held over the weekend of 21–23 November in Stafford, and marked a welcome return to form after being reduced to a couple of one-day events in London. Guests of Honour were Christopher Fowler and young-adult writer Catherine Fisher. The winners of the British Fantasy Awards, announced at the Banquet on the Sunday afternoon, were China Miéville's *The Scar* for Best Novel (The August Derleth Fantasy Award) and Mark Chadbourn's novella *The Fairy-Feller's Master Stroke* for Best Short Fiction, the latter from PS Publishing. The Best Anthology award went to another PS book, *Keep Out the Night* edited by Stephen Jones, as did the Best Collection Prize for *Ramsey Campbell, Probably: On Horror and Sundry Fantasies*. Best Artist was Les Edwards, Best Small Press was predictably PS Publishing, and Alan Garner was announced as the recipient of the Special Karl Edward Wagner Award.

There is too much stuff.

When Ramsey Campbell and I collaborated on the first Introduction to this series back in 1990, it took up seven pages in the book. This year's summation runs to more than ninety.

To be fair, over the past fifteen volumes we have expanded the scope of this round-up, and technological advances in e-books, print-on-demand and self-publishing have led to an explosion in the amount of material that is now available. These days, the listings from quality small-press publishers easily outweigh the number of horror titles from so-called "mainstream" publishing houses on both sides of the Atlantic, and we are just talking about the good material here. When you add all the other horror-related media into the mix, then it is no wonder that the modern horror fan is spoiled for choice.

For that small number of critics who complain about the length of this Introduction (one of whom, it just so happens, has a story in this volume), I would like to take this opportunity to point out that this, and all the other editorial material included in the book, should be considered as a *bonus*. I do not receive anything extra for compiling it throughout the year. If it was not included, or appeared in truncated form, then the total amount of fiction that I could afford to buy would remain basically the same. Far more people who come up to me at conventions, or communicate through e-mails and letters, tell me how much they enjoy this overview of the year in horror – invariably because they are unlikely to be aware of all the material themselves.

At the presentation of this year's International Horror Guild Awards in Phoenix, Arizona, Edward Bryant did us the honour of saying that the annual "Necrology" compiled by Kim Newman and myself is the most comprehensive in the field and is the first thing he turns to when he receives his copy of the book.

So for those who may be less interested in all the extraneous material, may I suggest that you simply skip over it and start reading the bumper amount of fiction. As for the rest of you, I hope you continue to find these articles and listings both informative and entertaining.

However, the sheer amount of material now available means that I am no longer able to cover *everything* – assuming of course that I ever did. It is simply an impossible (and, as you can see, sometimes thankless) task. I will continue to try to bring you a balanced overview of what is happening in horror out there, highlighting items of special interest and recommendation when and where I can.

I will also continue to keep my promise to give at least a mention to every publication (when appropriate) that is sent to me. It continues to be a disappointment that, after nearly a decade and a half, most publishers, editors and authors still do not submit their horror material for consideration. It is no good complaining that a particular book or magazine was not listed when those responsible could not even be bothered to send me a copy.

I try to be aware of as much material and as many sources as I can from each preceding year. But please remember, I cannot reprint your story or mention your publication if I have never seen it. And in the end, that is simply what it all comes down to.

The Editor
June 2004

RAMSEY CAMPBELL

Fear the Dead

RAMSEY CAMPBELL HAS BEEN named Grand Master by the World Horror Convention and has received a Lifetime Achievement Award from the Horror Writers Association. Tor Books recently reprinted his landmark collection *Alone With the Horrors*, and a new edition of his Arkham House collection *The Height of the Scream* has been reissued by California's Babbage Press.

His latest supernatural novel, *The Overnight*, is now available from PS Publishing, and forthcoming from Sutton Hoo Press of Winona is a limited edition of an original ghost story, "The Decorations", for Christmas 2004. The author is currently at work on a new novel, *Secret Stories*.

About the following story, Campbell explains: "I was asked to write a new tale for an anthology of stories about fear. I still have some I haven't told yet. I've published a few recently that touch on the afterlife. We must hope they're fiction."

S OMEONE ELSE HE DIDN'T think he'd ever seen before leaned down as if to let him count all her wrinkles. "I wish I'd had the chance to say goodbye to my grandmama, Jonathan."

Another lady dressed in at least as much black and holding her wineglass askew parted her pale lips, which looked as though they had once been stitched together. "Now you know she's at peace."

As he remembered how his grandmother's cheek had felt like a cold crumpled wad of paper he had to kiss, the winner of the wrinkle competition said "What a brave little soul. He's a credit to his mother."

"And his father."

"Careful or you'll drip."

The stitched lady straightened up her glass. "We don't want stains on your lovely carpet, do we, Jonathan? They don't make them like that any more."

He thought the elaborate carpet felt like the rest of the house – furtively chill and damp. "I can just hear her saying that, old Ire," his father joined him to remark.

"Her friends never called Iris that," the stitched mouth objected. "Oh, whatever's wrong, you poor little fellow?"

While Jonathan struggled to think of a reply that wouldn't be the truth, his mother hurried over to confront his father. "Are you upsetting him, Lawrence?"

"Only saying I could hear your mother pricing the contents of the house. Half of it Jonno wasn't supposed to touch," he confided to the wrinkled ladies. "You must have felt like you were living in a museum, did you, Jonno?"

Jonathan was yet more afraid to speak. The wineglass slouched again as its lady crooked her other thin arm around his shoulders and murmured "Don't worry, your daddy wasn't really hearing her. She's gone to Jesus and she'll be talking to him."

The mention of Jesus appeared to draw the priest, who smelled rather like an unlit candle wrapped in linen. He hoisted his tumbler of orange juice to acknowledge Jonathan's. "That's the right road. That's what real men drink."

"Is my grandma really talking to Jesus now?"

"I shouldn't be at all surprised, but it won't do any harm to pray she is."

"How long do you think she'll be?" Jonathan pleaded.

"That's one of the things God's keeping as a surprise for us. We won't know till we see her again."

"The father means till we're with Jesus too," Jonathan's mother made haste to say.

"Isn't she supposed to be there for ever?"

"If you keep your faith up," the priest said with a smile that was less than wholly aimed at Jonathan, "I'm sure she will be. You know Jesus has time for everyone."

How could Jesus deal with all the dead? God was meant to be able to see everyone at once, and perhaps his son had inherited the trick, but that wasn't the same as talking to them. If Jonathan's grandmother thought she didn't have Jesus's full attention, Jonathan could imagine her stalking off in search of someone who would have to notice her. He might have put some of this into words if the priest hadn't moved away, leaving Jonathan's parents to argue. "What are you trying to make Jonathan think of my mother?"

"Whatever's the truth, Essie."

"You didn't stay around to see it."

"Jonno knows why, don't you, Jonno? It's nobody's fault Ire and I didn't get on. I expect there are people you don't with."

"Maybe it was up to you to make the effort, Lawrence, considering it was her house."

"Well, now it's yours, and I don't feel any more welcome."

"I don't know how you'd expect me to change that."

"It's sounding like time I absented myself."

Jonathan thought he might leave it at that, having loaded his voice with dignity, but then his father swayed at him as though its weight had unbalanced him. "I'm sorry this had to be our day this week, Jonno. I'll take you somewhere better next weekend."

Jonathan watched his father's untypically sombre back view merge with the blackness of the crowd, and then he had to undergo a succession of pats on the head and kisses that felt like dried fruit brushing his cheek as mourners took their leave of his mother. Before long there was only Trudy, who also taught at the college. She ran her small hand several times up and down his mother's hefty arm. "You need to talk, I can tell."

"I could bear to," his mother admitted, and gave him a smile beneath a frown. "Don't bother helping clear up, Jonathan. You've had a long day and made us proud of you. I should go to bed."

He never understood why people said they should do things when they meant him. "I'm hungry," he said, not least in case he might be, and covered a plate with some of the remains of the buffet before sitting on a chair that protested like all his grandmother's furniture. When he'd managed to clear almost half of the plate, his mother intervened. "Don't stuff yourself for the sake of it or you won't be able to sleep."

That was something else to dread. He could only climb the stairs that were wider than his arms could stretch, and too dim under the yellowish chandelier, and creaked one by one as if they were playing a funeral tune. Until now he hadn't minded that the bathroom, which was almost big enough to be public and just as whitely tiled, echoed all his noises as if someone thinner than himself was hiding in it. He rushed through a token version of everything he had to do and fled next door to his bedroom.

Why did it need to be so big? It was at least twice the size of his room in the house where he'd lived with his parents until his grandmother had to be looked after at night – sometimes she'd prayed without seeming to breathe, and sometimes she'd wanted his mother to remember everything they'd done together and agree there had never been any bad times. Jonathan tried to feel grateful for the room, though it shrank his bed to a cot and his desk to a toddler's surrounded at a distance by furniture so gloomy – dressing-table, wardrobe, chest of drawers – he imagined it was waiting for him to misbehave. The books his grandmother had given him because she'd thought them suitable failed to welcome him; they just helped darken the room. The only one he could bring to mind concerned some children who made everyone believe an old lady was a witch, and it was too late for them to be sorry when she killed herself and couldn't go to heaven. He struggled to forget it as he inched under the bedclothes without pulling them free of the mattress, but already knew what the story brought back to him.

"Never speak ill of the dead," his grandmother used to warn him, "or they'll come back and haunt you." She'd gone into worse detail, especially during her last weeks. He would never say anything hurtful about her, and surely he needn't be afraid his mother had wanted him out of the way so that she could. She and Trudy were climbing the stairs now and saying nothing at all.

Trudy placed a moist kiss on top of the one his mother left on his forehead. The women moved to either side of the bed to tighten the sheets over him, then retreated to the door. "Sweet dreams or none at all," Trudy said, resting one black-varnished nail on the light switch. "Do we have the light out, Esther? I expect a big boy like Jonathan must."

"We won't be long. Trudy's staying over. *I* know," his mother said. "You have the light off and we'll come up and talk in my room."

He was afraid to aggravate her concern for him. "All right," he mumbled and turned his back.

The dark fell on him at once. He made himself wait until their footsteps began imitating one another on the stairs, then he twisted face up and jabbed his fingers together on his chest. What was he expected to say? He'd only started praying when his grandmother had assumed he did and asked him to on her behalf. Every night before he went to sleep he'd implored God not to take her away, but the idea of pleading for her to return terrified him. "Please God take care of my grandma," he muttered as he thought of it. "Please tell her she was the best grandma ever. And the best mum too," he felt compelled to blurt.

Surely that would make up for any criticisms his mother might let drop. She and Trudy were laughing in the kitchen, but that could hardly be about his grandmother. He was unable to think how long it was since he'd heard his mother laugh. He remembered the night his grandmother had emitted a snore so loud it had made him giggle in bed. "Mother?" his mother had called, though she was beside her, and more loudly "Mother?" suggesting that his grandmother had been retreating into the distance of the room. Then there was silence until she'd said "Oh" as if what she was seeing had almost robbed her of breath.

She and Trudy had finished laughing, perhaps because the house made them sound too small and shrill. Now they were lowering their voices as they came upstairs. They weren't scared to be overheard by anyone who'd been up here with him, he told himself: they were showing respect for his grandmother or trying not to waken him. Creaks marked their progress to his mother's room. Her door hadn't quite closed when he heard Trudy murmur "You say whatever you need to, Esther. It's part of dealing with your loss."

He couldn't distinguish what his mother said, even once he dragged himself free of the bedclothes and crouched against the headboard. When he lowered one reluctant foot, it was greeted with a creak by the floor, which felt as chill as his grandmother's face had last time he'd touched her. More than a dozen hasty paces took him through the dimness thick as the musty curtains, past the audience of hulking half-seen furniture, to the door. He inched it ajar and was confronted by his grandmother's room.

Her door was shut. That managed to seem reassuring until he thought of the darkness beyond it, even vaster than the dark behind him. Suppose that as he'd ventured to his door, his grandmother had reached hers with far longer strides of her spidery legs and was pressing her face against an upper panel? He was trying to find his next breath when he heard his mother say "I hate to admit it, but Lawrence was right. She was never happy till you knew how much everything she had was worth."

Jonathan sucked in air so that he could whisper "You were just proud of it, weren't you, grandma? I expect you still are. You should be, because it's so nice."

He was frightened to raise his voice, but equally frightened by the possibility that she was close enough to hear his whisper. He didn't realise he'd flinched from the prospect that her door might jerk open until the floor creaked beneath him. "Is that you, Jonathan?" his mother called.

He hung onto the door while he closed it as swiftly as he could without making a sound, then had to let go and turn to the glimmering slab of his bed. "I didn't hear anything. Have a top up so you sleep as well," he heard Trudy say, and a clink of glass. The creaks of his retreat obscured what the women said next, and once he was huddled in bed he couldn't understand them. "Please God don't let my grandma hear anything bad about her," he began to whisper, interspersed with words to her. "Mum thinks you were the best mum. She's just talking because she's upset like her friend said."

Soon the only word he was aware of uttering was mum. It must have lulled him to sleep, because he was awakened by his name creeping like a draught into his ear. A face was looming almost into his. He shrank across the mattress, dragging the bedclothes free, before he realised that daylight was showing him Trudy. "Shush now," she murmured. "We'll have to do something about those nerves of yours. Get up quietly and get ready and I'll run you to school. Esther's catching up on her sleep."

Once dressed, he found that Trudy had readied a bowl of cereal and some bread and jam, presumably because cookery might rouse his mother. Trudy watched with tentative fondness as he did his duty by the breakfast, then stopped just short of touching him while ushering him out to her car, which had front seats but no rear. Its smallness was a relief from the house, but drew the amusement of dozens of boys on the way to his school. The massive houses split amoeba-like along the route, and the school had undergone even more fission, separating into six unequal buildings that felt like a test the place was setting him. He was halfway through his first term, but the school still overwhelmed him. When Trudy left him at the gates with a wave of her fingertips that bore a kiss, he would have lost himself in the enormous crowded schoolyard if two boys a head taller than himself hadn't stopped him. "She your girlfriend?" said the one with a moustache or grime occupying sections of his upper lip.

"Could be his new ma," said his crony, the left side of whose chin boasted a single black curly hair.

"Gently now, gentlemen." This was Mr Foster, the long-faced English teacher who wore his greying hair in a ponytail. He pinched or massaged the backs of their necks until he'd finished saying "We don't harass our new fellows, do we? Especially when they've just lost a member of the family."

"Never mind touching us," one boy muttered as Mr Foster steered Jonathan away by an elbow to enquire "Are you fit to come back to school, Hastings?"

Being addressed by his surname was yet another aspect of the place Jonathan had still to accept. "I think so, sir," he said.

He'd hoped school would take his mind off his grandmother, but now he felt that anybody there might bring her up. Suppose she proved to be the the theme of the morning assembly? Once the pupils had been herded into the main building, however, and the staff had taken their seats onstage in the assembly hall, the headmaster lectured about the football team and how their performance should inspire the other pupils to try harder. Jonathan was trying to keep that in mind when Mr Foster singled him out at the beginning of the English lesson. "Is there anything you'd like to share with us, Hastings?"

"Like what, sir?"

"Such as, I believe you mean. About your bereavement."

"Such as what, sir?" Jonathan wished he didn't feel bound to ask.

"Forgive me if you think I'm prying." The teacher's face had managed to lengthen itself, and looked capable of pouting when Jonathan failed to answer. "Recollect in tranquillity," Mr Foster told himself, and seemed inspired. "That can be your subject for homework, all of you. Write about a loss, whatever it may be."

Could Jonathan's grandmother read what he wrote about her? In at least one way writing was different from talking – it was even harder – but surely it would give him more to say aloud about her. The trouble was that the prospect of writing drove all his thoughts for it out of his head. His skull felt emptied throughout the English lesson and the other classes, interrupted by lunch and larking in the schoolyard, activities that came no nearer reaching him than the questions teachers aimed at him. He assumed they toned down their responses to his uselessness because they knew about his grandmother.

None of the boys he'd made any kind of friends with lived near him. Soon his route home left him alone with the November dark, which he could have imagined the houses were hauling down from the sky. The dark had moved into his grandmother's house. The faltering light of the streetlamp beyond the unreasonably long drive showed him the key in his hand. The jerky shadow of a branch of the tree that hid the house from passers-by clawed at his wrist as he unlocked the front door.

Like his grandmother, it was half as tall again as Jonathan. The dimmest stretch of the glow from the streetlamp twitched underfoot as he sprinted to turn on the jangling chandelier. Its grudging illumination lent him the courage to shut himself in before dashing to switch on the kitchen light. He dropped his schoolbag on the table with a thump that seemed both too loud and dwarfed by the room, and hauled open the refrigerator to pour himself a drink. At once he knew what he could write.

He spread his books across the table and sat on the least creaky chair. "I'm going to say some nice things about you, grandma," he murmured. "I'll read you them when I've finished."

My loss is my grandmother who died last week. When I came home from school she'd always have a glass of juice and a plate of biscuits on the table for me. It must have been hard for her opening the fridge because I had to help her sometimes when I was in, but she did. She'd ask me all about the day at school and say I had to keep making her proud, then I'd have to start my homework now I'm at this school and she'd ask if it was quiet enough. She'd go about so quietly I couldn't hear where she

He wished he hadn't thought of that – it made him nervous of the silence around him and behind him. Having ceased its mousy scurrying across the page, the nib emitted a blot like an emphatic full stop. He crossed out the sentence that seemed eager to complete itself. Mr Foster said you had to show your first draft as well as your finished work, though Jonathan's grandmother had kept saying it looked untidy. The idea of her prowling soundlessly behind him to crane over his shoulder made him feel steeped in the lurking chill of the house. "I'll read you what I've written," he said as loudly as he dared.

He wanted to believe she was at least as distant as her room. He raised his voice so that it would be audible up there, and didn't realise it was deafening him to any sounds until he was asked "Have you brought someone home, Jonathan?"

"Just doing my homework," he found the breath to tell his mother as she and Trudy marched along the hall.

"Why, do you have to read it to your class?" She kissed his forehead before stooping to examine his homework while Trudy looked uncertain whether to do either. Eventually his mother straightened up and blinked at his forehead as though she had a mind to take back the kiss. "Well, if that's how you remember it, Jonathan."

"That's how grandma was."

"No need to shout. We're only here." He was hoping she would leave it at that when she said "I'd like to be home when you come in, you know, even if I mightn't give you snacks so close to dinner. Unfortunately I have to earn a living, particularly since my mother's attitudes got to be too much for your father. And by the way, I don't think you need to upset yourself over the fridge. If you can open it she could. Most of the time she wasn't quite as feeble as she liked to pretend."

"Go on, Esther, let it all come out." To Jonathan Trudy said "People have different ways of grieving, and this is how your mother has to. Are you finding yours?"

"I've got to go upstairs now."

"You can work better there, I expect," his mother said. "We'll call you when it's dinner."

He could tell she wanted to believe she hadn't distressed him, while Trudy thought he was off to grieve. Neither was the case. He loaded his schoolbag and climbed into the dimness that hung around the chandelier. Even when he switched on the upstairs light, gloom seemed to cling to the landing and the corridor. He felt as if his grandmother's disapproval had been roused: she used to say you shouldn't have more than one light on at a time. She'd just been trying to save money for her family, he told himself. "Mum only meant she wished she could be more like you, grandma," he muttered. "I expect that means she will be."

His voice faltered as he saw his blurred shadow growing smaller on a lower panel of his grandmother's door. Either he was unaware of shrinking from the notion that she was within arm's reach of the other side or the door was creeping open. The voice that made him see it lurch backwards because he had was his mother's. "Is that Jonathan talking to himself? What's wrong with him?"

"Will it be his way of coping, do you think?"

He should have closed the kitchen door. He shut himself in his room and moved his desk away from the wall so that he could sit facing the room with surely no space for anyone, no matter how thin, to sidle behind him. He didn't need to finish his English homework until the weekend. Instead he applied himself to sums that he was supposed to call arithmetic now that he'd changed schools. He was feeling sure enough of his pencilled answers to commit ink to them when Trudy called "It's waiting for you, Jonathan."

He left his bedroom light on so that it would be there for him, his mother's phrase that finally conveyed some meaning, and hurried to the dining-room. His mother was ladling out a lamb casserole as Trudy filled glasses with wine and his with juice while the sideboard and dresser kept their distance from the table yet helped it aggravate the disapproving sombreness. "Did you get much done?" his mother asked him.

"I won't do it about grandma after all."

"I hope that's not because of me." When he failed to think of a safe reply she said "What does your subject have to be?"

"Losing something."

"What else can you say you've lost beside your grandmother? Unless you're intending to tell your teacher how your father absconded."

Jonathan wasn't sure of the last word, but otherwise his thoughts seemed not to be hidden from anyone. "Are you still unhappy about him, Jonathan?" Trudy said, stroking his arm.

"Sometimes."

"Doesn't seeing him every week help?" Having watched until Jonathan repeated his nod, she said "Give it time and maybe there'll be someone extra in your life if that's what you'd like."

Just now he felt he had to concentrate all his liking on his grandmother. "I don't know," he mumbled.

Rather less than a look passed between Trudy and his mother. He could have done without the impression that another secret was at large in the house. Once dinner was finished he would have watched the Tuesday quiz shows with his mother, but their guest had to see a programme she'd told her history students to watch. The documentary about people being tortured by the Inquisition until they believed they were as bad as they were told only sharpened his unease. As soon as the credits began to crawl up the screen he retreated upstairs to talk to God and his grandmother.

He hadn't been in bed long when his mother came to give his forehead a lingering kiss, which she used to say was putting good dreams in. "Not asleep yet? I expect having the light off will help," she said. "Don't be surprised if you hear someone else upstairs."

"Who?" Jonathan gasped, scarcely a word.

"Trudy, of course. She'll be staying."

Since she would hardly be sleeping in his grandmother's old bed, presumably she would share his mother's – had shared it last night too. He wished he'd asked to sleep there instead of alone in the dark. Once his mother left him in it he found a solitary sentence to repeat. "Please God let my grandmother hear just nice things about her."

Shouldn't that settle everything? At last it let him sleep. He lurched awake, anxious not to be confronted by Trudy's face again, but only daylight had stolen into his room. While he was in the bathroom Trudy and his mother collaborated on breakfast before running him to school in his mother's car, which had space for all of them. Outside the school gates, as he leaned forward from the back seat to deliver a kiss he hoped would be too swift for his schoolfellows to see, both women turned to him. Their cheeks brushed together, and they exchanged smiles not unlike shy kisses, magnifying his awkwardness as he stumbled into the yard.

Yesterday's tormentors converged on him. "Found them yet?" said the boy with the tidemarked upper lip.

"What?" Jonathan was distracted enough to wonder.

"They're a what now, are they?" said the boy whose chin flourished a lone hair. "Thought it was a who you lost."

"She died," Jonathan said, hoping that would silence them. "My grandma."

"Was she old?" That sounded sympathetic until the greyish-lipped boy added "Did she smell?"

"Bet she does now," his friend said.

"He was right after all. She'll be a what by now."

"Like the dead cat we found with maggots for eyes."

"Looked like he was laughing about it."

"Those girls didn't laugh much when we threw—"

That was the last Jonathan heard as he dodged almost blindly through the crowd in search of somewhere he could be alone to talk to his grandmother. A smell of something like tobacco drifted out of the toilets, but even if they'd been deserted, how could he have invited her to follow him in there? He sneaked into the main school building by a side door and dashed along the overheated corridor to sit on the hard seat attached to his desk. "They don't know anything about you, grandma," he murmured urgently. "You'll never be like that. They were just making it up."

He couldn't hear her voice, he reassured himself, but remembering was close to hearing. "Never speak ill of the dead or they'll come back and haunt you. They'll come back and show you how ugly you've made them." When the bell shrilled he bruised his knees on the underside of the desk. He reached the hall in time to mingle with the others so that the staff wouldn't realise he'd skulked into the school rather than being healthy in the yard. Throughout the headmaster's address, and intermittently in all the lessons, he kept hearing his grandmother's words and could only respond with last night's prayer. More boys giggled each time he had to mutter. The teachers must be restraining themselves because of his grandmother – he had no idea how he might have responded if they'd spoken rather than merely frowning at him.

Tattered clouds like cobwebs laden with grime raced to meet him as he hurried home. They left the sky behind them no less dark. He let himself into the house and switched on the dimness before venturing upstairs. "You didn't hear anything bad today, did you, grandma?" he whispered at her door. "God wouldn't let you. Please God don't."

There was no sound from her room. If she'd been listening, the floorboards would surely have made her presence as apparent as they were making his. He was suddenly convinced he had been talking to nobody at all – for how long, he didn't know. He grabbed the chilly scalloped brass knob and threw open the door.

The room looked yet more enormous for its emptiness. He could have imagined all the heavy mournful furniture was huddling against the walls. A wedge of murky twilight had managed to slip between the ponderous sombre curtains to emphasise the isolation of the bed, on which a fat faded patchwork quilt was drawn over a flattened stack of pillows. "Aren't you there, grandma?" Jonathan barely said.

Perhaps he glimpsed the shadow of a cloud that was drifting unseen past the window, but the quilt appeared to stir as if something it concealed was trying to take shape and draw breath. He peered into the dimness until he grasped how terrified he was to see. Flinging himself backwards, he dragged the door shut and fled downstairs. "I'm sorry, grandma. I didn't mean to—" he cried, and interrupted himself. "Please God don't let her," he repeated while he spread his schoolbooks across the kitchen table and attempted to work.

He didn't know how his mother might react to his writing about his father. It could wait until the weekend, when Jonathan would be staying with him. The boy chanted his prayer as an accompaniment to copying a map of the world, and fell silent only when he heard Trudy and his mother at the front door.

Their wide smiles were virtually identical. "So how was your day?" Trudy asked.

It seemed safest not to be specific. "Just stuff."

"What did you learn, then?" said his mother.

All he could remember was praying. "More stuff."

"Never mind if you'd rather not tell us." Her smile drained into her face as she remarked to Trudy "I expect we'd hear it all if my mother was doing the asking."

Could his grandmother take that as a criticism? "I'm just . . ." Jonathan mumbled, and ran upstairs. "See, I said mum wants to be like you," he whispered from the top stair, and repeated his plea to God several times before descending to the kitchen.

"I didn't mean to upset you," his mother assured him. "Eat up your dinner and forget what I said."

He was able to achieve the first requirement and pretend the second was accomplished. Might she refrain from talking about his grandmother for fear of upsetting him? After dinner he finished his geography homework in the kitchen and then watched some of a television programme about how men were the cause of all conflict. He didn't mind if his mother and Trudy thought that included him so long as it drew blame away from his grandmother.

He still had to pray with every breath so as to fall asleep. He wakened in daylight to hear laughter downstairs – the night seemed to have renewed the women somehow. His tormentors didn't come to find him in the schoolyard, and his classmates had tired of giggling when he felt compelled to pray. He couldn't have predicted the question with which his mother greeted him that night. "Jonathan," she said, sitting down at the table to clasp his hands. "Aren't you happy at this school?"

"Why?" he blurted in case that gave him time to think.

"Just tell me. Tell us, Trudy's your friend too. What's disturbing you?"

He could think of nothing his grandmother mightn't be blamed for. It was Trudy who said "Shouldn't you explain . . ."

"You're right, I've missed a step. Jonathan, your headmaster rang me. He says you keep talking to yourself in class."

Barely in time he saw how to tell something like the truth. "I was just trying to get things right."

"So that's why you were reading out your essay the other night. You'll have to stop doing it at school, though, or you'll have people thinking you're—You'll put them off their own work."

He thought he'd convinced her all was well. He was on his way to bed when he overheard her saying "It's my mother again. Living with her, that's what's made him so nervy, and no wonder."

He dashed into his room and huddled in the bed to pray. He had to stop when he heard Trudy and his mother on the stairs: if his mother overheard him she would think he was mad – she'd almost said so – while explaining his behaviour seemed capable of making the situation even worse. At last his prayers under the bedclothes gave way to sleep and then to muddy daylight that smelled of hot food.

His mother and Trudy insisted on kissing him before he could escape from the car. He hastened through the gates to find his tormentors awaiting him. "How many mothers have you got?" enquired the boy with the grubby upper lip.

His singularly hairy crony imitated his disgusted grin. "Do they both live at your house?"

"Why shouldn't they?" Jonathan was confused enough to ask.

"Bet your grandma wouldn't like it."

"Bet they're glad she's dead."

"Bet they wouldn't want to smell her now, though."

All Jonathan's dismay and bewilderment surged like bile into his mouth. "Maybe you will."

The boys looked as if he'd shocked them by going further than they dared. "What do you reckon you'll do?" the boy with the sole hair spluttered.

"Nothing. You've done it," Jonathan told them and hid in the crowd.

He wasn't going to pray to protect them. He didn't mutter once in class. He mustn't ask his mother about Trudy in case his grandmother might indeed have disapproved of her – in case that made his mother say things he would have to rectify. Instead he could tell her about his day, except that when she and Trudy came home, holding hands just long enough for him to see, she surprised him by asking "Would you like Lawrence to pick you up from school tomorrow?"

"Don't you mind?"

"Why would anyone mind? That way you can spend a long weekend with him to make up for the last one and Trudy and I will sort out the house."

Would that include his grandmother's room? Tonight he had no sense of her presence. If the room was cleared out, mightn't that mean she would stay with Jesus, since she would have nowhere to return to? He thought it best to continue praying once he was in bed. "Please God don't let her hear us saying anything bad about her," he repeated on the way to sleep.

He felt as if he'd hidden the implications of his words from himself until he was back at school. He couldn't see his tormentors when he braved the yard. He left his suitcase full of clothes and other weekend items in the secretary's office and hurried out to search, only to be found by Mr Foster, who was on yard duty. "There's a pensive young face."

"Sorry, sir."

"No need to apologise for thinking." As Jonathan wondered if that was necessarily true, the teacher said "Feeling more at home now?"

"I think so, sir."

"You can expect a respite from the comedy, at any rate."

Jonathan had noticed none. "Which is that, sir?"

"The comedians. The young teasers you encountered earlier in the week. The school will have to do without their routines for a while."

That almost robbed Jonathan of the breath it took to demand "Why?"

"They appear to have taken up slapstick." Mr Foster frowned at himself or at Jonathan's terseness. "They climbed up on a roof they should have known wouldn't support them, not that they ought to have been anywhere near it."

What might they have been fleeing? Jonathan's grandmother would have said they'd brought it on themselves. Having thanked Mr Foster, who seemed to wonder why, he found a gap between two school buildings to hide in. "Please God look after my grandma now. Don't let her hear anything else bad," he added, and "I expect those boys have learned their lesson."

He wouldn't have minded if they had returned to school in time to see his father collect him in the Land Rover. His father had finished work early, having designed enough houses for one week. He'd once said Jonathan's grandmother's house was too big for today and itself, which she'd taken as an insult. "We'll have a lively weekend, shall we?" he said, shaking Jonathan's hand.

Jonathan tried as hard as he could tell his father's lady did. She was called but not spelled Zoh, and kept attempting to make her face even smaller and prettier while she acted girlish with his father or motherly with Jonathan. She and his father took him to restaurants and films and a museum and a game where they had to dodge through a maze and shoot one another with lasers, Zoh emitting a coy reproachful squeal whenever she was hit. Between some of these events he spent time in their apartment, where the rooms were uncluttered and elegantly plain and unobtrusively warm. He was sure they were just the right size, not least his bedroom, but he felt as if the place wasn't quite reaching him. Perhaps it was the other way round, since he couldn't stop wondering what was happening at his grandmother's house.

Wondering overwhelmed his English homework. The harder he struggled to resolve his uncertainty or to write, the more the page and his brain competed at blankness. He had to welcome the sight of half a car on Sunday, though it was only Trudy who had come for him. He even wished he hadn't greeted her with "Where's mum?"

"Making a welcome-home dinner."

Given the looks Trudy was exchanging with Zoh and his father, Jonathan felt all the more anxious to return to his grandmother's. "See you next weekend," he said, dealing his father's hand a shake and disappointing Zoh with one before scrambling into the car.

The fairground neon of the city centre had faded beyond the old and in some cases unbroken lamps standing guard throughout the suburb when Trudy said "Had a good break?"

"What from? I don't need a break from my mum."

"Nor from me either, I hope."

He felt bound to be polite while he tried to think. "No," he mumbled.

"That's good. Esther and I have had a chance to get a few things clearer."

All at once he was certain he knew why they'd wanted him out of the way – knew what he'd failed to realise. "You've been talking about my grandma."

"Among other issues."

"What did you say about her?"

"Me, nothing to speak of."

"What did mum?"

"Quite a flood. Everything she had to. It wasn't all bad."

"How much was?"

"Best if you discuss it together. I expect she'd like to share your memories now."

She mustn't until he'd remembered enough to counteract hers. Why hadn't he written about his grandmother while he'd had the chance? As the car turned along her street he felt like a small animal trapped inside his own head, darting about in search of a way of escape. He would have to flee upstairs and pray his hardest without being heard by his mother, but how long would she leave before coming to find him?

His suitcase dragged his arm down as he followed Trudy to the house. The shadow of a branch clutched at her wrist when she inserted his grandmother's key in the lock. He wished he were seeing his grandmother catch hold of her as the door swung inwards, revealing the dark.

Why was the house unlit if his mother was home? It didn't feel deserted, and her car was in the drive. He hung back until Trudy switched on the chandelier, illuminating a note in his mother's handwriting on the third stair. *Just run down the road for ingredients*, it said.

So it wasn't his mother he sensed waiting in the house. At once he was sure what to do. His grandmother's condition was Trudy's fault – she'd encouraged his mother to say all she could. Had his mother even finished? Perhaps she might have more and worse to say if Trudy stayed. He used his luggage to push the front door shut and dumped his suitcase in the hall. "Come and see something," he said.

"Is it a surprise?" Trudy said, widening her eyes and raising half her mouth.

"You'll have to say," he told her and turned hastily to the stairs.

The house felt as breathless with anticipation as he was. The creak of stairs counted the seconds and confirmed Trudy was following. The chandelier seemed to lower itself like a huge murkily luminous spider while the door of his grandmother's room held itself still as a trap. On the landing he halted, uncertain whether he'd heard the faintest sound beyond her door – a shuffling that grew thinner, increasingly less suggestive of feet, as it approached. "What is it, Jonathan?" Trudy said.

"Your surprise. Come and look."

On the whole she seemed pleased he'd grabbed her hand. She accompanied him willingly enough, even when he seized the icy knob and flung open his grandmother's door. "You put the light on," he said.

"Of course, if you want me to." Making it clear that she was puzzled but determined, she stepped through the doorway and pressed down the switch with a fingertip. "What am I meant to be seeing, Jonathan? It's just a room."

"Have a better look," he said, though he was tempted to believe her: the room was emptier than last time he'd seen it – the bed had been stripped to its stale piebald mattress. His grandmother wouldn't want to lie on that; perhaps she was hiding in one of the massive wardrobes, though she'd disliked games she considered to be childish. He urged himself into the room and swung around to catch Trudy's hand again. "Let's look in—"

His voice froze in his throat as he saw what was crouched behind her in the dimmest corner of the room. It could almost have been a swollen bunch of sticks, except that it was patched with rags of clothes or skin. Lolling on top of it was an object that looked pinched with chill and peeling with damp and distorted by worse than either. It hadn't much he would have liked to call a mouth or a nose, and was crowned with lumps of dust or hair. He might not have recognised it if his grandmother's eyes hadn't been glaring out of a section like an irregular piece of old toadstool. He hung onto Trudy and nodded at the corner. "There," he whispered.

She kept her gaze on him. "What now, Jonathan?"

"What you wanted. It's behind you, look."

"You mustn't do things like that. Even if you're still upset it isn't very pleasant, is it? You can tell me what's wrong. I'd like you to, it'd make me feel more like family. Just talk."

He saw his grandmother's eyes bulge in the remnant of a face while the rest of her crouched smaller and lower as if she was about to spring. He tried to drag Trudy to confront this – he was growing desperate enough to reach up for her head to twist it round. "I will if you look."

He felt her grow tense and make herself relax. She was beginning to turn her head when the shape in the corner unfolded itself and tottered to its full height. It jerked out a hand with little in the way of fingers, and he thought it was going to fasten on Trudy's shoulder. The next moment the light was gone, and Trudy clutched at him. "Did you—"

He wriggled free and dodged out of the room, snatching the door shut. If Trudy switched the light on she would come face to face with the thing she'd made of his grandmother, and otherwise she would be alone with it in the dark. It was suddenly apparent to him that his grandmother didn't want anyone to see her as she was now, and he wondered what she might do to gain control of the light-switch. He was hanging onto the doorknob with both hands when the front door slammed. "I'm back again," his mother called. "Where's everyone?"

"Could you come up?" Trudy responded rather less than steadily. "I'm shut in and I can't seem to find . . ."

"Where are you? Hold on." Jonathan's mother ran upstairs and halted at the top. "Where's Trudy?" she asked him. "What are you—"

"I'm in here, Esther."

"What on earth do you think you're doing, Jonathan? Let go at once."

He was afraid that if she opened the door she would see his grandmother. She had to prise his fingers off the knob in order to let Trudy out. As Trudy fled onto the landing, he saw that the room was still unlit. "Trudy, I'm sorry," his mother cried. "Tell me what happened."

"Just an attempt to scare me off," Trudy said more or less evenly. "I'm afraid someone doesn't want me here."

"My grandma doesn't. She doesn't like you making mum say bad things about her."

"I think you'd better get ready for bed and stay in it," his mother told him.

The women followed him into the hall and watched him trudge, weighed down by injustice and luggage, to his room. Was Trudy staying? His grandmother wouldn't have to go far to find her, then. The thought failed to lessen his dismay at his grandmother's state. He raced through preparing for bed and took as much refuge in it as he could. Trudy and his mother were murmuring downstairs, largely incomprehensibly. "He'll have to get used to it," he heard his mother say.

Did she mean Trudy or her own criticisms of his grandmother? How much would he have to pray to compensate for whatever she'd said over the weekend? He set about chanting his plea, only to wonder if it was too late. He couldn't bring any other prayers to mind. Before long his mind gave up being awake.

He dreamed Trudy was inciting his mother to say worse and

worse – at least, he hoped it was a dream. "That's right, keep pulling me to bits," he seemed to hear his grandmother complain. "Pull some more off me." She'd go to Trudy in the night, he thought, hoping she would. The idea transfixed him with panic. At first he couldn't understand why, even when he floundered awake – and then he realised how much of the fault was his. He'd willed his grandmother to look her worst for Trudy and his tormentors in the schoolyard.

He couldn't deny he was glad that Trudy had crept into his room and was stooping to rouse him. When he blinked his eyes wide, however, it wasn't Trudy's face he saw looming closer in the dimness. What the boys had said about his grandmother had overtaken her. Even if she couldn't see him, she could grope in search of him. He cowered under the bedclothes and tried to pray but could think of no words. Surely the noise he was making would bring his mother, or Trudy would do. Perhaps they were punishing him, because all it attracted was the sensation of less than hands plucking at the bedclothes. The time until dawn felt like for ever, and dawn might only show him what was waiting to be seen.

STEVE NAGY

The Hanged Man of Oz

STEVE NAGY LIVES IN Michigan with his wife and two daughters. He studied journalism at Kent State University in Ohio, and worked as a reporter and copy editor for several newspapers in the Midwest before becoming a phone support rep for a software company that services the newspaper industry. Nagy's story "The Revelation of St Elvis the Impersonator" recently appeared in *Electric Velocipede*, and he is working on various short stories and two novels.

One of the novels is a horror tale set during the First World War and the Roaring Twenties. The other tackles the issues of cloning and identity. When he isn't writing or spending his free time with his family, Nagy works as fiction editor for the fan lifestyle eZine *MarsDust*.

" 'The Hanged Man of Oz' is the first story I ever sold," reveals the author, "and its genesis was an unlikely series of coincidences. I had never heard the urban legend about the hanging until my wife Melissa and I went to a dinner party with some friends. One was a fanatic about the movie, and he played the tape for our kids while we ate dinner. As the video reached the scene at the Tin Man's cabin, he told me about the Hanged Man.

"When I saw the 'hanging' I wasn't sure whether the story was true or not. That day, I thought it was a bird. But the legend stayed with me and I couldn't stop thinking about how people let their imagination trick them. I wrote the tale thinking about those 'tricks' and the characters did take on a life of their own beyond the page. I know I can't watch the film any longer without pausing at the hanging scene, so I can understand the power found in obsession.

"I submitted the story several places before sending it to Dennis Etchison to consider for an HWA anthology he was editing. He turned it down for that book, but said he had another in mind for which he might want it. That anthology turned out to be *Gathering the Bones*. When I told my family I had sold the story, my oldest daughter Lindsey was especially excited because *Bones* had a story by Ray Bradbury in it and her freshman English class was reading *Fahrenheit 451*. She thought *that* was the coolest thing about my sale."

K NEE-HIGH GRASS DOMINATED *the scene, thick blades uprooting the foundation of a sagging cabin, pushing aside cobbles in the shaded road. trees circled the clearing and an abandoned orchard lay behind the cabin, straight rows masked by weeds and windrows of dead leaves and forgotten fruit.*

A pastoral display except for the people posed throughout – two middle-aged men, one dressed as a hobo, the second clad in a dirty threadbare uniform; an old woman sporting too much rouge and mascara, skinny legs visible beneath the hem of a little girl's dress; and a dead man, hanging from a tree, his feet twitching at odd moments in time with some unheralded tune raised by the wind whistling through the forest.

Obsession is an art form.

And if you're lucky it's contagious.

Denise and I got together for dinner and drinks at her place. Our first date, although we saw each other in the apartment hall every day. I lived in 2B. She had moved into 2C in February. I'd made great strides, starting with an occasional nod and shared rides to work. I'd eventually thrown out an off-the-cuff comment about her hair, which she'd shorn from its ponytail length to a flapper-style skullcap. Guys should notice changes like that; it's an easy way to score points.

After that first compliment, the progression from casual to intimate was natural. We left in the morning at the same time, talked about our days, compared notes on work. If you practice something enough, anything is possible. I knew the boy-next-door routine better than when to observe national holidays. And the Fourth of July doesn't change from year to year.

Besides dinner and drinks, Denise made me sit down and watch *The Wizard of Oz.*

"You've seen this before, Michael?"

"Lots of times," I said. "Not lately, though. Isn't it usually on around Easter?"

"Until recently," Denise said. "Ted Turner bought the rights and pulled it for theatrical release."

Oz? God save me. I already regretted the date and struggled to keep an interested expression as Denise gave me the inside scoop. It was like a psychotic version of *Entertainment Tonight.*

When I was in college I worked at a greasy spoon as a busboy. The chef was a compact Italian named Ricky Silva who came across as uneducated, unhealthy, and gullible. I stayed late one night, and I found Silva poring over a stamp collection in a back booth. I questioned him about it, saying something crass because the idea of Silva as a philatelist didn't match my preconceptions. He told me there were an infinite number of worlds. Each existed next to the other, always overlapping and occasionally intertwining. Learning about his deeper reality forced me to change my opinion of him.

Denise and *Oz* were like that. The places she went and the things she did contained wholly unexpected layers. Up until now I'd only seen her "hallway" face.

But I wasn't in Kansas anymore.

The trivia litany went like this:

Buddy Ebsen – the original Tin Man – almost died from pneumonia, suffering a bad reaction to aluminum dust from his make-up, which let Jack Haley jump into his metal shoes.

The Cowardly Lion's costume was so hot Bert Lahr passed out at least a dozen times.

The Munchkins raised so much holy hell on the set that Chevy Chase mined that aspect for *Under The Rainbow.*

Shirley Temple led the pack for Dorothy's role. Probably because everyone considered Judy Garland too old and a poor box-office draw. The movie lost money, costing about $4.6 million and earning only $4 million the first time out.

Studio executives cut a groundbreaking dance number that

showcased Ray Bolger. They believed audiences wouldn't sit through a "children's movie" if it was too long.

Faulty special effects burned Margaret Hamilton at the end of her first scene as the Wicked Witch. This was shortly after Garland arrived in Oz. Hamilton tried grabbing the ruby slippers, but was thwarted by the Good Witch, an actress named Billie Burke. Hamilton dropped below the stage and right into a badly timed burst of smoke and flame . . .

It went on and on and on, everything you never wanted to know. Peccadilloes, idiosyncrasies; in other words, crap.

Then Denise told me a story about the man who hanged himself during filming – and she claimed the final print showed the incident.

"What? You're kidding me. I've never seen a dead guy."

Denise licked her lips, imitating a poorly belled cat. "Not everybody does. It's like those 3-D pictures where you cross your eyes."

"Prove it."

Denise paused the video. Onscreen, Dorothy and the Scarecrow were in the midst of tricking the trees into giving up their apples, frozen seconds before stumbling across the Tin Man.

"It's at the end of this section. I'll run it through once at regular speed. Let me know if you catch it."

She hit PLAY. Dorothy and the Scarecrow freed the Tin Man, did a little song-and-dance, fought off the Wicked Witch, and continued their trek. I didn't see anything strange and shrugged when Denise paused it.

"Nothing, right?" She rewound the tape to a point immediately after the witch disappeared in a cloud of red-orange smoke (this time minus the hungry flames), then advanced the video frame by frame.

Our date had progressed from strange to surreal, and I couldn't wait for an excuse to leave.

Then I saw *him* – the hanged man.

Dorothy, the Scarecrow and the Tin Man skipped down the road. Before the scene cut away to the Cowardly Lion's forest, the jerky movement of the advancing frames highlighted activity inside the forest edge.

A half-shadowed figure moved in the crook of a tree about ten feet off the ground. I thought it might be one of the many birds spread throughout the clearing and around the cabin, but its shape looked too much like a man. The next frame showed him jumping from his perch. His legs were stiff, as if bound. Or maybe determination wouldn't let him go all loose and disjointed at this defining moment. Before his feet touched the ground, they wrenched to the right. Whatever held him to the upper branches swung his ill-lit body back into the shadows. I think I heard his neck snap, although with the tape playing at this speed there wasn't any sound. Even at regular speed I knew the only sound would come from the three actors, voicing in song their desire to see the Wizard.

My heart raced and for a minute I worried that its syncopated thrum might attract the Tin Man, prompting him to step into the apartment and take it for his own.

"I can't believe it," I said. "It's a snuff film."

"Awesome, isn't it?" Denise restarted the film. I couldn't picture her smile as kind; it seemed too satisfied. "I stay awake some nights," she said, "letting my mind experience what it was like. The studio buried the whole thing. Can you imagine the bad press? I even think Garland started drinking because of it."

On the television screen, Bert Lahr made his appearance. His growls matched the rough nature of Denise's monologue. As the film continued I offered small talk, made Denise vague promises that I would see her in the morning, and left as the credits rolled.

"I feel as if I've known you all the time, but I couldn't have, could I?"

"I don't see how. You weren't around when I was stuffed and sewn together, were you?"

"And I was standing over there rusting for the longest time . . ."

I knew I was asleep, sprawled on my couch. The past five days had stretched me to the limit. I always had a headache. Aspirin and whiskey didn't kill the pain. My conversations with Denise were forced; she mentioned the movie at every opportunity.

We'd had a second date. I agreed because Denise invited two friends from her work. Stan and Lora were smokers, rail-thin and shrouded in a pall of smoke. I think Denise brought them along (one) so she could look good in contrast and (two) so she had someplace to hide if things went sour. We hit a club and during a busy night on the dance floor I demonstrated I wasn't a klutz. I guess you could say it was the modern social equivalent of an

Army physical. Denise and Lora exchanged approving nods near the end and Stan loosened up enough so that he took a minute between shots of tequila and his chain-smoking to talk to me.

Between all the alcohol and nicotine, I got a contact buzz and found myself obsessing about the hanged man and the way he disappeared into the shadows. Denise was still attractive to me, but I couldn't forget how pleased she'd looked as she talked about the death.

My thoughts hid me beside the Tin Man's cabin, watching the trio skip past. I would move onto the road. The hanged man was visible ahead. They must have turned their eyes to follow the road as it bent to the right because they didn't see him.

But I did.

Denise had seemed like her old self in the mixed company, and I assumed I was overreacting. So I agreed to a third date. Instead of a rerun with the mystery man in the trees, I got Stan and Lora again and a nice restaurant. I was almost happy when I saw their wan faces.

Almost. Denise and Lora left to powder their noses, and Stan asked me a question.

"How did you like the movie?"

"What?"

"You know what I mean. You look like you haven't had a good night's sleep in a while."

"How do you know that?"

"Denise is predictable. I'd be more surprised if she hadn't shown you the film yet."

I gulped my beer. "You've . . . seen him?"

Stan shrugged. "What about it?"

"The guy hung himself. She seems so glad."

"Someone dies somewhere every second. Get used to it. Life will get a lot easier if you do."

Before I could ask what he meant, Denise and Lora returned from the bathroom.

I had the dream again the next night. It started at the same point. The Tin Man finished his dance, stumbled off the road, collapsed in a heap on a tree stump near the cabin. The others rushed to his side, Technicolor concern painting their expressions.

No one noticed me. I couldn't hear everything they said. It *did* seem to change night to night, probably because I couldn't remember the dialogue verbatim.

The Wicked Witch screeched at the three adventurers from her perch on the roof above, surprising me again. I crouched and prayed she wouldn't see me. She tossed a fireball at the Scarecrow and even from this distance I felt the heat. The Tin Man smothered the flames under his funnel hat, but not before the silver paint bubbled and blistered on the edge and on several of his fingers.

The Wicked Witch took off on her broom. Smoke billowed like a tumor in her wake. No trapdoors this time; my position offered an excellent view behind the cabin. Her flight left a rough scar across the sky that traced the road's path toward the Emerald City and beyond to the land of the Winkies.

"I wonder how many she'll kill when she gets home?"

I jumped from my crouch. The Scarecrow stood beside me. Dorothy and the Tin Man remained in the road. Instead of the concern I'd seen earlier, they appeared curious.

"What are you doing?" I glanced toward the trees. The hanged man swung from his rope, as solid as a mirage, flirting with the shadows. I turned back to the Scarecrow. "You're supposed to be on your way to the Emerald City."

The Scarecrow, who looked less and less like Bolger, dropped his gaze and shrugged. The simple gesture produced a sound reminiscent of dead leaves. "I'm not supposed to tell you," he said, his words more rustle than speech.

Dorothy and the Tin Man, poor doubles for Garland and Haley, edged towards the bend. "We have to go, Scarecrow," the not-Garland said. "There's not much time left and we're expected."

The Scarecrow joined them. "I'm not supposed to tell you, Michael," he repeated. "Talk to Stan." He glanced towards the trees one last time as he and his companions moved away. "Stay away from the Hanged Man."

I woke drenched with sweat. I don't know what happened after the three left. Maybe they found the Cowardly Lion, became a quartet, maybe not.

Stay away from the Hanged Man.

Even the memory of those words hurt.

Talk to Stan.

What was I involved in here? Were my dreams random sub-conscious processes? Talk to Stan? I didn't even know his last name. Denise introduced him by his first name. I only knew Denise's – Fleming – because the apartment glued labels to the lobby mailboxes. When we met, we exchanged greetings and first names. Surnames never came into it because right from the start we were always personal.

Hours remained until dawn. I left the apartment and hit Kroger. The big grocery on Carpenter stayed open all night – and its video selection included *The Wizard of Oz.*

I wanted a copy because . . . because I wanted privacy. I'd need Denise soon enough to find Stan, if I gathered the courage necessary to broach the subject. The hanged man was a drug and I was a junkie. If I had my own copy, I might control the addiction. I'd first seen him with Denise and everything stemmed from that. I'd entered one of Silva's infinite worlds; privacy might let me create a new perspective.

The shadowed streets looked different than they did during the day. The late-night wind didn't touch the trees. Each moved on its own, apple hoarders, ready for a rematch.

"Just wait," a voice rasped beside me. "It gets worse."

I shouted and slammed the brakes. My car swerved, shuddered to a halt and stalled. I turned and found myself facing the Scarecrow.

"What do you . . . what do you want?" I tried sounding angry, but my voice shook.

My Scarecrow smiled and the maw formed by his mouth – old burlap, leather, and rotting hay – made my stomach turn. "I won't hurt you, Michael." He nodded toward the back. "But I can't speak for her."

I twisted in my seat and craned to look. A shape huddled there, its outline weird and broken by too many angles. I fumbled to turn on the overhead dome light, but the person in the back actually *cackled* and I leaped from the car and into the deserted street.

I tripped before I'd gone half a dozen steps. Scrambling up, I looked over my shoulder, expecting pursuit – and saw nothing. The car door was open and the dome light revealed the empty interior. The only sound was the chime that signaled the keys were still in the ignition.

This isn't happening, I told myself. *The Scarecrow was in the passenger seat and the Witch – yes, the Witch – was in the back.*

A soft noise broke the breathless silence. I saw something slowly swinging in the tree shadows across the way. I knew the noise was a rope creaking under the strain of a dead man's weight. I retreated to my car, more scared of what hid outside than of my elusive passengers.

The residential speed limit was twenty-five. I did at least fifty and ran every red light getting home.

Two hours more till dawn.

I shredded the box wrap and popped the tape into my VCR. My head throbbed with too many ideas, as if I'd overdosed on coffee and Tylenol. I let it play and tried to clear my mind. I tried to tell myself there was no place like Oz. And this time the scene ran the same as I remembered it from my childhood.

The Tin Man stumbled and landed on the tree stump. Dorothy and the Scarecrow ran over to help. The Wicked Witch made her threats, threw her fireball, bolted in a puff of smoke. The three adventurers danced off down the road.

There wasn't any sign of the Hanged Man.

There was movement among the trees, but I could see it was a long-necked bird moving one of its wings. Was there something different on Denise's tape? I didn't consider myself gullible. Because I didn't trust my eyes. I rewound the tape and played it again, cursing myself for doing that.

The Tin Man collapsed on the tree stump. But he didn't resemble Haley. His fingers and hat were burned, warped by some tremendous heat, even though the fireball lay moments in the future. Dorothy and the Scarecrow ran to help him. But she looked middle-aged and the Scarecrow was the rotting bag from my car. Once, all three stared at me. The screen thinned to gauze as thin as the dust coating its surface.

And the Wicked Witch screamed to life on the roof – a gangrenous, misshapen version of Denise.

I stopped the tape.

I waited in my car for two hours before Denise left the apartment. I didn't want to meet her in the hall. She had started the avalanche of fear that had buried my senses, and I wasn't ready for a confrontation.

Stay away from the Hanged Man.

Talk to Stan . . .

I stayed at least a block behind her. She worked at a department store in the mall and liked to arrive early. I parked in the side lot. She was inside by the time I walked to the front entrance. I hung around there, wondering if I was too late. Entering the store wasn't an option. If Denise caught me inside, I didn't have any excuses. She'd know I'd followed her. Besides, I worked at a union job shop, creating ads on a computer, and I caught hell when I missed a shift.

Ten minutes later, Stan entered the lot.

I ran over and hovered as he locked his car. I'm not sure what I expected from him.

"I need help," I said.

"What are you doing here, Michael? Don't you have to work?"

"I'm taking a sick day."

Stan nodded, lit up a cigarette. I could blame my imagination, but I thought his hands shook. "So? What are you doing here?" he asked again. He didn't seem in any hurry to get to work.

"The Scarecrow told me to talk to you."

Stan didn't laugh. His mouth twitched, though.

"You know about it."

He shoved past me. "You're crazy," he said, walking briskly towards the store.

I followed, grabbed his arm. I glanced around the lot to see if anyone was watching. No one was close.

"Don't call me crazy," I said. "The Scarecrow popped in and out of my car like a damned ghost and he brought the Wicked Witch along for the ride and I'm scared. This is all Denise's fault and you know something. You asked me about the movie. Don't dare tell me you don't know what I'm talking about."

Stan jabbed his lit cigarette against my hand as I held his arm. I jerked it away, hissed with pain, put my mouth over the burn. Stan backed up and pinned a sneer on his pale face.

"Get away from me, Michael." He paused. "If you don't, I'll tell Denise."

I stood there, silent, and watched him leave.

*   *   *

This time I observed the speed limit on my way home. A ghostly Dorothy rode shotgun. Toto sat in her lap. I didn't recall seeing the mutt before. A taxidermist had worked him over, mounting him to a wood base, so he traveled well, no tongue-flapping out the window, no prancing from one side to the other, claws digging into your thighs. The Scarecrow and the Tin Man held the rear seats.

All four were quiet, which didn't bother me. Maybe the daylight silenced them. I parked in my slot, killed the engine. When I climbed out, chaff and aluminum dust and the ripe scent of a dead dog floated through the empty interior.

The apartment hall was empty. I pressed my hands against the cold surface of Denise's door. The number and letter glimmered as each reflected the fluorescent light, incandescent with a promise like prophecy. I knew now that I *wanted* to see. The knowledge might release me.

My fingers ached where I touched the door, as if the wood sucked at my bones, robbing them of warmth. The 2C pulsed and my breath frosted the air, crystallizing inside my chest until I forgot to breathe.

Then my legs buckled under fatigue and gravity, and the door answered my weakness with its own, selling its solid soul so I could fall through into the reality that lay beyond.

Dry grass rustled beneath me as I fell to my knees. A brick-paved road ran past, its surface a river of yellow pus baked solid under a neon-strobe sun. Disease festered in the scabbed cracks, more efficient as a contagion than as mortar.

The Tin Man's cabin sat across from me, wearing its abandonment like a badge. The logs sagged, eaten by dry rot and unable to sustain their weight. Years had passed since glass sealed the windows and thick cobwebs, choked with dead insects, served as the only curtains. The stone chimney wore moss and ivy like a fur coat, its only protection against the cold. Large gaps riddled the roof's green slate like open sores. In the places where there were not yet holes the sun glinted off shallow pools of water.

I stood and crossed the road, glancing left and right along its bumpy length – no one was visible in either direction. Not the intrepid trio or their hanged observer.

Light fell through the rear windows and the roof, illuminating the room. The sun had almost died in the west, but it was enough so I could pick out the familiar details of Denise's apartment.

From the front window to the door, I picked out the vague outlines of furniture. A mildewed couch slumped on broken legs. Two rickety crates supported several planks that served as a table, with an apish skull still wearing shreds of flesh as a centerpiece. Instead of the entertainment center, a cauldron sat before the fireplace, its mealy contents still bubbling.

A mask hung above the mantel like a trophy stuffed and mounted by a hunter. The facial lines were soft, cheeks frozen in a perpetual smile, spawning dimples on both corners. But the eyes were empty and soulless, the mouth a toothless hole, and they sucked away whatever resemblance to humanity the mask ever possessed.

It was Denise.

I backed away from the cabin, dazed by what I'd seen. Before I knew it, I'd crossed the road to my original entry point, just as a dark shape moved across the cabin roof, catching my eye. The Wicked Witch froze, straddling the peak like an Impressionist vision of the Statue of Liberty, broom held high in place of a torch.

"It took you long enough, Michael," she said, her smile as uneven as the road. "I thought I'd need to send someone out after you again."

"I don't know what you're thinking, Denise, but I'm finished with these dreams."

She cackled. "Stubborn to a fault, Michael. I love that. The longer you doubt, the closer I get. Eventually, it will be too late . . ."

I walked towards the cabin, my first steps tentative as loose bricks threatened to turn my ankles. I stopped once, crouched, pulled one broken piece loose, steeled myself against the slimy feel as I clenched it in my fist. I needed a weapon. I didn't think this ball-sized brick would hurt her, but it might serve as a distraction.

"You're right. I don't believe." Debris littered the yard between the cabin and the road and matched the landscape of my chaotic dreams. "You've drugged or hypnotized me. Whichever, I don't care. It's over."

From behind the trees the Scarecrow moved into the clearing. Dorothy and the Tin Man skulked in his shadow.

"Calling in your troops, Denise?" I asked.

Age lines shredded each of their faces, changing grins into something as old as the brown apples piled under the trees, something as calculated as the way the trees' prehensile branches reached out, straining against the roots that kept each woody demon in place.

"Her name isn't Denise," said the Tin Man, brandishing an ax that looked freshly honed. "I don't think she has one."

"Names don't matter here," the Scarecrow said.

"Is that why you told me to talk to Stan?"

The Scarecrow cringed, glanced at the Wicked Witch. His companions backed away. I looked at the Wicked Witch too, expecting her to nail his straw frame with a quick fireball.

"You warned him?" she asked.

"No! No! I was trying to prepare him!"

The Wicked Witch leaped off the roof, black dress billowing behind her like crows hovering around a fresh kill. She landed in the middle of the road, nimble as a black widow.

Forget the rock, I thought. I needed something bigger if I wanted to come out of this alive. I crouched beside rubble from the chimney, dropped my brick and grabbed a discarded axe handle where it lay half-buried among the weeds.

The Scarecrow trembled, begged. "Please don't hurt me! Please!"

The Wicked Witch formed her hand into a claw. Eldritch flames sprouted from her bitten nails, knotted into a pulsing globe.

"I release you, Scarecrow! I give you your freedom – in death!"

She hurled the fire and the Scarecrow tried to block it with upraised hands.

The ball hit him and ate his body up in seconds.

The Wicked Witch stepped into the yard, blocked my way to the road, as the Tin Man and Dorothy circled the Scarecrow's smoldering remains. If I braved the apple orchard, I'd have to fight them both, one armed with an ax, the other with a dead dog.

"This is taking too long," the Wicked Witch said. "It's time for you to join me, Michael."

"I'm not going anywhere, Denise." I waved the ax handle before me.

"My name is not Denise. I can't remember my name. It's been such a long time since I heard it."

"But if you're not Denise . . ."

My words trailed off. I let my eyes trace the lines in her face. I barely recognized the woman I'd flirted with in the hallway. She might be there under the thick cheeks, the warts, the bony chin and green skin, but there wasn't enough to convince me.

"Then . . . I must be the Wicked Witch!" she said.

I swung my weapon and reached for the roof. The handle cracked when it hit, cut my hands as it splintered. The Tin Man was nearest the cabin and he screamed. His voice squeaked. *You're going to need to oil more than that, buddy.* My blow shook the roof's remaining boards and the water puddles washed into the yard, striking the Tin Man. He scrambled into the road, metal limbs clanking, joints squealing from friction. The shower streaked Dorothy's make-up, washed her brown tresses blonde, knocked Toto from her arms.

The Wicked Witch smiled.

She raised her claws to meet the deluge running across her body, black rags clinging to her stick frame. The shape beneath was suddenly too skeletal and bulged in all the wrong places, cancerous and demonic. She licked the stagnant moisture off her lips with a leprous tongue, slurping at the algae.

"Yeah, right," she said. "Like no one's ever tried water before."

I ran but a tree stopped me. Not one of the apple trees. Those were back by the cabin.

The Wicked Witch screamed – "Get him! I won't lose two today!" – and I looked over my shoulder, trying to spot a pursuer. When I turned forward again I ran face first into a lightning-split oak.

As I lay there dazed, my audience assembled.

"You can't get away, Michael," the Wicked Witch said.

"What do you want?"

"I was thrown out of my land a long time ago and I can never go back." She gestured at the forest, the ramshackle cabin, and the rotting orchard. "This is my home. This is my reality. This is my dream."

I shook my head. "A dream?"

Dorothy wiped her face and left fingerprints in the wet mascara and rouge. "More than a dream. We play our parts, we keep her from loneliness."

"Stan was one of us," the Tin Man said. "He served his time. When she tired of him, she let him serve her outside."

"Be quiet, beehive!" said the Wicked Witch, pushing him aside. "You'll learn my ways soon enough, Michael. You're going to replace him."

"You're crazy!" I pulled myself up against the split trunk. "I'll never do anything you want!"

"That's why I love you, Michael." She motioned towards the tree. "Lift him up."

A noose dropped over my head and cinched tight. At the other end, hidden among the leaves, an orangutan jumped into the air, guiding its descent with spread wings as it hauled the rope across a thick branch.

My neck snapped.

The Witch's obsession traps us here, and her magic forces us into these forms. When I dream I'm still in my old life, but it fades as her obsession burns, tarnishing the memory. She watches and we try to amuse her. When she tires, I may stop hanging myself. And someday I will escape.

Her madness is contagious.

MICHAEL CHISLETT

Mara

MICHAEL CHISLETT HAS HAD his stories published in such magazines as *Ghosts & Scholars*, *Supernatural Tales* and *All Hallows*, along with anthologies published by the Oxford University Press and Ash-Tree Press. A collection is forthcoming from the latter imprint.

He is currently working on two novels, *Jane Dark's Garden* and *The Night Friends*, both of which are set in the same general area of London as "Mara", though they are contemporary, and another story, "Off the Map", appeared in *Best New Horror Volume Thirteen*.

As the author explains: "Axel Crescentius, the hero, if that is what he is, of the tale, features in some other stories, only one of which has so far been published.

"I wanted to write a Gothic vampire story with a London setting and the actual places described in the tale – the hill with its view of the River Thames, the creek and the cemetery – do exist, though not as close to each other as described in the text. Instead, they have come together in the geography of my mind to become one place – Mabbs Hill, which, I have been assured by one who claims to know, exists in some other alternative London in which we can travel usually and fortunately only in the imagination."

A FTER MY INVOLVEMENT IN the revolution of 1848 I was obliged to flee Germany and make my way to England and exile. For a time I resided just outside London, south of the River Thames, at a place called Mabbs End.

My custom was, after a day of study at the British Museum, to return by train from London and on reaching Mabbs End have a walk of about fifteen minutes to my lodgings. My journey would take me across a stone bridge spanning a creek, a narrow finger of the Thames that ran through the district. I then had to ascend a steep hill where the buildings gave way to hedges and market gardens.

This rise was called Mabbs Hill and, once on its crest, a short walk along an unpaved road led to my lodging, in a house newly built, one of a row as yet unconnected to the town other than by the way that I had come.

From this hill, on clear days, I had the most marvellous view of London. The dome of St Paul's would gleam in the sun and on the river there were more ships than had besieged Troy. Indeed, all of the Thames, both up-and downstream, then revealed itself to me in a most pleasing prospect. I say on clear days, for most often the metropolis was covered by that thick fog for which it is notorious. Mabbs Hill did not suffer so much from this but frequently, at night, the mist would creep from off the river to lie heavy over the creek so that I would have to cross blind to where a solitary lamp stood sentinel in the murk.

One such night the fog had travelled with me from London and rolled in great grey waves that increased by the moment. Shivering at its chill touch, I hurried along the High Street from the station. The glow of gas lamps did little to light my way, and those few others abroad flitted through the fume like phantoms with sinister, muffled footsteps, seeming to be about on fell missions which had but waited the chance of this complicit shroud to be done.

My native land was by the Baltic and I, Axel Crescentius, had been born to mist and fog, for it had haunted those shores. But I had travelled long and far since then.

Uncanny thoughts of how, on misty nights like this, when all becomes unreal, then we are in another world through which we travel not knowing what unseen companions walk with us, fretted me. After blindly crossing the bridge where the fog muffled the usual splash of water, I heard the sound of weeping, the cry of a child lost in murk-black night.

To my left, where the sound came from, lay an alley, narrow and dubious enough by daylight and certainly no place to linger by with this pall about. Sensing danger, I released the catch on my swordstick and held it ready to be drawn. Hearing another cry, sharp as a vixen's, I stepped back into a doorway where, doubly concealed, I stood to watch and listen.

There was a disturbance at the alley's fog-thick mouth and a woman passed barely an arm's length from me. Her movement disturbed the mist, scrims of which detached from the cottony mass to cling about her body, reminding me uneasily of feeding eels, or snakes. She pulled a hood over her head, but not before I had seen a coil of long dark hair hanging down over her breast. Then she vanished into night and fog, becoming one with them.

"Give it back to me!"

The voice wailed and I tensed as, from the alley, a young girl staggered. Her tear-stained face bore the look of one mortally stricken by some deadly pestilence, a wretch under sentence of death from which there could be no reprieve.

She fled toward the bridge, another wraith lost in the mist, but her voice still cried, lamenting whatever had been taken from her.

It was no more than an affair between street women, but that look of desolation on the girl's face – she was no more than a child – had been terrible to see. Brooding on this, I made a cautious way up the hill as the mist thinned somewhat until, at the crest, the air grew marvellously clear, the sky cloudless and I gazed down at the still and silent sea that covered the world below.

The heavens were all aglow with stars, the waxing moon their sovereign. I studied the firmament, bitterly regretting the loss of my telescope, abandoned with so many other things upon my abrupt departure from Germany.

For a while I watched the stars until my neck began to ache, then turned my gaze down to the mist. It was rising, steady as an incoming tide, toward me and I formed the conceit that I was some demigod who floated above these clouds which seemed solid enough for me to walk on.

I did not hear any footsteps in the mist until, with a shiver of surprise, I saw a hooded head rise from the cloudy mass, at first seeming to be curiously disembodied before the rest of the figure became visible, gliding through the grey air as though floating.

So uncanny was this apparition that my heart beat fast, but I recognized the woman who had emerged from the alley below by her cowl-like hood. The surprise of her appearance, with wraiths of mist still clinging to her body as if feeding, robbed me of speech and when, after walking a few paces in the clear air she stopped to boldly return my stare, I, who had lectured before congregations of the most learned men, blushed like a boy.

"Pardon me, miss," I said stupidly, "but can I be of assistance to you?"

"You are not English?" she said. Her voice, the contralto purr of some great cat, issued strangely from beneath the shadow of the hood, where her face was invisible.

"I am of German birth. Dr Axel Crescentius at your service."

The hood fell back to reveal full and sensual lips, eyes dark as night, face sharp and high-boned as a vixen's.

"I have no need of a doctor, or of your service, but if you wish to walk a little way with me then come."

Without waiting for a reply, she set off along the crest of the moonlit hill and I found myself following after.

"Do you live by here?" I asked, after catching up with her.

"Beneath the hill," she replied, pointing to a fork in the pathway.

The way that she indicated led down the far side of Mabbs Hill, a path untrod by me.

"Would you accompany me, down to my dwelling place?"

Her face glowed silver in the moonlight as she spoke these words and the mask it became dazzled my eyes. A wave of desire, the like of which I had never before felt, filled me as I closed my eyes to clear them of the uncanny glow that lit the woman's face.

"Yes, let me come with you."

She was, I told myself, but a streetwalker who, for a few pennies, I could slake my aroused passion upon. I reached out a hand to take her, but with a slight movement she evaded me.

"You think," she said, "that no honest woman would be out on such a night. But consider, I ask you, what good *man* would be abroad?"

The woman possessed a lively wit. Then again, without waiting for me, or another word, she walked down the path into the mist. I hesitated for but a second, then followed before she could be lost to me.

As we walked down and the mist covered us again I kept a firm hold on my swordstick, for I entertained a suspicion that there might lurk, somewhere in the obscurity, a bully in league with her to waylay and rob me.

The path fell sharply as the mist became icy, chilling with its touch. She turned a smile on my shivering, and I wondered at how she could show no apparent discomfort at the cold.

"I never feel the cold," she told me. "Once, long ago I did, but a fever of the blood took me, so now ice and fog are nothing to me." The woman smiled and her teeth showed sharp and white. "I am of those in whom blood turns to fire in their veins."

"Such conditions are not unknown," said I, nodding sagely. "I am, however, a doctor of philology, not medicine."

"Studying words and languages must be interesting. Though I have found" (she smiled knowingly) "that certain things can be understood by all, no matter what tongue they speak. You must be a clever man to know so much about words. My name is Mara."

I was surprised that she knew the meaning of the word "philology", and as the woman Mara spoke her name I thought to see, through the mist, a gleam as of smoky embers in her eyes.

"That," I said foolishly, "is a nice name."

"It is a terrible name."

Desire was strong within me, and I thought to take her there on the path, where she had stopped and smiled upon me. None would see us. In this place, concealed by the mist, we could do as we – as I – wished.

"Here is where I must leave you."

With a swift movement, her head darted forward and her lips sought mine. For a long moment we kissed, and the breath was drawn from my body as my head became peculiarly dizzy. I would have clipped her close to kiss again but she had gone, swallowed by the mist, leaving me alone and baffled at her abrupt disappearance.

My lips felt numb and I tasted blood – she had bitten me during our cold and foggy kiss. It had been long since I had been given a true and good love-kiss, one not bought and paid for. I held a hand before my eyes to see blood, black in the mist, stain the fingers. For she had bitten me on places other than my lips, though I could not exactly recall the bites, and I wondered what the price of her love and kisses might be.

All seemed unreal to me, the boundaries between worlds weak, but I took a resolute step forward, my swordstick held before me like a blind man's cane and I felt it strike and sound against metal.

Barely inches from my eyes I saw an iron gate, its tall bars vanishing up into the murky air. Padlocks secured it, three of them, rusty and obviously not opened for many a year. The strange sensation of being beneath the earth, in a vault, gripped me. The triple-locked gate the entrance to a place deeper yet.

"Mara!"

My voice was muffled in the foggy shroud but I heard and saw one of the locks open with a dry click and fall to the ground. I listened, but nothing else broke the stillness and silence.

The mist stifled me, choking my throat, and I made my way up the path, hurrying along its length like a grave-robber fleeing a necropolis until, after but a few minutes, not nearly so long as my descent had taken, I found myself once more on the crest of Mabbs Hill and in the clear air.

Through the icy moonlight I hurried to my lodgings, shivering as one possessed by an ague. I was soon abed, but it took a long while for sleep to claim me.

Strange thoughts flitted batlike through my brain, night-frights rising to vex and nag at me. When at last I fell into a restless slumber, my dreams were all of tomb and sepulchre, dreadful hollow vaults beneath the earth, in which I was lost. Something had me in a smothering embrace, pressing down on my chest. I thought myself to be immured in a grave, and that which lay atop me was feeding horribly upon my still-living corpse.

With the first light of dawn I lay awake, weak as one sucked dry, the woman Mara haunting my burning thoughts as my drained yet unappeased body hungered for her.

The day dawned bright and chill, and I resolved to explore the pathway that I had walked with Mara. The mist had gone, and I looked from the crest of Mabbs Hill toward London and wondered at how long it would be before the metropolis engulfed this quiet place and its environs.

Swinging my cane at the weeds by the side of the path, my night-fears forgotten, I made a way down. After but a minute the trees closed in above to turn the morning into twilight. I soon found the gate, set in a high wall that ran to either side for some distance. Thick spider webs, glistening with dew and long undisturbed, clung to the bars. With my cane I tore at them and looked within to see gravestones and broken tombs, all much worn by time.

Though I searched, no dwelling could I find. I saw the fallen lock and the two remaining. They, though rusted, seemed secure. I noted how the trees that twisted above and about me were oddly flourishing, even though it was winter. Perhaps their nourishment was drawn from that ground.

I soon left that place and stood again atop the hill. Looking down I could see nothing but the waving branches of trees, covering the graveyard on Mabbs Hill and wherever Mara dwelt.

Something odd struck me, for I realized that all the time I had been down there, by the cemetery, no noise of birds had I heard. But there was no leisure to confirm that, for I had a train to catch and so I set off, at a run, down the hill to the station.

The evening was bright with starlight. I stood on the bridge above the creek, watching the moon's reflection break in silver shards amid the flow, and I became lost in a reverie. Hearing a soft voice, I turned to see a girl staring intently at the moon-glade.

"Give it back to me, moon-witch. I can see you there, laughing at me."

It was the girl whom I had seen crying the night before. She leant over the bridge to throw a stone into the stream and the moon's face there shattered into a thousand pieces.

"Killed you!" she cried triumphantly. But her voice changed to a sob as the moon gathered up its shards to grin sardonically back at us.

She hurried away past me, and I held out my hand to stay her, asking if I could be of aid. She was a pretty thing, or would have been but for the look of utter desolation marring her face. Her red hair had been sheared short and uneven, sticking out at odd, uncombed angles about her head, and I was again reminded of one condemned.

"It's a mask." She pointed to the water below. "I know, the moon-witch told me. That grave-woman who said I was a moonchild . . . me who was just me mum's love child. The moon's a thief!" She screamed these words and buried her face in her hands. "I'm a dead one now because of what she took from me."

"What did she take?" I asked gently.

Her eyes peeped at me through parted fingers and she giggled, as though I had said something amusing.

"You've had yours taken too, I can tell. But you don't care. I hope you was happy with what you got for it. I didn't get nothing, nothing at all. I want it back."

Her distracted face was bathed white as a mask by the moonlight and she held out her hands towards me, as though making an offering. I looked and saw a moth sitting upon her palm, its wings fluttering ever so slightly. There was something unusual about it and I looked close.

"It's a strange thing, but the moon is really under the ground and no one knows that except me and you and her."

I could not look into the girl's eyes, so intently did they watch me as she spoke.

Then, lowering her hands, she fled away, across the bridge. Whether she still held the moth, or had dropped the thing, I did not know. But uselessly I searched the stone bridge, washed grey by moonlight, for it; and as I sought, the girl's voice was raised in a distant, wistful song:

> "I am just a love-child,
> "Lost in moon dreams am I."

Giving up my search for the moth, I listened for a space of time to the girl's song. It seemed that, though gone, she was still close by, but invisible, a ghost conjured by the moon to trill for its amusement.

I forced myself away and up the hill. My meeting with the girl had been distressing, bringing more disturbing thoughts and memories to my mind, for all that day the woman Mara had haunted me. Thoughts of her sensual mouth sucking on mine, biting with those sharp white teeth so hard that I bled. Strange and lurid sensations ran through me at the memory of it.

Mabbs Hill shone before me, lit by moonlight. A heavy frost sparkled the ground, a purse of silver thrown to Earth by the moon. No living thing had I seen since the girl and she, poor thing, bore the certain mark of one who soon would not be.

A footfall in a rime of frost sounded behind me, ominous as the snap of breaking bone.

I turned to see the hooded figure that followed.

"Is this not well met by moonlight?"

Her voice thrilled me as moonlight and starlight played with silver fire on the frost.

We stood regarding each other and the hood fell back. Eyes, dark as grapes, captured me, and her feline smile beguiled.

"I knew that we would meet again," she sighed, a sound almost a moan of pleasure as she looked up to let the moon bathe her face. "How I love the moon and so do you. I saw how you gazed at her last night. She is my mother. Ah! The mist and the moonlight, they are my elements."

"I have already met with a moonchild tonight," I said, "who told me that the moon is beneath the earth."

"That pretty little thing did not wish to give me a little pretty thing that I desired from her. Soon she will not be so pretty." Mara looked searchingly at me. "A moonchild indeed! Perhaps she is your wish-child? Would you rather her than me? Surely not!"

"What did you take from her, Mara? She said that the moon was a thief."

"Her hope, her youth, her flowering beauty. Her red hair was so long and lovely that I grew jealous of it and made her shear the tresses. Such a silly girl, so easy to beguile. She would never have missed her pretty little soul and I would have sent her out into the world to seek others for me."

A great fear seized me. Instinctively I released the catch on my swordstick and eased the blade slightly from its sheath. My action caused Mara some amusement, for she laughed.

"I shall leave you if you are so afraid and must draw your weapon on little me. But I promise that no great harm will befall you, on this night, unless you so wish it."

The blade slid back into its sheath as Mara's cold hand lightly brushed my face. She then took my hand and we walked up Mabbs Hill, at the top of which we looked down on the city below, the lights of which blazed – a town of fire lit by the flames of Hell – which, as the poet said, is a city much like London.

"All this could be yours," whispered Mara the temptress. "Better than knowledge, Herr Doctor Crescentius of the mouldy old books."

"No! There is nothing better than knowledge," I denied her.

"Shall I call you Faustus?" she mocked. "There is something better than that. Did not your hero sigh for the love of Helen?"

What was knowledge compared to the mystery of Mara's body? Mara, who could read my thoughts. For, secretly, I would often beguile myself with the conceit of being a new Faust, and learn the secrets of the natural world and of that occult one which is so close but yet so far from us.

Cold hand in mine, she led me down the path that led under the hill.

"You know who I am," Mara teased. "But you have put it from your mind. A wise fool indeed."

"You are Lilith, you are Hecate."

"Just Mara," she said, as clumsily I tried to kiss her and she easily evaded me.

A strange silver light, like a will-o'-the-wisp, danced before us as down, ever down we went, showing a way through what else would have been grave-dark. For it seemed that walls of earth surrounded us, until we came to the gate of that city of the dead, beneath the hill.

Mara fell into my arms at last, like one surrendering to a deep need whose satisfaction had been long denied to them. Her lips burnt mine with their cold as she bit and sucked, and a feeling of release from all care took hold of me as I let her drink.

"It is gone already."

Mara stepped back, out of my arms, and I saw the smear of blood on her lips.

"My soul, you mean. That is long gone," I answered truly. "Taken by another, freely given by me. Why, even your little moonchild knew that . . . recognized a similar loss in herself, perhaps."

A veil clouded my sight as I spoke, and Mara slipped away like a shadow.

Confounded, I peered into the dark, calling her name. Tearing at the spider web on the bars of the gate, I looked into the necropolis that was washed with a pale light like that from a subterranean moon. A place of luxurious foliage of horrid nurture it was, and I thought of how by day it was above ground, of that I was sure, but by night below.

Those who walk restless when by rights they should lie quiet made themselves known, drawing near between the tumbled graves to call and to beckon. None of them was Mara – she was not of those poor spirits, but a much more terrible thing.

A lock fell from the gate, leaving but one now to bar it. Those that walked within shuddered and drew closer. I recoiled from them, and hurried back up that tunnel through the hill, that grave-mound, until at last I was in the open with the light of moon and stars blazing above.

Soon I was home and abed, but again my night was one of fret.

An invisible bed-mate clung leech-close to me, draining my body. My tired eyes conjured shadows into phantasmagorical shapes, all becoming that of Mara, who tantalized me so that I cried out aloud for her. Until, with the dawn, I looked from my window to assure myself that I was still on the Earth and had not yet been taken below.

Later, as I approached the bridge over the creek, I saw that a crowd had gathered there and curiously joined them to look.

On the mud of the bank stood a group of men, who raised a figure covered by a sheet to silently bear it upon their shoulders. They used her more gently, I think, than anyone ever had in her poor life. The cover fell to reveal her face, the shorn red hair, the blank eyes that looked up at me. A woman cried out and another began a prayer; a man said what a shame it was that such a pretty thing had done that to herself.

The sheet was pulled back over her face, dead and white as the moon's, and I hurried down to the station, reaching it as the rain began to fall as tears of grief.

That evening, on my reluctant return to Mabbs End – I should not have returned at all, perhaps then Mara might have left me alone – the rain had become a downpour. I found my perversity in daring this danger, for that was what I knew it to be, quite frankly, amazing. By the time I reached the bridge I was soaked through, but I ignored this chilly discomfort for I anticipated meeting Mara. That we would encounter each other again I did not doubt.

I stood on the beach watching the torrent of water run down the creek and the reflection of a gas lamp flickering in the flood. Or was it the pale face of a lost girl, a moonchild, a dream child, a love child, my wish-child, seeking for her soul?

Wearily, I climbed Mabbs Hill, looking all around me for Mara. But the murk-black rain fell in sheets, and I could see little. I kept vigil under the shelter of an oak until, when I was on the point of giving up, I felt her presence by me and saw that she stood near, watching me with a raptorial smile. Her uncovered hair gleamed slick with the rain that ran down the valley between her breasts.

"I cannot escape you," she purred. "We meet together in mist and frost, now rain, you strange man without a soul. I am curious about what you were given for it. Was it a good price?"

"That is no business of yours. It is long gone and there is nothing that you could give me that I would want."

"I have a web, cunningly fashioned, in which souls are trapped. When I wish to feed, I pluck one out and drink." She laughed, and her teeth showed sharp. "I like to play with them too, pull their wings off. For they take the form of moths, each with a human face, and yours, I think, is one among them."

Mara came close to me, and I was like to fall into the trap of her eyes but turned mine away. Her lips touched my ear as she whispered, and I thought of those sharp teeth and my blood in that mouth, and could not help but flinch from them.

"Come with me," tempted Mara, "and I shall show you such wonders. I know where your soul is. Shall I give it back?"

"It is not yours to give," I answered, and remembered the red-haired girl, the moonchild, with her pale-dead face, and knew what I must do. "But you may take me there with you, under the hill to see, for I am curious."

The earth of Mabbs Hill parted before her, it seemed, and we were at the gate of the necropolis, a city for those dead interred deeper than any could imagine, save in nightmare.

The third lock fell from the gate and it drew open, pulled, it seemed, by invisible hands. Through the gate we went and to a great tomb about which, shining silver in the light of that mock-moon, a thick web clung. Pale as bone, the orb shining below ground. I knew it for the face of Mara by the smear of blood, the Grave-Queen's mask watching over her dominion.

In the web were held poor struggling things, those caught in the moon-spider's net, trawled by that Mara.

I looked closely, on the web. Seeing her, I plucked the moth-girl carefully from the holding strands and blew my breath on her until a shiver throbbed there. Unsteadily, with beating wings, she rose from my hand and flitted about, unsure of which way to turn.

I watched her unsteady flutter, willing her to fly away. But, after a few moments of confused flitting, the moth-girl fell back, straight as an arrow, to the web, willingly caught again in its toils.

"You should have taken her with you," said Mara. "Perhaps put her in a bottle to look at when it pleased you to. A curiosity to show your friends – a moth with a girl's flower-face. No better off than she is in my web. I could have given her to you, your little red witch, bound with thongs made of her own hair. It was very long, and there was more than enough for that."

Enough, too, to tie a tether about my heart. Though my soul was gone, I still had that to my sorrow. I knew that between myself and Mara there could be but one thing. My hand shook as I unsheathed the swordstick's blade, and she looked at me with such terrible desire.

"Would you like to cut me with your steel?" she mocked as I hesitated. "See me bleed? I can always obtain a sufficiency of blood, so will take no harm. I will scream most prettily for you too, if that is your need. You may do anything to me, anything you desire, and all I want from you is but a kiss."

The guise fell from her like a discarded garment, and she snarled like a beast – the fangs that bite, the lips that suck, and the tongue to lap the blood.

I did not hesitate but, with one swift motion, sunk my sword into the creature's body. Cold iron is a sovereign remedy against the powers of the air, the undead, those too much alive for the good of mankind.

She uttered a groan at my thrust, the sound of one far gone in passion. Then, to my horror, with a mocking and ironic bow, she herself withdrew the blade from her own flesh to hand it back to me. In a moment the deep wound that I had caused her miraculously healed itself before my eyes, leaving not a mark there.

"You have had your will of me," purred Mara. "Now I will take from you. That is only fair."

She seized me, and I was held helpless as she bit. I felt a brief instant of vertigo, sickening in its intensity, followed by a burning joy that was too soon over. My head spinning, I fell to the ground and lay there, looking up at her like a drunkard gazing at the moon.

"You are mine for ever, but then you always have been – all men are."

I saw my blood smearing her grinning lips, and staggered to my feet. Again, in a frenzy, I struck at her with my sword, slashing at the flesh as she mocked. Her blood steamed molten as those fires within the earth. At last my arm grew weary, and the glamour fell from my eyes to reveal what had been destroyed.

Hacked and black with blood, the poor carrion lay before me. I was no longer beneath the mound of Mabbs Hill, as it had seemed, but upon our middle earth where the rain had ceased and the betraying moon burst through cloud to reveal what I had done. A hand, completely severed, pointed up in accusation at me, and I shuddered in horror at my crime.

Then, uttering a laugh such as demons give, Mara rose up before me, bearing no trace of a wound upon her bare body. Again I was in that netherworld where she ruled her get, who gathered about to mock and jeer me.

I fled, uselessly trying to pull shut the gates against her, but they would not move. Three locks had fallen and now naught could keep them down.

Wildly I ran. Reaching the crest of Mabbs Hill, all out of breath, I had to stop. Mara danced past me, leading her children – dancing like moths then changing before my eyes to human form – beautiful and tempting to a man . . . and to a woman too. Her sons and daughters who mockingly saluted me, their liberator, as they passed to plague the world with their dreadful appetites.

Mara had been playing a game with me, using me for sport and to free her progeny, who now walk among us, another legion among the many who torment humanity. The moonchild was among them, her red hair was long again, enough to bind a man's heart and soul, and she tried to take my hand. But I fled from her, though she cried out a promise to always follow . . .

I soon left London, and at Cambridge I found one of Mara's spawn. She tried to drink from me, but I overwhelmed her and threw the body into the river Cam. I can never look down over a bridge since, nor into water, for she revealed her true form as Mara's long dark hair spread out like a Medusa and her black eyes stared at me.

In Berlin I carefully dissected and left parts of her body scattered about the city. While about this task, she accosted me in the Alexandraplatz and laughed at her joke.

I have tried so many times but should know this: one cannot slay the slayer, the cruel mother, bringer of nightmare, blood-drinking grave-queen, the moon-witch Kali, Mater Tenebrarum, call her as you will. She who rules the dark places, Our Lady of Shadow and Darkness, who is after all the true queen of this world and of the one below.

MARC LAIDLAW

Cell Call

MARC LAIDLAW WAS BORN in Los Angeles, spent many years in San Francisco, and currently lives in Redmond, Washington, with his wife and daughters.

His novels include *Dad's Nuke*, *Neon Lotus*, *Kalifornia*, *The Orchid Eater*, *The Third Force* and *The 37th Mandala* (winner of the International Horror Guild Award for Best Novel). In 1997, he joined Valve Software in order to write and design computer games, beginning with the very successful *Half-Life*.

"It must be a writer's reflex to encounter a new piece of technology and wonder impulsively, 'How can I get a story out of this?'" speculates Laidlaw. "More specifically, for this writer, a ghost story. The attraction is to figure out the latest twist on something very old. The danger is that such stories may age very poorly – especially if the object of the piece is something faddish and prone to fade.

"I wrote this story in an evening and didn't show it to a soul for four years. I suppose I was waiting to see if it might be rendered obsolete before I pinned any hopes on it. Also, it is a story that depresses me immensely, but since that was sort of the point, I can't blame the poor story for the fact that I couldn't bring myself to touch it again until very recently."

H E WASN'T USED TO the cell phone yet, and when it rang in the car there was a moment of uncomfortable juggling and panic as he dug down one-handed into the pocket of his jacket, which he'd thrown onto the passenger seat. He nipped the end of the antenna in his teeth and pulled, fumbling for the "on" button in the dark, hoping she wouldn't hang up before he figured this out. Then he had to squeeze the phone between ear and shoulder because he needed both hands to finish the turn he'd been slowing to make when the phone rang. He realized then that for a moment he'd had his eyes off the road. He was not someone who could drive safely while conducting a conversation, and she ought to know that. Still, she'd insisted he get a cell phone. So here he was.

"Hello?" he said, knowing he sounded frantic.

"Hi." It was her. "Where are you?"

"I'm in the car."

"Where?"

"Does it matter that much?"

"I only meant, are you on your way home? Because if you are I wanted to see if you could pick up a pack of cigarettes. If you have money."

"I'm on my way home, yes." He squinted through the window for a familiar landmark, but considering the turn he'd just taken, he knew he was on a stretch of older suburban road where the streetlights were infrequent. There was parkland here, some-where, and no houses visible. "But I don't think there's a store between here and home."

"You'll pass one on the way."

"How do you know which way I went?"

"There's only one way to go."

"No, there isn't."

"If you have any sense, there is."

"I have to get off. I can't drive and talk at the same time. I'm driving the stick-shift, remember?"

"If you don't want to then forget it."

"No, I don't mind. I'll take a detour."

"Just forget it. Come home. I'll go out later."

"No, really. I'll get them."

"Whatever. Goodbye."

He took the phone out of the vice he'd made with jaw and shoulder. His neck was already starting to cramp, and he didn't feel safe driving with his head at such an angle, everything leaning on its side. He had to hold the phone out in front of him a bit to be sure the light had gone out. It had. The read-out still glowed faintly, but the connection was broken. He dropped the phone onto the seat beside him, onto the jacket.

The parkland continued for another few blocks. The headlights caught in a tangle of winter-bared hedges and stripped branches thrusting out into the street so far that they hid the sidewalk. It would be nice to find a house this close to woods, a bit of greenbelt held in perpetuity for when everything else had been bought up and converted into luxury townhouses. If all went well then in the next year, maybe less, they'd be shopping for a house in the area. Something close to his office but surrounded by trees, a view of mountains, maybe a stream running behind the house. It was heaven here but still strange, and even after six months most of it remained unfamiliar to him. She drove much more than he did, keeping busy while he was at work; she knew all the back roads already. He had learned one or two fairly rigid routes between home and office and the various shopping strips. Now with winter here, and night falling so early, he could lose himself completely the moment he wandered from a familiar route.

That seemed to be the case now. In the dark, without any sort of landmark visible except for endless bare limbs, he couldn't recognize his surroundings. The houses that should have been lining the streets by now were nowhere to be seen, and the road itself was devoid of markings: No center line, no clean curb or gutter. Had he turned into the parkland, off the main road? He tried to think back, but part of his memory was a blank – and for good reason. When the phone rang he'd lost track of everything else. There had been a moment when he was fumbling around in the dark, looking at the seat next to him, making a turn at a traffic light without making sure it was the right light. He could have taken the wrong turn completely.

But he hadn't turned since then. It still wasn't too late to backtrack.

He slowed the car, then waited to make sure no headlights were coming up behind him. Nothing moved in either direction. The road was narrow – definitely not a paved suburban street. Branches scraped the hood as he pulled far to the right, readying the car for a tight turn, his headlights raking the brittle shadows. He paused for a moment and rolled the window down, and then turned back the key in the ignition to shut off the motor. Outside, with the car quieted, it was hushed. He listened for the barking of dogs, the sigh of distant traffic, but heard nothing. A watery sound, as if the parkland around him were swamp or marsh, lapping at the roots of the trees that hemmed him in. He wasn't sure that he had room to actually turn around; the road was narrower than he'd thought. He had better just back up until it widened.

He twisted the key and heard nothing. Not even a solenoid click. He put his foot on the gas and the pedal went straight to the floor, offering no resistance. The brake was the same. He stamped on the clutch, worked the gearshift through its stations – but the stick merely swiveled then lolled to the side when he released it. The car had never felt so useless.

He sat for a moment, not breathing, the thought of the repair bills surmounting the sudden heap of new anxieties. A walk in the dark, to a gas station? First, the difficulty of simply getting back to the road. Did he have a flashlight in the glove-box? Was he out of gas? Would he need a jump-start or a tow? In a way, it was a relief that he was alone, because his own fears were bad enough without hers overwhelming him.

He started again, checking everything twice. Ignition, pedals, gears. All useless. At least the headlights and the dashboard were still shining. He rolled up the window and locked the door. How long should he sit here? Who was going to come along and . . .

The phone.

Jesus, the cell phone. How he had put off buying one, in spite of her insistence. He didn't care for the feeling that someone might always have tabs on him, that he could never be truly alone. What was it people were so afraid of, how could their lives be so empty, and their solitude of so little value, that they had to have a phone with them at every minute, had to keep in constant chattering contact with someone, anyone? Ah, how he had railed at every driver he saw with the phone in one hand and the other lying idly on the steering wheel. And now, for the first time, he turned to the damned thing with something like hope and relief. He wasn't alone in this after all.

The cell phone had some memory but he'd never programmed it because he relied on his own. He dialed his home number and waited through the rings, wondering if she was going to leave the answering machine to answer, as she sometimes did – especially if they had been fighting and she expected him to call back. But she answered after three rings.

"It's me," he said.

"And?" Cold. He was surprised she hadn't left the machine on after all.

"And my car broke down."

"It what?"

"Right after you called me, I got . . ." He hesitated to say lost; he could anticipate what sort of response that would get out of her. "I got off the regular track and I was looking to turn around and the engine died. Now it won't start."

"The regular track? What's that supposed to mean?"

"Just that I, uh—"

"You got lost." The scorn, the condescension. "Where are you?"

"I'm not sure."

"Can you look at a street sign? Do you think you could manage that much or am I supposed to figure out everything myself?"

"I don't see any," he said. "I'm just wondering if something happened to the engine. Maybe I could take a look."

"Oh, right. Don't be ridiculous. What do you know about cars?"

He popped the hood and got out of the car. It was an excuse to move, to pace. He couldn't sit still when she was like this. It was as if he thought he'd be harder to hit if he made a moving target of himself. Now he raised the hood and leaned over it, saying, "Ah," as if he'd discovered something. But all he could see beneath the hood was darkness, as if something had eaten away the workings of the car. The headlights streamed on either side of his legs, losing themselves in the hedges, but their glare failed to illuminate whatever was directly before his eyes.

"Uh . . ."

"You don't know what you're looking at."

"It's too dark," he said. "There aren't any streetlights here."

"Where the hell are you?"

"Maybe I got into a park or something. Just a minute." He slammed the hood, wiped his gritty-feeling fingers on his legs, and went back to the door. "There are lots of roads around here with no lights . . . it's practically . . ." He pressed the door handle. ". . . Wild . . ."

At his lengthy silence, she said, "What is it?"

"Uh . . . just a sec."

The door was locked. He peered into the car, and could see the keys dangling in the ignition. He tried the other doors, but they were also locked. They were power doors, power windows, power locks. Some kind of general electrical failure, probably a very small thing, had rendered the car completely useless. Except for the headlights?

"What is it?" she said again.

"The keys . . . are in . . . the car." He squeezed hard on the door handle, wrenching at it, no luck.

"Do you mean you're locked out?"

"I, uh, do you have the insurance card? The one with the emergency service number on it?"

"I have one somewhere. Where's yours?"

"In the glove-box."

"And you're locked out."

"It looks that way."

Her silence was recrimination enough. And here came the condescension: "All right, stay where you are. I'll come get you. We can call the truck when I'm there, or wait until morning. I was just about to get in bed, but I'll come and bring you home. Otherwise you'll just get soaked."

Soaked, he thought, tipping his head to the black sky. He had no sense of clouds or stars, no view of either one. It was just about the time she'd have been lying in bed watching the news; there must have been rain in the forecast. And here he was, locked out, with no coat.

"How are you going to find me?" he asked.

"There are only so many possible wrong turns you could have taken."

"I don't even remember any woods along this road."

"That's because you never pay attention."

"It was right past the intersection with the big traffic light."

"I know exactly where you are."

"I got confused when you called me," he said. "I wasn't looking at the road. Anyway, you'll see my headlights."

"I have to throw on some clothes. I'll be there in a few minutes."

"Okay."

"Bye."

It was an unusually protracted farewell for such a casual conversation. He realized that he was holding the phone very tightly in the dark, cradling it against his cheek and ear as if he were holding her hand to his face, feeling her skin cool and warm at the same time. And now there was no further word from her. Connection broken.

He had to fight the impulse to dial her again, instantly, just to reassure himself that the phone still worked – that she was still there. He could imagine her ridicule: he was slowing her down, she was trying to get dressed, he was causing yet another inconvenience on top of so many others.

With the conversation ended, he was forced to return his full attention to his surroundings. He listened, heard again the wind, the distant sound of still water. Still water which made sounds only when it lapped against something, or when something waded through it. He couldn't tell one from the other right now. He wished he were still inside the car, with at least that much protection.

She was going to find him. He'd been only a few minutes, probably less than a mile, from home. She would be here any time.

He waited, expecting raindrops. The storm would come, it would short out his phone. There was absolutely no shelter on the empty road, now that he had locked himself out of the car. He considered digging for a rock, something big enough to smash the window, so he could pull the lock and let himself in. But his mistake was already proving costly enough; he couldn't bring himself to compound the problem. Anyway, it wasn't raining yet. And she would be here any minute now.

It was about time to check in with her, he thought. She had to be in her car by now. Did he need a better excuse for calling her?

Well, here was one: The headlights were failing.

Just like that, as if they were on a dimmer switch. Both at once, darkening, taken down in less than a minute to a dull stubborn glow. It was a minute of total helpless panic; he was saved from complete horror only by the faint trace of light that remained. Why didn't they go out all the way? By the time he'd asked himself this, he realized that his wife had now lost her beacon. That was news. It was important to call her now.

He punched the redial number. That much was easy. The phone rang four times and the machine answered, and then he had to restrain himself from smashing the phone on the roof of the car. She wouldn't be at home, would she? She'd be on the road by now, looking for him, cruising past dark lanes and driveways, the entrance to some wooded lot, hoping to see his stalled headlights – and there would be none.

What made all this worse was that he couldn't remember the number of her cell phone. He refused to call her on it, arguing that she might be driving if he called her, and he didn't want to cause an accident.

Should he . . . head away from the car? Blunder back along the dark road without a flashlight until he came in sight of the street? Wouldn't she be likely to spot him coming down the road, a pale figure stumbling through the trees, so out of place?

But he couldn't bring himself to move away. The car was the only familiar thing in his world right now.

There was no point breaking the window. The horn wouldn't sound if the battery had died. No point in doing much of anything now. Except wait for her to find him.

Please call, he thought. Please please please call. I have something to tell—

The phone chirped in his hand. He stabbed the on button.

"Yes?"

"I'm coming," she said.

"The headlights just died," he said. "You're going to have to look closely. For a . . . a dark road, a park entrance, maybe . . ."

"I know," she said, her voice tense. He pictured her leaning forward, driving slowly, squinting out the windshield at the street-sides. "The rain's making it hard to see a damn thing."

"Rain," he said. "It's raining where you are?"

"Pouring."

"Then . . . where are you? It's dry as a bone here." Except for the sound of water, the stale exhalation of the damp earth around him.

"I'm about three blocks from the light."

"Where I was turning?"

"Where you got turned around. It's all houses here. I thought there was park. There is some park, just ahead . . . that's what I was thinking off. But . . ."

He listened, waiting. And now he could hear her wipers going, sluicing the windshield; he could hear the sizzle of rain under her car's tires. A storm. He stared at the sky even harder than before. Nothing up there. Nothing coming down.

"But what?" he said finally.

"There's a gate across the road. You couldn't have gone through there."

"Check it," he said. "Maybe it closed behind me."

"I'm going on," she said. "I'll go to the light and start back, see if I missed anything."

"Check the gate."

"It's just a park, it's nothing. You're in woods, you said?"

"Woods, marsh, parkland, something. I'm on a dirt road. There are . . . bushes all around, and I can hear water."

"Ah . . ."

What was that in her voice?

"I can . . . wait a minute . . . I thought I could see you, but . . ."

"What?" He peered into the darkness. She might be looking at him even now, somehow seeing him while he couldn't see her.

"It isn't you," she said. "It's a car, like yours, but . . . it's not yours. That . . . that's not you, that's not your . . ."

"What's going on?" The headlights died all the way down.

"Please, can you keep on talking to me?" she said. "Can you please just keep talking to me and don't stop for a minute?"

"What's the matter? Tell me what's going on?"

"I need to hear you keep talking, please, please," and whatever it was in her voice that was wrenching her, it wrenched at him too, it was tearing at both of them in identical ways, and he knew he just had to keep talking. He had to keep her on the phone.

"Don't be afraid," he said. "Whatever it is. I won't make you stop and tell me now, if you don't want to talk, if you just want to listen," he said. "I love you," he said, because surely she needed to hear that. "Everything's going to be fine. I'm just, I wish you could talk to me but—"

"No, you talk," she said. "I have to know you're all right, because this isn't, that's not, it can't be . . ."

"Sh. Shhh. I'm talking now."

"Tell me where you are again."

"I'm standing by my car," he said. "I'm in a dark wooded place, there's some water nearby, a pond or marsh judging from the sound, and it's not raining, it's kind of warm and damp but it's not raining. It's quiet. It's dark. I'm not . . . I'm not afraid," and that seemed an important thing to tell her, too. "I'm just waiting, I'm fine, I'm just waiting here for you to get to me, and I know you will. Everything will be . . . fine."

"It's raining where I am," she said. "And I'm . . ." She swallowed. "And I'm looking at your car."

Static, then, a cold blanket of it washing out her voice. The noise swelled, peaked, subsided, and the phone went quiet. He pushed the redial button, then remembered that she had called him and not the other way round. It didn't matter, though. The phone was dead. He wouldn't be calling anyone, and no one would be calling him.

I'll walk back to that road now, he thought. While there's still a chance she can find me.

He hefted the cell phone, on the verge of tossing it overhand out into the unseen marshes. But there was always a chance that some faint spark remained inside it; that he'd get a small blurt of a ring, a wisp of her voice, something. He put it in a pocket so he wouldn't lose it in the night.

He tipped his face to the sky and put out his hand before he started walking.

Not a drop.

It's raining where I am, and I'm looking at your car.

PAULINE E. DUNGATE

In the Tunnels

PAULINE E. DUNGATE LIVES in Birmingham, England, and is a teacher at the local Nature Centre. Her stories have appeared in such anthologies as *Skin of the Soul*, *Narrow Houses*, *Swords Against the Millennium*, *Birmingham Noir*, *Birmingham Nouveau*, *Merlin*, *Victorious Villains* and *Warrior Fantastic*.

She has won awards for her poetry and has also written numerous critical articles and reviews under the name "Pauline Morgan". One of the leaders of the Cannon Hill Writers' Group, her other interests include gardening, cooking, truck driving and bat watching.

As the author explains, " 'In the Tunnels' is a drawing-together of a number of things seen around Birmingham or garnered over the years. Often, I start with an image and let the other things fall into place around it. In this case it was a pupil I used to teach. When he left school, at sixteen, he was still only about five feet tall. He had a round, gnome-like face and his front teeth were pointed. And he often wore wellingtons to school."

T HE PLATFORM OF BIRMINGHAM'S Moor Street Station was crowded. Late shoppers and office workers stood crushed together waiting for the Leamington train. Bernie, who wanted the one that followed, stood out of the way near the mouth of the tunnel. It fascinated him, this dark cavern that ran under the city and disgorged trains at regular intervals. He had walked through it once, just before they had reopened the rail link between Moor

Street and Snow Hill, the station at its far end. But there had been too many people on that special trek for him to be able to appreciate fully its echoing magnificence.

Just a minute or so before the train arrived, there was a disturbance. Shouting distracted Bernie from his contemplation of underground places. As he turned he saw a ripple of movement and a child-sized figure belting along the platform towards him, weaving and barging between commuters. Vaguely registering the cries of "Stop, thief!" Bernie prepared to make a grab for the boy. The child slowed, grinned at him and leapt onto the rails.

"Ilyas!" Bernie would have plunged after him if someone hadn't grabbed him from behind.

The figure disappeared into the tunnel moments before the lights of the train became visible round the curve in the track. He tensed, waiting for the impact. But the carriages drew quietly into the station. Doors banged open as passengers scrambled for seats, emptying the platform of all but those waiting for the Stratford train, and a small knot of people halfway along.

"D'ya know the kid, sir?" the porter who had restrained him asked Bernie.

"Yes . . . no . . . it couldn't have been," he stuttered.

"But yer got a good look?"

"Yes, but . . ."

"An' yer'd know 'im agin?"

"I think so."

"Could yer come an' 'ave a word with the station manager, then?"

Bernie glanced at the clock. The yellow numbers flicked over to show 17:39, one minute to his train. His mother would hardly notice if he was late for tea. She never did. "If you think I can help," he said.

There was a policeman in the Station Manager's office when they finally showed Bernie in. A tearful woman was being led out as he entered.

"Now, young man, the constable would like you to answer a few questions if you don't mind."

Bernie nodded and gave his name and address.

"Do you know the bag-snatcher?" the policeman asked.

"No, sir. He just looked a bit like someone I knew at school."

"What was his name?"

"Ilyas. I can't remember his other name. He was in my class, that's all."

"This lad was about twelve," the manager said.

That's why it couldn't be him, Bernie thought. He wouldn't recognize most of the kids from school, just the few he saw sometimes down the market, like Javad who'd nick things off the stall if he wasn't watching, or Shazad who had a club foot. In six years, Ilyas was sure to have grown a bit, and changed.

The phone rang part-way through the interview. The manager listened, nodding his head from time to time. When he cradled the receiver he spoke to the constable.

"He hasn't come out at Snow Hill yet. And none of the drivers have seen anyone on the track."

The policeman wrote it down in his notebook.

Finally, they let Bernie go, just in time to catch the 18:40, the manager saying, "Thank you so much for your help, young man."

It was dark and raining when the train pulled out. Bernie sat staring at his reflection in the window, seeing the round, grinning face of Ilyas as he passed under the bridges that muted the sound of the wheels. Whoever the boy was, he couldn't have disappeared.

Bernie found himself searching crowds for familiar faces, especially those pushing their way through the market towards the subway leading to the station. He found it easy to superimpose features on his customers at the fruit stall. Once he was sure he caught sight of the small, dark-haired figure of Ilyas disappearing behind an unloading lorry. When the boy re-emerged he could see clearly that it wasn't. But from the back . . .

"Stop daydreaming, lad. We've got customers," his boss told him.

Bernie blinked and stared down at the change he was clasping tightly. He grinned nervously and handed it to the old lady who counted the coins carefully before stowing them in her purse.

"Where's me oranges?" she said.

Bernie passed her the bag, thankful that no one could see his blushes.

"I don't know what's got into you recently, lad," his boss said later when they were clearing away. "You've been a pretty good worker up till now. Don't spoil it."

Bernie gave himself a mental shake and resolved to concentrate.

At the station, Bernie took to standing as close to the tunnel entrance as he could. He remembered the Station Manager's words about the boy not coming out at the other end. There were caverns under Birmingham, he had heard. Vast concrete hangars where they had stored supplies in the war. Perhaps there was a way in through the tunnel. He couldn't remember any side branches on the day he had walked through.

Bernie decided that he had to go through the tunnel again. Instead of heading for Moor Street as he usually did, he set off across town, deliberately choosing a roundabout route to take him through as many underpasses as possible. He liked the enclosed spaces and wished there were fewer people around. He wanted to hear his own footsteps echo from the walls.

There was a busker in the underpass leading to the main-line station, a bald, elderly violinist whose squeaky music followed Bernie as he passed.

He walked through Old Square. They were just locking the basement doors to Lewis's. He could see the security man of the department store through the heavy plate glass as he slid the bolts into place. Then down the ramp and past the toilets. Bernie hadn't realized there were so many small men in the city centre. There was another of them leaning on a broom in the entrance to the gents'. He looked like a gnome.

Bernie glanced at his watch and began to hurry. He didn't want to miss the train.

The trip was a little disappointing. He managed to get a seat at the front so that he could see through the driver's cab and out onto the track but it was difficult to watch both sides at once. There were lights strung all along the tunnel and although he could see the shadows of archways set into the walls he missed any dark opening leading away.

Under Colmore Circus, he saw Ilyas again. Bernie had taken to staying later and later in the market area, taking the most circuitous route he could devise to the station and lingering in the empty subways. Some were shabby and rubbish-filled and stank of urine. Others had murals painted on them or incised in the tiles. He was surprised how little graffiti was added to those pictures; the street artists seemed to confine their efforts to the railway, scarring the walls along the lines with their spray-on paint.

Sometimes a subway would open out into an oasis of green.

The walls of the Horsefair had a delicate mosaic depicting the old market, and plants grew unmolested in the centre. Bernie had almost forgotten his search for Ilyas in his growing delight at the variety of underground passages.

Then he saw him. The small figure had his back to him as he crossed the open space under the traffic island. Ilyas disappeared behind a supporting pillar. Bernie hurried after him.

"Ilyas!" he called.

The boy stopped and turned. Ilyas was exactly as he had been six years before, when they had both walked out of school for the last time. They had never been friends, and Bernie remembered him most for his broken front teeth and the fact that he only ever seemed to wear wellies to school.

"It *is* Ilyas, isn't it?" Bernie said.

Ilyas grinned.

"It's me. Bernie Robinson. From school."

"Hi," Ilyas said.

"What are you doing these days?" It was an inane question but Bernie couldn't think of anything else to say. He couldn't very well ask if the other boy had been stealing handbags.

Ilyas shrugged. "Working for my uncle."

"I've got a job in the market," Bernie said. "Selling fruit."

"That's nice. See you around." And Ilyas disappeared into the shadows so quickly that Bernie hardly saw him go. Bernie started after him, reluctant to lose him after all this time; but the doorway he thought Ilyas had gone through was only a locked service duct. Bernie looked round, expecting to see Ilyas hurrying up one of the ramps. There was a movement to his left that quickly stilled when he turned that way and an echo that might have been laughter, or the tail end of a whistled tune. The only other person in sight was an old tramp whom Bernie was now used to seeing around town. He believed he slept on the steps outside the NatWest bank.

People didn't disappear into walls. Only ghosts did that and Bernie didn't believe in ghosts. Ilyas was real. The more he thought about it, the more he was convinced that there was a way underground. Probably several ways.

He made up his mind and bought himself the most powerful torch he could find, and some spare batteries. He chose a Saturday night for his exploration, after the trains had ceased to run on the branch line, and caught the night-service bus into town. If graffiti artists could get onto the railway line so, Bernie reasoned, could he.

The subways, now totally deserted, resounded to the echoes of his footsteps. Bernie was torn between increasing the resonance of the sounds by stamping his feet and a desire for silence – since he was about to break the law.

The station was locked up as expected but next to the old part was a rutted car-parking lot surrounded by a high chain-link fence. Bernie glanced around quickly before sauntering in through the gate. He had expected to have to climb the swaying fence but it lay trampled in the dirt by other feet. He crossed boldly. To his left the old part of the station was secured from intruders, the fencing topped with vicious twists of barbed wire.

Bernie stepped over the rusting rails and walked round, past the sign that warned NO PASSENGERS BEYOND THIS POINT.

Finally, he stood between the rails, looking into the maw of the tunnel. It was lightless. A solid wall of dark, facing him. Beckoning. His heart thudded with excitement – and with fear. Bernie took two steps inside, then another two. The sound of the gravel beneath his feet was loud but muffled, as though the black air tried to erase his presence while the curved walls wanted to advertise it. He felt everything was being focused back on him.

He looked back and was reassured by the paler arch that marked the cavernous mouth, an orange-tinted grey fed by the lights of the city above. Bernie switched on his torch and began to walk slowly, swinging the beam from side to side, scanning the soot-coloured brickwork for doorways, anything that would suggest a way underground. A rat, startled by the light, scuttled along the bottom of the wall and vanished into a recess. Bernie ran his hands over the brickwork, hunting for an opening. Nothing.

He went on.

At one point he switched off the torch and just stood. The darkness was total. Out of sight of either tunnel mouth it enfolded him gently. Far above he could hear the occasional rumble of passing cars. There was the odd tick of metal and mortar contracting. Bernie shivered. It was cooler than he had expected. It was supposed to get warmer, the further you went underground.

He found it almost by accident. A streamer of paper had caught on the cable that was strung between the lamps. It stirred in a ghostly breeze as the torch beam flashed past it. Bernie looked upwards, expecting to see some shaft burrowing from the tunnel's roof to the surface and creating a draught. There was none. Neither was there a discernible wind blowing through the tunnel itself. He stood still wondering if his own movements had caused the fluttering. But no – the strip still jigged about in the torchlight.

Bernie crouched next to it, feeling for the airstream. He traced it to a crack at the base of the wall in another of the alcoves. He pushed tentatively. The brickwork seemed solid until he tapped it. It had a hollow ring. There was no fastening that he could see. He pushed harder, in all the places and directions that he could think of.

He grinned in the darkness as a panel slipped suddenly sideways. He shone the torch through the opening. It was a service passage running parallel with the tunnel and connected with it by a short linking corridor, five paces long. Cables and pipes stretched in both directions, but there was room for a small man to move carefully between them.

Bernie jumped as the panel slid and snicked back into place. He felt a momentary rise of panic as his beam caught the blank, closed wall. A quick check showed how easy it was to open again.

Bernie turned right towards Snow Hill. It was damp here, condensation forming and dripping from the ducts to form intermittent puddles. Some pipes gurgled with the passage of water through them.

There was a grille in the wall a little way along that slid to the side like the door of an old-fashioned lift. Peering through, Bernie could see steps spiralling down. The passage was tiled with pale blue. It reminded him of the steps leading down to the lower levels of some of London's Underground stations. He'd spent a week's holiday there two years ago, haunting the network and wishing he could follow the trains that burrowed into the earth like giant worms.

The gate was secured by a rusted padlock. Bernie stared longingly into the inviting gloom before searching for something to break it with. The penknife he always carried was too flimsy, the blade bending as he twisted it in the catch. He needed a more sturdy length of metal, like a screwdriver. He cast around, without much hope, for something suitable. The piece of wood he found snapped the moment he applied force to it.

Bernie tugged viciously at the padlock in his frustration. The loop snapped. It lay in the palm of his hand for a few moments before he realized what had happened. Then he carefully put it in his pocket. Passing through the gate, he pulled it almost closed behind him, satisfied that he could get out easily.

His footsteps echoed, the sound bouncing and reflecting from the curving walls, continuing after he stopped. It was almost as if there were someone simultaneously in front of and behind him.

There *was* someone behind him. Another pair of shoes keeping time with him. But not quite. The click of the heels was slightly different to the slap of his trainers.

"Who's there?" Bernie called. The cry stretched. Amplified by the stairs, it was returned to him altered: "Hoos sair".

Bernie dithered, knowing he was trespassing. As long as he remained still, so did the other. He tried tiptoeing down, then, flashing the torch suddenly behind him, miscalculated and bashed it against the wall. The light flickered.

"You don't scare me," he whispered into the darkness.

"Scairee," it came back.

The torch went out.

"Scairee," the echo repeated.

Bernie froze. Being underground wasn't quite so much fun any more.

He started to creep back up the steps, fingers of one hand touching the tiles, the other holding the torch up as a club.

He encountered no one.

He stumbled on the top step and sprawled across the floor, hitting his head on the gate. He hauled himself to his feet and pulled at the grid. It didn't move. He tugged again. And heard laughing.

He thought it was just the gurgle in the pipes above him, but it continued. Chuckling at first, then louder. A demented sound. Bernie shook and rattled the gate.

"Let me out," he shouted.

"Ow, ow, ow," came the reply from behind him.

He clasped his hands over his ears to shut out the sounds.

He could wait, he thought, wait until morning. Until someone came.

But perhaps no one ever came.

He brushed a tickle from his cheek. It was wet. A tear. He wiped his face on his sleeve. Men didn't cry. And there must be another way. Besides, whoever it was had been behind him.

Without light, Bernie picked his way down the stairs again, feeling for every step with his toes before committing himself. It made his legs ache. But there were no echoes.

As he descended he became aware that he could see. Not clearly. Just the dim outline of his outstretched hand. There were lights below. People.

Bernie stopped. People had locked him in. His throat was dry, his head sore and he could smell his own sweat. He edged round the last bend.

It wasn't much of a light. A pale glowing in the distance, its source blocked by a dark shadow. Bernie sank down, his back to the wall, shivering. He was in a cavern, he realized, the roof held up by massive columns.

The wartime caverns. Now empty. What was it he had read in the newspaper? If the idea had been to convert them into a huge bus depot then there must be another way out. And the light must be a bonfire lit by vagrants. They would know.

Bernie bent his head to rest it on his knees. To calm down. To still the fear. He would walk across to them. Warm himself, ask the way. It was nothing to get fretted about.

He was right up to them before he saw them. Grey figures stooping over a pile of burning sticks. One picked up a brand and straightened. He was no taller than a twelve-year-old boy. None of them were. Slowly they reached for the flaming torches. The flames illuminated only their faces. They were round and wrinkled and ugly. Like goblins.

One smiled. His teeth were small and sharp and pointed. Bernie spun round. They were behind him too. He panicked.

He screamed. He ran, heedless of the fact that he couldn't see.

He hit a pillar with his shoulder. He held his arms out before him and ran into another.

"Bernie, Bernie." Someone was shaking his shoulder.

"The alarm's not gone off," he muttered trying to pull the blankets over his head. There weren't any. He was cold.

"Bernie."

His head throbbed. His shoulder ached and there was pain in one of his wrists. He knew his eyes were open but he couldn't see.

"It's Ilyas, Bernie. Do you remember me?"

"I can't see you," Bernie said.

"What are you doing here?" Ilyas asked. There was a babble of unintelligible voices around him.

"Exploring," Bernie said.

One of the other people spoke to him. He couldn't understand. Ilyas answered in his own tongue, then spoke to Bernie in English. "I've told them we were at school together. That they cannot have you."

"What do you mean?" The feeling of panic was coming back, seeping through the pain of Bernie's hurts. He remembered the leering faces, the pointed, eager teeth.

"You must go," Ilyas said. "Can you stand?"

"I'm locked in. Someone locked the gate." Bernie heard himself whining.

"I'll show you the way." Ilyas put his arm under Bernie's shoulder and helped him to his feet. Bernie swayed, disorientated. He felt invisible walls pressing in on him and the weight of Birmingham descending slowly to crush him. He whimpered.

The voice in the darkness spoke again, sharply, insistently. Ilyas replied and began to lead Bernie forward.

Bernie felt hands pawing him, long nails touching his face. Ilyas spoke and they withdrew. Bernie could hear feet shuffling after them and somewhere a squeaky sound as a violin began to play. It was a dirge.

They splashed into water, which became deeper, soaking his trainers and numbing his legs inside wet trousers. The sound changed as though they were entering a narrow, enclosed space. "This is the river Rea," Ilyas said. "It runs underground here, down through Digbeth."

"What're you doing here?" Bernie asked, partly to drown out the sound of the scuffles of their followers. He felt slightly safer now. The air around was a bit warmer, though it smelt a little of sewage.

"I live here. My people always have. We steal from above when we have to, and eat what comes down to us."

"But we were at school together."

"Times change. We have to adapt."

Progress was slow. Bernie staggered when he tried to walk unaided. He blundered into the tunnel wall. Pain shot up his arm from the damaged wrist.

He leant heavily on Ilyas, though it was uncomfortable due to the other's lack of stature. There were splashings and squealings from the water.

"Just rats," Ilyas said, "squabbling over food."

Bernie shuddered. He would have felt happier if he could have seen the animals. Something soft brushed by him. Far behind he thought he heard howling, the kind that could emanate from human throats.

Then Bernie could see. The end of the tunnel was a small orange-grey circle in the distance. It looked much too tiny for him to get through. The shaft they were traversing began to narrow. Old brick was replaced by smooth concrete. The water, concentrated into the compressed space, was deeper and swirled faster, tugging at his legs.

"You will have to crawl," Ilyas said. "There was no time to fetch the raft."

He tried, but his wrist gave way, throwing him into the water. He screamed with pain and swallowed foul-tasting liquid. He surfaced, spluttering and sobbing.

"I can't," he said.

"You must. I can't keep them away for ever. There's a grid at the end but it lifts up easy. I used to come this way to school most days."

Bernie dragged himself through the tube. Cold and soaked, he kept watching the patch of light.

Ilyas started back the other way, whispering a hasty, "Goodbye."

Bernie peered through bars set about nine inches apart. Beyond them the river ran between steep banks, above which were silhouetted buildings outlined by sodium lights. The fringes of the water were studded with the debris of city life. He could hear the sound of an occasional car.

A piece of chicken wire stretched across the bottom of the bars, catching paper, twigs and gnawed bones as the river flowed out of he culvert. The gate itself had been repaired recently and was held in place by shiny new bolts. By reaching through, Bernie could just reach them. He had drawn one when he heard the snuffling behind him, and a whispering. He stretched for the other. Refusing to glance behind, he stared out at freedom, and at the four men who were walking towards him.

A street lamp created a brighter pool of light, illuminating the round wizened face and the pointed teeth.

DALE BAILEY

Hunger: A Confession

DALE BAILEY LIVES IN Hickory, North Carolina, with his wife Jean and daughter Carson. A frequent contributor to *The Magazine of Fantasy & Science Fiction*, he has also published stories in *SciFiction, Amazing Stories, Pulphouse, The Year's Best Fantasy and Horror, Nebula Awards 31*, and the two most recent collections of *The Best from Fantasy & Science Fiction*.

His short fiction has been collected in *The Resurrection Man's Legacy and Other Stories* from Golden Gryphon Press. In addition to the Nebula-nominated title story, presently under option to Twentieth Century Fox, the collection includes "Death and Suffrage", a winner of the International Horror Guild Award.

The author has also published two novels, *The Fallen*, a nominee for the International Horror Guild Award, and *House of Bones* (both from Signet). A crime novel, *Sleeping Policemen*, is forthcoming from Golden Gryphon, written in collaboration with Jack Slay, Jr., and a study of contemporary horror fiction, *American Nightmares: The Haunted House Formula in American Popular Fiction* is published by Bowling Green State University Popular Press.

Bailey also writes a regular column on death and grieving for *The Dodge Magazine*, published by one of the world's leading manufacturers of embalming equipment and chemicals.

As the author recalls: "I started writing 'Hunger: A Confession' by longhand during a six-hour airport delay following the 2001 World Science Fiction Convention, and continued drafting the piece during the flight that followed. By the time the plane touched down, I had the first draft well in hand." He adds that he is terrified of flying and cannot help wondering if some element of his own anxiety might have infected the piece in question.

M E, I WAS NEVER afraid of the dark.

It was Jeremy who bothered me – Jeremy with his black rubber spiders in my lunchbox, Jeremy with his guttural demon whisper (*I'm coming to get you, Simon*) just as I was drifting off to sleep, Jeremy with his stupid Vincent Prince laugh (*Mwha-ha-ha-ha-ha*), like some cheesy mad scientist, when he figured the joke had gone far enough. By the time I was walking, I was already shell-shocked, flinching every time I came around a corner.

I remember this time, I was five years old and I had fallen asleep on the sofa. I woke up to see Jeremy looming over me in this crazy Hallowe'en mask he'd bought: horns and pebbled skin and a big leering grin, the works. Only I didn't realize it was Jeremy, not until he cut loose with that crazy laugh of his, and by then it was too late.

Things got worse when we left Starkville. The new house was smaller and we had to share a bedroom. That was fine with me. I was seven by then, and I had the kind of crazy love for my big brother that only little kids can feel. The thing was, when he wasn't tormenting me, Jeremy was a great brother – like this one time he got a Chuck Foreman card in a package of Topps and he just handed it over to me because he knew the Vikings were my favorite team that year.

The room thing was hard on Jeremy, though. He'd reached that stage of adolescence when your voice has these alarming cracks and you spend a lot of time locked in the bathroom tracking hair growth and . . . well, you know, *you* were a kid once, right? So the nights got worse. I couldn't even turn to Mom for help. She was sick at that time, and she had this frayed, wounded look. Plus, she and Dad were always talking in these strained whispers. You didn't want to bother either one of them if you could help it.

Which left me and Jeremy alone in our bedroom. It wasn't much to look at, just this high narrow room with twin beds and an old milk crate with a lamp on it. Out the window you could see one half-dead crab-apple tree – a crap-apple, Jeremy called it –

and a hundred feet of crumbling pavement and a rusting 1974 El
Camino which our neighbor had up on blocks back where the
woods began. There weren't any street lights that close to the edge
of town, so it was always dark in there at night.

That was when Jeremy would start up with some crap he'd seen
in a movie or something. "I heard they found a whole shitload of
bones when they dug the foundation of this house," he'd say, and
he'd launch into some nutty tale about how it turned out to be an
Indian burial ground, just crazy stuff like that. After a while, it
would get so I could hardly breathe. Then Jeremy would unleash
that crazy laugh of his. "C'mon, Si," he'd say, "you know I'm
only kidding."

He was always sorry – genuinely sorry, you could tell by the look
on his face – but it never made any difference the next night. It was
like he forgot all about it. Besides, he always drifted off to sleep,
leaving me alone in the dark to ponder open portals to Hell or
parallel worlds or whatever crazy stuff he'd dreamed up that night.

The days weren't much better. The house was on this old
winding road with woods on one side and there weren't but a few
neighbors, and none of them had any kids. It was like somebody
had set off a bomb that just flattened everybody under twenty –
like one of those neutron bombs, only age-specific.

So that was my life – interminable days of boredom, torturous
insomniac nights. It was the worst summer of my life, with
nothing to look forward to but a brand-new school come the
fall. That's why I found myself poking around in the basement
about a week after we moved in. Nobody had bothered to unpack
– nobody had bothered to do much of anything all summer – and
I was hoping to find my old teddy bear in one of the boxes.

Mr Fuzzy had seen better days – after six years of hard use, he
literally had no hair, not a single solitary tuft – and I'd only
recently broken the habit of dragging him around with me
everywhere I went. I knew there'd be a price to pay for back-
sliding – Jeremy had been riding me about Mr Fuzzy for a year –
but desperate times call for desperate measures.

I'd just finished rescuing him from a box of loose Legos and
Jeremy's old *Star Wars* action figures when I noticed a bundle of
rags stuffed under the furnace. I wasn't inclined to spend any more
time than necessary in the basement – it smelled funny and the light
slanting through the high dirty windows had a hazy greenish

quality, like a pond you wouldn't want to swim in – but I found myself dragging Mr Fuzzy over toward the furnace all the same.

Somebody had jammed the bundle in there good, and when it came loose, clicking metallically, it toppled me back on my butt. I stood, brushing my seat off with one hand, Mr Fuzzy momentarily forgotten. I squatted to examine the bundle, a mass of grease-stained rags tied off with brown twine. The whole thing was only a couple feet long.

I loosened the knot and pulled one end of the twine. The bundle unwrapped itself, spilling a handful of rusty foot-long skewers across the floor. There were half a dozen of them, all with these big metal caps. I shook the rag. A scalpel tumbled out, and then a bunch of other crap, every bit of it as rusty as the skewers. A big old hammer with a wooden head and a wicked-looking carving knife and one of those tapered metal rods that butchers use to sharpen knives. Last of all a set of ivory-handled flatware.

I reached down and picked up the fork.

That was when I heard the stairs creak behind me.

"Mom's gonna kill you," Jeremy said.

I jumped a little and stole a glance over my shoulder. He was standing at the foot of the stairs, a rickety tier of backless risers. That's when I remembered Mom's warning that I wasn't to fool around down here. The floor was just dirt, packed hard as concrete, and Mom always worried about getting our clothes dirty.

"Not if you don't tell her," I said.

"Besides, you're messing around with the furnace," Jeremy said.

"No, I'm not."

"Sure you are." He crossed the room and hunkered down at my side. I glanced over at him. Let me be honest here: I was nobody's ideal boy next door. I was a scrawny, unlovely kid, forever peering out at the world through a pair of lenses so thick that Jeremy had once spent a sunny afternoon trying to ignite ants with them. The changeling, my mother sometimes called me, since I seemed to have surfaced out of somebody else's gene pool.

Jeremy, though, was blond and handsome and already broad-shouldered. He was the kind of kid everybody wants to sit with in the lunchroom, quick and friendly and capable of generous strokes of kindness. He made such a gesture now, clapping me on the shoulder. "Geez, Si, that's some weird-looking shit. Wonder how long it's been here?"

"I dunno," I said, but I remembered the landlord telling Dad the house was nearly a hundred and fifty years old. *And hasn't had a lick of work since*, I'd heard Dad mutter under his breath.

Jeremy reached for one of the skewers and I felt a little bubble of emotion press against the bottom of my throat. He turned the thing over in his hands and let it drop to the floor. "Beats the hell out of me," he said.

"You're not gonna tell Mom, are you?"

"Nah." He seemed to think a moment. "Course I might use that scalpel to dissect Mr Fuzzy." He gazed at me balefully, and then he slapped my shoulder again. "Better treat me right, kid."

A moment later I heard the basement door slam behind me.

I'd been clutching the fork so tightly that it had turned hot in my hand. My knuckles grinned up at me, four bloodless white crescents. I felt so strange that I just let it tumble to the floor. Then I rewrapped the bundle, and shoved it back under the furnace.

By the time I'd gotten upstairs, I'd put the whole thing out of my mind. Except I hadn't, not really. I wasn't thinking about it, not consciously, but it was there all the same, the way all the furniture in a room is still there when you turn out the lights, and you can sense it there in the dark. Or the way pain is always there. Even when they give you something to smooth it out a little, it's always there, a deep-down ache like jagged rocks under a swift-moving current. It never goes away, pain. It's like a stone in your pocket.

The bundle weighed on me in the same way, through the long night after Jeremy finally fell asleep, and the next day, and the night after that as well. So I guess I wasn't surprised, not really, when I found myself creeping down the basement stairs the next afternoon. Nobody saw me steal up to my room with the bundle. Nobody saw me tuck it under my bed. Mom had cried herself to sleep in front of the TV (she pretended she wasn't crying, but I knew better) and Dad was already at work. Who knew where Jeremy was?

Then school started and Mom didn't cry as often, or she did it when we weren't around. But neither one of our parents talked very much, except at dinner Dad always asked Jeremy how freshman football was going. And most nights, just as a joke, Jeremy would start up with one of those crazy stories of his, the minute we turned out the light. He'd pretend there was a vampire in the room or something and he'd thrash around so that I could hear him over the narrow space between our beds. "Ahhh," he'd say, "Arrggh," and, in a strangled gasp, "When it finishes with me, Si, it's coming for you." I'd hug Mr Fuzzy tight and tell him not to be afraid, and then Jeremy would unleash that nutty mad-scientist laugh.

"C'mon, Si, you know I'm only kidding."

One night, he said, "Do you believe in ghosts, Si? Because as old as this house is, I bet a whole shitload of people have died in it."

I didn't answer, but I thought about it a lot over the next few days. We'd been in school a couple of weeks at this point. Jeremy had already made a lot of friends. He talked to them on the phone at night. I had a lot of time to think.

I even asked Dad about it. "Try not to be dense, Si," he told me. "There's no such thing as ghosts, everybody knows that. Now chill out, will you, I'm trying to explain something to your brother."

So the answer was, no, I didn't believe in ghosts. But I also thought it might be more complicated than that, that maybe they were like characters in a good book. You aren't going to run into them at the Wal-Mart, but they seem real all the same. I figured ghosts might be something like that. The way I figured it, they had to be really desperate for something they hadn't gotten enough of while they were alive, like they were jealous or hungry or something. Otherwise why would they stick around some crummy old cemetery when they could go on to Heaven or whatever? So that's what I ended up telling Jeremy a few nights later, after I'd finished sorting it all out inside my head.

"*Hungry?*" he said. "Christ, Si, that's the stupidest thing I've ever heard." He started thrashing around in his bed and making these dumb ghost noises. "Ooooooooh," he said, and, "Ooooooooooh, I'm a ghost, give me a steak. Ooooooooooh, I want a bowl of Cheerios."

I tried to explain that that wasn't what I meant, but I couldn't find the words. I was just a kid, after all.

"Christ, Si," Jeremy said, "don't tell anybody anything that stupid. It's like that stupid bear you drag around everywhere, it makes me ashamed to be your brother."

I knew he didn't mean anything by that – Jeremy was always

joking around – but it hurt Mr Fuzzy's feelings all the same. "Don't cry, Mr Fuzzy," I whispered. "He didn't mean anything by it."

A few days later, Jeremy came home looking troubled. I didn't think anything about it at first because it hadn't been a very good day from the start. When Jeremy and I went down to breakfast, we overheard Dad saying he was taking Mom's car in that afternoon, the way they had planned. Mom said something so low that neither one of us could make it out, and then Dad said, "For Christ's sake, Mariam, there's plenty of one-car families in the world." He slammed his way out of the house, and a few seconds later we heard Mom shut the bedroom door with a click. Neither one of us said anything after that except when Jeremy snapped at me because I was so slow getting my lunch. So I knew he was upset and it didn't surprise me when he came home from football practice that day looking a bit down in the mouth.

It turned out to be something totally different, though, because as soon as we turned out the light that night, and he knew we were really alone, Jeremy said, "What happened to that bundle of tools, Si?"

"What bundle of tools?" I asked.

"That weird-looking shit you found in the basement last summer," he said.

That was when I remembered that I'd put the bundle under my bed. What a crazy thing to do, I thought, and I was about to say *I*'d taken them – but Mr Fuzzy kind of punched me. He was so sensitive, I don't think he'd really forgiven Jeremy yet.

I thought it over, and then I said, "Beats me."

"Well, I went down the basement this afternoon," Jeremy said, "and they were gone."

"So?"

"It makes me uncomfortable, that's all."

"Why?"

Jeremy didn't say anything for a long time. A car went by outside, and the headlights lit everything up for a minute. The shadow of the crap-apple danced on the ceiling like a man made out of bones, and then the night swallowed him up. That one little moment of light made it seem darker than ever.

"I met this kid at school today," Jeremy said, "and when I told him where I lived he said, 'No way, Mad Dog Mueller's house?'

'Mad Dog who?' I said. 'Mueller,' he said. 'Everyone knows who Mad Dog Mueller is.' "

"I don't," I said.

"Well, neither did I," Jeremy said, "but this kid, he told me the whole story. 'You ever notice there aren't any kids that live out that end of town?' he asked, and the more I thought about it, Si, the more right he seemed. There *aren't* any kids."

The thing was, he was right. That's when I figured it out, the thing about the kids. It was like one of those puzzles with a picture hidden inside all these little blots of color and you stare at it and you stare at it and you don't see a thing, and then you happen to catch it from just the right angle and – *Bang!* – there the hidden picture is. And once you've seen it, you can never unsee it. I thought about the neighbors, this scrawny guy who was always tinkering with the dead El Camino and his fat wife – neither one of them really old, but neither one of them a day under thirty, either. I remember how they stood out front watching us move in, and Mom asking them if they had any kids, her voice kind of hopeful. But they'd just laughed, like who would bring kids to a place like this?

They hadn't offered to pitch in, either – and people *always* offer to lend a hand when you're moving stuff inside. I *know*, because we've moved lots of times. I could see Dad getting hotter and hotter with every trip, until finally he turned and said in a voice just dripping with sarcasm, "See anything that strikes your fancy, folks?" You could tell by the look on Mom's face that she didn't like that one bit. When we got inside she hissed at him like some kind of animal, she was so mad. "Why can't you ever keep your mouth shut, Frank?" she said. "If you kept your mouth shut we wouldn't *be* in this situation."

All of which was beside the point, of course. The point was, Jeremy was right. There wasn't a single kid in any of the nearby houses.

"See," Jeremy said, "I told you. And the reason is, this guy Mad Dog Mueller."

"But it was some old lady that used to live here," I said. "We saw her the first day, they were moving her to a nursing home."

"I'm not talking about her, stupid. I'm talking like a hundred years ago, when this was all farm land, and the nearest neighbors were half a mile away."

"Oh."

I didn't like the direction this was going, I have to say. Plus, it seemed even darker. Most places, you turn out the light and your eyes adjust and everything turns this smoky blue color, so it hardly seems dark at all. But here the night seemed denser somehow, weightier. Your eyes just never got used to it, not unless there was a moon, which this particular night there wasn't.

"Anyway," Jeremy said, "I guess he lived here with his mother for a while and then she died and he lived here alone after that. He was a pretty old guy, I guess, like forty. He was a blacksmith."

"What's a blacksmith?"

"God you can be dense, Si. Blacksmiths make horseshoes and shit."

"Then why do they call them *black*smiths?"

"I don't know. I guess they were black or something, like back in slavery days."

"Was *this* guy black?"

"No! The point is, he makes things out of metal. That's the point, okay? And so I told this kid about those tools I found."

"*I'm* the one who found them," I said.

"Whatever, Si. The point is, when I mentioned the tools, the kid who was telling me this stuff, his eyes bugged out. 'No way,' he says to me, and I'm like, 'No, really, cross my heart. What gives?'"

Jeremy paused to take a deep breath, and in the silence I heard a faint click, like two pieces of metal rubbing up against each other. That's when I understood what Jeremy was doing. He was "acting out", which is a term I learned when I forgot Mr Fuzzy at Dr Bainbridge's one day, back at the clinic in Starkville, after I got suspended from school. When I slipped inside to get him, Dr Bainbridge was saying, "You have to understand, Mariam, with all these pressures at home, it's only natural that he's acting out."

I asked Dr Bainbridge about it the next week, and he told me that sometimes people say and do things they don't mean just because they're upset about something else. And now I figured Jeremy was doing it because he was so upset about Mom and stuff. He was trying to scare me, that was all. He'd even found the little bundle of tools under my bed and he was over there clicking them together. I'd have been mad if I hadn't understood. If I hadn't understood, I might have even been afraid – Mr Fuzzy was, I could feel him shivering against my chest.

"Did you hear that?" Jeremy said.

"I didn't hear anything," I said, because I wasn't going to play along with his game.

Jeremy didn't answer right away. So we lay there, both of us listening, and this time I really *didn't* hear anything. But it seemed even darker somehow, darker than I'd ever seen our little bedroom. I wiggled my fingers in front of my face and I couldn't see a thing.

"I thought I heard something." This time you could hear the faintest tremor in his voice. It was a really fine job he was doing. I couldn't help admiring it. "And that would be bad," Jeremy added, "because this Mueller, he was crazy as a shithouse rat."

I hugged Mr Fuzzy close. "Crazy?" I said.

"Crazy," Jeremy said solemnly. "This kid, he told me that all the farms around there, the farmers had about a zillion kids. Everybody had a ton of kids in those days. And one of them turned up missing. No one thought anything about it at first – kids were always running off – but about a week later *another* kid disappeared. This time everybody got worried. It was this little girl and nobody could figure out why *she* would run off. She was only like seven years old."

"She was my age?"

"That's right, Si. She was just your age."

Then I heard it again: this odd little clicking like Grandma's knitting needles used to make. Jeremy must have really given that bundle a shake.

"*Shit*," Jeremy said, and now he sounded really scared. Somebody ought to have given him an Oscar or something.

He switched on the light. It was a touch of genius, that – his way of saying, *Hey, I'm not doing anything!*, which of course meant he was. I stared, but the bundle was nowhere in sight. I figured he must have tucked it under the covers, but it was hard to tell without my glasses on. Everything looked all blurry, even Jeremy's face, blinking at me over the gap between the beds. I scooched down under the covers, holding Mr Fuzzy tight.

"It was coming from over there," he said. "Over there by your bed."

"I didn't hear anything," I said.

"No, I'm serious, Si. I heard it, didn't you?"

"You better turn out the light," I said, just to prove I wasn't afraid. "Mom'll be mad."

"Right," Jeremy said, and the way he said it, you could tell he knew it was an empty threat. Mom had told me she was sick when I'd knocked on her bedroom door after school. I opened the door, but it was dark inside and she told me to go away. The room smelled funny, too, like the stinging stuff she put on my knee the time Jeremy accidentally knocked me down in the driveway. "I just need to sleep," she said. "I've taken some medicine to help me sleep."

And then Jeremy came home and made us some TV dinners. "She must have passed out in there," he said, and that scared me. But when I said maybe we should call the doctor, he just laughed. "Try not to be so dense all the time, okay, Si?"

We just waited around for Dad after that. But Jeremy said he wouldn't be surprised if Dad *never* came home again, the way Mom had been so bitchy lately. Maybe he was right, too, because by the time we went up to bed, Dad still hadn't shown up.

So Jeremy was right. Nobody was going to mind the light.

We both had a look around. The room looked pretty much the way it always did. Jeremy's trophies gleamed on the little shelf that Dad had built for them. A bug smacked the window screen a few times, like it really wanted to get inside.

"You sure you didn't hear anything?"

"Yeah."

Jeremy looked at me for a minute. "All right, then," he said, and turned out the light. Another car passed and the crab-apple man did his little jig on the ceiling. The house was so quiet I could hear Jeremy breathing these long even breaths. I sang a song to Mr Fuzzy while I waited for him to start up again. It was this song Mom used to sing when I was a baby, the one about all the pretty little horses.

And then Jeremy started talking again.

"Nobody got suspicious," he said, "until the third kid disappeared – a little boy, he was about your age too, Si. And then someone happened to remember that all these kids had to walk by this Mueller guy's house on their way to school. So a few of the parents got together that night and went down there to see if he had seen anything."

It had gotten colder. I wished Jeremy would shut the window and I was going to say something, but he just plowed on with his stupid story. "Soon as he answered the door," Jeremy said, "they could tell something was wrong. It was all dark inside – there wasn't a fire or anything – and it smelled bad, like pigs or something. They could hardly see him, too, just his eyes, all hollow and shiny in the shadows. They asked if he'd seen the kids and that's when things got really weird. He said he hadn't seen anything, but he was acting all nervous, and he tried to close the door. One of the men held up his lantern then, and they could see his face. He hadn't shaved and he looked real thin and there was this stuff smeared over his face. It looked black in the light, like paint, only it wasn't paint. You know what it was, Si?"

I'd heard enough of Jeremy's stories to be able to make a pretty good guess, but I couldn't seem to make my mouth say the word. Mr Fuzzy was shaking he was so scared. He was shaking real hard, and he was mad, too. He was mad at Jeremy for trying to scare me like that.

"It was blood, Si," Jeremy said.

That was when I heard it again, a whisper of metal against metal like the sound the butcher makes at the grocery store when he's putting the edge on a knife.

Jeremy gasped. "Did you hear that?"

And just like that the sound died away.

"No," I said.

We were silent, listening.

"What happened?" I whispered, because I wanted him to finish it. If he finished he could do his dumb little mad-scientist laugh and admit he made it all up.

"He ran," Jeremy said. "He ran through the house and it was all dark and he went down the basement, down where you found those rusty old tools. Only it wasn't rust, Si. It was blood. Because you know what else they found down there?"

I heard the whisper of metal again – *shir shir shir*, that sound the butcher makes when he's putting the edge on a knife and his hands are moving so fast the blade is just a blur of light. But Jeremy had already started talking again.

"They found the missing kids," he said, but it sounded so far away. All I could hear was that sound in my head, *shir shir shir*. "They were dead," Jeremy was saying, "and pretty soon Mueller was dead, too. They killed the guy right on the spot, he didn't even get a trial. They put him down the same way he'd killed those kids."

I swallowed. "How was that?"

"He used those long nails on them, those skewer things. He knocked them on the head or something and then, while they were out, he just hammered those things right through them – *wham wham wham* – so they were pinned to the floor, they couldn't get up. And then you know what he did?"

Only he didn't wait for me to answer, he couldn't wait, he just rolled on. He said, "Mueller used the scalpel on them, then. He just ripped them open and then—" Jeremy's voice broke. It was a masterful touch. "And then he started eating, Si. He started eating before they were even dead—"

Jeremy broke off suddenly, and now the sound was so loud it seemed to shake the walls – *SHIR SHIR SHIR* – and the room was so cold I could see my breath fogging up the dark.

"Christ, what's that sound?" Jeremy whimpered, and then he started making moaning sounds way down in his throat, the way he always did, like he wanted to scream but he was too afraid.

Mr Fuzzy was shaking, just shaking so hard, and I have to admit it, right then I hated Jeremy with a hatred so pure I could taste it, like an old penny under my tongue. The darkness seemed heavy suddenly, an iron weight pinning me to my bed. It was cold, too. It was so cold. I've never been so cold in my life.

"Christ, Si," Jeremy shrieked. "Stop it! *Stop it! STOP IT!*"

Mr Fuzzy was still shaking in my arms, and I hated Jeremy for that, I couldn't help it, but I tried to make myself get up anyway, I really tried. Only the dark was too thick and heavy. It seemed to flow over me, like concrete that hadn't quite formed up, binding me to my mattress with Mr Fuzzy cowering in my arms.

Jeremy's whole bed was shaking now. He was grunting and wrestling around. I heard a *pop*, like a piece of taut rubber giving way, and a metallic *wham wham wham*. There was this liquidy gurgle and Jeremy actually screamed, this long desperate scream from the bottom of his lungs. I really had to admire the job he was doing, as much as I couldn't help being mad. He'd never taken it this far. It was like watching a master at the very peak of his form. There was another one of those liquidy thumps and then the sound of the hammer and then the whole thing happened again and again. It happened so many times I lost track. All I knew was that Jeremy had stopped screaming, but I couldn't remember when. The only sound in the room was this muffled thrashing sound, and that went on for a little while longer and then it stopped, too. Everything just stopped.

It was so still. There wasn't any sound at all.

The dark lay heavy on my skin, pinning me down. It was all I could do to open my mouth, to force the word out—

"Jeremy?"

I waited then. I waited for the longest time to hear that stupid Vincent Price laugh of his, to hear Jeremy telling me he'd gotten me this time, he was only joking, *Mwah-ha-ha-ha-ha*.

But the laugh never came.

What came instead was the sound of someone chewing, the sound of someone who hadn't had a meal in ages just tucking right in and having at it, smacking his lips and slurping and everything, and it went on and on and on. The whole time I just lay there. I couldn't move at all.

It must have gone on for hours. I don't know how long it went on. All I know is that suddenly I realized it was silent, I couldn't hear a thing.

I waited some more for Jeremy to make that stupid laugh of his. And then a funny thing happened. I wasn't lying in my bed after all. I was standing up between the beds, by the milk crate we used for a nightstand, and I was tired. I was so tired. My legs ached like I'd been standing there for hours. My arms ached, too. Every part of me ached. I ached all over.

I kept having these crazy thoughts as well. About ghosts and hunger and how hungry Mad Dog Mueller must have been, after all those years down in the basement. About how maybe he'd spent all that time waiting down there, waiting for the right person to come along, someone who was just as hungry as he was.

They were the craziest thoughts, but I couldn't seem to stop thinking them. I just stood there between the beds. My face was wet, too, my whole face, my mouth and everything. I must have been crying.

I just stood there waiting for Jeremy to laugh that stupid mad-scientist laugh of his and tell me it was all a game. And I have to admit something: I was scared, too. I was so scared.

But it wasn't the dark I was scared of.

God help me, I didn't want to turn on the light.

CHRISTOPHER FOWLER

Seven Feet

CHRISTOPHER FOWLER LIVES AND works in central London, where he is a director of the Soho movie-marketing company The Creative Partnership, producing TV and radio scripts, documentaries, trailers and promotional shorts. He spends the remainder of his time writing short stories and novels, and he contributes a regular column about the cinema to *The 3rd Alternative*.

His books include the novels *Roofworld, Rune, Red Bride, Darkest Day, Spanky, Psychoville, Disturbia, Soho Black, Calabash, Full Dark House* and *The Water House*, and such short-story collections as *The Bureau of Lost Souls, City Jitters, Sharper Knives, Flesh Wounds, Personal Demons, Uncut, The Devil in Me* and *Demonized*. *Breathe* is a new novella from Telos Publishing.

Fowler's short story "Wageslaves" won the 1998 British Fantasy Award, and he also scripted the 1997 graphic novel *Menz Insana*, illustrated by John Bolton.

"I wrote this story when I was researching feral animals in London," the author explains, "and found that proximity to rats was changing in cities because of fast-food outlets. During the hot summer of 2003, I noticed that at 2:00 a.m. every morning I could hear scampering noises across my bedroom ceiling. I went up on the roof (it's a terraced street) but didn't see anything. However, a few nights later, a rat came into my kitchen from the open back door and I found myself battling it with a broom.

"My hysterical overreaction to what was basically a small terrified rodent is apparently normal. The rat-catcher relies on this to charge me £200.00 for putting poison down while telling me horror stories about rats, some of which I've included here."

C LEETHORPES WAS A CRAP mouser. She would hide underneath the sink if a rodent, a squirrel or a neighbour's cat even came near the open back door. Clearly, sleeping sixteen hours a day drained her reserves of nervous energy, and she was forced to play dead if her territory was threatened. She was good at a couple of things: batting moths about until they expired with their wings in dusty tatters, and staring at a spot on the wall three feet above the top of Edward's head. What could cats see, he wondered, that humans couldn't?

Cleethorpes was his only companion now that Sam was dead and Gill had gone. He'd bought her because everyone else had bought one. That was the month the price of cats skyrocketed. Hell, every cats' home in the country sold out in days, and pretty soon the mangiest strays were changing hands for incredible prices. It was the weirdest form of panic-buying that Edward had ever seen.

He'd lived in Camden Town for years, and had been thinking of getting out even before he met Gill; the area was being compared to Moscow and Johannesburg after eight murders on its streets in as many weeks earned the area a new nickname: "Murder Mile". There were 700 police operating in the borough, which badly needed over a thousand. It was strange, then, to think that the real threat to their lives eventually came not from muggers, but from fast-food outlets.

Edward lived in a flat in Eversholt Street, one of the most peculiar roads in the neighbourhood. In one stretch of a few hundred yards there was a Roman Catholic church, a sports centre, a legendary rock pub, council flats, a bingo hall, a juvenile detention centre, an Italian café, a Victorian men's hostel for transients and an audacious green-glass development of million-pound loft apartments. Edward was on the ground floor of the council block, a bad place to be as it turned out. The Regent's Canal ran nearby, and most of the road's drains emptied into it.

The council eventually riveted steel grilles over the pipe covers, but by then it was too late.

Edward glanced over at Gill's photograph, pinned on the cork noticeboard beside the cooker. Once her eyes had been the colour of cyanothus blossom, her hair saturated in sunlight, but now the picture appeared to be fading, as if it was determined to remove her from the world. He missed Gill more than he missed Sam, because nothing he could do would ever bring Sam back, but Gill was still around, living in Hackney with her two brothers. He knew he was unlikely ever to see her again. He missed her to the point where he would say her name aloud at odd moments for no reason at all. In those last days after Sam's death, she had grown so thin and pale that it seemed she was being erased from her surroundings. He watched helplessly as her bones appeared beneath her flesh, her clothes began hanging loosely on her thin arms. Gill's jaw-length blonde hair draped forward over her face as she endlessly scoured and bleached the kitchen counters. She stopped voicing her thoughts, becoming barely more visible than the water stains on the walls behind her. She would hush him with a raised finger, straining to listen for the scurrying scratch of claws in the walls, under the cupboards, across the rafters.

Rats. Some people's worst nightmare, but the thought of them no longer troubled him. What had happened to their family had happened to people all over the city. "*Rats!*" thought Edward as he welded the back door shut, "*they fought the dogs and, killed the cats, and bit the babies in the cradles . . .*" He couldn't remember the rest of Robert Browning's poem. It hadn't been quite like that, because Camden Town was hardly Hamelin, but London could have done with a pied piper. Instead, all they'd got was a distracted mayor and his dithering officials, hopelessly failing to cope with a crisis.

He pulled the goggles to the top of his head and examined his handiwork. The steel plates only ran across to the middle of the door, but were better than nothing. Now he could sort out the chewed gap underneath. It wasn't more than two inches deep, but a cat-sized rat was capable of folding its ribs flat enough to slide through with ease. He remembered watching thousands of them one evening as they rippled in a brown tapestry through the back gardens. There had been nights when he'd sat in the darkened lounge with his feet lifted off the floor and a cricket bat across his knees, listening to the scampering conspiracy passing over the roofs, feet pattering in the kitchen, under the beds, under his chair. He'd watched as one plump brown rat with eyes like drops of black resin had fidgeted its way between books on a shelf, daring him into a display of pitifully slow reactions.

The best solution would be to rivet a steel bar across the space under the door, but the only one he had left was too short. He thought about risking a trip to the shops, but most of the ones in the high street had closed for good, and all the hardware stores had sold out of stock weeks ago. It was hard to imagine how much a city of 8 million people could change in just four months. So many had left. The Tubes were a no-go zone, of course, and it was dangerous to move around in the open at night. The rats were no longer frightened by people.

He was still deciding what to do when his mobile buzzed its way across the work counter.

"Is that Edward?" asked a cultured, unfamiliar voice.

"Yeah, who's that?"

"I don't suppose you'll remember me. We only met once, at a party. I'm Damon, Gillian's brother." The line fell warily silent. Damon, sanctimonious religious nut, Gill's older brother, what was the name of the other one? Matthew. Fuck. *Fuck*.

"Are you still there?"

"Yeah, sorry, you caught me a bit by surprise."

"I guess it's a bit of a bolt from the blue. Are you still living in Camden?"

"One of the last to leave the epicentre. The streets are pretty quiet around here now."

"I saw it on the news, didn't recognize the place. Not that I ever really knew it to begin with. Our family's from Hampshire, but I expect you remember that."

Stop being so damned chatty and tell me what the hell you want, thought Edward. His next thought hit hard: *Gill's condition has deteriorated, she's made him call me.*

"It's about Gillian, isn't it?"

"I'm afraid – she's been a lot worse lately. We've had a tough time looking after her. She had the problem, you know, with dirt and germs—"

Spermophobia, thought Edward, *Mysophobia*. A lot of people had developed such phobias since the rats came.

"Now there are these other things, she's become terrified of disease."

Nephophobia, Pathophobia. Once arcane medical terms, now almost everyday parlance. They were closely connected, not so surprising when you remembered what she'd been through.

"It's been making life very difficult for us."

"I can imagine." Everything had to be cleaned over and over again. Floors scrubbed, handles and counters sprayed with disinfectant, the air kept refrigerated. All her foodstuffs had to be washed and vacuum-sealed in plastic before she would consider eating them. Edward had watched the roots of fear digging deeper within her day by day, until she could barely function and he could no longer cope.

"She's lost so much weight. She's become frightened of the bacteria in her own body. She was living on the top floor of the house, refused to take any visitors except us, and now she's gone missing."

"What do you mean?"

"It doesn't seem possible, but it's true. We thought you should know."

"Do you have any idea where she might have gone?"

"She couldn't have gone anywhere, that's the incredible part of it. We very badly need your help. Can you come over tonight?" *This is a turnaround*, Edward thought. *Her family spent a year trying to get me to clear off, and now they need me.*

"I suppose I can come. Both of you are still okay?"

"We're fine. We take a lot of precautions."

"Has the family been vaccinated?"

"No, Matthew and our father feel that The Lord protects us. Do you remember the address?"

"Of course. I can be there in around an hour."

He was surprised they had found the nerve to call at all. The brothers had him pegged as a man of science, a member of the tribe that had helped to bring about the present crisis. People like him had warmed the planet and genetically modified its harvests, bringing abundance and pestilence. Their religion sought to exclude, and their faith was vindictive. Men who sought to accuse were men to be avoided. But he owed it to Gill to go to them.

He used the short steel bar to block the gap in the door, and covered the shortfall by welding a biscuit-tin lid over it. Not an ideal solution, but one that would have to do for now. The sun would soon be setting. The red neon sign above the Kentucky Fried Chicken outlet opposite had flickered on. It was the only part of the store that was still intact. Rioters had smashed up most of the junk-food joints in the area, looking for someone to blame.

Pest-controllers had put the massive rise in the number of rats down to three causes: the wetter, warmer winters caused flooding that lengthened the rats' breeding periods and drove them above ground. Councils had reduced their spending on street cleaning. Most disastrously of all, takeaway litter left the street-bins over-flowing with chicken bones and burger buns. The rat population rose by thirty per cent in a single year. They thrived in London's Victorian drainage system, in the sewers and canal outlets, in the Tube lines and railway cuttings. Beneath the city was a maze of interconnected pipework with openings into almost every street. They moved into the gardens and then the houses, colonizing and spreading as each property became vacant.

One much-cited statistic suggested that a single pair of rats could spawn a maximum number of nearly a hundred billion rats in just five years. It was a sign of the burgeoning rodent popula-tion that they began to be spotted during the day; starvation drove them out into the light, and into densely populated areas. They no longer knew fear. Worse, they sensed that others were afraid of them.

Edward had always known about the dangers of disease. As a young biology student he had been required to study pathogenic microbes. London had not seen a case of plague in almost a century. The Black Death of the Middle Ages had wiped out a third of the European population. The bacterium *Yersinia pestis* had finally been eradicated by fire in London in 1666. Plague had returned to consume 10 million Indians early in the twentieth century, and had killed 200 as recently as 1994. Now it was back in a virulent new strain, and rampant. It had arrived via infected rat fleas, in a ship's container from the East, or perhaps from a poorly fumigated cargo plane, no one was sure, and everyone was anxious to assign blame. Rats brought leptospirosis, hantavirus and rat-bite fever, and they were only the fatal diseases.

Edward drove through the empty streets of King's Cross with the windows of the Peugeot tightly closed and the air-condition-ing set to an icy temperature. Lying in the road outside McDonald's, a bloated, blackened corpse had been partially covered by a cardboard standee for Caramel McFlurrys. The gesture, presumably intended to provide some privacy in death, had only created further indignity. It was the first time he'd seen a body on the street, and the sight shocked him. It was a sign that the services could no longer cope, or that people were starting not to care. Most of the infected crept away into private corners to die, even though there were no red crosses to keep them in their houses this time.

The plague bacillus had evolved in terms of lethality. It no longer swelled the lymph glands of the neck, armpits and groin. It went straight to the lungs and caused catastrophic internal haemorrhaging. Death came fast as the lungs filled with septicaemic pus and fluid. There was a preventative vaccine, but it proved useless once the outbreak began. Tetracycline and streptomycin, once seen as effective antibiotics against plague, also failed against the emerging drug-resistant strains. All you could do was burn and disinfect; the city air stank of both, but it was preferable to the smell of death. It had been a hot summer, and the still afternoons were filled with the stench of rotting flesh.

Edward had been vaccinated at the college. Gill had blamed him for failing to vaccinate their son in time. Sam had been four months old when he died. His cradle had been left near an open window. They could only assume that a rat had entered the room foraging for food, and had come close enough for its fleas to jump to fresh breeding grounds. The child's pale skin had blackened with necrosis before the overworked doctors of University College Hospital could get around to seeing him. Gill quickly developed a phobic reaction to germs, and was collected by her brothers a few weeks after.

Edward dropped out of college. In theory it would have been a good time to stay, because biology students were being drafted in the race to find more powerful weapons against the disease, but he couldn't bear to immerse himself in the subject, having so recently watched his child die in the very same building.

He wondered why he hadn't fled to the countryside like so many others. It was safer there, but no one was entirely immune. He found it hard to consider leaving the city where he had been born, and was fascinated by this slow decanting of the population. An eerie calm had descended on even the most populous districts. There were no tourists; nobody wanted to fly into Britain. People had become terrified of human contact, and kept their outside journeys to a minimum. *Mad-cow disease was a comparative picnic*, he thought, with a grim chuckle.

The little car bounced across the end of Upper Street, heading toward Shoreditch. The shadows were long on the gold-sheened tarmac. A blizzard of newspapers rolled across the City Road, adding to the sense of desolation. Edward spun the wheel, watching for pedestrians. He had started to think of them as survivors. There were hardly any cars on the road, although he was surprised to pass a bus in service. At the junction of Old Street and Pitfield Street, a shifting amoeba-shape fluctuated around the doorway of a closed supermarket. The glossy black rats scattered in every direction as he drove past. You could never drive over them, however fast you went.

There were now more rats than humans, approximately three for every man, woman and child, and the odds kept growing in their favour. They grew bolder each day, and had become quite brazen about their battle for occupancy. It had been said that in a city as crowded as London you were never more than fifteen feet away from a rat. Scientists warned that when the distance between rodent and human lowered to just seven feet, conditions would be perfect for the return of the plague. The flea, *Xenopsylla cheopis*, sucked up diseased rat blood and transported it to humans with shocking efficiency.

A great black patch shimmered across the road like a boiling oil slick, splitting and vanishing between the buildings. Without realising it, he found himself gripping the sweat-slick wheel so tightly that his nails were digging into his palms.

Rattus rattus. No one knew where the black rat had originated, so their Latin name was suitably unrevealing. The brown ones – the English ones, *Rattus norvegicus* – lived in burrows and came from China. They grew to nearly a foot and a half, and ate anything at all. They could chew their way through brick and concrete; they had to keep chewing to stop their incisors from growing back into their skulls. The black ones were smaller, with larger ears, and lived off the ground in round nests. Edward had woken in the middle of the night two weeks ago and found a dozen of them in his kitchen, feeding from a waste bin. He had run at them with a broom, but they had simply skittered up the curtains and through a hole they had made in the ceiling to the drainpipes outside. The black ones were acrobats; they loved heights. Although they were less aggressive, they seemed to be outnumbering their brown cousins. At least, he saw more of them each day.

He fumigated the furniture and carpets for ticks and fleas, but still developed clusters of painful red welts on his ankles, his arms, his back. He was glad that Gill was no longer here, but missed her terribly. She had slipped away from him, her mind distracted by a future she could not imagine or tolerate.

Damon and Matthew lived with their father above offices in Hoxton, having bought the building at the height of the area's property boom. These had once been the homes of well-to-do Edwardian families, but more than half a century of neglect had followed, until the district had been rediscovered by newly wealthy artists. That bubble had burst too, and now the houses were in fast decline as thousands of rats scampered into the basements.

As Edward climbed the steps, spotlights clicked on. He could hear movement all around him. He looked up and saw the old man through a haze of white light. Gill's father was silently watching him from an open upstairs window.

There was no bell. Edward slapped his hand against the front door glass and waited. Matthew answered the door. What was it about the over-religious that made them keep their hair so neat? Matthew's blond fringe formed a perfect wave above his smooth scrubbed face. He smiled and shook Edward's hand.

"I'm glad you could make it," he said, as though he'd invited Edward to dinner. "We don't get many visitors." He led the way upstairs, then along a bare white hall into an undecorated space that served as their living quarters. There were no personal effects of any kind on display. A stripped-oak table and four chairs stood in the centre of the bright room. Damon rose to shake his hand. Edward had forgotten how alike the brothers were. They had the eyes of zealots, bright and black and dead. They spoke with great intensity, weighing their words, watching him as they spoke.

"Tell me what happened," Edward instructed, seating himself. He didn't want to be here any longer than was strictly necessary.

"Father can't get around any more, so we moved him from his quarters at the top of the house and cleaned it out for Gillian. We thought if we couldn't cure her we should at least make her feel secure, so we put her up there. But the black rats . . ."

"They're good climbers."

"That's right. They came up the drainpipes and burrowed in through the attic, so we had to move her. The only place we could think where she'd be safe was within our congregation." *Ah yes,* thought Edward, *the Church of Latter-Day Nutters. I remember all too well.* Gill had fallen out with her father over religion. He had raised his sons in a far-right Christian offshoot that came with more rules than the Highway Code. Quite how he had fetched up in this biblical backwater was a mystery, but Gill was having none of it. Her brothers had proven more susceptible, and when the plague rats moved in the two of them had adopted an insufferably smug attitude that drove the children further apart. Matthew was the father of three immaculately coiffed children whom Edward had christened "the Midwich Cuckoos". Damon's wife was the whitest woman Edward had ever met, someone who encouraged knitting as stress therapy at Christian coffee mornings. He didn't like them, their politics or their religion, but was forced to admit that they had at least been helpful to his wife. He doubted their motives, however, suspecting that they were more concerned with restoring the family to a complete unit and turning Gill back into a surrogate mother.

"We took her to our church," Matthew explained. "It was built in 1860. The walls are three feet thick. There are no electrical cables, no drainpipes, nothing the smallest rat could wriggle its way into. The vestry doors are wooden, and some of the stained-glass windows are shaky, but it's always been a place of safety."

Edward had to admit that it was a smart idea. Gill's condition was untreatable without access to a psychiatrist and medication, and right now the hospitals were nightmarish no-go areas where rats went to feast on the helpless sick.

Matthew seated himself opposite. "Gillian settled into the church, and we hoped she was starting to find some comfort in the protection of the Lord. Then some members of our congregation started spending their nights there, and she began to worry that they were bringing in plague fleas, even though we fumigated them before entering. We couldn't bear to see her suffer so we built her a special room, right there in the middle of the apse—"

"—We made her as comfortable as we could," Damon interrupted. "Ten feet by twelve. Four walls, a ceiling, a floor, a lockable door and a ventilation grille constructed from strong fine mesh." He looked as sheepish as a schoolboy describing a woodwork project. "Father directed the operation because he'd had some experience in carpentry. We moved her bed in there, and her books, and she was finally able to get some sleep. She even stopped taking the sleeping pills you used to give her." *The pills to which she had become addicted when we lived together*, thought Edward bitterly. *The habit I was blamed for creating.*

"I don't understand," he said aloud. "What happened?"

"I think we'd better go over to the church," said Matthew gently.

It wasn't far from the house, smaller than he'd imagined, slim and plain, without buttresses or arches, very little tracery. The former Welsh presbytery was sandwiched between two taller glass buildings, commerce dominating religion, darkening the streets with the inevitability of London rain.

Outside its single door sat a barrel-chested black man who would have passed for a nightclub bouncer if it weren't for the cricket pads strapped on his legs. He lumbered aside as Damon and Matthew approached. The small church was afire with the light of a thousand coloured candles looted from luxury stores. Many were shaped like popular cartoon characters: Batman, Pokemon and Daffy Duck burned irreverently along the altar and apse. The pews had been removed and stacked against a wall. In the centre of the aisle stood an oblong wooden box bolted into the stone floor and propped with planks, like the back of a film set. A small door was inset in a wall of the cube, and that was guarded by an elderly woman who sat reading in a high-backed armchair. In the nave, a dozen family friends were talking quietly on orange plastic chairs that surrounded a low oak table. They fell silent with suspicion as Edward passed them. Matthew withdrew a key from his jacket and unlocked the door of the box, pushing it open and clicking on a light.

"We rigged a bulb to a car battery because she wouldn't sleep in the dark," Damon explained, waving a manicured hand at the room, which was bare but for an unfurled white futon, an Indian rug and a stack of dog-eared religious books. The box smelled of fresh paint and incense.

"You built it of wood," said Edward, thumping the thin wall with his fist. "That makes no sense, Damon. A rat would be through this in a minute."

"What else could we do? It made her feel safer, and that was all that counted. We wanted to take away her pain. Can you imagine what it was like to see someone in your own family suffer so much? Our father worshipped her."

Edward detected an undercurrent of resentment in Damon's voice. He and Gill had chosen not to marry. In the eyes of her brothers, it was a sin that prevented Edward from ever being treated as a member of the family. "You're not telling me she disappeared from inside?" he asked. "How could she have got out?"

"That's what we thought you might be able to explain to us," snapped Matthew. "Why do you think we asked you here?"

"I don't understand. You locked her in each night?"

"We did it for her own good."

"How could it be good to lock a frightened woman inside a room?"

"She'd been getting panic attacks – growing confused, running into the street. Her aunt Alice has been sitting outside every night since this thing began. Anything Gillian's needed she's always been given."

"When did she go missing?"

"The night before last. We thought she'd come back."

"You didn't see her leave? Edward asked the old lady.

"No," replied Alice, daring him to defy her. "I was here all night."

"And she didn't pass you. Are you sure you never left your chair?"

"Not once. And I didn't fall asleep, either. I don't sleep at night with those things crawling all over the roof."

"Did you let anyone else into the room?"

"Of course not, Alice said indignantly. "Only family and regular worshippers are allowed into the church. We don't want other people in here." *Of course not*, thought Edward. *What's the point of organized religion if you can't exclude unbelievers?*

"And no one except Gillian used the room," Damon added. "That was the point. That was why we asked you to come."

Edward studied the two brothers. He could just about understand Damon, squeaky clean and neatly groomed in a blazer and a pressed white shirt that provided him with an aura of faith made visible, but Matthew seemed in a state of perpetual anger, a church warrior who had no patience with the unconverted. He remained a mystery.

"Why me?" Edward asked. "What made you call me?"

Momentarily stumped, the brothers looked at each other awkwardly. "Well – you slept with her." Presumably they thought he must know her better for having done so.

"I knew her until our son died, but then – well, when someone changes that much, it becomes impossible to understand how they think any more." Edward hoped they would appreciate his point of view. He wanted to make contact with them just once. "Let me take a look around. I'll see what I can do."

The brothers stepped back, cognisant of their ineffectiveness, their hands awkwardly at their sides. Behind them, the church door opened and the congregation slowly streamed in. The men and women who arranged themselves at the rear of the church looked grey and beaten. Faith was all they had left.

"I'm sorry, it's time for our evening service to begin," Damon explained.

"Do what you have to do." Edward accepted the red plastic torch that Matthew was offering him. "I'll call you if I find anything."

A series of narrow alleys ran beside the church. If Gill had managed to slip past the old lady, she would have had to enter them. Edward looked up at the dimming blue strip of evening sky. Along the gutters sat fat nests constructed of branches and bin bags, the black plastic shredded into malleable strips. As he watched, one bulged and disgorged a family of coal-eyed rats. They clung to the drainpipes, staring into his torch beam before suddenly spiralling down at him. He moved hastily aside as they scurried over his shoes and down the corridor of dirt-encrusted brick.

The end of the alley opened out into a small litter-strewn square. He hardly knew where to begin his search. If the family had failed to find her, how would he succeed? On the steps of a boarded-up block of flats sat an elderly man swathed in a dirty green sleeping bag. The man stared wildly at him, as if he had just awoken from a nightmare.

"All right?" asked Edward, nodding curtly. The old man beckoned him. Edward tried to stay beyond range of his pungent stale aroma, but was summoned nearer. "What is it?" he asked, wondering how anyone dared to sleep rough in the city now. The old man pulled back the top of his sleeping bag as if shyly revealing a treasure, and allowed him to look in on the hundred or so hairless baby rats that wriggled over his bare stomach like maggots, pink and blind.

Perhaps that was the only way you could survive the streets now, thought Edward, riven with disgust: you had to take their side. He wondered if, as a host for their offspring, the old man had been made an honorary member of their species, and was therefore allowed to continue unharmed. Although perhaps the truth was less fanciful: rats sensed the safety of their surroundings through the movement of their own bodies. Their spatial perception was highly attuned to the width of drains, the cracks in walls, the fearful humans who moved away in great haste. Gill might have been panicked into flight, but she was weak and would not have been able to run for long. She must have stopped somewhere to regain her breath. But where?

He searched the dark square. The wind had risen to disturb the tops of the plane trees, replacing the city's ever-present bass-line of traffic with natural susurration. It was the only sound he could now hear. Lights shone above a corner shop. Slumped on the windowsill, two Indian children stared down into the square, their eyes half-closed by rat bites.

Edward returned to the church, slipping in behind the ragged congregation, and watched Matthew in the dimly illuminated pulpit.

"For this is not the end but the beginning," said Matthew, clearly preaching a worn-in sermon of fire and redemption. "Those whom the Lord has chosen to keep in good health will be free to remake the land in His way." It was the kind of lecture to which Edward had been subjected as a child, unfocused in its promises, peppered with pompous rhetoric, vaguely threatening. "Each and every one of us must make a sacrifice, without which there can be no admittance to the Kingdom of Heaven, and he who has not surrendered his heart to Our Lady will be left outside, denied the power of reformation."

It seemed to Edward that congregations always required the

imposition of rules for their salvation, and desperate times had
forced them to assume that these zealous brothers would be
capable of setting them. He moved quietly to the unguarded
door of the wooden box and stepped inside, shutting himself in.

The sense of claustrophobia was immediate. A locked room,
guarded from outside. Where the hell had she gone? He sat on the
futon, idly kicking at the rug, and listened to the muffled litany of
the congregation. A draught was coming into the room, but not
through the door. He lowered his hand down into darkness, and
felt chill air prickle his fingers. At first he failed to see the corner of
the hatch, but as he focused the beam of the torch more tightly he
realized what he was looking at: a section of flooring, about three
feet by two, that had been sawn into the wooden deck beside the
bed. The flooring was plywood, easy to lift. The hatch covered the
spiral stairwell to the crypt. A black-painted Victorian iron
banister curved away beneath his feet. Outside, Matthew was
leading a catechism that sounded more like a rallying call.

Edward dipped the light and stepped onto the fretwork wedges.
Clearly Gill had been kept in the wooden room against her will,
but how had she discovered the staircase to the chamber beneath
her prison? Perhaps its existence was common knowledge, but it
had not occurred to anyone that she might be able to gain access
to it. The temperature of the air was dropping fast now; could this
have been its appeal, the thought that germs would not be able to
survive in such a chill environment?

He reached the bottom of the steps. His torch beam reflected a
fracturing moon of light; the flagstones were hand-deep in icy
water. A series of low stone arches led through the tunnelled crypt
ahead of him. He waded forward and found himself beneath the
ribbed vault of the main chamber. The splash of water boomed in
the silent crypt.

With freezing legs and visible breath, Edward stood motionless,
waiting for the ripples to subside. Something was wrong. Gillian
might have lost her reason, but she would surely not have
ventured down here alone. She knew that rats were good swim-
mers. It didn't make sense. Something was wrong.

Above his head in the church, the steeple bell began to ring,
cracked and flat. The change in the congregation was extraordinary. They dropped to their knees unmindful of injury, staring
toward the tattered crimson reredos that shielded the choir stall.

Damon and Matthew had reappeared in sharp white surplices, pushing back the choir screen as their flock began to murmur in anticipation. The dais they revealed had been swathed in shining gold brocade, discovered in bolts at a Brick Lane saree shop. Atop stood the enshrined figure, a mockery of Catholicism, its naked flesh dulled down with talcum powder until it resembled worn alabaster, its legs overgrown with plastic vines.

The wheels of the wooden dais creaked as Damon and Matthew pushed the wobbling tableau toward the altar. The voices of the crowd rose in adulation. The figure on the dais was transfixed in hysterical ecstasy, posed against a painted tree with her knees together and her palms turned out, a single rose stem lying across the right hand, a crown of dead roses placed far back on her shaved head, her eyes rolled to a glorious invisible heaven. Gillian no longer heard the desperate exultation of her worshippers; she existed in a higher place, a vessel for her brothers' piety, floating far above the filthy, blighted Earth, in a holy place of such grace and purity that nothing dirty or harmful would ever touch her again.

Edward looked up. Somewhere above him the bell was still ringing, the single dull note repeated over and over. He cocked his head at the ribs of the vault and listened. First the trees, then the church bell, and now this, as though the forgotten order of nature was reasserting itself. He heard it again, the sound he had come to know and dread, growing steadily all around him. Raising the torch, he saw them scurrying over the fine green nylon webbing that had been stretched across the vault ceiling, thousands of them, far more than he had ever seen in one place before: black rats, quite small, their bodies shifting transversely, almost comically, as they weighed and judged distances.

They had been summoned to dinner.

They gathered in the roof of the main chamber, directly beneath the ringing bell, until they were piling on top of each other, some slipping and swinging by a single pink paw, and then they fell, twisting expertly so that they landed on Edward and not in the water, their needle claws digging into the flesh of his shoulders to gain purchase, to hang on at all costs. Edward hunched himself instinctively, but this exposed a broader area for the rats to drop onto, and now they were releasing themselves from the mesh and falling in ever greater numbers, more and more, until the sheer weight of their solid, sleek bodies pushed him down into the filthy water. This was their cue to attack, their indication that the prey was defeatable, and they bit down hard, pushing their heads between each other to bury thin yellow teeth into his soft skin. He felt himself bleeding from a hundred different places at once, the wriggling mass of rat bodies first warm, then hot, now searing on his back until they made their way through his hair, heading for the tender prize of his eyes.

Edward was determined not to scream, not to open his mouth and admit their poisonous furred bodies. He did the only thing he could, and pushed his head deep under the water, drawing great draughts into his throat and down into his lungs, defeating them in the only way left to him, cheating them of live prey.

Gill, I love you, was his final prayer. *I only ever loved you, and wherever you are I hope you are happy*. Death etched the thought into his bones and preserved it for ever.

In the little East End church, a mood of satiated harmony fell upon the congregation, and Matthew smiled at Damon as they covered the tableau once more, content that their revered sister was at peace. For now the enemy was assuaged, the commitment had been made, the congregation appeased.

Science had held sway for long enough. Now it was time for the harsh old gods to smile down once more.

SUSAN DAVIS

The Centipede

SUSAN DAVIS'S SHORT STORIES have been broadcast on BBC Radio 4 and widely published in anthologies and magazines. These include *Panurge*, *Metropolitan*, *Mslexia* and *Staple*. Three ghost stories have also appeared in *All Hallows*.

The author's comic-horror trilogy for Young Adults comprises *The Henry Game*, *Delilah and the Dark Stuff* and *Mad, Bad and Totally Dangerous*, published by Random House/Corgi Books.

"'The Centipede' grew out of a holiday in remote rural Spain," recalls Davis. "The insect was disturbed during a track maintenance procedure and smartly chopped in half by the workman's spade. The subsequent tales I heard about the creature, also the oppressive atmosphere of the place, combined to haunt me, and this was the result."

S HE WISHED ELSA HADN'T told them about the poisonous centipede. Annie kept her head down, negotiating the track like a minefield. The centipede could be right here, coiled in the long grasses with purple vetch and lilies fluttering. It could be tunnelled beneath those stones, or down where the old garden gave way to scrub, the silly Mickey Mouse ears of the prickly pears.

"You go on inside," she called out to her husband and sister-in-law who stood below, on the terrace of Pepe's old cottage.

"Okay. We'll go and do the recce." Elsa's voice boomed up at

her. Elsa was swinging Pepe's great key from her hand. She
looked as if she were doing the pendulum test over the belly
of a pregnant woman. "We'll have to holler to frighten the rats,"
she added cheerfully.

Left alone, Annie paused to sneeze. The drifts of flowers
released a hot peppery tang, which irritated her nose. The air
was so dry. She might shrivel up out here: defenceless, her skin
would slough off. The centipede knew this. The centipede was
waiting just for her.

"Friend of mine met up with one of the things in the shower." It
was one of Elsa's dinner-party anecdotes. Last night, as she'd
cracked open mussel shells and decapitated prawns, she'd told
them of the malevolent habits of the centipede.

"Had to prise it off her arm with the shower head." Elsa sucked
at the squid until the black ink oozed at the corners of her mouth.
"They won't let go once they get a grip on you. They stick like
leeches, hang on for grim death."

Elsa would probably never have mentioned the creature. But
earlier that week, just before Mark and Annie arrived in Anda-
lucia, a neighbouring *campesino* had disturbed one while digging
a hole for a water pipe,

"Chopped it into three separate pieces, every piece still squirming all by itself." She waggled inky fingers at them. "Poor thing. I
was quite pissed off about it. What are you frowning at, Annie?"

"I was just thinking . . ." Annie hesitated, knowing that con-
tradicting Elsa was a reckless act. "I read somewhere that over
thirty thousand bulls are tormented to death in this country, every
year. Surely that's something to get upset about?"

Elsa shrugged. Bulls? What of it? Dull, lumbering great creatures bred for entertainment. But the centipede was beautiful.
"The way I see it," Elsa said, "anything beautiful has the right to
life."

Annie continued down the track. She could hear Elsa's voice now,
echoing in the emptiness of Pepe's cottage. The cottage was for
sale. Elsa's idea was that Mark and Annie should buy it and move
to Spain for good.

Inside, the three rooms smelled of rats and mouldy garlic and
damp. Mark reached out and pulled Annie close, as if they were

newly-weds inspecting their new home, as if the decision were already made.

"What d'you think, love? It's a snip, Elsa says. Did you see the olive trees, and the almonds?"

In Elsa's presence Mark seemed to shrink. Annie felt a pang of sympathy and irritation. This air of bravado was thrown on for Elsa's benefit, like the linen jacket and Panama hat. They could not disguise what he really was: timid, unfit, an ineffectual schoolteacher.

Elsa was striding about, wrenching the shutters open as if she owned the place herself.

"It takes imagination, that's all. A good airing; it needs living in again." Elsa's bare feet in their flip-flops shuffled carelessly through the rat droppings and dead leaves which had blown in under the door.

"You don't think they might be nesting here?" Annie glanced nervously about.

"What? The rats? Oh, more than likely."

Elsa feared nothing, it seemed. Not rats, nor spiders, nor snakes, nor poisonous centipedes. Nothing. Look at her now, peering into cupboards, into cavernous fireplaces, dodging a shower of debris with a kind of elegant flamenco move. The Carmen-style blouse revealed an opera singer's cleavage, the same weathered texture as those pots on the terrace: her legs were ropy with veins. And yet Elsa carried herself, straight-backed Spanish style, bosom thrust forwards, head thrown back, so that she seemed to be looking down upon everything.

It was strange. Annie was the younger of the two women, yet, in her sister-in-law's presence, she felt faded and frail. She knew that in the southern sun she would not flesh out like Elsa into a tawny handsome woman; she would simply frizzle up like an empty seed-pod and grow old.

"The garden needs work, naturally." Elsa pushed past them to the terrace. "But you can take cuttings from my place."

Annie said mildly that she hadn't got as far as thinking about gardens just yet.

"Why not?" Elsa swung around to face her, small amber eyes piercing, demanding explanations.

Annie raised her head and blinked. It was always like this.

Confronted by Elsa she felt as if she were gazing into the sun. Black spots danced before her eyes. She felt suddenly drowsy.

"Well, there are things to be considered . . ." She glanced toward Mark for support, but he stood smiling vacantly out at the view, content to allow his big sister to make the decisions.

"Like what?"

"Oh . . . money for one thing . . ."

"Sod the money!" Elsa spat the words as if she had something between her teeth. "I have money. I want to help."

"Oh well, that's very kind . . . but the children . . ."

"What children? You're not pregnant again, are you?"

"Of course not. I mean Bethan and Simon, well, I know Simon's in his last year at college, and Bethan lives with her boyfriend, but they still need . . ."

"They're all grown up!" Elsa roared, not letting her finish even. Dismissing Annie's children, Elsa strode to the lower terrace to inspect the olives. "You can't mollycoddle them for ever, Annie."

"That's what I keep telling her." Surfacing from his trance, Mark sounded petulant. "We should put ourselves first for once."

Annoyed, Annie started back up the track. What did Elsa know about families? She had married a Galician poet who gave her no children, who was her child himself. The poet had died four years ago. Elsa, who had guarded him like a lioness from journalists, fans and interruptions of any sort, saw him off with an elaborate funeral.

Did Elsa now have lovers? Pondering this a little jealously, Annie forgot to look where she was walking. Halfway up the track, she screamed: "I've been bitten, I've been bitten by something!" She shrieked shamelessly, hopping on one foot. Her fault. Thinking of Elsa's lovers, she'd forgotten about the danger lurking in the grass . . . the centipede. "I didn't see what it was. I didn't see it!"

In an instant Elsa was beside her. For such a large woman she moved rapidly, darting to Annie's side, grasping her shin, "Let's have a look, then . . . ah, that's all it is, horse fly. My God, what a bloody fuss!"

Feebly, Annie explained, "I thought it might be that thing you told us about, you know, the centipede . . ." She trembled upon one leg, frail as a stork.

Elsa laughed, "Listen, my darling girl, if it had been the

centipede, you'd be writhing on the ground in bloody agony, I
assure you. And anyway, the last person to be killed by the bite in
this country was four years ago. Did you know that?"

"No. No, I didn't." Once again, Annie squinted as if to protect
her eyes from the sun.

"Well, there you are then!"

The poet had left Elsa in some style. Inside, the hacienda was all
polished Gothic gloom, great thronelike chairs and chests with
rusting iron locks; chests that might have been brimming with
Conquistador gold rather than spare bedding. The dining table
was sombre, immense; its glassy surface relieved by a gaunt
candelabra and a shallow dish of medlars.

Through these rooms, Elsa blazed in her gaudy kaftans, a fire
catching. She suffered, it seemed, no ill effects from her bare feet on
cold marble floors. Annie watched enviously. She herself would
surely have developed a kidney infection at once. She was careful
always to wear her sandals or canvas shoes inside the house.

"You used to hate her once." Annie had tracked Mark down in
the study. "You told me. Even your mother told me . . . she once
tried to smother you in your pram by getting the cat to sit on your
face."

"Did she? I don't remember that."

"She smeared fish paste on your chin."

"Hmmmm . . .?" Mark watched the TV screen doggedly. He
had the look of a man in denial while ships sank, while houses
burned around him.

"She must've been about seven, love. I don't think she'd want
the cat to sit on my face now, do you?"

"But why, why is she so keen for us to take Pepe's cottage?"

"Is it the rats you're scared of? It's all right, Elsa left Paco
instructions to put poison down – he's cleared them out, apparently."

"It's not the rats, it's the thought of living two miles away from
your sister. She's . . . she's . . ."

But what could she honestly say about Elsa? Elsa, who was the
perfect hostess, feeding and entertaining them, even wanting to
help buy them a house in the sun, and refusing any contribution
towards their keep; Elsa with her jokes and stories and her great
crushing bear hugs and her temper.

"Annie . . . Annie, are you there?" Now the summons brought her trotting, trit-trot along the passage towards the open door of Elsa's room, and the furious rattling of clothes hangers. Elsa was having a clear-out.

"These are for you, madam. Try them on. I can't wear them bloody all, and I hate waste!"

Flashing her amber eyes at Annie as if she suspected her of harbouring butter mountains, of compulsive shopping orgies. The dresses were like cosmic accidents: bright floral splodges, violent starbursts in gold and flame.

Annie held one against herself. She looked as if she were being swallowed whole by some gigantic jungle man-eating flower. "Thank you, Elsa." What else could she say? Elsa's generosity always disarmed her. "You're too good to us, really. Thank you."

They were supposed to be staying for a month. Mark was convalescing from a mild breakdown. Arriving in this country strained and jittery, now he seemed almost tranquil, lulled both by the heat and his sister's motherly attentions.

Elsa was "motherly" in her way. Always up before them in the mornings, humming a strident flamenco as she stirred the porridge. Into the porridge she dripped a stream of golden honey, the precious *Miel de Canna*, produced exclusively in one of the white Moorish villages thereabouts. Then she would stand with her arms folded, watching until Mark had licked his spoon clean.

"He can't go back to teaching, Annie, it will kill him," Elsa told her. More of a proclamation, really. She had packed Mark off on a walk with map and picnic. From the terrace, they could see him, leaping goatlike on a distant hillside across the valley. No, not a hillside, a mountain. Annie could hardly bear to look. She held her breath as Mark ascended to a brittle precipice, crimped and fragile as pastry edging.

"He'll fall," she had whispered, "Oh my God! It makes me dizzy just watching."

"Don't be pathetic," Elsa roared. "It's only a pimple. We should all learn to live a little dangerously from time to time."

With Mark packed off for the day, Annie had to accompany her sister-in-law to the market, where Elsa would haggle over vegetables, silk blouses, lace tablecloths, waving her fleshy arms about, exclaiming in her exuberant Spanish. Later, the market produce would reappear in a paella with everything thrown in: fish heads, or claws, or eyeballs goggling up at them from the plate. Elsa would tuck in heartily. There was not much that she considered inedible. Once, a guest joined them for dinner, a handsome Spaniard who flicked his napkin with a bullfighter's grace. Elsa lowered her head and spoke to this guest in a throaty flirtatious whisper. Her amber eyes flickered dangerously. Elsa's lover. Of this, Annie had no doubt. It was not surprising. After all, her sister-in-law was a woman of large appetites.

The paella did not agree with Annie. After frequent trips to the loo, she felt she must be growing thinner and frailer. Her body remained greenish white, sappy like a bluebell stalk; her head weighed heavy. Elsa's very presence exhausted her. The energy radiating from the magnificent woman had sapped Annie's own strength. She could only fidget listlessly on the terrace, viewing the distant figure of her husband as he cavorted about the hills, growing bronzer and fitter on mountain air and his sister's honeyed porridge.

Strange how Annie felt most alive at siesta, when Elsa retired behind the great oak door of her room, curled up in her kaftan like some voluptuous beast. At these times, Annie felt like a bird who sees the cage door open and fidgets on its perch, uncertain whether to chance flying into the light.

Outside the light was dazzling. There were strange rustlings among the geraniums; lizards basked in the heat, crickets chirped.

Inside the house, Annie rustled in the cool of Elsa's study, finding the book she wanted with its picture of the centipede, the thickness of a man's two middle fingers. There it was with its waspy stripe. The book was written in Spanish. But she recognized the word *muerte*. Death. The centipede meant death. How could she come to live in a country where such things existed?

They were waiting for Elsa. The town was beginning to stir slowly into life after siesta. Men clustered in the bars. The abrupt gunfire of their conversation reached Annie as she sat with Mark at the fountain.

An old woman passed with that stoical waddle common to the

locals, arms laden with gladioli. She was making her way toward
the church where all about the crumbly stucco of the tower the
swifts dived, darted endlessly. The men's voices, the swifts, the
smooth hiss of the fountain were soothing.

Annie was thinking that, yes, she could grow comfortable here;
even perhaps live in Pepe's cottage. It would please Mark. He sat
now, twirling his sunglasses in his hands, gazing towards the
abogado's office for his sister. If only she could relax. If only she
could give herself up to it, to the sweet drowsy heat . . . to Elsa
. . . No, not to Elsa! At once Annie sat upright, grasped the rim of
the fountain, for here she was, Elsa, crossing the plaza, bouncing
toward them.

"*Hola! Hola, Maria!*" Elsa called gaily to the gladioli lady, who
appeared startled and murmured something. Did Annie imagine
it, or did the woman cross herself as Elsa passed? Elsa waved
triumphantly at Annie and Mark, flourishing a wad of papers,
then halted by Juan's bar to call to the little lame dog which
always skulked there: "Here, *perro*! Look, see what mummy's got
. . ." The mutt limped forward as Elsa crumbled stale blood
sausage which she always kept for this purpose in her bag.
Nervously it suffered her caress, her croonings, before shrinking
back to the doorway.

Elsa rose, dazzling as a sunflower in her kaftan, her strings of
amber beads, bronzed arms chinking with bangles. Annie could
almost smell her from across the square. Or was it the acacia
trees, releasing a fragrance so strong she almost swooned? She
clutched harder at the fountain, feeling the lukewarm spray in her
face. Elsa bounded toward them now, and it seemed the swifts
dive-bombed the church tower in a kind of panic; some German
tourists at one of the pavement tables seemed suddenly to flag in
the heat beneath striped awnings.

"Darlings!" Elsa was upon them, thrusting her warm solid
flesh between them both. "It's all settled. Nothing for you two to
worry about. I've signed the papers myself." She beamed at them,
"I've bought Pepe's old place in my name, but God, what do I
need of it? It's for you two. A present."

Annie could remember little after that, just Mark's wittering
gratitude. And being almost crushed by Elsa's thigh next to her,
the heavy scent of her, the energy . . . and she . . . Annie, clinging
and clutching at the damp stone rim to stop from falling. The

water gave off a rancid scent. It was evaporating in the heat. Soon there would be nothing left but a greenish vapour.

Annie's first thought on waking was that she was in jail. But she was looking at the iron grille at her bedroom window. Mark was leaning over her: "Elsa says you've had a touch of sunstroke. She says with your fair colouring it's madness to go out without a hat. And look . . . she found you one. She thinks of everything."

The hat smelt of dog basket. The great flopping brim was wound about with a bronzy chiffon scarf. Turn it upside down and you could sail the Atlantic, across the choppy Bay of Biscay, all the way to Dover, safe from the sun and Elsa and centipedes . . . Annie's eyes closed again.

"What time is it?"

"Nearly eight. We thought we'd take an evening stroll over to the cottage. Our cottage, I mean. Not Pepe's. God, I can't get used to the idea. Annie and Mark's cottage . . . how does it sound?"

"You mean Elsa's cottage," she said dully. "It belongs to Elsa."

But he was drifting towards the door, telling her to stay there and rest. He was drifting away from her, from England, into Elsa's burning stratosphere, into Spain. She called out after him: "Watch out for the centipede." But he was gone.

The centipede burrows below ground to hatch its grubs. It prefers undisturbed land, the thatch of dead grasses, skeleton leaves, powdered seed heads; it lurks in cracks and craters, in the dust beneath the bony roots of olive trees. You might never see one in your whole life, except in a book. You might go hunting it out deliberately, turning every stone, peeping into crevices, and yet find only ants and spiders. Or – and no one can rule out this possibility – you might just be one of the very few who come upon it suddenly, its deadly amber stripe flashing its warning . . . too late. You might be an unlucky statistic, a few lines in the newspaper, the wrong place, the wrong time. Statistically it's rare. But not impossible. Nothing is impossible.

The sun was low as Annie started towards Pepe's cottage. She was wearing the pale blue sundress, and Elsa's straw hat, and sandals. To the west, the sun brushed the mountaintops, turning the land the colour of *Miel de Canna*, porridge honey.

Things were biting her shins, mean little pinpricks of pain which she ignored. She had grown tired of it, this fear she had of wild dogs and sickness and insects; of this bright burning landscape, of skulking in Elsa's shadow. Somehow she must steal back the initiative, show Elsa that she was no frail sappy Englishwoman to be dried out and crushed.

A slight breeze ruffled the grass as she descended to the cottage. The purple and yellow wild flowers undulated like a quilt.

"Elsa!" she sang out bravely, "Elsa . . . are you down there?" Then, as Elsa appeared, "This hat you gave me is too big!"

They were looking up at her, Elsa and Mark, as she flung the hat into the grass. There! That would show Elsa what she could do with her gifts. Big generous Elsa, now so silent. Both of them. As if they didn't want her there.

Something twitched, just beneath the brim of the hat, tilting it up slightly . . . shifting. Annie looked down, noticing her own toes, vulnerable in the sandals. There was a moment almost of relief that she had come face to face with it at last.

It was the hat, of course, that had disturbed its nesting place. She recalled quite coolly what the book had said, how fast they moved, the centipedes, full of a mad voracious energy, poison flowing like ink from tiny steel-trap jaws.

"Once they get a grip," Elsa had said, "you can't shake them off."

Elsa and Mark were clambering towards her. They seemed to be moving in slow motion. The sun going down lit Elsa's hair in a curious two-tone of dark honey with an amber stripe. Funny how she had never noticed before, that stripe in Elsa's hair.

As they drew closer to her, the sun vanished altogether; the eucalyptus trees shivered in the breeze. The pain was really no worse than she'd expected.

JAY LAKE

The Goat Cutter

JAY LAKE LIVES IN Portland, Oregon, with his family and their books. In 2004 his short stories appeared in dozens of markets, including *Asimov's*, *Chiaroscuro*, *Postscripts* and *Realms of Fantasy*. His collection *Greetings from Lake Wu* was a *Locus* Recommended book for 2003 and his follow-up collection, *Dogs in the Moonlight*, is available from Prime Books.

About "The Goat Cutter", Lake explains: "Everything in this story is true in one form or another, except that the Bible bus sits a bit up the road from my mother's old farm instead of on the middle of her property.

"While I never personally met the Devil in the Texas woods, I'm pretty sure I heard him shouting on moonless nights. Life in Caldwell County can be, if anything, stranger than fiction."

T HE DEVIL LIVES IN Houston by the ship channel in a high-rise apartment fifty-seven stories up. They say he's got cowhide sofas and a pinball machine and a telescope in there that can see past the oil refineries and across Pasadena all the way to the Pope in Rome and on to where them Arabs pray to that big black stone.

He can see anyone anywhere from his place in the Houston sky, and he can see inside their hearts.

But I know it's all a lie. Except about the hearts, of course. 'Cause I know the Devil lives in an old school bus in the woods

outside of Dale, Texas. He don't need no telescope to see inside
your heart, on account of he's already there.

This I know.

Central Texas gets mighty hot come summer. The air rolls in
heavy off the Gulf, carries itself over two hundred miles of cow
shit and sorghum fields and settles heavy on all our heads. The
katydids buzz in the woods like electric fans with bad bearings,
and even the skeeters get too tired to bite most days. You can
smell the dry coming off the Johnson grass and out of the bar
ditches.

Me and my best friend Pootie, we liked to run through the
woods, climbing bob wire and following pipelines. Trees is
smaller there, easier to slip between. You gotta watch out in
deer season, though. Idiots come out from Austin or San Antone
to their leases, get blind drunk and shoot every blessed thing that
moves. Rest of the time, there's nothing but you and them turkey
vultures. Course, you can't steal beer coolers from turkey vultures.

The Devil, he gets on pretty good with them turkey vultures.

So me and Pootie was running the woods one afternoon
somewhere in the middle of summer. We was out of school,
waiting to be sophomores in the fall, fixing to amount to something. Pootie was bigger than me, but I already got tongue off
Martha Dempsey. Just a week or so ago back of the church hall, I
even scored a little titty squeeze inside her shirt. It was over her
bra, but that counts for something. I knew I was coming up good.

Pootie swears he saw Rachel MacIntire's nipples, but she's his
cousin. I reckoned he just peeked through the bathroom window
of his aunt's trailer house, which ain't no different from me
watching Momma get out of the shower. It don't count. If there
was anything to it, he'd a sucked on 'em, and I'd of never heard
the end of *that*. Course I wouldn't say no to my cousin Linda if
she offered to show me a little something in the shower.

Yeah, that year we was big boys, the summer was hot, and we
was always hungry and horny.

Then we met the Devil.

Me and Pootie crossed the bob wire fence near the old bus wallow
on county road 61, where they finally built that little bridge over

the draw. Doug Bob Aaronson had that place along the south side of 61, spent his time roasting goats, drinking tequila and shooting people's dogs.

Doug Bob was okay, if you didn't bring a dog. Three years back, once we turned ten, he let me and Pootie drink his beer with him. He liked to liquor up, strip down to his underwear and get his ass real warm from the fire in his smoker. We was just a guy and two kids in their shorts drinking in the woods. I'm pretty sure Momma and Uncle Reuben would of had hard words, so I never told.

We kind of hoped, now that we was going to be sophomores, he'd crack some of that *Sauza Conmemorativo Anejo* for us.

Doug Bob's place was all grown over, wild rose and stretch vine and beggar's lice everywhere, and every spring a huge-ass wisteria wrapped his old cedar house with lavender flowers and thin whips of wood. There was trees everywhere around in the brush, mesquite and hackberry and live-oak and juniper and a few twisty old pecans. Doug Bob knew all the plants and trees, and taught 'em to us sometimes when he was less than half drunk. He kept chickens around the place and a mangy duck that waddled away funny whenever he got to looking at it.

We come crashing through the woods one day that summer, hot, hungry, horny and full of fight. Pootie'd told me about Rachel's nipples, how they was set in big pink circles and stuck out like little red thumbs. I told him I'd seen that picture in *Hustler* same as him. If'n he was gonna lie, lie from a magazine I hadn't stole us from the Triple E Grocery.

Doug Bob's cedar house was bigger than three double wides. It was set at the back of a little clearing by the creek that ran down from the bus wallow. He lived there, fifty feet from a rusted old school bus that he wouldn't never set foot inside. Only time I asked him about that bus, he cracked me upside the head so hard I saw double for days and had to tell Uncle Reuben I fell off my bike.

That would of been a better lie if I'd of recollected that my bike'd been stolen three weeks gone. Uncle Reuben didn't beat me much worse than normal, and we prayed extra long over the Bible that night for forgiveness.

Doug Bob was pretty nice. He about never hit me, and he kept his underpants on when I was around.

*   *   *

That old smoker was laid over sidewise on the ground, where it didn't belong. Generally, Doug Bob kept better care of it than anything except an open bottle of tequila. He had cut the smoker from a gigantic water-heater, so big me and Pootie could of slept in it. Actually, we did a couple of times, but you can't never get ash out of your hair after.

And Pootie snored worse than Uncle Reuben.

Doug Bob roasted his goats in that smoker, and he was mighty particular about his goats. He always killed his goats hisself. They didn't usually belong to him, but he did his own killing. Said it made him a better man. I thought it mostly made him a better mess. The meat plant over in Lockhart could of done twice the job in half the time, with no bath in the creek afterward.

Course, when you're sweaty and hot and full of piss and vinegar, there's nothing like a splash around down in the creek with some beer and one of them big cakes of smelly purple horse soap me and Pootie stole out of barns for Doug Bob. Getting rubbed down with that stuff kind of stings, but it's a good sting.

Times like that, I knew Doug Bob liked me just for myself. We'd all smile and laugh and horse around and get drunk. Nobody got hit, nobody got hurt, everybody went home happy.

Doug Bob always had one of these goats, and it was always a buck. Sometimes a white Saanen, or maybe a creamy La Mancha or a brown Nubian looked like a chubby deer with them barred goat eyes staring straight into your heart. They was always clean, no socks nor blazes nor points, just one colour all over. Doug Bob called them *unblemished*.

And Doug Bob always killed these goats on the north side of the smoker. He had laid some rocks down there, to make a clear spot for when it was muddy from winter rain or whatever. He'd cut their throats with his jagged knife that was older than sin, and sprinkle the blood all around the smoker.

He never let me touch that knife.

Doug Bob, he had this old grey knife without no handle, just rags wrapped up around the end. The blade had a funny shape like it got beat up inside a thresher or something, as happened to Momma's sister Cissy the year I was born. Her face had that funny shape until Uncle Reuben found her hanging in the pole barn one morning with her dress up over her head.

They puttied her up for the viewing at the funeral home, but I recall Aunt Cissy best with those big dents in her cheek and jaw and the one brown eye gone all white like milk in coffee.

Doug Bob's knife, that I always thought of as Cissy's knife, it was kind of wompered and shaped all wrong, like a corn leaf the bugs been at. He'd take that knife and saw the head right off his goat.

I never could figure how Doug Bob kept that edge on.

He'd flay that goat, and strip some fatback off the inside of the hide, and put the head and the fat right on the smoker where the fire was going, wet chips of mesquite over a good hot bed of coals.

Then he'd drag the carcass down to the creek, to our swimming hole, and sometimes me and Pootie could help with this part. We'd wash out the gut sack and clean off the heart and lungs and liver. Doug Bob always scrubbed the legs specially well with that purple horse soap. We'd generally get a good lot of blood in the water. If it hadn't rained in a while, like most summers, the water'd be sticky for hours afterward.

Doug Bob would take the carcass and the sweetbreads – that's what he called the guts, sweetbreads. I figured they looked more like spongy purple and red bruises than bread, kind of like dog food fresh outta the can. And there wasn't nothing sweet about them.

Sweetbreads taste better than dog food, though. We ate dog food in the winter sometimes, ate it cold if Uncle Reuben didn't have work and Momma'd been lazy. That was when I most missed my summers in the woods with Pootie, calling in on Doug Bob.

Doug Bob would drag these goat parts back up to the smoker, where he'd take the head and the fat off the fire. He'd always give me and Pootie some of that fat, to keep us away from the head meat, I guess. Doug Bob would put the carcass and the sweetbreads on the fire and spit his high-proof tequila all over them. If they didn't catch straight away from that, he'd light 'em with a bic.

We'd watch them burn, quiet and respectful like church on account of that's what Doug Bob believed. He always said God told him to keep things orderly, somewhere in the beginning of Leviticus.

Then he'd close the lid and let the meat cook. He didn't never clean up the blood around the smoker, although he would catch some to write Bible verses on the sides of that old school bus with.

The Devil lives in San Francisco in a big apartment on Telegraph Hill. Way up there with all that brass and them potted ferns and naked women with leashes on, he's got a telescope that can see across the Bay, even in the fog. They say he can see all the way to China and Asia, with little brown people and big red demon gods, and stare inside their hearts.

The Devil, he can see inside everybody's heart, just about.

It's a lie, except that part about the hearts. There's only one place in God's wide world where the Devil can't see.

Me and Pootie, we found that smoker laying over on its side, which we ain't never seen. There was a broken tequila bottle next to it, which ain't much like Doug Bob neither.

Well, we commenced to running back and forth, calling out "Doug Bob!" and "Mister Aaronson!" and stuff. That was dumb 'cause if he was around and listening, he'd of heard us giggling and arguing by the time we'd crossed his fence line.

I guess we both knew that, 'cause pretty quick we fell quiet and starting looking around. I felt like I was on TV or something, and there was a bad thing fixing to happen next. Them saloon doors were flapping in my mind and I started wishing mightily for a commercial.

That old bus of Doug Bob's, it was a long bus, like them revival preachers use to bring their people into town. I always thought going to Glory when you died meant getting on one of them long buses painted white and gold, with Bible verses on the side and a choir clapping and singing in the back and some guy in a powder-blue suit and hair like a raccoon pelt kissing you on the cheek and slapping you on the forehead.

Well, I been kissed more than I want to, and I don't know nobody with a suit, no matter the color, and there ain't no choir ever going to sing me to my rest now, except if maybe they're playing bob-wire harps and beating time on burnt skulls. But Doug Bob's bus, it sat there flat on the dirt with the wiry bones of tires wrapped over dented black hubs grown with morning glory, all yellow with the rusted old metal showing through, with the windows painted black from the inside and crossed over with duct tape. It had a little vestibule Doug Bob'd built over the double doors out of wood from an old church in Rosanky. The entrance to that vestibule was crossed over with duct tape just like the windows. It was but number seven, whatever place it had come from.

And bus number seven was covered with them Bible verses written in goat's blood, over and over each other to where there was just red-brown smears on the cracked windshield and across the hood and down the sides, scrambled scribbling that looked like Aunt Cissy's drool on the lunch table at WalMart. And they made about as much sense.

I even seen Doug Bob on the roof of that bus a few times, smearing bloody words with his fingers like a message to the turkey vultures, or maybe all the way to God above looking down from His air-conditioned heaven.

So I figured, the smoker's tipped, the tequila's broke, and here's my long bus bound for glory with Bible verses on the side, and the only choir is the katydids buzzing in the trees and me and Pootie breathing hard. I saw the door of the wooden vestibule on the bus, that Doug Bob never would touch, was busted open, like it had been kicked out from the inside. The duct tape just flapped loose from the door frame.

I stared all around that bus, and there was a new verse on the side, right under the driver's window. It was painted fresh, still shiny and red. It said, "Of the tribe of Reuben were sealed twelve thousand."

"Pootie."

"Huh?" He was gasping pretty hard. I couldn't take my stare off the bus, which looked as if it was gonna rise up from the dirt and rumble down the road to salvation any moment, but I knew Pootie had that wild look where his eyes get almost all white and his nose starts to bleed. I could tell from his breathing.

Smelled like he wet his pants, too.

"Pootie," I said again, "there ain't no fire, and there ain't no fresh goat been killed. Where'd the blood come from for that there Bible verse?"

"Reckon he talking 'bout your Uncle?" Pootie's voice was duller than Momma at Christmas.

Pootie was an idiot. Uncle Reuben never had no twelve thousand in his life. If he ever did, he'd of gone to Mexico and to hell with me and Momma. "Pootie," I tried again, "where'd the blood come from?"

I knew, but I didn't want to be the one to say it.

Pootie panted for a little while longer. I finally tore my stare off that old bus, which was shimmering like summer heat, to see Pootie bent over with his hands on his knees and his head hanging down. "It ain't his handwritin' neither," Pootie sobbed.

We both knew Doug Bob was dead.

Something was splashing around down by the creek. "Aw, shit," I said. "Doug Bob was – is – our friend. We gotta go look."

It ain't but a few steps to the bank. We could see a man down there, bending over with his bare ass toward us. He was washing something big and pale. It weren't no goat.

Me and Pootie, we stopped at the top of the bank, and the stranger stood up and turned around. I about shit my pants.

He had muscles like a movie star, and a gold tan all the way down, like he'd never wore clothes. The hair on his chest and his short-and-curlies was blond, and he was hung good. What near to made me puke was that angel's body had a goat head. Only it weren't no goat head you ever saw in your life.

It was like a big heavy ram's head, except it had *antlers* coming up off the top, a twelve-point spread off a prize buck, and baby's eyes – big, blue and round in the middle. Not goat's eyes at all. That fur kind of tapered off into golden skin at the neck.

And those blue eyes blazed at me like ice on fire.

The tall, golden thing pointed to a body in the creek. He'd been washing the legs with purple soap. "Help me with this. I think you know how it needs to be done." His voice was windy and creaky, like he hadn't talked to no one for a real long time.

The body was Doug Bob, with his big gut and saggy butt, and a bloody stump of a neck.

"You son of a bitch!" I ran down the bank, screaming and swinging my arms for the biggest punch I could throw. I don't know, maybe I tripped over a root or stumbled at the water's edge, but that golden thing moved like summer lightning just as I slipped off my balance.

Last thing I saw was the butt end of Doug Bob's ragged old

knife coming at me in his fist. I heard Pootie crying my name when my head went all red and painful.

The Devil lives in your neighborhood, yours and mine. He lives in every house in every town, and he has a telescope that looks out the bathroom mirror and up from the drains in the kitchen and out of the still water at the bottom of the toilet bowl. He can see inside of everyone's heart through their eyes and down their mouth and up their asshole.

It's true, I know it is.

The hope I hold secret deep inside my heart is that there's one place on God's green Earth the Devil can't see.

I was naked, my dick curled small and sticky to my thigh like it does after I've been looking through the bathroom window. A tight little trail of come itched my skin. My ass was on dirt, and I could feel ants crawling up the crack. I opened my mouth to say, "Fine," and a fly buzzed out from the inside. There was another one in the left side of my nose that seemed ready to stay a spell.

I didn't really want to open my eyes. I knew where I was. My back was against hot metal. It felt sticky. I was leaning against Doug Bob's bus and part of that new Bible verse about Uncle Reuben under the driver's window had run and got Doug Bob's heart blood all down my back. I could smell mesquite smoke, cooked meat, shit, blood, and the old oily metal of the bus.

But in all my senses, in the feel of the rusted metal, in the warmth of the ground, in the stickiness of the blood, in the sting of the ant bites, in the touch of the fly crawling around inside my nose, in the stink of Doug Bob's rotten little yard, there was something missing. It was an absence, a space, like when you get a tooth busted out in a fight, and notice it for not being there.

I was surrounded by absence, cold in the summer heat. My heart felt real slow. I still didn't want to open my eyes.

"You know," said that windy, creaky voice, sounding even more hollow and thin than before, "if they would just repent of their murders, their sorceries, their fornication, and their thefts, this would be a lot harder."

The voice was sticky, like the blood on my back, and cold, coming from the middle of whatever was missing around me. I opened my eyes and squinted into the afternoon sun.

Doug Bob's face smiled at me. Leastwise it tried to. Up close I could tell a whole lot of it was burnt off, with griddle marks where his head had lain a while on the smoker. Blackened bone showed through across the cheeks. Doug Bob's head was duct-taped to the neck of that glorious, golden body, greasy black hair falling down those perfect shoulders. The head kept trying to lop over as he moved, like it was stuck on all wompered. His face was puffy and burnt-up, weirder than Doug Bob mostly ever looked.

The smoker must of been working again.

The golden thing with Doug Bob's head had Pootie spread out naked next to the smoker. I couldn't tell if he was dead, but sure he wasn't moving. Doug Bob's legs hung over the side of the smoker, right where he'd always put the goat legs. Cissy's crazy knife was in that golden right hand, hanging loose like Uncle Reuben holds his when he's fixing to fight someone.

"I don't understand . . ." I tried to talk, but burped up a little bit of vomit and another fly to finish my sentence. The inside of my nose stung with the smell, and the fly in there didn't seem to like it much neither. "You stole Doug Bob's head."

"You see, my son, I have been set free from my confinement. My time is at hand." Doug Bob's face wrinkled into a smile, as some of his burnt lip scaled away. I wondered how much of Doug Bob was still down in the creek. "But even I cannot walk the streets with my proud horns."

His voice got sweeter, stronger, as he talked. I stared up at him, blinking in the sunlight.

"Rise up and join me. We have much work to do, preparations for my triumph. As the first to bow to my glory you shall rank high among my new disciples, and gain your innermost desire."

Uncle Reuben taught me long ago how this sweet bullshit always ends. The old Doug Bob liked me. Maybe even loved me a little. He was always kind to me, which this golden Doug Bob ain't never gonna be.

It must be nice to be loved a lot.

I staggered to my feet, farting ants, using the ridges in the sheet metal of the bus for support. It was hot as hell, and even the katydids had gone quiet. Except for the turkey vultures circling low over me, I felt like I was alone in a giant dirt coffin with a huge blue lid over my head. I felt expanded, swollen in the heat like a dead coyote by the side of the road.

The thing wearing Doug Bob's head narrowed his eyes at me. There was a faint crinkling sound as the lids creased and broke.

"Get over here, *now*." His voice had the menace of a Sunday-morning twister headed for a church, the power of a wall of water in the arroyo where kids played.

I walked toward the Devil, feet stepping without my effort.

There's a place I can go, inside, when Uncle Reuben's pushing into me, or he's using the metal end of the belt, or Momma's screaming through the thin walls of our trailer the way he can make her do. It's like ice cream without the cone, like cotton candy without the stick. It's like how I imagine Rachel MacIntire's nipples, sweet and total, like my eyes and heart are in my lips and the world has gone dark around me.

It's the place where I love myself, deep inside my heart.

I went there and listened to the little shuffling of my pulse in my ears.

My feet walked on without me, but I couldn't tell.

Cissy's knife spoke to me. The Devil must of put it in my hand.

"We come again to Moriah," it whispered in my heart. It had a voice like its metal blade, cold from the ground and old as time.

"What do you want?" I asked. I must of spoke out loud, because Doug Bob's burned mouth was twisting in screaming rage as he stabbed his golden finger down toward Pootie, naked at my feet next to the smoker. All I could hear was my pulse, and the voice of the knife.

Deep inside my heart, the knife whispered again. "Do not lay a hand on the boy."

The golden voice from Doug Bob's face was distant thunder in my ears. I felt his irritation, rage, frustration building where I had felt that cold absence.

I tried again. "I don't understand."

Doug Bob's head bounced up and down, the duct tape coming loose. I saw pink ropy strings working to bind the burned head to his golden neck. He cocked back a fist, fixing to strike me a hard blow.

I felt the knife straining across the years toward me. "You have a choice. The Enemy promises anything and everything for your help. I can give you nothing but the hope of an orderly world. You choose what happens now, and after."

I reckoned the Devil would run the world about like Uncle Reuben might. Doug Bob was already dead, and Pootie was next, and there wasn't nobody else like them in my life, no matter what the Devil promised. I figured there was enough hurt to go around already and I knew how to take it into me.

Another one of Uncle Reuben's lessons.

"Where you want this killing done?" I asked.

The golden thunder in my ears paused for a moment, the tide of rage lapped back from the empty place where Doug Bob wasn't. The fist dropped down.

"Right here, right now," whispered the knife. "Or it will be too late. Seven is being opened."

I stepped out of my inside place to find my eyes still open and Doug Bob's blackened face inches from my nose. His teeth were burnt and cracked, and his breath reeked of flies and red meat. I smiled, opened my mouth to speak, but instead of words I swung Cissy's knife right through the duct tape at the throat of Doug Bob's head.

He looked surprised.

Doug Bob's head flew off, bounced into the bushes. The golden body swayed, still on its two feet. I looked down at Pootie, the old knife cold in my hands.

Then I heard buzzing, like thunder made of wires.

I don't know if you ever ate a fly, accidental or not. They go down fighting, kind of tickle the throat, you get a funny feeling for a second, and then it's all gone. Not very filling, neither.

These flies came pouring out of the ragged neck of that golden body. They were big, the size of horseflies. All at once they were everywhere, and they came right at me. They came pushing at my eyes and my nose and my ears and flying right into my mouth, crawling down my throat. It was like stuffing yourself with raisins till you choke, except these raisins crawled and buzzed and bit at me.

The worst was they got all over me, crowding into my butt crack and pushing on my asshole and wrapping around my balls like Uncle Reuben's fingers right before he squeezed tight. My skin rippled, as if them flies crawled through my flesh.

I jumped around, screaming and slapping at my skin. My gut heaved, but my throat was full of flies and it all met in a knot at the back of my mouth. I rolled to the ground, choking on the rippling mess that I couldn't spit out nor swallow back down. Through the flies I saw Doug Bob's golden body falling in on itself, like a balloon that's been popped. Then the choking took me off.

I lied about the telescope. I don't need one.

Right after, while I was still mostly myself, I sent Pootie away with that old knife to find one of Doug Bob's kin. They needed that knife, to make their sacrifices that would keep me shut away. I made Pootie seal me inside the bus with Doug Bob's duct tape before he left.

The bus is hot and dark, but I don't really mind. There's just me and the flies and a hot metal floor with rubber mats and huge stacks of old Bibles and hymnals that make it hard for me to move around.

It's okay, though, because I can watch the whole world from in here.

I hate the flies, but they're the only company I can keep. The taste grows on me.

I know Pootie must of found someone to give that old knife to. I try the doors sometimes, but they hold firm. Somewhere one of Doug Bob's brothers or uncles or cousins cuts goats the old way. Someday I'll find him. I can see every heart except one, but there are too many to easily tell one from another.

There's only one place under God's golden sun the Devil can't see into, and that's his own heart.

I still have my quiet place. That's where I hold my hope, and that's where I go when I get too close to the goat cutter.

MICHAEL MARSHALL SMITH

Maybe Next Time

MICHAEL MARSHALL SMITH LIVES in North London and Brighton with his wife Paula and two cats. His first novel, *Only Forward*, won the August Derleth and Philip K. Dick Awards; his second, *Spares*, was optioned by Steven Spielberg and translated in seventeen countries worldwide; his third, *One of Us*, was optioned by Warner Brothers.

His most recent novels, *The Straw Men* and *The Lonely Dead* (a.k.a. *The Upright Man*), published under the name "Michael Marshall", have been international best-sellers, and he is currently working on a third volume in the series.

Smith's short fiction has won the British Fantasy Award three times, and is collected in *What You Make It* and the International Horror Guild Award-winning *More Tomorrow & Other Stories*. Six of his tales are currently under option for television.

About the following story, the author reveals: "Every now and then the reality of time hits you: the fact that it really is passing, and that there will come a point where the seemingly random things that happen every day will reach a conclusion, and stop, and then they will be all that ever happened.

"The act structure of one's life will then finally become evident – but only when it is too late to do anything about it: too late to punch up the action in the middle section, or spread some more laughs throughout, to take it all just a bit more seriously – or perhaps less seriously. This story came from one of those realizations, and wonders what it might be like if the universe worked otherwise."

A T FIRST, WHEN DAVID began to consider the problem, he wondered if it was related to the start of a new year. January in London is not an exciting time. You'd hardly contend the month showed any part of the country at its best, but there were places – the far reaches of Scotland, perhaps, or the stunned emptiness of the midland fens – where you could at least tell it was winter, a season with some kind of character and point. In London, the period was merely still-grey and no-longer-New Year and Spring-not-even-over-the-horizon. A pot of negatives, a non-time of non-events in which you trudged back to jobs that the festive break had drunkenly blessed with purpose, but which now felt like putting on the same old overcoat again. But still, however much David unthinkingly lived a year that began in the Autumn – as did most who had soldiered their way through school and college, where promise and new beginnings came with the term after the summer – he could see that January was the real start of things. He thought at first that might be it, but he was wrong. The feelings were not coming after something, but pointing the way forward. To May, when he would have his birthday.

To May, when he would be forty years old.

The episodes came on quietly. The first he remembered happened one Thursday afternoon when he was at his desk in Soho, pen hovering over a list of things to do. The list was short. David was good at his job, and believed that a list of things to do generally comprised of a list of things that should already have been done.

His list said he had to (1) have a quick and informal chat with the other participants in the next day's new-business meeting (2) have a third and superfluous scan through the document explaining why said potential clients would be insane not to hand their design needs over to Artful Bodgers Ltd (3) make sure the meeting room had been tidied up and (4) . . .

David couldn't think what (4) might be. He moved his pen back, efficiently preparing to cross out the numeral and its businesslike brackets, but didn't. He dimly believed that his list was incomplete, in the same way you know, when wandering around the kitchen periodically nibbling a biscuit, whether you finished it in the last bite or if there's a portion still lying around.

There was something he was supposed to do . . . nope, it had gone.

He went home, leaving the list behind. When he covertly glanced at it towards the end of the meeting the following morning, his sense of mild satisfaction (the pitch was going well, the new clients in the bag) was briefly muted by the sight of that (4), still there, still unfilled. The list now had a (5), a (6) and a (7), all ticked, but still no (4).

For a moment he was reminded of the old routine—

    Item 1: do the shopping
    Item 2: mow the lawn
    Item 4: where's item 3?
    Item 3: ah, there it is . . .

—and smiled. He was disconcerted to realize that the most senior of the clients, a man with a head which looked carved out of a potato, was looking at him, but the smile was easily converted into one of general commercial warmth. The deal was done. By lunchtime he was on to other things, and the list was forgotten.

This, or something like it, happened a couple more times that month. David would find himself in the kitchen, wiping his hands after clearing away the dinner that Amanda had cooked, thinking that he could sit down in front of the television just as soon as he had . . . and realize there was nothing else he had to do. Or he would take five minutes longer doing the weekly shop in Waitrose, walking the aisles, not looking for anything in particular but yet not quite ready to go and take his position in the checkout line. In the end he would go and pay, and find himself bagging only the things he had come out looking for, the things on his and Amanda's list.

February started with a blaze of sunshine, as if the gods had been saving it for weeks and suddenly lost patience with clouds and grey. But it turned out that they hadn't stocked as much as they thought, and soon London was muted and fitful again. David worked, put up some shelves in the spare bedroom, and went out once a week to a restaurant with his wife. They talked of things in the paper and on the news, and Amanda had two glasses of wine while he drank four. But plenty of mineral water too, and so the walk home was steady, his arm around her shoulders for part of the way. Artful Bodgers continued to make money, in a quiet, unassuming fashion. The company's job was to take other companies' corporate identities and make them better. Spruce up or rethink the logo, make typeface decisions, provide a range of stationery to cater for all contingencies: business cards, letter-heads, following-page sheets (just the logo, no address), docu-ment folders, fax sheets, envelope labels, cassette boxes for the video companies. They had the latest Macs and some decent young designers. Their accounts department was neither menda-cious nor incompetent. Everyone did their job, well enough to weather the periodicity of corporate confidence and wavering discretionary spend. His company was a success, but sometimes David thought the only interesting thing about it was the name. He'd chosen it personally, on start-up, seven years before. Every-one else – including Amanda – had thought it a bad idea. All too easy to take the second word and run with it. Who wants to hire bodgers, even if you know it's a little joke? David fought, arguing that it showed a confident expectation that clients would never feel the need to make the association. He won, and it worked, and there were other times when David thought that the name was probably the most boring thing about the company, too.

One evening in February he found himself in Blockbuster, looking for a film he couldn't name. He was twice becalmed at pub bars, both times with clients, having remembered what he wanted to drink, but then forgotten it again. On both occasions he bought a glass of Chardonnay, which was what he always drank.

Once again, too, David found himself hesitating in the midst of jotting a note at work: apparently unsure not so much of what he was going to write as of the precise physical nature of the act. He hadn't forgotten how to use a pen, of course. It was more a question of choice, like recalling whether one played a tennis backhand with one or two hands on the racket. When he eventually started writing, his handwriting looked odd for a while.

But it was not until the next month that he could honestly say that he started to think about any of these things.

*   *   *

On 4 March David dreamed. This was not in itself unusual. He dreamed as much as the next man, the usual intermittent cocktail of machine-like anxiety or amusing but forgettable trivia. On the fourth of March he dreamed of something different. He didn't know what it was; could not, when he awoke, remember. But he was distracted as he sat with his first cup of the day, feeling as if some recollection was hidden just behind a fold in his brain. He stood, stared out of the window, and did not move even after Amanda had come down after her shower.

She rummaged in the cupboard, looking for a new box of her current brand of herbal tea. "What are you thinking about?"

"I don't know," he said.

"Why have we got so many olives?"

"Hmm?" He turned to look at her. The memory felt neither closer nor further away. She held up a jar of green olives.

"There's three of these in there."

"You didn't buy them?"

"No." She held the jar so he could see the label: Waitrose own-brand. He always did the Waitrose shop, and did it alone. Supermarkets made Amanda irritable.

"Then I must have bought them."

"You don't like olives."

"I know."

Ten minutes later she was gone, off to work. David was still in the kitchen, sitting now with a second cup of tea, no closer to remembering his dream. All he could recall was an atmosphere of affectionate melancholy. It reminded him of another dream from five or six years before. This had been of his college, of returning there alone and walking the halls and corridors which had shaped three years of his life, back when the future seemed deliciously malleable. In the dream he'd met none of his friends from that period, and had notably not encountered the girl with whom he'd spent most of that time. The dream hadn't been about them, but about him. It was about absence. About some distance he had travelled, or perhaps had failed to come, since those days: a period now backlit by its passing, at the time merely the day-to-day. The dream he could not now remember had something of this about it too, but it wasn't the same. It wasn't about college. It wasn't about anything he could recall.

It was enough to nudge him into awareness, however, and at

the end of the day he sat in the living room, after Amanda had gone upstairs, and thought back over the previous couple of months. He considered the missing (4), the drinks without a name, remembered also standing one afternoon in Soho Square and gazing at the shapes of the buildings that surrounded it, as if they should mean something more to him than they did. At the time each of these non-incidences, these failures to mean, had seemed distinct from each other, distinct from anything at all. Now they did not. Once gathered together, they referred to a whole. There was something on his mind, that was clear. He just didn't know what it was.

It was then that he tried connecting them with the start of the year, with the feeling of something beginning. Though in general a level-headed man, David was sometimes surprised to find himself prey to rather New Age notions. Perhaps this year, this 2004, was trying to tell him something. Maybe some celestial timepiece, some combination of shadow and planetary sphere, had reached its predetermined mark. Perhaps 2004 was the year of . . .

He couldn't make the thought go anywhere, and soon zoned out into watching the television screen. It showed a crazy-haired old gent tramping around an undistinguished patch of country-side. He couldn't remember selecting the channel, and with the sound off it really wasn't very interesting. Was it worth turning the sound up? Probably not. It increasingly seemed to him that television was being created for someone else. He was welcome to watch it, of course, but it was not he whom the creators had in mind.

As David left the room he passed one of the bookcases, and paused a moment when a book caught his eye. He took it down, opened it. It was a first edition of *Conjuring and Magic* by Robert Houdin, published in 1878, bought some months before at a stall in Covent Garden. He'd told himself it was merely an investment – at fifty pounds for a vg+ copy, it was certainly a bargain – but actually he'd bought it in the hope that going back to the classics might help. In fact, it had yielded no better results than the small handful of cheap paperbacks he'd desultorily acquired over the last few years, since he'd realized that a little magic was some-thing he'd very much like to be able to do. The problem with magic, he'd discovered, was that there was no trick to it. There was practice, and hard work – and the will to put these things into practice. Even buying the little gewgaws of the trade didn't help. All but the most banal still required sleight of hand, which had to be acquired the old-fashioned way. If you learned how a trick worked, all you actually gained was confirmation that it required a skill you didn't have and lacked the time and energy to acquire. Learning how a trick worked was the same as being told you couldn't do it. You gained nothing, and lost everything.

He flicked through the book for a few moments, admiring the old illustrations of palming techniques, and then put the volume back on the shelf. It wasn't worth even trying tonight. Maybe tomorrow.

Instead he went into the kitchen and ate half a jar of olives while he waited for the kettle to boil.

David dreamed a few more times in March, but remained unable to take anything from them. All he was left with the next morning was absence and the unnameable smell of open water. An absence, too, was what he felt during most of the last weekend of the month, which they spent down in Cornwall. It was the third time they'd taken a romantic mini-break in Padstow. Both previous occasions had been great successes. They'd walked along the craggy coast, bought a couple of little paintings which now graced the bathroom, enjoyed a superlative dinner in Rick Stein's restaurant (having taken efficient care to book ahead). Good, clean, adult fun. This time David couldn't seem to get into it. They did the same things, but it wasn't the same, and it wasn't merely the repetition which made the difference. Amanda was in good form, braced by the wind and the sky. To him they seemed merely there. In some way it all reminded him of an experience he'd had a couple of weeks previously, during a meeting at work. A creative powwow, with, as it happened, the clients with the potato-headed boss. There had come a point when David had found himself talking. He had been talking for a little while, he realized, and knew that he could keep going for as long as he wanted. The other people around the table were either his employees or clients gathered to take advantage of his keen design brain, his proven insights into the deep mysteries of corporate identity. Their gazes were all on him. This didn't frighten him, merely made him wonder if they were in fact listening, or rather staring at him and wondering who he was, and what he was talking about. They were all nodding in the right places, so this seemed unlikely. Presumably it was only David, therefore, who was wondering these things. And wondering too whether it was ever worth speaking, if no one wanted you to stop.

On the second evening in Padstow they paid their tribute to the god of seafood. Amanda seemed happy, perky in a new Karen Millen and smelling faintly of expensively complimentary shampoos and unguents. David knew that it was remarkable that a woman of thirty-seven should look so good in fashion tailored for the young and slim, and was glad. Not delighted – because, to be honest, he had grown accustomed to Amanda looking good – but glad. The food was predictably excellent. David ate it. Amanda ate it. They talked of things in the news and in the papers. They were benignly tolerant of the next table, which featured two well-behaved but voluble children. Neither had anything against children. They didn't have any because it had been discussed, seven or eight years before, when David was launching the business and Amanda had just switched companies and embarked on the route to her current exalted position in publishing. At the time it would have been a mistake to complicate their lives, or might have been a mistake. It was then still more or less appropriate, too, for Amanda to make that amusing joke about not needing children just yet, because she was married to one. David did little to sustain this idea now bar an occasional hangover and a once-in-a-while good-humoured boisterousness, but having children wasn't something they discussed at the moment. Maybe later.

They went back to their room after dinner and made love. This was nice, if a little self-conscious and laden with implicit self-congratulation. They'd still got it, still knew how to have a good time. That much was clear.

In the middle of the night David awoke. Amanda was sound asleep beside him, and remained so for the two hours he spent lying on his back, staring up at the ceiling. This time he'd brought something more back with him than an atmosphere. An image of long grasses near somewhere watery. Of somewhere not close, but not far away.

A sense that this was not the beginning of something after all.

* * *

By the second week of April David was waking almost once a night to find himself lying in a strange bed. Familiarity closed in rapidly, but for a moment there was a sense of inexplicability, like moving on from the missing (4) to the comfort of the present (5). He could remember things about the dreams now. Very small things. The long grasses, often, though sometimes they seemed more like reeds. The sense of water: not moving fast, not a river or stream, but present nonetheless.

Finally, a building, or the remains of one.

He knew it was a building, and that it was ruined, though in the dream his point of view was too close up to make out anything more than lichened stone and clouded blue sky above. As if he was crouched down low, and glancing up.

That morning Amanda look at him over her cup of mint tea. "Where did all those olives go?"

"I ate them," he said.

She raised an eyebrow. "Are you sleeping okay?"

"Why do you ask?"

"You don't seem to be. You look tired. And sometimes you thrash about The other night I thought I heard you say 'Goodbye, love' in your sleep."

" 'Goodbye, love'? That doesn't sound like me."

"Quite."

David shrugged. He knew that he should tell her about what was happening. He hated films in which a character keeps secrets from the very people or person who should be on his side: a source of cheap tension that had more to do with padding the plot than representing real life. But he didn't tell her, all the same. It didn't seem relevant. Or she didn't, perhaps.

He went to work, and came home, and went to work again. He went to the gym, as usual: moving weights nowhere, running the same rolling yard, strutting and fretting his half-hour on the elliptical trainer. Artful Bodgers won more business, and he gave everyone a little bonus. He considered taking over one of their suppliers, then shelved the decision for another day. He came home, he went to work again. He dreamed of the building once more, this time from a little further away. The fact that it was ruined was clearly apparent. And that it was somewhere in England. There was nothing about it that proved that. David simply knew it.

*   *   *

"You spoke in your sleep again," Amanda said, at another breakfast. "You said, 'I can't hear what you're saying.'"

He looked at her. "But what does that mean?"

She turned a page in this morning's manuscript. "You tell me," she said. "God, this novel's shite."

He started visiting bookstores in his lunch breaks, and stopping off at Borders on his way home from work. He wasn't sure what he was looking for, so he just browsed. He looked in the travel sections (domestic); he looked at books on the English countryside. Nothing seemed to help. He didn't have enough to work with, and there was a sense, when he looked at pictures, that he shouldn't need to. Whatever this was, it wasn't a puzzle. It wasn't supposed to be hard.

In the last week of April, now only a week from his birthday, Amanda sometimes worked in her study with her door shut. He knew that she would be wrapping little presents for him. David knew that they would be nice. He had no desire to know what they were yet. He liked surprises. They came along seldom enough.

Amanda surprised him in another way, before the day. She asked if he was going to visit his mother. He realized both that he should, and that he should do it on the day itself. Without her, after all, there wouldn't be forty years to mark. He called her, and arranged it. She said she'd put on a little lunch.

He was dreaming now, almost constantly, but through a veil. He felt sick some mornings, as if he had failed to digest something. Nothing he looked at seemed to be what he should be seeing. None of his lists had anything on them except numerals in brackets.

He finally mentioned this to Amanda. She kissed him, and put her arms around him. She was his wife. She understood, or thought she did.

David got up at the usual time on the fourth of May, though he had taken the day off work. He had breakfast in bed, then came down in a dressing gown to a kitchen table on which his presents had been laid. They were all very nice, and Amanda left for work fifteen minutes later than usual. She sat with him, and had an extra cup of tea, and they smiled and laughed.

After she'd gone he showered and dressed and then went out

and got in his car. He forged a route out of London and onto the M11, taking it up past Cambridge and into the countryside. He tried to find something on the radio to listen to, some CD in the glove compartment, but none of them sounded right. He could remember buying them, but none of them seemed to be his.

He reached Willingham a little before midday, on time. His mother was standing at the door to her house, steel-haired, compact and smiling. Once the land on which she stood had been part of a farm, a larger holding belonging to one of her ancestors. Like everything else, it had been made smaller by time.

His mother had made sandwiches and cake. While she laid them out he wandered around the house where he had grown up, trying to remember how long it had been since he'd visited. A couple of years, certainly. She occasionally made it down to London, and that tended to be where they met. Tea at the Ritz, sometimes. An overnight or two in the house he owned with Amanda, tucked up safe in the spare bed. Not so very often, for the person who had been his mother, but that tended to be the way it went. You moved further from the start, and towards something else: eyes turned always forward, the past something you only remembered once in a while, generally through something heard. Things weren't about beginnings any more. They were about persistence, and endings, for the most part. Persistence, above all.

He found himself drawn to one room in particular. His parents' old room; his mother's still. He stood in the centre, unsure of what he was doing there. He looked up at the ceiling. Off-white, as it always had been. If you allowed your eyes to fall out of focus then the imperfections blurred away, and its colour became all you could see.

His mother's voice floated upstairs.

After lunch he asked her about her bedroom. Had something changed? She said no. Nothing had changed for her in several years.

David shrugged, took a risk: told her how he'd felt compelled to stand in there. She was a woman. She'd understand.

She did, and perhaps more than he'd expected. More than he did. "Well," she said, "it's your birthday."

He shook his head, not comprehending. She smiled, as if it were self-evident. "That's where it happened, up there in that room.

That's where you were born," she said, and then winked. "You can live down in that London all you like," she added. "But this is where you're from."

He barely heard anything else she said, and left twenty minutes later. When he reached the end of the village, he did not take the left turn which would lead to the A-road and later back to the M11. Instead he turned right, and kept driving.

He drove for an hour, out into the countryside, out beyond the villages and into the country proper, to where the fens began. To the place where water became as much a part of the world as earth, to where grass and reeds and flatness were all the land had to say.

After a while he turned again, not back on himself, but at an angle, and headed in a different direction. A little later, he did so once more.

He could have driven for hours, for days. He could have looked for weeks and never found it, were it not for the church. That, presumably, had been the point. It had worked, in the end.

It was half-ruined, and stood by itself in the middle of a field. David knew enough to understand this meant it most likely represented the last lingering sign of a lost village. Seen from above, from a low-flying plane, there would have been crop marks to show where domestic buildings had once been, a previous lay of the land. But that had been long, long ago.

When he saw the two remaining walls, the jagged half-steeple, it took his breath away and every unremembered dream came back at once.

He lurched the car over to the side of the road and parked chaotically on the verge. Then he got out, stepped gingerly over the low barbed-wire fence, and started to walk towards the ruin. It was probably private land. He didn't care. Twice he disappeared up to one knee in the boggy ground. He didn't care about that either. His mobile phone went once. He didn't even hear it.

He walked slowly around the church. He knew it only meant one thing to him, that he had only been here once before. He approached it, finally, and stood close up against the wall. The sky was blue above, flecked with cloud. It looked the same wherever you stood, whether inside the remains of the structure or without, and at any point along the walls. But again, he had planned well, and eventually he found the heavy stone.

He went down on one knee and prised his fingers around the sides. Gym savvy told him to protect his back, and he took his time to pull the big flat stone out of place. Underneath was a small metal box.

He lifted it out, and sat down on the grass.

Inside the box was a small old sack, stained with time and wrapped over itself. David waited for a while, wishing for a cigarette, though he had never smoked. He thought about the ceiling in his mother's bedroom, knowing it not to be the first thing he had ever seen. Finally he opened the bag, and pulled out the envelope inside.

He recognized the handwriting, from a list he had written back in February. The letter said:

To whoever I might be—

I hope this time it has worked, and I'm young, that I've caught me in time. Better still I hope I will find this and smile, knowing it was unnecessary, knowing I can palm anything, make coins appear out of people's ears, and that I have not come here alone. But just in case:

1) Do things. Do everything. Learn, explore, open the world's boxes while you're young and time stretches out infinitely far.
2) Make mistakes, and make them early, not late. Too soon can be undone. Too late cannot.
3) Marry the one who could break your heart.
4) There is no (4). The first three will be enough.

Good luck,
Yourself.

Ten minutes later David put the letter back in the bag. He wished he had known to bring the Houdin book with him. He could have put it in there as well, for next time. But if he remembered this late then too, there would be little point. He might as well sell it, hope it would find, someone who would use it in time.

When the stone was back in place he spent a while standing close to the wall of the ruined church, memorizing the shape of the road, the pattern of the water inlets in the distance: anything he might reasonably hope would be here next time. Finally he walked back over to the car, climbed in, and sat for a while looking out at the flat fens.

Then he started the drive back to London, where he knew a surprise party was waiting for him.

JOHN FARRIS

Story Time With the Bluefield Strangler

JOHN FARRIS IS BEST known as the author of *The Fury* (filmed by Brian De Palma in 1978, starring Kirk Douglas and Amy Irving). He followed it with the belated sequels *The Fury and the Terror*, *The Fury and the Power* and the forthcoming *Avenging Fury*.

Described by Stephen King as "America's premier novelist of terror", the author's other books include *When Michael Calls* (filmed as a TV movie), *All Heads Turn When the Hunt Goes By*, *Catacombs*, *Son of the Endless Night*, *Wildwood*, *Nightfall*, *Fiends*, *Soon She Will Be Gone* and *Phantom Nights*. His short stories have been collected in *Scare Tactics* and *Elvisland*, the latter published by California's Babbage Press. Farris has also recently collaborated with his son Peter on a screenplay entitled *Class of 1347*.

It is a pleasure to welcome him to the pages of *Best New Horror*. As you would expect from an author of his skill and experience, the following story about an imaginary friend has a killer twist . . .

S IX-YEAR-OLD ALISON on the candy-striped swing set in the side yard of the big white house on the hill. Turning her head at the sound of tires on the gravel drive. Daddy's home. Alison holds Dolly in the crook of one arm, holds the swing chain with her other hand. Alison has many dolls that Daddy and Mommy have given her but Dolly was the first and will always be special, in spite of wear and tear.

Alison turns her head when Daddy calls. He comes across the bright green lawn of the white house on the hill, smiling at her. Daddy smiles a lot. He doesn't frown. One hand is behind his back. Of course he has a present for her. He brings home something every day. There is one huge tree on the lawn at the top of the hill (Alison sometimes forgets that). The leaves of the tree are dark green. They shade the swing set and play area where she spends her day. Every day. Because it never rains in the daytime on the hill with the big white house.

Daddy sets his briefcase down. Some days he wears a blue suit to work, some days it's brown. His shoes are always black and shiny. One day Daddy had a mustache but Alison decided she didn't like it so Daddy doesn't wear it any more.

"Here's my girl!" Daddy says, crouching and waiting for her to run into his arms. It's what he says every afternoon when he comes home.

("Where does your daddy work?" Lorraine asks Alison, and after a few moments Alison says, "In an office," as if it isn't important to her. "Do you know what kind of work he does?" Lorraine asks then. Alison shakes her head with a hint of displeasure. Lorraine smiles, and doesn't ask more questions.)

Alison reaches around Daddy, trying to find out what he has for her. Daddy laughs and teases for the few seconds Alison will put up with it. Then he offers her the present. It's tissue-wrapped, and tied with a pink ribbon. Alison allows Daddy to hold Dolly, which is a special privilege on the occasion of gift-bringing, while she unwraps her present.

It's a glass jar in the form of a girl with pigtails. Like Alison herself. And it's filled with candy. Red candies. Daddy shows Alison how to open the jar. The glass girl's head twists off.

Mommy comes out to the back steps of the porch and waves. "Hey, you two." Mommy wears her blue apron. Mommy is beautiful. She is so blonde her hair looks silver in the sunlight. She wears it in a bun on the back of her head. Alison calls back, as she always does, "Daddy's home!" (as if Mommy can't see that for herself). And he brought me a present." (As if Mommy couldn't guess.) They love Alison *so much*. Mommy calls out, "Just one of those before supper, Alison!"

"Just one," Daddy repeats to Alison, and she nods obediently. Daddy picks up his briefcase and walks across the lawn as if he has forgotten that he has Dolly in one hand. Alison runs after him and tugs Dolly away from him. Privilege revoked. She hugs Dolly and the glass girl against her breast and watches Daddy give Mommy a big hug. They love each other, a whole lot. Alison watches them and smiles. But then she looks up from the porch, way way up, to the third floor of the big white house and *he*'s up there in one of the rooms looking out the window. Alison can't smile any more. She takes a deep breath. Big Boy is home. The day is spoiled.

("Why haven't you said anything to Daddy and Mommy about Big Boy?" Lorraine asks, after an unusually long, glum silence on Alison's part. Sometimes Alison isn't willing to talk about Big Boy. Today she shifts Dolly from the crook of one arm to another, picks at a flaking lower lip while she slides down until almost horizontal in the big leather chair in Lorraine's office. Staring at her feet straight out in front of her. Her shoes are red slip-on Keds sneakers. "Because they'd be scared," Alison says finally.)

After dinner. After her bath. Mommy undoes Alison's pigtails and brushes her hair smooth down over her shoulders while Alison reads to both of them from her storybook. Daddy comes upstairs to Alison's room with cookies and milk. Then it's lights out and time for sleep. Mommy forgets and shuts the bedroom door all the way. Alison calls her back. The door is left open a few inches. Mommy and Daddy go down the hall to their own bedroom. Alison lies awake with Dolly on her breast and waits for Big Boy.

("How long has Big Boy been in the house?" Lorraine asks. Alison fidgets. "A long time. It's his house." Lorraine nods. "You mean Big Boy was there before you and Daddy and Mommy moved in." Alison mimics Lorraine's sage nod. She fiddles with her box of crayons. The lid remains closed. Alison hasn't drawn anything today. Not in the mood. "Only nobody knew about him," Lorraine says. "So does that mean he hides during the day?" Alison nods again. She opens the Crayola box and pulls an orange crayon half out and looks at it with one eye squinched shut. "Do you know where?" Lorraine continues. Now Alison shrugs. "Oh, in the walls." "So he lives in the walls." "Yes," Alison says, turning around so that she is on her knees in the big leather chair with her back to Lorraine. Well-traveled Dolly continues to stare at Lorraine with a single button eye. The other eye is missing. Dolly has yellow yarn curls around a sewn-on face.)

Tell me a story, Big Boy says. It's always the first thing he says to Alison on those nights when he comes out of the walls. The second thing is, *Or I'll go down the hall to their room and hurt them*.

Alison holds herself rigid beneath the covers so that he can't see her shudder. She looks at his shadow on the section of wall between the windows with the shades half pulled down on the tree of night and stars so bright beyond the hill where the big white house is. She doesn't look at Big Boy's face very often, even when he comes to stand at the foot of her bed, lean against one of the bedposts with folded arms. One hand tucked into an armpit, the other, the hand with the missing finger, on his elbow. Big Boy's hair is dark, short, mussed-looking. He's only fifteen, but already he has a man's shoulders and strength.

Alison clears her throat.

There was a beautiful butterfly, Alison begins, a thrum of desperation in her heart, *who – who lived in a glass jar shaped like a little Dutch girl with pigtails.*

(Bluefield detective sergeant Ed Lewinski says to Lorraine, over coffee in the cafeteria of the children's hospital, "I did a global on the street name 'Big Boy'. Nothing turned up. No wants, no arrest record, juvenile or adult." Lorraine sips her coffee. "What about the missing finger? That's an interesting detail, even for an imaginative six-year-old." But Lewinski shakes his head. He's having a doughnut with his coffee. The doughnut's stale. After two bites he shoves the plate away. "Maybe that wasn't just the kid's imagination, Doc. She could've seen someone on staff here at the Med who has a missing finger. That could be a traumatic thing, for a kid who may have been traumatized already." "*May* have been?" Lorraine says with a wry smile. "Traumatized? Oh, yes, deeply. Alison is quite a challenge, Ed." Lewinski nods sympathetically. "Three months, but nobody's come forward. Kids get abandoned all the time; we have to assume that's what happened to Alison." Lorraine doesn't disagree. "How long before Family Services takes over?" he asks. Lorraine says firmly, "She's not emotionally prepared to go into a foster home. Alison

shows no willingness to interact with other children here. Abandonment can crush a child. In Alison's case her psychic refuge, her
protection, is a vivid imagination. Betrayed by her real mother
and/or father, she's blanked them from her mind and created new
ones – parents who adore her and never, never, would do such a
terrible thing to her." Lewinski thinks this over. "I understand her
need to invent new parents. But what's all this about 'Big Boy'?
How does he fit into her, what d'ya call it, psychological sche-
matic?" Lorraine checks her watch, says, "Let you know when I
know, Ed. I have a couple of ideas I want to explore." They walk
out of the cafeteria together. "Do something different with your
hair this weekend, Doc?" "I cut it. *Two* weeks ago. Some
detective you are." Lewinski has a fair face that blushes easily.
"Seeing our girl this afternoon? Sorry I couldn't turn up 'Big Boy'
for real; might've been some help to you. Bad for Alison, but a
break for us cops." Lorraine, already on her way to the elevators,
turns and stares at him. Lewinski laughs. "I mean, Bluefield
doesn't need another teenage strangler, no matter what his name
is.")

Three a.m.
The low drone of a siren in the night. Alison wakes up on her
back, looking at the flush of ambulance light on the ceiling of the
small room. Dolly in the crook of a thin arm. Alison knowing
instantly that she's in the Wrong Place, where they keep the crazy
children. She must get back to the White House on the Hill, to her
beautiful room with wallpaper and the white cases filled with
dolls and books that Daddy made for her in his workshop. But
something bad has happened. Out There. On a lonely street. With
trees to hide behind, shadows. The red light swirling on her
ceiling, a crackle of radio voices too distant to be understood
distracts her; she can't leave the Wrong Place.
Alison trembles.
And becomes aware of someone standing in a corner opposite
the iron bed in this bleak room that smells like medicines, stale
peepee.
Oh no.
"Wake you up?" Big Boy says.
"What are you doing h-here? You're never s'posed to be *here*."
"Tell me about it," Big Boy says; and he moves a couple of
steps, to where the light from the single window with its chicken-

wire glass and shabby shade bathes his face in a hellfire glow. "But if you're here, then I have to be here, don't I?"

"No! I don't know. Just go away."

Big Boy, grinning. Closer.

"Don't you want to know what I did tonight? Out There?"

Alison flinches, cold from terror. "No no no! Not Mommy and Daddy!"

"Whoa. I'll never hurt them. Not as long as you tell me stories."

"But I'm in the Wrong Place!"

"So what?"

"I can't think of any stories here, it – it isn't pretty and smells like peepee!"

"Oh." He sighs, a big show of regret. "That's too bad, Alison. I really wanted to hear a story tonight." Big Boy shrugs, on his way to the door.

"W-where're you going?"

"The only other place I *can* go," Big Boy says with a glance over his shoulder.

"Oh no *please* don't!"

Big Boy hesitates at the door.

"It'll be dark for a few more hours. I'll find another pretty head to twist off."

"No no no wait!"

"Alison. It's what I like to do."

"Tell you – tell you a story if you don't!"

That sly Big Boy grin. "But you said you couldn't think of a story. Because you're in the Wrong Place."

"I'll try I'll really try!"

Big Boy considers her appeal, then nods.

"Know you will, Alison. Because the one thing you don't want is for me to twist Mommy and Daddy's heads off. Because without Mommy and Daddy to go to, where would you be? You'll just have to stay with the Crazy Children forever. *And nobody loves you here.*"

"I'll . . . try . . ."

"Okay, okay, Alison. Don't cry any more. Tell you what. I'll help you out." Big Boy sits on the side of the bed with her. "Let me put my thinking cap on, now. Umm-hmmm. Hey, I know! I've got a swell idea for a story. Want me to start? Then you can pitch in."

"Oh – kay."

"It's a story about . . . Dolly, and how she got lost." And before Alison can react, tighten her grip on one-eyed Dolly, Big Boy has mischievously snatched her away with the hand that has the missing finger. He holds Dolly high in the air, letting her swing by a stuffed lanky leg, delightedly watching Alison's mouth open and close in horror.

("His name was Walter Banks," Ed Lewinski says to Lorraine. They've stopped at a Wendy's for burgers after the movie. "I heard about him from an old-timer at the jail; the case file went into dead storage twenty years ago. I thought old Eb was just yarning, so I looked up Banks in the *Tribune*'s morgue. Sure 'nuff. Between 1943 and 1945 Banks may have murdered as many as eight women in Bluefield. Same m.o. every time. He broke their necks. He was all of sixteen when he started his career as a serial killer. Eighteen when he disappeared, and the stranglings stopped, about the same time as World War Two ended." Lorraine adds ketchup to her double with cheese, takes a bite, stares thoughtfully at Lewinski until he smilingly waves a hand through her line of concentration. "Sorry," Lorraine says. Ed says, "Your eyes turn a different color when you do that." Lorraine nods but she's already out of focus again, thinking. "Is there a photo of Walter Banks in the *Trib*'s file?" "From his high-school yearbook. I copied it for you." "I don't suppose you know where the Banks kid lived." Lewinski takes an envelope from his inside jacket pocket and lays it on the table. "Two-oh-four Columbine Street. The house is still there, but it's badly run-down." Lorraine gives him a questioning look. "I drove by this afternoon and took some pictures. Two-oh-four Columbine is occupied, but they all look like slackers and drifters. Take better care of their Harleys than they do their own selves." He shakes his head before Lorraine can ask. "Yeah, Doc, I showed the present occupants Alison's picture. They didn't know her. But like I said: drifters.")

Six-year-old Alison on the candy-striped swing set in the side yard of the big white house on the hill. Drawing tablet in her lap, crayons in a pocket of her apron, blue like the one Mommy always wears. Alison has been drawing furiously all afternoon: bears, dragons, spaceships. But now Mommy calls from the steps of the back porch: it's time to go shopping.

("Alison? How about some lemonade now?" A few minutes before the close of their hour together, during which Alison has been deeply involved with her artwork and uncommunicative, she sighs and closes her drawing tablet, careful not to let Lorraine see what she was working on – that's a special intimate privilege when things are going well between them, but not today – and replaces all of her crayons in the box. She looks at the pitcher on Lorraine's desk. There's nothing Alison likes more than lemonade when she's thirsty. Lorraine pours a cupful for each of them. "Alison, I wonder if you'd mind looking at a couple of pictures for me?" Alison nods, sipping. Lorraine places one of Ed Lewinski's shots of two-oh-four Columbine Street on the edge of her desk. Alison leans forward in her chair, needing to crane a little to see. She doesn't touch the digital photo. Studies it with no change of expression. "Is that where *you* live, Lorraine?" "No. I thought you might—" "I'm glad. Because it isn't pretty." Alison's nose wrinkling. "*I* wouldn't live there." There is a hint of something in the girl's face that gives Lorraine a reason to press on. "But have you ever been to this house?" "No," Alison says, with a show of revulsion to close the subject. "It looks like it has rats." Lorraine smiles and withdraws the photo of two-oh-four Columbine Street. "Could be." She replaces it with a murky copy of Walter Banks's old yearbook photo. "Do you know this boy?" Alison stares at the likeness of Walter Banks for almost ten seconds before blinking, twice. Then she sits back in the deep leather chair and closes her eyes. "Alison?" "I have to go home now," Alison says. A small hand twitches in her lap. There is a sighing in her throat, a windy plaintive sound. "I have to . . . help Mommy bake the cake. Because today is . . . Daddy's birthday.")

And what a wonderful party they have, in the big white house on the hill! Surprises galore for Daddy after his special birthday dinner. And the cake, oh, oh, she can't *count* how many candles blazing in thick swirls of icing. Alison did most of the frosting herself.

With tears in his eyes, Daddy gathers Mommy and Alison into his arms and kisses them both. He loves them *so* much. Alison knows that they are the happiest family that ever lived. If Lorraine could be there she would see that, and never ask another question. But there are barriers that Lorraine cannot cross. Alison won't permit that. And this has made Lorraine jealous. Alison is fearful of her jealousy, afraid of what she might do. Because somehow she has found out. She *knows*.

"She knows who you are," Alison tells Big Boy later, after everyone is in bed. Alison treated to a cool breeze from the open windows, nightingale's trill, treasure-house of stars.

Big Boy is silent for quite a long time. Silence making Alison nervous. She plays with the yarn curls of Dolly's stuffed and sewn head.

"So what?" Big Boy says at last.

"Well . . . I thought . . ."

Big Boy, arms folded, waits. Alison arranges the yarn curls this way and that.

"What?"

"You might want to . . . do something about Lorraine."

Unexpectedly he grins. "Having Bad Thoughts, Alison?"

Alison thrusts Dolly away, face down, in a tangle of curls. A seam, twice restitched, is popping again where Dolly's head joins her neck. Alison looks at it, face filled with dread. No, she doesn't think Bad Thoughts in the big white house under the stars, because . . . because otherwise what good is it to be there at all? Shuddering, she recalls one of the smudgy photographs Lorraine showed her. That shabby brick bungalow with its mildew and greasy kitchen smells. It's what Lorraine wants her to go back to, instead of to her real home, Mommy and Daddy's clean, airy house. The place where instead of stars shining into her bedroom there were the eyes of prowling rats. She wants Alison to go back to *that*. Lorraine is not her friend any more, if she ever was. Alison's heart beats furiously at the thought, she feels a flush of outrage in her cheeks. No, *never*! And rising blood forces a flood of tears.

"She wants to . . . send me back to that stinking ol' place! And if I have to go . . . you'll have to go back there too!"

Alison grabs a corner of bedsheet to wipe her streaming eyes. Big Boy sits beside her.

"There's some snot on your upper lip," he says.

Alison wipes it away, glaring at him.

"Well . . . what can you do?"

But Big Boy shakes his head.

"It's only what *you* can do that matters, Alison."

(Lorraine gets up slowly from her side of the bed so as not to wake Ed Lewinski, who is sleeping on his stomach. She bends to kiss a naked shoulder, then pulls on a nightshirt from her chest of drawers before walking downstairs to the kitchen of her garden condo to get something to drink. Mouth parched from all the kissing and those other things she did with him, after more years than she cares to remember new meaning to *going all the way*; around the moon and back with sweet Eddie Lew. Carton of tomato juice on the top shelf in the fridge. She pours a glass, adds a squeeze from the fat plastic lime-juice container, adds Tabasco: Virgin Mary. Leans against the sink smiling to herself as she sips, probably could use a shower but relishes the smell of her lover on her still-tingling body.

The phone. It's the hospital. *Damn.*)

By the time Lorraine walks into Alison's room in the children's wing Alison has been sedated and is half-asleep.

"Must've been a nightmare," the charge nurse says. "She woke up hysterical, and what a time we had with her. She wet the bed."

Alison's head moves on the pillow. Her face is nearly colorless except for the small cherry bow of her mouth.

"Rats and bugs. Fights . . . all the time. She *hurts* me."

Lorraine looks sharply at her. "How are you doing, Sweetie?"

Alison can open her milky eyes only part way. "Headache."

Lorraine holds her hand. "Can you tell me what you were dreaming about?"

"Nuh."

"That's okay. We'll talk about it later. You rest now."

Instead of closing her eyes and subsiding into her sedative cocoon, Alison trembles.

"*Where's Dolly?*"

"Oh," Lorraine says, noting that Dolly isn't in her usual place in the crook of Alison's arm, "I don't see her."

In spite of the rockabye sedative more hysteria threatens. "*Dolly!*"

Lorraine glances at the charge nurse, who shrugs. Alison begins to wail. Lorraine has a quick look around the spartan room but Dolly isn't lurking anywhere. Then she remembers: Alison wet the bed, so the sheets would've been changed . . . she questions the nurse, who nods. Possible. Dolly could've left the room in a wad of soiled sheets. Lorraine moves swiftly to Alison's side.

"I think I know where Dolly's gone. She's not lost. I'll bring her to you." She holds the girl close.

"P-promise?"

"Just give me a few minutes."

Lorraine takes the elevator to the second-basement level.

Dead quiet down there, no working in the laundry at one-thirty in the morning. The machinery of the elevator seems unnaturally loud to her ears in the quiet of the cavernous basement. Corridors criss-crossing beneath the entire hospital complex. The concrete walls are painted grey and pale green. Yellow ceiling bulbs in wire baskets. Signs point to different areas. Crematory, Electrical, Maintenance, Storage.

Laundry.

The metal door, twenty feet from the elevator, is closed. Lorraine pushes it open.

There's a windowless outer room with a couple of tables, chairs, vending machines for the laundry workers. The room would be full dark except for the illuminated facades of the machines. By their glow she sees, inside the laundry itself, a dumpster-size canvas hamper on wheels that sits beneath the drop chute. And there's a dim light deep inside the shadowy room. She hears a lone clothes-dryer thumping dully as it makes its rounds.

Lorraine draws a breath that burns her throat, eases around the canteen tables into the laundry. The big room has glass-block windows on one wall, above the pipe complex that grids the ceiling. The one dim bulb is behind pebbled glass in an office door eighty feet away; not enough light to cast her shadow. She tries a wall switch inside the door but nothing much happens to the fluorescent fixtures overhead: a cloudy flickering in two or three of the five-foot tubes.

She draws another breath and begins to search the hamper, pulling out sheets one at a time, shaking them. There are sheets recently peed on, all right, but no Dolly.

"I think I have what you're looking for," he says.

Lorraine turns with a jolt that has her skin sparking.

"*Who's there?*"

She hears a phlegmy chuckle, then the quavering voice again.

"It's only me. Did I scare you?"

"Did you—? Hell, yes," Lorraine says, shaking her head in annoyance. She is unable to tell where his voice is coming from.

Next she hears a dry reedy sucking sound, like someone pulling on a straw to get the last drops from a container of soda or fruit juice. That gets on her nerves fast. "Who are you?"

"Oh – I work nights around here. Just washed my old sneakers, now I'm waiting for them to come out of the dryer."

"What did you mean, you have what I'm looking for? How would you know why—"

She sees him then, shadowy, as he rises from a stool behind a long sorting table; his head, in silhouette against the glass of the office door, looks shaggy. "I believe you come down here for her doll. Throwed out by mistake, was it?"

"Yes. But—"

"Come and get it, then," he says, chuckling, his amusement causing him to wheeze at the end.

"No. Bring it to me," Lorraine says. And adds, "Please."

"All right. All right." Sounding a little cross. The stool legs scrape on the concrete floor. He comes toward Lorraine, slowly, soundlessly. His sneakers clunking around in the dryer. "How's little Missy doing? She calm down some from her bad dreams?"

"Were you upstairs earlier? In the children's wing?"

"That I was. That I was."

"I see. But how did you know Alison's doll was missing?"

"Oh, I know things. I know lots of things. Been here almost all my life."

"Do I know you? What's your name?"

At the instant she asks, the fluorescent tubes flare overhead with the violence of lightning, the laundry is garishly illuminated, and he is closer than she thought, white-haired, stooped, unkempt head thrust forward of his shoulders as he shuffles toward her. Alison's Dolly offered in his right hand. Chuckling fit to kill, is Walter Banks. The thumping of old sneakers round and round the dryer tub is like an echo of the accelerated tempo of her heart. She stares in hammering fright at the missing finger on the veiny hand that grips the doll.

"Oh Jesus—!"

The door is only a few feet away, he is old now, and slow and obviously not strong, she can get away easily; Lorraine turns but—

There is no room for her to run.

Because Alison is standing in the doorway in her nightie, arms folded, looking up at Lorraine, rigid in her purpose, baleful.

"Oh Alison! But – you can't do this!"

Alison shakes her head slowly, unyielding. Then Lorraine feels the hand with the missing digit on her shoulder. She glances at it. Not an old man's juiceless spidery spotted claw, the skin is smooth, unblemished, large, strong: strong enough to grind her bones. Even with a finger gone.

"Alison – *God* – it's wrong – listen to me!"

Alison in a quiet kind of huff shuts the door in her face and is gone.

Big Boy bears down and Lorraine screams. He pulls her slowly around to face him. He smiles fondly at Lorraine.

"You don't want to go yet," he says. "It's storytime."

GENE WOLFE

Hunter Lake

GENE WOLFE WAS BORN in New York City and raised in Houston, Texas. He began writing in 1956, and his first sale was "The Dead Man" to *Sir* magazine in 1965.

The author of hundreds of short stories and dozens of novels, including *The Fifth Head of Cerberus*, *The Devil in a Forest*, *Free Live Free*, *There Are Doors*, *Castleview*, *Pandora by Holly Hollander*, the World Fantasy Award, Nebula Award and British Science Fiction Award-winning "Book of the New Sun" sequence, "The Long Sun" tetralogy and "The Short Sun" trilogy, his story "The Death of Doctor Island" (collected in *The Island of Doctor Death and Other Stories and Other Stories*) also won the Nebula, his novel *Peace* won the Chicago Foundation for Literature Award and "The Computer Iterates the Greater Trumps" was awarded the Rhysling Award for SF poetry. He is also a recipient of the World Fantasy Award for Lifetime Achievement.

Wolfe has recently published *The Knight* and *The Wizard*, a two-part novel under the umbrella title "The Wizard Knight". *Innocents Aboard* is a new collection with another, *Starwater Strains*, forthcoming. Also due are the novels *Pirate Freedom* and *The Soldier of Sidon*, the latter the third book in the "Soldier" series (after *Soldier of the Mist* and *Soldier of Arete*).

He writes five pages each day, often rising at 5:00 or 5:30 a.m. to work before breakfast, and sometimes completing the fifth page around midnight. Every page of his stories receives at least three drafts and some go through ten or more.

As Wolfe reveals: "I had written a story called 'My Name is

Nancy Wood' in which I attempted a female narrator; I liked the result; and wanted to try another in which most of the characters were women or girls.

"I combined that ambition with a dream – a sort of mild nightmare – involving my own mother, and wrote 'Hunter Lake'. The old farmhouse recurs in my dreams with some frequency. In part it is surely my grandmother Wolfe's house, which she inherited and which predated the American Civil War. The other elements are (I think) drawn from houses I visited as a child. England may well be the most haunted country on Earth, but the US is not far behind – New England and the old Confederacy particularly."

"**Y**OU'LL GET ARTHRITIC EYES," Susan declared, "if you keep watching that thing. Turn it off and listen a minute."

Ettie pressed MUTE.

"Off!"

Obediently, Ettie pressed the red button. The screen went dark.

"You know what Kate told us. There's a lake here – a beautiful lake that isn't on anybody's map."

"I did the Internet search, Mom. Remember?"

"And you sit watching an old TV with rabbit ears in a rented cabin." Susan was not to be distracted. "You know what your father says – people who get eyeball arthritis see only what they're supposed to see, like that TV screen. Their eyes stiffen—"

Ettie brought out the artillery. "If Dad's so smart and such a good father, why did you divorce him?"

"I didn't say he was a good husband. Come on! Get your coat. Don't you want to look for a haunted lake?"

Thinking it over, Ettie decided she did not. For one thing, she did not care for ghosts. For another, she was pretty sure this was a dream, and it might easily turn into a bad one. A haunted lake would give it entirely too much help. Aloud she said, "You're going to write a magazine article and get paid. What's in it for me?"

"I'll take pictures, too," Susan declared. "Lots of pictures. It's supposed to be very scenic. If a ghost shows up in one of my pictures, the sale will be a . . ."

"Snap," Ettie supplied.

"Foregone conclusion."

The car door slammed, and the car pulled smoothly away from the one-room log cabin that had been their temporary home. Ettie wondered whether she had left the TV on and decided she had. Would Nancy Drew have remembered to turn it off? Absolutely.

"The Indians performed unspeakable rites there," Susan continued. Studying Ettie from the corner of her eye, she concluded that more selling was in order. "They tortured their white prisoners, gouging out their eyes and scalping them while they were still alive. Isn't that exciting?"

"Native Americans never did anything like that." Ettie sounded positive, even to herself.

"Oh yes, they did! A hunter found the lake hundreds of years afterward, and took his family there for a picnic because it was so pretty. His little daughter wandered away and was never seen again."

"I knew I wasn't going to like this."

"Her spirit haunts it, walking over the water and moaning," Susan declared with relish.

"You can't possibly know that."

"It's what everybody says, Kate says. So today we'll find it – you and me, Ettie – and we'll stay out there all night and take lots and lots of pictures. Then I can write about how a sudden chill descended at midnight, a chill our struggling little fire could not dispel, seeming to rise from the very waters that—"

"*Mother!*"

"Harbor the ghosts of hundreds of Mohicans massacred by the Iroquois and thousands – no, innumerable – Iroquois massacred by white settlers, waters said to harbor pike of enormous size, fattened for centuries upon— Ah! There's the farmhouse."

It looked horrible, Ettie decided. "Burning that down would be an improvement."

"They're old and poor. It's not polite to make fun of old people. Or poverty." A wrench at the wheel sent the car gliding into a farmyard from which no chicken fled in terror.

"They're dead, if you ask me." Ettie pointed toward the little cemetery that should have been the front yard. Its cast-iron fence was rusting to pieces, and its thin limestone monuments leaned crazily.

Susan took her key from the ignition. "Just a private burying-ground, Ettie. Lots of old farms have them."

"Right in front of the house?"

"I think that's touching. They cared about their dead." They were climbing broken steps to a ramshackle porch innocent of paint. "Probably they sat out here on rockers and talked to them."

"Cozy."

"It is, really. The dead are nearer the living than you know, Ettie."

You're dead yourself, Ettie thought rebelliously, and ohmyGod how I miss you.

Susan knocked. The knocks echoed inside the old farmhouse. There was no other sound.

"Let's go," Ettie suggested.

"I'm right here, dear."

"I know you are," Ettie said. "I'm scared anyway. Let's go. Please?"

"Kate says there's an old man here who knows precisely where Hunter's Lake is. I'm going to question him and tape everything he says. I'm going to take his picture, and take pictures of this house."

Somebody behind them said, "No, you're not."

Ettie found that she had turned to look, although she had not wanted to. The woman behind them was old and bent, and looked blind.

Susan smiled, laid a hand on Ettie's shoulder and tried to grasp that shoulder in a way that would make it clear to Ettie that she, Susan, was counting on her not to misbehave. "Mrs Betterly?"

"Ain't no business of yours, young woman."

"My name's Susan Price," Susan continued bravely, "and my daughter and I are friends – good friends – of Kate Eckert's. We're looking for Hunter's Lake—"

The old woman moaned.

"And Kate said your husband would help us."

"He won't talk to no women," the old woman declared. "He hates women. All of us. Been fifty years since he spoke civil to a woman, he tolt me once."

Susan looked thoughtful. "My daughter isn't a woman yet."

"*Mother!*"

"Really now, Ettie. What would Nancy Drew say?"

" 'I'm getting out of here,' if she had any sense."

"He won't hurt you. How old is he, Mrs Betterly?"

"Eighty-seven." The old woman sounded proud. "He's ten year old'n me, and won't never die. Too mean."

Susan gave Ettie her very best smile. "You see? What are you afraid of? That he'll hit you with his walker? He might call you a name, at worst."

"Or shoot me."

"Nonsense. If he shot little girls for asking polite questions, he'd have been sent to prison long ago." Susan turned to the old woman. "All right if Ettie tries?"

"Door's not locked," the old woman said. After a moment she added grudgingly, "That's a brave little gal."

As though by magic, Ettie found that her hand was on the doorknob.

"He'll be in the parlor listenin' to us. Or if he ain't, in the sittin' room. If he ain't in the sittin' room, he'll be in the kitchen for sure."

The hinges are going to squeak, Ettie told herself. I just know it.

They did, and the floorboards creaked horribly under her feet. She closed the door so that her mother would not see her fear and pressed her back against it.

Outside, Susan endeavored to peep through several windows, returned to her car, and got her camera. "All right for me to take your picture, Mrs Betterly?"

"Just fog your film," the old woman said. "Always do."

"Then you don't mind." Susan snapped the picture, being sure to get in a lot of the house.

In it (it appeared immediately on the back of her camera) the old woman was holding a bouquet of lilies. "Where did you get the flowers?" Susan asked.

"Picked 'em," the old woman explained. "Grow wild 'round here. Buttercups, mostly."

"Where did they go?" Susan tried to hide her bewilderment.

"Threw 'em away once your picture was took."

Inside, Ettie was poking around the parlor, pausing every few seconds to look behind her. The carpet, she noticed, was too small for the room, torn and moth-eaten. Dust covered the bare floor, and there were no footprints in the dust save her own.

He isn't here, she thought. He hasn't been here for a long, long time.

And then: I could take something. A souvenir. Anything. None of this stuff is doing anybody any good, and I've earned it.

There was a glass-topped case at the end of one of the divans. It held old coins and arrowheads, and the top was not locked. She selected a worn little coin with a crude picture of a Native American on it, and slipped it into her pocket. It had not looked valuable, and she would have it always to remember this day and how frightened she had been.

There was no one in the sitting room and no one in the kitchen. No one in the dining room, either.

A crude stair took her upstairs as effortlessly as an escalator. He's old, she thought, I'll bet he's sick in bed.

There were three very old-fashioned bedrooms, each with its own small fireplace. All were empty.

He's gone, Ettie told herself happily. He's been gone for years and years. I can tell Mother anything.

Outside again, speaking to Susan from the porch, she said, "Do you want everything, or just the important parts?"

"Just the important parts."

"Where's the old lady?"

"She went away." For an instant, Susan forgot to look perky. "I turned around, and she wasn't there. Did her husband call you names?"

That was easy. Ettie shrugged. "You said you just wanted the important stuff. Here it is. He said for us to go home."

Susan sighed. "That's not what I sent you in to find out."

"Well, that was the important thing." Ettie did her best to sound reasonable.

"All right, everything. But leave out the names."

"Okay. He said, 'Little lady, that lake's a real bad place, so don't you ever forget you're a grown woman and got a Ph.D. and a daughter of your own.' Am I supposed to do the dialect?"

"No."

"Fine. He also said, 'If you got to go there, you time it so your alarm goes off before anything bad happens. You go home. One way or the other. That's all I'm going to tell you. Get on home.'"

Curious, Susan asked, "Did he really call you 'little lady'?"

"Heck, no. You said to leave out the names so I did."

Susan sighed. "I suppose it's better that way. How did he say to get to the lake?"

"He didn't." Ettie shrugged. "Want me to go in and ask him again?"

"Will you?"

"Not unless you tell me to."

"All right. Ettie, you get yourself back in there and tell him we *must* find Hunter Lake. Don't take no for an answer. You have to be firm with men, and you might as well learn now."

Nodding, Ettie went back inside. It would be smart, she told herself, to spend quite a bit of time in there. She pulled a book off the shelf in the parlor and opened it. *The Alhambra* by Washington Irving. It looked as though it had never been read.

After a minute or two, she realized that her mother was trying to peer through the very dirty window-pane and the filthy curtains, and went into the sitting room. There was a nice old rocker in there. She sat in it and rocked a while, reading Washington Irving.

Outside again, blinking in the sunlight, she realized that she had never really decided what to say when she came out. To buy time, she cleared her throat. "You really want to hear this?"

"Yes. Of course."

"Okay, first he asked me all about you. That was after I had said you kept sending me back in. He said you sounded like a real bitch, and if you came in he'd get the chamber pot and throw shit at you."

"Ettie!"

"Well, you said you wanted to hear it. After that he explained to me about Hunter Lake. He said didn't I know why they called it that? I said because a hunter found it. He said that was wrong. He said it was 'cause it hunted people. He said it could move all around just like bear and climb trees—"

Susan stamped her foot. "We want directions."

"What do you mean, 'we'?"

"Did he give you any directions? Any directions at all?"

"Just go home. I told you that the first time."

"We need directions, not stories. Go back in there and tell him so."

Ettie walked through the empty house, slowly, stopping to stare at things and open drawers, until she felt that something was following her. When she did, she hurried back outside, slamming the door and running down off the porch. "I'm not going back in there! Never! Never any more. You can ground me forever! I won't!"

Susan studied her, her lips pursed. "That bad, huh?"

"*Yes!*"

"Did he give you directions?"

Mutely, Ettie went to the car and got in. Two minutes passed before Susan slipped into the driver's seat next to her. "Ettie?"

Ettie said nothing, and Susan started the engine.

"Get out of here," Ettie told her. "Pull out onto the road again. Turn left."

"That's away from the cabin. I thought you wanted to go home."

"Home-home," Ettie said. "Not away-home. Turn left."

"Our bags are back at the cabin."

"Left."

Susan turned left.

"Go down this road," Ettie said, " 'til you see a road off to the right through the corn field. There's no sign and it's easy to miss."

Wanting to do more than glance at her, Susan slowed instead. Twenty miles an hour. Fifteen. Ten.

"Slower," Ettie told her. "Follow it to the woods. Stop the car and get out. Look for the path. Follow the path to the house. A Injun named George Jones lives in the house. He knows. Give him ten dollars."

"You said 'Injun'," Susan muttered. "You never even say *Indian*."

Ettie said nothing.

Half a mile later, Susan saw the road, braked too late, backed up, and turned down it – a red-dirt road barely wide enough for a farm truck, two ruts flanking a strip of grass and weeds.

When the road would take them no farther, she and Ettie got out.

"Please don't lock the car," Ettie said. "I've got a feeling we might want to get in and get away quick."

Susan stared, then shrugged. "I think I see the path. I'm going down it. You can wait in the car if you want to, but it may be quite a while."

"You won't leave the keys?"

"No."

"Two will be safer than one," Ettie said.

The house was a shack, perhaps ten feet by fifteen. An Indian woman was tending a tiny plot of vegetables. Susan said, "We're looking for George Jones," and the Indian woman straightened up and stared at her.

"We need his help. We'll pay him for it."

The Indian woman did not speak, and Ettie wanted to cheer.

Susan opened her purse and took a ten-dollar bill from her wallet. She showed it to the Indian woman. "Here it is. Ten dollars. That's what we'll pay him to guide us to Hunter Lake."

Something that was no expression Susan had ever seen before flickered in the Indian woman's eyes. And was gone. "He fish," she said.

"In Hunter Lake?"

Slowly, the Indian woman nodded.

Susan breathed a sigh and gave Ettie one triumphant glance. "Then take us to him, or tell us how to find him."

The Indian woman held out her hand, and Susan dropped the ten into it. The Indian woman clutched it, wadding it into a tiny ball.

"How do we get there?"

The Indian woman pointed. The path was so narrow as to be almost invisible even when they were on it. A game trail, Susan decided. "Deer made this," she told Ettie.

If Ettie spoke, twenty or thirty feet behind her, she could not be heard.

"They need water," Susan explained, "just like us. They must go to Hunter Lake to drink." Privately, she wondered how far it was, and whether her feet would hold up. She was wearing her jogging shoes, but she rarely jogged more than a couple of blocks. Ettie, in jeans, T-shirt, and loafers, was probably worse off still. But younger, Susan told herself. Ettie's a lot younger, and that counts for a lot. "Ettie?" She had stopped and turned.

"Yes, mother?"

"Am I going too fast for you? I can slow down."

"A little bit."

Susan waited for her to catch up. "What are you thinking about?"

"Nothing."

Susan bent and kissed her. "Really, dear. I love you. You know that. I'll always love you."

Ettie shook her head. "That's not how it will be. Not really. I'll always love you, Mom."

Susan kissed her again. "Now tell me what's troubling you."

"I was wondering if I'd turned off the TV before we left."

"Really, dear?"

Ettie nodded.

"Is that all?"

"Why I'd told you that stuff. About the Native American. All this. I could have just said he wouldn't tell, only I didn't."

"Because you're an honest, decent person, Ettie."

Ettie shook her head. "Because he made me. I don't know how he did it, but he did."

"Well, come on." Susan turned and began to walk again. "It's probably right over the next hill."

"It's a long, long way," Ettie said despondently. "Besides, this path doesn't even go there. We'll walk until we're too tired to walk any more, and be lost in the woods. Nobody will ever find us."

In point of fact, Susan was right. The path skirted the crest of the hill and descended sharply through close-packed hardwoods. For almost twenty minutes Susan and Ettie picked their way through these, Susan holding up branches for Ettie, who hurried under them, waving away mosquitoes.

As abruptly as the explosion of a firework, they emerged into sunlight. Water gleamed at the bottom of a steep hillside thick with ferns. On the other side of the gleam, water like molten silver cascaded down the face of a miniature cliff.

Susan raised her camera. A hundred yards or so down to the water – from here, she could only suggest that by showing a few fern fronds at the bottom of the picture. Then the water, then the cliff with its waterfall, then white clouds in the blue sky, and thank God for sky filters.

She snapped the picture and moved to her left.

"Are we really going to stay here?" Ettie asked.

"Only overnight, dear. We'll have to carry some gear from the car – not the tent, just the sleeping bags and a little food. It won't be all that hard. Will you want to swim?"

Ettie shook her head, but Susan was looking through her viewfinder and did not see her. It wasn't really a hundred yards, she decided. More like fifty. She snapped the picture, and decided the next should be taken at the water's edge.

"Mom . . ."

She stopped and turned. "Yes, Ettie? What is it?"

"I wish you wouldn't go down there."

"Afraid I'll fall in? I won't, and I doubt that it's very deep close to shore." Susan turned and began walking downhill again. She was a little tired, she decided; even so, walking down a gentle slope over fern was remarkably easy.

"Mom!"

She stopped again.

"Where's the Native American man, Mom? Where's George Jones? He was supposed to be down here fishing. I can see the whole lake. There's nobody here but us."

Suddenly, Ettie was tugging at her arm. "It's coming up! Get back!"

It was, or at least it seemed to be. Surely the lake had not been that large.

"It's a natural phenomenon of some kind," Susan told Ettie, "like the tide. I'm sure it's harmless."

Ettie had released her arm. Ettie was running up the slope like the wind. A loafer flew off one foot as Susan watched, but Ettie never paused. She walked up the slope to the spot, found the loafer, and looked back at the water.

In a moment more it would be lapping her feet.

She turned and ran, pausing for a moment at the highest point of the path to watch the water and take another picture. That was probably a mistake, as she realized soon after. The water had circled the hill, not climbed it. She ran then, desperately, not jogging but running for all that she was worth, mouth wide and eyes bulging, her camera beating her chest until she tore it off and dropped it. The Indian shack was nowhere in sight; neither was her car. Woods gave way to corn, and corn to woods again, and the water was still behind her. When the land over which she staggered and stumbled rose, she gained on the water, when it declined, the water gained on her with terrifying rapidity.

Ettie had turned back to look for her, limping on tender feet. She met the water before she had gone far, and thereafter ran as desperately, leaving a trail of blood the water soon washed away. Twice she fell, and once crashed straight though a tangle of briars whose thorns did nothing at all to hold back the water behind her.

"Here, Ettie! Over here!"

She looked to her left, and tried to shout *Mom*. There was precious little breath left for Mom.

"It's our cabin! Over here!"

It was not. The cabin they had rented had been of logs. This was white clapboard.

"Get in!" Susan was standing in the doorway. (Behind Susan, Ettie glimpsed the flickering television screen.) Ettie stumbled in, and fell.

Susan slammed the door and locked it. "It'll try to get in under it," she said, "but we'll pack it with towels. Clothes. Anything." She had thrown her suitcase on the bed. She opened it.

Ettie raised her head. "I've got to wake up, Mom."

"We'll beat it!" Briefly, Susan bent to kiss her. "We've got to!"

Then Ettie faded and was gone, and Susan was alone in the clapboard cabin. Water crept past the towels and her terrycloth robe to cover the cabin floor. When the water outside had risen higher than the windowsills, it crept under and around the sashes to dribble on the floor.

Henrietta woke sweating, terrified of something she could not name. Through the closed door, Joan said, "Everything's ready, Mom. You want to have your Mother's Day breakfast in bed?"

"No," Henrietta whispered. More loudly, "No. I don't want to stay in here. I'll be out in a minute, Honey."

There were two robes in her closet, terrycloth and silk. Henrietta put the silk one on over her nightgown and tied its belt with a sudden violence she could not have explained.

The bed was a mess, sheet and blanket twisted and half on the floor. Pausing to straighten it up before she left the bedroom, her eyes caught the dull red of old copper. Once the worn little coin was in her hand, memories came flooding back.

Bacon and waffles, real butter and almost-real maple syrup in the sunshine-yellow breakfast nook, and Joan spraying Pam on the waffle iron. "Coffee's on the stove," Joan announced.

Henrietta sat, put the penny on her plate, and stared at it. A minute passed, then two. At last she picked it up and dropped it into a pocket of her robe.

"Do you know," she told Joan, "I've just recalled how your grandmother died, after being wrong about it all these years. She drowned."

"Sure." Joan held the steaming coffee pot. She filled Henrietta's cup. "Fluid in her lungs. Uncle Ed told me."

SCOTT EMERSON BULL

Mr Sly Stops for a Cup of Joe

SCOTT EMERSON BULL PLIES his dark trade in the rural charms of Carroll County, Maryland. When he's not keeping an eye out for ghosts or suspicious-looking types at his local convenience store, he scribbles stories, some of which have appeared in *Darkness Rising: Caresses of Nightmare*, *Outer Darkness*, *Night to Dawn* and *chizine.com*. He lives with his wife Deb, his two step-kids, a cat and a proud little puppy.

"It amazes me how many people love the character, Mr Sly," admits Bull. "He's even getting some fan mail! I mean, he's not a very nice guy, although he does have a wicked sense of humour.

"I guess we would all like to have his sense of fearlessness, but I doubt we'd want to run into him . . ."

M R SLY AND FEAR were old acquaintances, though when they usually met it was at Mr Sly's invitation and on his terms. He never expected to run into fear at twelve-thirty on a Tuesday night in a Quik-stop convenience store while he chose between the Rich Colombian Blend and the De-Caf Hazel Nut coffees. But then, fear always did have a mind of its own.

A kid had ushered in fear. He did it when he yelled, "Everybody in back. This is a robbery."

Mr Sly crushed the empty coffee cup in his hand and dropped it to the floor. Dammit, he thought. He knew he should've just got what he needed and skipped the coffee. If he had, perhaps he'd have avoided this, but he had to have his fix, didn't he? Now his work at home would have to wait. He'd have to deal with this first.

"Come on, Fat Man. That means you, too."

He turned towards the direction of the voice. The first thing he saw was the gun. The kid holding it wasn't much, just some local Yo-boy wannabe with bleached hair and a bad attitude. The gun, however, was big as a cannon. Mr Sly hated guns. Blam blam blam and all you had left was a big ugly mess. Mr Sly preferred knives. Knives required skill and demanded intimacy. Kind of like fucking without all the post-coital chit-chat.

"As you wish," he said. "You seem to be in charge."

The kid pointed him towards an office in the back, where Mr Sly joined the Indian girl who ran the register and a well-dressed woman of about thirty who'd also been buying coffee. He looked for a window or a second door, but there was no other exit. Not good.

"Okay. On the floor!"

Mr Sly turned to the kid. He had to look downward, since he had a good eight inches on the boy.

"Do you want us sitting or face down?" he asked.

"Huh?"

Mr Sly looked into the boy's bloodshot eyes. He didn't see much sign of intelligence.

"Do you want us to sit on the floor or lie on it face down?"

"Face down," the kid said.

The two women complied. Mr Sly remained standing.

"Why would you want us to do that?" he asked.

"Because I fucking said so, okay?"

Mr Sly shrugged. "That's not how I would do it. I'm assuming you plan on shooting us in the back of the head."

"Maybe," the kid said. One of the women sobbed.

Mr Sly shook his head. "For what? Maybe a hundred bucks in the register? Where's the fun in that?" He made a gun with his index and forefinger and aimed it at his own temple. "Don't you want to see our faces when you pull the trigger?"

The kid's eyes widened.

"Why the hell would I want to do that?"

"You don't have a clue, do you?"

"Fuck you, man. On the floor! Now!"

"Okay, but I'm going to do you a favor and stay sitting up. If you shoot me, I want you to see my face."

"Just fucking sit down."

Mr Sly did as he was told, keeping his anger in check. At six eight, three hundred and fifty pounds, he could easily crush this punk's head with his bare hands, but the gun equalized the situation. He lowered his bulk and sat cross-legged on the floor.

"Now don't move. I'm gonna be right out here. I hear anyone move, you're all dead, okay?"

Mr Sly nodded.

The kid left the room and started banging on what sounded like the register. The well-dressed woman sat up and turned to Mr Sly.

"What the hell's wrong with you?"

Mr Sly smiled at her. He could see she was in the first stage of fear, what he liked to call disbelief. That was when your mind still refused to come to grips with what was happening, although your body had accepted it fully. He could see that by the sweat on the woman's brow and the red splotches on her cheeks. He wondered if she'd wet herself yet. Most of them did and Mr Sly hated that. How could you enjoy the deliciousness of dread with soggy panties?

"I must tell you that I thought you were rather rude a few minutes ago," he said.

"What?"

Mr Sly didn't like this woman. He didn't like her at all.

"I thought you were rather rude when you reached in front of me to get that coffee cup. You could have been more patient."

"Are you insane? Any minute that kid's going to blow our brains out and you're lecturing me on patience? Is that all you're worried about?"

"Perhaps not the only thing."

"Well, good. Now will you please cooperate so we'll have a chance of getting out of this alive."

He felt an urge to slap this woman across the mouth, but fought it off.

"Either way he's going to shoot us," he said. "So why do you want to deny me a little fun in the last minutes of my life?"

"My God, you're insane."

"As the day is long," he said, smiling.

They could hear the kid returning, so the woman lay back down on the floor. When the kid came in, he looked agitated.

"There's only seventy-five dollars in the cash drawer. Where's the rest of the money?"

"Told you so," Mr Sly said.

"Shut up." The kid motioned with his gun to the Indian girl. "Get up and open the safe."

"I'm not sure I can open it," the girl said, rising to her feet. Tears dampened her delicate brown face. Now Mr Sly liked her. He loved the diamond stud in her nose and the way her small breasts pushed against her Quik Stop T-shirt. She displayed an intoxicating blend of terror and submission. In the end, these were the ones that really fought back or at least took some dignity in suffering.

"Just relax and give it a try," Mr Sly said.

"Did I ask you for any help?" the kid said.

"No, you did not. I apologize. I hate it when someone interferes with my work, too."

"Man, you're fucked in the head."

"You don't know the half of it."

They left the room. Mr Sly could hear them talking, but couldn't make out the words. The woman sat up again.

"You want us to get killed, don't you?"

"Not particularly. I'm just trying to feel him out."

"And your opinion is?"

"I'd say one of us is going to die."

"Oh, terrific. And this doesn't bother you?"

"Not really. Not when I figure you're the one that's going to take a bullet."

The woman's mouth dropped open.

"Excuse me?"

Mr Sly leaned closer and whispered.

"The way I see it, our best shot is for you to make a move on him. He'll have to react to you, most likely by blowing your head off, but at least I'd be able to subdue him."

"You're insane."

"Perhaps, but it's a good plan."

"It sucks. I end up getting killed."

"I didn't say it was perfect."

"Well, why do I have to be the brave one? Why don't *you* make a move on him?"

"Because if he shoots me, you'll never be able to take him down. Then you get shot and most likely so does the girl. If I get a hold of him, I'll twist the little bastard's head off. Then at least the girl and I make it."

"It still sucks."

"Look, lady. If you have a better idea, I'm waiting to hear it."

The gun appeared at the door, followed in by the kid.

"What the hell are you doing?"

"Plotting your death," Mr Sly said.

"Man, I am this fucking close to shooting you. And you." He pointed the gun at the woman. "Back on the floor."

"No." The woman straightened her back "If he sits up, then I sit up, too."

The room exploded with a hail of smoke and coffee grounds. The kid had blasted a four-inch hole in a can of Colombian mix on the shelf above their heads. Mr Sly's ears rang from the noise. He suppressed a smile when he saw the woman face down on the floor again.

The kid had the gun pointed at Mr Sly.

"Next one's gonna be lower. You get my drift?"

"Loud and clear."

The kid left the room. Mr Sly could smell piss.

"Fear should be our friend," he told the woman.

"Dear God, we're going to die," she said.

Yes, they were, Mr Sly thought, unless he thought of something soon. He closed his eyes and thought of his walnut chest at home, the one he kept his knives in. He wished he had one now, but he never took them out of the house, because of the risk they presented if he was caught with one. After tonight, he might have to rethink that policy, if he got the chance.

"Fear brings clarity," he said. "It fires the brain. I don't mind admitting that I'm scared, but I'm trying to enjoy this experience and learn from it. I don't often get this perspective."

The woman looked up at him, her face a series of red splotches on a pale white canvas.

"I don't want to know what you do in your spare time, do I?"

Mr Sly smiled. As he did, they heard the gun go off out in the store.

"I guess she couldn't get the safe open," he said.

The woman put her face in her hands and wept.

The kid rushed back into the room. His gun seemed bigger now, as if reacting to some exhilaration it got from firing its shiny missiles. The kid looked wired. Either the drug he'd taken had finally peaked or he finally understood what this was all about.

"All right. Wallets. Jewelry. Anything you got. Dump it on the floor."

The woman sat up and dumped out her purse. Mr Sly eyed the contents: a wallet, eyeliner, lipstick. A container of Mace landed near his foot. He looked at the woman, catching her eye, then looked back at the Mace.

"Not all that shit. Just the money and credit cards." The kid aimed the gun at Mr Sly. "You, too. Get your wallet out now."

Mr Sly studied the gun, figuring the bullet's probable trajectory and the distance between himself and the kid. He reached towards his left back pocket where he kept his wallet. Then he stopped.

"I only have twelve dollars. I really only needed a cup of coffee and some maxi pads."

The kid's grip tightened on the gun.

"Maxi pads?"

"Let's just say I'm entertaining tonight and she's in no position to pick them up herself."

"Just give me your wallet."

Mr Sly looked back at the gun. He wondered if he'd survive taking a bullet in the gut. Given all his fat, he probably stood a pretty good chance of making it, but doing time in a hospital wasn't something he could afford, nor could he afford a few days of questioning by the police. That was all he'd need, some bright cop putting two and two together.

"I can't get it out," he said.

"What?"

Mr Sly switched hands and reached towards his right rear pocket.

"It's the problem with being fat," he said. "My pants are too tight. I'll have to stand up if you want me to take out my wallet."

The kid took a step back. Mr Sly could see him sizing up the situation. The kid didn't seem to like it, but luckily greed was still foremost in his mind.

"All right, but get up real slow."

Mr Sly laughed. He had no choice but to get up slow. His leg muscles strained as they lifted his weight from the floor. He felt like an old grizzly bear raring up for one final attack. He only hoped he looked that way, too.

"That feels much better," he said, stretching up to full height. "My legs were going to sleep."

The kid looked up at Mr Sly, who now dwarfed him. Some of the kid's cockiness seemed to drain away, but that didn't stop him from sticking his hand out for the wallet.

"You have no sense of fun, do you?" Mr Sly reached for his right rear pocket. "A man should love his work no matter what line he chooses. Don't you think?"

The kid cocked the trigger.

"Just give me your wallet."

"As you requested."

Mr Sly stopped time. He could do this when he wanted to, just like a quarterback when he gets into the zone or a racing driver when he pushes his car towards two hundred-plus miles per hour. Everything slows down when you're in total control. He watched as his arm came from behind his back. Watched the look of horror on the kid's face, then the split second of consternation when he saw that the big man's weapon was a comb, a simple plastic comb. He watched as it tore into the kid's cheek.

The gun went off, but the bullet missed. The kid slumped back against the door and screamed when he saw a generous portion of his skin hanging from the broken plastic teeth of the comb. The woman picked up the Mace and sprayed it in the kid's face. Ouch, that had to hurt on an open wound. The gun fell to the floor and Mr Sly kicked it away. Then he delivered a finishing blow to the kid's head, letting him drop like the proverbial sack of potatoes.

"Only good thing my drunken daddy ever taught me," Mr Sly said, shaking the flesh loose from the comb. "A plastic comb can come in handy if you ever find yourself in a bar fight without a weapon."

"Charming," the woman said. She pointed the Mace at Mr Sly. "Now I think it's time for you to leave."

"Fair enough," he said. "Just let me tie him up first."

The woman kept the Mace pointed at Mr Sly as he bound the kid's feet and hands together with packing tape.

"We should check on the girl," he said. "See if she's dead."

"You first."

They walked into the store with Mr Sly leading. They found the girl behind the counter, a purplish welt rising on her forehead. There was a bullet hole in the safe.

"He really was an amateur, wasn't he?" Mr Sly said, as he turned to face the woman. "I'm glad she's okay, aren't you?"

Before the woman could answer, Mr Sly had grabbed the Mace from her.

"Sorry, but I don't like people pointing things at me."

The woman shrunk back against the counter. Mr Sly read the concern on her face and laughed.

"You didn't believe all that stuff I said back there, did you?"

"Well."

"You needn't worry." He picked up some maxi pads and threw them into a plastic Quik Stop bag. "Think I'll skip the coffee. I'm keyed up enough already, aren't you?"

The woman stared at him.

Mr Sly went to leave, but when he reached the front door and looked out at the empty street, he turned around.

"Mind if I take something with me?"

"By all means," the woman said.

He went back into the storage room and came out with the kid thrown over his shoulder. "And just in case you get a sudden bout of sympathy for our attacker here." Mr Sly held up the woman's driver's license.

"I can't imagine that happening," she said.

He walked with the boy over his shoulder towards the door.

"Wait," the woman called. "I suppose I should say thank you."

He turned and smiled. "No need," he said. "Most fun I've had in years."

Then Mr Sly went out the door and disappeared into the night.

STEVE RASNIC TEM

The Bereavement Photographer

A REGULAR CONTRIBUTOR TO the *Best New Horror* series, Steve Rasnic Tem's stories and poetry have recently appeared in the revived *Argosy* magazine and the anthologies *Quietly Now*, *Taverns of the Dead*, *The Many Faces of Van Helsing* and *The Devil's Wine*.

A chapbook entitled *The World Recalled* was published by Wormhole Books, and a collection of his selected poetry, *The Hydrocephalic Ward*, appeared from Dark Regions Press.

"I've wanted to write this story for a long time," explains Tem about his contribution to this volume. "I was looking for a container for some of the things I had observed with grieving parents, with people dealing with loss in general.

"I've also always been fascinated by those photographs of the dead taken in the early years of this country – often retouched by painting pupils on the permanently closed eyelids. Dead children dressed up like 'little angels'. Dead children looking as if they'd been unable to stay awake for their important, formal portraits. The way parents deal with what cannot be dealt with, finally, without being changed for ever.

"When I found out that a contemporary version of these photographs exists today, the story came about not without effort, but also without my ability to halt it."

"**S**o, have you been doing this a while now?"

"A few years."

"Sorry for asking, and tell me if I'm out of line, but you can't possibly be making a full-time living doing this can you?"

I actually almost say, "It's a hobby," which would be disastrous. But I don't. I look at the fellow: sandy-haired, a beard whose final length appears to be forever undecided. He looks terrible in the suit – either long outgrown or borrowed for the occasion. And it is an occasion – a grim occasion but an occasion none the less. He watches me as I set up, without a glance for his child. The young wife fusses with her to make ready for this picture, this family portrait.

I'm used to this. Who could blame him?

"I'm a volunteer. They reimburse me for film and lab costs. It's a way . . . of being of service."

He glances down, gazes at his wife rearranging the baby in her arms, glances away again, with no place to look.

Me, I have only one place to look. I peer through the lens, musing on composition issues, the light, the shadows, the angles of their arms. "Could you move her a little to the left?" The husband and father stares at me, puzzled, then bends to move his wife's chair. She blushes.

"No, sorry. You, ma'am." I straighten up behind the camera. "Could you move the baby a little to the left?" Notice how I said "the" baby, not "your". I try to avoid upsetting words. These are family portraits, after all. Just like all families have. Most parents don't want to be crying. I have folders full of photographs of mothers and fathers wailing, faces split in the middle. Believe me, they don't want to keep those. Sometimes I have taken roll after roll until there is sufficient calm for me to make the picture that will go into some leather-bound matte, slipped into some nondescript manila folder, or, if they're so inclined, up on the living room mantel in a place of honor, there, oh so much *there*, for the whole world to see.

I've been doing this for years. But still I find that hard to imagine.

I feel bad that I haven't found the right words for this father, the words that will soothe, or at least minimize his discomfort and embarrassment. But sometimes there are just no right words. At least, I can't always find them.

"I'll be taking the shot in a few minutes," I say. "Just make yourself comfortable. This isn't going to be flash flash flash and me telling you to smile each time. The most important thing is to try to make yourselves comfortable. Try to relax and ease into this shared moment."

This shared moment. Whatever words I say to my subjects, I always include these. Even though I've never been sure they were accurate, or fair. The moment is shared in that it happens to both of them. But most of the time, I think, the experience is so personal and large it will soon split the marriage apart if they're not careful.

I've seen it happen so much. I've seen so much.

"Okay, then," I say in warning and again I move behind the camera, almost as if I expect it to protect me from what is to come. As I peer into the electronic viewfinder, so like a small computer screen, so distancing in that same way, I see the mother's smile, and it is miraculous in its authenticity. I've seen it before in my portraits, this miraculous mother's smile, and it never fails to surprise me.

And I see the father at last look down upon his dead baby girl and reach out two fingers, so large against the plump, pale arm, and he lets them linger, a brief time but longer than I would have expected, and I realize this touch is for the first, and last, time.

I again shift my focus to the light, to the shadows and the play of shadows, and ready myself to shoot. The father attempts a dignified smile, but of course goes too broadly with it. The mother holds the child a bit too tightly. And I trigger the camera once, then twice, the baby looking as if she were merely sleeping. The baby looking. Then I take a shot for the photographer, a shot I will never show the parents, an image to add to the growing collection I keep hidden in a file drawer at home, the one in which the baby opens its eyes and fixes its gaze upon me.

I should explain, I suppose, that I've never had much talent for photography. I have the interest, sometimes I've had the enthusiasm, but I've never had the eye. I got this volunteer position because my next-door neighbor is a nurse, and she used to see me in my back yard with camera and tripod shooting birds, trash, leaves, whatever happened to land in front of me. Inconsequential subjects, but I was afraid I'd screw up a more significant one, which would have broken my heart, maybe even have prevented me from ever taking another photograph. I didn't want to risk that.

Not that I wanted to risk taking such an important photograph in a family's life, either. But Liz had talked about how temporary this was, how they just needed someone to man the camera now, and every time I tried to tell her I really wasn't that good at it, she said I didn't have to be – the families just wanted the photograph – having it was the idea and they wouldn't care how good it was, technically.

But I told her no anyway. Even unpaid, I would have felt like an impostor. Not only was I not that good as a photographer, but I wasn't that good with kids.

Maybe that sounds terrible under the circumstances. It seemed to me at the time that the appropriate person for this kind of sensitive task would be someone with a strong empathy and dedication to and involvement with children. And I didn't have that. Of course I used to be a child, and my sister Janice and I had pretty good parents, but I don't remember childhood as being a particularly happy time. I could hardly wait for it to be over so I could be out on my own. And I can't say that I've ever *enjoyed* children. I've never particularly liked spending time with them. My nephews are okay – I've taken them to ballgames and movies and such and I think they're great kids now that they're older. When they were little I didn't know what to say to them and, frankly, they scared me a little. They seemed so needy and fragile and that was pretty much the extent of their personalities.

As far as other kids go, I'd have to say I've basically ignored them. Their concerns are not my concerns. Most of the time I haven't even been aware they were there.

That weekend I was in the city park taking bad pictures. I tried shooting couples, failing – everything looked fuzzy and poorly framed. Composition was eccentric at best, whatever I tried. A number of families were barbecuing. I noticed one small group in particular: really young parents, kids themselves, with a huge, dish-shaped barbecue looking hundreds of years old.

Suddenly there was an explosion of shouts, barking, shapes racing through the crowd. Then several large dogs burst from the wall of people to my right, followed by a half-dozen teenage boys, red-faced, barking like hyenas, and all of them converging on that young family.

I shouted a warning, but too late. One of the dogs knocked the unwieldy barbecue over, and several others a few feet away. The little kids started screaming, the mother and father running toward them, but the air was full of thick, white, choking smoke. The mother grabbed up two of their kids and folded them into her. But the little one . . . "Jose!" the young father screamed. "Jose!"

I could not breathe in the smoke, but I could not close my eyes. And almost as if to protect my eyes I raised my camera in front of my face and started taking pictures of the turmoil and the panic, the father gesturing as if mad, and I'm wondering how could this be, all this over some kids and their pets, but these poor people, their lives changing forever. And then the little boy appears out of the smoke like some apparition from the mists, some ghost back to rejoin his family because the taking of him had been a mistake, arms reaching up for his daddy, crying and sobbing and the father sobbing as well.

It was at that moment I decided to say yes to my neighbor, and became the hospital's bereavement photographer. Even before I saw the photographs I had taken: the looks on the young couple's faces on their rapid descent into despair, and that small boy appearing out of the clouds like a tragedy retrieved from the fierce and unforgiving eddies of time.

"Oh, Johnny, those poor people!" Janice is my older sister, my confessor, and, I'm a little embarrassed to say, my barometer as to what's normal or abnormal, what's okay and what's not okay.

The day after I'd made that decision to volunteer my photographic services she had a barbecue of her own. (Would I have changed my mind if she'd responded negatively? I still don't know.) I was invited, of course. With no family or even regular girlfriend, I usually ate at her house three, four times a week. Tom didn't seem to mind, but of course you never really know when you visit married couples. They might have been fighting for hours before you got there, but when they open the front door they're like a glossy advertisement for the connubial life.

"Sounds like pretty sad work to me," Tom said morosely.

"Tom!"

"I'm not criticizing him, Janice. It just sounds like it'd be pretty grim stuff, and he's not even being paid to do it."

"Well, I wouldn't be doing it every day," I said, somewhat off the point. I just wanted them both to believe that, contrary to appearances, I lead a pretty balanced life. Despite the fact that I had no girlfriend, spent most of my spare time at their house, and obsessively took photographs even *I* didn't think were very good.

Janice snorted. "Don't listen to him, Johnny. It's a noble way to spend your time. We should *all* do at least one activity like that."

The subject mercifully disappeared into a conversational salad of new movies, music, old friends recently seen, what my twin nephews were doing (now fifteen, athletic, and a deadly combination with an alarmingly broad age range of females), and, of course, the pregnancy.

"You should have one of your own, sometime," Janice said, smiling and rubbing her belly as if it were silk.

"Wrong equipment, sis."

"I meant with a *girl*."

"Oh, duh, I didn't *understand*."

"You guys." Tom, an only child, didn't get it.

"Actually I think I would, even have it myself, if it made me half as happy as you look every time you're pregnant."

"Every *time*? *Two times*, little brother."

"Could be more," Tom said, and ducked when she tossed the ketchup squeeze-bottle at his head.

I looked around. The angle of the light had changed, deepening some colors, brightening others. There had always been an intensity and vividness about my sister's life. It was almost unnatural the way the environment shifted its spectrum to suit her. The bright blue stucco house, the grass green as Astroturf, the red- and white-checkered cloth over the redwood table, laden with matching yellow plates and cups and a rainbow of food. A few feet away the tanned blond boys passing the football through the jeweled spray from the sprinkler. Unexpectedly, the sight made me hold my breath. My beautiful nephews. I could have been a better uncle. But perhaps for the first time, their connection to me seemed sharp and undeniable, and it didn't seem to matter that I didn't understand them most of the time.

All of it like one of those Kodachrome photographs from the

1960s: colors so intensely unrealistic, so vividly assaultive, they dazzled the eyes.

The job was meant to be only temporary. That actually increased my stress over the whole affair, because I felt I didn't have that much time to figure out how to do things right. I'd spend a long time with the camera, framing the shot, then suddenly I'd feel everything was wrong, that I'd be leaving this family with nothing to remember their dead child by. So I'd compulsively start all over again adjusting, readjusting, my fingers shaking and sliding off the controls.

Invariably I'd take too long and the family's understandable nervousness would increase tenfold. They'd suddenly be anxious to let go of this child or they would slip over some invisible line and would act as if they might hold onto him or her forever. The mothers, mostly. The fathers would usually just be irritated, but most of them started out irritated, angry. They were being asked or pressured into doing something they weren't really sure they could do.

Liz could see what was happening. She let me struggle a little at first, scoping out the boundaries of my difficulty, and then she finally stepped in, talking to these parents, letting them know what to expect, helping me set up, letting *me* know what to expect, by example teaching me what to say, what to look out for, how to pace things so the experience wasn't too much, wasn't too little.

Despite all my worries, I never took a bad picture for any of these people. Oh, some shots were better than others, certainly, but I don't think I ever took a really *bad* shot. As morbid as it sounds, I had found my subject.

And my subject had found me.

Taking pictures of dead children – well, as I've said, the work generated the expected tension in both the families and the photographer. I'd spend so much time trying to get a pose that looked natural. Sometimes I'd be working so hard to make everything look just right that I'd forget why these people were looking so sad and I'd catch myself hoping that the baby would wake up and look at the camera.

And when one of them finally did, I went on with what I was doing and took the shot without a thought about what had just occurred.

Then minutes later – I stood up and looked over the camera at the couple and their tiny, tiny baby. Dead baby – I could not have imagined that a creature so small who looked so like a miniature human being could have survived our comparatively brutal, everyday air.

The couple looked at me uneasily. Finally the man said, "Are we done here? Something wrong?"

Everything's wrong, I wanted to say. *Your baby is dead. How much wronger could things possibly get?*

"No," I said. "No." And I looked closely at this child, hoping to see that it was sleeping, but immediately knew it was not.

Dead children, at least the really small ones, have an unformed, stylized quality even though there may be nothing missing anatomically. Their tiny bodies recall some unusual piece of art, perhaps of an animal that's never been seen before, some part-human, part-bird thing, or some new breed of feral pig or rodent. They are like remnants of the long, involved dream you just had, mysteriously conveyed to our waking world. They are like hope petrified and now you have no idea where to put the thing.

That was what sat perched against the young mother's swollen breasts, a sad reminder of her fullness craving release.

Of course I decided almost immediately that what I was sure I had seen hadn't even happened at all. One of the things that occurs when you spend a great deal of time staring into a camera lens is that stationary things appear to move, moving things freeze, and a variety of other optical illusions may occur. Things appear, disappear, change color and shape. Of course you don't have to use a camera to see this – stare at almost anything in the real world long enough and these kinds of phenomena occur. That's true enough, isn't it? I mean, it isn't just me, right?

The great photographers are great because they see things differently from the rest of us. So from our perspective they see things that aren't there. I've long had this notion, not quite a theory, that the world changes when a great photographer looks through the lens.

As I said before, I'm not a great photographer. But when I took those first rolls home and developed them I think I got just a glimpse of what the great photographer sees. In three of the shots the baby's eyes were open, looking at me.

*   *   *

I admit that upon occasion I do fall prey to a certain suggestibility. I'm wound pretty tightly at times. I get somewhat anxious in the darkroom. I'm interested in shadows in an aesthetic sense, but I'm also uncomfortable with them. Unexpected sounds can make me jump out of my skin. I don't care for scary movies. And I'll believe almost anything that comes out of the mouth of a well-spoken man or woman.

So I wasn't about to let myself believe what the pictures were telling me. Not without a fight.

"Liz, did you ever notice the babies' eyes? How sometimes they're . . . open just a little?"

I don't know if I expected her to ask me if I'd been drinking, or suggest that I get more sleep, or maybe just stare at me with that evaluating look I'd seen her give some of the patients. But I didn't expect the calmness, the matter-of-factness. "Sometimes the eyes don't close all the way. When they get to the embalmer, sometimes he'll sew the lids down, or glue them maybe. Whatever seems necessary for the viewing. Occasionally I'll warn the parents, if I think it will upset them. Why, has it been bothering you, or is it just something you noticed?"

Relieved, I almost told her what I'd been thinking, what I'd been imagining, but I didn't. "I just noticed," I said.

So for a while I refocused myself on just taking the pictures, trying to relax the couples (or in some cases, single moms, and in one very complicated case, a single dad, who seemed angry about the whole thing, and frowned during the picture, but still insisted that the picture with his son was something he *had* to have. Liz was obviously nervous about that one, and hung around outside the room while I hurried the session.) My composition got better; the pictures improved.

Sometimes there would be something different about a baby: a certain slant to the shoulders, a small hand frozen in a gesture, an ambiguous expressiveness in the face that tugged at my imagination, but I withheld any response. I knew that if I brought any of these details to Liz's attention she would give me some simple, calm, rational answer, and I would feel that I was only making myself suspect in her eyes.

Yet I felt almost guilty not to be paying more notice to these small details, as if I were ignoring the appeals of some damaged or frightened child. And what did I know of these things? I'd never been a parent, never hoped to be a parent. I knew nothing, really, of children. I had learned a little about grieving parents: how they held their dead babies, how they looked at the camera, how they held themselves.

And I could see clearly, now, the way the eyelids sometimes loosened a bit, sliding up to expose crescent-shaped slivers of greyish eyeball. I'd seen this look in people who were napping – there was nothing unusual about it. But I still didn't like seeing this in the babies. For in the babies it didn't look like napping at all – it looked like additional evidence of their premature deaths.

I had become more relaxed in my volunteer work. I didn't expect any surprises and no surprises occurred. And yet still I would occasionally take those special pictures out of their folders and examine them. And it did not escape my notice that the babies in the pictures, the ones who appeared to be staring at me, had eyes which remained wide open, with an aspect of deliberate and unmistakable intention.

This vocation of bereavement photography is hardly a new one. From the earliest days of photography you will find pictures of dead people staring at the camera, sometimes with the surgeon's or embalmer's stitches all too visible around the scalp or chest. The adults are in their best clothing, sometimes slouched in a chair, sometimes propped up in bed, a Bible underneath one hand. Sometimes the women are holding flowers.

Many, of course, appear to be sleeping, caught by the sneaky photographer as they nap the afternoon away. Others look terrified: eyes wide and impossibly white, the enlarged dots of their pupils fixing you in a mean, unforgiving gaze.

These gazes are artificial, of course: the eyes painted onto the closed, dead lids. They look, I think, like stills from some badly animated cartoon.

In those days portraiture was quite a bit more formal, and sittings a special occasion. Few families owned cameras of their own, and you might have only two or three photographs taken of yourself over the course of a lifetime. Sometimes a grieving relative's only chance for a photographic record of a beloved's life was after the beloved was dead.

This was particularly true in the case of children. Infant mortality in the days of our great-grandparents was so high that without the photographic proof people might not ever know you'd ever been a parent. You dressed them up as angels and paid the man good money to take their everlasting portraits, money you doubtless could not spare. You put those portraits up on the mantel or in an honored place on the parlor wall, and you showed them to friends and neighbors, even salesmen come to call. And you alternately preened and choked with grief when they commented "How precious," "How handsome," and "How terribly, terribly sad."

The issue returned with the Wilson child.

Did I mention before that most of the children I photographed were stillborns? Of course that would make sense as there would be no opportunities for school pictures or family portraits or any of the other usual domestic photo opportunities. The need for my services was greater.

But occasionally an older child of one or two years would be signed up for the service, accompanied by parents who were always a bit ashamed for not having engaged in that normal parental obsession of incessant snapshots and home movies.

I have to say I was glad this particular age group didn't come up too often. It was awful enough to take pictures of parents devastated by the loss of a dream – a child who might have been anything, whose likes and dislikes, the sound of the voice, were completely unknown. Worse was the child who had developed a personality, however roughly formed, who liked toy trucks and hated green beans, who smelled of a dozen different things, whose eyes had focus.

The Wilsons were older than the usual couples I saw. She was in her early forties; he had to be on the far side of fifty. They had a small chicken farm twenty miles outside the city. Mrs Wilson smelled of flour and of make-up carelessly and too thickly applied. In fact I think make-up was a rare accessory for her. She had pupils like little dark peas, washed up in a cup of milk. There was something wrong with her hip; she shuffled and bobbed across the room to the metal chair I'd set up for her. The nice chair was being cleaned, and the appointment had been hastily arranged. I felt bad about that. I knew nothing about her, but I would have liked to have photographed her in the finest hotel in the city.

This reaction was all silliness on my part, of course. She wouldn't have cared – she was barely aware of her surroundings. Her eyes were focused on another piece of furniture in the room: a gurney bearing a small swaddled bundle, an elderly nurse stationed nearby as if to prevent its theft or escape.

Mr Wilson also came to me in layers. Floating above it all was the stink of chickens, of years of too much labor with too little reward. Under that was a face like sheared-off slabs of rock, and eyes scorched from too little crying, no matter what. Unlike Mrs Wilson, there appeared to be nothing wrong with his body, but he shuffled across the floor just the same, a rising tide of anger impeding forward progress. He stopped dutifully by the rigid metal chair, gripping the back with narrow, grease-stained fingers, a little too tightly because he thought no one would notice. He watched as his wife made her way painfully over to the gurney and stood there patting and stroking – not the sunken little bundle, but the sheets surrounding it.

He didn't move another step. He knew his place.

The nurse asked if they'd like to "get situated", and then she'd bring them their son. I couldn't imagine what she meant – it sounded as if they were moving into a new place, or starting a new job. They appeared to understand her better, however. Mrs Wilson dropped into the chair and held on to her knees. Mr Wilson straightened up as if to verify the height listed on his driver's license.

The nurse carried the package over, whispering comforting things into its open top. She unwrapped the child and fussed with him in mock-complaint, trying to position him in his mother's lap so that the large dent in the side of his head wouldn't show. She almost managed it by laying the dent against his mother's chest and twisting his pelvis a little. She pretended not to notice the mother's profound shudder.

Then the nurse quickly backed away from the house of cards she'd just constructed, holding her breath as if even that might trigger collapse. She retreated to the back of the room, with a gesture toward the family as if presenting some magic trick or religious tableau.

The couple stared straight ahead, slightly above me at the dark wall behind. I didn't bother telling them to look at or reposition the child. They were done with me and what I represented.

All that was left for me to do was to gaze at the child and snap the shutter.

Even slumped inwards like that, he was actually a pretty sturdy kid. Broad-faced with chubby arms and legs. The head a little large, and I wondered briefly if there had been a spreading due to impact and I shook slightly, a bit disgusted with myself. This couple's beautiful little boy.

But the head wasn't quite right, and the composition was made worse by the couple's hunched-forward, intense stares. I moved the camera and tripod a little to the left while gazing through the viewfinder, ready to stop moving when things looked right.

The little boy opened his eyes, the pupils following me.

I looked up from the viewfinder. The eyes remained closed.

Back with my eye to the lens and the boy's eyes were following me again, as I moved further left, than back right again. It was probably just the position of his head and the slump of the shoulders, but he looked angry. He looked furious.

Finally I stopped. The eyes closed. But as I started to press the button they opened again. Bore down on me. Impatient, waiting.

I took shot after shot that afternoon. Most of them were unusable. What was he so angry about? It was as if he didn't want his picture taken with these people and he was blaming me for it.

After that day the children opened their eyes for me now and then, although certainly not during the majority of these sessions. I don't believe I'd still be doing this work today if it had happened with every child. Most of the time my volunteer work consisted of calming the parents without actually counseling them – I don't have the temperament or training for it. Positioning them, feeling out what they would be comfortable with, and finally taking the shot. That's what it's all about, really: taking the shot.

The children who opened their eyes to me hampered that work, since obviously I couldn't send those poor couples home with that kind of photograph. Increasingly they seemed angry with me, and increasingly I was irritated with them for the obstacle they had become.

"Okay . . . uh, could you move her to the left just a bit? There, that's good. That's perfect."

And she is. This child, this Amy, my flesh, my blood, my niece. Tom grips Janice's shoulders a little too firmly. I can see the small wince of discomfort playing with the corners of my sister's mouth. I look at Tom, he looks back at me, relaxes his hands. He looks so pale – I think if I don't take this family portrait soon he might faint. The twin boys stand to each side of him, beautiful and sullen, yet they pull in closer to his body for his support and theirs.

Janice looks up at me, her little brother, not sure what she should do. I offer her a smile; she takes it, attempts to make it her own, and almost succeeds.

Then I look through the lens. I look at Amy, and she's otherworldly, beautiful as her mother. And then she opens her eyes, giving me that stare I've seen a hundred times before, but it's different this time, because this is Amy, this is one of my own. I see the anger coming slowly into her eyes, but I smile at her anyway. I make a kiss with my mouth, and I hope she understands it is just for her. And I take the shot, this one for me, and she closes her eyes again, and I take the other shot for them.

GEMMA FILES

Kissing Carrion

THOUGH SHE RECENTLY BETRAYED her Gothic roots by beginning to wear colours, Gemma Files still often invites all and sundry to, as Susan Musgrave puts it, "bite into [her]/and open [their] mind to blood."

Previously a freelance film critic, she now teaches screenwriting and Canadian film history at the Toronto Film School, and has adapted two of her own stories for The Showtime Network's *The Hunger* cable TV series. Her short story "The Emperor's Old Bones" won the International Horror Guild Award for Best Short Story of 1999.

"Kissing Carrion" is the title story from her first collection of short stories, available from Prime Books. A second collection, *The Worm in Every Heart*, is currently available from the same publisher.

"I first got the germ for 'Kissing Carrion' back in 1993," Files remembers, "when I'd just quit my job as Vibrator Room floor attendant at Lovecraft, Toronto's most upscale sex shop. The virulent combination of having an eighty per cent employee discount but no significant other to share the spoils with had already begun to screw with my ideas about 'healthy' sexuality. I also spent a fair amount of time listening to early Nine Inch Nails while reading underground comics and 'zines, simultaneously jealous and admiring of their creators' capacity to self-publish material which seemed to come straight from the same vein of icky, suppurating, intensely private darkness I was becoming somewhat afraid to tap into myself.

"The turning point came when I discovered an article in one of said 'zines about those wacky folks down at Survival Research Laboratories (whose self-destructive industrial antics would later inspire NIN's 'Happiness in Slavery' video), which led me to rent their performance tapes from Suspect Video – I was particularly struck by the infamous "rabbot", a rotting bunny corpse hooked up to a system of rods and pistons and technical what-have-you which puppeted it around, making it parade itself back and forth until it started to fall apart. Mix well with the Pixies, and Pat Calavera's Bone Machine was born.

"But things soon slid to a halt, as they often do with me, and the story lay fallow for years . . . I had vague ideas of submitting it for a zombie anthology, like John Skipp and Craig Spector's *The Book of the Dead*, which is how the whole 'triangle between a man, a woman and a corpse splits apart when the corpse objects to the arrangement' theme came into play.

"Still and all, it took until 2000 for me to finally realize that the narrative perspective should come from Mr Stinky, rather than Pat or Ray. A deadline was proffered by Ellen Datlow, for which I'll be eternally grateful, even though the story itself didn't turn out to meet her needs for the anthology in question. And the rest is history."

Q: *Are we living in a land where sex and horror are the new Gods?*
A: *Yeah.*

– Frankie Goes To Hollywood

I AM PERSECUTED BY angels, huge and silent – marble-white, rigid-winged, one in every corner. Only their vast eyes speak, staring mildly at me from under their painful halos, arc-weld white crowns of blank. They say: *Lie down.* They say: *Forgive, forget. Sleep.*

Forget, lie down. Drift away into death's dream. Make your . . . final . . . peace.

But being dead is nothing peaceful – as they must know, those God-splinter-sized liars. It's more like a temporal haematoma, time pooling under the skin of reality like sequestered blood. Memory looping inward, turning black, starting to stink.

A lidless eye, still struggling to close. An intense and burning contempt for everything you have, mixed up tight with an absolute – and absolutely justified – terror of losing it all.

Yet here I am, still. Watching the angels hover in the ill-set corners of Pat Calavera's Annex basement apartment, watching me watch *her* wash her green-streaked hair under the kitchen sink's lime-crusted tap. And thinking one more time how funny it is I can see them, when she can't: They're far more "here" than I am, one way or another, especially in my current discorporant state – an eddying tide of discontent adding one more vague chill to the mouldy air around her, stirring the fly-strips as I pass. Pat's roommate hoards trash, breeding a durable sub-race of insects who endure through hot, cold and humid weather alike; he keeps the bathtub full of dirty dishes and the air full of stink, reducing Pat's supposed bedroom to a mere way-stop between gigs, an (in)convenient place to park her equipment till the next time she needs to use it.

Days, she teaches socks to talk cute as a trainee intern on *Ding Dong the Derry-o*, the world-famous Hendricks Family Conglomerate's longest-running preschool puppet-show. Nights, she spins extra cash and underground performance art out of playing with her Bone Machine, getting black-market-fresh cadavers to parade back and forth on strings for the edification of bored ultra-fetishists. "Carrionettes", that's what she usually calls them whenever she's making them dance, play cards or screw some guy named Ray, a volunteer post-mortem porn star whose general necrophiliac bent seems to be fast narrowing to one particular corpse, and one alone . . . mine, to be exact.

Pat can't see the angels, though – can't even sense their presence like an oblique, falling touch, a Seraph's pinion-feather trailed quick and light along the back of my dead soul. And really, when you think about it, that's probably just as well.

I mean, they're not here for *her*.

Outside, life continues, just like always: Jobs, traffic, weather. It's February. To the south of Toronto there's a general occlusion forming, a pale and misty bee-swarm wall vorticing aimlessly back and forth across the city while a pearly, semi-permeable lace of nothingness hangs above. Soft snow to the ankles, and rising. Snow falling all night, muffling the world's dim lines, half-choking the city's constant hum.

Inside, Pat turns the tap off, rubs her head hard with a towel and leans forward, frowning at her own reflection in the sink's chipped back-mirror. Her breath mists the glass. Behind her, I float unseen over her left shoulder, not breathing at all.

But not leaving, either. Not as yet.

And: *Sleep*, the angels tell me, silently. And: *Make* me, I reply. Equally silent.

To which they say nothing.

I know a lot about this woman, Pat Calavera – more than she'd want me to, if she only knew I knew. How there are days she hates every person she meets for not being part of her own restless consciousness, for making her feel small and useless, inappropriate and frightened. How, since she makes it a habit to always tell the truth about things that don't matter, she can lie about the really important things under almost any circumstances – drunk, high, sober, sobbing.

And the puppets, I know about them too: How Pat's always liked being able to move things around to her own satisfaction, to make things jump – or not – with a flick of her finger, from Barbie and Ken on up. To pull the strings on *something*, even if it's just a dead man with bolts screwed into his bones and wires fed along his tendons.

Because she can. Because it's an art with only one artist. Because she's an extremist, and there's nothing more extreme. Because who's going to stop her, anyway?

Well. Me, I guess. If I can.

(Which I probably can't.)

A quick glance at the angels, who nod in unison: No, not likely.

Predictable, the same way so much of the rest of this – experience of mine's been, thus far; pretty much exactly like all the tabloids say, barring some minor deviations here and there. First the tunnel, then the light – you rise up, lift out of your shell, hovering mothlike just at the very teasing edge of its stinging sweetness. After which, at the last, most wrenching possible moment – you finally catch and stutter, take on weight, dip groundwards. Go down.

Further and further, then further still. Down where there's a Bridge of Sighs, a Bridge of Dread, a fire that burns you to the bone. Down where there's a crocodile with a human face, ready and waiting to weigh and eat your heart. Down where there's a room full of dust where blind things sit forever, wings trailing, mouths too full to speak.

I have no name now, not that I can remember, since they take our names first of all – name, then face, then everything else, piece by piece by piece. No matter that you've come down so fast and hard, fighting it every step; for all that we like to think we can conquer death through sheer force of personality, our mere descent alone strips away so much of who we were, who we *thought* we were, that when at last we've gotten where we're going, most of us can't even remember why we didn't want to get there in the first place.

The truism's true: It's a one-way trip. And giving everything we have away in order to make it, up to and including ourselves, is just the price – the going rate, if you will – of the ticket.

Last stop, everybody off; elevator to . . . not Hell, no. Not exactly . . .

. . . Goin' down.

Why would I belong in Hell, anyway, even if it did exist? Sifting through what's left of me, I still know I was average, if that: Not too good, not too bad, like Little Bear's porridge. I mean, I never *killed* anybody, except myself. And that—

—that was only the once.

Three years back, and counting: An easy call at the time, with none of the usual hysterics involved. But one day, I simply came home knowing I didn't ever want to wake up the next morning, to have to go to work, and talk to people, and do my job, and act as though nothing were wrong – to see, or know, or worry about anything, ever again. The mere thought of killing myself had become a pure relief, sleep after exhaustion, a sure cure after a long and disgusting illness.

I even had the pills already – for depression, naturally; thank you, Doctor. So I cooked myself a meal elaborate enough to use up everything in my fridge, finally broke open that dusty bottle of good white wine someone had once given me as a graduation present and washed my last, best hope for oblivion down with it, a handful at a time.

When I woke up I had a tube down my throat, and I was in too much pain to even cry about my failure. Dehydration had shrunk my brain to a screaming point, a shaken bag of poison jellyfish. I knew I'd missed my chance, my precious window of opportunity, and that it would never come again. I felt like I'd been lied to. Like I'd lied to myself.

So, with a heavy heart, I resigned myself once more – reluctantly – to the dirty business of living. I walked out the hospital's front doors, slipped back into my little slot, served out my time. Until last week, when I keeled over while reaching for my notebook at yet one more Professional Development Retreat lecture on stress management in the post-Millennial workplace: Hit the floor like a sack of salt with a needle in my chest, throat narrowing – everything there, then gone, irised inward like some silent movie's Vaseline-smeared final dissolve. Dead at twenty-nine of irreparable heart failure, without even enough warning to be afraid of what –

– or who, in my case –

– came next.

Am I the injured party here? I hover, watching, inside and out; I can hear people's thoughts, but that doesn't mean I can judge their motives. My only real option, at this point, is just what the angels keep telling me it is: Move on, move on, move on. But I'm not ready to do that, yet.

There were five of us in the morgue, after all, but the body-snatchers only took two for her to choose from. And of those two . . .

. . . Pat chose me.

Lyle turns up at one, punctual as ever, while Pat's still dripping. She opens the door for him, then drops her towel and stalks nearly naked back to her room, rooting through her bed's top-most layers in search of some clean underwear; though he's obviously seen it all before, neither of them shows any interest in extending this bodily intimacy beyond the realm of the purely familial.

Which only makes sense, now I think about it. In Pat's mind – the only place I've ever encountered Lyle, up till now – their relationship rarely goes any further than strictly business. He's her prime "artistic" pimp, shopping the act she and Ray have been working so hard to perfect to a truly high-class clientele: One time only, supposedly. Though by Lyle's general demeanour, I get the feeling he may already be developing his own ideas about that part.

Pat discards a Pixies concert T with what looks like mould-stains all over the back in favor of her Reg Hartt's Sex And Violence Cartoon Festival one, and returns to find Lyle grimacing over a cup of coffee that's been simmering since at least eight.

"Jesus Corpse, Pats. You could clean cars with this shit."

"Machine's on a timer, I'm not." Then, grabbing a comb, bending over, worrying through those last few knots: "Tonight all set up, or what?"

He shrugs. "Or what." She shoots him a glance, drawing a grin. "Look, I told you it was gonna be one of two places, right? So on we go to Plan B, 's all. The rest's still pretty much as wrote."

" 'Pretty much.' "

"Pretty, baby. Just like you."

And: Is she? I suppose so. Black hair and deep, dark eyes – a certain eccentric symmetry of line and feature, a clever mind, a blind and ruthless will. Any and all of which would've certainly been enough to pull *me* in, back when I was still alive enough to want pulling.

The angels tell me I'm bound for something better now, though. Some form of love precious far beyond the bodily, indescribable to anyone who hasn't tasted it at least once before. Which means there's no earthly way I can possibly know if I *want* to till I'm already there and drinking my fill, already immersed soul-deep in restorative, White Light-infused glory . . .

Convenient, that. As *Saturday Night Live*'s Church Lady so often used to say.

Oh – and "earthly", ha; didn't even catch that one, first time round. Look, angels! The corpse just made a funny.

(I said, *look*.)

But they don't.

Pat tops her shirt with a sweater, and starts in filling the many pockets of army pants with all the various Bone Machine performance necessities: Duct tape, soldering wire, extra batteries. Lyle, meanwhile, drifts away to the video rack, where he amuses himself scanning spines.

"This that first tape he sent you?" he demands suddenly, yanking one.

"Who?"

He waggles it, grinning. "Your boyfriend. RAY-mond."

A shrug. "Pop it and see."

"Pass." Which seems to remind him: "So, Patty – realize you two are sorta tight and this comes sorta late, but exactly how much research you actually do on this freak-o before you signed him up for the program?"

Pat's bent over now, hauling her semi-expensive boots up with both mittened hands. "Enough to know he'll fuck dead bodies if I ask him to," she says, shortly.

" 'Cause he *wants* to."

A short, sharp smile, orthodontic-straight except for that one canine her wisdom teeth pushed out of line, coming in. "Best way to get anyone to do anything, baby. As you should know."

Of course, Pat's hardly objective. Seeing how she's in lust with Ray . . . love, maybe, albeit of a perversely limited sort. Much the same way *he* is, truth be told—

—With "me".

But Lyle, obviously, doesn't feel he can argue the point. So he just returns her smile, talk-show bland and throat-slitting bright, as she reaches for the door handle: Lets them both out, side by side, into a world of gathering cold. All bundled up like Donner Party refugees, and twice as hungry.

And: *Don't follow*, the angels advise me, uselessly. *Don't watch. Don't care.*

But the fact is, I . . . don't. I really don't. Don't feel, or know what I don't feel. Let alone what I do.

D-E-A-D, but way too much still left of me. I'm DEAD, so let me lie. Let me *lie*.

Please.

Pat and Lyle, struggling up the alley and down to the nearest curb. Ray, his obtrusively unobtrusive car – the Rich Pervert-mobile itself, far too clean and anonymous to be used for anything but life's dirtiest little detours – already there to meet them, pluming steam.

And somewhere, awaiting its cue, the reluctant third party in this little triangle-cum-foursome: My body, a water-clock full of blood and other fluids, forever counting down to an explosion that's already happened. A psychic plague-bomb oozing excess pain, a hive for flies, all slick, lily-waxen and faintly bruised in the wake of rigor mortis's ebb, even before Ray's hot mouthings gave birth to that starburst of pale lavender hickeys around what used to be my trachea.

It's not *me*, not in any way that counts – but it's not NOT me, either. And I just, I just . . .

. . . don't . . .

. . . want . . .

. . . them *touching* it anymore.

Either of them.

Going back – as far back as he can, at least – Ray tells Pat that he thinks the first time he really began to understand the true nature of his personal . . . distinction . . . must have been when his parents insisted he visit his beloved grandfather's freshly dead body at the local hospital: Washed, laid out, neatly johnny-clad. His parents had already forewarned him it would look like a mannequin, like something made of plaster, an empty husk. But it wasn't like that, not even vaguely. It looked oddly magnetic, oddly tactile; nothing rotten, or gross, or potentially contagious – soothing, like an old friend. And its only smell was the familiar odor of shed human skin.

Ray wanted to lie down with his head on its sternum, breathe deep and let it cool his fever, this constant ceaseless hammering in his head and heart. To free him, for once and for all, of the febrile hum and spark of his own life.

Since then, Ray's never been able to decide what arouses him more: The concept itself, or the sheer impossibility of its execution. Because anyone can fuck the dead, if they only try hard enough – but the dead, by their very nature, can never fuck *back*. Which is why it has to be guys, though he himself is – in every other way than this – "straight". If that term even applies, under these circumstances.

Their superiority. Their otherness. To him, it's only natural: The dead know more, and knowledge is power. And power, as that old politician once boasted . . . is sexy.

So: Fucked in slaughterhouses, under the hanging racks of meat. Fucked with decay smeared all over them both, in grave-yards, animal cemeteries; sure, buddy – just gimme my cut, you freak, and bend on over. Fucked in mortuaries, the "other" corpses watching impassively. Corpses taking part in his own taking, silent voyeurs, sad puppets in countless sweaty *ménages à mort*. Fucked by guys wearing corpses' skins – and wow, was *that* expensive, mainly because it went against so many kinds of weird sanitation strictures; public health, and all that. Same reason you can't just drop your Grandad in the garden if he happens to croak at your house – or die at home at all, these days, for that matter.

Fucked by the dying – guys so far gone, so far in the financial hole, that they'd do anything to make their next medical bill. A charge, but not quite the same; not the same, and never enough. And finally, back to the morgue alone with condoms and trocar in hand – here's an extra hundred to leave the door ajar, I'll lock up as I leave. No worries.

Money's no problem; Ray *has* money. Too much, some might say – too much free time, and a bit too little to do with it except obsess, jerk off, plan. The idle rich are hard to entertain, Vinnie . . .

Things do keep on escalating, though, often and always. And escalation can bring a bad reputation, especially in some quarters.

Which made it all the more lucky that Ray and Pat happened to find each other, I suppose – for them both.

And for Lyle, of course, albeit from a very different point of view . . . Lyle, to whom falls the onerous yet lucrative task of facilitating this gender-switched post-Millennial Death And The Maiden tableau they've played out every day this week, give or take; same one that would surely rerun itself constantly behind my eyelids if only I still had either eyes to see with, or lids to close on what I didn't want to see. Same one you might well have seen already, if you're just hip and sick enough to have paid Lyle's "finder's fee" up front – or bought the bootleg DV8 tapes he peddles over the Internet, thus far unbeknownst to either of his silent partners.

Like Lyle, I never saw that original "audition" tape on Pat's shelf, either. But as the rundown above should prove, I've certainly heard its précis often enough: Why I Like To Get Screwed By Dead Bodies For The Amusement Of Total Strangers Even When The Money Involved's My Own, in fifty thousand words or more. Ray's confession/manifesto, re-spilled at intervals – after various post-post-mortem Bone Machine-aided orgies, usually – over binges of beer and weed which sometimes culminate in fumbling, gratitude- and guilt-ridden, mutually unsatisfying attempts at "normal" sex. Pat lying slack beneath a sweating, huffing Ray, trying to will her internal temperature down far enough to maintain his shamed half-erection even as her own orgasm builds, inexorably. Cursing the demeaning depths this idiot hunger for him can make her sink to, while simultaneously feeling her fingers literally itch to seize the Machine's controls again and do the whole damn thing over *right*.

Part of me wonders exactly how much detail I need – or care – to go into here, vis-à-vis Pat's "art" and my rather uncomfortable place in its embrace. But then again, close as "I" may get to it in flesh, most of the Bone Machine's complex structural workings will probably always remain a mystery to me. Bolts screwed directly into bones, wires strung like tendons, electrical impulses jumping from brain to finger to keypad to central animatronic switchboard . . .

Pat pulls the strings here, as in all else. When my dead body's making "love" to Ray, it's her moves, her ideas, her smoothing, gentle touch translated through my flesh, which keeps him coming back time and time again; I'm just the medium for her message, a clammy six-foot dildo powered by rods and pistons. A deadweight sex-aid soaked in scented lube to hide the growing spoiled-meat smell, the inevitable wear and tear of Ray's increasingly desperate affections.

But Ray, like any true fetishist, ignores whatever doesn't contribute directly to the fulfillment of his motivating fantasy. He knows our time together's on a (necessarily) tight schedule, so he tries to wring every extra ounce of pleasure he can out of the experience while Pat watches and fumes, trapped behind her rows of switches. He loves the mask, not the face; the made, not the maker. Decay's his groom, and he doesn't want even the shadow of anything else getting in the way of this so-devoutly-desired consummation, this last great graveyard gasp.

It'd be sort of tragic, if it wasn't so – mordantly – funny. Together, Pat and Ray have all the requisite common interests and obsessions, plus a heaping helping of that brain-to-groin combustive spark which so many other relationships are made from; if she was dead (or had the right equipment required to rock his world), they'd be perfect for each other. But her hole just doesn't fit his socket, or vice versa. So the only way she can touch him . . . and make him *want* her to, at least . . .

. . . is with *my* hands.

And more and more, that very fact is already making her dream happy dreams of someday taking a bone-saw to "my" wrists. Of burning them in some Haz-Mat crematorium's fire, like plague-infected monster grasshoppers.

Ray told Pat that he was literally up for her ultimate piece of performance art, to bravely go where none of her other co-conspirators were ever willing to, not even with three condoms' worth of protection. She told Lyle, who instantly cheered her on, visions of Ben Franklin dancing in his money-colored eyes; he paged his pals down at the ME's office, and the deal was struck – cash for flesh, tickets at the door and a fresh new co-star every week, after the old one finally started to rot.

And so it went, a neat little cycle, a perverse new rhythm method. Pat called the shots, Ray did the dance, Lyle racked up the take; they soon got into the habit of partying later, while Lyle was on his way to the bank. Pat, using Ray's addiction to feed her own, like any pusher trading "free" product for not-so-free favors, while Ray replays his own earlier performance for both thair benefits.

It was, and is, a match made in Gomorrah, or maybe Gehenna: Pimp meets girl meets boy meets corpse(s). And everybody's happy.

Everybody alive enough to count, that is.

All that changed once Pat and Lyle fixed Ray up with my mortal coil, though, and he "fell for" it . . . telling her, feverishly, and repeatedly, how this hunk of otherwise nondescript white male meat which just happened to come with my restless spirit attached was the end of his search, the literal em*bodi*ment of all his most cadaver-centric daydreams. Suddenly, his fetish had narrowed and shifted to allow for only this one particular corpse or nothing at all.

And: "You know tomorrow night's gonna have to be curtains for Mr Stinky, right?" She asked him, briskly, after yesterday's post-show pas de deux.

Ray, frowning: "How so?"

Pat reclipped her bra, sponged sweat from her cleavage; I saw the angels' halos reflected in her throat's shiny hollow, a wet white crackle of phantom jewelry. "'Cause he's starting to fall apart, same as the others. Already had to rewire his joints twice just to get him limber enough to limbo – and his scalp's starting to peel, too. Now it's just a matter of time."

"But if you're keeping him refrigerated . . ."

"Yeah, sure. But there's only so far that goes, Ray. No freezer in the world's totally fly-tight; nature of the beast, man."

A pause. Ray stood silent as Pat wriggled back into her jeans, then shot him the raised eyebrow: You comin', or what? Shook his head. And replied, finally—

"Then I guess we're looking at goodbye for me too, Pat."

At that, Pat turned fully, *both* eyebrows up. "You're kidding."

"No."

Because . . . this is the *one*. Remember? The one and only. No substitutes need apply, not even—

(Well, *you*, sweetheart)

Ahhhh, true love.

He feels like he's having a dialogue with it, that's what he's always told her. Like he's finally being privileged, through this nightly series of gag-makingly contortionate sex-show antics, to vicariously experience the ecstatic transformation that my corpse is already undergoing – the transition from flesh to fleshlessness, an all-expenses-paid tour through time's metaphorical flensing chamber. To share in the experience as it sloughs the residue of its own mortality off like a scab, revealing some clean, invisible new form lurking beneath.

My body, my husk. My shucked, slimy former skin.

It's not *pure*, though, for fuck's sweet sake. It's not *perfected*. It has no "secret wisdom" to impart. And as for powerful, well . . .

If it really *was* powerful – if *I* was – then we wouldn't be here, would we?

Any of us.

The argument went on for some time, back and forth: Pat's voice soaring snappishly while Ray stayed quiet but firm, unshakable. There was an element of betrayal to her mounting disbelief, as both of them well knew. Suffice to say, Lyle probably wouldn't have been too happy to find out that his star attraction had decided to retire either. Not that Pat even seemed to be thinking of things from that particular angle.

"It's just a fucking *corpse*, Ray. You've done fifty of 'em already, most of 'em long before you ever met me—"

Ray nodded. "Because I was looking for the *right* one."

"And this is it?"

"In my opinion."

She stared, snorted.

"Lyle won't like it."

"Fuck Lyle."

A sigh: "Been there."

The unsaid implication – goodbye to it, to this, the nightly grind. To Lyle's meal ticket. And, by extension, goodbye . . .

(To me?)

Me meaning her. As well as me meaning "me".

Before, whenever Ray's beaux got too pooped to preserve, the routine took over. Lyle got on the pager again, handing out more of Ray's money; the bodies made their exit, stage wherever. Parts in a dump, an acid-soaked tub-ring, concrete at the bottom of a lake, with all trace of Ray's touch, or Pat's – or Lyle's, for that matter, not that Lyle ever *touches* the Bone Machine's prey – salved away in disposal.

Which should be enough, surely: Enough to wash this lingering wisp of me clean and let me rise. Sponge the fingerprints from my soul, and all that good, metaphorical stuff. But—

(but)

At first I just hovered above, horrified, longing for the angels to cover my see-through face with their equally see-through wings. So grotesquely helpless to do anything but watch, and wait, and watch some more. Wait some more. Watch some more. Repeat, repeat, repeat.

But then, slowly . . . through sheer, profane will alone, one assumes, while my constant companions loomed ever closer in (literally) holier-than-thou disapproval . . .

Don't look.

But I have to.

Move on.

But – I CAN'T.

(Not yet.)

. . . I found myself starting to be able to feel it once more, from the inside out. The ghost of a ghost of a ghost of a sensation. Ray's mouth on "mine", sucking at my cold tongue like a formaldehyde-flavored lollipop. "My" muscles on his, bunching like poisoned tapeworms.

Taking shaky repossession part by part; hacking back into my own former nervous system synapse by painful synapse, my shot neural net fizzing at cross purposes like that eviscerated eight-track we used to have in the student lounge back at my old high school – the one you could only make change tapes by reaching inside and touching two stripped wires together, teeth gritted against the inevitable shock.

Pat sends her commands and I . . . resist, just a fraction of a micro-inch; she's offput, suspects that her callibrations aren't quite as exact as she'd thought. But even as she reworks them, Ray strains towards me and I . . . strain back. Rise to meet him, halfway. I know he sees what I'm doing, if only on a subconscious level. Her too.

Because: It's like cheating, isn't it? Always is, when love's involved. And lovers *always* know.

"I want to do it," he told her in the car, on the way home. "I want to be the one, this time."

"The one to do what?"

"You know. Finish it."

Pat narrowed her dark, dark eyes. "Finish it," she repeated. "Like – get rid of it? Destroy it yourself?"

Rip it apart, tear it limb from limb, eat it (un) alive. If he couldn't have it . . .

Dark eyes, with green sliding to meet them: Money-colored too, in a far more vivid way. Because it's not that Ray's unattractive, that he couldn't possibly indulge himself any other way. In fact, if you look at it too closely – closer than he probably wants you to, or wants to himself – you'd have to conclude that the *indulgence* is doing things the way he's chosen to.

"You're worried about what Lyle'd think?"

She shrugged. "His customers, maybe."

"Should be a hell of a show, though."

. . . Should be.

Another cool look, another pause – silence between them, smooth as a stone. All that frustrated longing, that self-bemused *ache*; enough to power a city, to set both their carefully constructed internal worlds on fire.

The angels ruffle their pinions, disapprovingly. But I was human once, just flawed and impermanent enough to understand.

I mean, we all want what we want, don't we? Even when it's impossible, perverse, ridiculous, we want just what WE want. And nothing else will do.

Move ON.

Be at PEACE.

But: I can't, can't. Won't. Because I want . . . what I want. Nothing else.

(Nothing.)

"You're the last of the red-hot Romantics, Ray," Pat told him, eventually, knowing what she was agreeing to, but not caring. Or thinking she knew, at least. But knowing only the half of it.

She's had her dance, after all, like Ray's had his: Now I'll have mine, and be done with it. Change partners mid-song; no harm in that. And if there is . . .

. . . If there *is*, well – it's not like anyone'll be complaining.

And now it's past midnight, the zero hour. Showtime. Lyle's customers file in as he sets up the cameras, trance-silent with anticipation: Stoned suburbanites, jaded superfan ultra-scene-sters, unsocialized Western *otaku* with bad BO and worse fashion sense. Teens who followed the wrong set of memes and ended up somewhere way too cool for school, let alone anywhere else. Many seem breathless, barely able to sit still. Some – few, thankfully – have actually brought dates, rummaging absently between each other's thighs as they lick their lips, eyes firmly on the prize: The Bone Machine itself, a slumped mantis of hooks and cords; Pat, strapping "my" body in for its final run around Ray's block, suturing it fast with duct tape. Slipping the requisite genital prosthetic mini-bladder tube up the corpse's urethral tract and pumping it erect before condoming the whole package shut once more . . .

The Machine – model number five, rebuilt on site by Pat herself, due to be broken down to component parts and blue-prints when the spectacle's dollar-value finally wears itself thin – occupies a discontinued butchering lab somewhere in the Hospi-tality area of a shut-down community college campus: Ray's coin bought a deal with security guards who let them in at night after the campus manager goes home, as well as access to a walk-in fridge/freezer just big enough to keep their mutual "carrionette" pliant. It's a vast, slick cave of a place whose dark-toned walls are hung with 1960s charts of cartoon pigs and cows tattooed with dotted "cut here" lines, whose sloping concrete floor still sports drains and runnels to catch blood already congealed into forty years' worth of collective grease-stink. Under the heat of Lyle's lights the air is hot and close, smell thick enough to cut: Meat, sweat, anticipation.

Transgression a-comin'. That all-purpose po/mo word poseurs of every description love so well. But there are all kinds of transgressions, aren't there? Transgression against society's standards, the laws of God and man, against others, against yourself . . .

Here's Pat, gearing up – eyes intent, face studiously deadpan. Here's Lyle, all sleaze and charm, spinning his strip-club barker's spiel. Here's "me", slug-pale and seeping slightly, yet already beginning to stir as the connections flare, the cables pull, the hip-pistons give a tentative little preliminary thrust and grind. And—

—Here's Ray, nude, gleaming with antibacterial gel. Right on cue.

See the man, see the corpse. See the man see the corpse. See the man? See the *corpse*?

Okay, then.

. . . Let's get this party started, shall we?

Jolt forward, pixilate, zoom in – not much foreplay, at this stage of the game. Just wind and wipe into Ray bent l-shaped and hooking his heels in the small of my jouncing avatar's back, clawing passion-sharp down its slack sides. Pat puppets the Machine's load forward, digging deep, straining for that magic buried trigger; Ray scissors himself and "me" together even harder, so hard I hear something crack. And blood comes welling: Fluid, anyway, tinged darker with decay. Blood already starbursting the cillia of "my" upturned eyes, broken vessels knit in a pinky-red wash of old petecchial haemorrhaging—

Ray groaning, teeth bared. Lyle leaning in for the all-important ECU. Pat, bent to the board, her hair lank and damp across her frowning forehead.

Ray, grabbing at "my" hair, feeling its mooring slip and slide like rotten chicken-skin. Taking a big, biting tug at "my" bile-soaked lower lip, swapping far more than spit, before rearing back again for a genuine chomp. Starting to – *chew*.

Pat gags: Ewwww, rubbery. You kiss your girlfriend with that mouth?

(Not any more, I guess.)

First the bottom lip, then the upper. A bit of "my" cheek. Sticky cuspids and canines like stars in a gum-pink evening sky. Ray's tearing at "my" sides, "my" chest, "my" throat, as the audience coos and gasps; Lyle's still filming. And Pat's twisting knobs like a maniac, trying to match Ray's growing frenzy, fighting with all her might to keep the show's regularly scheduled action on track: Destruction, ingestion, transgression with a capital "T". Fighting *Ray*, really, as he guides "my" exposed jaws to his own neck again and again, like he's daring "me" to – somehow – bite in, bite down, pop his jugular and give all his fans the ultimate perverted thrill of their collective lives.

Because: Ray feels himself going now, in the Japanese sense. Knows just how late it's getting, how soon the high from this last wrench and spurt will fade. Knows that no possible climax to this drama will ever seem good enough, *climactic* enough, no matter WHAT he does to "me". I can see it in his eyes. I can—

(*see* it)

See it. "I" *can*. And "I", I, *I* . . .

I feel myself. Feel *myself*. Coming, too.

Feel myself *there*. At last.

Feel Ray hug me to him and hug him back, arms contracting floppily – feel that pin Pat put in my shoulder last time snap as the joint finally pulls free, and tighten my grip with the other before Ray can start to slip. Feel my clotty lashes bat, a wet cough in my dry throat; the sudden gasp of breath comes out like a sneeze, spraying his face with reddish-brown gunk. See Ray goggle up at me, as Lyle gives a girly little scream: Cry to God and Pat's full name, reduced to panicked consonants. HolyshitPahtriSHA-FUCK!

Pat's head comes up fast, hair flipping. Eyes so wide they seem square.

My tongue creaks and Ray hasn't left me much lip to shape words with, but I know we understand each other. Like I said, I can SEE it.

Gotta go, Ray. You want to come with?

Well, *do* you?

And Ray . . . nods.

And I . . .

. . . I give him. What he wants.

And oh, but the angels are screaming at me now like a Balkan choir massacre, all at once – glorious, polyphonic, chanting chains of scream: Sing *No*, sing *stop*, sing *thou shalt thou shalt thou shalt NOT.* Their halos flare like sunspots, making the whole room pulse – hiss and pop, paparazzi flashbulb storm, a million-sparkler overdrip curtain of angry white light.

(Sorry, guys. Looks like revenge comes before redemption, this time round.)

Ray pulls me close, spasming, as my front teeth find his Adam's apple. Blood jets up. The audience shrieks, almost in unison.

I look over Ray's shoulder at Pat, frozen, her board so hot that it's starting to smoke. And I smile, with Ray's blood all over my mouth.

So hook *him* up to the Bone Machine now, Pats – make a movie, while you're at it. Take a picture, it'll last longer. Take your turn. Take your time.

But this is how it breaks down: He's gone, long gone, like I'm gone, too. Like *we*'re gone, together. Gone.

Gone to lie down.

Gone to forgive, to forget.

Gone, gone, finally—

—To sleep.

Aaaaaah, *yes.*

The sheep look up, the angels down. And I'm done, at long, long last – blown far, far away, the last of my shredded self trailing behind like skin, like wings, a plastic bag blowing.

Done, and I'm out: Forgiven, forgotten, sleeping. Loving nothing. Being nothing. Feeling none of your pain, fearing none of your anger, craving none of your – anything. Anymore.

Down here where things settle, down below the bridge, the weighing-room, the House of Dust itself – down here, where our faces fall away, where we lose our names, where we no longer care what brought us here, or why . . . I don't care, finally, because (finally) I don't have to. And in this way, I'm just the same as every other dead person – thank that God I've never met, and probably never will: No longer mere trembling meaty prey for the thousand natural shocks that flesh is heir to; no longer cursed to live with death breathing down my neck, metaphoric or literal.

Which only makes the predicament of people like Ray – or like Pat, for that matter – seem all the crueller, in context. Since the weakness of the living is their enduring need to still love us, and to

feel we still love them in return; to believe that we are still the
same people who were once capable of loving them back. Even
though we're, simply . . .

. . . Not.

Down here, down here: The psychic sponge-bed, the hole at the
world's heart, that well of poison loneliness every cemetery elm
knows with its great tap-root. Here's where we float, my fellow
dead and I – one of whom might *be* Ray, not that he or I would
recognize each other now.

The keenest irony of all being that I suppose Ray killed himself
for *me*, in a way – killed himself, by letting me kill him. Even
though . . . until that very last moment we shared together . . .
we'd never really even met.

Come with me, I said. Not caring if he could, but suspecting—

(rightly, it turns out)

—I'd probably never know, in the final analysis, if he actually
did.

Down here, where we float in a comforting soup of nonde-
scription – charred and eyeless, Creation's joke. Big Bang detritus
bought with Jesus' blood.

Ash, drifting free, from an eternally burning heaven.

MARK SAMUELS

The White Hands

MARK SAMUELS IS THE author of two short-story collections, *The White Hands and Other Weird Tales* from Tartarus Press, and *Black Altars*, published by Rainfall Books. New stories were recently published in *A Walk on the Darkside* edited by John Pelan, and *Strange Attractor Journal* #2, edited by Mark Pilkington.

When not writing weird fiction, the author often spends his time wandering the London streets in search of scenes of glamorous decay with his wife, the acclaimed Mexican writer Adriana Diaz-Enciso.

About "The White Hands", Samuels explains: "For editorial reasons it was not possible to include the complete text of this story in my Tartarus book, so I'm therefore delighted to see it finally appear here in the form which I consider most satisfactory."

YOU MAY REMEMBER Alfred Muswell, whom devotees of the weird tale will know as the author of numerous articles on the subject of literary ghost stories. He died in obscurity just over a year ago.

Muswell had been an Oxford don for a time, but left the cloisters of the University after an academic scandal. A former student (now a journalist) wrote of him in a privately published memoir:

Muswell attempted single-handedly to alter the academic criteria of excellence in literature. He sought to eradicate what he termed the "tyranny of materialism and realism" from his teaching. He would loom over us in his black robes at lectures and tutorials, tearing prescribed and classic books to shreds with his gloved hands, urging us to read instead work by the likes of Sheridan Le Fanu, Vernon Lee, M.R. James and Lilith Blake. Muswell was a familiar sight amongst the squares and courtyards of the colleges at night and would stalk abroad like some bookish revenant. He had a very plump face and a pair of circular spectacles. His eyes peered into the darkness with an indefinable expression that could be somewhat disturbing.

You will recall that Muswell's eccentric theories about literature enjoyed a brief but notorious vogue in the 1950s. In a series of essays in the short-lived American fantasy magazine *The Necrophile*, he championed the supernatural tale. This was at a time when other academics and critics were turning away from the genre in disgust, following the illiterate excesses of pulp magazines such as *Weird Tales*. Muswell argued that the anthropocentric concerns of realism had the effect of stifling the much more profound study of infinity. Contemplation of the infinite, he contended, was the faculty that separated man from beast. Realism, in his view, was the literature of the prosaic. It was the quest for the hidden mysteries, he contended, which formed the proper subject of all great literature. Muswell also believed that literature, in its highest form, should unravel the secrets of life and death. This latter concept was never fully explained by him but he hinted that its attainment would involve some actual alteration in the structure of reality itself. This, perhaps inevitably, led to him being dismissed in academic circles as a foolish mystic.

After his quiet expulsion from Oxford, Muswell retreated to the lofty heights of Highgate. From here, the London village that had harboured Samuel Taylor Coleridge during the final phase of his struggle against opium addiction, Muswell continued his literary crusade. A series of photographs reproduced in the fourth issue of *The Necrophile* show Muswell wandering through the leafy streets of Highgate clad in his black three-piece suit, cigarette jammed between lips, plump and bespectacled. In one of his gloved hands is a book of ghost stories by the writer he most admired, Lilith Blake. This Victorian author is perhaps best known for her collection of short stories, *The Reunion and Others*. Then, as now, fabulously rare, this book was printed in an edition of only one hundred copies. Amongst the cognoscenti, it has acquired legendary status. Muswell was undoubtedly the greatest authority on her life and works. He alone possessed the little that remained of her extant correspondence, as well as diaries, photographs and other personal effects.

In moving to Highgate, Muswell was perhaps most influenced by the fact that Blake had been resident in the village for all of the twenty-two years of her brief life. Her mortal remains were interred in the old West Cemetery in Swain's Lane.

I first met Alfred Muswell after writing a letter to him requesting information about Lilith Blake for an article I was planning on supernatural writers of the late nineteenth and early twentieth centuries. After an exchange of correspondence he suggested that we should meet one afternoon in the reading room of the Highgate Literary and Scientific Institution. From there he would escort me to his rooms, which, apparently, were difficult to find without help, being hidden in the maze of narrow brick passageways beyond Pond Square.

It was a very cold, clear winter afternoon when I alighted at Highgate Underground station and made my way up Southwood Lane. Snow had fallen since the night before and the lane was almost deserted. Only the sound of my footsteps crunching in the brittle snow broke the silence. When I reached Highgate Village I paused for a while to take in my surroundings. The Georgian houses were cloaked in white and glittered in the freezing sunshine. A sharp wind blew chilly gusts across the sagging roofs and chimney pots. One or two residents, clad in greatcoats and well muffled, plodded warily along.

I accosted one of these pedestrians and was directed by him towards the Institute. This was a whitewashed structure, two floors high, facing the square on the corner of Swain's Lane. Through one of the ground-floor windows I could see the glow of a coal fire within and a plump man reading in an easy chair. It was Alfred Muswell.

After dusting the snowflakes from my clothes, I made my way inside and introduced myself to him. He struggled out of his chair,

stood upright like a hermit crab quitting its shell, and threw out a
gloved hand for me to grasp. He was dressed in his habitual black
suit, a cigarette drooping from his bottom lip. His eyes peered at
me intensely from behind those round glasses. His hair had
thinned and grown white since the photographs in *The Necrophile*. The loss of hair was mainly around the crown, giving him a
somewhat monkish appearance.

I hung up my duffel coat and scarf and sat down in the chair
facing him.

"We can sit here undisturbed for a few more minutes at least,"
he said. "The other members are in the library attending some
lecture about that charlatan James Joyce."

I nodded as if in agreement, but my attention was fixed on
Muswell's leather gloves. He seemed always to wear them. He had
worn a similar pair in *The Necrophile* photographs. I noticed the
apparent emaciation of the hands and long fingers that the gloves
concealed. His right hand fidgeted constantly with his cigarette
while the fingers of his left coiled and uncoiled repeatedly. It was
almost as if he were uncomfortable with the appendages.

"I'm very pleased to talk with a fellow devotee of Lilith Blake's
tales," he said, in his odd, strained voice.

"Oh, I wouldn't describe myself as a devotee. Her work is
striking, of course, but my own preferences are for Blackwood
and Machen. Blake seems to me to lack balance. Her world is one
of unremitting gloom and decay."

Muswell snorted at my comment. He exhaled a great breath of
cigarette smoke in my direction and said:

"Unremitting gloom and decay? Rather say that she makes
desolation glorious! I believe that De Quincey once wrote: 'Holy
was the grave. Saintly its darkness. Pure its corruption.' Words
that describe Lilith Blake's work perfectly. Machen indeed! That
red-faced old coot with his deluded Anglo-Catholic rubbish! The
man was a drunken clown obsessed by sin. And Blackwood?
Pantheistic rot that belongs to the Stone Age. The man wrote
mainly for money and he wrote too much. No, no. Believe me, if
you want the truth beyond the frontier of appearances it is to
Lilith Blake that you must turn. She never compromises. Her
stories are infinitely more than mere accounts of supernatural
phenomena . . ."

His voice had reached a peak of shrillness and it was all I could do not to squirm in my chair. Then he seemed to regain his composure and drew a handkerchief across his brow.

"You must excuse me. I have allowed my convictions to ruin my manners. I so seldom engage in debate these days that when I do I become overexcited." He allowed himself to calm down and was about to speak again when a side door opened and a group of people bustled into the room. They were chatting about the Joyce lecture that had evidently just finished. Muswell got to his feet and made for his hat and overcoat. I followed him.

Outside, in the cold afternoon air, he looked back over his shoulder and crumpled up his face in a gesture of disgust.

"How I detest those fools," he intoned.

We trudged through the snow, across the square and into a series of passageways. Tall buildings with dusty windows pressed upon us from both sides and, after a number of twists and turns, we reached the building that contained Muswell's rooms. They were in the basement and we walked down some well-worn steps outside, leaving the daylight above us.

He opened the front door and I followed him inside.

Muswell flicked on the light switch and a single bulb suspended from the ceiling and reaching halfway towards the bare floor revealed the meagre room. On each of the walls were long bookcases stuffed with volumes. There was an armchair and footstool in one corner along with a small, circular table on which a pile of books teetered precariously. A dangerous-looking Calor gas fire stood in the opposite corner. Muswell brought another chair (with a canvas back and seat) from an adjoining room and invited me to sit down. Soon afterwards he hauled a large trunk from the same room. It was extremely old and bore the mono-gram "L.B." on its side. He unlocked the trunk with some ceremony, and then sat down, lighting yet another cigarette, his stare fixed on my face.

I took a notebook from my pocket and, drawing sheaves of manuscripts from the trunk, began to scan them. It seemed dark stuff, and rather strange, but just what I needed for the article. And there was a mountain of it to get through. Muswell, mean-while, made a melancholy remark, apropos of nothing, the significance of which I did not appreciate until much later.

"Loneliness," he said, "can drive a man into mental regions of extreme strangeness."

I nodded absently. I had found a small box and, on opening it, my excitement mounted. It contained a sepia-coloured photographic portrait of Lilith Blake, dated 1890. It was the first I had seen of her, and must have been taken just before her death. Her beauty was quite astonishing.

Muswell leaned forward. He seemed to be watching my reaction with redoubled interest.

Lilith Blake's raven-black and luxuriant hair curled down to her shoulders. Her face was oval, finished with a small pointed chin. The eyes, wide apart and piercing, seemed to gaze across the vastness of the time that separated us. Her neck was long and pale, her forehead rounded and stray curls of hair framed the temples. The fleshy lips were slightly parted and her small, sharp teeth gleamed whitely. Around her neck hung a string of pearls and she wore a jet-black velvet dress. The most delicate and lovely white hands that I had ever seen were folded across her bosom. Although the alabaster skin of her face and neck was extremely pale, her hands were paler. They were whiter than the purest snow. It was as if daylight had never touched them. The length of her graceful fingers astonished me.

I must have sat there for some time in silent contemplation of that intoxicating image. Muswell, becoming impatient, finally broke my reverie in a most violent and unnecessary manner. He snatched the photograph from me and held it in the air while he spoke, his voice rising to a feverish pitch:

"Here is the hopeless despair of one haunted by the night. One who had gone down willingly into the grave with a black ecstasy in her heart instead of fear!"

I could only sit there in stunned silence. To me, Muswell seemed close to a complete nervous breakdown.

Later, Muswell must have helped me to sort through the various papers in the trunk. I remember little of the detail. I do know that by the time I finally left his rooms and found my way back to the square through the snow, I had realized that my research into Blake's work would be of the utmost importance to my academic career. Muswell had treasure in his keeping, a literary gold mine, and, given the right handling, it could make my name.

After that, my days were not my own. Try as I might, I could not expunge the vision of Blake from my mind. Her face haunted my thoughts, beckoning me onwards in my quest to discover the true meaning of her work. The correspondence between Muswell and myself grew voluminous as I sought to arrange a time when I would be enabled to draw further on his collection. For a while he seemed to distrust my mounting interest, but at last he accepted my enthusiasm as genuine. He welcomed me as a kindred spirit. By a happy chance, I even managed to rent a room in his building.

And so, during the course of the winter months, I shut myself away with Muswell, poring over Blake's letters and personal effects. I cannot deny that the handling of those things began to feel almost sacrilegious. But as I read the letters, diaries and notebooks I could see that Muswell had spoken only the truth when he described Blake as supreme in the field of supernatural literature.

He would scuttle around his library like a spider, climbing stepladders and hauling out volumes from the shelves, passing them down through the gloomy space to me. He would mark certain passages that he believed furthered a greater understanding of Blake's life and work. Outside, the frequent snow showers filled the gap between his basement window and the pavement above with icy whiteness. My research was progressing well, my notebook filling up with useful quotations and annotations, but somehow I felt that I was failing to reach the essence of Lilith; the most potent aspect of her vision was eluding my understanding. It was becoming agonizing to be so close to her, and yet to feel that her most secret and beautiful mysteries were buried from my view.

"I believe," Muswell once said, "that mental isolation is the essence of weird fiction. Isolation when confronted with disease, with madness, with horror and with death. These are the reverberations of the infinity that torments us. It is Blake who delineates these echoes of doom for us. She alone exposes our inescapable blind stumbling towards eternal annihilation. She alone shows our souls screaming in the darkness with none to heed our cries. Ironic, isn't it, that such a beautiful young woman should possess an imagination so dark and riddled with nightmare?"

Muswell took a deep drag on his cigarette and, in contemplating his own words, seemed to gaze through everything into a limitless void.

Sometimes, when Muswell was away, I would have the collection to myself. Blake's personal letters became as sacred relics to me. Her framed photograph attained a special significance, and I was often unable to prevent myself from running my fingers around the outline of her lovely face.

As time passed, and my research into Lilith Blake's oeuvre began to yield ever more fascinating results, I felt that I was now ready to afford her the posthumous attention that she so richly deserved. Whereas previously I had planned to merely include references to her work in my lengthy article on supernatural fiction during the late nineteenth and early twentieth centuries, I now realized that she had to be accorded a complete critical book of her own, such was the importance of the literary legacy I had stumbled across through my association with Muswell. It seemed obvious to me that the man had little real idea of the prime importance of the materials in his possession and that his reclusive lifestyle had led him to regard anything relating to this dead and beautiful creature as his own personal property. His understanding was hopelessly confused by the unsubstantiated assertion that he made of the importance of the "work behind the works", which I took to mean some obscure mystical interpretation he had formulated in his own muddled, ageing brain.

One afternoon he came across me working on my proposed book and took an apparent polite interest in my writing, but mingled in with that interest was an infuriating sarcasm. I voiced my contention that Blake deserved a much higher place in the literary pantheon. The only reasonable explanation for the failure of her work to achieve this was, I had discovered, the almost total lack of contemporary interest in it. I could trace no extant reviews of *The Reunion and Others* in any of the literary journals of the time nor any mention of her in the society columns of the period. At this statement Muswell actually laughed out loud. Holding one of his cigarettes between those thin, gloved fingers he waved it in the air dismissively, and said:

"I should have thought that you would have found the silence surrounding her person and work suggestive, as I did. Do not mistake silence for indifference. Any imbecile might make that erroneous conclusion and indeed many have done so in the past. Lilith Blake was no Count Stenbock, merely awaiting rediscovery. She was *deliberately* not mentioned; her work was specifically excluded from consideration. How much do you think was paid simply to ensure that she had a fitting tomb in Highgate Cemetery? But pray continue, tell me more of your article and I shall try to take into consideration your youthful naivety."

As I continued to expand on my theories I saw clearly that Muswell began to smirk in a most offensive fashion. Why, it was as if he were humouring me! My face flushed and I stood up, my back rigid with tension. I was close to breaking point and could not tolerate this old fool's patronizing attitude any longer. He took a step backwards and bowed, rather affectedly, in some idiotic gentlemanly gesture. But as he did so, he almost lost his footing, as if a bout of dizziness had overcome him. I was momentarily startled by the action and he took the opportunity to make his exit. But before he did so he uttered some departing words:

"If you knew what I know, my friend, and perhaps you soon will, then you would find this literary criticism as horribly amusing as I do. But I am extremely tired and will leave you to your work."

It seemed obvious to me at that point that Muswell was simply not fit to act as the trustee for Lilith Blake's estate. Moreover, his theatrics and lack of appreciation for my insights indicated progressive mental deterioration. I would somehow have to wrest control over the estate from his enfeebled grasp, for the sake of Blake's reputation.

The opportunity came more quickly than I could have dared hope.

One evening in February Muswell returned from one of his infrequent appointments looking particularly exhausted. I had noticed the creeping fatigue in his movements for a number of weeks. In addition to an almost constant sense of distraction he had also lost a considerable amount of weight. His subsequent confession did not, in any case, come as a shock.

"The game is up for me," he said. "I am wasting away. The doctor says I will not last much longer. I am glad that the moment of my assignation with Blake draws near. You must ensure that I am buried with her."

Muswell contemplated me from across the room, the light of the dim electric bulb reflecting off the lenses of his spectacles and veiling the eyes behind. He continued:

"There are secrets that I have hidden from you, but I will reveal

them now. I have come to learn that there are those who, though
dead, lie in their coffins beyond the grip of decay. The power of
eternal visions preserves them: there they lie, softly dead and
dreaming. Lilith Blake is one of these and I shall be another. You
will be our guardian in this world. You will ensure that our bodies
are not disturbed. Once dead, we must not be awakened from the
eternal dream. It is for the protection of Lilith and myself that I
have allowed you to share in my thoughts and her literary legacy.
Everything will make sense once you have read her final works."

He climbed up the steepest stepladder to the twilight of the
room's ceiling and took a metal box from the top of one of the
bookcases. He unlocked it and drew from within an old writing
book bound in crumpled black leather. The title page was written
in Lilith Blake's distinctive longhand style. I could see that it bore
the title *The White Hands and Other Tales*.

"This volume," he said, handing it to me, "contains the final
stories. They establish the truth of all that I have told you. The
book must now be published. I want to be vindicated after I die.
This book will prove, in the most shocking way, the supremacy of
the horror tale over all other forms of literature. As I intimated to
you once before, these stories are not *accounts* of supernatural
phenomena but are supernatural phenomena in themselves.

"Understand this: Blake was dead when these stories were
conceived. But she still dreams and transmitted these images from
her tomb to me so that I might transcribe them for her. When you
read them you will know that I am not insane. All will become
clear to you. You will understand how, at the point of death, the
eternal dream is begun. It allows dissolution of the body to be
held at bay for as long as one continues the dreaming."

I realized that Muswell's illness had deeply affected his mind. In
order to bring him back to some awareness of reality I said: "You
say that Blake telepathically dictated the stories and you tran-
scribed them? Then how is it that the handwriting is hers and not
your own?"

Muswell smiled painfully, paused, and then, for the first and
last time, took off his gloves. The hands were Lilith Blake's, the
same pale, attenuated forms I recognized from her photograph.

"I asked for a sign that I was not mad," said Muswell, "and it
was given to me."

*   *   *

Four weeks later Muswell died.

The doctor's certificate listed the cause of death as heart failure. I had been careful, and as he was already ill, there was little reason for the authorities to suspect anything.

Frankly, I had never countenanced the idea of fulfilling any of Muswell's requests and I arranged for his body to be cremated and interred at Marylebone and St Pancras Cemetery, amongst a plain of small, anonymous graves and headstones. He would not rest at Highgate Cemetery alongside Lilith Blake.

The ceremony was a simple one and beside myself there were no other mourners in attendance. Muswell's expulsion from Oxford had ensured that his old colleagues were wary of keeping in touch with him and there were no surviving members of his family who chose to pay their last respects. The urn containing his ashes was interred in an unmarked plot and the priest who presided over the affair muttered his way through the rites in a mechanical, indifferent fashion. As the ceremony concluded and I made my way across that dull sepulchral plain, under a grey and miserable sky, I had a sense of finality. Muswell was gone for ever and had found that oblivion he seemed so anxious to avoid.

It was a few days later that I made my first visit to Lilith Blake's vault. She had been interred in the old west section of Highgate Cemetery and I was unable to gain access alone. There were only official tours of the place available and I attended one, but afterwards I paid the guide to conduct me privately to Blake's vault. We had to negotiate our way through a tangle of over-grown pathways and crumbling gravestones. The vault was located in a near-inaccessible portion of the hillside cemetery and as we proceeded through the undergrowth, with thick brambles catching on our trousers, the guide told me that he had only once before visited this vault. This had been in the company of another man whose description led me to conclude that it had been Muswell himself. The guide mentioned that this particular area was a source of some curiosity to the various guides, volunteers and conservationists who worked here. Although wildlife flourished in other parts of the cemetery, here it was conspicuous by its absence. Even the birds seemed to avoid the place.

I remember distinctly that the sun had just set and that we reached the tomb in the twilight. The sycamores around us only added to the gloom. Then I caught sight of an arched roof covered with ivy just ahead, and the guide told me that we had reached our destination. As we approached it and the structure came fully into view I felt a mounting sense of anticipation. Some of the masonry had crumbled away but it was still an impressive example of High Victorian Gothic architecture. The corners of its square exterior were adorned with towers and each side boasted a miniature portico. On one of the sides, almost obliterated by neglect and decay, was a memorial stone, bearing the epitaph: LILITH BLAKE. BORN 25 DECEMBER 1874. DIED 1 NOVEMBER 1896.

"It is getting late," the guide whispered to me. "We must get back."

I saw his face in the gloom and he had a restless expression. His words had broken in on the strange silence that enveloped the area. I nodded absently, but made my way around to the front of the vault and the rusty trellis gates blocking the entrance to a stairway that led down to Lilith's coffin. Peering through the gates I could see the flight of stairs, covered by lichen, but darkness obscured its lower depths. The guide was at my elbow now and tugging my jacket sleeve.

"Come on, come on," he moaned. "I could get in real trouble for doing this."

There was something down there. I had the unnerving sensation that I was, in turn, being scrutinized by some presence in that perpetual darkness. It was almost as if it were trying to communicate with me, and images began to form in my mind, flashes of distorted scenes, of corpses that did not rot, of dreams that things no longer human might dream.

Then the guide got a grip of my arm and began forcibly dragging me away. I stumbled along with him as if in a trance, but the hallucinations seemed to fade the further away we got from the vault and by the time we reached the main gate I had regained my mental faculties. Thereafter the guide refused any request that I made for him to again take me to the vault and my attempts to persuade his colleagues were met with the same response. In the end I was no longer even granted access to the cemetery on official tours. I later learned that my connection with Muswell had been discovered and that he had caused much trouble to the cemetery authorities in the past with his demands for unsupervised access. On one occasion there had even been threats of legal action for trespassing.

As indicated, Muswell had informed me that I was to be his literary executor and thus his collection of Blakeiana was left in my control. I also gained possession of his rooms. So I turned again to the study of Blake's work, hoping therein to further my understanding of the enigma that had taken control of my life. I had still to read *The White Hands and Other Tales* and had been put off doing so by Muswell's insistence that this would enlighten me. I still held to the view that his mystical interpretation was fallacious and the thought that this book might be what he actually claimed it to be was almost detestable to me. I wanted desperately to believe that Muswell had written the book himself, rather than as a conduit for Blake. And yet, even if I dismissed the fact of his peculiar hands, so like Blake's own, even if I put that down to some self-inflicted mutilation due to his long-disordered mental state, not to mention the book's comparatively recent age, still there remained the experience at the vault to undermine my certainty. And so it was to *The White Hands and Other Tales* that I turned, hoping there to determine matters once and for all.

I had only managed to read the title story. Frankly, the book was too hideous for anyone but a lunatic to read in its entirety. The tale was like an incantation. The further one progressed the more incomprehensible and sinister the words became. They were sometimes reversed and increasingly obscene. The words in that book conjured visions of eternal desolation. The little that I had read had already damaged my own mind. I became obsessed with the idea of Blake lying in her coffin, dreaming and waiting for me to liberate her.

During the nights of sleeplessness her voice would call across the dark. When I was able to sleep strange dreams came to me. I would be walking among pale shades in an overgrown and crumbling necropolis. The moonlight seemed abnormally bright and even filtered down to the catacombs where I would follow the shrouded form of Lilith Blake. The world of the dead seemed to be replacing my own.

For weeks, I drew down the blinds in Muswell's library, shutting out the daylight, lost in my speculations.

As time passed I began to wonder just why Muswell had been so insistent that he must be interred with Blake at all costs? My experiences at her vault and the strange hallucinations that I had suffered: might they not have been authentic after all? Could it be that Muswell had actually divined some other mode of existence beyond death, which I too had gleaned only dimly? I did not reach this conclusion lightly. I had explored many avenues of philosophical enquiry before coming back again and again to the conclusion that I might have to rely on Muswell's own interpretation. The critical book on Blake that I proposed to write floundered, lost in its own limitations. For, incredible as it seemed, the only explanation that lay before me was that the corpse itself did harbour some form of unnatural sentience, and that close contact with it brought final understanding of the mystery.

I sought to solve a riddle beyond life and death yet feared the answer. The image that held the solution to the enigma which tormented me was the corpse of Lilith Blake. I had to see it in the flesh.

I decided that I would arrange for the body to be exhumed and brought to me here in Muswell's – *my* – rooms. It took me weeks to make the necessary contacts and raise the money required. How difficult it can be to get something done, even something so seemingly simple! How tedious the search for the sordid haunts of the necessary types, the hints dropped in endless conversations with untrustworthy strangers in dirty public houses. How venal, how mercenary is the world at large. During the nights of sleeplessness Lilith Blake's voice would sometimes seem to call to me across the darkness. When I was able to sleep I encountered beautiful dreams, where I would be walking among pale shades in an overgrown and crumbling necropolis. The moonlight seemed abnormally bright and even filtered down to the catacombs where I would find Lilith's shrouded form.

At last terms were agreed. Two labourers were hired to undertake the job, and on the appointed night I waited in my rooms. Outside, the rain was falling heavily and in my mind's eye, as I sat anxiously in the armchair smoking cigarette after cigarette, I saw the deed done: the two simpletons, clad in their raincoats and with crowbars and pickaxes, climbing over the high wall which ran along Swain's Lane, stumbling through the storm and the overgrown grounds past stone angels and ruined monuments, down worn steps to the circular avenue, deep in the earth, but open to the mottled grey-and-black sky. Wet leaves must have choked the passageways. I could see the rain sweeping over the hillside cemetery as they levered open the door to her vault, their coats flapping in the wind. The memory of Lilith Blake's face rose before me through the hours that passed. I seemed to see it in every object that caught my gaze. I had left the blind up and watched the rain beating at the window above me, the water streaming down the small Georgian panes. I began to feel like an outcast of the universe.

As I waited, the eyes in the clock on the mantelpiece stared back at me. I thought I saw two huge and thin white spiders crawling across the books on the shelves.

At last there were three loud knocks on the door and I came to in my chair, my heart pounding in my chest. I opened the door to the still-pouring rain, and there at last, shadowy in the night, were my two grave-robbers. They were smiling unpleasantly, their hair plastered down over their worm-white faces. I pulled the wad of banknotes from my pocket and stuffed them into the nearest one's grasp.

They lugged the coffin inside and set it down in the middle of the room.

And then they left me alone with the thing. For a while, the sodden coffin dripped silently onto the rug, the dark pools forming at its foot spreading slowly outwards, sinking gradually into the worn and faded pile. Although its wooden boards were decrepit and disfigured with dank patches of greenish mould, the lid remained securely battened down by a phalanx of rusty nails. I had prepared for this moment carefully; I had all the tools I needed ready in the adjoining room, but something, a sudden sense of foreboding, made me hesitate foolishly. At last, with a massive effort of will, I fetched the claw hammer and chisel, and knelt beside the coffin. Once I had prised the lid upwards and then down again, leaving the rusted nail-tops proud, I drew them out one by one. It seemed to take for ever – levering each one up and out and dropping it onto the slowly growing pile at my feet. My lips were dry and I could barely grip the tools in my slippery hands. The shadows of the rain still trickling down the window were thrown over the room and across the coffin by the orange glow of the street lamp outside.

Very slowly, I lifted the lid.

Resting in the coffin was a figure clothed in a muslin shroud that was discoloured with age. Those long hands and attenuated fingers were folded across its bosom. Lilith Blake's raven-black hair seemed to have grown whilst she had slept in the vault and it reached down to her waist. Her head was lost in shadow, so I bent closer to examine it. There was no trace of decay in the features, which were those in the photograph, and yet they now had a horrible aspect, quite unlike that decomposition I might have anticipated. The skin was puffy and white, resembling paint applied on a tailor's dummy. Those fleshy lips that had so attracted me in the photograph were now repulsive. They were lustreless and drew back from her yellowed, sharp little teeth. The eyes were closed and even the lashes seemed longer, as if they too had grown, and they reminded me of the limbs of a spider. As I gazed at the face and fought back my repulsion, I had again the sensation that I had experienced at the vault.

Consciousness seemed to mingle with dreams. The two states were becoming one and I saw visions of some hellish ecstasy. At first I again glimpsed corpses that did not rot, as if a million graves had been opened, illuminated by the phosphoric radiance of suspended decay. But these gave way to wilder nightmares that I could glimpse only dimly, as if through a billowing vapour; nightmares that to see clearly would result in my mind being destroyed. And I could not help being reminded of the notion that what we term sanity is only a measure of success in concealing underlying madness.

Then I came back to myself and saw Lilith Blake appearing to awaken. As she slowly opened her eyes, the spell was broken, and I looked into them with mounting horror. They were blank and repugnant, no longer belonging in a human face: the eyes of a thing that had seen sights no living creature could see. Then one of her hands reached up and her long fingers clutched feebly against my throat as if trying to scratch, or perhaps caress, me.

With the touch of those clammy hands I managed to summon up enough self-control to close the lid and begin replacing the coffin nails, fighting against the impulses that were driving me to gaze again upon the awakened apparition. Then, during a lull in the rain, I burned the coffin and its deathly contents in the back yard. As I watched the fire build I thought that I heard a shrieking, like a curse being invoked in the sinister and incomprehensible language of Blake's tale. But the noise was soon lost in the roar of the flames.

It was only after many days that I discovered that the touch of Lilith Blake's long white fingers had produced marks that, once visible, remained permanently impressed upon my throat.

I travelled abroad for some months afterwards, seeking southern climes bathed in warm sunshine and blessed with short nights. But my thoughts gradually returned to *The White Hands and Other Tales*. I wondered if it might be possible to achieve control over it, to read it in its entirety and use it to attain my goal. Finally, its lure proved decisive. I convinced myself that I had already borne the darkest horrors, that this would have proved a meet preparation for its mysteries, however obscenely they were clothed. And so, returning once more to Highgate, I began the task of transcribing and interpreting the occult language of the book, delving far into its deep mysteries. Surely I could mould the dreams to my own will and overcome the nightmare. Once I had achieved this, I would dwell for ever in Paradise . . .

Text of a letter written by John Harrington whilst under confinement in Maudsley Psychiatric Hospital:

> *My dearest wife Lilith,*
> *I do not know why you have not written or come to see me.*
> *The gentlemen looking after me here are very kind but will not allow any mirrors. I know there is something awful about my face. Everyone is scared to look at it.*
> *They have taken your book away. They say it is gibberish. But I know all the secrets now.*
> *Sometimes I laugh and laugh.*
> *But I like the white hands that crawl around my bed at night like two spiders. They laugh with me.*
> *Please write or come.*
> *With all my heart,*
>
> *—John*

CAITLÍN R. KIERNAN

Waycross

CAITLÍN R. KIERNAN WAS BORN in Ireland and now lives in Atlanta, Georgia. She has published five novels: *Silk*, *Threshold*, *The Five of Cups*, *Low Red Moon* and, most recently, *Murder of Angels*, and her short fiction has been collected in *Tales of Pain and Wonder*, *From Weird and Distant Shores*, *Wrong Things* (with Poppy Z. Brite) and *To Charles Fort, With Love*. She is currently writing her sixth novel, *Daughter of Hounds*.

"Dancy Flammarion, the protagonist (or, depending on your point of view, antagonist) of 'Waycross', first appeared in my novel *Threshold*," reveals the author. "But she's one of those characters I keep coming back to because I want to know more, and the only way of learning more about her is to write more about her."

"Waycross" was originally published by Subterranean Press as a chapbook, illustrated by Ted Naifeh. Dancy also appears in Kiernan's stories "In the Garden of Poisonous Flowers", "The Well of Stars and Shadow" and "Alabaster".

"**R**ISE AND SHINE, SNOW WHITE," the Gynander growls, and so the albino girl slowly opens her pink eyes, the dream of her dead mother and sunlight and the sheltering sky dissolving to the bare earth and meat-rot stink of the cellar.

Go back to sleep, and I'll be home again, she thinks. *Close my eyes, and none of this has ever happened.* Not the truth, nothing like the truth, but cold comfort better than no comfort at all in this hole behind the place where the monster sleeps during the day. Dancy blinks at the darkness, licks her dry, chapped lips, and tries hard to remember the story her mother was telling her in the dream. Lion's den, whale belly, fiery-furnace Bible story, but all the words and names running together in her head, the pain and numbness in her wrists and ankles more real and the dream growing smaller and farther away with every beat of her heart.

The red thing crouching somewhere at the other side of the cellar makes a soft, wet sound and strikes a match to light the hurricane lamp gripped in the long, raw fingers of its left hand. Dancy closes her eyes, because the angel has warned her never to look at its face until after it puts on one of the skins hanging from the rusted steel hooks set into the ceiling of the cellar. All those blind and shriveled hides like deflated people, deflated animals, and it has promised Dancy that some day very soon she'll hang there, too, one more hollow face, one more mask for it to wear.

"What day . . . what day is it?" Dancy whispers, hard to talk because her throat's so dry, hard even to swallow, and her tongue feels swollen. "How long have I been down here?"

"Why?" the Gynander asks her. "What difference does it make?"

"No difference," Dancy croaks. "I just wanted to know."

"You got some place to be? You got someone else to kill?"

"I just wanted to know what day it is."

"It isn't any day. It's *night*."

Yellow-orange lantern light getting in through Dancy's eyelids, warm light and cold shadows, and she squeezes them shut tighter, turns her head to one side so her face is pressed against the hard dirt floor. Not taking any chances because she promised she wouldn't ever look, and if she starts lying to the angel he might stop coming to her.

"Sooner or later, you're gonna *have* to take a look at me, Dancy Flammarion," the Gynander says and laughs its bone-shard, thistle laugh. "You're gonna have to open them rabbity little eyes of yours and have a good, long look, before we're done."

"I was having a dream. You woke me up. Go away so I can go back to sleep. Kill me, or go away."

"You're already dead, child. Ain't you figured that out yet? You been dead since the day you came looking for me."

Footsteps, then, the heavy, stumbling sounds its splayed feet make against the hard-packed floor, and the clank and clatter of the hooks as it riffles through the hides, deciding what to wear.

"Kill me, or go away," Dancy says again, gets dirt in her mouth and spits it back out.

"Dead as a doornail," it purrs. "Dead as a dodo. Dead as I want you to be," and Dancy tries not to hear what comes next, the dry, stretching noises it makes stuffing itself into the skin suit it's chosen from one of the hooks. If her hands were free she could cover her ears; if they weren't tied together behind her back with nylon rope she could shove her fingers deep into her ears and maybe block it out.

"You can open your eyes now," the Gynander says. "I'm decent."

"Kill me," Dancy says, not opening her eyes.

"Why do you keep saying that? You don't want to die. When people want to die, when they *really* want to die, they get a certain smell about them, a certain brittle *incense*. You, you smell like someone who wants to live."

"I failed, and now I want this all to end."

"See, now *that*'s the truth," the Gynander says, and there's a ragged, zipping-up sort of sound as it seals the skin closed around itself. "You done let that angel of yours down, and you're ashamed, and you're scared, and you sure as hell don't want what you got coming to you. But you *still* don't want to die."

Dancy turns her head and opens her eyes, and now the thing is squatting there in front of her, holding the kerosene lamp close to its face. Borrowed skin stitched together from dead men and dogs, strips of diamond-backed snake hide, and it pokes at her right shoulder with one long black claw.

"This angel, he got hisself a name?"

"I don't know," Dancy says, though she knows well enough that all angels have names. "He's never told me his name."

"Must be one bad motherfucker, he gotta send little albino bitches out to do his dirty work. Must be one mean-ass son-of-a-whore."

When it talks, the Gynander's lips don't move, but its chin jiggles loosely, and its blue-grey cheeks bulge a little. Where its eyes should be there's nothing at all, blackness to put midnight at the bottom of the sea to shame. And Dancy knows about eyes, windows to the soul, so looks at the lamp instead.

"Maybe he ain't no angel. You ever stop and let yourself think about that, Dancy? Maybe he's a monster, too."

When she doesn't answer it pokes her again, harder than before, drawing blood with its ebony claw: warm, crimson trickle across her white shoulder, precious drops of her life wasted on the cellar floor, and she stares deep into the flame trapped inside the glass chimney. Her mother's face hidden in there somewhere, and a thousand summer-bright days, and the sword her angel carries to divide the truth from lies.

"Maybe you got it turned round backwards," the Gynander says and sets the lamp down on the floor. "Maybe what you *think* you know, you don't know at all."

"I knew right where to find you, didn't I?" Dancy asks it, speaking very quietly and not taking her eyes off the lamp.

"Well, yeah, now that's a fact. But someone like me, you know how it is. Someone like me always has enemies. Besides the angels, I mean. And word gets around, no matter how careful—"

"Are you *afraid* to kill me? Is that it?"

And there's a loud and sudden flutter from the Gynander's chest, then, like a dozen mockingbirds sewn up in there and wanting out, frantic wings beating against that leather husk. It leans closer, scalding carrion breath and the fainter smell of alcohol, the eager *snik snik snik* of its sharp white teeth, but Dancy keeps staring into the flickering heart of the hurricane lamp.

"Someone like you," she says, "needs to know who its enemies are. Besides the angels, I mean."

The Gynander hisses through its teeth and slips a hand around her throat, its palm rough as sandpaper, its needle claws spilling more of her blood.

"Patience, Snow White," it sneers. "You'll be dead a long, long time. I'll wear your pretty alabaster skin to a thousand slaughters, and your soul will watch from Hell."

"Yeah," Dancy says. "I'm starting to think you're gonna talk me to death," and she smiles for the beast, shuts her eyes and the afterimage of the lamp flame bobs and swirls orange in the dark behind her lids.

"You're still alive 'cause I still got things to *show* you, girl," the

Gynander growls. "Things those fuckers, those *angels*, ain't ever bothered with, 'cause they don't want you to know how it is. But if you're gonna fight with monsters, if you're gonna play saint and martyr for cowards that send children to do their killing, you're gonna have to see it *all*."

Its grip on her throat tightens, only a little more pressure to crush her windpipe, a careless flick of those claws to slice her throat, and for a moment Dancy thinks maybe she's won after all.

"This whole goddamn world is *my* enemy," the thing says. "Mine and yours both, Dancy Flammarion."

And then it releases her, takes the lamp and leaves her alive, alone, not even capable of taunting a king of butchers into taking her life. Dancy keeps her eyes closed until she hears the trapdoor slam shut and latch, until she's sure she's alone again, and then she rolls over onto her back and stares up at the blackness that may as well go on forever.

After the things that happened in Bainbridge, Dancy hitched the long asphalt ribbon of US 84 to Thomasville and Valdosta, following the highway on to Waycross. Through the swampy, cypress-haunted south Georgia nights, hiding her skin and her pink eyes from the blazing June sun when she could, hiding herself from sunburn and melanoma and blindness. Catching rides with truckers and college students, farmers and salesmen, rides whenever she was lucky and found a driver who didn't think she looked too strange to pick up, maybe even strange enough to be dangerous or contagious. And when she was unlucky, Dancy walked.

The last few miles, gravel and sandy, red-dirt back roads between Waycross and the vast Okefenokee wilderness, *all* of those unlucky, all of those on foot. She left the concrete and steel shade of the viaduct almost two hours before sunset, because the angel said she should. This time it wouldn't be like Bainbridge. This time there would be sentries, and this time she was expected. Walking right down the middle of the road because the weedy ditches on either side made her nervous; anything could be hiding in those thickets of honeysuckle and blackberry briars, anything hungry, anything terrible, anything at all. Waiting patiently for her beneath the deepening slash-pine and magnolia shadows, and Dancy carried the old carving knife she usually kept tucked way down at the bottom of her duffel bag, held it gripped in her right hand and watched the close and darkening woods.

When the blackbird flapped noisily out of the twilight sky and landed on the dusty road in front of her, Dancy stopped and stared at it apprehensively. Scarlet splotches on its wings like fresh blood or poisonous berries, and the bird looked warily back at her.

"Oh Jesus, you gotta be pullin' my leg," the blackbird said and frowned at her.

"What's your problem, bird?" Dancy asked, gripping the knife a little tighter than before.

"I mean, we wasn't expecting no goddamn St George on his big white horse or nothin', but for crying out loud."

"You knew I was coming here tonight?" she asked the bird and glanced anxiously at the trees, the sky, wondering who else might know.

"Look, girly, do you have any idea what's waitin' for you at the end of this here road? Do you even have the foggiest—"

"This is where he sent me. I go where my angel sends me."

The blackbird cocked its head to one side and blinked at her.

"Oh Lord and butter," the bird said.

"I go where my angel tells me. He shows me what I need to know."

The blackbird glanced back over the red patch on its shoulder at the place where the dirt road turned sharply, disappearing into a towering cathedral of kudzu vines. It ruffled its feathers and shook its head.

"Yeah, well, this time I think somebody up there musta goofed. So you just turn yourself right around and get a wiggle on before anyone notices."

"Are you testing me? Is this a temptation? Did the monsters send you?"

"*What*?" the bird squawked indignantly and hopped a few inches closer to Dancy; she raised her carving knife and took one step backwards.

"Are you trying to stop me, bird? Is that what you're doing?"

"No. I'm trying to *save* your dumb ass, you simple twit."

"Nobody can save me," Dancy said and looked down at her knife. In the half-light, the rust on the blade looked like old, dried blood. "Maybe once, a long, long time ago, but no one can save me now. That's not the way this story ends."

"Go *home*, little girl," the bird said and hopped closer. "Run away home before it smells you and comes lookin' for its supper."

"I don't have a home. I go where the angel tells me to go, and he told me to come here. He said there was something terrible hiding out here, something even the birds of the air and the beasts of the field are scared of, something I have to stop."

"With *what*? That old knife there?"

"Did you call me here, blackbird?"

"Hell, no," the bird cawed at her, angry, and glanced over its shoulder again. "Sure, we been prayin' for someone, but not a crazy albino kid with a butcher knife."

"I have to hurry now," Dancy said. "I don't have time to talk anymore. It's getting dark."

The bird stared up at her for a moment, and Dancy stared back at it, waiting for whatever was coming next, whatever she was meant to do or say, whatever the bird was there for.

"Jesus, you're really goin' through with this," it said finally, and she nodded. The blackbird sighed a very small, exasperated sigh and pecked once at the thick dust between its feet.

"Follow the road, past that kudzu patch there, and the old well, all the way to down to—"

"I know where I'm going, bird," Dancy said and shifted the weight of her duffel bag on her shoulder.

"Of course you do. Your *angel* told you."

"The old blue trailer at the end of the road," Dancy whispered. "The blue house trailer with three old refrigerators in the front yard." In the trees, fireflies had begun to wink on and off, off and on, a thousand yellow-green beacons against the gathering night. "Three refrigerators and a broken-down truck."

"Then you best shove in your clutch, girl. And don't think for a minute that they don't know you're comin'. They know everything. They know the number of stars in the heavens and how many days left till the end of time."

"This is what I do," she told the bird and stepped past him, following the road that led to the blackness coiled like a jealous, ancient serpent beneath the summer sky.

Sometime later, when the Gynander finally comes back to her, it's carrying a small wooden box that it holds out for Dancy to see. Wood like sweet, polished chocolate and an intricate design worked into the lid – a perfect circle filled in with a riot of intersecting lines to form a dozen or more triangles, and on either side of the circle a waning or waxing half-moon sickle. She blinks at the box in the unsteady lantern light, wondering if the design is supposed to mean something to her, if the monster thinks that it will.

"Pretty," Dancy says without enthusiasm. "It's a pretty box."

The Gynander makes a hollow, grumbling sound in its throat, and the dead skin hiding its true face twitches slightly.

"You never saw that before?" it asks her and taps at the very center of the circular design with the tip of one claw. "You never saw that anywhere else?"

"No. Can I please have a drink of water?"

"Your *angel* never showed it to you?"

"No," Dancy says again, giving up on the water, and she goes back to staring at the rootsy ceiling of the cellar. "I never saw anything like that before. Is it some sort of hex sign or something? My grandma knew a few of those. She's dead—"

"But you've never seen it before?"

"That's what I said."

The Gynander sits down in the dirt beside her, sets the lamp nearby, and she can feel the black holes where its eyes should be watching her, wary nothingness peering suspiciously out from the slits in its mask.

"This box belonged to Sinethella."

"Who?"

"The woman that you *killed* last night," the Gynander growls, beginning to sound angry again.

"I didn't kill a woman," Dancy says confidently. "I don't kill people."

"It's carved from a type of African cedar tree that's been extinct for two thousand years," the Gynander says, ignoring Dancy, and its crackling voice makes her think of dry autumn leaves and fire. "And she carried this box for eleven millennia. You got any idea what that means, child?"

"That she was a lot older than she looked," Dancy replies, and the Gynander grunts and puts the box down roughly on her chest. Heavy for its size, and cold, like a small block of ice, and suddenly the musty cellar air smells like spices – cinnamon, basil, sage, a few others that Dancy doesn't immediately recognize or has never smelled before.

"Get that thing off me," she tells the monster. "Whatever it is, I don't want it touching me. It isn't clean."

"Next to Sinethella," the Gynander says, "I'm nothing, nothing at all. Next to her, I'm just a carny freak. So why did you come for me instead of her?"

"I go where my angel leads me. He shows me—"

"In a moment, Dancy Flammarion, I'm going to open up this box here and show you what's inside."

"Get it off me. It stinks."

The Gynander grunts, then leans very close to Dancy and sniffs at her; something almost like a tongue, the dark, un-healthy color of indigo or polk-salad berries, darts out from between its shriveled lips and tastes the cellar air.

"That's sorta the stew pot callin' the kettle black, don't you think? When's the last time *you* had a bath, Snow White?"

And Dancy shuts her eyes, praying that her angel will come, after all, that he'll appear in a whirling storm of white, white feathers and hurricane wind and take her away from this awful place. She imagines herself in his arms, flying high above the swamps and pine barrens, safe in the velvet and starlight spaces between the moon and Earth. *I've done my best*, she thinks, trying not to imagine what's waiting for her inside the freezing wooden box pressing painfully down on her chest. *I've done my best, and none of these things can ever touch my immortal soul.*

"When men still huddled in their own filth and worshipped the sun because they were too afraid to face the night, she walked the wide world, and nobody and nothin' stood against her. She was a goddess, almost."

"I saw her with my own eyes," Dancy whispers. "I saw exactly what she was."

"You saw what you were told to see."

Sailing with her angel high above the winding black waters of the Okefenokee, above the booming voices of bull alligators and the nervous ears of marsh rabbits, safe in his arms because she's done the best that she can do. And he would tell her that, and that she doesn't have to be strong anymore. Time now to lay down and die, finally, time to be with her grandmother and mother in Paradise, no more lonely roads, no more taunts for her pink eyes and alabaster skin, and no more monsters. The angel's wings would sound like redemption, and she might glance down between her feet to see the Gynander's blue house trailer blazing in the night. "It'll be nothing but ashes by morning," she'd say and the angel would smile and nod his head.

"The first time Sinethella brought this box to me, first time she opened it and let me have a peek inside, I thought that I would surely die. I thought my heart would burst."

There are no more monsters left in the world, the angel would say to her as they flew across the land, east towards the sea. *You don't have to be afraid anymore. You can rest now, Dancy.*

"She read me a poem, before she let me look inside," the Gynander says. "I never was much for poetry, but I still remember this one. Hell, I'll remember this one till the day I die."

She would ask her angel about the box, and he would tell her not to worry. The box was destroyed. Or lost in the swamp in some pool so deep only the catfish will ever see it. Or locked away forever in the inviolable vaults of Heaven.

"*But from my grave across my brow,*" the Gynander whispers, "*plays no wind of healing now, and fire and ice within me fight, beneath the suffocating night.*"

Open your eyes, Dancy, the angel says, and she does, not afraid of falling anymore, and the Gynander opens the box sitting on her chest. Far, far away, there's a sound like women crying, and the ebony and scarlet light that spills from the cedar box wraps Dancy tight in its searing, squirming tendrils, and slowly, bit by bit, drags her away.

Dancy walked through the long, dark tunnel formed by the strangling kudzu vines, the broad green leaves muffling her footsteps, the heavy lavender flowers turning the air to sugar. She moved as quickly as she dared, wishing now that the black-bird had come with her, wishing she'd gotten an earlier start and then there would still be a few bright shafts of late-afternoon sunlight to pierce the tunnel of vines. Surrounded by the droning scream of cicadas, the songs of crickets and small, peeping frogs hidden in amongst the rotten branches and trunks of the oaks that the kudzu had taken long ago for its skeleton, she counted her paces, like rosary beads, something to mark distance and occupy her mind, something to keep her focused and moving. No more than a hundred feet from one end to the next, a hundred feet at the most, but it might as well have been a mile. And halfway through, a spot where the air was as cold as a January morning, air so cold that her breath fogged, and Dancy jumped backwards, hugging herself and shivering.

Too late, she thought. *It knows I'm coming now*, realizing that the forest around her had gone completely quiet, not one insect or amphibian voice, no twilight birdsongs left to break the sudden silence.

Reluctantly, she held a hand out, penetrating the frigid curtain of air again, a cold that could burn, that could freeze living flesh to stone; she drew a deep breath and stepped quickly through it.

Beyond the vines, the blue house trailer was sitting there alone in a small, weedy clearing, just like she'd seen it in her dreams, just exactly the way the angel had shown it to her. Light spilled from the windows and the door standing wide open like a welcome sign – *Come on in, I've been waiting for you, Dancy Flammarion*.

She set her duffel bag down in the sand and looked first at her knife and then back to the blue trailer. Even the shimmering, mewling things she'd killed back in Bainbridge, even they were afraid of this haunted place, something so terrible inside those aluminum walls that even boogeymen and goblins were afraid to whisper its name. Dancy glanced up at the summer sky, hoping the angel might be there, watching over her, but there were only a few dim and disinterested stars.

Well, what are you waiting on? the trailer seemed to whisper.

"Nothing," she said. "I'm not waiting on anything."

She walked past the three refrigerators, the burned-out carcass of the old Ford pickup, and climbed the cinder-block steps to stand in the open doorway. For a moment, the light was so bright that she thought it might blind her, might shine straight into her head and burn her brain away, and Dancy squinted through the tears streaming from the corners of her eyes. Then the light seemed to ebb, dimming enough that she could make out the shoddy confusion of furniture crammed into the trailer: a sofa missing all its cushions, a recliner the color of Spanish moss, and a coffee table buried beneath dirty plates, magazines, chicken bones, beer cans, and overflowing ashtrays. A woman in a yellow raincoat was sitting in the recliner, watching Dancy and smiling. Her eyes were very green and pupilless, a statue's jade-carved eyes, and her shaggy black hair fell about her round face in tangled curls.

"Hello there, Dancy," she said. "We were beginning to think that you wouldn't make it."

"Who are you?" Dancy asked, confused, and raised her knife so she was sure the woman could see it. "You're not supposed to be here. No one's supposed to be here but—"

"I'm not? Well, someone should have told me."

The woman stood up, slipping gracefully, slowly, from the grey recliner, her bare feet on the linoleum floor, and Dancy could see that she wasn't wearing anything under the coat.

"Not exactly what you were expecting, am I?" she asked and took a single step towards Dancy. Beneath the bright trailer lights, her bare olive skin glinted wetly, skin as smooth and perfect as oil on deep, still water, and "Stop," Dancy warned her and jabbed the knife at the air between herself and the woman.

"No one here wants to hurt you," she said and smiled wider so that Dancy could see her long, sharp teeth.

"I didn't come for you," Dancy said, trying hard to hide the tremble in her voice, because she knew the woman wanted her to be afraid. "I don't even know who you are."

"But I know who *you* are, Dancy. News travels fast these days. I know all about what you did in Bainbridge, and I know what you came here to do tonight."

"Don't make me hurt you, too."

"No one has to get hurt. Put the knife down and we can talk."

"You're just here to distract me, so *it* can run, so it can escape, and then I'll have to find it all over again."

The woman nodded and looked up at the low ceiling of the trailer, her green eyes staring directly into the flood of white light pouring down into the tiny room.

"You have a hole inside you," she said, her smile beginning to fade. "Where your heart should be, there's a hole so awfully deep and wide, an abyss in your soul."

"That's not true," Dancy whispered.

"Yes, it is. You've lost everything, haven't you? There's nothing left in the world that you love and nothing that loves you."

And Dancy almost turned and ran then, back down the cinder-block steps into the arms of the night, not prepared for this strange woman and her strange, sad voice, the secret things she had no right to know or ever say out loud. Not fair, the angel leaving this part out, not fair, when she's always done everything he asked of her.

"You think that *he* loves you?" the woman asked. "He doesn't. Angels love no one but themselves. They're bitter, selfish things, every one of them."

"Shut up."

"But it's the truth, dear. Cross my heart. Angels are nothing but spiteful—"

"I said to *shut up.*"

The woman narrowed her eyes, still staring up at the ceiling, peering into the light reflecting off her glossy skin.

"You've become their willing puppet, their doll," she said. "And, like the man said, they have made your life no more than a tale told by an idiot, full of sound and fury, signifying nothing. Nothing whatsoever."

Dancy gripped the carving knife and took a hesitant step towards the woman.

"You're a liar," she said. "You don't have any idea what you're talking about."

"Oh, but I *do*," the woman replied, lowering her head and turning to gaze at Dancy with those startling, unreal eyes. "I know so very many things. I can show you, if you want to see. I can show you the faces of God, the moment you will die, the dark places behind the stars," and she shrugged off the yellow raincoat, and it slipped to the linoleum floor.

Where her breasts should have been there were wriggling, tentacled masses instead, like the fiery heads of sea anemones, surrounding hungry, toothless mouths.

"There is almost no end to the things I can show you," the woman said. "Unless you're too afraid to see."

Dancy screamed and lunged towards the naked woman, all of her confusion and anger and disgust, all of her fear, flashing like steam to blind, forward momentum, and she swung the rusty knife, slashing the woman's throat open a couple of inches above her collarbones. The sudden, bright spray of blood across Dancy's face was as cold as water drawn from a deep well, and she gasped and retreated to the door of the trailer. The knife slid from her hand and clattered against the aluminum threshold.

"You *cut* me," the woman croaked, dismayed, and now there was blood trickling from her lips, too, blood to stain those sharp teeth pink and scarlet. Her green eyes had gone wide, swollen with surprise and pain, and she put one hand over the gash in her throat, as if to try and hide the wound hemorrhaging in time to her heart.

"You did it," she said. "You really fucking did it," and then the tentacles on her chest stopped wriggling, and she crumpled to the floor beside the recliner.

"Why didn't you tell me?" Dancy asked the angel, as if she expected an answer. "Why didn't you tell me she would be here too?"

The woman's body shuddered violently and then grew still, lying on top of the discarded raincoat, her blood spreading out across the floor like a living stain. The white light from the ceiling began to dim and, a moment later, winked out altogether, so that Dancy was left standing in the dark, alone in the doorway of the trailer.

"What have you done to her?" the Gynander growled from somewhere close, somewhere in the yard behind Dancy, its heavy, plodding footsteps coming closer, and she murmured a silent, doubtful prayer and turned to face it.

Unafraid of falling, but falling nonetheless, as the living light from the wooden box ebbs and flows beneath her skin, between the convolutions of her brain. Collapsing into herself, that hole where her heart should be, that abyss in her soul, and all the things she's clung to for so long, the handholds clawed into the dry walls of her mind, melt beneath the corrosive, soothing voices of the light.

Where am I going? she asks, and the red and black tendrils squeezing her smaller and smaller, squeezing her away, reply in a hundred brilliant voices – *Inside*, they say, and *Down*, and *Back*, and finally, *Where the monsters come from.*

I don't have my knife, she says.

You won't need it, the light reassures her.

And Dancy watches herself, a white streak across a star-dappled sky, watches her long fall from the rolling deck of a sailing ship that burned and sank and rotted five hundred years ago. A sailor standing beside her curses, crosses himself, and points at Heaven.

"Did ye see it?" he asks in a terrified whisper, and Dancy can't tell him that she did and that it was only the husk of her body burning itself away, because now she's somewhere else, high above the masts and stays, and the boat is only a speck in the darkness below, stranded forever in a place where no wind blows and the sea is as still and flat as glass. *As idle as a painted ship, upon a painted ocean.*

Falling, not up or down, but falling farther in, and *Is there a bottom, or a top? Is there ever an end?*, she wonders and *Yes*, the voices reply, *Yes and no, maybe and that depends.*

Depends on what?

On you, my dear. That depends on you.

And she stands on a rocky, windswept ledge, grey stone ground smooth and steep by eons of frost and rain, and the mountains rise up around her until their jagged peaks scrape at the low-slung belly of the clouds. Below her is a long, narrow lake, black as pitch, and in the center of the lake the ruins of a vast, shattered temple rise from its depths. There are things stranded out there among the ruins, nervous orange eyes watching the waters from broken spires and the safety of crumbling archways. Dancy can hear their small and timorous thoughts, no one desire among them but to reach the shore, to escape this cold, forgotten place – and they *would* swim, the shore an easy swim for even the weakest among them, but, from time to time, the black waters of the lake ripple, or a stream of bubbles rises suddenly to the surface, and there's no knowing what might be waiting down there. What might be hungry. What might have lain starving since time began.

"I want to go back now," Dancy says, shouting to be heard above the howling wind.

There's only one way back, the wind moans, speaking now for the light from the Gynander's box. *And that's straight on to the center.*

"The center of what?" Dancy shouts, and in a moment her voice has crossed the lake and echoed back to her, changed, mocking. *The center of when? Center of where? Of who?*

On the island of ruins, the orange-eyed things mutter ancient, half-remembered supplications and scuttle away into deeper shadows. Dancy's voice has become the confirmation of their every waking nightmare, reverberating God-voice to rain the incalculable weight of truth and sentence. And the wind sweeps her away like ash . . .

"What about her bush?" the orderly asks the nurse as the needle slips into Dancy's arm, and then he laughs.

"You're a sick fuck, Parker, you know that?" the nurse tells him, pulling the needle out again and quickly covering the tiny hole she's left with a cotton ball. "She's just a kid, for Christ's sake."

"Hey, it seems like a perfectly natural question to me. You don't see something like her every day of the week. Guys are curious about shit like that."

"Is that a fact?" the nurse asks the orderly, and she removes the cotton ball from Dancy's arm, stares for a moment at the single drop of crimson staining it.

"Yeah. Something like that."

"If you tell anyone, I swear to fucking—"

"Babe, this shit's between me and you. Not a peep, I swear."

"Jesus, I oughta have my head examined," the nurse whispers and drops the cotton ball and the syringe into a red plastic container labeled INFECTIOUS WASTE, then checks Dancy's restraints one by one until she's sure they're all secure.

"Is that me?" Dancy asks the lights, but they seem to have deserted her, left her alone with the nurse and the orderly in this haze of antiseptic stink and Thorazine.

"Is that me?"

The nurse lifts the hem of Dancy's hospital gown and, "There," she says and licks her lips. "Are you satisfied? Does that answer your question?" She sounds nervous and excited at the same time, and Dancy can see that she's smiling.

"Goddam," the orderly numbles, rubs at his chin and shakes his head. "Goddam, that's a sight to see."

"Poor kid," the nurse says and lowers Dancy's gown again.

"Hey, wait a minute, I was gonna get some pictures," the orderly protests and laughs again.

"Fuck you, Parker," the nurse says.

"Anytime you're ready, baby."

"Go to hell."

And Dancy shuts her eyes, shuts out the white tile walls and fluorescent glare, pretends that she can't smell the nurse's flowery perfume or the orderly's sweat, that her arm doesn't ache from the needle and her head isn't swimming from the drugs.

Closing her eyes. Shutting one door and opening another.

The night air is very cold and smells like pine sap and dirt, night in the forest, and Dancy runs breathless and barefoot over sticks and stones and pine straw, has been running so long now that her feet are raw and bleeding. But she can hear the men on their horses getting closer, shouting to one another, the men and their hounds, and if she dares stop running they'll be on top of her in a heartbeat.

She stumbles and almost falls, cracks her left shoulder hard against the trunk of a tree and the force of the blow spins her completely around so that she's facing her pursuers, the few dark boughs left between them and her, and one of the dogs howls. The eager sound of something that knows it's almost won, that can taste her even before its jaws close around her throat.

The light from the box swirls about her like a nagging swarm of nocturnal insects, whirring black wings and shiny, scarlet shells to get her moving again. Each step fresh agony now, but the pain in her feet and legs and chest is nothing next to her terror, the hammer of hooves and the barking hounds, the men with their guns and knives. Dancy cannot remember why they want her dead, what she might have done, if this is only some game or if it's justice; she can't remember when this night began or how long she's been running. But she knows that none of it will matter in the end, when they catch her, and then the earth drops suddenly away beneath her, and she's falling, really falling, the simple, helpless plummet of gravity. She crashes headlong through the branches of a deadfall and lands in a shallow, freezing stream.

The electric shock of cold water to rip the world around her open once again, the slow burn before it numbs her senseless, the fire before sleep and death to part the seams; she looks back to see the indistinct, frantic tumble of dog bodies already coming down the steep bank after her. Above them, the traitorous pines seem to part for the beautiful man on his tall black horse, his antique clothes, the torch in his hand as bright as the sun rising at midnight. His pale face is bruised with the anger and horror of everything he's seen and done, and everything he will see and do before the dawn.

"*Je l'ai trouvé!*" he shouts to the others. "*Dépêchez-vous!*"

Words Dancy doesn't know, but she *understands* them perfectly well, just the same.

"*La bête! Je l'ai trouvé!*"

And then she looks down at the reflection of the torch-light dancing in the icy, gurgling water, and her reflection there, as well, her albino's face melting in the flowing mirror, becoming the long snout and frightened, iridescent eyes of a wolf, melting again and now the dead woman from the Gynander's trailer stares back at her. She tries to stand, but she can't feel her legs anymore, and the dogs are almost on top of her, anyway.

"Is this me?" she asks the faces swirling in the stream. "Is this my face, too?" But this *when* and *where* slides smoothly out from beneath her before the light can reply, before snapping dog teeth tear her apart; caught up in the implosion again, swallowed whole by her own disintegration.

"They're all dead," the nurse says, and her white shoes squeak loud against the white floor. "Cops up in Milligan think maybe she had something to do with it."

"No shit?" the orderly says. He's standing by the window, looking out at the rain, drawing circles in the condensation with his index finger. Circles and circles inside circles. "Where the hell's Milligan?"

"If you don't know already, trust me, you don't want to know."

Far away, the beautiful man on his black horse fires a rifle into the night.

"How old were you then?" the psychiatrist asks Dancy, and she doesn't answer him right away, stares instead at the clock on the wall, wishing she could wait him out. Wishing there was that much time in the universe, but he has more time than she does. He keeps it nailed like Jesus to his office wall and doles it out in tiny paper cups, a mouthful at a time.

"Dancy, how old were you that night your mother took you to the fair?"

"Does it matter?" she asks him, and the psychiatrist raises his eyebrows and shrugs his bony, old-man shoulders.

"It might," he says.

And the fair unfurls around her, giddy violence of colored lights and calliope wails, cotton-candy taffy air, saw-dust air, barkers howling like drunken wolves, and the mechanical thunk and clank and wheeze of the rides. Her mother has an arm around her, holding her close as the sea of human bodies ebbs and surges about them, and Dancy thinks this must be Hell. Or Heaven. Too much of everything good or everything bad all shoved together into this tiny field, a deafening, swirling storm of laughter and screams; she wants to go home, but this is a birthday present, so she smiles and pretends that she isn't afraid.

"You didn't want to hurt your mother's feelings," the psychiatrist says and chews on the end of a yellow pencil. "You didn't want her to think you weren't having fun."

"Look, Dancy," her mother says. "Have you ever seen anything like that in your whole life?"

And the clown on stilts, tall as a tree, strides past them, wading stiffly through the crowd. He looks down as Dancy looks up and the clown smiles at her, real smile behind his painted smile, but she doesn't smile back. She can see his shadow, the thing hiding in his shadow, its stilt-long legs and half-moon smile, its eyes like specks of molten lava burning their way out of its skull.

Dancy looks quickly down at the ground, trampled sawdust and mud, cigarette butts and a half-eaten candy apple, and "Get a load of her, will you?" a man says and laughs.

"Hey, girly. You part of the freak show or what?"

"Oh, you know she is. She's one of the albinos. I saw a poster. They got a whole albino family. They got a boy that's half-alligator and a stuffed cow with two heads. They got a Chinese hermaphrodite—"

"They ain't got no cow with two heads. That's a damn fake."

"Well, *she* ain't no fake, now is she?"

And then Dancy's mother is shoving a path roughly through the crowd, towing Dancy behind her, trying to get away from the two men, but they follow close behind.

"Slow up, lady," one of them shouts. "We just want to get a good look at her. We'll pay you."

"Yeah, that's right," the other one shouts, and now everyone is staring and pointing. "We'll pay. How much just to look? We ain't gonna touch."

The psychiatrist taps his pencil against his chin and helps Dancy watch the clock. "Were you mad at her afterwards, for taking you to the fair?" he asks.

"That was a long time ago," Dancy replies. "It was my birthday present."

He takes a deep breath and exhales slowly, makes a whistling sound between his front teeth.

"We never went anywhere, so she took me to the fair for my birthday."

"Did you know about freak shows, Dancy? Did your mother tell you about them before you went to the fair?"

"What's the difference between freaks and monsters?" she asks the psychiatrist.

"Monsters aren't real," he says. "That's the difference. Why? Do you think you're a monster? Has anyone ever told you that you're a monster?"

She doesn't answer him. In only five more minutes she can go back to her room and think about anything she wants, anything but fairs and grinning clowns on stilts and the way the two men chased them through the crowd, anything but freaks and monsters. In the forest, the man fires his rifle again, and this time the shot tears a hole in the psychiatrist's face, so Dancy can see shattered bone and torn muscle, his sparkling silver teeth and the little metal gears and springs that move his tongue up and down. He drops the pencil, and it rolls underneath his desk; she wants to ask him if it hurts, being shot, having half your face blown off like that, but he hasn't stopped talking, too busy asking her questions to care if he's hurt.

"Have you ever been afraid that she took you there to get rid of you, to leave you with the freaks?"

And all the world goes white, a suffocating white where there is no sky and no earth, nothing to divide the one from the other, and the Arctic wind shrieks in her ears, and snow stings her bare skin. Not the top of the world, but somewhere very near it, a rocky scrap of land spanning a freezing sea, connecting continents in a far-off time of glaciers. Dancy wants to shut her eyes; then, at least, it would only be black, not this appalling, endless white, and she thinks about going to sleep, drifting down to someplace farther inside herself, the final still-point in this implosion, down beyond the cold. But she knows that would mean death, in this place, this *when*, some mute instinct to keep her moving, answering to her empty belly when she only wants to be still.

"*Ce n'est pas un loup!*" the man on his horse shouts to the others in his company, and Dancy peers over her shoulder, but she can't see him anywhere. Nothing at all back there but the wind-blown snow, and she wonders how he could have possibly followed her, when he won't even be born for another thirteen thousand years. The storm picks his voice apart and scatters it across the plains.

With the impatient wind at her back, hurrying her along, Dancy stumbles on ahead, helpless to do otherwise.

She finds the camp just past a line of high granite boulders, men and women huddled together in the lee of the stones, a ragged, starving bunch wrapped in bear hides. She smells them before she sees them – the soot of their small, smoky fires, the oily stink of their bodies, the faint death smell from the skins they wear. She slips between the boulders, sure-footed, moving as quietly as she can, though, over the wind, they could never hear her coming. The wind that blows her own scent away, and she crouches above them and listens. The men clutching their long spears, the women clutching their children, and all eyes nervously watching the white-out blur beyond the safety of the fires.

Dancy doesn't need to understand their language to read their minds, the red and ebony light coiled tight inside her head to translate their hushed words, their every fearful thought, to show her the hazy nightmares they've fashioned from the shadows and the wailing blizzard. They whisper about the strange white creature that has been trailing them for days, tracking them across the ice, the red-eyed demon like a young girl carved from the snow itself. Their shaman mumbles warnings that they must have trespassed into some unholy place protected by this spirit of the storms, but most of the men ignore him. They've never come across any beast so dangerous that it doesn't bleed.

Crouched there among the boulders, her teeth chattering, Dancy gazes up into the swirling snow. The light leaks out of her nostrils and twines itself in the air above her head like a dozen softly glowing serpents.

They will come for you soon, it says. *If you stay here, they'll find you and kill you.*

"Will they?" Dancy asks, too cold and hungry and tired to really care, one way or the other, and *Yes*, the light replies.

"Why? I can't hurt them. I couldn't hurt them if I wanted to."

The light breaks apart into a sudden shower of sparks, bright drops of fire that splash against each other and bounce off the edges of the boulders. In a moment, they come together again and the woman from the Gynander's trailer, the woman in the yellow raincoat that she knows isn't a woman at all, steps out of the gloom and stands nearby, watching Dancy with her green eyes.

"It only matters that they are *afraid* of you," she says. "Maybe you could hurt them, and maybe you could not, but it only matters that they are afraid."

"I killed you," Dancy says. "You're dead. Go away."

"I only wanted you to see," the woman says and glances down at the camp below the boulders. "Sometimes we forget what we are and why we do the things we do. Sometimes we never learn."

"It won't make any difference," Dancy growls at her, and the woman smiles and nods her head. Her raincoat flutters and flaps loudly in the wind, and Dancy tries hard not to look at the things writhing on her bare chest.

"It might," the woman says. "Someday, when you can't kill the thing that frightens you. When there's nowhere left to run. Think of it as a gift—"

"Why would you give *me* a gift?"

"Because you gave me one, Dancy Flammarion," and then the woman blows apart in the wind, and Dancy shivers and watches as the glittering pieces of her sail hight into the winter sky and vanish.

"Is it over now?" Dancy asks the light, and in a moment it answers her. *That depends*, it says, and *Is it ever over?* it asks, but Dancy is already tumbling back the way she's come. Head over heels, ass over tits, and when she opens her eyes, an instant later, an eternity later, she's staring through the darkness at the ceiling of the Gynander's root cellar.

Dancy coughs and rolls over onto her left side, breathing against the stabbing, sharp pain in her chest, and there's the box sitting alone in the dust, its lid closed now. The dark, varnished wood glints dull in the orange light from the hurricane lantern hanging nearby, and whatever might have come out of the box has been locked away again. She looks up from the floor, past the drooping, empty husks on their hooks and the Gynander's work-benches, and the creature is watching her from the other side of the cellar.

"What did you see?" it asks her, and she catches a guarded hint of apprehension in its rough voice.

"What was I supposed to see?" Dancy asks back, and she coughs again. "What did you think I'd see?"

"That's not how it works. It's different for everyone."

"You wanted me to see things that would make me doubt what the angel tells me."

"It's different for everyone," the Gynander says again and draws the blade of a straight razor slowly across a long leather strap.

"But that's what you wanted, wasn't it? That's what you hoped I'd see, because that's what you saw when she showed you the box."

"I never talked to no angels. I made a point of that."

And Dancy realizes that the nylon ropes around her ankles and wrists are gone, and her own knife is lying on the floor beside the box. She reaches for it, and the Gynander stops sharpening its razor and looks at her.

"Sinethella wanted to die, you know. She'd been wanting to die for ages," it says. "She'd heard what you did to them folks over in Bainbridge, and down there in Florida. I swear, child, you're like something come riding out of a Wild West movie, like goddamn Clint Eastwood, you are."

Dancy sits up, a little dizzy from lying down so long, and wipes the rusty blade of her carving knife on her jeans.

"Like in that one picture, *High Plains Drifter*, where that nameless stranger fella shows up acting all holier than thou. The whole town thinks they're using him, but turns out it's really the other way round. Turns out, maybe he's the most terrible thing there is, and maybe good's a whole lot worse thing to have after your ass than evil. Course, you have a name—"

"I haven't seen too many movies," Dancy says, though, in truth, she's never seen a single one. She glances from the Gynander to the wooden box to the lantern and back to the Gynander.

"I just want you to understand that she wasn't no two-bit backwoods haint," it says and starts sharpening the straight razor again. "Not like me. I just want you to know ain't nothing happened here she didn't *want* to happen."

"Why did you untie me?"

"Why don't you trying asking that angel of yours? I thought it had all the answers. Hell, I thought that angel of yours was all over the truth like flies on dog shit."

"She told you to let me go?"

The Gynander makes a sound like sighing and lays the leather strap aside, holds the silver razor up so that it catches a little of the stray lantern light. Its stolen face sags and twitches slightly.

"Not exactly," it says. "Ain't nothing that easy, Snow White."

Dancy stands up, her legs stiff and aching, and she lifts the hurricane lantern off its nail.

"Then you want to die, too," she says.

"Not by a long sight, little girl. But I do like me some sport now and then. And Sinethella said you must be a goddam force of nature, a regular shatterer of worlds, to do the things you been getting away with."

"What I saw in there," Dancy says, and she cautiously prods at the box with the toe of one shoe. "It doesn't make any difference. I know it was just a trick."

"Well, then what're you waiting for?" the thing whispers from the lips of its shabby, patchwork skin. "Show me what you got."

The fire crackles and roars at the night sky lightening slowly towards dawn. Dancy sits on a fallen log at the side of the red-dirt road leading back to Waycross and watches as the spreading flames begin to devour the leafy walls of the kudzu tunnel.

"Well, I guess you showed me what for," the blackbird says. It's perched on the log next to her, the fire reflected in its beady eyes. "Maybe next time I'll keep my big mouth shut."

"You think there's ever gonna be a next time?" Dancy asks without looking away from the fire.

"Lord, I hope not," the bird squawks. "That was just, you know, a figure of speech."

"Oh. I see."

"Where you headed next?" the bird asks.

"I'm not sure."

"I thought maybe the angels—"

"They'll show me," Dancy says, and she slips the carving knife back into her duffel bag and pulls the drawstrings tight again. "When it's time, they'll show me."

And then neither of them says anything else for a while, just sit there together on the fallen pine log, as the fire she started in the cellar behind the trailer burns and bleeds black smoke into the hyacinth sky.

CHARLES COLEMAN FINLAY

Lucy, In Her Splendor

CHARLES COLEMAN FINLAY LIVES in Columbus, Ohio, and he is
the administrator for the Online Writing Workshop for Science
Fiction, Fantasy, and Horror.

His first story, "Footnotes", a series of footnotes to an article
about a future disaster, appeared in the August 2001 issue of *The
Magazine of Fantasy & Science Fiction*, where he has since
become a regular contributor.

In 2003, he was a finalist for the Nebula, Hugo, Sidewise and
John W. Campbell Awards. His fiction has appeared in *Year's
Best Science Fiction Volume 20* (a.k.a. *The Mammoth Book of
Best New SF #16*) edited by Gardner Dozois, and *Year's Best
Fantasy #4*, edited by David Hartwell.

"'Lucy, In Her Splendor' was inspired by my vacations on
Kelleys Island in Lake Erie," Finlay reveals. "When I wrote it, I
didn't realize that one of my friends, who owns a bed-and-
breakfast there, was nicknamed 'Lucy'. Fortunately, she enjoyed
the story and took the ribbing she got in good spirit."

W HEN THEY WERE DONE, they sat in the plastic lawn chairs
by the lake and listened in the dark to waves lapping the
sharp white boulders mounded along the shore.

The first moth came fluttering from the direction of the pumphouse. It slapped into Lucy's cheek almost accidentally and startled them both. She raised her hand against it and the moth settled on one white-tipped nail. As she flicked her fingertip, it lifted into the air and hurtled back at her face.

A second and a third moth followed seconds later, followed in time by others until a tiny halo of insects swirled around her short platinum-blonde hair.

"Could be worse," Martin said, trying to wave them off. "Could be mosquitoes."

She smiled at him, shifted her chair closer, and leaned against his shoulder.

"God, Lucy, you're hot," he said.

She laughed, a little sadly, making a warm vibration that resonated in his chest. "I'm glad you still think so."

"No," he said. "Are you sure you haven't turned into a bug lamp? I swear you're hot enough to zap those bugs to ashes."

"You—"

She lifted her hand to slap him, but he caught it and folded her fingers within his own. Her skin was dry, caked with grit. He gave it a little squeeze and looked around, but rows of trees blocked the view of their neighbors. More bugs flew at Lucy's head.

Her voice trembled. "I'm really sick, aren't I?"

"It's just a fever. That's all it is." He placed her hand in his lap, and tried to wave the bugs away. One of the moth's wings buzzed harshly while the stones tapped against each other in the susurration of the waves. "Let's go inside."

"I don't know what I'd do without you," she whispered.

Without saying anything to reassure her, he helped her to her feet, propping her up as they strolled back to the house. When they passed the hand-carved sign that read CROW'S NEST BED & BREAKFAST, LITTLE LIMESTONE ISLAND, he flipped the board. SORRY, NO VACANCY.

Lucy's fever burned all night. Martin sat on the edge of the bed, feeding her tablets of aspirin and ice chips.

A single moth had followed them inside the house, tickling Lucy out of her rest until Martin turned on the lamp and the tiny creature flew to rest, panting, on the white shade. He smashed it, leaving a smear of grey dust and wings.

Walking over to the gable window, he gazed out of their attic apartment at the lake. All their life's savings were encompassed by these few acres of land, bounded on one end by the stone jetty covered with zebra-mussel shells and on the other by the apple tree with the bench swing. When insects began collecting at the screen, he stepped away.

Lucy shuddered in her sleep, sucking air through her mouth. Martin bent over and slipped his tongue – briefly – between her teeth. He expected the sour-sweet taste of sickness, but it wasn't there.

That only made it worse.

In the morning, Martin puttered in the kitchen even though they had no guests, making himself a cappuccino and sitting at the dining-room table beside the double-hung windows facing the lake. An ore carrier moved sluggishly away from the island, heading past Put-in Bay for the Ohio shore.

A tall, silver-haired man in gold pants and shirt – their neighbor, Bill – walked along the shore with a little girl about four or five years old. Martin's heart began to skip. He set his cup down so fast that it splashed, and ran through the screened-in porch, the door clapping shut behind him.

Sunrise glinted off the water. Martin shielded his eyes with his hand as he walked barefoot over the dew-damp grass. "Hey, neighbor!"

"Good morning, Marty," Bill replied. He gestured at the little girl. "This here's our granddaughter, Kelsey. Say hi, darling."

The little girl looked up at Martin. Panic flashed across her eyes, and she spun away from him to look at the lake.

"Hi, Kelsey," Martin said. He noticed the cappuccino running down his arm, and absent-mindedly lifted his wrist to his mouth to lick it off.

Bill shrugged. "Kids, huh. Folks don't teach 'em any manners these days." He pointed to the pumphouse, a squat slab of concrete that sat on the edge of the lake. "When did you block that up?"

"Oh." The farmhouse was over a hundred years old. Before the island built its water supply, the farmers pumped it in directly from the lake. "A couple days ago."

"I thought you were going to turn it into a sauna."

"That's still the plan. But one of our guests was poking around in it after he came back from the winery. Fell and cut his head. Pretty big gash. He didn't need stitches, but we figured—"

"Liability?"

"Yeah."

"That's a shame, people not being responsible." Bill looked up to the porch. "Say, where are your guests? Isn't it about breakfast time?"

"We had to cancel all our reservations," Martin said. He watched Kelsey closely. She poked around the rocks, searching for a way into the pumphouse. "Lucy's been sick."

"Gosh, I'm sorry to hear that. What's wrong?"

"She came down with this fever—"

"Hey, there she is."

Martin turned. Lucy stood outlined in the attic window. The glass caught the sun, casting it in such a way that she was surrounded by a corona of jagged, golden light.

Bill waved to the attic window and cupped his hands to his mouth. "Get well soon, Lucy!"

She returned the greeting.

"You have an awful pretty wife there," Bill said.

Martin frowned. "Some days she's more awful than—"

Kelsey pounded on the side of the pumphouse with a rock. Martin hurried toward her, hand outstretched, stepping carefully in his bare feet across the stones. "Hey, Kelsey, come here. I want to show you something neat."

The little girl looked to her grandfather, who nodded permission.

"Shhh." Martin pressed his forefinger to his lips. With exaggerated tiptoeing, he led her onto their other neighbor's property. It was a small cabin, seldom used. Its lake pump had been more modern, an eight-foot cube of concrete that jutted out from the shore like a single tooth in a child's mouth. Algae-slick boulders, driftwood branches, and other debris heaped around it.

The two inched slowly out on the slab until they reached the edge and saw the snakes – a dozen or more of them, ranging in length from one to three feet. Their scales glistened black as they sunned themselves on the rocks.

Kelsey gasped and clung to Martin's leg, pressing her face against his thigh and peeking out. Martin wrapped his hand around the top of her head and pointed out to the water, where a new snake sinuated across the rippled surface toward the shore. It lifted its nose, turning it like a submarine periscope.

Bill crept up behind them and stomped his foot on the concrete, chuckling as they jumped. The snakes immediately disappeared among the rocks and driftbrush. The snake in the water dived beneath the surface.

Kelsey lifted her head. "Grampa!"

Martin straightened, letting her go. "They're harmless," he said. "Lake Erie water snakes. Endangered."

Bill wrapped his arms around his granddaughter. "Just 'cause they're endangered don't mean they're not dangerous. Tigers are endangered too, but they're still dangerous."

Martin smiled and stepped off the slab. "You come back any time you want to see my snakes now, Kelsey."

They said goodbye to one another. Martin watched until they were off the property, then went inside and watched out the window to be sure they didn't come back.

The setting sun sheened off the windshield, causing Martin to slow the car as he passed the black-clad teenagers strolling down the road, trading cigarettes. A pink-haired boy sneered at Martin and Lucy, shaping his hand into a claw and gouging at them. The other kids laughed.

"Are you sure you feel well enough to do this?" Martin asked Lucy.

She ran her fingertips over her face to smooth the skin. "It's been long enough. We have to get back to normal some time. And I do feel better."

"Good." Martin pulled into the lot of the Limestone Island Winery, tires crunching on the gravel. He jumped out and opened the door for her.

They walked up the steps. The winery sat on the waterfront, within walking distance of the docks. The terrace faced the lake so that was where the tourists gathered. A Jimmy Buffet song started over the speakers, an impromptu singalong shaking the walls as Lucy and Martin went into the pub.

Martin traded nods with a few locals watching the TVs and waved to the fortyish woman behind the bar. She wore a tight T-shirt, logoed with a bottle of Two Worms Tequila, a picture of a lemon, and the slogan SUCK THIS.

She waved back as Lucy and Martin took their usual booth in the corner. Then she yelled something into the kitchen, threw the towel over her shoulder, and came to join them.

"God, Lucy," she said, sliding in across the booth. "You're *radiant*. You look wonderful. You sure you've been sick?"

An enthusiastic chorus of "Wasting away again" came through the wall from the terrace outside.

"Hi, Kate," Martin said above the singing.

"I don't look nearly as wonderful as you," Lucy answered, smiling. "Is that a new perm?"

Kate struck a pose, vamping the hairdo for them. "What do you think, Marty?"

"Looks terrific."

Kate's daughter, Maya, a high-school senior, stepped to the kitchen door, looked around, and then carried over a bottle of red wine and three glasses. "Thanks, honey," Kate said. "Now don't serve anyone else. Make Mike do it."

"He hates coming out of the kitchen, Mom."

Kate wagged her finger. "I'm not kidding." As Maya stepped away, Kate snapped the towel at her butt. She twisted around, frowning. Martin winked at her.

"Now don't go making eyes at my daughter, Mr Marty Van Wyk," Kate said, threatening him with the towel.

"Here, give me the bottle," he said. "I'll open it."

"What happened to Christie and Boyko?" Lucy asked, looking around. All summer long, Christie had waited tables while Boyko worked the kitchen.

Kate curled her lip dramatically. "The Vulgarians?"

"Bulgarians," Martin corrected.

"You ever notice the way they pawed each other all the time?" Kate asked.

Lucy leaned her head on Martin's shoulder. "They're in love with each other. It's very sweet."

"It was out of control."

The cork popped out of the bottle. Martin poured the dark red liquid into their three glasses. He slid the first one over to Kate. "Why are you talking about them in the past tense?"

"Didn't you hear? Hristina" – Kate pronounced it with the accent – "and Boyko disappeared two weeks ago. Not a word – we were worried! But then someone saw them over at Sandusky

Pointe, running the roller coasters at the park. They said the pay was better over there, and they had some other job at night. They're trying to make as much as they can before their green cards expire and they have to go home."

Lucy sipped her wine.

"Everybody disappeared at once," Kate said. "First it was those two, then you, then Pitr. We all suspected—" She dropped her voice and lifted her eyebrows. "—Foul play."

Martin swallowed his wine the wrong way and coughed. Pitr was Czech, from some small town with a castle south of Brno; he came over through the same agency that hired the other foreign workers. "Pitr?" he rasped. "He go over to the mainland too?"

"Probably." Kate leaned forward, elbows on the table, eyes glittering. "Say, did he ever come out to your place to fill that hole of yours?"

Lucy pressed her leg against Martin's. "He wasn't interested in doing any yardwork."

"Who's talking about yardwork?" Kate laughed. "Pitr's not interested in *any* work, but he's still good for business. God, he's gorgeous! Every woman who came in here wanted him."

Lucy put a hand against her throat. "He has such a lovely, full mouth," she said, just above a whisper.

"Uh-huh," added Kate, who overheard. "And what was his mouth full of? I bet Marty knows." She glanced down at his crotch and winked at him.

"If I did," Martin said, "I certainly wouldn't tell you."

"Oh, pooh! You two are no fun tonight."

Martin dipped his finger in his wine and pressed it against Lucy's forehead. The droplets sizzled. "We're just tired," he said. "And Lucy's not quite as well as we thought."

They left the winery, sitting at the island's only traffic light just outside the parking lot. A tiny beetle of some sort, attracted to Lucy, buzzed around the inside of the dark car.

"Oh, that was so awful," she said, trying to chase it away.

Martin reached up and flicked the overhead light on. The beetle flew to it, rested a second, then buzzed back at Lucy. "We've got a little money left. Enough to get away somewhere."

"No, we can't."

"Let's go over to the mainland, then. See if we can find a doctor—"

"No! I'll get better."

Martin could see the light getting ready to change, but he waited while a couple of trucks full of quarry workers sped through the intersection and parked across the street in front of the Ice Cellar, a rougher bar where locals hung out.

"I suppose it has to get better," he said, turning on to the road that led to the other side of the island and their house.

Lucy swatted at the beetle. "It can't get worse."

The next morning Lucy was too weak from the fever to rise from bed. Martin sat in the easy chair by the bed and popped the tape into the VCR. He turned the sound off so he wouldn't disturb her, and hit the play button.

Despite what Kate thought, Martin only liked to watch. He had been hiding in the closet under the stairs the day that Lucy invited Pitr over to do the yardwork.

The peephole made the picture hazy around the edges. Lucy stepped into the room – the "special" guest bedroom, next to the closet stairs – shook off her robe, and turned around right in front of the camera. Performing for it. Underneath she wore only a black corset, black stockings, high heels. She had rings on her thumbs and fingers, bracelets on her arms.

She looked as gorgeous as Martin had ever seen her, ten years younger than her actual age, timelessly beautiful.

The second figure stepped into view from the left. Pitr. Prettier than Kate's description. Scrumptious. "To die for," Lucy had said. And Martin had agreed. Dark skin, all muscle, pale blond hair, and lips so full they looked as though they would burst like bubbles if you touched them.

Lucy touched Pitr's lips. First with her fingernails. Then with her mouth, as her hands began to undress him. Still performing.

Martin hit pause on the tape. When he closed his eyes, he could still hear their sounds come through the walls. He could still smell the candles that Lucy had burned.

Blankets rustled, a foot bumped against the wall. Lucy tossed, mumbling in her delirium. He stroked her leg once.

Scooting forward to the edge of his seat, he hit the forward button. On the tape, Lucy straddled Pitr, her favorite position, but he grabbed her arms and flipped her over, forcing himself on top of her, roaring as he bulled away between her legs. Neither she nor Martin minded the roughness. Martin had parted his bathrobe and taken his cock in hand by then, watching everything on the little camcorder screen – it was an old camera, one they had used for years.

Lucy, still performing, bit into Pitr's dark, hairless chest.

Martin liked to see her hurt the other men. But this time something went beyond the normal rough play. Grabbing her arms and pinning them above her head, Pitr slammed into her so hard that she clamped her teeth down, twisting her head as if possessed, until the skin tore. Martin, so intent on his own desire, realized it only when he saw the blood trickling from her mouth.

He had sat there, then, in the closet, still holding himself loosely, frozen with the thought of viruses; they'd been exposed before and escaped okay—

Pitr pounded away until he groaned and pulled away. Lucy rolled over on her side, spitting out the blood, scrubbing her mouth with the sheets. Pitr stepped back from the bed, out of view of the camera, and spoke to her in some language that didn't sound like Czech to Martin, but something far older, harsher. He slammed the closet door.

Martin snatched up the remote and hit pause.

A full-length mirror hung on the closet door. When Pitr stepped in front of it, there was no sign of his bare flesh, only a vague, indefinite mist.

Rewind, play, pause. Again. Martin watched it over and over, frame by frame, but there was never anything there but the mist. Finally he clicked forward.

Pitr stepped away from the mirror. Lucy leaned back, bare-breasted chest heaving like that of a B-movie diva. Pitr grew to the height of the room, cackling at her, wiping blood from the wound on his chest with clawed fingers and anointing her like a priest at a baptism. She screamed.

Blankets rustled. "What are you doing?" Lucy asked in a weak, sleepy voice.

"Nothing," Martin said. He hit the eject button. Yanking the tape out of the cassette, he piled it at his feet until the reels were empty. Then he carried it downstairs and burned it all in the fireplace.

*   *   *

Martin stood at the kitchen counter, making soup for Lucy, when he saw the rat outside on the rocks. It crawled all around the pumphouse, trying to scale the sides. Martin went out to the screened-in porch to watch it.

Finally the rat fell exhausted, lethargic.

Martin went out and picked up a large flat rock from the herb garden beside the foundation. He crept slowly out to the pumphouse, expecting the rat to bolt away at any minute. But it crouched there, on the concrete base, facing the blank wall. Martin slammed down the rock.

There was a wet crunch as it connected with the concrete pad; blood squirted out one side.

A ferocious tapping, faint but unmistakable, came from inside the pumphouse. Martin cupped his hands to the stone.

"Shut up, Pitr!" he shouted.

Then he went back inside.

It was late afternoon before Martin gathered the courage to find a pair of gloves and a shovel. He went back to the pumphouse and tossed the bloody stone among the other boulders piled up where the waves licked the shore. Then he buried the rat. He covered the bloodstain on the concrete with dirt, and scuffed it in as well as he could with his deck shoes.

When he was done, he cupped his hands to the stone. "How do I make her well again, Pitr?" He leaned his ear to the concrete to hear the answer.

"Let me to come out and I will tell you," the voice croaked, so faint that Martin could barely make it out. "She is burning, with the fire. Only I can help her."

"Fuck you, Pitr."

"I am come out and you can do that do." Laughter. Or choking. Martin rather hoped it was choking. "You want young again, Martin?" the voice cracked through the stone. "I can give you the young again."

"Yeah, you and Viagra. Go to hell, Pitr."

Something hard pounded on the inside wall. "You cannot keep me here. You cannot run far enough. When I—"

Martin lifted his ear from the concrete and heard nothing except the sound of the waves and the cries of a few gulls.

The sky was the color of faded jeans. Jet contrails seamed the blue, taking other people to some point far away. Martin walked wearily back to the house.

Lucy sat up in bed. The blankets were shoved against the footboard, but she was wrapped in a kimono. The glow inside her lit it up like a Japanese lantern.

"You upset him," she said, her voice cold.

Martin grabbed his wallet from the dresser, and started changing his clothes. "You know, he was already pissed. Something about being hit on the head while you were su—"

"No, I mean it." Her cold voice shattered with panic like ice in the sun. "He's going to hurt me, Martin. You promised you wouldn't let him hurt me."

"He's not going to hurt you." He pulled on clean pants.

"Where are you going?"

"Into town for a drink."

She grabbed the lamp on the bedside table and shoved it onto the floor. The base cracked. "Are you going to go see Kate? Are you going to go *fuck* Kate? Is that it, Martin?"

"I don't even like Kate," he said softly. He leaned over and kissed her forehead, then pushed her gently onto the bed. "If it makes you any happier, I'll go to the Ice Cellar. Won't even see her."

"I'm sorry, Martin. I didn't mean that. It's just—"

"I know." Rising, he took their bank-deposit bag from its hiding place and emptied the cash into his pocket. Then he took the rest of their bills and did the same.

She clutched at his sleeve. "You're running away! Omigod, Martin. You're going to catch the ferry and leave me. You can't do that."

"I just need time to think," he said.

He pried her fingers loose and left the house before he lost his nerve.

It was after midnight before Martin returned, driving down the long dirt driveway through the woods to their house. He was drunk. Two other trucks followed his.

Lucy waited for him on the porch, in the papa-san chair, sitting directly under the one bright light.

The trucks pulled up and parked beside him. Martin lifted the case of beer off the front seat and carried it over to the picnic table. "I'm going to go get some ice to keep this cold, guys," he shouted over his shoulder, staggering to the porch.

Doors slammed in the dark. "Ain't gonna last that long," a harsh voice said. A can popped open. The others laughed.

Lucy rose and pressed herself against the screen. Insects pinged against it, trying to reach her. Bats screeched through the air, feasting.

"Is that really you, Martin? Who are those men?"

"Just some guys who work, from the quarry," he said, his tongue thick in his mouth. "I ran into them down at the Ice Cellar. They're good guys. We had a few, a few beers."

"What are they doing, Martin?"

"Shhh." His forefinger smashed his lips. "They're doing us a l'il favor."

Lucy's nostrils flared. Her mouth flattened out in a ruby "O" against the screen as she strained to see what they were doing. She took a step toward the door and sank to her knees, too weak to go any further.

A stocky, bearded man walked stiffly over to the porch. "Howdy, Missus Van Wyk," he said, sounding a little more sober than Martin. "Your husband told us 'bout the problem with the water stagnating in the pumphouse, making you sick and alla that. Well, this ought to take care of it."

"Can't tell you how much I 'preciate this," Martin said.

The man grinned and patted a wad of bills in his shirt pocket. "You already did. Just remember, it wasn't us who did it."

As he turned and walked away, Lucy whispered, "What are—"

"It's self the fence," Martin slurred.

The bats veered suddenly from their random feeding and began to swoop and shriek at the quarry men. Martin stepped over, blocked Lucy's view. The bats flew with less purpose. The men finished their work and ran back towards their trucks a hundred and fifty feet away. One of them grabbed the beer.

Lucy scraped at the screen, making it sing, her face a mixture of anguish and hope. "He said we couldn't kill him. He said he could turn into—"

One man shouted something as she spoke, then a second, then the explosion, a sharp blast that was mostly dark, not at all like the movies, followed by the pebbled drum of debris pattering on the lake.

Someone whistled, a note of appreciation.

"That ought about do it," someone said, and the others laughed. They climbed back into their trucks and drove off into the night with their headlights off.

Martin and Lucy leaned against each other, not touching, the screen between them.

Nursing a hangover, having hardly slept at all, Martin walked up and down the shore at the first hint of dawn, searching for bones or other pieces of Pitr. He thought the gulls might come for them, the way they sometimes came for dead fish. But the gulls stayed way offshore and he found nothing.

Bill came over at sunrise. The island's sheriff and his only deputy arrived shortly after. Martin, prepared to confess everything, instead heard himself repeating the story about some guest injuring himself, with Bill corroborating. Telling them how they bricked-in the pumphouse to be safe. Speculating that maybe there was some kind of gas build-up or something.

The sheriff and his deputy seemed pretty skeptical about that last part. They climbed all over the rocks, examining the pieces. The deputy waded down into the water's edge. The flat rock from the garden stood out among all the water-smoothed boulders. The deputy grabbed it, flipped it over. The rat's blood made a dark stain on the bottom.

Martin's heart stuck in his throat.

"Say, is Lucy feeling any better yet?" Bill asked.

"Her fever broke last night, after almost a week," Martin answered, his voice squeaking.

The deputy let go of the rock. It splashed into the water. "What's that? Mrs Van Wyk's been sick?"

Martin explained how sick she'd been, what a strain it had been on him, with no guests, not able to get out of the house. The sheriff and the deputy both liked Mrs Van Wyk, appreciated the volunteer work she did for the island's Chamber of Commerce.

The sheriff's radio squawked. Some tourist had woken up on his yacht this morning missing his wallet and wanted to report it stolen. The two men left their regards for Lucy and headed back into town.

The deputy's eyes stared at Martin from the rear-view mirror as the car pulled away.

Lucy stood by the window, wearing a long dress, a sweater on top of that, with a blanket around her shoulders. A slight breeze ruffled the lace curtains, slowly twisting them. Martin pressed his hand to her forehead. Her temperature felt normal; the glow had dissipated.

"I destroyed the camera," he told her. "And all the other tapes. I patched up the hole beneath the stairs."

"I'll never be warm again, Martin."

"I'll keep you warm." He wrapped his arms around her.

She turned her back against his touch. "I'll never be beautiful again," she whispered.

"You're lovely." He fastened his lips on the rim of her ear. "You're perfect."

She jerked her head away from his mouth. Outside, a remnant of oily mist layered the surface of the lake, tiny wisps that coalesced, refusing to burn away in the morning sun.

CHRISTOPHER BARZAK

Dead Boy Found

CHRISTOPHER BARZAK HAS PUBLISHED stories in a variety of magazines and anthologies including *Nerve*, *Realms of Fantasy*, *Lady Churchill's Rosebud Wristlet*, *Strange Horizons*, *The Vestal Review*, *The Year's Best Fantasy and Horror*, *Descant* and *Trampoline*. He lives in Youngstown, Ohio. Recently Barzak completed a novel, *One for Sorrow*, which continues the narrative begun in "Dead Boy Found".

"I wrote this story during the summer I turned twenty-five," recalls the author. "At the time several friends had either died suddenly or had some life-damaging event happen to them, and quickly the world became a scary, uncomfortable place for me to live in. I couldn't help wondering what horrible thing would happen next, and if I would survive it.

"The only other time in my life that I'd felt that way was when I was a kid and a young boy who lived in the next town over was brutally tortured and murdered by two men whom he'd stumbled upon in the woods while walking home from his Boy Scout meeting. His death sent ripples through the surrounding area, and for months I was obsessed with what had happened. I couldn't comprehend how such a thing could occur. I kept imagining the scene, trying to give his murder some sort of rational coherence, but I always utterly failed.

"When death came crashing too close for comfort once more, I began thinking about that boy again, and what had happened to him. And again I started to try and make sense of these losses we all face.

"I don't think I ended up making any sense out of the death of that boy from my childhood. Nor do I think I made any sense out of the death and damage that struck my circle of friends when I was twenty-five. The only thing I managed to do was to make this story out of that failure to comprehend their sudden absences."

A LL THIS STARTED WHEN my father told my mother she was a waste. He said, "You are such a waste, Linda," and she said, "Oh, yeah? You think so? We'll see about that." Then she got into her car and pulled out of our driveway, throwing gravel in every direction. She was going to Abel's, or so she said, where she could have a beer and find herself a real man.

Halfway there, though, she was in a head-on collision with a drunk woman named Lucy, who was on her way home, it happened, from Abel's. They were both driving around that blind curve on Highway 88, Lucy swerving a little, my mother smoking cigarette after cigarette, not even caring where the ashes fell. When they leaned their cars into the curve, Lucy crossed into my mother's lane. Bam! Just like that. My mother's car rolled three times into the ditch and Lucy's car careened into a guardrail. It was Lucy who called the ambulance on her cellular phone, saying, over and over, "My God, I've killed Linda McCormick, I've killed that poor girl."

At that same moment, Gracie Highsmith was becoming famous. While out searching for new additions to her rock collection, she had found the missing boy's body buried beneath the defunct railroad tracks just a couple of miles from my house. The missing boy had been missing for two weeks. He disappeared on his way home from a Boy Scout meeting. He and Gracie were both in my class. I never really talked to either of them much, but they were all right. You know, quiet types. Weird, some might say. But I'm not the judgmental sort. I keep my own counsel. I go my own way. If Gracie Highsmith wanted to collect rocks and if the missing boy wanted to be a Boy Scout, more power to them.

We waited several hours at the hospital before they let us see my mother. Me, my brother Andy, and my father sat in the lobby, reading magazines and drinking coffee. A nurse finally came and got us. She took us up to the seventh floor. She pointed to room number 727 and said we could go on in.

My mother lay in the hospital bed with tubes coming out of her nose. One of her eyes had swelled shut and was already black and shining. She breathed with her mouth open, a wheezing noise like snoring. There were bloodstains on her teeth. Also several of her teeth were missing. When she woke, blinking her good eye rapidly, she saw me and said, "Baby, come here and give me a hug."

I wasn't a baby, I was fifteen, but I didn't correct her. I figured she'd been through enough already. A doctor came in and asked my mother how she was feeling. She said she couldn't feel her legs. He said that he thought that might be a problem, but that it would probably work itself out over time. There was swelling around her spinal cord. "It should be fine after a few weeks," he told us.

My father started talking right away, saying things like, "We all have to pull together. We'll get through this. Don't worry." Eventually his fast talking added up to mean something. When we brought my mother home, he put her in my bed so she could rest properly, and I had to bunk with Andy. For the next few weeks, he kept saying things like, "Don't you worry, honey. It's time for the men to take over." I started doing the dishes and Andy vacuumed. My father took out the trash on Tuesdays. He brought home pizza or cold cuts for dinner.

I wasn't angry about anything. I want to make that clear right off. I mean, stupid stuff like this just happens. It happens all the time. One day you're just an average fifteen-year-old with stupid parents and a brother who takes out his aggressions on you because he's idiotic and his friends think it's cool to see him belittle you in public, and suddenly something happens to make things worse. Believe me, morbidity is not my specialty. Bad things just happen all at once. My grandma said bad things come in threes. Two bad things had happened: My mother was paralyzed and Gracie Highsmith found the missing boy's body. If my grandma was still alive, she'd be trying to guess what would happen next.

I mentioned this to my mother while I spooned soup up to her trembling lips. She could feed herself all right, but she seemed to like the attention. "Bad things come in threes," I said. "Remember Grandma always said that?"

She said, "Your grandma was uneducated."

I said, "What is that supposed to mean?"

She said, "She didn't even get past eighth grade, Adam."

I said, "I knew that already."

"Well, I'm just reminding you."

"Okay," I said, and she took another spoonful of chicken broth.

At school everyone talked about the missing boy. "Did you hear about Jamie Marks?" they all said. "Did you hear about Gracie Highsmith?"

I pretended like I hadn't, even though I'd watched the news all weekend and considered myself an informed viewer. I wanted to hear what other people would say. A lot of rumors were circulating already. Our school being so small made that easy. Seventh through twelfth grade all crammed into the same building, elbow to elbow, breathing each other's breath.

They said Gracie saw one of his fingers poking out of the gravel, like a zombie trying to crawl out of its grave. They said that after she removed a few stones, one of his blue eyes stared back at her, and that she screamed and threw the gravel back at his eye and ran home. They said, sure enough, when the police came later, they found the railroad ties loose, with the bolts broken off of them. So they removed them, dug up the gravel, shoveling for several minutes, and found Jamie Marks. Someone said a cop walked away to puke.

I sat through Algebra and Biology and History, thinking about cops puking, thinking about the missing boy's body. I couldn't stop thinking about those two things. I liked the idea of seeing one of those cops who set up speed traps behind bushes puking out his guts, holding his stomach. I wasn't sure what I thought about Jamie's dead body rotting beneath railroad ties. And what a piece of work, to have gone to all that trouble to hide the kid in such a place! It didn't help that at the start of each class all the teachers said they understood if we were disturbed, or anxious, and that we should talk if needed, or else they could recommend a good psychologist to our parents.

I sat at my desk with my chin propped in my hands, chewing an eraser, imagining Jamie Marks under the rails staring at the undersides of trains as they rumbled over him. Those tracks weren't used anymore, not since the big smash-up with a school bus back in the 1980s, but I imagined trains on them anyway. Jamie inhaled each time a glimpse of sky appeared between boxcars and exhaled when they covered him over. He dreamed when there were no trains rolling over him, when there was no metallic scream on the rails. When he dreamed, he dreamed of trains again, blue sparks flying off the iron railing, and he gasped for breath in his sleep. A ceiling of trains covered him. He almost suffocated, there were so many.

After school, my brother Andy said, "We're going to the place, a bunch of us. Do you want to come?" Andy's friends were all seniors and they harassed me a lot, so I shook my head and said no. "I have to see a friend and collect five dollars he owes me," I said, even though I hadn't loaned out money to anyone in weeks.

I went home and looked through school yearbooks and found Jamie Marks smiling from his square in row two. I cut his photo out with my father's Exacto knife and stared at it for a while, then turned it over. On the other side was a picture of me. I swallowed and swallowed until my throat hurt. I didn't like that picture of me anyway, I told myself. It was a bad picture. I had baby fat when it was taken, and looked more like a little kid. I flipped the photo over and over, like a coin, and wondered, *If it had been me, would I have escaped?* I decided it must have been too difficult to get away from them – I couldn't help thinking there had to be more than one murderer – and probably I would have died just the same.

I took the picture outside and buried it in my mother's garden between the rows of sticks that had, just weeks before, marked off the sections of vegetables, keeping carrots carrots and radishes radishes. I patted the dirt softly, inhaled its crisp dirt smell, and whispered, "Don't you worry. Everything will be all right."

When my mother started using a wheelchair, she was hopeful, even though the doctors had changed their minds and said she'd never walk again. She told us not to worry. She enjoyed not always having to be on her feet. She figured out how to pop wheelies, and would show off in front of guests. "What a burden legs can be!" she told us. Even so, I sometimes found her wheeled into dark corners, her head in her hands, saying, "No, no, no," sobbing.

That woman, Lucy, kept calling and asking my mother to forgive her, but my mother told us to say she wasn't home and that she was contacting lawyers and that they'd have Lucy so broke within seconds; they'd make her pay real good. I told Lucy, "She isn't home," and Lucy said, "My God, tell that poor woman I'm so sorry. Ask her to please forgive me."

I told my mother that Lucy was sorry, and the next time Lucy called, my mother decided to hear her out. Their conversation sounded like when my mom talks to her sister, my Aunt Beth, who lives in California near the ocean, a place I've never visited. My mother kept shouting, "No way! You too?! I can't believe it! Can you believe it?! Oh Lucy, this is too much."

Two hours later, Lucy pulled into our driveway, blaring her horn. My mother wheeled herself outside, smiling and laughing. Lucy was tall and wore red lipstick, and her hair was permed real tight. She wore plastic bracelets and hoop earrings, and stretchy hot pink pants. She bent down and hugged my mother, then helped her into the car. They drove off together, laughing, and when they came home several hours later, I smelled smoke and whiskey on their breath.

"What's most remarkable," my mother kept slurring, "is that I was on my way to the bar, sober, and Lucy was driving home, drunk." They'd both had arguments with their husbands that day; they'd both run out to make their husbands jealous. Learning all this, my mother and Lucy felt destiny had brought them together. "A virtual Big Bang," said my mother.

Lucy said, "A collision of souls."

The only thing to regret was that their meeting had been so painful. "But great things are born out of pain," my mother told me, nodding in a knowing way. "If I had to be in an accident with someone," she said, patting Lucy's hand, which rested on one of my mother's wheels, "I'm glad that someone was Lucy."

After I buried Jamie's and my photo, I walked around for a few days, bumping into things. Walls, lockers, people. It didn't matter what, I walked into it. I hadn't known Jamie all that well, even though we were in the same class. We had different friends. Jamie liked computers; I ran track. Not because I like competition, but because I'm a really good runner, and I like to run, even though my mom always freaks because I was born premature, with undersized lungs. But I remembered Jamie: a small kid with stringy, mouse-colored hair and pale skin. He wore very round glasses and kids sometimes called him Moony. He was supposed to be smart, but I didn't know about that. I asked a few people at lunch, when the topic was still hot, "What kind of grades did he get? Was he an honors student?" But no one answered. All they did was stare like I'd stepped out of a spaceship.

My brother Andy and his friends enjoyed a period of extreme popularity. After they went to where Jamie had been hidden, everyone thought they were crazy but somehow brave. Girls asked Andy to take them there, to be their protector, and he'd pick out the pretty ones who wore makeup and tight little skirts. "You should go, Adam," Andy told me. "You could appreciate it."

"It's too much of a spectacle," I said, as if I were above all that.

Andy narrowed his eyes. He spit at my feet. He said I didn't know what I was talking about, that it wasn't offensive at all, people were just curious, nothing sick or twisted. He asked if I was implying that his going to see the place was sick or twisted. "Cause if that's what you're implying, you are dead wrong."

"No," I said, "that's not what I'm implying. I'm not implying anything at all."

I didn't stick around to listen to the story of his adventure. There were too many stories filling my head as it was. At any moment Andy would burst into a monologue of detail, one he'd been rehearsing since seeing the place where they'd hidden Jamie, so I turned to go to my room and – bam – walked right into a wall. I put my hand over my aching face and couldn't stop blinking. Andy snorted and called me a freak. He pushed my shoulder and told me to watch where I was going, or else one day I'd kill myself. I kept leaving, and Andy said, "Hey! Where are you going? I didn't get to tell you what it was like."

Our town was big on ghost stories, and within weeks people started seeing Jamie Marks. He waited at the railroad crossing on Sodom-Hutchins road, pointing farther down the tracks, toward where he'd been hidden. He walked in tight circles outside of Gracie Highsmith's house, with his hands clasped behind his back and his head hanging low and serious. In these stories he was always a transparent figure. Things passed through him. Rain was one example; another was leaves falling off the trees, drifting through his body. Kids in school said, "I saw him!" the same eager way they did when they went out to Hatchet Man Road to see the ghost of that killer from the 1970s, who actually never used hatchets but a hunting knife.

Gracie Highsmith hadn't returned to school yet, and everyone said she'd gone psycho, so no one could verify the story of Jamie's ghost standing outside her house. The stories grew anyway, without her approval, which just seemed wrong. I thought if Jamie's ghost was walking outside Gracie's house, then no one should tell that story but Gracie. It was hers, and anyone else who told it was a thief.

One day I finally went to the cemetery to visit him. I'd wanted to go to the funeral, just to stand in the back where no one would notice, but the newspaper said it was family only. If I *was* angry about anything at all, it was this. I mean, how could they just shut everyone out? The whole town had helped in the search parties, had taken over food to Jamie's family during the time when he was missing. And then no one but family was allowed to be at the funeral? It just felt a little selfish.

I hardly ever went to the cemetery. Only once or twice before, and that was when my Grandma died, and my dad and Andy and I had to be pallbearers. We went once after my mom came home in her wheelchair. She said she needed to talk to my grandma, so we drove her there on a surprisingly warm autumn day, when the leaves were still swinging on their branches. She sat in front of the headstone, and we backed off to give her some private time. She cried and sniffed, you could hear that. The sunlight reflected on the chrome of her wheelchair. When she was done we loaded her back into the van, and she said, "All right, who wants to rent some videos?"

Now the cemetery looked desolate, as if ready to be filmed for some Hallowe'en movie. Headstones leaned toward one another. Moss grew green over the walls of family mausoleums. I walked along the driveway, gravel crunching beneath my shoes, and looked from side to side at the stone angels and pillars and plain flat slabs decorating the dead, marking out their spaces. I knew a lot of names, or had heard of them, whether they'd been relatives or friends, or friends of relatives, or ancestral family enemies. When you live in a town where you can fit everyone into four churches – two Catholic, two Methodist – you know everyone. Even the dead.

I searched the headstones until I found where Jamie Marks was buried. His grave was still freshly turned earth. No grass had had time to grow there. But people had left little trinkets, tokens or reminders, on the grave, pieces of themselves. A handprint. A piece of rose-colored glass. Two cigarettes standing up like fence posts. A baby rattle. Someone had scrawled a name across the bottom edge of the grave: Gracie Highsmith. A moment later I heard footsteps, and there she was in the flesh, coming toward me.

I was perturbed, but not angry. Besides his family, I thought I'd be the only one to come visit. But here she was, this girl, who'd drawn her name in the dirt with her finger. Her letters looked soft; they curled into each other gently, with little flourishes for decoration. Did she think it mattered if she spelled her name pretty?

I planted my hands on my hips as she approached and said, "Hey, what are you doing here?"

Gracie blinked as if she'd never seen me before in her life. I could tell she wanted to say, "Excuse me? Who are you?" But what she did say was, "Visiting. I'm visiting. What are *you* doing here?"

The wind picked up and blew hair across her face. She tucked it back behind her ears real neatly. I dropped my hands from my hips and nudged the ground with my shoe, not knowing how to answer. Gracie turned back to Jamie's tombstone.

"Visiting," I said finally, crossing my arms over my chest, annoyed that I couldn't come up with anything but the same answer she'd given.

Gracie nodded without looking at me. She kept her eyes trained on Jamie's grave, and I started to think maybe she was going to steal it. The headstone, that is. I mean, the girl collected rocks. A headstone would complete any collection. I wondered if I should call the police, tell them, "Get yourselves to the cemetery, you've got a burglary in progress." I imagined them taking Gracie out in handcuffs, making her duck her head as they tucked her into the back seat of the patrol car. I pinched myself to stop daydreaming, and when I woke back up I found Gracie sobbing over the grave.

I didn't know how long she'd been crying, but she was going full force. I mean, this girl didn't care if anyone was around to hear her. She bawled and screamed. I didn't know what to do, but I thought maybe I should say something to calm her. I finally shouted, "Hey! Don't do that!"

But Gracie kept crying. She beat her fist in the dirt near her name.

"Hey!" I repeated. "Didn't you hear me? I said, Don't do that!" But she still didn't listen.

So I started to dance. It was the first idea that came to me.

I kicked my heels in the air and did a two-step. I hummed a tune to keep time. I clasped my hands together behind my back and did a jig, or an imitation of one, and when still none of my clowning distracted her, I started to sing the Hokey Pokey.

I belted it out and kept on dancing. I sung each line like it was poetry. "You put your left foot in/You take your left foot out/You put your left foot in/And you shake it all about/You do the Hokey Pokey and you turn yourself around/That's what it's all about! Yeehaw!"

As I sang and danced, I moved toward a freshly dug grave just a few plots down from Jamie's. The headstone was already up, but there hadn't been a funeral yet. The grave was waiting for Lola Peterson to fill it, but instead, as I shouted out the next verse, I stumbled in.

I fell in the grave, singing, "You put your whole self in—" and about choked on my own tongue when I landed. Even though it was still light out, it was dark in the grave, and muddy. My shoes sunk, and when I tried to pull them out, they made sucking noises. The air smelled stiff and leafy. I started to worry that I'd be stuck in Lola Peterson's grave all night, because the walls around me were muddy too; I couldn't get my footing. Finally, though, Gracie's head appeared over the lip of the grave.

"Are you okay?" she asked.

Her hair fell down toward me like coils of rope.

Gracie helped me out by getting a ladder from the cemetery toolshed. She told me I was a fool, but she laughed when she said it. Her eyes were red from crying, and her cheeks looked wind-chapped. I thanked her for helping me out.

I got her talking after that. She talked a little about Jamie and how she found him, but she didn't say too much. Really, she only seemed to want to talk about rocks. "So you really do collect rocks?" I asked, and Gracie bobbed her head.

"You should see them," she told me. "Why don't you come over to my place tomorrow? My parents will be at marriage counseling. Come around five."

"Sure," I said. "That'd be great."

Gracie dipped her head and looked up at me through brown bangs. She turned to go, then stopped a moment later and waved. I waved back.

I waited for her to leave before me. I waited until I heard the squeal and clang of the wrought-iron front gates. Then I knelt down beside Jamie's grave and wiped Gracie's name out of the dirt. I wrote my name in place of it, etching into the dirt deeply.

My letters were straight and fierce.

I went home to find that I'd missed dinner. My father was already in the living room, watching TV, the Weather Channel. He could watch the weather report for hours, listening to the muzak play over and over. He watched it every night for a couple of hours before Andy and I would start groaning for a channel switch. He'd change the channel but never acknowledge us. Usually he never had much to say anyway.

When I got home, though, he wanted to talk. It took him only a few minutes after I sat down with a plate of meatloaf before he changed the channel, and I about choked. There was a news brief on about the search for Jamie's murderers. I wondered why the anchorman called them "Jamie's murderers", the same way you might say, "Jamie's dogs" or "Jamie's Boy Scout honors". My dad stretched out on his reclining chair and started muttering about what he'd do with the killers if it had been his boy. His face was red and splotchy.

I stopped eating, set my fork down on my plate.

"What would you do?" I asked. "What would you do if it had been me?"

My dad looked at me and said, "I'd tie a rope around those bastard's armpits and lower them inch by inch into a vat of piranhas, slowly, to let the little suckers have at their flesh."

He looked back at the TV.

"But what if the police got them first?" I said. "What would you do then?"

Dad looked at me again and said, "I'd smuggle a gun into the courtroom, and when they had those bastards up there on the stand, I'd jump out of my seat and shoot their God-damned heads off." He jumped out of his recliner and made his hands into a gun shape, pointing it at me. He pulled the fake trigger once, twice, a third time. Bam! Bam! Bam!

I nodded with approval. I felt really loved, like I was my dad's favorite. I ate up all this great attention and kept asking, "What if?" again and again, making up different situations. He was so cool, the best dad in the world. I wanted to buy him a hat: Best Dad in the World! printed on it. We were really close, I felt, for the first time in a long time.

Gracie Highsmith's house was nestled in a bend of the railroad tracks where she found Jamie. She'd been out walking the tracks looking for odd pieces of coal and nickel, when she found him. All of this she told me in her bedroom, on the second floor of her house. She held out a fist-sized rock that was brown with black speckles embedded in it. The brown parts felt like sandpaper, but the black specks were smooth as glass. Gracie said she'd found it in the streambed at the bottom of Marrow's Ravine. I said, "It's something special all right," and she beamed like someone's mother.

"That's nothing," she said. "Wait till you see the rest."

She showed me a chunk of clear quartz and a piece of hardened blue clay; a broken-open geode filled with pyramids of pink crystal; a seashell that she'd found, mysteriously, in the woods behind her house, nowhere near water; and a flat rock with a skeletal fish fossil imprinted on it. I was excited to see them all. I hadn't realized how beautiful rocks could be. It made me want to collect rocks too, but it was already Gracie's territory. I'd have to find something of my own.

We sat on her bed and listened to music by some group from Cleveland that I'd never heard of, but who Gracie obviously loved because she set the CD player to replay the same song over and over. It sounded real punk. They sang about growing up angry and how they would take over the world and make people pay for being stupid idiots. Gracie nodded and gritted her teeth as she listened.

I liked being alone in the house with her, listening to music and looking at rocks. I felt eccentric and mature. I told Gracie this, and she knew what I meant. "They all think we're children," she said. "They don't know a God-damned thing, do they?"

We talked about growing old for a while, imagining ourselves in college, then in mid-life careers, then when we were so old that we couldn't walk without a walker. Pretty soon we were so old we both clutched our chests like we were having heart attacks, fell back on the bed, and choked on our own laughter.

"What sort of funeral will you have?" she wondered.

"I don't know, what about you? Aren't they all the same?"

"Funerals are all different," she said. "For instance, Mexican cemeteries have all these bright, beautifully colored decorations for their dead; they're not all serious like ours." I asked her where she had learned that. She said, "Social Studies. Last year."

"Social Studies?" I asked. "Last year?" I repeated. "I don't remember reading about funerals or cemeteries last year in Social Studies." Last year I hadn't cared about funerals. I was fourteen and watched TV and played video games a lot. What else had I missed while lost in the fog of sitcoms and fantasy adventures?

I bet Mexicans never would have had a private funeral. Too bad Jamie wasn't Mexican.

"I see graves all the time now," Gracie told me. She lay flat on her back, head on her pillow, and stared at the ceiling. "They're everywhere," Gracie said. "Ever since—"

She stopped and sighed, as if it was some huge confession she'd just told me. I worried that she might expect something in return, a confession of my own. I murmured a little noise I hoped sounded supportive.

"They're everywhere," she repeated. "The town cemetery, the Wilkinson family plot, that old place out by the ravine, where Fuck-You Francis is supposed to be buried. And now the railroad tracks. I mean, where does it end?"

I said, "Beds are like graves, too," and she turned to me with this puzzled look. "No," I said, "really." And I told her about the time when my grandmother came to live with us, after my grandfather's death. And how, one morning my mother sent me into her room to wake her for breakfast – I remember, because I smelled bacon frying when I woke up – and so I went into my grandma's room and told her to wake up. She didn't, so I repeated myself. But she still didn't wake up. Finally I shook her shoulders, and her head lolled on her neck. I grabbed one of her hands, and it was cold to touch.

"Oh," said Gracie. "I see what you mean." She stared at me hard, her eyes glistening. Gracie rolled on top of me, pinning her knees on both sides of my hips. Her hair fell around my face, and the room grew dimmer as her hair brushed over my eyes, shutting out the light.

She kissed me on my lips, and she kissed me on my neck. She started rocking against my penis, so I rocked back. The coils in her bed creaked. "You're so cold, Adam," Gracie whispered, over and over. "You're so cold, you're so cold." She smelled like clay and dust. As she rocked on me, she looked up at the ceiling and bared the hollow of her throat. After a while, she let out several little gasps, then collapsed on my chest. I kept rubbing against her, but stopped when I realized she wasn't going to get back into it.

Gracie slid off me. She knelt in front of her window, looking out at something.

"Are you angry?" I asked.

"No, Adam. I'm not angry. Why would I be angry?"

"Just asking," I said. "What are you doing now?" I said.

"He's down there again," she whispered. I heard the tears in her voice already and went to her. I didn't look out the window. I wrapped my arms around her, my hands meeting under her breasts, and hugged her. I didn't look out the window.

"Why won't he go away?" she said. "I found him, yeah. So fucking what? He doesn't need to fucking follow me around forever."

"Tell him to leave," I told her.

She didn't respond.

"Tell him you don't want to see him anymore," I told her.

She moved my hands off her and turned her face to mine. She leaned in and kissed me, her tongue searching out mine. When she pulled back, she said, "I can't. I hate him, but I love him, too. He seems to, I don't know, understand me, maybe. We're on the same wavelength, you know? As much as he annoys me, I love him. He should have been loved, you know. He never got that. Not how everyone deserves."

"Just give him up," I said.

Gracie wrinkled her nose. She stood and paced to her doorway, opened the door, said, "I think you should go now. My parents will be home soon."

I craned my neck to glance out the window, but her voice cracked like a whip.

"Leave, Adam."

I shrugged into my coat and elbowed past her.

"You don't deserve him," I said on my way out.

I walked home through wind, and soon rain started up. It landed on my face cold and trickled down my cheeks into my collar. Jamie hadn't been outside when I left Gracie's house, and I began to suspect she'd been making him up, like the rest of them, to make me jealous. Bitch, I thought. I thought she was different.

At home I walked in through the kitchen, and my mother was waiting by the doorway. She said, "Where have you been? Two nights in a row. You're acting all secretive. Where have you been, Adam?"

Lucy sat at the dinner table, smoking a cigarette. When I looked at her, she looked away. Smoke curled up into the lamp above her.

"What is this?" I said. "An inquisition?"

"We're just worried, is all," said my mother.

"Don't worry."

"I can't help it."

"Your mother loves you very much," said Lucy.

"Stay out of this, paralyzer."

Both of them gasped.

"Adam!" My mother sounded shocked. "That's not nice. You know Lucy didn't mean that to happen. Apologize right now."

I mumbled an apology.

My mother started wheeling around the kitchen. She reached up to cupboards and pulled out cans of tomatoes and kidney beans. She opened the freezer and pulled out ground beef. "Chili," she said, just that. "It's chilly outside, so you need some warm chili for your stomach. Chili will warm you up." She sounded like a commercial.

Then she started in again. "My miracle child," she said, pretending to talk to herself. "My baby boy, my gift. Did you know, Lucy, that Adam was born premature, with underdeveloped lungs and a murmur in his heart?"

"No, dear," said Lucy. "How terrible!"

"He was a fighter, though," said my mother. "He always fought. He wanted to live so much. Oh, Adam," she said. "Why don't you tell me where you've been? Your running coach said you've been missing practice a lot."

"I haven't been anywhere," I said. "Give it a rest."

"It's everything happening at once, isn't it?" Lucy asked. "Poor kid. You should send him to see Dr Phelps, Linda. Stuff like what happened to the Marks boy is hard on kids."

"That's an idea," said my mother.

"Would you stop talking about me in front of me?" I said. "God, you two are ridiculous. You don't have a God-damned clue about anything."

My father came into the kitchen and said, "What's all the racket?"

I said, "Why don't you just go kill someone!" and ran outside again.

At first I didn't know where I was going, but by the time I reached the edge of the woods, I figured it out. The rain still fell steadily, and the wind crooned through the branches of trees. Leaves shook and fell around me. It was dusk, and I pushed my way through the brambles and roots back to the old railroad tracks.

His breath was on my neck before I even reached the spot, though. I knew he was behind me before he even said a thing. I felt his breath on my neck, and then he placed his arms around my stomach, just like I had with Gracie. "Keep going," he said. And I did. He held onto me, and I carried him on my back all the way to the place where Gracie had found him.

That section of the railroad had been marked out in yellow police tape. But something was wrong. Something didn't match up with what I expected. The railroad ties – they hadn't been pulled up. And the hole where Jamie had been buried – it was there all right, but *next* to the railroad tracks. He'd never been under those railroad tracks, I realized. Something dropped in my stomach. A pang of disappointment.

Stories change. They change too easily and too often.

"What are you waiting for?" Jamie asked, sliding off my back. I stood at the edge of the hole and he said, "Go on. Try it on."

I turned around and there he was, naked, with mud smudged on his pale white skin. His hair was all messed up, and one lens of his glasses was shattered. He smiled. His teeth were filled with grit.

I stepped backward into the hole. It wasn't very deep, not like Lola Peterson's grave in the cemetery. Just a few feet down. I stood at eye level with Jamie's crotch. He reached down and touched himself.

"Take off your clothes," he told me.

I took them off.

"Lay down," he told me.

I lay down.

He climbed in on top of me, and he was so cold, so cold. He said there was room for two of us in here and that I should call him Moony.

I said, "I never liked that name."

He said, "Neither did I."

"Then I won't call you that."

"Thank you," he said, and hugged me. I let him. He said she never let him hug her. She didn't understand him. I told him I knew. She was being selfish.

I said, "Don't worry. I've found you now. You don't have to worry. I understand. I found you."

"I found *you*," he said. "Remember?"

"Let's not argue," I said.

He rested his cheek against my chest, and the rain washed over us. After a while I heard voices, faraway but growing closer. I stood up and saw the swathes of light from their flashlights getting bigger. My dad and Andy and Lucy. All of them moved toward me. I imagined my mother wheeling in worried circles back in the kitchen.

"Adam!" my father shouted through the rain.

I didn't move. Not even when they came right up to me, their faces white and pale as Jamie's dead body. Andy said, "I told you he'd be here. The little freak."

Lucy said, "My Lord, your poor mother," and her hand flew to her mouth.

My father said, "Adam, come out of there. Come out of that place right now."

He held his hand out to me, curling his fingers for me to take it.

"Come on, boy," he said. "Get on out of there now." He flexed his fingers for emphasis.

I grabbed hold of his hand, and he hauled me out onto the gravel around the hole and I lay there, naked, like a newborn. They stood around me, staring. My father took off his coat and put it on me. He told me to come on, to just come on back to the house. He put his arm around me, and we started walking down the tracks.

I decided right then that's I wasn't a freak, not really. I took my father's hand, sure, but not because of anything remotely like defeat. I hadn't "come to my senses". I hadn't "realized I needed help." I took it to make them feel better about themselves and to get them off my back.

What I was thinking as they walked me home was: You silly people, I'm already finished. I'm already dead and gone. All you have is some mess of a zombie shambling through your kitchens and your living rooms, turning on your showers and kissing you goodnight. All you have is a dead boy, only it's hard to tell, because I won't rot. I'll be like one of those bodies that people in South America pry out of old coffins, the ones whose hair and fingernails continue to grow in death. The ones who smell of rose petals, whose skin remains smooth and lily white. They call those corpses saints, but I won't aspire to anything so heavenly. I'll wash the dishes and do my homework and wheel my mother around in her chair. I'll do all of these things, and no one will notice that there's no light behind my eyes and no heat in my step. They'll clothe me and feed me and tell me what good grades I get. They'll give me things to make me happy, when all I'll be wanting is a cold grave to step into. I'll grow up and go to college, marry a beautiful woman and have three kids. I'll make a lot of money and age gracefully, no pot belly. I'll look youthful when I'm fifty-eight.

What I knew right then was that everyone I'd ever know from here on out would talk about me and say, He's so lucky. He has everything a person could want.

JOYCE CAROL OATES

The Haunting

JOYCE CAROL OATES IS one of the most prolific and respected
writers in the United States today. A member of the American
Academy of Arts and Letters since 1978, she teaches creative
writing at Princeton University, New Jersey, and publishes the
small press and literary magazine *The Ontario Review* with her
husband, Raymond J. Smith.

A winner of the O. Henry Prize and the National Book Award,
her published works include *Blonde, Wonderland, Them, Broke
Heart Blues, Black Water, We Were the Mulvaneys, Beasts,
Middle Age: A Romance, I'll Take You There* and *The Falls*.
The author's short fiction has appeared in publications as diverse
as *Harpers, Playboy, Granta* and *The Paris Review*, and has been
anthologized in *The World's Finest Mystery and Crime Stories*
and *The Best American Short Stories of the 20th Century*.

Over the years, Oates's keen interest in Gothic literature and
psychological horror has led her to contribute stories to genre
anthologies ranging from Kirby McCauley's *Dark Forces* to
Ellen Datlow's *The Dark: New Ghost Stories*. She has written
dark suspense novels under the pseudonym "Rosamond Smith",
edited the collection *Tales of H.P. Lovecraft: Major Works*, and
some of her more recent short stories have been collected in *The
Collector of Hearts: New Tales of the Grotesque*. Oates's short
novel *Zombie* won the Bram Stoker Award, and she is a
recipient of the Life Achievement Award of the Horror Writers
Association.

It is a privilege to welcome her to the pages of *Best New Horror* with the following dark and surreal story involving ghostly rabbits . . .

T here's nothing! you hear nothing. It's the wind. It's your dream. You know how you dream. Go back to sleep. I want to love you, stop crying, let go of me, let me sleep for sweet Jesus's sake I'm somebody too not just your Mommy don't make me hate you.

In this new place Mommy has brought us to. Where nobody will know us, Mommy says.

In this new place in the night when the rabbits' cries wake us. In the night my bed pushed against a wall and through the wall I can hear the rabbits crying in the cellar in their cages begging to be freed. In the night there is the wind. In this new place at the edge of a river Mommy says is an Indian name – *Cuy-a-hoga*. In the night when we hear Mommy's voice muffled and laughing. Mommy's voice like she is speaking on a phone. Mommy's voice like she is speaking, laughing to herself. Or singing.

Calvin says it might not be Mommy's voice. It's a ghost-voice of the house Mommy brought us to, now Mommy is a widow.

I ask Calvin is it Daddy? Is it Daddy wanting to come back?

Calvin looks at me like he'd like to hit me. For saying some wrong dumb thing like I am always doing. Then he laughs.

"Daddy ain't coming back, dummy. Daddy is dead."

Daddy is dead. Dead Daddy. Daddy-dead.

Daddydeaddead. Deaaaaaddaddy.

If you say it enough times faster and faster you start giggling. Calvin shows me.

In this new place a thousand miles Mommy says from the old place where we have come to make a *new start*. Already Mommy has a job, in sales she says. Not much but only temporary. Some nights she has to work, Calvin can watch me. Calvin is ten: old enough to watch his little sister Mommy says. Now that Daddy is gone.

Now that Daddy is gone we never speak of him. Calvin and me, never when Mommy might hear.

At first I was worried: how would Daddy know where we were, if he wanted to come back to us?

Calvin flailed his fists like windmills he'd like to hit me with. Told and told and told you Daddy is D-E-A-D.

Mommy said, "Where Randy Malvern has gone is his own choice. He has gone to dwell with his own cruel kin." I asked where, and Mommy said scornfully, "He has gone to Hell to be with his own cruel kin."

Except for the rabbits in the cellar, nobody knows me here.

In their ugly rusted old cages in the cellar where Mommy says we must not go. There is nothing in the cellar Mommy says. Stay out of that filthy place. But in the night through the wall I can hear the rabbits' cries. It starts as whimpering at first like the cooing and fretting of pigeons then it gets louder. If I put my pillow over my head still I hear them. I am meant to hear them. My heart beats hard so that it hurts. In their cages the rabbits are pleading *Help us! Let us out! We don't want to die.*

In the morning before school Mommy brushes my hair, laughs and kisses the tip of my nose. In the morning there is a Mommy who loves me again. But when I ask Mommy about the rabbits in the cellar Mommy's face changes.

Mommy says she told me! The cellar is empty. There are no rabbits in the cellar, she has shown me hasn't she?

I try to tell Mommy the rabbits are real, I can hear them in the wall in the night but Mommy is exasperated brushing my hair, always there are snarls in my curly hair especially at the back of my neck, Mommy has to use the steel comb that makes me whimper with pain saying, "No. It's your silly dream, Ceci. I'm warning you: no more dreams."

Now that Daddy is gone we are learning to be cautious of Mommy.

Always it was Daddy to look out for. Daddy driving home, and the sound of the pickup motor running off. And the door slamming. And Daddy might be rough lifting us to the ceiling in his strong arms but it was all right because Daddy laughed and tickled with his mustache, and Daddy brought us presents and took us for fast swerving drives in the pickup playing his CDs loud so the music thrummed and walloped through us like we were rag dolls. But other times Daddy was gone for days and when Daddy came back Mommy tried to block him from us and he'd grab her hair saying, What? What the fuck you looking at me like that? Those fucking kids are *mine*. He'd bump into a chair and curse and kick it and if Mommy made a move to set the chair straight he'd shove her away. If the phone began to ring he'd yank it out of the wall socket. Daddy's eyes were glassy and had like red cobwebs in them and his fingers kept bunching into fists, and his fists kept striking out like he couldn't help himself. Especially Calvin. Poor Calvin if Daddy saw him holding back or trying to hide. Little shit! Daddy shouted. What the fuck you think you're doing, putting something over on your fucking Dad-*dy*? And Mommy ran to protect us then, and hid us.

But now Daddy is gone, it's Mommy's eyes like a cat's eyes jumping onto us. Mommy's fingers twitchy like they want to be fists.

I want to love you, honey. You and your brother. But you're making it so hard . . .

Our house is a row house Mommy calls it. At the end of a block of row houses. These are brick houses you think but up close you see it's asphalt siding meant to look like brick. Red brick with streaks running down like tears.

This is a city we live in now, it's a big city and far away from where we used to live. Mommy says nobody will follow us here, and nobody will know us here.

Mommy says don't talk to neighbors. Ever.

Mommy says don't talk to anybody at school. Any more than you need to talk. Understand, kids?

Mommy smiling at us. Mommy's eyes shining she's so happy.

Nothing was ever proved against Mommy.

Mommy says, Know why? Because there was nothing to be proved.

When Daddy rode away the last time in the pickup we saw from the front windows. We saw the red taillights rapidly receding into the night. We were meant to be sleeping but we never slept, the voices through the floorboards kept us awake.

Later there was Mommy running outside where a car was waiting. Whoever came to pick her up, we didn't know. They drove away and later I would think maybe I had dreamt it because Mommy said she had not left the house and how do you know what's real and what you have dreamt? When they asked me I shook my head, I shut my eyes not-knowing. Calvin told them Mommy was with us all that night. Mommy slept with us, and held us.

I was only five then. I cried a lot. Now I'm six, and in first grade. Calvin is in fourth grade. Calvin had to be kept back a year, for *learning disability*. That's all right with him Calvin says, he doesn't get picked on so much now. He's one of the big boys now, nobody better pick on *him*.

Whoever came to question my brother, if it was the nice social worker lady bringing us oatmeal cookies she baked herself, or the sheriff calling us by our names like he knew us, Calvin would say the same thing.

Mommy held us all that night long.

The cellar. That is forbidden to Calvin and me.

Mommy says nothing is down there. No rabbits! For Christ's sake will you stop, both of you. *There are no rabbits in this house*.

The cages are still in the cellar, though. There are some outside in the back yard almost hidden by weeds but there are more in the cellar, rabbit hutches Calvin says they are. Mommy has called about the cages in the cellar, and the smell in the cellar, and the cellar walls that ooze oily muck when it rains, and the roof too that leaks, and Mommy starts to cry over the phone but the man hasn't come yet.

The cellar! I wish I didn't think about it so much. In the night when the rabbits cry for help it's because they are in the cages in the cellar trapped.

Let us go! We don't want to die.

In our other house built on a concrete slab there was no cellar. Then Daddy moved into a mobile home as he called it, that was on just wheels. Here the cellar is like a big square dug in the ground. The first time Mommy went away and we were alone in the house, we went into the cellar giggling and scared. Calvin turned on the light – it was just one light bulb overhead. The steps were wood, and wobbly. The furnace was down there, and a smell of oil, and pipes. In a corner were the rabbit hutches, Calvin called them. Ugly old rusted wire cages stacked together almost to the ceiling. We counted eight of them. The cellar smelled bad, especially the cages smelled. You could see bits of soft grey fur stuck in the wires. On the concrete floor were dried rabbit turds Calvin said they were, little black pellets. Oily dark stains on the concrete and stains Calvin teased me about saying they were blood.

A smell down here of old musty things. Muck oozing through

the walls after a heavy rain. Calvin said, Mommy would kill us if she knew we were down here. He scolded me when I reached inside one of the cages, where the door was open, saying, "Hey! If you cut yourself on that, if you get tet'nus, Mommy will give me hell."

I asked Calvin what *tet'nus* is.

In a sneering voice like he was so smart, because he was in fourth grade and I was only in first, Calvin said, "Death."

I was afraid Calvin would see, I had scratched my arm on the cage door. I don't know how, it just happened. Not a deep cut but like a cat's scratch, it was bleeding a little and it stung. I would tell Mommy I'd scratched my arm on the sharp edge of a packing crate.

It was then I saw something move in one of the cages farthest back in the corner. A shadowy furry shape. A gleam of small close-set eyes. I gave a little cry, and grabbed at Calvin, but he shook off my arm.

Calvin made a scornful snorting noise he'd got from Daddy. When Daddy would say drawing the word out like he liked it – *Bull-shit.*

I told Calvin that almost you could see a rabbit there. You could see the other rabbits in their cages. Almost.

Calvin called me a dumb dopey girl. Yanking at my arm to make me come with him, back upstairs.

Lots of times now Calvin calls me worse things. Nasty things to make me cry. Words I don't know the meaning of except they're meant to be nasty like words Daddy called Mommy in the last days Daddy was living with us.

Saying now, "If she finds out we're down here I'm gonna break your ass. Anything she does to me, I'm gonna do to you, cunt."

Calvin doesn't mean it, though. Calvin loves me. At school where we don't know anybody, Calvin stays close to me. It's just that words fly out of his mouth sometimes like stinging wasps. Like with Daddy, and Daddy's fists.

They don't mean to hurt. It just happens.

Now Daddy is gone it's so strange to us, Mommy plays his music.

Daddy's music she complained of. His CDs. Heavy metal mostly, Calvin calls it. Like somebody kicking kicking kicking a door. Low and mean like thunder.

Now Daddy is gone Mommy buys bottles like Daddy used to bring home. One of them has a mean-looking wild boar head on it Calvin says is a giant pig living in a swamp that's been known to eat up a little girl *alive and kicking*.

Now Daddy is gone Mommy has his guitar, picking at the strings and trying to strum chords. Daddy's old guitar he hadn't touched in years he'd left behind when he moved away. One of the strings is broke but Mommy doesn't care. Mommy gets loud and happy singing *on the banks of the O-hi-o* and *yonder stands little Mag-gie, suitcase in her hand*. Mommy has a way some nights in the kitchen straddling the guitar across her legs and strumming it and moving her head so her long beet-colored hair ripples to almost her waist. Songs Mommy doesn't know the words to she sings anyway. *Yonder stands little Mag-gie, suitcase in her hand, little Mag-gie was made for lovin', cheatin' another man another man man man!* Calvin says Mommy can't play that old guitar worth shit but Mommy's so pretty now her face is mostly mended and her hair grown out, nobody's gonna notice.

In school I'm so sleepy my eyelids keep shutting. My head falls onto my folded arms on my desk top and there's a woman asking is something wrong. I don't recognize her right away then I see she's my teacher, leaning over me.

I can't remember her name. She smells like erasers not like Mommy who smells so sweet and sharp when she goes out.

"Ceci? You can tell me, dear. If there's anything you wish to confide. If . . ."

I shut my eyes tight. It's like wood smoke in my eyes, how they burn and sting. I feel myself freezing like a scared rabbit.

". . . there's anything wrong at home. Every morning you look so . . ." My teacher pauses licking her lips. Not knowing what she means to say. When Daddy went away, and we were told he would not be coming back you could see in people's eyes how they didn't know what words to use. They could not bring themselves to say *Your father is dead*. They could not say like Calvin *Daddy is dead. Dead-daddy*. My teacher can't bring herself to say *Every morning you look so haunted* for this is not anything you would say to a little girl whose father has gone to Hell to dwell with his own cruel kin.

". . . look so hollow-eyed, dear. Don't you sleep well at night?"

I shake my head the way Calvin does. Tears spill from my eyes. I'm not crying, though. Before anybody can see I wipe my face with both my hands.

In the infirmary the nurse removes my shoes and pulls a blanket up over me so that I can sleep. I'm shivering and my teeth are chattering I'm so cold. I hold myself tight against sleep but it's like the bulb in the cellar suddenly switched off and everything is dark and empty like there's nobody there. And after a while somebody else comes into the infirmary. Her voice and the nurse's voice I can hear through the gauzy curtain pulled around my cot. One voice saying, "This isn't the place for that child to sleep. Not at school. She's missing her school work."

The other voice is the nurse's. Saying quietly like there's a secret between them. "She's the Malvern girl. You know . . ."

"Her! The one whose father . . ."

"It must be. I checked the name."

" 'Malvern.' Of course. The boy Calvin is in fourth grade. He's fidgety and distracted, too."

"Do you think they know? How their father died?"

"God help us, I hope not."

Nasty things were said about Mommy. Like she'd been arrested by the sheriff's deputies. That was not true. Mommy was never arrested. Calvin ran hitting and kicking at kids who said that, jeering at us. Mommy was taken away for questioning. But Mommy was released, and was not ever arrested. *Because there was not one shred of evidence against her.*

During that time Mommy was away a day and a night and part of a day, we stayed with Aunt Estelle. Mommy's older sister. Half-sister. Mommy spoke of her with a hurt twist of her mouth. We didn't have to go to school. We were told not to play with other children. Not to wander from the house. We watched videos not TV and when the TV was on, it was after we went to bed. In that house there was no talk of Daddy. The name *Malvern* was not heard. Later we would learn that there had been a funeral, Calvin and I had been kept away. Aunt Estelle smoked cigarettes and was on the phone a lot and said to us your mother will be back soon, you'll be back home soon. And that was so.

I hugged Auntie Estelle hard, when we left. But afterward Mommy and Aunt Estelle quarreled and when Mommy drove us a thousand miles away in the pickup with the U-Haul behind she never said good-bye to Aunt Estelle. That bitch, Mommy called her.

When Mommy came home from what was called *questioning* her face was sickly and swollen and there were fine white cracks in it like a plaster of Paris face that has been broken but mended again. Not too well mended, but mended. You could hardly see the cracks.

Eventually we would cease seeing them. Mommy grew her hair out long to shimmer and ripple over her shoulders. There was a way Mommy had of brushing her hair out of her eyes in a sweeping gesture that looked like a drowning swimmer suddenly shooting to the surface of the water. *Ah-ah-ah* Mommy filled her lungs with air.

With a lipstick pencil Mommy drew a luscious red-cherry mouth on her pale twisty mouth. Mommy drew on black-rimmed eyes we had not seen before.

Mommy strummed her guitar. It was her guitar now, she'd had the broken string mended. Saying, "It was his own choice. When one of their own comes to dwell with them there is rejoicing through Hell."

By Christmastime in this new place Mommy has quit her job at the discount shoe store and works now at a café on the river. Most nights she's a cocktail waitress but some nights she plays her guitar and sings. With her face bright and made up and her hair so glimmering you don't notice the cracks in Mommy's skin, in the drifting smoky light of the café they are invisible. Mommy's fingers have grown more practiced. Her nails are filed short and polished. Her voice is low and throaty with a little burr in it that makes you shiver. In the café men offer her money which she sometimes accepts. Saying quietly, Thank you. I will take this as a gift for my music. I will take this because my children have no father, I am a single mother and must support two small children. But I will not accept it if you expect anything more from me than this: my music, and my thanks.

At the River's Edge Mommy calls herself Little Maggie. In time she will be known and admired as Little Maggie. She's like a little girl telling us of the applause. Little Maggie taking up her guitar that's polished now and gleaming like the smooth inside of a chestnut after you break off the spiky rind. Strumming chords and letting her long beet-colored hair slide over her shoulders,

Mommy says when she starts to sing everybody in the café goes silent.

In the winter the rabbits' cries grow more pleading and piteous. Calvin hears them, too. But Calvin pretends he doesn't. I press my pillow over my head not wanting to hear. *We don't want to die. We don't want to die.* One night when Mommy is at the café I slip from my bed barefoot and go downstairs into the cellar that smells of oozing muck and rot and animal misery and there in the dim light cast by the single light bulb are the rabbits.

Rabbits in each of the cages! Some of them have grown too large for the cramped space, their hindquarters are pressed against the wire and their soft ears are bent back against their heads. Their eyes shine in apprehension and hope seeing me. A sick feeling comes over me, each of the cages has a rabbit trapped inside. Though this is only logical as I will discover through my life. *In each cage, a captive.* For why would adults who own the world manufacture cages not to be used. I ask the rabbits, Who has locked you in these cages? But the rabbits can only stare at me blinking and twitching their noses. One of them is a beautiful pale powder-grey, a young rabbit and not so sick and defeated as the others. I stroke his head through the cage wire. He's trembling beneath my touch, I can feel his heartbeat. Most of the rabbits are mangy and matted. Their fur is dull grey. There is a single black rabbit, heavy and misshapen from his cage, with watery eyes. The doors of the cages are latched and locked with small padlocks. Both the cages and the padlocks are rusted. I find an old pair of shears in the cellar and holding the shears awkwardly in both hands I manage to cut through the wires of all the cages, I hurt my fingers peeling away openings for the rabbits to hop through but they hesitate, distrustful of me. Even the young rabbit only pokes his head through the opening, blinking and sniffing nervously, unmoving.

Then I see in the cellar wall a door leading to the outside. A heavy wooden door covered in cobwebs and the husks of dead insects. It hasn't been opened in years but I am able to tug it open, a few inches at first, then a little wider. On the other side are concrete steps leading up to the surface of the ground. Fresh cold air smelling of snow touches my face. "Go on! Go out of here! You're free."

The rabbits don't move. I will have to go back upstairs, and leave them in darkness, before they will escape from their cages.

"Ceci? Wake up."

Mommy shakes me, I've been sleeping so hard.

It's morning. The rabbit cries have ceased. Close by running behind our backyard is the Cuyahoga & Erie train with its noisy wheels, almost I don't hear the whistle any longer. In my bed pushed against the wall.

When I go downstairs into the cellar to investigate, I see that the cages are gone.

The rabbit cages are gone! You can see where they've been, though, there's empty space. The concrete floor isn't so dirty as it is other places in the cellar.

The door to the outside is shut tight. Shut, and covered in cobwebs like before.

Outside, where cages were dumped in the weeds, they've been taken away, too. You can see the outlines in the snow.

Calvin is looking, too. But Calvin doesn't say anything.

Mommy says, lighting a match in a way Daddy used to, against her thumb, and raising it to the cigarette dipping from her mouth, "At last those damn stinking cages have been hauled away. It only took five months for that bastard to move his ass."

Burned alive were words that were used by strangers but we were not allowed to hear. *Burned alive in his bed* it was said of our father on TV and elsewhere but we were shielded from such words.

Unless Calvin heard. And Calvin repeated to me.

Burned alive drunk in his bed. Gasoline sprinkled around the trailer and a match tossed. But Randy Malvern was a man with enemies, in his lifetime that was thirty-two years he'd accumulated numerous enemies and not a one of these would be linked to the fire and not a one of these was ever arrested in the arson death though all were questioned by the sheriff and eventually released and some moved away, and were gone.

Now the cages are gone. And now I hear the rabbits' cries in the wind, in the pelting rain, in the train whistle that glides through my sleep. Miles from home I hear them, through my life I will hear them. Cries of trapped creatures who have suffered, who have died, who await us in Hell, our kin.

GLEN HIRSHBERG

Dancing Men

GLEN HIRSHBERG LIVES IN the Los Angeles area with his wife and children. He is the author of a novel, *The Snowman's Children*, and a collection of ghost stories, *The Two Sams*, both published by Carroll & Graf in the United States.

His work has appeared in numerous anthologies, including *The Mammoth Book of Best New Horror*, *The Year's Best Fantasy and Horror*, *Dark Terrors 6*, *Trampoline: An Anthology* and *The Dark: New Ghost Stories*, where "Dancing Men" made its original appearance. Both this story and *The Two Sams* received International Horror Guild Awards in 2004. He is currently completing a new novel and a second set of ghost stories.

"It's gratifying and a relief to see 'Dancing Men' finding some sort of home for itself," admits the author. "It took dozens of drafts and most of a year to complete, and remains an uncomfortable piece for me. I think I was so concerned with honouring the subject matter that I kept strangling the fiction.

"In terms of people lost, the Holocaust touched my family far less directly than it did so many millions of others. But it has been impossible not to notice the scars that event has left in people I love, the ongoing effects it has had on the way nations interact, the jagged holes it has ripped in language and cultural perspective and our mutual sense of what we can expect from each other."

*"These are the last days of our lives so we give a signal maybe
there still will be relatives or acquaintances of these persons
. . . They were tortured and burnt goodbye . . ."*
                                    —Testimonial found at Chelmno

I

W E'D BEEN ALL AFTERNOON in the Old Jewish Cemetery,
where green light filters through the trees and lies atop the
tumbled tombstones like algae. Mostly I think the kids were tired.
The two-week Legacy of the Holocaust tour I had organized had
taken us to Zeppelin Field in Nuremberg, where downed electrical wires slither through the brittle grass, and Bebelplatz in East
Berlin, where ghost-shadows of burned books flutter in their
chamber in the ground like white wings. We'd spent our nights
not sleeping on sleeper trains east to Auschwitz and Birkenau and
our days on public transport, traipsing through the fields of dead
and the monuments to them, and all seven high-school juniors in
my care had had enough.

From my spot on a bench alongside the roped-off stone path
that meandered through the grounds and back out to the streets
of Josefov, I watched six of my seven charges giggling and
chattering around the final resting place of Rabbi Loew. I'd told
them the story of the Rabbi, and the clay man he'd supposedly
created and then animated, and now they were running their
hands over his tombstone, tracing Hebrew letters they couldn't
read, chanting *"Amet"*, the word I'd taught them, in low voices
and laughing. As of yet, nothing had risen from the dirt. The
Tribe, they'd taken to calling themselves, after I told them that the
Wandering Jews didn't really work, historically, since the essential characteristic of the Wanderer himself was his solitude.

There are teachers, I suppose, who would have been considered
members of the Tribe by the Tribe, particularly on a summer trip,
far from home and school and television and familiar language.
But I had never been that sort of teacher.

Nor was I the only excluded member of our traveling party.
Lurking not far from me, I spotted Penny Berry, the quietest
member of our group and the only Goy, staring over the graves
into the trees with her expressionless eyes half closed and her
lipstickless lips curled into the barest hint of a smile. Her auburn

hair sat cocked on the back of her head in a tight, precise ponytail. When she saw me watching, she wandered over, and I swallowed a sigh. It wasn't that I didn't like Penny, exactly. But she asked uncomfortable questions, and she knew how to wait for answers, and she made me nervous for no reason I could explain.

"Hey, Mr Gadeuszki," she said, her enunciation studied, perfect. She'd made me teach her how to say it right, grind the s and z and k together into that single Slavic snarl of sound. "What's with the stones?"

She gestured at the tiny grey pebbles placed across the tops of several nearby tombstones. Those on the slab nearest us glinted in the warm, green light like little eyes. "In memory," I said. I thought about sliding over on the bench to make room for her, then thought that would only make both of us even more awkward.

"Why not flowers?" Penny said.

I sat still. listening to the clamor of new-millennium Prague just beyond the stone wall that enclosed the cemetery. "Jews bring stones."

A few minutes later, when she realized I wasn't going to say anything else, Penny moved off in the general direction of the Tribe. I watched her go and allowed myself a few more peaceful seconds. Probably, I thought, it was time to move us along. We had the Astronomical Clock left to see today, puppet-theatre tickets for tonight, the plane home to Cleveland in the morning. And just because the kids were tired didn't mean they would tolerate loitering here much longer. For seven summers in a row, I had taken students on some sort of exploring trip. "Because you've got nothing better to do," one member of the Tribe cheerfully informed me one night the preceding week. Then he'd said, "Oh my God, I was just kidding, Mr G."

And I'd had to reassure him that I knew he was, I always looked like that.

"That's true. You do," he'd said, and returned to his tripmates.

Now, I rubbed my hand over the stubble on my shaven scalp, stood, and blinked as my family name – in its original Polish spelling – flashed behind my eyelids again, looking just the way it had this morning amongst all the other names etched into the Pinkas Synagogue wall. The ground went slippery underneath me, the tombstones slid sideways in the grass, and I teetered and sat down hard.

When I lifted my head and opened my eyes, the Tribe had swarmed around me, a whirl of backwards baseball caps and tanned legs and Nike symbols. "I'm fine," I said quickly, stood up, and to my relief found I did feel fine. I had no idea what had just happened. "Slipped."

"Kind of," said Penny Berry from the edges of the group, and I avoided looking her way.

"Time to go, gang. Lots more to see."

It has always surprised me when they do what I say, because mostly, they do. It's not me, really. The social contract between teachers and students may be the oldest mutually accepted enacted ritual on this earth, and its power is stronger than most people imagine.

We passed between the last of the graves and through a low stone opening. The dizziness or whatever it had been was gone, and I felt only a faint tingling in my fingertips as I drew my last breath of that too-heavy air, thick with loam and grass springing from bodies stacked a dozen deep in the ground.

The side street beside the Old-New synagogue was crammed with tourists, their purses and backpacks open like the mouths of grotesquely overgrown chicks. Into those open mouths went wooden puppets and embroidered kepot and Chamsa hands from the rows of stalls that lined the sidewalk; the walls, I thought, of an all-new, much more ingenious sort of ghetto. In a way, this place had become exactly what Hitler had meant for it to be: the Museum of a Dead Race, only the paying customers were descendants of the Race, and they spent money in amounts he could never have dreamed. The ground had begun to roll under me again, and I closed my eyes. When I opened them, the tourists had cleared in front of me, and I saw the stall, a lopsided wooden hulk on bulky brass wheels. It tilted toward me, the puppets nailed to its side leering and chattering while the gypsy leaned out from between them, nose studded with a silver star, grinning.

He touched the toy nearest him, set it rocking on its terrible, thin wire. "*Loh-ootkawve divahd-law*," he said, and then I was down, flat on my face in the street.

I don't know how I wound up on my back. Somehow, somebody had rolled me over. I couldn't breathe. My stomach felt squashed, as though there was something squatting on it, wooden and heavy, and I jerked, gagged, opened my eyes, and the light blinded me.

"I didn't," I said, blinking, brain flailing. I wasn't even sure I'd been all the way unconscious, couldn't have been out more than a few seconds. But the way the light affected my eyes, it was as though I'd been buried for a month.

"*Dobry den, dobry den,*" said a voice over me, and I squinted, teared up, blinked into the gypsy's face, the one from the stall, and almost screamed. Then he touched my forehead, and he was just a man, red Manchester United cap on his head, black eyes kind as they hovered around mine. The cool hand he laid against my brow had a wedding ring on it, and the silver star in his nose caught the afternoon light.

I meant to say I was okay, but what came out was "I didn't" again.

The gypsy said something else to me. The language could have been Czech or Slovakian or neither. I didn't know enough to tell the difference, and my ears weren't working right. In them I could feel a painful, persistent pressure.

The gypsy stood, and I saw my students clustered behind him like a knot I'd drawn taut. When they saw me looking, they burst out babbling, and I shook my head, tried to calm them, and then I felt their hands on mine, pulling me to a sitting position. The world didn't spin. The ground stayed still. The puppet stall I would not look at kept its distance.

"Mr G, are you all right?" one of them asked, her voice shrill, slipping toward panic.

Then Penny Berry knelt beside me and looked straight into me, and I could see her formidable brain churning behind those placid grey-green eyes, the color of Lake Erie when it's frozen.

"Didn't what?" she asked.

And I answered, because I had no choice. "Kill my grandfather."

II

They propped me at my desk in our *pension* not far from the Charles Bridge and brought me a glass of "nice water", which was one of our traveling jokes. It was what the too-thin waitress at Terezin – the "town presented to the Jews by the Nazis," as the old propaganda film we saw at the museum proclaimed – thought we were saying when we asked for ice.

For a while, The Tribe sat on my bed and talked quietly to each other and refilled my glass for me. But after thirty minutes or so, when I hadn't keeled over again and wasn't babbling and seemed my usual sullen, solid, bald self, they started shuffling around, playing with my curtains, ignoring me. One of them threw a pencil at another. For a short while, I almost forgot about the nausea churning in my stomach, the trembling in my wrists, the puppets bobbing on their wires in my head.

"Hey," I said. I had to say it twice more to get their attention. I usually do.

Finally, Penny noticed and said, "Mr Gadeuszki's trying to say something," and they slowly quieted down.

I put my quivering hands on my lap under the desk and left them there. "Why don't you kids get back on the metro and go see the Clock?"

The Tribe members looked at each other uncertainly. "Really," I told them. "I'm fine. When's the next time you're going to be in Prague?"

They were good kids, and they looked unsure for a few seconds longer. In the end, though, they started trickling toward the door, and I thought I'd gotten them out until Penny Berry stepped in front of me.

"You killed your grandfather," she said.

"Didn't," I snarled, and Penny blinked, and everyone whirled to stare at me. I took a breath, almost got control of my voice. "I said I didn't kill him."

"Oh," Penny said. She was on this trip not because of any familial or cultural heritage but because this was the most interesting experience she could find to devour this month. She was pressing me now because she suspected I had something more startling to share than Prague did at the moment. And she was always hungry.

Or maybe she was just lonely, confused about the kid she had never quite been and the world she didn't quite feel part of. Which would make her more than a little like me, and might explain why she had always annoyed me as much as she did.

"It's stupid," I said. "It's nothing."

Penny didn't move. In my memory, the little wooden man on his wire quivered, twitched, and began to rock, side to side.

"I need to write it down," I said, trying to sound gentle. Then I lied. "Maybe I'll show you when I'm done."

Five minutes later, I was alone in my room with a fresh glass of nice water and a stack of unlined blank white paper I had scavenged from the computer printer downstairs. I picked up my black pen, and in an instant, there was sand on my tongue and desert sun on my neck and that horrid, gasping breathing like snake-rattle in my ears, and for the first time in many, many years, I was home.

III

In June 1978, on the day after school let out, I was sitting in my bedroom in Albuquerque, New Mexico, thinking about absolutely nothing when my dad came in and sat down on my bed and said, "I want you to do something for me."

In my nine years of life, my father had almost never asked me to do anything for him. As far as I could tell, he had very few things that he wanted. He worked at an insurance firm and came home at exactly 5:30 every night and played an hour of catch with me before dinner or, sometimes, walked me to the ice-cream shop. After dinner, he sat on the black couch in the den reading paperback mystery novels until 9:30. The paperbacks were all old with bright yellow or red covers featuring men in trench coats and women with black dresses sliding down the curves in their bodies like tar. It made me nervous, sometimes, just watching my father's hands on the covers. I asked him once why he liked those kinds of books, and he just shook his head. "All those people," he said, sounding, as usual, like he was speaking to me through a tin can from a great distance. "Doing all those things." At exactly 9:30, every single night I can remember, my father clicked off the lamp next to the couch and touched me on the head if I was up and went to bed.

"What do you want me to do?" I asked that June morning, though I didn't much care. This was the first weekend of summer vacation, and I had months of free time in front of me, and I never knew quite what to do with it anyway.

"What I tell you, okay?" my father said.

Without even thinking, I said, "Sure."

And he said, "Good. I'll tell Grandpa you're coming." Then he left me gaping on the bed while he went into the kitchen to use the phone.

My grandfather lived seventeen miles from Albuquerque in a red adobe hut in the middle of the desert. The only sign of humanity anywhere around him was the ruins of a small pueblo maybe half a mile away. Even now, what I remember most about my grandfather's house is the desert rolling up to and through it in an endless red tide that never receded. From the back steps, I could see the pueblo, honeycombed with caves like a giant beehive tipped on its side, empty of bees but buzzing as the wind whipped through it.

Four years before, my grandfather had told my parents to knock off the token visits. Then he'd had his phone shut off. As far as I knew, none of us had seen him since.

All my life, he'd been dying. He had emphysema and some kind of weird allergic condition that turned swatches of his skin pink. The last time I'd been with him, he'd just sat in a chair in a tank top, breathing through a tube. He'd looked like a piece of petrified wood.

The next morning, a Sunday, my father packed my green camp duffel bag with a box of new, unopened wax packs of baseball cards and the transistor radio my mother had given me for my birthday the year before, then loaded it and me into the grimy green Datsun he always meant to wash and didn't. "Time to go," he told me in his mechanical voice, and I was still too baffled by what was happening to protest as he led me outside. Moments before, a morning thunderstorm had rocked the whole house, but now the sun was up, searing the whole sky orange. Our street smelled like creosote and green chili and adobe mud and salamander skin.

"I don't want to go," I said to my father.

"I wouldn't either, if I were you," he told me, and started the car.

"You don't even like him," I said.

My father just looked at me, and for an astonishing second I thought he was going to hug me. But he looked away instead, dropped the car into gear, and drove us out of town.

All the way to my grandfather's house, we followed the thunderstorm. It must have been traveling at exactly our speed, because we never got any closer, and it never got further away. It just retreated before us, a big black wall of nothing, like a shadow the whole world cast, and every now and then streaks of lightning flew up the clouds like signal flares but illuminated only the sand and mountains and rain.

"Why are we doing this?" I asked when my dad started slowing, studying the sand on his side of the car for the dirt track that lead to my grandfather's.

"Want to drive?" he answered, gesturing to me to slide across the seat into his lap.

Again, I was surprised. My dad always seemed willing enough to play catch with me. But he rarely generated ideas for things we could do together on his own. And the thought of sitting in his lap with his arms around me was too alien to fathom. I waited too long, and the moment passed. My father didn't ask again. Through the windshield, I watched the thunderstorm retreating, the wet road already drying in patches in the sun. The whole day felt distant, like someone else's dream.

"You know he was in the war, right?" my father said, and despite our crawling speed he had to jam on the brakes to avoid passing the turnoff. No one, it seemed to me, could possibly have intended this to be a road. It wasn't dug or flattened or marked, just a rumple in the earth.

"Yeah," I said.

That he'd been in the war was pretty much the only thing I knew about my grandfather. Actually, he'd been in the camps. After the war, he'd been in other camps in Israel for almost five years while Red Cross workers searched for living relatives and found none and finally turned him loose to make his way as best he could.

As soon as we were off the highway, sand ghosts rose around the car, ticking against the trunk and hood as we passed. Thanks to the thunderstorm, they left a wet, red residue like bug smear on the hood and windshield.

"You know, now that I think about it," my father said, his voice flat as ever but the words clearer, somehow, and I found myself leaning closer to him to make sure I heard him over the churning wheels. "He was even less of a grandfather to you than a father to me." He rubbed a hand over the bald spot just beginning to spread over the top of his head like an egg yolk being squashed. I'd never seen him do that before. It made him look old.

My grandfather's house rose out of the desert like a Druid mound. There was no shape to it. It had exactly one window, and that couldn't be seen from the street. No mailbox. Never in my life, I realized abruptly, had I had to sleep in there.

"Dad, please don't make me stay," I said as he stopped the car fifteen feet or so from the front door.

He looked at me, and his mouth turned down a little, and his shoulders tensed. Then he sighed. "Three days," he said, and got out.

"You stay," I said, but I got out, too.

When I was standing beside him, looking past the house at the distant pueblo, he said, "Your grandfather didn't ask for me, he asked for you. He won't hurt you. And he doesn't ask for much from us, or from anyone."

"Neither do you," I said.

After a while, and very slowly, as though remembering how, my father smiled. "And neither do you, Seth."

Neither the smile nor the statement reassured me.

"Just remember this, son. Your grandfather has had a very hard life, and not just because of the camps. He worked two jobs for twenty-five years to provide for my mother and me. He never called in sick. He never took vacations. And he was ecstatic when you were born."

That surprised me. "Really? How do you know?"

For the first time I could remember, my father blushed, and I thought maybe I'd caught him lying, and then I wasn't sure. He kept looking at me. "Well, he came to town, for one thing. Twice."

For a little longer, we stood together while the wind rolled over the rocks and sand. I couldn't smell the rain anymore, but I thought I could taste it, a little. Tall, leaning cacti prowled the waste around us like stick figures who'd escaped from one of my doodles. I was always doodling, then, trying to get the shapes of things.

Finally, the thin, wooden door to the adobe clicked open, and out stepped Lucy, and my father straightened and put his hand on his bald spot again and put it back down.

She didn't live there, as far as I knew. But I'd never been to my grandfather's house when she wasn't in it. I knew she worked for some foundation that provided care to Holocaust victims, though she was Navajo, not Jewish, and that she'd been coming out here all my life to make my grandfather's meals, bathe him, keep him company. I rarely saw them speak to each other. When I was little and my grandmother was still alive and we were still welcome, Lucy used to take me to the pueblo after she'd finished with my grandfather and watch me climb around on the stones and peer into the empty caves and listen to the wind chase thousand-year-old echoes out of the walls.

There were grey streaks now in the black hair that poured down Lucy's shoulders, and I could see semi-circular lines like tree rings in her dark, weathered cheeks. But I was uncomfortably aware, this time, of the way her breasts pushed her plain white denim shirt out of the top of her jeans while her eyes settled on mine, black and still.

"Thank you for coming," she said, as if I'd had a choice. When I didn't answer, she looked at my father. "Thank you for bringing him. We're set up out back."

I threw one last questioning glance at my father as Lucy started away, but he just looked bewildered or bored or whatever he generally was. And that made me angry. "Bye," I told him, and moved toward the house.

"Goodbye," I heard him say, and something in his tone unsettled me; it was too sad. I shivered, turned around, and my father said, "He want to see me?"

He looked thin, I thought, just another spindly cactus, holding my duffel bag out from his side. If he'd been speaking to me, I might have run to him. I wanted to. But he was watching Lucy, who had stopped at the edge of the square of patio cement outside the front door.

"I don't think so," she said, and came over to me and took my hand.

Without another word, my father tossed my duffel bag onto the miniature patio and climbed back in his car. For a moment, his gaze caught mine through the windshield, and I said, "Wait," but my father didn't hear me. I said it louder, and Lucy put her hand on my shoulder.

"This has to be done, Seth," she said.

"What does?"

"This way." She gestured toward the other side of the house, and I followed her there and stopped when I saw the hogan.

It sat next to the squat grey cactus I'd always considered the edge of my grandfather's yard. It looked surprisingly solid, its mud walls dry and grey and hard, its pocked, stumpy wooden pillars firm in the ground, almost as if they were real trees that had somehow taken root there.

"You live here now?" I blurted, and Lucy stared at me.

"Oh, yes, Seth. Me sleep-um ground. How." She pulled aside the hide curtain at the front of the hogan and ducked inside, and I followed.

I thought it would be cooler in there, but it wasn't. The wood and mud trapped the heat but blocked the light. I didn't like it. It reminded me of an oven, of Hansel and Gretel. And it reeked of the desert: burnt sand, hot wind, nothingness.

"This is where you'll sleep," Lucy said. "It's also where we'll work." She knelt and lit a beeswax candle and placed it in the center of the dirt floor in a scratched glass drugstore candlestick. "We need to begin right now."

"Begin what?" I asked, fighting down another shudder as the candlelight played over the room. Against the far wall, tucked under a miniature canopy constructed of metal poles and a tarpaulin, were a sleeping bag and a pillow. My bed, I assumed. Beside it sat a low, rolling table, and on the table were another candlestick, a cracked ceramic bowl, some matches, and the Dancing Man.

In my room in this *pension* in the Czech Republic, five thousand miles and twenty years removed from that place, I put my pen down and swallowed the entire glass of lukewarm water my students had left me. Then I got up and went to the window, staring out at the trees and the street. I was hoping to see my kids returning like ducks to a familiar pond, flapping their arms and jostling each other and squawking and laughing. Instead, I saw my own face, faint and featureless, too white in the window glass. I went back to the desk and picked up the pen.

The Dancing Man's eyes were all pupil, carved in two perfect ovals in the knottiest wood I had ever seen. The nose was just a notch, but the mouth was enormous, a giant "O", like the opening of a cave. I was terrified of the thing even before I noticed that it was moving.

Moving, I suppose, is too grand a description. It . . . leaned. First one way, then the other, on a wire that ran straight through its belly. In a fit of panic, after a nightmare, I described it to my college roommate, a physics major, and he shrugged and said something about perfect balance and pendulums and gravity and the rotation of the earth. Except that the Dancing Man didn't just move side to side. It also wiggled down its wire, very slowly, until it reached the end. And then the wire tilted up, and it began to wiggle back. Slowly. Until it reached the other end. Back and forth. Side to side. Forever.

"Take the drum," Lucy said behind me, and I ripped my stare away from the Dancing Man.

"What?" I said.

She gestured at the table, and I realized she meant the ceramic bowl. I didn't understand, and I didn't want to go over there. But I didn't know what else to do, and I felt ridiculous under Lucy's stare.

The Dancing Man was at the far end of its wire, leaning, mouth open. Trying to be casual, I snatched the bowl from underneath it and retreated to where Lucy knelt. The water inside the bowl made a sloshing sound but didn't splash out, and I held it away from my chest in surprise and noticed the covering stitched over the top. It was hide of some kind, moist when I touched it.

"Like this," said Lucy, and she leaned close and tapped on the skin of the drum. The sound was deep and tuneful, like a voice. I sat down next to Lucy. She tapped again, in a slow, repeating pattern. I put my hands where hers had been, and when she nodded at me, I began to play.

"Okay?" I said.

"Harder," Lucy said, and she reached into her pocket and pulled out a long wooden stick. The candlelight flickered across it, and I saw the carvings there. A pine tree, and underneath, roots that bulged along the stick's base like long, black veins.

"What is that?" I asked.

"A rattle stick. My grandmother made it. I'm going to rattle it while you play. So if you would. Like I showed you."

I beat on the drum, and the sound came out dead in that airless space.

"For God's sake," Lucy snapped. "Harder." She had never been exceptionally friendly to me. But she'd been friendlier than this.

I slammed my hands down harder, and after a few beats Lucy

leaned back and nodded and watched. Not long after, she lifted her hand, stared at me as though daring me to stop her, and shook the stick. The sound it made was less rattle than buzz, as though it had wasps inside it. Lucy shook it a few more times, always at the same half-pause in my rhythm. Then her eyes rolled back in her head, and her spine arched. My hand froze over the drum, and Lucy snarled, "Don't stop."

After that, she began to chant. There was no tune to it, but a pattern, the pitch sliding up a little, down some, up a little more. When Lucy reached the top note, the ground under my crossed legs seemed to tingle, as though there were scorpions sliding out of the sand, but I didn't look down. I thought of the wooden figure on its wire behind me, but I didn't turn around. I played the drum, and I watched Lucy, and I kept my mouth shut.

We went on for a long, long time. After that first flush of fear, I was concentrating too hard to think. My bones were tingling, too, and the air in the hogan was heavy. I couldn't get enough of it in my lungs. Tiny tide-pools of sweat had formed in the hollow of Lucy's neck and under her ears and at the throat of her shirt. Under my palms, the drum was sweating, too, and the skin got slippery and warm. Not until Lucy stopped singing did I realize that I was rocking side to side. Leaning.

"Want lunch?" Lucy said, standing and brushing the earth off her jeans.

I put my hands out perpendicular, felt the skin prickle and realized my wrists had gone to sleep even as they pounded out the rhythm that Lucy had taught me. When I stood, the floor of the hogan seemed unstable, like the bottom of one of those balloon tents my classmates sometimes had at birthday parties. I didn't want to look behind me, and then I did. The Dancing Man rocked slowly in no wind.

I turned around again, but Lucy had left the hogan. I didn't want to be alone in there, so I leapt through the hide curtain and winced against the sudden blast of sunlight and saw my grandfather.

He was propped on his wheelchair, positioned dead center between the hogan and the back of his house. He must have been there the whole time, I thought, and somehow I'd managed not to notice him when I came in, because unless he'd gotten a whole lot better in the years since I'd seen him last, he couldn't have wheeled himself out. And he looked worse.

For one thing, his skin was falling off. At every exposed place on him, I saw flappy folds of yellow-pink. What was underneath was uglier still, not red or bleeding, just not skin. Too dry. Too colorless. He looked like a cornhusk. An empty one.

Next to him, propped on a rusty blue dolly, was a cylindrical silver oxygen tank. A clear tube ran from the nozzle at the top of the tank to the blue mask over my grandfather's nose and mouth. Above the mask, my grandfather's heavy-lidded eyes watched me, though they didn't seem capable of movement, either. Leave him out here, I thought, and those eyes would simply fill up with sand.

"Come in, Seth," Lucy told me, without any word to my grandfather or acknowledgement that he was there.

I had my hand on the screen door, was halfway into the house when I realized I'd heard him speak. I stopped. It had to have been him, I thought, and couldn't have been. I turned around and saw the back of his head tilting toward the top of the chair. Retracing my steps – I'd given him a wide berth – I returned to face him. The eyes stayed still, and the oxygen tank was silent. But the mask fogged, and I heard the whisper again.

"*Ruach*," he said. It was what he always called me, when he called me anything.

In spite of the heat, I felt goosebumps spring from my skin, all along my legs and arms. I couldn't move. I couldn't answer. I should say hello, I thought. Say something.

I waited instead. A few seconds later, the oxygen mask fogged again. "*Trees*", said the whisper-voice. "*Screaming. In the trees.*" One of my grandfather's hands raised an inch or so off the arm of the chair and fell back into place.

"Patience," Lucy said from the doorway. "Come on, Seth." This time, my grandfather said nothing as I slipped past him into the house.

Lucy slid a bologna sandwich, a bag of Fritos and a plastic glass of apple juice in front of me. I lifted the sandwich, found that I couldn't imagine putting it in my mouth, and dropped it on the plate.

"Better eat," Lucy said. "We have a long day yet."

I ate a little. Eventually, Lucy sat down across from me, but she didn't say anything else. She just gnawed a celery stick and watched the sand outside change color as the sun edged west. The house was silent, the countertops and walls bare.

"Can I ask you something?" I finally asked.

Lucy was washing my plate in the sink. She didn't turn around, but she didn't say no.

"What are we doing? Out there, I mean."

No answer. Through the kitchen doorway, I could see my grandfather's living room, the stained wood floor and the single brown armchair lodged against a wall, across from the TV. My grandfather had spent every waking minute of his life in this place for fifteen years or more, and there was no trace of him in it.

"It's a Way, isn't it?" I said, and Lucy shut the water off.

When she turned, her expression was the same as it had been all day: a little mocking, a little angry. She took a step toward the table.

"We learned about them at school," I said.

"Did you," she said.

"We're studying lots of Indian things."

The smile that spread over Lucy's face was ugly, cruel. Or maybe just tired. "Good for you," she said. "Come on. We don't have much time."

"Is this to make my grandfather better?"

"Nothing's going to make your grandfather better." Without waiting for me, she pushed through the screen door into the heat.

This time, I made myself stop beside my grandfather's chair. I could just hear the hiss of the oxygen tank, like steam escaping from the boiling ground. When no fog appeared in the blue mask and no words emerged from the hiss, I followed Lucy into the hogan and let the hide curtain fall shut.

All afternoon and into the evening, I played the water drum while Lucy sang. By the time the air began to cool outside, the whole hogan was vibrating, and the ground, too. Whatever we were doing, I could feel the power in it. I was the beating heart of a living thing, and Lucy was its voice. Once, I found myself wondering just what we were setting loose or summoning, and I stopped for a single beat. But the silence was worse. The silence was like being dead. And I thought I could hear the Dancing Man behind me. If I inclined my head, stopped drumming, I almost believed that I'd hear him whispering.

When Lucy finally rocked to her feet and walked out again without speaking to me, it was evening, and the desert was alive. I sat shaking as the rhythm spilled out of me and the sand soaked it up. Then I stood, and that unsteady feeling came over me again, stronger this time, and the air was too thin, as though some of the atmosphere had evaporated. When I emerged from the hogan, I saw black beetles on the wall of my grandfather's house, and I heard wind and rabbits and the first coyotes yipping somewhere to the west. My grandfather sat slumped in the same position he had been in hours and hours ago, which meant he had been baking out here all afternoon. Lucy was on the patio, watching the sun melt into the horizon's open mouth. Her skin was slick, and her hair was wet where it touched her ear and neck.

"Your grandfather's going to tell you a story," she said, sounding exhausted. "And you're going to listen."

My grandfather's head rolled upright, and I wished we were back in the hogan, doing whatever it was we'd been doing. At least there I was moving, pounding hard enough to drown out sounds. Sounds that weren't us, and weren't supposed to be there. The screen door slapped shut, and my grandfather looked at me. His eyes were deep, deep brown, almost black, and horribly familiar. Did my eyes look like that?

"*Ruach*," he whispered, and I wasn't sure, but his whisper seemed stronger than it had before. The oxygen mask fogged and stayed fogged. The whisper kept coming, as though Lucy had spun a spigot and left it open. "*You will know . . . Now . . . Then the world . . . won't be yours . . . anymore.*" My grandfather shifted like some sort of giant, bloated sand-spider in the center of its web, and I heard his ruined skin rustle. Overhead, the whole sky went red.

"*At war's end . . .*" my grandfather hissed. "*Do you . . . understand?*" I nodded, transfixed. I could hear his breathing now, the ribs rising, parting, collapsing. The tank machinery had gone strangely silent. Was he breathing on his own, I wondered? Could he, still?

"*A few days. Do you understand? Before the Red Army came . . .*" He coughed. Even his cough sounded stronger. "*The Nazis took . . . me. And the Gypsies. From . . . our camp. To Chelmno.*"

I'd never heard the word before. I've almost never heard it since. But as my grandfather said it, another cough roared out of his throat, and when it was gone, the tank was hissing again. Still, my grandfather continued to whisper.

"*To die. Do you understand?*" Gasp. Hiss. Silence. "*To die. But not yet. Not . . . right away.*" Gasp. "*We came . . . by train, but open train. Not cattle car. Wasteland. Farmland. Nothing. And then trees.*" Under the mask, the lips twitched, and above it, the eyes closed completely. "*That first time. Ruach. All those . . . giant . . . green . . . trees. Unimaginable. To think anything . . . on the Earth we knew . . . could live that long.*"

His voice continued to fade, faster than the daylight. A few minutes more, I thought, and he'd be silent again, just machine and breath, and I could sit here in the yard and let the evening wind roll over me.

"*When they took . . . us off the train,*" my grandfather said, "*for one moment . . . I swear I smelled . . . leaves. Fat, green leaves . . . the new green . . . in them. Then the old smell . . . The only smell. Blood in dirt. The stink . . . of us. Piss. Shit. Open . . . sores. Skin on fire. Hnnn.*"

His voice trailed away, hardly-there air over barely moving mouth, and still he kept talking. "*Prayed for . . . some people . . . to die. They smelled . . . better. Dead. That was one prayer . . . always answered.*

"*They took us . . . into the woods. Not to barracks. So few of them. Ten. Maybe twenty. Faces like . . . possums. Stupid. Blank. No thoughts. We came to . . . ditches. Deep. Like wells. Half full already. They told us 'Stand still' . . . 'Breathe in'.*"

At first, I thought the ensuing silence was for effect. He was letting me smell it. And I did, the earth and the dead people, and there were German soldiers all around, floating up out of the sand with black uniforms and white, blank faces. Then my grandfather crumpled forward, and I screamed for Lucy.

She came fast but not running and put a hand on my grandfather's back and another on his neck. After a few seconds, she straightened. "He's asleep," she told me. "Stay here." She wheeled my grandfather into the house. She was gone a long time.

Sliding to a sitting position, I closed my eyes and tried not to hear my grandfather's voice. After a while I thought I could hear bugs and snakes and something larger padding out beyond the cacti. I could feel the moonlight, too, white and cool on my skin. The screen door banged, and I opened my eyes to find Lucy moving toward me, past me, carrying a picnic basket into the hogan.

"I want to eat out here," I said quickly, and Lucy turned with the hide curtain in her hand.

"Why don't we go in?" she said, and the note of coaxing in her voice made me nervous. So did the way she glanced over her shoulder into the hogan, as though something in there had spoken.

I stayed where I was, and eventually Lucy shrugged and let the curtain fall and dropped the basket at my feet. From the way she was acting, I thought she might leave me alone out there, but she sat down instead and looked at the sand and the cacti and the stars.

Inside the basket I found warmed canned chili in a tupperware container and fry bread with cinnamon sugar and two cellophane-wrapped broccoli stalks that reminded me of uprooted miniature trees. In my ears, my grandfather's voice murmured. To drown out the sound more than anything else, I began to eat.

As soon as I was finished, Lucy began to pack up the basket, but she stopped when I spoke. "Please," I said. "Just talk to me a little."

She gave me the same look she'd given me all day. As though we'd never even met. "Get some sleep. Tomorrow . . . well, let's just say tomorrow's a big day."

"For who?"

Lucy pursed her lips, and all at once, inexplicably, she seemed on the verge of tears. "Go to sleep."

"I'm not sleeping in the hogan," I told her.

"Suit yourself."

She was standing, her back to me now. I said, "Just tell me what kind of Way we're doing."

"An Enemy Way."

"What does it do?"

"It's nothing, Seth. Jesus Christ. It's silly. Your grandfather thinks it will help him talk. He thinks it will sustain him while he tells you what he needs to tell you. Don't worry about the goddamn Way. Worry about your grandfather, for once."

My mouth flew open, and my skin stung as though she'd slapped me. I started to protest, then found I couldn't, and didn't want to. All my life, I'd built my grandfather into a figure of fear, a gasping, grotesque monster in a wheelchair. And my father had let me. I started to cry.

"I'm sorry," I said.

"Don't apologize to me." Lucy walked to the screen door.

"Isn't it a little late?" I called after her, furious at myself, at my father, at Lucy. Sad for my grandfather. Scared and sad.

One more time, Lucy turned around, and the moonlight poured down the white streaks in her hair like wax through a mold. Soon, I thought, she'd be made of it.

"I mean, to hurt my grandfather's enemies," I said. "The Way can't really do anything to them. Right?"

"His enemies are inside him," Lucy said, and left me.

For hours, it seemed, I sat in the sand, watching constellations explode out of the blackness like firecrackers. In the ground, I heard night-things stirring. I thought about the tube in my grandfather's mouth and the unspeakable hurt in his eyes – because that's what it was, I thought now, not boredom, not hatred – and the enemies inside him. And then, slowly, exhaustion overtook me. The taste of fry bread lingered in my mouth, and the starlight got brighter still. I leaned back on my elbows. And finally, at God knows what hour, I crawled into the hogan, under the tarpaulin-canopy Lucy had made me, and fell asleep.

When I awoke, the Dancing Man was sliding down its wire toward me, and I knew, all at once, where I'd seen eyes like my grandfather's, and the old fear exploded through me all over again. How had he done it, I wondered? The carving on the wooden man's face was basic, the features crude. But the eyes were his. They had the same singular, almost oval shape, with identical little notches right near the tear ducts. The same too-heavy lids. Same expression, or lack of any.

I was transfixed, and I stopped breathing. All I could see were those eyes dancing toward me. Halfway down the wire, they seemed to stop momentarily, as though studying me, and I remembered something my dad had told me about wolves. "They're not trial-and-error animals," he'd said. "They wait and watch, wait and watch, until they're sure they know how the thing is done. And then they do it."

The Dancing Man began to weave again. First to one side, then the other, then back. If it reached the bottom of the wire, I thought – I *knew* – I would die. Or I would change. That was why Lucy was ignoring me. She had lied to me about what we were doing here. That was the reason they hadn't let my father stay.

Leaping to my feet, I grabbed the Dancing Man around its clunky wooden base, and it came off the table with the faintest little suck, as though I'd yanked a weed out of the ground. I wanted to throw it, but I didn't dare. Instead, bent double, not looking at my clenched fist, I crab-walked to the entrance of the hogan, brushed back the hide curtain, slammed the Dancing Man down in the sand outside, and flung the curtain closed again. Then I squatted in the shadows, panting. Listening.

I crouched there a long time, watching the bottom of the curtain, expecting to see the Dancing Man slithering beneath it. But the hide stayed motionless, the hogan shadowy but still. I let myself sit back, and eventually I slid into my sleeping bag again. I didn't expect to sleep anymore, but I did.

The smell of fresh fry bread woke me, and when I opened my eyes Lucy was laying a tray of bread and sausage and juice on a red, woven blanket on the floor of the hogan. My lips tasted sandy, and I could feel grit in my clothes and between my teeth and under my eyelids, as though I'd been buried overnight and dug up again.

"Hurry," Lucy told me, in the same chilly voice as yesterday.

I threw back the sleeping bag and started to sit up and saw the Dancing Man gliding back along its wire, watching me. My whole body clenched, and I glared at Lucy and shouted, "How did that get back here?" Even as I said it, I realized that wasn't what I wanted to ask. More than how, I needed to know *when*. Exactly how long had it been hovering over me without my knowing?

Without raising an eyebrow or even looking in my direction, Lucy shrugged and sat back. "Your grandfather wants you to have it," she said.

"I don't want it."

"Grow up."

Edging as far from the nightstand as possible, I shed the sleeping bag and sat down on the blanket and ate. Everything tasted sweet and sandy. My skin prickled with the intensifying heat. I still had a piece of fry bread and half a sausage left when I put my plastic fork down and looked at Lucy, who was arranging a new candle, settling the water drum near me, tying her hair back with a red rubber-band.

"Where did it come from?" I asked.

That got Lucy to look at me, at least, and this time, there really were tears in her eyes. "I don't understand your family," she said.

I shook my head. "Neither do I."

"Your grandfather's been saving that for you, Seth."

"Since when?"

"Since before you were born. Before your father was born. Before he ever imagined there could be a you."

This time, when the guilt came for me, it mixed with my fear rather than chasing it away, and I broke out sweating. I thought I might be sick.

"You have to eat. Damn you," said Lucy.

I picked up my fork and squashed a piece of sausage into the fry bread and put it in my mouth. My stomach convulsed, but it accepted the food.

As soon as I'd finished, Lucy shoved the drum onto my lap. I played while she chanted, and the sides of the hogan seemed to breathe in and out, very slowly. I felt drugged. Then I wondered if I had been. Had they sprinkled something over the bread? Was that the next step? And toward what? Erasing me, I thought, almost chanted. Erasing me, and my hands flew off the drum and Lucy stopped.

"All right," she said. "That's probably enough." Then, to my surprise, she actually reached out and tucked some of my hair behind my ear, touched my face for a second as she took the drum from me. "It's time for your Journey," she said.

I stared at her. The walls, I noticed, had stilled. I didn't feel any less strange, but a little more awake. "Journey where?"

"You'll need water. And I've packed you a lunch." She slipped through the hide curtain, and I followed, dazed, and almost walked into my grandfather, parked right outside the hogan with a black towel on his head, so that his eyes and splitting skin were in shadow. On his peeling hands, he wore black leather gloves. His hands, I thought, must be on fire.

Right at the moment I noticed that Lucy was no longer with us, the hiss from the oxygen tank sharpened, and my grandfather's lips moved beneath the mask. "*Ruach*." This morning, the nickname sounded almost affectionate.

I waited, unable to look away. But the oxygen hiss settled again, like leaves after a gust of wind, and my grandfather said nothing more. A few seconds later, Lucy came back carrying a red backpack, which she handed to me.

"Follow the signs," she said, and turned me around until I was facing straight out from the road into the empty desert.

Struggling to life, I shook her hand off my shoulder. "Signs of what? What am I supposed to be doing?"

"Finding. Bringing back."

"I won't go," I said.

"You'll go," said Lucy coldly. "The signs will be easily recognizable and easy to locate. I have been assured of that. All you have to do is pay attention."

"Assured by who?"

"The first sign, I am told, will be left by the tall flowering cactus."

She pointed, which was unnecessary. A hundred yards or so from my grandfather's house, a spiky green cactus poked out of the rock and sand, supported on either side by two miniature versions of itself. A little cactus family staggering in out of the waste.

I glanced at my grandfather under his mock cowl, then at Lucy with her ferocious black eyes trained on me. Tomorrow, I thought, my father would come for me, and with any luck I would never have to come here again.

Suddenly, I felt ridiculous and sad and guilty once more. Without even realizing what I was doing, I stuck my hand out and touched my grandfather's arm. The skin under his thin cotton shirt depressed beneath my fingers like the squishy center of a misshapen pillow. It wasn't hot. It didn't feel alive at all. I yanked my hand back, and Lucy glared at me. Tears sprang to my eyes.

"Get out of here," she said, and I stumbled away into the sand.

I don't really think the heat intensified as soon as I stepped away from my grandfather's house. But it seemed to. Along my bare arms and legs, I could feel the little hairs curling as though singed. The sun had scorched the sky white, and the only place to look that didn't hurt my eyes was down. Usually when I walked in the desert, I was terrified of scorpions, but not that day. It was impossible to imagine anything scuttling or stinging or even breathing out there. Except me.

I don't know what I expected to find. Footprints, maybe, or animal scat, or something dead. Instead, stuck to the stem by a cactus needle, I found a yellow stick-'em note. It said *Pueblo*.

Gently, avoiding the rest of the spiny needles, I removed the note. The writing was black and blocky. I glanced toward my grandfather's house, but he and Lucy were gone. The ceremonial hogan looked silly from this distance, like a little kid's pup tent.

Unlike the pueblo, I thought. I didn't even want to look that way, let alone go there. Already I could hear it calling for me in a whisper that sounded way too much like my grandfather's. I could head for the road, I thought. Start toward town instead of the pueblo and wait for a passing truck to carry me home. There would have to be a truck, sooner or later.

I did go to the road. But when I got there, I turned in the direction of the pueblo. I don't know why. I didn't feel as if I had a choice.

The walk, if anything, was too short. No cars passed. No road signs sprang from the dirt to point the way back to town and the world I knew. I watched the asphalt rise out of itself and roll in the heat like the surface of the sea, and I thought of my grandfather in the woods of Chelmno, digging graves in long, green shadows. Lucy had put ice in the thermos she gave me, and the cubes clicked against my teeth when I drank.

I walked, and I watched the desert, trying to spot a bird or a lizard. Even a scorpion would have been welcome. What I saw was sand, distant, colorless mountains, white sky, a world as empty of life and its echoes as the surface of Mars, and just as red.

Even the lone road sign pointing to the pueblo was rusted through, crusted with sand, the letters so scratched away that the name of the place was no longer legible. I'd never seen a tourist trailer here, or another living soul. Even calling it a pueblo seemed grandiose.

It was two sets of caves dug into the side of a cliff-face, the top one longer than the bottom, so that together they formed a sort of gigantic cracked harmonica for the desert wind to play. The roof and walls of the top set of caves had fallen in. The whole structure seemed more monument than ruin, a marker of a people who no longer existed rather than a place where they had lived.

The bottom stretch of caves was largely intact, and as I stumbled toward them along the cracking macadam I could feel their pull in my ankles. They seemed to be sucking the desert inside them, bit by bit. I stopped in front and listened.

I couldn't hear anything. I looked at the cracked, nearly square window openings, the doorless entryways leading into what had once been living spaces, the low, shadowed caves of dirt and rock. The whole pueblo just squatted there, inhaling sand through its dozens of dead mouths in a mockery of breath. I waited a while longer, but the open air didn't feel any safer, just hotter. If my grandfather's enemies were inside him, I suddenly wondered, and if we were calling them out, then where were they going? Finally, I ducked through the nearest entryway and stood in the gloom.

After a few seconds, my eyes adjusted. But there was nothing to see. Along the window openings, blown sand lay in waves and mounds, like miniature relief maps of the desert outside. At my feet lay tiny stones – too small to hide scorpions – and a few animal bones, none of them larger than my pinky, distinguishable primarily by the curve of them, their stubborn whiteness.

Then, as though my entry had triggered some sort of mechanical magic show, sound coursed into my ears. In the walls, tiny feet and bellies slithered and scuttled. Nothing rattled a warning. Nothing hissed. And the footsteps came so softly that at first I mistook them for sand shifting along the sills and the cool clay floor.

I didn't scream, but I staggered backwards, lost my footing, slipped down, and I had the thermos raised and ready to swing when my father stepped out of the shadows and sat down cross-legged across the room from me.

"What . . ." I said, tears flying down my face, heart thudding.

My father said nothing. From the pocket of his plain yellow button-up shirt, he pulled a packet of cigarette paper and a pouch of tobacco, then rolled a cigarette in a series of quick, expert motions.

"You don't smoke," I said, and my father lit the cigarette and dragged air down his lungs with a rasp.

"Far as you know," he answered. The red-orange light looked like an open sore on his lips. Around us, the pueblo lifted, settled.

"Why does Grandpa call me *ruach*?" I snapped. And still my father only sat and smoked. The smell tickled unpleasantly in my nostrils. "God, Dad. What's going on? What are you doing here, and—"

"Do you know what *ruach* means?" he said.

I shook my head.

"It's a Hebrew word. It means ghost."

Hearing that was like being slammed to the ground. I couldn't get my lungs to work.

My father went on. "Sometimes that's what it means. It depends what you use it with, you see? Sometimes it means spirit, as in the spirit of God. Spirit of life. What God gave to his creations." He stubbed his cigarette in the sand, and the orange light winked out like an eye blinking shut. "And sometimes it just means wind."

By my sides, I could feel my hands clutch sand as breath returned to my body. The sand felt cool, soft. "You don't know Hebrew, either," I said.

"I made a point of knowing that word."

"Why?"

"Because that's what he called me, too," my father said. He rolled a second cigarette but didn't light it. For a while we sat. Then my father said, "Lucy called me two weeks ago. She told me it was time, and she said she needed a partner for your . . . ceremony. Someone to hide this, then help you find it. She said it was essential to the ritual." Reaching behind him, he produced a brown paper grocery bag with the top rolled down and tossed it to me. "I didn't kill it," he said.

I stared at him, and more tears stung my eyes. Sand licked along the skin of my legs and arms and crawled up my shorts and sleeves as though seeking pores, points of entry. Nothing about my father's presence here was reassuring. Nothing about him had ever been reassuring, or anything else, I thought furiously, and the fury felt good. It helped me move. I yanked the bag to me.

The first thing I saw when I ripped it open was an eye. It was yellow-going-grey, almost dry. Not quite, though. Then I saw the folded black, ridged wings. A furry, broken body twisted into a "J". Except for the smell and the eye, it could have been a Hallowe'en decoration.

"Is that a bat?" I whispered. Then I shoved the bag away and gagged.

My father glanced around the walls, back at me. He made no move toward me. *He's part of it,* I thought wildly. *He knows what they're doing.* I pushed the thought away. It couldn't be true. "Dad, I don't understand," I pleaded.

"I know you're young," my father said. "He didn't do this to me until I left for college. But there's no more time, is there? You've seen him."

"Why do I have to do this at all?"

My father's gaze swung down on me. He cocked his head and pursed his lips, as though I'd asked something completely incomprehensible. "It's your birthright," he said, and stood up.

We drove back to my grandfather's adobe in silence. The trip lasted less than five minutes. I couldn't even figure out what else to ask, let alone what I might do. I kept glancing at my father. I wanted to scream at him, pound on him until he told me why he was acting this way.

Except that I wasn't sure he was acting anything but normal, for him. He didn't speak when we played catch or when he walked me to the ice-cream shop, either. When we arrived at the adobe, he leaned across me to push my door open, and I grabbed his hand.

"Dad. At least tell me what the bat is for."

My father straightened, moved the air-conditioning lever right, then hard back to the left, as though he could surprise it into working. He always did this. It never worked. My father and his routines. "Nothing," he said. "It's a symbol."

"For what?"

"Lucy will tell you."

"But you know." I was almost snarling at him now.

"It stands for the skin at the tip of the tongue. It's the Talking God. Or part of it, I think. I don't know, exactly. I'm sorry."

Gently, hand on my shoulder, he eased me out of the car before it occurred to me to wonder what he was apologizing for. But he surprised me by calling after me. "I promise you this, Seth," he said. "This is the last time in your life that you'll have to come here. Shut the door."

Too stunned and confused and scared to do anything else, I did as he told me, then watched as my father's car disintegrated into the first far-off shadows of twilight. Already, too soon, I felt the change in the air, the night chill seeping through the gauze-dry day like blood through a bandage.

My grandfather and Lucy were waiting on the patio. She had her hand on his shoulder, her long hair gathered on her head, and without its dark frame her face looked much older. And his – fully exposed now, without its protective shawl – looked like a rubber mask on a hook, with no bones inside to support it.

Slowly, my grandfather's wheelchair squeaked over the patio onto the hard sand as Lucy propelled it. I could do nothing but watch. The wheelchair stopped, and my grandfather studied me.

"*Ruach*," he said. There was still no tone in his voice. But there were no holes in it either, no gaps where last night his breath had failed him. "*Bring it to me.*"

It was my imagination, surely, or the first hint of breeze, that made the paper bag seem to squirm in my hands. This would be the last time, my father had said. I stumbled forward and dropped the bag in my grandfather's lap.

Faster than I'd ever seen him move, but still not fast, my grandfather crushed the bag against his chest. His head tilted forward, and I had the insane idea that he was about to sing to the dead bat as if it were a baby. But all he did was close his eyes and clutch the bag.

"All right, that's enough," Lucy said, and took the bag from him. She touched him gently on the back but didn't look at me.

"What did he just do?" I asked, challenging her. "What did the bat do?"

Once more, Lucy smiled her slow, nasty smile. "Wait and see."

Then she was gone, and my grandfather and I were alone in the yard. The dark came drifting down the distant mountainsides like a fog bank, but faster. When it reached us, I closed my eyes and felt nothing except an instantaneous chill. I opened my eyes to find my grandfather still watching me, head cocked a little on his neck. A wolf, indeed.

"*Digging,*" he said. "*All we did, at first. Making pits deeper. The dirt so black. So soft. Like sticking your hands . . . inside an animal. All those trees leaning over us. Pines. Great white birches. Bark as smooth as baby skin. The Nazis gave us nothing to drink. Nothing to eat. But they paid us no attention, either. I sat next to the gypsy I had slept beside all through the war. On a single slab of rotted wood. We had shared body heat. Blood from each other's cuts and wounds. Infections. Lice.*

"*I never . . . even knew his name. Four years six inches from each other . . . never knew it. Couldn't understand each other. Never really tried. He'd saved—*" A cough rattled my grandfather's entire body, and his eyes got wilder, began to bulge, and I thought he wasn't breathing and almost yelled for Lucy again, but he gathered himself and went on. "*Buttons,*" he said. "*You understand? From somewhere. Rubbed their edges on rocks. Posts. Anything handy. Until they were . . . sharp. Not to kill. Not as a weapon."* More coughing. *"As a tool. To whittle."*

"Whittle," I said automatically, as though talking in my sleep.

"When he was starving. When he woke up screaming. When we had to watch children's . . . bodies dangling from gallows . . . until the first crows came for their eyes. When it was snowing, and . . . we had to march . . . barefoot . . . or stand outside all night. The gypsy whittled."

Again, my grandfather's eyes ballooned in their sockets as though they would burst. Again came the cough, shaking him so hard that he almost fell from the chair. Again, he fought his body to stillness.

"Wait," he gasped. *"You will wait. You must."*

I waited. What else could I do?

A long while later, he said, *"Two little girls."* I stared at him. His words wrapped me like strands of a cocoon. "What?"

"Listen. Two girls. The same ones, over and over. That's what . . . the gypsy . . . whittled."

Dimly, in the part of my brain that still felt alert, I wondered how anyone could tell if two figures carved in God knows what with the sharpened edge of a button were the same girls.

But my grandfather just nodded. *"Even at the end. Even at Chelmno. In the woods. In the rare moments . . . when we weren't digging, and the rest of us . . . sat. He went straight for the trees. Put his hands on them like they were warm. Wept. First time, all war. Despite everything we saw, everything we knew . . . no tears from him, until then. When he came back, he had . . . strips of pine bark in his hands. And while everyone else slept . . . or froze . . . or died . . . he worked. All night. Under the trees.*

"Every few hours . . . shipments came. Of people, you understand? Jews. We heard trains. Then, later, we saw creatures . . . between tree trunks. Thin. Awful. Like dead saplings walking. When the Nazis . . . began shooting . . . they fell with no sound. Pop-pop-pop from the guns. Then silence. Things lying in leaves. In the wet.

"The killing wasn't . . . enough fun . . . for the Nazis, of course. They made us roll bodies . . . into the pits, with our hands. Then bury them. With our hands. Or our mouths. Some-

GLEN HIRSHBERG

times our mouths. Dirt and blood. Bits of person in your teeth. A few of us lay down. Died on the ground. The Nazis didn't have . . . to tell us. What to do with them. We just . . . pushed anything dead . . . into the nearest pit. No prayers. No last look to see who it was. It was no one. Do you see? No one. Burying. Or buried. No difference.

"And still, all night, the gypsy whittled.

"For the dawn . . . shipment . . . the Nazis tried . . . something new. Stripped the newcomers . . . then lined them up . . . on the lip of a pit . . . twenty, thirty at a time. Then they played . . . perforation games. Shoot up the body . . . down it . . . see if you could get it . . . to flap apart . . . before it fell. Open up, like a flower.

"All through the next day. All the next night. Digging. Waiting. Whittling. Killing. Burying. Over and over. Sometime . . . late second day, maybe . . . I got angry. Not at the Nazis. For what? Being angry at human beings . . . for killing . . . for cruelty . . . like being mad at ice, for freezing. It's just . . . what to expect. So I got angry . . . at the trees. For standing there. For being green, and alive. For not falling when bullets hit them.

"I started . . . screaming. Trying to. In Hebrew. In Polish. The Nazis looked up, and I thought they would shoot me. They laughed instead. One began to clap. A rhythm. See?"

Somehow, my grandfather lifted his limp hands from the arms of the wheelchair and brought them together. They met with a sort of crackle, like dry twigs crunching.

"The gypsy . . . just watched. Still weeping. But also . . . after a while . . . nodding."

All this time, my grandfather's eyes had seemed to swell, as though there were too much air being pumped into his body. But now, the air went out of him in a rush, and the eyes went dark, and the lids came down. I thought maybe he'd fallen asleep again, the way he had last night. But I still couldn't move. Dimly, I realized that the sweat from my long day's walking had cooled on my skin, and that I was freezing.

My grandfather's lids opened, just a little. He seemed to be peering at me from inside a trunk, or a coffin.

"I don't know how the gypsy knew . . . that it was ending. That it was time. Maybe just because . . . it had been hours . . . half a day . . . between shipments. The world had gone . . . quiet. Us.

Nazis. Trees. Corpses. There had been worse places . . . I thought . . . to stop living. Despite the smell.

"Probably, I was sleeping. I must have been, because the gypsy shook me . . . by the shoulder. Then held out . . . what he'd made. He had it . . . balanced . . . on a stick he'd bent. So the carving moved. Back and forth. Up and down."

My mouth opened and then hung there. I was rock, sand, and the air moved through me and left me nothing.

" 'Life,' the gypsy said to me, in Polish. Only Polish I ever heard him speak. 'Life. You see?'

"I shook . . . my head. He said it again. 'Life.' And then . . . I don't know how . . . but I did . . . see.

"I asked him . . . 'Why not you?' He took . . . from his pocket . . . one of his old carvings. The two girls. Holding hands. I hadn't noticed . . . the hands before. And I understood.

" 'My girls,' he said. 'Smoke. No more. Five years ago.' I understood that, too.

"I took the carving from him. We waited. We slept, side by side. One last time. Then the Nazis came.

"They made us stand. Hardly any of them, now. The rest gone. Fifteen of us. Maybe less. They said something. German. None of us knew German. But to me . . . at least . . . the word meant . . . run.

"The gypsy . . . just stood there. Died where he was. Under the trees. The rest . . . I don't know. The Nazi who caught me . . . laughing . . . a boy. Not much . . . older than you. Laughing. Awkward with his gun. Too big for him. I looked at my hand. Holding . . . the carving. The wooden man. 'Life,' I found myself chanting . . . instead of Shma. 'Life.' Then the Nazi shot me in the head. Bang."

And with that single word, my grandfather clicked off, as though a switch had been thrown. He slumped in his chair. My paralysis lasted a few more seconds, and then I started waving my hands in front of me, as if I could ward off what he'd told me, and I was so busy doing that that I didn't notice, at first, the way my grandfather's torso heaved and rattled. Whimpering, I lowered my hands, but by then, my grandfather wasn't heaving anymore, and he'd slumped forward further, and nothing on him was moving.

"Lucy!" I screamed, but she was already out of the house,

wrestling my grandfather out of his chair to the ground. Her head dove down on my grandfather's as she shoved the mask up his face, but before their mouths even met, my grandfather coughed, and Lucy fell back, sobbing, tugging the mask back into place.

My grandfather lay where he'd been thrown, a scatter of bones in the dirt. He didn't open his eyes. The oxygen tank hissed, and the blue tube stretching to his mask filled with wet mist.

"How?" I whispered

Lucy swept tears from her eyes. "What?"

"He said he got shot in the head." And even as I said that, I felt it for the first time, that cold slithering up my intestines into my stomach, then my throat.

"Stop it," I said. But Lucy slid forward so that her knees were under my grandfather's head and ignored me. Overhead, I saw the moon half-embedded in the ridged black of the sky like the lidded eye of a Gila monster. I stumbled around the side of the house and, without thinking about it, slipped into the hogan.

Once inside, I jerked the curtain down to block out the sight of Lucy and my grandfather and that moon, then drew my knees tight against my chest to pin that freezing feeling where it was. I stayed that way a long while, but whenever I closed my eyes, I saw people splitting open like peeled bananas, limbs strewn across bare, black ground like tree branches after a lightning storm, pits full of naked dead people.

I'd wished him dead, I realized. At the moment he tumbled forward in his chair, I'd hoped he was dead. And for what, exactly? For being in the camps? For telling me about it? For getting sick, and making me confront it?

But with astonishing, disturbing speed, the guilt over those thoughts passed. And when it was gone, I realized that the cold had seeped down my legs and up to my neck. It clogged my ears, coated my tongue like a paste, sealing the world out. All I could hear was my grandfather's voice like blown sand against the inside of my skull. *Life.* He was inside me, I thought. He had erased me, taken my place. He was becoming me.

I threw my hands over my ears, which had no effect. My thoughts flashed through the last two days: the drumming and chanting; the dead bat in the paper bag; my father's goodbye. All the while, that voice beat in my ears, attaching itself to my pulse. *Life.* And finally, I realized that I'd trapped myself. I was alone in the hogan in the dark. When I turned around, I would see the Dancing Man. It would be wiggling toward me with its mouth wide open. And it would be over, too late. It might already be.

Flinging my hands behind me, I grabbed the Dancing Man around its thin black neck. I could feel it bob on its wire, and I half-expected it to squirm as I fought to my feet. It didn't, but its wooden skin gave where I pressed it like real skin. Inside my head, the new voice kept beating.

At my feet lay the matches that Lucy had used to light her ceremonial candles. I snatched up the matchbook, then threw the carved thing to the ground, where it smacked on its base and tipped over, face up, staring at me. I broke a match against the matchbox, then another. The third match lit.

For one moment, I held the flame over the Dancing Man. The heat felt wonderful crawling toward my fingers, a blazing, living thing chasing back the cold inside me. I dropped the match, and the Dancing Man disintegrated in a spasm of white-orange flame.

And then, abruptly, there was nothing to be done. The hogan was a dirt and wood shelter, the night outside the plain old desert night, the Dancing Man a puddle of red and black ash that I scattered with my foot. Still cold but mostly tired, I staggered outside, sat down hard against the side of the hogan and closed my eyes.

Footsteps woke me, and I sat up and found, to my amazement, that it was daylight. I waited, tense, afraid to look up, and then I did.

My father was kneeling beside me on the ground.

"You're here already?" I asked.

"Your grandpa died, Seth," he said, in his zombie-Dad voice, though he touched my hand the way a real father would. "I've come to take you home."

IV

The familiar commotion in the hallway of the *pension* alerted me that my students had returned. One of them, but only one, stopped outside my door. I waited, holding my breath, wishing I'd snapped out the light. But Penny didn't knock, and after a few seconds, I heard her careful, precise footfall continuing toward her room. And so I was alone with my puppets and my memories and my horrible suspicions, the way I always have been.

I remember rousing myself out of the malaise I couldn't quite seem to shake – have never, for one instant, shaken since – during that last ride home from my grandfather's. "I killed him," I told my father, and when he glanced at me, expressionless, I told him all of it, the Dancing Man and the ceremony and the thoughts I'd had.

My father didn't laugh. He also didn't touch me. All he said was, "That's silly, Seth" And, for a while, I thought it was.

But today I am thinking of Rabbi Loew and his golem, the creature he infected with a sort of life. A creature that walked, talked, thought, saw, but couldn't taste. Couldn't feel. I'm thinking of my father, the way he always was. If I'm right, then of course it had been done to him, too. And I'm thinking of the way I only seem all the way real, even to me, when I see myself in the vividly reflective faces of my students.

It's possible, I realize, that nothing happened to me those last few days. It could have happened years before I was born. The gypsy had offered what he offered, and my grandfather had accepted, and as a result become what he was. Might have been. If that's true, then my father and I are unexceptional in a way. Natural progeny. We simply inherited our natures and our limitations, the way all earthly creatures do.

But I can't help thinking about the graves I saw on this summer's trip, and the millions of people in them, and the millions more without graves. The ones who are smoke.

And I find that I can feel it, at last. Or that I've always felt it, without knowing what it was: the Holocaust, roaring down the generations like a wave of radiation, eradicating, in everyone it touches, the ability to trust people, experience joy, fall in love, believe in love when you see it in others. And I wonder what difference it makes, in the end, whether it really was my grandfather, or the approximation of him that the gypsy made, who finally crawled out of the woods of Chelmno.

NEIL GAIMAN

Bitter Grounds

NEIL GAIMAN HORROR-HOSTED the Fox Channel's *13 Nights of Fear* during the fortnight before Hallowe'en 2004 and got to introduce movies from inside a coffin. He thought it was cool.

His 2002 novel *American Gods* won science fiction's Hugo Award and horror's Bram Stoker Award, while *Coraline*, a dark fantasy for children which he had been writing for a decade, was a huge success on both sides of the Atlantic and even managed to beat its predecessor in the awards stakes.

On the illustrated front, his first *Sandman* graphic novel in seven years, entitled *Endless Nights*, is published by DC Comics and illustrated by seven different artists; *1602* is a new alternate history miniseries from Marvel, and he has collaborated with artist Dave McKean on the children's picture book *The Wolves in the Walls*.

As well as all the above, the *New York Times* best-selling author has somehow also found the time to make a short vampire film entitled *A Short Film About John Bolton*, and he has recently started writing a new novel, with the working title of *Anansi Boys*.

" 'Bitter Grounds' was written for Nalo Hopkinson," explains Gaiman, "for her anthology *Mojo: Conjure Stories*. I wondered if I could say anything new or interesting about zombies, and several things sort of came together at once when I wrote it. It's set in the hotel the 1994 World Fantasy Convention was held in.

"I read a review of the story recently, which pointed out that it was trickier than it seems on the surface, which seemed like a wise observation to me."

I
"Come back early or never come"

I N EVERY WAY THAT counted, I was dead. Inside – somewhere, maybe – I was screaming and weeping and howling like an animal, but that was another person deep within, another person who had no access to the face and lips and mouth and head, so on the surface I just shrugged and smiled and kept moving. If I could have physically passed away, just let it all go, like that, without doing anything, stepped out of life as easily as walking through a door, I would have done. But I was going to sleep at night and waking in the morning, disappointed to be there and resigned to existence.

Sometimes I telephoned her. I let the phone ring once, maybe even twice, before I hung up.

The me who was screaming was so far inside that nobody knew he was even there at all. Even I forgot that he was there, until one day I got into the car – I had to go to the store, I had decided, to bring back some apples – and I went past the store that sold apples and I kept driving, and driving. I was going south, and west, because if I went north or east I would run out of world too soon.

A couple of hours down the highway my cellphone started to ring. I wound down the window and threw the cellphone out. I wondered who would find it, whether they would answer the phone and find themselves gifted with my life.

When I stopped for gas I took all the cash I could on every card I had. I did the same for the next couple of days, ATM by ATM, until the cards stopped working.

The first two nights I slept in the car.

I was halfway through Tennessee when I realized I needed a bath badly enough to pay for it. I checked into a motel, stretched out in the bath and slept in it until the water got cold and woke me. I shaved with a motel courtesy-kit plastic razor and a sachet of foam. Then I stumbled to the bed, and I slept.

Awoke at 4:00 a.m., and knew it was time to get back on the road.

I went down to the lobby.

There was a man standing at the front desk when I got there: silver-grey hair although I guessed he was still in his thirties, if only just, thin lips, good suit rumpled, saying "I *ordered* that cab an *hour* ago. One *hour* ago." He tapped the desk with his wallet as he spoke, the beats emphasizing his words.

The night manager shrugged. "I'll call again," he said. "But if they don't have the car, they can't send it." He dialled a phone number, said, "This is the Night's Out Inn front desk again . . . Yeah, I told him . . . Yeah, I told him."

"Hey," I said. "I'm not a cab, but I'm in no hurry. You need a ride somewhere?"

For a moment the man looked at me like I was crazy, and for a moment there was fear in his eyes. Then he looked at me like I'd been sent from Heaven. "You know, by God, I do," he said.

"You tell me where to go," I said. "I'll take you there. Like I said, I'm in no hurry."

"Give me that phone," said the silver-grey man to the night clerk. He took the handset and said, "You can *cancel* your cab, because God just sent me a Good Samaritan. People come into your life for a reason. That's right. And I want you to think about that."

He picked up his briefcase – like me, he had no luggage – and together we went out to the parking lot.

We drove through the dark. He'd check a hand-drawn map on his lap, with a flashlight attached to his key ring, then he'd say, *Left here*, or *This way*.

"It's good of you," he said.

"No problem. I have time."

"I appreciate it. You know, this has that pristine urban-legend quality, driving down country roads with a mysterious Samaritan. A Phantom Hitch-hiker story. After I get to my destination, I'll describe you to a friend, and they'll tell me you died ten years ago, and still go round giving people rides."

"Be a good way to meet people."

He chuckled. "What do you do?"

"Guess you could say I'm between jobs," I said. "You?"

"I'm an anthropology professor." Pause. "I guess I should have introduced myself. Teach at a Christian College. People don't believe we teach anthropology at Christian Colleges, but we do. Some of us."

"I believe you."

Another pause. "My car broke down. I got a ride to the motel from the Highway Patrol, as they said there was no tow truck going to be there until morning. Got two hours of sleep. Then the Highway Patrol called my hotel room. Tow truck's on the way. I got to be there when they arrive. Can you believe that? I'm not there, they won't touch it. Just drive away. Called a cab. Never came. Hope we get there before the tow truck."

"I'll do my best."

"I guess I should have taken a plane. It's not that I'm scared of flying. But I cashed in the ticket, I'm on my way to New Orleans. Hour's flight, four hundred and forty dollars. Day's drive, thirty dollars. That's four hundred and ten dollars spending money, and I don't have to account for it to anybody. Spent fifty dollars on the motel room, but that's just the way these things go. Academic conference. My first. Faculty doesn't believe in them. But things change. I'm looking forward to it. Anthropologists from all over the world." He named several, names that meant nothing to me. "I'm presenting a paper on the Haitian coffee girls."

"They grow it, or drink it?"

"Neither. They sold it door-to-door in Port-au-Prince, early in the morning, in the early years of the century."

It was starting to get light now.

"People thought they were zombies," he said. "You know. The walking dead. I think it's a right turn here."

"Were they? Zombies?"

He seemed very pleased to have been asked. "Well, anthropologically there are several schools of thought about zombies. It's not as cut-and-dried as populist works like *The Serpent and the Rainbow* would make it appear. First we have to define our terms: are we talking folk belief, or zombie dust, or the walking dead?"

"I don't know," I said. I was pretty sure *The Serpent and the Rainbow* was a horror movie.

"They were children, little girls, five to ten years old, who went door to door through Port-au-Prince selling the chicory-coffee mixture. Just about this time of day, before the sun was up. They belonged to one old woman. Hang a left just before we go into the next turn. When she died, the girls vanished. That's what the books tell you."

"And what do you believe?" I asked.

"That's my car," he said, with relief in his voice. It was a red Honda Accord, on the side of the road. There was a tow truck beside it, lights flashing, a man beside the truck smoking a cigarette. We pulled up behind the recovery vehicle.

The anthropologist had the door of the car opened before I'd stopped. He grabbed his briefcase and got out.

"Was giving you another five minutes, then I was going to take off," said the tow-truck driver. He dropped his cigarette into a puddle on the tarmac. "Okay, I'll need your triple-A card, and a credit card."

The man reached for his wallet. He looked puzzled. He put his hands in his pockets. He said, "My wallet." He came back to my car, opened the passenger-side door and leaned back inside. I turned on the light. He patted the empty seat. "My wallet," he said again. His voice was plaintive and hurt.

"You had it back in the motel," I reminded him. "You were holding it. It was in your hand."

He said, "God *damn* it. God fucking *damn* it to Hell."

"Everything okay there?" called the tow-truck driver.

"Okay," said the anthropologist to me, urgently. "This is what we'll do. You drive back to the motel. I must have left the wallet on the desk. Bring it back here. I'll keep him happy until then. Five minutes, it'll take you five minutes." He must have seen the expression on my face. He said, "Remember. People come into your life for a reason."

I shrugged, irritated to have been sucked into someone else's story.

Then he shut the car door, and gave me a thumbs-up.

I wished I could just have driven away and abandoned him, but it was too late – I was driving to the hotel. The night clerk gave me the wallet, which he had noticed on the counter, he told me, moments after we'd left.

I opened the wallet. The credit cards were all in the name of Jackson Anderton.

It took me half an hour to find my way back, as the sky greyed into full dawn. The tow truck was gone. The rear window of the red Honda Accord was broken, and the driver's-side door hung open. I wondered if it were a different car, if I had driven the wrong way to the wrong place; but there were the tow-truck driver's cigarette stubs, crushed on the road, and in the ditch nearby I found a gaping briefcase, empty, and beside it, a manila folder containing a fifteen-page typescript, a prepaid hotel reservation at a Marriott in New

Orleans in the name of Jackson Anderton, and a packet of three condoms, ribbed for extra pleasure.

On the title page of the typescript was printed:

> "This was the way Zombies are spoken of: They are the bodies without souls. The living dead. Once they were dead, and after that they were called back to life again."
>
> Hurston. Tell My Horse.

I took the manila folder, but left the briefcase where it was. I drove south under a pearl-coloured sky.

People come into your life for a reason. Right.

I could not find a radio station that would hold its signal. Eventually I pressed the scan button on the radio and just left it on, left it scanning from channel to channel in a relentless quest for signal, scurrying from gospel to oldies to Bible talk to sex talk to country, three seconds a station with plenty of white noise in between.

. . . Lazarus, who was dead, you make no mistake about that, he was dead, and Jesus brought him back to show us, I say to show us . . .

. . . What I call a Chinese dragon, can I say this on the air? Just as you, y'know, get your rocks off, you whomp her round the backatha head, it all spurts outta her nose, I damn near laugh my ass off . . .

. . . If you come home tonight I'll be waiting in the darkness for my woman with my bottle and my gun . . .

. . . When Jesus says will you be there will you be there? No man knows the day or the hour so will you be there . . .

. . . President unveiled an initiative today . . .

. . . Fresh-brewed in the morning. For you. For me. For every day. Because every day is freshly ground . . .

Over and over. It washed over me, driving through the day, on the back roads. Just driving and driving.

They become more personable as you head south, the people. You sit in a diner, and, along with your coffee and your food, they bring you comments, questions, smiles and nods.

It was evening, and I was eating fried chicken and collard greens and hush puppies, and a waitress smiled at me. The food seemed tasteless, but I guessed that might have been my problem, not theirs.

I nodded at her, politely, which she took as an invitation to come over and refill my coffee cup. The coffee was bitter, which I liked. At least it tasted of something.

"Looking at you," she said, "I would guess that you are a professional man. May I enquire as to your profession?" That was what she said, word for word.

"Indeed you may," I said, feeling almost possessed by something, and affably pompous, like W.C. Fields or the Nutty Professor (the fat one, not the Jerry Lewis one, although I am actually within pounds of the optimum weight for my height). "I happen to be . . . an anthropologist, on my way to a conference in New Orleans, where I shall confer, consult and otherwise hobnob with my fellow anthropologists."

"I knew it," she said. "Just looking at you. I had you figured for a professor. Or a dentist, maybe."

She smiled at me one more time. I thought about stopping for ever in that little town, eating in that diner every morning and every night. Drinking their bitter coffee and having her smile at me until I ran out of coffee and money and days.

Then I left her a good tip, and went south and west.

II
"Tongue brought me here"

There were no hotel rooms in New Orleans, or anywhere in the New Orleans sprawl. A Jazz Festival had eaten them, every one. It was too hot to sleep in my car, and, even if I'd cranked a window and been prepared to suffer the heat, I felt unsafe. New Orleans is a real place, which is more than I can say about most of the cities I've lived in, but it's not a safe place, not a friendly one.

I stank, and I itched. I wanted to bathe, and to sleep, and for the world to stop moving past me.

I drove from fleabag motel to fleabag motel, and then, at the last, as I had always known I would, I drove into the parking lot of the downtown Marriott on Canal Street. At least I knew they had one free room. I had a voucher for it in the manila folder.

"I need a room," I said to one of the women behind the counter.

She barely looked at me. "All rooms are taken," she said. "We won't have anything until Tuesday."

I needed to shave, and to shower, and to rest. *What's the worst she can say?* I thought. *I'm sorry, you've already checked in?*

"I have a room, prepaid by my university. The name's Anderton."

She nodded, tapped a keyboard, said "Jackson?" then gave me a key to my room, and I initialled the room rate. She pointed me to the elevators.

A short man with a ponytail, and a dark, hawkish face dusted with white stubble cleared his throat as we stood beside the elevators. "You're the Anderton from Hopewell," he said. "We were neighbours in the *Journal of Anthropological Heresies.*" He wore a white T-shirt that said ANTHROPOLOGISTS DO IT WHILE BEING LIED TO.

"We were?"

"We were. I'm Campbell Lakh. University of Norwood and Streatham. Formerly North Croydon Polytechnic. England. I wrote the paper about Icelandic spirit-walkers and fetches."

"Good to meet you," I said, and shook his hand. "You don't have a London accent."

"I'm a Brummie," he said. "From Birmingham," he added. "Never seen you at one of these things before."

"It's my first conference," I told him.

"Then you stick with me," he said. "I'll see you're all right. I remember my first one of these conferences, I was scared shitless the entire time that I'd do something stupid. We'll stop on the mezzanine, get our stuff, then get cleaned up. There must have been a hundred babies on my plane over, I swear to God. They took it in shifts to scream, shit and puke, though. Never less than ten of them screaming at a time."

We stopped on the mezzanine, collected our badges and programmes. "Don't forget to sign up for the ghost walk," said the smiling woman behind the table. "Ghost walks of Old New Orleans each night, limited to fifteen people in each party, so sign up fast."

I bathed, and washed my clothes out in the basin, then hung them up in the bathroom to dry.

I sat naked on the bed, and examined the contents of Anderton's briefcase. I skimmed through the paper he had intended to present, without taking in the content.

On the clean back of page five he had written, in a tight, mostly legible, scrawl, *In a perfect world you could fuck people without giving them a piece of your heart. And every glittering kiss and every touch of flesh is another shard of heart you'll never see again.*

Until walking (waking? calling?) on your own is unsupportable.

When my clothes were pretty much dry I put them back on and went down to the lobby bar. Campbell was already there. He was drinking a gin and tonic, with a gin and tonic on the side.

He had out a copy of the conference programme and had circled each of the talks and papers he wanted to see. ("Rule one, if it's before midday, fuck it unless you're the one doing it," he explained.) He showed me my talk, circled in pencil.

"I've never done this before," I told him. "Presented a paper at a conference."

"It's a piece of piss, Jackson," he said. "Piece of piss. You know what I do?"

"No," I said.

"I just get up and read the paper. Then people ask questions, and I just bullshit," he said. "Actively bullshit, as opposed to passively. That's the best bit. Just bullshitting. Piece of utter piss."

"I'm not really good at, um, bullshitting," I said. "Too honest."

"Then nod, and tell them that that's a really perceptive question, and that it's addressed at length in the longer version of the paper, of which the one you are reading is an edited abstract. If you get some nut-job giving you a really difficult time about something you got wrong, just get huffy and say that it's not about what's fashionable to believe, it's about the truth."

"Does that work?"

"Christ, yes. I gave a paper a few years back about the origins of the Thuggee sects in Persian military troops – it's why you could get Hindus and Moslems alike becoming Thuggee, you see; the Kali worship was tacked on later. It would have begun as some sort of Manichaean secret society—"

"Still spouting that nonsense?" She was a tall, pale woman with a shock of white hair, wearing clothes that looked both aggressively, studiedly Bohemian, and far too warm for the climate. I could imagine her riding a bicycle, the kind with a wicker basket in the front.

"Spouting it? I'm writing a fucking book about it," said the

Englishman. "So, what I want to know is, who's coming with me to the French Quarter to taste all that New Orleans can offer?"

"I'll pass," said the woman, unsmiling. "Who's your friend?"

"This is Jackson Anderton, from Hopewell College."

"The Zombie Coffee Girls paper?" She smiled. "I saw it in the programme. Quite fascinating. Yet another thing we owe Zora, eh?"

"Along with *The Great Gatsby*," I said.

"Hurston knew F. Scott Fitzgerald?" said the bicycle woman. "I did not know that. We forget how small the New York literary world was back then, and how the colour bar was often lifted for a genius."

The Englishman snorted. "Lifted? Only under sufferance. The woman died in penury as a cleaner in Florida. Nobody knew she'd written any of the stuff she wrote, let alone that she'd worked with Fitzgerald on *The Great Gatsby*. It's pathetic, Margaret."

"Posterity has a way of taking these things into account," said the tall woman. She walked away.

Campbell stared after her. "When I grow up," he said, "I want to be her."

"Why?"

He looked at me. "Yeah, that's the attitude. You're right. Some of us write the bestsellers, some of us read them, some of us get the prizes, some of us don't. What's important is being human, isn't it? It's how good a person you are. Being alive."

He patted me on the arm. "Come on. Interesting anthropological phenomenon I've read about on the Internet I shall point out to you tonight, of the kind you probably don't see back in Dead Rat, Kentucky. *Id est*, women who would, under normal circumstances, not show their tits for a hundred quid, will be only too pleased to get 'em out for the crowd for some cheap plastic beads."

"Universal trading medium," I said. "Beads."

"Fuck," he said. "There's a paper in that. Come on. You ever had a jello shot, Jackson?"

"No."

"Me neither. Bet they'll be disgusting. Let's go and see."

We paid for our drinks. I had to remind him to tip.

"By the way," I said. "F. Scott Fitzgerald. What was his wife's name?"

"Zelda? What about her?"

"Nothing," I said.

Zelda. Zora. Whatever. We went out.

III
"Nothing, like something, happens anywhere"

Midnight, give or take. We were in a bar on Bourbon Street, me and the English anthropology prof, and he started buying drinks – real drinks, this place didn't do jello shots – for a couple of dark-haired women at the bar. They looked so similar that they might have been sisters. One wore a red ribbon in her hair, the other wore a white ribbon. Gauguin might have painted them, only he would have painted them bare-breasted, and without the silver mouse-skull earrings. They laughed a lot.

We had seen a small party of academics walk past the bar at one point, being led by a guide with a black umbrella. I pointed them out to Campbell.

The woman with the red ribbon raised an eyebrow. "They go on the Haunted History tours, looking for ghosts. You want to say, dude, this is where the ghosts come, this is where the dead stay. Easier to go looking for the living."

"You saying the tourists are *alive*?" said the other, mock-concern on her face.

"When they *get* here," said the first, and they both laughed at that.

They laughed a lot.

The one with the white ribbon laughed at everything Campbell said. She would tell him, "Say 'fuck' again," and he would say it, and she would say, "Fook! Fook!" trying to copy him, and he'd say, "It's not *fook*, it's *fuck*," and she couldn't hear the difference, and would laugh some more.

After two drinks, maybe three, he took her by the hand and walked her into the back of the bar, where music was playing, and it was dark, and there were a couple of people already, if not dancing, then moving against each other.

I stayed where I was, beside the woman with the red ribbon in her hair.

She said, "So you're in the record company too?"

I nodded. It was what Campbell had told them we did. "I hate telling people I'm a fucking academic," he had said, reasonably, when they were in the Ladies' Room. Instead he had told them that he had discovered Oasis.

"How about you? What do you do in the world?"

She said, "I'm a priestess of Santeria. Me, I got it all in my blood, my papa was Brazilian, my momma was Irish-Cherokee. In Brazil, everybody makes love with everybody and they have the best little brown babies. Everybody got black slave blood, everybody got Indian blood, my poppa even got some Japanese blood. His brother, my uncle, he looks Japanese. My poppa, he just a good-looking man. People think it was my poppa I got the Santeria from, but no, it was my grandmomma, said she was Cherokee, but I had her figgered for mostly high yaller when I saw the old photographs. When I was three I was talking to dead folks, when I was five I watched a huge black dog, size of a Harley-Davidson, walking behind a man in the street, no one could see it but me, when I told my mom, she told my grandmomma, they said, she's got to know, she's got to learn. There's people to teach me, even as a little girl.

"I was never afraid of dead folk. You know that? They never hurt you. So many things in this town can hurt you, but the dead don't hurt you. Living people hurt you. They hurt you so bad."

I shrugged.

"This is a town where people sleep with each other, you know. We make love to each other. It's something we do to show we're still alive."

I wondered if this was a come-on. It did not seem to be.

She said, "You hungry?"

I said, "A little."

She said, "I know a place near here they got the best bowl of gumbo in New Orleans. Come on."

I said, "I hear it's a town you're best off not walking on your own at night."

"That's right," she said. "But you'll have me with you. You're safe, with me with you."

Out on the street college girls were flashing their breasts to the crowds on the balconies. For every glimpse of nipple the onlookers would cheer and throw plastic beads. I had known the red-ribbon woman's name earlier in the evening, but now it had evaporated.

"Used to be they only did this shit at Mardi Gras," she said. "Now the tourists expect it, so it's just tourists doing it for the tourists. The locals don't care. When you need to piss," she added, "you tell me."

"Okay. Why?"

"Because most tourists who get rolled, get rolled when they go into the alleys to relieve themselves. Wake up an hour later in Pirate's Alley with a sore head and an empty wallet."

"I'll bear that in mind." She pointed to an alley as we passed it, foggy and deserted. "Don't go there," she said.

The place we wound up in was a bar with tables. A TV on above the bar showed *The Tonight Show* with the sound off and subtitles on, although the subtitles kept scrambling into numbers and fractions. We ordered the gumbo, a bowl each.

I was expecting more from the best gumbo in New Orleans. It was almost tasteless. Still, I spooned it down, knowing that I needed food, that I had had nothing to eat that day.

Three men came into the bar. One sidled, one strutted, one shambled. The sidler was dressed like a Victorian undertaker, high top hat and all. His skin was fish-belly pale; his hair was long and stringy; his beard was long and threaded with silver beads. The strutter was dressed in a long black leather coat, dark clothes underneath. His skin was very black. The last one, the shambler, hung back, waiting by the door. I could not see much of his face, nor decode his race: what I could see of his skin was a dirty grey. His lank hair hung over his face. He made my skin crawl.

The first two men made straight for our table, and I was, momentarily, scared for my skin, but they paid no attention to me. They looked at the woman with the red ribbon, and both of the men kissed her on the cheek. They asked about friends they had not seen, about who did what to whom in which bar and why. They reminded me of the fox and the cat from *Pinocchio*.

"What happened to your pretty girlfriend?" the woman asked the black man.

He smiled, without humour. "She put a squirrel tail on my family tomb."

She pursed her lips. "Then you better off without her."

"That's what I say."

I glanced over at the one who gave me the creeps. He was a filthy thing, junkie-thin, grey-lipped. His eyes were downcast. He barely moved. I wondered what the three men were doing together: the fox and the cat and the ghost.

Then the white man took the woman's hand and pressed it to his lips, bowed to her, raised a hand to me, in a mock salute, and the three of them were gone.

"Friends of yours?"

"Bad people," she said. "Macumba. Not friends of anybody."

"What was up with the guy by the door? Is he sick?"

She hesitated, then she shook her head. "Not really. I'll tell you when you're ready."

"Tell me now."

On the TV, Jay Leno was talking to a thin blonde woman. IT &S NOT .UST T½E MOVIE said the caption. SO H.VE SS YOU SE¾N THE AC ION F!GURE? He picked up a small toy from his desk, pretended to check under its skirt to make sure it was anatomically correct. [LAUGHTER], said the caption.

She finished her bowl of gumbo, licked the spoon with a red, red tongue, and put it down in the bowl. "A lot of kids they come to New Orleans. Some of them read Anne Rice books and figure they learn about being vampires here. Some of them have abusive parents, some are just bored. Like stray kittens living in drains, they come here. They found a whole new breed of cat living in a drain in New Orleans, you know that?"

"No."

SLAUGHTER S] said the caption, but Jay was still grinning, and *The Tonight Show* went to a car commercial.

"He was one of the street kids, only he had a place to crash at night. Good kid. Hitch-hiked from LA to New Orleans. Wanted to be left alone to smoke a little weed, listen to his Doors cassettes, study up on Chaos magick and read the complete works of Aleister Crowley. Also get his dick sucked. He wasn't particular about who did it. Bright eyes and bushy tail."

"Hey," I said. "That was Campbell. Going past. Out there."

"Campbell?"

"My friend."

"The record producer?" She smiled as she said it, and I thought, *She knows. She knows he was lying. She knows what he is*.

I put down a $20 and a $10 on the table, and we went out onto the street to find him. But he was already gone.

"I thought he was with your sister," I told her.

"No sister," she said. "No sister. Only me. Only me."

We turned a corner and were engulfed by a crowd of noisy tourists, like a sudden breaker crashing onto the shore. Then, as fast as they had come, they were gone, leaving only a handful of people behind them. A teenaged girl was throwing up in a gutter, a young man nervously standing near her, holding her purse and a plastic cup half-full of booze.

The woman with the red ribbon in her hair was gone. I wished I had made a note of her name, or the name of the bar in which I'd met her.

I had intended to leave that night, to take the Interstate west to Houston and from there to Mexico, but I was tired and two-thirds drunk, and instead I went back to my room, and when the morning came I was in still in the Marriott. Everything I had worn the night before smelled of perfume and rot.

I put on my T-shirt and jeans, went down to the hotel gift shop, picked out a couple more T-shirts and a pair of shorts. The tall woman, the one without the bicycle, was in there, buying some Alka Seltzer.

She said, "They've moved your presentation. It's now in the Audubon Room, in about twenty minutes. You might want to clean your teeth first. Your best friends won't tell you, but I hardly know you, Mister Anderton, so I don't mind telling you at all."

I added a travelling toothbrush and toothpaste to the stuff I was buying. Adding to my possessions, though, troubled me. I felt I should be shedding them. I needed to be transparent, to have nothing.

I went up to the room, cleaned my teeth, put on the Jazz Festival T-shirt. And then, because I had no choice in the matter, or because I was doomed to confer, consult and otherwise hobnob, or because I was pretty certain Campbell would be in the audience and I wanted to say goodbye to him before I drove away, I picked up the typescript and went down to the Audubon Room, where fifteen people were waiting. Campbell was not one of them.

I was not scared. I said hello, and I looked at the top of page one.

It began with another quote from Zora Neale Hurston:

> "Big Zombies who come in the night to do malice are talked about. Also the little girl Zombies who are sent out by their owners in the dark dawn to sell little packets of roasted coffee. Before sun-up their cries of "Café grillé" can be heard from dark places in the streets and one can only see them if one calls out for the seller to come with the goods. Then the little dead one makes herself visible and mounts the steps."

Anderton continued on from there, with quotations from Hurston's contemporaries, several extracts from old interviews with older Haitians, the man's paper leaping, as far as I was able to tell, from conclusion to conclusion, spinning fancies into guesses and suppositions and weaving those into facts.

Half-way through, Margaret, the tall woman without the bicycle, came in and simply stared at me. I thought, *She knows I'm not him. She knows.* I kept reading, though. What else could I do?

At the end, I asked for questions.

Somebody asked me about Zora Neale Hurston's research practices. I said that was a very good question, which was addressed at greater length in the finished paper, of which what I had read was essentially an edited abstract.

Someone else, a short, plump woman, stood up and announced that the zombie girls could not have existed: zombie drugs and powders numbed you, induced deathlike trances, but still worked fundamentally on belief – the belief that you were now one of the dead, and had no will of your own. How, she asked, could a child of four or five be induced to believe such a thing? No. The coffee girls were, she said, one with the Indian Rope Trick, just another of the urban legends of the past.

Personally I agreed with her, but I nodded, and said that her points were well made and well taken. And that, from my perspective – which was, I hoped, a genuinely anthropological perspective – what mattered was not that it was easy to believe, but, much more importantly, the truth.

They applauded, and afterwards a man with a beard asked me whether he might be able to get a copy of the paper for a journal he edited. It occurred to me that it was a good thing that I had come to New Orleans, that Anderton's career would not be harmed by his absence from the conference.

The plump woman, whose badge said her name was Shanelle Gravely-King, was waiting for me at the door. She said, "I really enjoyed that. I don't want you to think that I didn't."

Campbell didn't turn up for his presentation. Nobody ever saw him again.

Margaret introduced me to someone from New York, and mentioned that Zora Neale Hurston had worked on *The Great Gatsby*. The man said yes, that was pretty common knowledge these days. I wondered if Margaret had called the police, but she seemed friendly enough. I was starting to stress, I realized. I wished I had not thrown away my cellphone.

Shanelle Gravely-King and I had an early dinner in the hotel, at the beginning of which I said, "Oh, let's not talk shop," and she agreed that only the very dull talked shop at the table. So we talked about rock bands we had seen live, fictional methods of slowing the decomposition of a human body, and about her partner, who was a woman older than she was and who owned a restaurant, and then we went up to my room. She smelled of baby powder and jasmine, and her naked skin was clammy against mine.

Over the next couple of hours I used two of the three condoms. She was sleeping by the time I returned from the bathroom, and I climbed into the bed next to her. I thought about the words Anderton had written, hand-scrawled on the back of a page of the typescript, and I wanted to check them, but I fell asleep, a soft-fleshed jasmine-scented woman pressing close to me.

After midnight, I woke from a dream, and a woman's voice was whispering in the darkness.

She said, "So he came into town, with his Doors cassettes and his Crowley books, and his handwritten list of the secret URLS for Chaos magick on the Web, and everything was good, he even got a few disciples, runaways like him, and he got his dick sucked whenever he wanted, and the world was good.

"And then he started to believe his own press. He thought he was the real thing. That he was the dude. He thought he was a big mean tiger-cat, not a little kitten. So he dug up . . . something . . . someone else wanted.

"He thought the something he dug up would look after him. Silly boy. And that night, he's sitting in Jackson Square, talking to the tarot readers, telling them about Jim Morrison and the kabalah, and someone taps him on the shoulder, and he turns, and someone blows powder into his face, and he breathes it in.

"Not all of it. And he is going to do something about it, when he realizes there's nothing to be done, because he's all paralysed, there's fugu-fish and toadskin and ground bone and everything else in that powder, and he's breathed it in.

"They take him down to emergency, where they don't do much for him, figuring him for a street-rat with a drug problem, and by the next day he can move again, although it's two, three days until he can speak.

"Trouble is, he needs it. He wants it. He knows there's some big secret in the zombie powder, and he was almost there. Some people say they mixed heroin with it, some shit like that, but they didn't even need to do that. He wants it.

"And they told him they wouldn't sell it to him. But if he did jobs for them, they'd give him a little zombie powder, to smoke, to sniff, to rub on his gums, to swallow. Sometimes they'd give him nasty jobs to do that no one else wanted. Sometimes they'd just humiliate him because they could – make him eat dog shit from the gutter, maybe. Kill for them, maybe. Anything but die. All skin and bones. He'd do anything for his zombie powder.

"And he still thinks, in the little bit of his head that's still him, that he's not a zombie. That he's not dead, that there's a threshold he hasn't stepped over. But he crossed it a long time ago."

I reached out a hand, and touched her. Her body was hard, and slim, and lithe, and her breasts felt like breasts that Gauguin might have painted. Her mouth, in the darkness, was soft and warm against mine.

People come into your life for a reason.

IV
*"Those people ought to know who we are
and tell that we are here"*

When I woke, it was still almost dark, and the room was silent. I turned on the light, looked on the pillow for a ribbon, white or red, or for a mouse-skull earring, but there was nothing to show that there had ever been anyone in the bed that night but me.

I got out of bed and pulled open the drapes, looked out of the window. The sky was greying in the east.

I thought about moving south, about continuing to run, continuing to pretend that I was alive. But it was, I knew now, much too late for that. There are doors, after all, between the living and the dead, and they swing in both directions.

I had come as far as I could.

There was a faint tap-tapping on the hotel-room door. I pulled on my jeans and the T-shirt I had set out in, and, barefoot, I pulled the door open.

The coffee girl was waiting for me.

Everything beyond the door was touched with light, an open, wonderful predawn light, and I heard the sound of birds calling on the morning air. The street was on a hill, and the houses facing me were little more than shanties. There was mist in the air, low to the ground, curling like something from an old black and white film, but it would be gone by noon.

The girl was thin and small; she did not appear to be more than six years old. Her eyes were cobwebbed with what might have been cataracts, her skin was as grey as it had once been brown. She was holding a white hotel cup out to me, holding it carefully, with one small hand on the handle, one hand beneath the saucer. It was half-filled with a steaming mud-coloured liquid.

I bent to take it from her, and I sipped it. It was a very bitter drink, and it was hot, and it woke me the rest of the way.

I said, "Thank you."

Someone, somewhere, was calling my name.

The girl waited, patiently, while I finished the coffee. I put the cup down on the carpet, then I put out my hand and touched her shoulder.

She reached up her hand, spread her small grey fingers, and took hold of my hand. She knew I was with her. Wherever we were headed now, we were going there together.

I remembered something that somebody had once said to me. "It's okay. Every day is freshly ground," I told her.

The coffee girl's expression did not change, but she nodded, as if she had heard me, and gave my arm an impatient tug. She held my hand tight with her cold, cold fingers, and we walked, finally, side by side into the misty dawn.

PAUL McAULEY

Child of the Stones

PAUL McAULEY LIVES IN North London. He is a winner of the Philip K. Dick, Arthur C. Clarke, John W. Campbell, Sidewise and British Fantasy Awards for his novels and short stories.

A former university researcher and lecturer in biology, his most recent novel is the biotech thriller *White Devils*. His *Doctor Who* novella, *The Eye of the Tyger*, was published by Telos Books in November 2003, exactly forty years after the author was scared behind the sofa by William Hartnell's minatory Time Lord, and a new short-story collection, *Little Machines*, is available from PS Publishing.

"Child of the Stones" is the most recent in a series of stories featuring McAuley's enigmatic occult investigator Mr Carlyle. Previous tales have appeared in *Best New Horror Volumes Eleven*, *Twelve* and *Fourteen*.

"Many of my own walks through London follow in the footsteps of Mr Carlyle," reveals the author. "While researching this story, I took a long walk up the River Thames, past Cheyne Walk, where there are possibly more blue plaques attached to houses in commemoration of famous former residents than in any other street in London. But there's still one notable resident who isn't acknowledged: isn't it time that Bram Stoker, father of Dracula, got his own plaque?"

A T NIGHT, THE PAST has a stronger hold on London than the present. The urgent beat of daily business stalls and drifts backwards. The city's inhabitants lock themselves in the prisons of their homes and the vacant streets stretch away in every direction under the thin orange glow cast by long, regular lines of street lamps, their silence haunted by echoes of the dramas of past generations. But some of London's streets are never quiet. Queensway; Hyde Park Corner; Old Compton Street in Soho; the streets around Victoria Station; the Embankment; Upper Street in Islington: people are drawn to these places at night, and it is to these unsleeping streets that many of the dead are also drawn, by habit, hunger, and forlorn curiosity. Lately, it was where I spent most of my nights, too, walking amongst the living and the dead.

Although the matter of the dead has been my business for as long as I have lived in London, during those nocturnal rambles I was interested not in the ghosts, imps, and other ordinary revenants I encountered, but in what they might attract. Six months previously, I had discovered that there were new and terrible things awakening into the world. Things that preyed on the dead, and drew strength from them; things that were beginning to prey on the living. Lions and tigers and bears. The unsleeping streets where the cities of the living and the dead intersected were beginning to draw the attention of these new predators, just as a watering hole in the African veldt draws the big cats that prey on the buffalo and zebra and gazelles that come there to drink. It was while I was mapping this strange new bestiary that I discovered that not only monsters were awakening in these strange times. And a door onto my past opened and an old enemy stepped through it.

Islington, Upper Street, summer, two hours past midnight:

A bare-chested young man with a bright green Mohican hair-cut, his arms ropy with tattoos and track marks, was sitting in the doorway of an estate agent's office and sharing a can of lager with a young woman in a ragged black dress and army boots. Imps clustered around their eyes like tiny scorpions, pale, articulated, and fat with the venom of heroin dreams.

In another doorway, a man slept jackknifed under a filthy blanket, guarded by a starveling mongrel who looked at me calmly when I dropped a couple of pound coins beside his master's head. The man, an old acquaintance, stirred and without waking mumbled, "Mr Carlyle. Take care."

It was good advice, and I should have taken it. For the past three nights, I had been intercepted by a pair of men in an immaculately restored blood-red Mark 1 Jaguar. Each night, the big car had purred up to me as I was making my way home, and the man in the passenger seat had leaned at the open window and spoken to me about a book in my possession, a rare volume that his employer wished to buy. Each night he had offered more money for the book, and each night I had refused his offer. I knew that sooner or later he would try another tactic – most probably some kind of violence. I had not yet seen the Jaguar that night, but I was certain it would appear before I gained the safety of my house, and anticipation of that encounter was like an electric itch at the back of my neck.

A club was closing a little way down the street. People stumbled past two black-suited bouncers into the night. A woman in a short white dress hunched on the kerb, crying. Another woman in an even shorter white dress had an arm around her shoulder and was trying to comfort her, unaware of imps clustered in her friend's hair, thick as fleas on a sick cat. A woman pulled away from a man in a grey suit, tried and failed to hail a passing taxi, and walked away unsteadily while he shouted insults at her, angry black sparks jumping around his face. Three men in football shirts, arms linked around each other's waists, walked past me with the mechanical stagger of the very drunk. When I stepped aside to let them pass, the outermost gave me a flat stare that suddenly clouded with confusion when I pinched out the jagged little thing that had prompted his hostility.

Even as I completed the gesture, something caught my eye on the other side of the road. A small, scant figure slouched in the doorway of a restaurant, wearing tracksuit bottoms and a grey top, its hood drawn over a baseball cap. An imp as fat and sleek as a graveyard rat crouched on his shoulder, the end of its long tail knotted around his wrist.

I felt a prick of curiosity, and walked on for a little way before crossing the road, doubling back and finding a vantage point of my own in the doorway of another restaurant. An old woman drifted out of the wedge of darkness behind me. She wore an old-fashioned bonnet and a shawl over a ragged black dress, and was so thin I could see right through her. Cast off long ago by an out-of-work seamstress who'd starved to death in some nearby attic or basement, this ghost was familiar, harmless, and occasionally useful to me. I asked her about the figure lurking in the doorway up the street, but she knew nothing about him, knew only that she was weak with hunger, if she could only get something to eat she would be as right as rain. I brushed her aside over and again, as an ordinary man might fan away smoke, and each time she forgot my dismissal and drifted back, hoping that I was the kind of gent who might oblige with a penny or two toward the necessary, it had been so very long since she'd had so much as a crust to chew. At last, the hooded figure stepped out of his doorway and set off down the street. When I started after him, the poor little ghost trailed after me for only a few steps before retreating to her haunt.

The hooded fellow was following an unsteady couple who, with their arms around each other, wove south down Upper Street, pausing to embrace and kiss at the point of Islington Green's triangle before turning along Camden Passage. He slouched along with hands in his pockets, stopping whenever they stopped to kiss, pausing at each street corner to check the lie of the land before moving on. Anyone else would have thought him no more than an ordinary cutpurse or thug intent on robbery or some other mischief, for they could not have seen the fat imp squatting on his left shoulder. I wondered if this young cutpurse was possessed by it, or if it was a kind of pet or familiar. And if it was a familiar, how had he tamed it, and for what purpose?

With mounting curiosity and more than a little eagerness, I followed the cutpurse as he tracked the couple through a street of early Victorian houses that ran parallel to the Grand Union canal. (A man sat on the steps of one of the houses, sobbing over the bloody hammer in his lap; a woman stood at the window of another, her face a mask of triumph and despair as she cradled a baby's skeleton to her breast.) The couple waltzed around the corner at the end of the street; the cutpurse paused for a moment before following them. I heard loud, angry voices disturb the profound quiet of the night, and hurried after him, pausing where he had paused, peeking around the corner. The road crossed the canal a few dozen yards ahead; the couple stood at the crown of the bridge, confronting their pursuer. A locked gate to one side of the bridge guarded an access ramp to the canal towpath, and something lurked in the shadows there. It was the revenant of something or someone very old and, once upon a time, very powerful. It was possessed by an appalling hunger, and its attention was fixed on the imp that squatted on the cutpurse's shoulder.

The girl was telling him to leave her alone, her voice ringing shrill in the night. She was fifteen or sixteen, wearing a skimpy top and a short skirt that left her belly bare. Her fists shook on either side of her face. She was angry and afraid. "Just piss off, all right? It ain't anything to do with you."

Her companion, a shaven-headed, thuggish man in his thirties, took a step forward and threatened violence, but the cutpurse stood his ground. The imp on his shoulder vibrated with a sudden eager pulse, like a clockwork toy wound too tight. A nimbus of spiky black energies crackled around it, as a dog will bristle before it bites, while its master told the girl that she was making a mistake. "You shouldn't be going with him, Liz. It ain't right." His voice was high-pitched but steady and sincere, and it was exactly the wrong thing to say.

"Leave her alone, you little freak," Liz's shaven-headed companion said. He took two quick steps and threw a punch.

The cutpurse dodged the blow and flung out his left arm, like a hawker loosing his bird of prey. For all its sleek bulk, the imp was quick and eager, and flew straight at the man's face. But the thing behind the gate was quicker still. It had a long smooth pale neck and a small head with jaws that disarticulated like a snake's, stretching wide and snapping the fat imp from the air and gulping it down whole. The cutpurse, connected by the imp's tail to the revenant which had devoured it, yelped with shock; the girl's companion saw his chance and hit him square in the face. The cutpurse sat down flat, his hood fell down and his baseball cap fell off, and I saw that he was a girl, with a thin pale face and blonde hair unevenly hacked short.

The revenant's ghastly head quested towards her; she screamed and tried to pull away. The shaven-headed man, completely unaware of the apparition, kicked her in the side, and would have kicked her again if I had not stepped out, drawing my blade from my hollow cane.

"You have to be fucking kidding," the man said, staring at the yard of engraved steel in my right hand.

I stepped up and with a short stroke severed the umbilicus that linked the cutpurse to the revenant. It slurped up the cut end like a length of spaghetti and turned towards me. Whatever human qualities it might once have possessed had worn away long ago, leaving little more than a blind, bottomless appetite. For a moment, as I menaced it with my blade and tried and failed to dismiss it, it stood within my head, and I was jolted by a sudden, freezing headache. It reared back and stared at me; then its tiny, wide-mouthed head, like that of some species of deep-sea fish all maw and stomach, whipped sideways and snapped at the cutpurse.

"Your familiar," I said, countering the revenant's quick, sinuous moves with my blade. "It wants what's left of your familiar."

The man, still completely oblivious to the drama, believed that I was menacing him, and said he'd give me a right good kicking if I didn't fuck off. His girlfriend pulled at his arm and told him to leave it; after a moment he spat at his feet, said that if he saw me again he'd make me eat my fucking sword, and, honour satisfied, allowed himself to be led away.

The revenant lunged at the cutpurse with jaws that were now as wide as a shark's. I caught her wrist, broke off the knotted remnant of the imp's tail, and threw it at the monster, which snapped up the trifle and withdrew as swiftly as thought. I ran to the crown of the bridge, looked over the parapet and saw something faintly luminous and very long pour into the canal's black water.

The cutpurse sat in the middle of the road, watching me walk back to her. My nose had started to bleed when the thing had briefly inhabited my head. I mopped up the blood with my handkerchief, folded it away, held out a hand, and told the girl that she had best come with me.

Although she had suffered a bad shock, the girl was blessed with youth's resilience, and soon began to recover what I had to suppose was her usual sullen defiance. From her more or less monosyllabic answers to my questions I learnt that her name was Miranda, that she was sixteen, that she lived with her mother in a nearby council flat, and that she and the other girl, Liz, were neighbours, and had both been left to fend for themselves because their mothers had gone away on holiday together.

"That bloke she was with only wants her for one thing," Miranda said. "That's why . . ."

"You wished to help her. There's no shame in that. To care for others is an admirable quality."

"I was stupid," she muttered. "I could have got my head kicked in."

"And you lost your familiar, but I'm sure you can find another easily enough."

She glanced up at me from beneath the brim of her baseball cap. She was small and skinny, and already hardened to the ways of the world; hers was a type that had not changed since the Romans had first made London the capital of the northernmost tip of their empire, a child 'brought up on the stones', armoured with soul-scabs and premature cynicism.

"How long have you been able to see things that others cannot?" I said.

"Don't know what you're on about. Don't even know who you are."

"I am Mr Carlyle. I have the honour of being a consultant in the matter of the dead."

"Like a bloke that buries people?"

"In a way. And something like a private detective, too."

"Yeah, you look a bit like what's-his-name. Sherlock Holmes. Was that a real sword? Where are we going?"

"My blade is Damascus steel, and very old. Some say that its kind were quenched after their final forging by being run through the body of a slave, although I myself do not believe this fancy. In any case, it derives its strength from more than its steel, which is why I was able to help you. I won it a hundred years ago – you don't believe me, but it is true. As to where we are going, why, here we are."

We stood at the head of a short paved alley. When London had been no more than a huddle of herders' huts in a clearing on the hill now called Ludsgate, this spot had been the beginning of a path that had linked two sacred groves. Now it was blocked by a crooked little house whose ground floor was given over to a café. Warm light fell from its plate-glass window onto the plastic tables and chairs on the flagstones in front of it. A neon sign boasted that it was open all hours.

"I haven't been here for a long time," I said, "but tonight it's the nearest haven. Even if you don't want any refreshment, we can at least sit comfortably while we talk."

"What have we got to talk about?"

"I can see everything that you can see. We can talk about that, to begin with," I said, and stepped inside the café. After a moment, to my immense relief, the girl followed me.

Fluorescent light shone on worn wooden tables and chapel chairs, the glass-fronted counter and its polished steel top. A man in a grey suit sat in one corner, toying with an espresso in a doll's-house-sized china cup; in another, a taxi driver studied an old copy of the *Financial Times*, his laminated licence on a chain around the neck of his short-sleeved shirt.

Rose, the pleasant, round-faced woman of indeterminate age who had owned this place for more than a century, materialized from the shadows behind the massive coffee machine. Her silver hair was caught up in a bun with a pencil stuck through it. Her lipstick was bright red. Her smile was wide and warm and welcoming. "Mr C! What a pleasant surprise. Will you be having your usual? And what about your friend? You both look in need of a refresher."

"We ran into a little local difficulty."

"Down by the canal, I expect," Rose said, as she bustled behind the counter, slapping bacon rashers on a griddle, buttering two slices of white bread.

"You know of it?"

"It's been lying low in the Hackney Marshes ever since I've been running this place, Mr C, but recently it's been growing bolder, if you know what I mean. Change is in the air, isn't it? Yours isn't the only old face I've seen recently," she added in a more confidential tone, nodding towards the man in the grey suit as he threw down some coins and left. "Foreigner, he is, but I've a feeling I know him from way back when."

I watched him walk away down the little alley. He was unfamiliar, but I could not help wondering if he had anything to do with the two men in the red Jaguar.

"He's been coming in about this time for the past week," Rose said. "Sits in the corner, drinks his coffee, doesn't say a word to a soul." She smiled at Miranda, who was staring at the taxi driver. "And what will you be having, dear? A Coke, perhaps. A little sugar does you good after you've had a shock. Much better than coffee or alcohol. You're lucky you fell in with Mr C. He looks a little odd, I know, what with that black suit of his, and his bow tie and his hat and his cane, but he's the best of us."

I took off my Homburg and executed a small bow. "Why, thank you, Rose."

"Pish-posh, Mr C, I wouldn't say it if it wasn't true. That's why I'm pleased to see you out and about again."

While Miranda sucked on the straw stuck in her can of Coca-Cola, I squeezed brown sauce from the plastic bottle into my bacon sandwich, stirred three spoonfuls of brown sugar into my tea, and added a dash of brandy from my flask. I asked her about the imp she had made into her familiar, where she had found it and how she had mastered it, but she shrugged off my questions, and took out a crushed pack of cigarettes and lit one. The left side of her face was reddened, beginning to swell from the blow she'd received. She blew out smoke and said, "You think you're a character, don't you? What with your fancy words and your funny clothes."

"Something happened just now, on the canal bridge. Something attacked you."

"If that bloke tries it on again," Miranda said with sudden cold ferocity, "I'll cut off his dick. I swear I will."

"You know quite well that I do not mean Liz's boyfriend. Did you see it, Miranda, when it took your familiar?"

"Don't know what you're talking about," Miranda said, but the hand holding her cigarette was shaking. I saw thin white lines on the skin inside her wrist. I saw oval white scars.

"You can see imps, and you can make them obey you. Your familiar was one such. You found it and trained it to do your bidding. That attachment grew a kind of leash or umbilicus between you and your pet, and it nearly caused your downfall. The revenant that ate your familiar swallowed the umbilicus too, and for that reason you were briefly attached to it. You may not have seen it, Miranda, but I know that you must have felt its hunger."

The girl shrugged, and would not meet my gaze.

"You tried to use the imp you had captured and trained against the man. He wouldn't be able to see it, but it would have scared him away. I believe that you wanted to do it for a good reason. You wanted to help the girl. Is that how you always use the imps you make into your familiars?"

Miranda drew so hard on her cigarette that its tip crackled, and gave me a flat, challenging stare. She said, "What do they look like to you?"

"They are mostly black, and most of them are no bigger than insects. They are spawned by discharge of violent emotion, or by delirium induced by drink or drugs. The one you had tamed was exceptionally large."

"There's a bloke that lives near me. He drinks a lot, and he's always angry at something or other. His flat is full of 'em. Law courts are good places too. Lots of fear and anger there. I get 'em to follow me, feed 'em up, get 'em to do what I want. It ain't so different from training a dog." Miranda drew on her cigarette again. "I suppose you're gonna give me grief about it."

"There are worse things in the world than imps," I said. "You met one of them just now."

"I see all kinds of things. People who aren't really there. Dead people. Ghosts. There's one over there, reading a newspaper. He's one of the harmless ones. I try to make them do stuff too, but they don't listen. How about you? Can you make them do what you want?"

"You have a rare gift, Miranda, and it frightens you. It makes you feel that you are different – that there is something wrong with you. You punish yourself because of it. You cut your flesh with razor blades. You stub cigarettes out on your skin. You punish your body because you believe that it is betraying you. I understand, because I have that gift too. I see the things that you see—"

"You don't understand nothing," Miranda said. She crushed out her cigarette on the table's scarred red Formica and stood up. Her can of Coca-Cola fell over, spilling a fizzing slick. "I don't know what your game is, but I want you to leave me alone. All right?"

I was surprised to discover that I felt disappointed by her rejection. As she turned away, I said, "If you want to talk to me again, come here and ask about Mr Carlyle. Will you do that?"

She kicked the door open, and walked straight out.

Behind the counter, Rose looked at me and shook her head slightly, but whether in amusement, sympathy, or disapproval it was impossible to tell.

Ever since my parents died and I quit Edinburgh for London, I have spent most of my life alone, and for most of that time I have lived in a tall, narrow Georgian house in Spitalfields, at the edge of the City of London. It is a quiet, comfortably shabby place. The only modern improvements are the gas lighting and the gas geyser that, when lit, with much volcanic rumbling spits a miserly stream of hot water into the bath. The few ghosts that inhabit the house are harmless; they, and the mice in the walls, are my only company. I make sure that every threshold is well protected, and I do not advertise for clients. Anyone in need of my services must find their own way to me.

The two men in the vintage Jaguar had not yet found my house, but for the fourth night in a row, as I was making my way home after my unsatisfactory conversation with Miranda, they found me.

Their blood-red motor car was parked at a bus stop opposite Shoreditch Town Hall. As I approached it, ready to draw my blade, the passenger door opened and the man who had accosted me three times before climbed out. He was in his forties, tall and wide, with a seamed complexion and a boxer's broken nose. His cream linen suit and mauve silk shirt looked expensive, but were rumpled and sweated through. He was beginning to get a beard, and had a dull, haggard expression. When I stepped around him, he walked after me. He did not quite dare lay hands on me – not yet.

"You're a stubborn man," he said, "but my boss is very patient."

"Others might say he is foolishly persistent."

"My boss wants that book very badly. He told me to do everything I can to make you see sense. You understand what I mean, Mr Carlyle?"

He spoke flatly and mechanically, as if reciting something he had memorized.

"You can tell him that he is wasting his time. The book is not for sale."

I quickened my pace, but the man easily matched it. The Jaguar crawled alongside us. I glanced at the driver, but couldn't see his face through the slick of light reflected from the windscreen.

"My boss is generous with my time," the man said. "He's altogether a very generous man. And as such, he's prepared to consider any price you care to name. He told me to tell you that. I warned him, I said the man will rook you, but he doesn't care. Money means nothing to him. Why don't you get in the motor, Mr Carlyle? We can discuss this in comfort."

"I think not."

"You don't trust me?"

"Of course I do not trust you. Also, I find all modes of modern transport uncomfortable."

"I noticed that you like to walk everywhere. Dangerous, that. Anything could happen."

We had reached the junction with the A10, five lanes of newly laid tarmacadam as black as deep water. A handful of pale ghosts were spaced alongside it, like herons along a river bank. I stopped beside the traffic light, and the Jaguar stopped too. The light was green; a white van sounded its horn as it swerved past and shot across the junction.

"You live somewhere near here," the man said. "Why don't we go to your place and talk about it?"

"Why does your boss send a puppet to talk to me?"

The traffic light above us turned red, and I started across the A10, moving between the handful of vehicles that accelerated away from the junction, racing each other towards the City. The man started after me, but had to jump back when a black cab nearly ran him down. I stepped past another black cab into the diesel wind of an enormous trailer truck and gained the far side of the road.

The man had retreated, and was standing impotently beside the Jaguar. He shouted at me, his voice torn by the brute noise of the traffic. "We'll find you where you live! My boss, he doesn't give up!"

I could not resist lifting my Homburg in salute. I walked for another hour until the feeling of being followed finally slipped away, and I could turn at last for home.

I wasted the next evening in a fruitless search for Miranda. A few of my usual informants knew of a girl who was followed about by tame imps, but none knew where she lived. "She spends a lot of time down King's Cross," one of them said. "Chases off punters with those pets of hers. They cruise up in their motors, looking for some short-time fun and games, and she leans in and lets them have it. They're all over the road when they drive off, crying and screaming."

It seemed that she had been frightening away kerb-crawlers for several months. When I asked my informant why he hadn't told me about her before, he gave the equivalent of a shrug and said that I hadn't asked.

"You must know that I would be interested in someone like that."

"Someone like you, you mean. I suppose so. But I see all kinds, Mr Carlyle, especially these days. Things are waking up that should be long gone. *Hungry* things. I try to keep myself to myself these days, but it isn't easy, even here."

We had met at the edge of a patch of waste ground. On the far side, three men sat at a little fire they'd built from scraps of wood and cardboard, passing around a bottle of jake.

"Poor sods," my informant said. He was as thin as a wisp of smoke, and leaned at an angle, as if bent by a high wind. "They'll be joining me soon enough."

I made my ritual offer to put him to rest; he made his ritual refusal. "I'm still interested in what's goin' on, Mr Carlyle. Day I ain't, then maybe I'll call on your services and you can unmake me or whatever it is you do to make my kind vanish. But I ain't by no means ready yet."

I steeled myself to search the noisome streets of King's Cross, had no luck, and walked up the hill to Islington. I failed to find Miranda there, either, and at last gave up and returned home. It was three in the morning. For once, there was no sign of the blood-red Jaguar, and when I reached the street where my house stood I knew why. I went carefully, as if walking barefoot on broken glass, to my house. All the wards I had set in place were broken, screaming in my mind like common burglar alarms. I had never felt the need to lock my front door in more than a century, but I locked it behind me after I had stepped into the familiar gloomy clutter of my hallway.

The three ghosts that shared the house with me were all in retreat. I drew out the Huguenot silkmaker, but he claimed not to have seen anything, and fled towards the attic as soon as I released him. I lit a candle and climbed the stairs after him. I was certain that I knew who had broken into my house; sure enough, several dozen books of my little library of esoterica had been swept from their shelves, and lay tumbled like the corpses of a flock of lightning-struck birds on the worn Turkish rug that covered most of the age-blackened oak floor. I lit the gas mantles and after a few minutes determined that only one book was missing.

It was the book that the man in the red Jaguar had wished to purchase, of course – the rarest, most valuable, and most dangerous of my collection. I had bought it at a public auction only twenty years ago, finally completing my recreation of the library which had been destroyed, with so much else, in the accident that had killed my parents.

My father had searched out and purchased most of the books in that library, but in most cases he had been carrying out my mother's instructions. She had inherited from her mother my family's interest and talent in the matter of the dead, and although he was as blind to revenants as any ordinary man, my father was happy to help her in any way he could. He was a small, neat man, and something of a dandy, famous for his crushed velvet suits and his elaborately carved pipes (I cannot pass the tobacconist shop on Charing Cross Road without pausing to breathe in the earthy odour that reminds me of him). Once I was old enough to accompany him on his rambles about Edinburgh, I quickly learned that he was on first-name terms with everyone from crossing sweepers to the Provost, and knew every obscure nook and cranny of the old town. Although he had many friends, none were close to him, and most believed him to be some sort of a poet. He was not, but he was a great writer of letters, and included Byron and Keats amongst his regular correspondents; almost every evening would find him in his favourite armchair, wrapped in a silk dressing gown, a tasselled cap on his head, scratching away at a letter on the writing board propped in his lap, a pipe hanging from one corner of his mouth, a glass of whisky at his elbow.

Although I have inherited so much from her, I have fewer memories of my mother. She was a practical, briskly decisive woman, absent-mindedly affectionate, busy with her clients or in her elaboratory, with its sharp chemical reek, scarred wooden bench and hand-blown glassware, stained porcelain crucibles, a furnace built of brick and firestones, and intricate diagrams drawn on one whitewashed wall in black chalk and haematite. She provided me with a good grounding in our family business, giving me formal lessons each morning of my childhood and, when I was older, allowing me to attend the sessions with her clients. I remember best her sharply intent gaze, and her shapely hands with their bitten fingernails, and nicks and burns and chemical stains.

My mother and my father were as different as chalk and cheese, but they loved each other more than I am able to describe. They collaborated in experiments to augment my mother's natural ability; they died together when their last and most elaborate work released something feral and uncontrollably powerful. They had known of the danger and had taken the precaution of sending me away to help a client in St Andrews, and so my life was saved. I have dedicated it to their memory ever since.

I had just finished reshelving the fallen books when I heard a sound elsewhere in the house, a rap on the front door only a little louder than a mouse's scratch. I drew my blade, picked up my candle and crept back downstairs where I unlocked the door and opened it a scant inch. Miranda stood there, her pale face set like stone under the bill of her baseball cap.

"I know who took it," she said.

She gave up her story over a cup of hot chocolate in my kitchen. It was an assured performance, and even though I was certain that almost everything she told me was a lie, I had to admire her cool nerve, even though I could barely control my anger and anxiety. She told me that the night before she had hung around outside the café until I had left, and had followed me as I had walked homeward. She had seen the encounter with the Jaguar, and had managed to keep on my tail as I had walked a long widdershins spiral to shake off any pursuers.

"I am growing careless," I said. "A few years ago I would have discovered you at once."

Miranda shrugged. She sat at the scrubbed pine table in my basement kitchen, her baseball cap in her lap, her hood pulled back from her cropped blonde hair. There was a sprinkling of acne on her pale, sharp face, a faint moustache of chocolate foam on her upper lip. She was working on her third cigarette, stabbing it between her lips, blowing thin streams of smoke from the side of her mouth, tapping off the growing ash with her forefinger into the saucer I had provided.

"I'm good at following people," she said flatly, as if stating her height or the colour of her eyes.

"And tonight you followed me again."

I was angry and anxious, and I was also more than a little afraid of her. In the wrong hands, her raw talent could be very dangerous, and I was certain that she had already fallen into the wrong hands, that she was working for the man who wanted my book.

She shook her head. "I kept watch right here. I heard what that guy Halliwell said, so I thought I'd keep a lookout."

"Halliwell? Is that the man in the Jaguar? How do you know his name?"

The little minx had her answer ready; she did not even blink. "Donny Halliwell used to be a well-known face in Islington," she said, and mentioned a family that ran most of the protection rackets in the area.

"I presume that he is not working for them now."

"I heard what he said about finding where you lived, so I thought I'd better keep an eye out. I was right, too."

She looked at me when I laughed, and asked what was so funny.

"While you were here, keeping watch on my house, I was looking for you."

"Yeah? Why's that, then?"

"Many people have a touch of our ability, Miranda, but a few have something more than a touch. In most cases, they are either driven mad by it, or they do their best to deny it and allow it to wither, like an unused limb. But one or two, although untutored, find a use for their gift. Usually, they become charlatans, preying on the gullible and the grief-stricken, and any good that they do is by accident. Very rarely, they actively try to use their ability for the good of others. That is why I was looking for you."

She shrugged.

"You wanted to help your friend last night. I believe that you have tried to help others. And you want to help me."

"I want to find out what you were about. I've never met anyone like you before."

"No, I don't suppose you have."

"And now I've seen where you live, I know you're the kind of man who likes to keep himself to himself. You were looking for me because you were curious about me. You wanted to find out about me because you were worried about me – about what I was doing, about what I could do. But it's not like you want to be friends or anything like that, is it? You're not the kind of man who has friends."

I was startled by how clearly she saw me.

"On the contrary. I have many friends."

"You let 'em come here? You hang out with them, chat with them about this and that over a drink? No, I thought not. You know people, but you don't have what you'd call real friends. What were you planning to do, if you found me? Give me some advice about how to live my life, like you did at that café last night?"

"I can help you, Miranda, if you'll let me."

"I can look after myself. Don't need no man telling me what to do. I was going to break into your house myself," she said, with a look that dared me to contradict her. "I would've, too, if that guy hadn't come along."

"Forgive me, Miranda, but I don't believe you. You were able to follow me without my knowledge, and that is no small achievement. But I don't think you could have overcome the wards I left in place."

"*He* managed it," Miranda said.

Someone had, at any rate. I doubted that it had been Mr Donny Halliwell, of the glazed expression, the expensive, slept-in clothes, the sleepwalking menace. "If he did," I said, "then I am guilty of having grievously underestimated him."

"The way you talk. It's like the way you dress."

"You think that my clothes and my locution are affectations. I can assure you that they are not."

"Locution? What's that when it's at home?"

"It's the way I talk."

"It's a funny old word, is what it is. Old-fashioned. Like your clothes. Like this place. All this old furniture, and candles and such instead of proper lights." Miranda lit her fourth cigarette with a quick snap of flame. "You don't have a proper cooker, or a fridge . . . I bet you don't even have a telly."

"When you are a little older, Miranda, you'll find that many people prefer the time in which they grew up to the time in which they find themselves."

"Maybe. But you didn't grow up in, like, Victorian times."

"That's quite true. When I first came to London, Queen Victoria had yet to ascend to the throne."

She looked at me. She wanted to sneer, but in her heart she was beginning to believe me. I took it as a hopeful sign: a sign that she could yet be saved. And even if I could not save her, I thought, it was always best to keep your enemy close.

"Those of us who know something of the matter of the dead can be quite long-lived," I said. "If you are more careful in how you use your talent, Miranda, you might discover the trick."

"I could live a hundred years, could I? And not grow old?"

"Or you could step into the road tomorrow, and be run over by a bus."

Her smile was more like a grimace, there and gone. "I followed you, and you didn't have any idea, did you? Man like you, hiding away in this old place, you're not streetwise. I bet there's all sorts of things I can help you with. Maybe we can come to an arrangement."

When she had entered my house, squeezing past me at the door, I had taken the opportunity to pick the pocket of her hooded top. I placed her mobile phone and travel card on the table, and said, "You don't live as long as I do without learning a few tricks necessary for survival."

"I knew you took those," she said, but could not quite hide her twitch of alarm, and clearly did not know what I had done to her mobile phone, for otherwise she would not have put it straight in her pocket.

"You think that I am old-fashioned, which in a way is true enough, but it does not mean that I am out of touch with the world. And there is a good, practical reason why I do not have electricity here, nor a telephone nor any of the paraphernalia of modern life. Electricity attracts imps and other nuisances. You must know this. Look at any street lamp at night, and you will see more than moths whirling around the light."

"You didn't know who that the bloke who talked to you last night was. And I bet you don't know who Donny Halliwell works for these days, do you?"

"I am sure that I can find that out without your help. I have extensive resources, and a man who is able break my wards will be well known in the circles in which I move."

Miranda rose to my bait. "My mum knows all about him, and I bet she doesn't move in those 'circles'. "

"You wish to make a bargain, is that it? You will help me, and I will help you, turn and turn about."

"Shake on it," Miranda said, and stuck out her hand.

I smiled at her boldness and took her hand and shook it, knowing that the bargain meant nothing to either of us.

Miranda told me that Donny Halliwell had met a pop star while he was in prison. The pop star, Rainer Sue, had been serving a short sentence for possession of a variety of Class A drugs; Donny Halliwell had been coming to the end of a longer sentence for extracting money with menaces from restaurants in North London. When he had been freed, he'd gone to work for Rainer Sue, now a recluse in his house in Cheyne Walk, one of Chelsea's most exclusive addresses, as a bodyguard and a general fixer.

"How do you know so much about these people?"

"My mum was keen on old Rainer when she was my age, back in the 1980s. But he ain't done nothing in years and years except go to parties and film premieres and like that. My mum, she comes home with a few inside her or she sees his picture in *Hello!* or whatever, and she puts on one of his CDs and goes all smoochy. It's real bad stuff though, tinny synthesizers and like a drum machine and saxophones. Bad as in shit, not like in good."

"I know what bad means."

"I bet you don't. Anyway, that's why I know about Donny Halliwell, and about the Jag too."

"The Mark I Jaguar."

Miranda pretended to be surprised.

"I do try to keep up," I said.

"Has personalized number plates, doesn't it? RA 1 NR. I see that straight away, and know who owns it. Anyway, the thing about Rainer Sue is that he's famous for being into weird shit. He wasn't exactly a Goth back in the day, but he dressed like Christopher Lee in those old Dracula movies, had skulls and coffins and lots of candles on stage, shit like that, yeah? I suppose he found out about you, thought you had something he wanted, is that it?"

"He wished to purchase a book that I own."

"Yeah? Like a book of spells?"

"In a way. The *Stenographia* is the masterwork of a monk and magician who called himself Trithemius, and contains codes and conjurations and various prayers which its author claimed could cause angels to act on behalf of those deploying them. My copy is not of the much corrupted edition that was published long after

Trithemius's death, in 1676, but one of only five volumes printed in 1504, the year before he was summoned before Maximillian I and interrogated on matters of faith. Mr Halliwell – or the man for whom he works – probably traced it through the records of the auction house where I purchased it some twenty years ago."

"Ever tried any of those spells out?" Miranda tried to sound casual, but her eyes were shining.

"Of course not. If you were in possession of a bomb, would you try to detonate it to see if it worked?"

" 'Course I would. And I wouldn't leave it in a house with an unlocked door, neither."

"The house was protected by more than mere locks, as you well know, but I will admit that you have a valid point."

"He had a briefcase," Miranda said. "Donny Halliwell, I mean. The kind City gents take to work with them. My mate Wayne nicked one once, thinking he was on to a good thing, and all he found in it was a sandwich from Pret À Manger. Couldn't even sell the briefcase, 'cause he broke the locks getting it open."

"You saw Mr Halliwell walk into the house."

Her gaze was bold and unflinching. She really did possess an admirable faculty for untruths. "He burned a piece of paper on the front step first. It went off like a firework, made a sort of greenish smoke. Then he walked in, and about two minutes later he walked out. Got in the car, and off he drove."

"He was, I presume, still carrying the briefcase."

"With your book inside it. So now we have to get it back before he does something bad with it."

"*I* have to get it back, Miranda. You have already done more than enough."

"No problem, Mr Carlyle. You got to do what you got to do."

She met my gaze boldly, and I saw the glint of triumph in her eyes. She believed that she had succeeded in fooling me, but it was not yet time to disabuse her.

After Miranda left, I slept for a few hours, breakfasted in a café, and walked against the swelling tide of commuters to the Thames and followed the path beside it upriver, towards Chelsea. Public transport is so thickly infested with imps and other revenants that I am forced to walk everywhere, and these days even the streets are so crowded with remnants of moments of frustration and anger that at times it is like plunging head first into the mephitic smuts and fumes of a factory chimney.

Ordinarily, I would have waited and watched before acting. I would have consulted various contacts. I would have made sure that I knew as much as possible about my enemy before making the first move. But this was no time for temperate contemplation. My house had been violated; one of my most precious possessions had been stolen; my temper had been roused. And I feared that the stolen book would be put to immediate use – why else would Donny Halliwell's boss have resorted to such desperate measures to obtain it? I did make one stop along the way, however, to use (after spending a good five minutes clearing it of the residue of its previous occupants) one of the few public telephone kiosks that still accepted coins to call my old friend, Chief Superintendent Rawles. He had recently retired from the Metropolitan Police, but told me that he could find out the answers to my questions easily enough.

"I will telephone you again, in an hour or so," I said, and hung up the receiver before he could ask any questions of his own.

I reached Chelsea just after midday, hot, footsore, and beginning to feel a pinching anxiety about the task ahead of me. I found refuge in a public house, bought a Ploughman's Lunch and a half-pint of beer, and, after the usual chore of cleansing it, used the public telephone to call Rawles.

He told me what he had found out about Miranda, confirmed what she had told me about Donny Halliwell, gave me Rainer Sue's address, and asked if I was in trouble again.

"It is nothing serious," I said, regretting the lie.

"Call me if you need any real help," Rawles said. "And promise me that you'll tell me what this is all about when it finished."

I said that I would, and meant it; Rawles was a kind and generous friend who had been a great help to me many times in the past. I left the pub and strolled through the neat, pretty streets of Chelsea to Cheyne Walk, with its ghosts and memories and heavy mantle of history. Here was the house where the young engineer who had shared my first adventure in this city had once lived with his father; here was the house where the irascible old painter, known to his neighbours only as either the Admiral or "Puggy" Booth had ended his days in hiding from his public. Here was the house of John Martyn, whose ability to glimpse a little of the city of the dead that surrounds and interpenetrates the city of the living had informed his apocalyptic paintings (his brother, who once had tried to burn down York Minster, had been driven insane by the same gift); and here the house where one memorable evening I once visited Hilaire Belloc in the company of Gilbert Chesterton.

The address Rawles had given me was at the eastern end of Cheyne Walk, in the middle of a row of old, red-brick houses shielded from the headlong roar of traffic along the Chelsea Embankment by a narrow public garden of shrubbery and grass. Expensive motor vehicles stood nose to tail at the kerb of the narrow road that ran between the houses and the park. There was a quiet, dignified air of prosperity, the smell of fresh paint.

I found a bench in the public garden and studied Rainer Sue's house through a gap in the shrubbery. There was no sign of the blood-red Mark 1 Jaguar. A huge wisteria flopped pale green leaves and spikes of purple flowers over the black railings of the front garden. The curtains were closed at every window, as if in mourning, or as if those who ordinarily lived in it had picked up and moved elsewhere for the season, and I quickly realized that in one sense it really was uninhabited. Unlike all the other houses in this old, much-haunted street, it was quite without ghosts or any kind of revenant, and none came near it; not even the smallest batsqueak of an imp clung anywhere close. It was as quiet as a tomb set under a bell jar in the middle of a busy thoroughfare, so completely still that its silence vibrated in the ear like a gnat. Sealed deep in that silence, like a fly in amber, was a tiny, dense knot of impacted energies that would have escaped the attention of someone only a little less skilled than I.

The ghost of a sulky young housemaid who had drowned herself more than a century ago, after she had become pregnant from a dalliance with a coachman, loitered by the river wall on the far side of the Embankment. I called her over (she drifted across the busy road quite oblivious to the traffic), but she would not do my bidding, said that she'd do anything else for me, anything at all, but not that. I felt a sudden spark of exasperation at this unhappy remnant's simpering refusal and dismissed her – erased her entire, as easily as blowing out a candle, and allowed my anger to balloon, sucking up all the discarded emotions that blew about the street like scraps of litter. Prickly shards of anger, suffocating rags of distress; flecks of shock and fear bright as fragments of glass; slimy strands of disgust; even a few pure motes of joy, that most effervescent of emotions: I drew in all of them. The baggy crowd whirled about me like a pocket thunderstorm, growing ever darker and denser. The leaves of the dusty young plane tree under which I sat began to tremble. On the Embankment road, drivers unconsciously tapped on their accelerators to speed past.

When I had called up every imp within reach, I threw the entire flock at the front door of the house, straight into the heart of its bubble of preternatural quiet. The house swallowed the thick, lively rope whole. For several minutes nothing happened. Traffic continued to chase itself along the Embankment. An aeroplane made a dull roar above the low grey clouds that sagged over the trees on the other side of the river. Then I felt a swelling pressure, and the ordinary fabric of the house – the red-brick walls, the wrought-iron balcony, the slate roof – was overlaid by a filmy black wave, like a photograph blistering in the heat of a fire. Things seethed within it, shadows on shadows, imps of every kind twisting around each other like a myriad of snakes eating each other's tails, many more than I had poured into the house, released from the trap buried deep in its fabric and flying outward in every direction. I dissolved hundreds of imps as the expanding wavefront boiled over me, but it was like trying to flick away every drop of rain that pelts you in a thunderstorm. I felt a moment of intense dislocation as several dozen surviors passed straight through me, and managed to save a few of them. The rest flew on, across the road, across the river. A white van broadsided by the impalpable storm swerved and smashed into an oncoming car; the car spun around and its rear slammed into a tree. Broken branches collapsed onto it, fell into the road. A bus braked with an explosive sneeze; horns sounded along the two lanes of stalled traffic.

I had no doubt that the trap had been designed to collapse had I entered the house unprepared; and if I had been caught in the midst of thousands of suddenly freed imps, I would have been stripped bare by their frenzy of anger and fear and delirium and disgust. It would have taken me days to recover, and meanwhile I would have been quite helpless. As it was, there would be a sudden and inexplicable increase in violence in this part of the city tonight – arguments, fights, perhaps even murders – but I had escaped the worst of the trap.

Traffic was building up on either side of the road accident. The driver of the car which had smashed into the tree was climbing out of his wrecked vehicle. Two men wrenched back the door of the van; the driver slumped into their arms. And the front door of Rainer Sue's house opened and a woman in a nylon housecoat walked down the steps, unlocked the gate, sat down at the kerb, put her head between her knees and was sick. I ducked through the shrubbery and walked straight past her, into the house.

A vacuum cleaner moaned in the hallway, whispering into silence when I pulled out its plug. I called out Rainer Sue's name, called out Donny Halliwell's, and when there was no reply walked into the living room. Its pale yellow walls were hung with framed gold records and intricate paintings by Australian aboriginals that whispered of landscapes I would never know, dreams I would never have. There was a huge white couch facing a widescreen TV. There were vases of white lilies, vases of eucalyptus branches. There was a tall bookcase crammed with leather-bound volumes, mostly fake grimoires and incunabulae, although amongst the rubbish was a worm-eaten set of the three volumes of del Rio's *Disquisitionum Magicarum*, and a rather fine copy of Casiano's *Summa Diabolica* in Moroccan leather. The raised wing of a grand piano gave back my reflection as I hurried past it, through open French windows and down a flight of steps into the garden. A gravel path ran between raised beds of white lavender, white roses, grey thistles and tiger-striped grasses to a pergola grown over with an enormous, ancient grape vine that was perhaps as old as the house. Glassy bunches of grapes, transparent as teardrops, dangled amongst hand-shaped leaves. In one corner a plywood construct not much bigger than a coffin stood on its end. I opened its door. It was lined with wards and layers of soil and tinfoil – it was a form of orgone box, although infinitely more sophisticated – and the man who squatted inside on a narrow bench seat blinked at me.

He was in his early forties, bare-chested and barefoot, wearing only white jeans and a deep tan, and possessed of a delicate, androgynous beauty. His face was unlined; his blond quiff artfully dishevelled. There were marks like little bee stings along the insides of his forearms, yet no imps of delirium clung to him.

He smiled tremulously at me, his eyes clouded and vague, and said, "Do I know you?"

I had no doubt that this was the former pop star Rainer Sue, and knew at once that he could have had nothing to do with the theft of my book, or the trap left for me in his house. "You must come with me at once," I said, and tugged at his arm when he was slow to rise. I was fizzing with impatience and fear – I knew that the man who had set the trap would be nearby, eager to see if it had caught me.

Rainer Sue followed me compliantly and unquestioningly. When I asked him about Donny Halliwell, he shrugged.

"He is not here?"

Rainer Sue shrugged again. I was sure that he was drugged – those bee stings – but he had also been made safe, made docile. We were walking away from the house now, and for a moment his attention was caught by the flashing blue lights of the ambulance and the two police cars that had arrived at the scene of the accident on the Embankment.

"Someone got hurt," he said.

"It isn't as bad as it could have been. Apart from Mr Halliwell, who else lives with you?"

Rainer Sue considered this. Thoughts rose to the surface of his face like trout in a still pool. "I have a guy who cooks for me and looks after the garden. And this woman comes in and cleans, she should be around, I guess. Wakes me up with her vacuum cleaner . . ."

"I saw her. Where is Donny Halliwell? And where is your driver?"

"Donny drives me. Or we get a limo, and a driver comes with it."

I thought of the two people in the Jaguar. If Donny Halliwell had been the man who had confronted me – and I had only Miranda's word that it was, just as I had only Miranda's word that Donny Halliwell had broken into my house – then who was the driver? Someone who was skilled in the matter of the dead, that much was certain – someone who had made Donny Halliwell into his servant and had turned Rainer Sue into an amiable zombie, cleaned his house of revenants, and packed thousands of imps into the trap.

I said, "Does Mr Halliwell have a friend? Someone who is perhaps staying with you?"

"He's my friend," Rainer Sue said simply.

"And who is he, this friend of yours?"

"We like the same things. Books – that's how we became friends." The pop star's attempt to look sly made him seem imbecilic. "We like the same books."

"Does he have a name, this friend of yours?"

"Cagliostro." Rainer Sue frowned when I laughed. "What's wrong? You know him?"

"I know of the man whose name your friend has assumed. How long has he been staying with you?"

Rainer Sue scratched at his bare chest while thoughts came and went under the surface of his face. At last he said, "A few days. A week, something like that. He's a very together guy, you know. He helped me. Helped me get rid of some very heavy psychic luggage. Made me feel a whole lot better, you know?"

"I'm sure he did." I felt a touch of nausea at the thought of what had been done to this poor foolish man, and asked, "Can you drive?"

"Sure. I love driving." His eyes lit up for a moment; then his face fell. "But Donny doesn't let me."

"I will let you. Do you have a motor car other than the Jaguar?"

"Sure."

"Then lead on, Mr Sue," I said. "Take me to your car."

It was cached in a lock-up garage at the rear of a nearby mansion block: a Mini in racing green, with white leather seats and tinted windows. It took me fifteen minutes, trembling with concentration, to purge it of every imp and residue, and make certain that there were no hidden traps or surprises. All the while, Rainer Sue hugged himself and hopped from one bare foot to the other like an incontinent child, murmuring *Boy oh boy, boy oh boy*.

It turned out that he was not a bad driver, and in any case it was not possible for him to drive at any great speed in the traffic-clogged streets, but I kept my eyes closed most of the way, opening them only to give directions or to try to work out where we were on the four or five occasions when he lost his bearings. He grinned from ear to ear, beating brief rhythms on the steering wheel and humming to himself as the little car lurched and scuttled and crept along. At least he had been left with the capacity for happiness; not out of charity on the part of the man who called himself Cagliostro, but because it made him more amenable to instruction.

It took more than two hours to drive across the city to the second address Rawles had given me: the mean block of council flats where Miranda lived. I left Rainer Sue in the Mini – I was fairly certain that he would not drive off, and was also fairly certain that he would fail to remember to sound the horn if he saw Donny Halliwell or the red Jaguar – and climbed three flights of a concrete stairway. The usual graffiti, the usual stink of urine, the usual litter of discarded needles and soft-drink cans and poly-styrene clamshells, the usual little infestations.

Like Rainer Sue's house, Miranda's flat possessed an eerie, empty quiet. There were no wards or traps; apart from a single nest of imps, it had been swept clean. No one came to the door when I knocked. The window beside it was blanked with a lace curtain; inside, the ledge was thick with the husks of flies, which have the same mindless attraction to certain residues as to excrement, rotten food, and corpses.

The door was armed with three cheap locks that took only a couple of minutes to pick. It was hot inside, the air thickened by a stale human smell. The kitchen counter was piled with fast-food containers, pizza boxes, cartons of a generic protein powder, and crushed soft-drink cans; the living room was stacked with loot. Small televisions and portable stereos; video and DVD players; microwaves and laptop computers; dozens of boxes of trainers. The sofa glittered with drifts of CDs and DVDs. A shoebox heavy with loose jewellery and wristwatches sat on top of a pile of neatly folded tracksuits. I imagined Miranda waiting outside a house while a tame imp inspected every room; I imagined her inter-rogating imps or even ghosts cast off by householders, discover-ing where spare sets of keys were cached, the codes for alarms.

I steeled myself for the worst, and went towards the place where the little nest of imps was lodged. The door to one bedroom – Miranda's – was sealed with a padlocked metal bar. The door to the other stood open. It was very dark inside, and smelt worse than the stairwell. Someone lay on the bed, breathing with a steady rasping snore.

I assumed that it was Miranda's mother, but when I cracked the curtains I saw that it was a man, very thin, heavily bearded, and naked apart from a pair of urine-sodden underpants. Imps of delirium clustered thickly around his head. They were like fat, pale grubs, satiated, sluggish, and as vulnerable as newborn kittens, but it cost me much to disperse them. I had to sit on the edge of the bed afterwards, feeling my blood moving through me, slow and thick. The man was as pale as paper, all bone and sinew, and he stank like a corpse. His hair tangled in greasy ropes around his face. His skin was tight on the bones of his skull. His shallow breath rasped in the black slot of his mouth. As I stared at him, he made a small movement, averting his face as if in shame.

I rinsed grey fur from a coffee mug in the kitchen, fed the man sips of water with my wetted handkerchief. I asked him gently how long he had been held like this. He could not or would not speak, but when I told him the date, tears leaked from his sunken eyes. The insides of his forearms were raw with track marks. Disposable hypodermic syringes in clear plastic envelopes and disposable needles in brown plastic sleeves lay on the bedside table. There was a cellophane wrap of gritty white powder, a bent, blackened spoon, several disposable cigarette lighters, a baby's bottle. Miranda had kept this man prisoner a long time, quietening him with heroin and the attentions of the imps, feeding him on protein mix. I had a pretty good idea who he must be, and wondered what he had done to her (or what she thought he had done to her) to deserve such a dreadful punishment.

I found a working mobile phone on the kitchen table and used it to make two calls, then made inquiries amongst the neighbouring flats, explaining that I was a private investigator trying to trace Miranda on behalf of lawyers who were administering a small bequest due to her. A garrulous old woman in a bright red wig said that she felt sorry for the girl – her mother had disappeared, and her father was a nasty piece of work. A no-nonsense black woman who stood in her doorway with a small girl embracing her knees and a delicious smell of baking wafting around her, told me she thought that Miranda was living alone, confirmed that her father possessed the skull tattoo I had seen on the shoulder of the man on the bed, and said that she had not seen him for six months, good riddance as far as she was concerned. She leaned closer and whispered that I should be careful of his daughter, she was a duppy girl. "Spooky little creature. Give you a look like she want to try stop your heart, you know?"

I said that I did, and thanked her. As I descended the noisome stairs, I saw a familiar head of auburn hair climbing towards me: it was Liz, the girl Miranda had followed two nights ago. She fled when I called her name, unlocked the door of a flat and slid through it and slammed it in my face. I called through the letter box and told her that I wanted to ask her about Miranda; she said that if I didn't go away she'd call the police. I reached out and combed away her fear. I told her that I knew now that I had been wrong about the other night, and wanted to make amends. I said, "I will make sure that she does not trouble you again."

There was a long silence, and then Liz said, "She's mad, she is. Someone should do something about her."

"I intend to. Perhaps you can help me, young lady. Perhaps you can tell me about Miranda's father."

"Him? He's a right devil. Used to beat up her mother something awful, until she had enough and ran back to Ireland. Then he started on Miranda. He'd hit her with the telephone book, or his belt. Police would come round sometimes, but they didn't do anything. I used to feel sorry for her, but then her dad ran off too, and she went funny. She changed."

Liz told me that Miranda had stopped going to school six months ago, that she had been hurting herself ever since her mother ran off.

"She said it was the only thing that made her feel real. But then she started trying to hurt other people."

Liz was crying on the other side of the door, half-suppressed sobs like hiccups.

I said, "When did you last see her father?"

"About the same time. Miranda said he went to look for her mother. She's been living on her own ever since. The social people came snooping around once, but they left her alone. Everyone leaves her alone now. She scares them. Who are you, mister? Are you with the social, or the police?"

"I am trying to find out how I can help Miranda," I said. I was thinking of the man on the bed. I suspected that she had been punishing her father for something a good deal nastier than a few beatings.

"She follows people around," Liz whispered through the letter box. "Like she followed me, the other night. She's jealous, I reckon. Doesn't like people who have ordinary lives. Someone should make her stop it, but everyone's frightened of her."

"Where does she spend her time, during the day?"

"I told you, she doesn't go to school any more. Got suspended, didn't she? She hangs around here, pops up when you don't expect her . . ."

"If she said to you, 'I'll be at the usual place,' where would that be?"

"You know the pub in the market where they sell the antiques and stuff? She nicks stuff, and she sells some of it there. Doesn't care who knows it, either. Gets drunk on beer she pays this old wino to buy for her."

"Thank you, Elizabeth. You have been most helpful."

"She wants putting away somewhere. Somewhere where she can get better. Is that what you're going to do?"

"I am going to try to help her," I said.

As Rainer Sue drove me away in his Mini, an ambulance twinkled past in the other direction, towards the block of flats. One of the calls I had made had been to the emergency services; the other had been to Miranda's mobile phone, in which I had cached an imp during my demonstration of my pickpocketing skills. It was a very small and very stupid imp, but after Miranda had spat a swear word into my silence and rung off, it had maintained the connection and recited the various conversations it had overheard. There had been several bits of business about the disposal of stolen property and the purchase of heroin, and there had been this:

UNKNOWN MAN: The trap has fired.
MIRANDA: I told you I'd get him to go there. So he's out of the picture, right?
UNKNOWN MAN: Unfortunately, he has escaped from the house. However, I imagine that he is seriously weakened, and I will deal with him later, when we have concluded our business.
MIRANDA: It doesn't change what we agreed about the book.
UNKNOWN MAN: It would be unwise to anger me, young woman.
MIRANDA: Well, don't *you* piss *me* off, either, or I might find someone else interested in what I took. (*A pause.*) You still there?

UNKNOWN MAN: We will meet as agreed.

MIRANDA: The usual place I meet everyone, out in the open, no tricks. I'll give you what you want, and you'll pay me what you promised.

UNKNOWN MAN: As agreed, yes.

MIRANDA: And you'll show me things.

UNKNOWN MAN: Of course. I am a man of honour.

I had Rainer Sue park a little way from Camden Passage, and told him that he was free to go.

"Can't I stay? This is kind of exciting." He wriggled in his seat and looked at me with shining eyes, like a puppy eager to play.

I wrote the name and address of a psychologist on a slip of paper, a good man with an open mind who had sought my help once or twice, and folded it into the hand of the former pop star. "This man will help you, if you let him. Go home, Mr Sue, and get on with the rest of your life. And if the man who calls himself Cagliostro comes back to your house, don't let him in," I said, and climbed out of the Mini and walked away, towards Camden Passage.

It was Thursday, the day that antique traders set up their stalls in the spaces amongst the small shops that line the lane. It was late in the afternoon and most of them were packing up now, wrapping unsold goods in newspaper, carrying laden cardboard boxes and plastic bakery trays to Volvos and people carriers double-parked on Essex Road. I saw Miranda on the wall of the terrace outside the public house in the middle of the market, swigging from a bottle of beer, idly kicking her legs while she talked with one of the blanket traders who make their pitches on the pavement outside. Her baseball cap was perched on her head. A briefcase was set on the wall beside her.

I waited and watched for more than an hour. At last, she went inside the public house to use its lavatory. I caught her in the corridor when she came out, and pushed her into a cupboard full of cleaning materials. At first she denied that she had anything to do with the theft of my book, but after I drew my blade and put it to her throat and convinced her that I meant business, she said that Donny Halliwell had made her do it.

"Mr Halliwell is merely a stooge for the man who wants my copy of the *Stenographia*. The man with whom you conversed on your mobile phone a few hours ago. The man who calls himself Cagliostro. Who is he, Miranda?"

The girl tried to twist away but stilled when I pricked her throat with the point of my blade. We were jammed together in the close dark of the cupboard. She smelt of fear and alcohol; fear oozed out of her in a discrete package that clung inside her hood, and she tried and failed to use this newborn imp against me.

"It will not obey you as long as I am here," I said. "Did you really think you were more powerful than me?"

"I fooled you, didn't I?"

"For a little while, but no longer. When did you start to work for Cagliostro?"

"I don't work for anyone."

"You made a compact with him. You told him that you had found out where I lived, and you agreed to steal my book for him."

"I told you, I don't work for anyone."

Keeping the point of my blade at her throat, I pulled the briefcase from her grasp. "What would I find, Miranda, if I looked in here?"

She looked at me, sullen and defiant and scared.

"The man who wants the book you stole could not find my house, attempted to lure me into an insultingly obvious trap, and hides behind a foolish pseudonym. If you had the benefit of a proper education, Miranda, you would know that the Count of Cagliostro was a charlatan who died more than two hundred years ago, a peddler of quack remedies whose chief fame is that he was immortalized in the writings of Alexander Dumas. I doubt that I have anything to fear from the man who has taken his name, and I also doubt that he has anything to teach you."

"He showed me how to break your wards, and he said he'd show me other stuff, too. He's a powerful man," Miranda said sullenly, "so you better watch out."

"We will soon see how powerful he is – you arranged to meet him here, did you not, in your 'usual place'? I warned you about the affinity of imps for telephones. One inhabits your mobile phone, and has been listening to your conversations. You arranged to meet Cagliostro. Very well. We will wait for him together."

"He'll hurt you."

"No, he won't. And I won't let him hurt you, either."

"I can look after myself."

"I know that you can," I said. "But the way you are going about it will only do you harm. I know about your father, Miranda. I know what he did to you, and I know what you did to him. I understand—"

She twisted in my grip again, started to shout bloody murder, the perennial cry of the London mob, and kicked at the door of the cupboard. I twisted the key and stood aside and let her run.

A large man in one of the green sweatshirts worn by the public house's staff stood at the top of the stairs, wanting to know what all the noise was about. I plucked up an imp and flung it at him and left him there, whimpering some nonsense about rats, and followed Miranda. I knew that she would go straight to Cagliostro. It was time to meet him.

The red Jaguar was waiting at the end of Camden Passage. Donny Halliwell eased out of it like a cork from a champagne bottle.

I raised the briefcase, and told him that I would deal only with the man for whom he was working. The driver of the Jaguar said something; Donny Halliwell reached into the pocket of his crumpled jacket and showed me a small black pistol. His smile was a grimace, as if wires had pulled up the corners of his mouth. One of his front teeth was gold. "Get in the car," he said.

I climbed into the back. Miranda was hunched in the corner, small and scared. She looked at me, her lower lip caught between her teeth, and looked away when I told her that everything would be all right.

"There is a sword in his cane," the man behind the steering wheel said. "Deal with it."

Donny Halliwell took my cane from me, unsheathed the blade, stuck it between two paving stones, and put a right angle in it. He left it quivering there like a broken Excalibur, and levered himself into the car, making the back seat unpleasantly crowded and enveloping me in a yeasty smell of old sweat. The driver put his arm on the back of the passenger seat and looked at me. I realized that I had seen him two nights ago, in the café, and knew that he must be the man who called himself Cagliostro.

"You can let the girl go," I said. "She has nothing to do with this."

"She tried to cheat me," Cagliostro said. His was the kind of clipped English accent that had been the norm on BBC radio until about twenty years ago. With his square, handsome face and black polo-neck sweater worn under a black corduroy jacket, he looked like a philosophy professor who has written a bestselling book traducing the ideas of his colleagues. His black hair, almost certainly dyed, was cut very short, showing the white scalp beneath; his eyes were the pale blue of sunlight seen through snow, and unblinkingly intent. He looked older than me, but he was not.

Beside me, Miranda stirred and said, "I never cheated you. I was going to give you the book, but he found me, didn't he? He took it back."

"You should have given it to me straight away," Cagliostro said.

"We had a deal. You said you'd teach me stuff."

"And so I will," Cagliostro said. "Such wonders. What a pity that you and Mr Carlyle will not survive them." He looked at Donny Halliwell and said, "Show me the book."

The big man took the briefcase from me and snapped its locks. Cagliostro touched the book with long white fingers, then told his servant to close the briefcase and set it on the front seat. He smiled at me and said, "You do not recognize me."

"We have met before?"

"In 1941," Cagliostro said, and put the car in gear and pulled out into the traffic, ignoring the outraged horn blast of a bus.

"Which side were you on?"

"You must ask?"

"I suppose not."

"I was a mere boy then. And because it took me some time to learn how to prolong my life, I have aged somewhat. You, however, look much as you did then. You even wear the same silly costume."

"It is not a costume," I said, remembering the young man who had given me a calm look of pure hatred as he stood between two military policemen, in a room hazed with the smoke of the one-time code pads that he had burnt while soldiers had fought a gun battle with his associates. I told him now, "You had some small talent in the matter of the dead. You believed it to be a form of magic when we first met, and I thought you foolishly deluded. If you still believe it, then I am afraid that my opinion has not changed."

"See how he talks," Miranda said to Cagliostro. The poor girl was still trying to win his favour. "He thinks he's more important than anyone. That's why I helped you."

"This man was an enemy agent in the Second World War," I told her. "A Nazi spy. He bound ghosts to important buildings. The ghosts acted as markers or beacons for others of his kind, who rode in bombers."

"Sounds cool," Miranda said.

"It was very cool," Cagliostro said. He was a skilful and ruthless driver, riding hard on the rear of the car in front of the Jaguar, overtaking it on the inside at the big roundabout as he aimed the big car into Old Street. "Unfortunately, flattery will not undo the damage you have caused."

"He called himself Count Roemheld then," I said. "It was no more his real name than Cagliostro."

"Names are powerful things, Mr Carlyle," Cagliostro said. "I do not give up mine lightly."

"I did everything you asked," Miranda said. "I got him to go to Rainer Sue's house."

"Yet Mr Carlyle escaped the trap. I wonder, young lady, if it was because you told him about it."

"I never!"

"I escaped," I said, "because your trap was so very crude. I defeated you once, and I will do so again."

But despite my brave words and the voluptuous feeling of calm that had possessed me ever since I had committed myself to this confrontation, I was not certain that either I or Miranda would survive it. I did not know how much power Cagliostro had gained since we had last met, and I had not counted on Donny Halliwell being armed. Miranda had been right. I was no longer wise to the ways of the streets. I did not assume that English criminals would carry pistols as casually as Wild West cowboys.

The Jaguar sped under the railway bridge where I had been stopped two nights before, and turned sharply onto Kingsland Road. A pedestrian levitated himself out of the way. We drove past the Geffrye Museum. We drove past the new mosque. The gold cap of its tower shone in the late-afternoon sunlight.

Cagliostro looked at me in the rear-view mirror and said, "Perhaps you are wondering why I need the book."

"As a matter of fact, I am wondering why you believe that you need me. You went to a great deal of trouble with your silly little trap, and you did not ask your creature to kill me just now, after you took possession of the book."

"Times are changing, Mr Carlyle. We are at the end of one age and the beginning of another. It is time to choose sides. Those like you, who attempt to remain neutral, who pretend that they are aloof from the world, will be the first casualties. Do you not think that poetic justice?"

"I see no justice here, only the tired cliché of an old, defeated Nazi attempting revenge on his former nemesis."

"If I had wanted revenge, Mr Carlyle, I would have found you more than fifty years ago. This is no more than a happy coincidence. I discovered that you had something I wanted, and when you would not accept my very reasonable offer I was forced to take it."

"I believe it was Miranda who stole the book. You were not able to find my house, although you tried several times to follow me home."

"A foolish piece of deception, nothing more."

"A deception you were unable to see through, although Miranda managed it well enough. Of the three of us, who has the most of what you call 'power'?"

"I broke your wards. I laid the trap."

"Which did not quite catch me. You have the book, and you have me. Why not let the girl go? She has no part in this foolishness."

"I can look after myself," Miranda said.

"I wish it was true," I told her.

We passed through Hackney, driving beneath the flyovers of the motorway junction beyond Victoria Park to an industrial estate named after Shakespeare's gloomy, haunted prince. Donny Halliwell heaved out of the Jaguar and unlocked the gate.

"The man in charge of the security of this place is one of Mr Halliwell's associates," Cagliostro said. "Remarkably easy to bribe. We will not be disturbed."

He drove past long low brick sheds housing businesses that mostly had something to do with the motor trade, and stopped the Jaguar beside a fence that, sagging in front of a strip of weeds and straggling elder trees, ran along the boundary of the industrial estate, at the edge of the junction with the Hereford Union Canal and the navigational cut of the River Lea. Menaced by Donny Halliwell's gun, Miranda and I scrambled through the narrow belt of scrub to the towpath.

"Christ's cross was made from elder wood," Cagliostro said, as he followed us. "And Judas hanged himself from an elder tree. A nice symmetry, don't you think?"

"More likely he hanged himself from a fig tree," I said, "since fig trees are native to his country and elder trees are not. Still, if you believe in that kind of thing, elder wood is said to be a protection from witchcraft. I find the idea encouraging."

The air was hot and close, thick with the smell of open water and fecund vegetation. To the west, the low clouds were breaking up, and the sun burned in the middle of a ragged patch of blue sky. On the dual carriageway that was elevated beyond a snaggled sprawl of roofs, fugitive shards of sunlight gleamed on the roofs of speeding cars and trucks. Cagliostro, holding the briefcase in one hand, turned a full circle, taking in the view of the backs of industrial buildings and brick walls on the other side of the canal. It was one of those mournful, scruffy places that belong to no one except the dead, but there were no revenants there – not so much as the smallest imp.

"A quiet place," he said. "I have made sure that we will not be disturbed, too. Any walkers or cyclists will discover that they have a pressing need to turn back if they approach too closely."

He set the briefcase between his feet, reached inside his jacket, lifted out a white mouse by its naked tail, and tossed it to the ground. It ran off along the towpath, cheeping like a sparrow. He smiled when he saw my dismay and said, "I believe you have already met the entity my little sacrifice will summon. Shoot him."

Donny Halliwell stirred like a man jerked out of sleep, raised his little pistol and fired. The bullet punched me in my left thigh. It passed straight through the meat without hitting bone, but even so I felt as if I had been struck with a red-hot poker. I grabbed the spot reflexively, lost my balance, and fell on my backside amongst dry weeds.

"You should have sold me the book," Cagliostro said. "I made you an excellent offer, and I would have honoured it. I even had another sacrifice marked out for this business. But you were too stubborn, Mr Carlyle, and it has brought you to this."

"So that was why you were at the café," I said. It was a small consolation that I had saved its kindly owner.

"But instead you walked in, with the girl. You were trying to help her, but later that night she betrayed you and made a bargain with me. And now I have the book, and I have you, and I have her. Miranda, I will make good my promise to teach you something useful. Find four branches of elder wood, each about as thick as your thumb. Break them off and use your knife, the one you think I do not know about, to sharpen the broken ends into points."

"What for?"

"Because I tell you to."

They stared at each other. Miranda was searching for any revenant she could use against him, but apart from something with a cold remorseless hunger that was flowing towards us from the west, none were within reach.

"He wishes to stake me out," I told Miranda. "As a sacrifice to the thing that has taken up residence in this stretch of water. The thing that took your pet two nights ago. Can you feel it draw near?"

"Very good, Mr Carlyle," Cagliostro said.

"You hope to make it more powerful, and then bind it with incantations from the *Stenographia*. I should warn you that it will not work."

"The book has puissance."

"It has nothing of the kind."

"I believe your parents would disagree."

"They are in no position to disagree."

They had been dead for more than a hundred and seventy years, but it still hurt me to speak about them to a stranger.

"You will soon be at the same disadvantage. Four pieces of wood, young woman. Do it now, or Mr Halliwell will shoot you dead and I'll feed your ghost to my pet."

Miranda looked at him from beneath the bill of her baseball cap. She was slight and so very young, but was stiffened by a core of irreducible defiance. "I know you're gonna do that anyway," she said, "so don't expect me to do your work for you."

Cagliostro shrugged, and told Donny Halliwell to deal with her. As the big man stepped towards Miranda, I used the connection I still had with the imp in her mobile phone, and made the little machine ring. Cagliostro pinched the imp out, as I knew he would, and I used the momentary distraction to loose the imps that I had saved from the trap at Rainer Sue's house. I had pinched them as small as a full stop and swallowed them. Now I coughed them up and threw them as hard as I could.

Not at Cagliostro – he would have dismissed them in an instant – but at Donny Halliwell.

They slammed into the big man and clung, covering him with crackling sparks of panic and disgust that burnt away the calm of his trance in an instant. His face cleared and he turned to Cagliostro and raised the little black pistol and shot him, shot him again as he pitched forward, blood all over his face. As the two gunshots echoed off the brick wall on the other side of the canal, Cagliostro's prone body blurred, like a double-exposed photographic image. But even as the ghost, shocked from him by the violent moment of his death, began to get to its feet, a smooth white snake whipped up from the canal and opened its jaws wide and snapped it down. Miranda screamed, and something as massive and fast as an express train blasted over my head and smashed into the ancient revenant. It blew apart like a snowman hit square by a howitzer round. For an instant, a thousand fragments skittered away in every direction across the calm black water of the canal, and then they smoked into the air and were gone.

Miranda had fallen to her knees. The red blood that ran from her nose was shockingly bright against her white skin. She dabbed at it with the back of her hand, saw me looking at her, and said, "It took him. I saw it. I saw it eat his soul."

"It took the ghost he created at the moment of dying. If there are such things as souls, I have never seen one."

Donny Halliwell said, "I don't know what you two are talking about. I don't want to know. Just tell me he was going to kill you."

"Something of the sort," I said. My leg was hurting quite badly now, a swelling, bone-deep ache. My trouser leg was soaked with blood. My shoe was filled with blood.

Donny Halliwell stuck the pistol in his jacket pocket. His hand was shaking so badly that it took him three tries. "He made me shoot you," he said.

"I know."

"It wasn't my idea. None of this was my idea. I don't even know where I am. Last thing I remember properly is opening the door to him. And then everything sort of fell away. It was like I was in the back of my head, watching things happen on a very small TV."

"He hypnotized you," I said.

"Where's Rainer?"

"He helped me, and then I sent him home."

"He was so excited when this bloke wrote to him – something about those stupid books of his. He trusts people too much. Are you sure he's okay? At some point I think I gave him some kind of drug."

"I gave him the name of a man who can help him," I said.

"I better go and see how he is," Donny Halliwell said. "He isn't too good on his own."

"Of course," I said, and was relieved when the big man crashed away through the belt of scrubby trees.

Miranda shuddered once, all over, and said, "I thought he was going to finish us off."

"So did I. Is your mobile phone working?"

"'Course. I'll call an ambulance."

"That won't be necessary," I said, and gave her the telephone number of a sympathetic doctor. After she had made the call, I told her to open the briefcase and bring me my book.

She could not quite meet my gaze when she handed it to me. It was a heavy quarto volume bound in the hide of an unborn calf tanned by age to an uneven buttery colour, its pages made of good-quality linen paper. I ran my fingers over the intricate knot embossed in the leather under the stamped gold title. "After my parents died, it was important to me to recreate their library. This was the last volume I needed – the rarest, and the most expensive. You would not believe me if I told you how much I paid for it," I said, and threw it into the canal.

It made quite a splash.

"You're mad," Miranda said.

"I should have done it some time ago. Our dead friend was right about one thing: times have changed. And it is time to let go of the past. Now, would you be so kind as to cut a branch from one of those elders?"

"What are you going to do? Stake him through the heart?"

"Cagliostro was no vampire. I do not want Dr Barrow to find us here, with the body. If I am to hobble to the road, I will need a crutch."

"Then what?"

"Dr Barrow will take me to his home, he will treat my wound, and I will make up a story for the police."

"I mean, what about me?"

"The police will want to talk to you about your father, but I can vouch for you."

"He hurt me," she said, plainly and simply. "After Mum left, he came into my room every night and hurt me."

"And when you could, you hurt him in turn. I understand. But by destroying him in that way, by dedicating your life to his punishment, you would also have destroyed yourself."

"I wanted to kill him," she said. "But I didn't want his ghost haunting me. I can see them sometimes, ghosts, but I can't do anything with them."

"You did quite well with Cagliostro's pet."

"They'll put me away, won't they?"

"I have never before taken on an apprentice, Miranda. I have lived a solitary life ever since I moved to London. Last night, you said that I had no real friends. That I did not let anyone get close to me. And you were right. But times have changed, much more than I believed when I first began to walk the streets at night. You have a powerful gift, and I can teach you how to use it, if you will let me. But I should warn you that it will not be an easy path."

"Teach me."

She said it with a sudden, raw, naked passion, and in that moment I had my first glimpse of the real Miranda, the human being who hid behind the sullen, wary mask of a child brought up on the stones.

"Teach me," she said. "Teach me stuff."

MIKE O'DRISCOLL

The Silence of
the Falling Stars

BORN IN LONDON, BROUGHT up in the south-west of Ireland and
living in Wales for the last seventeen years, Mike O'Driscoll
remains uncertain about where he really belongs.

He has worked in construction, transport and recruitment, and
owned his own business (a video rental store) for five years, this
last being an enjoyable experience apart from the near-bank-
ruptcy. For the last four years he has worked in childcare,
combining the terrors of fostering with the less rigorous demands
of working part-time towards a Master's degree in Literature.

O'Driscoll has been writing short stories for fifteen years, and
his fiction has appeared in *The 3rd Alternative, Interzone, BBR,
Crime Wave, Peeping Tom, Nemonymous, Albedo One, Indi-
genous Fiction* and *Fear*, plus online at *Infinity Plus, Eclectica*
and *Gothic.net*. He has also contributed to such anthologies as
*Off Limits, Lethal Kisses, Darklands, Last Rites and Resurrec-
tions, Decalog 5, The Sun Rises Red, The Dark: New Ghost
Stories, Gathering the Bones, Thackery Lambshead's Pocket
Guide to Eccentric or Discredited Diseases* and all three volumes
of *Cold Cuts*. His regular comment column on the horror genre,
"Night's Plutonium Shore", which has appeared for over two
years at the *Alien Online* website, was recently transferred to a
new home in the pages of *The 3rd Alternative*.

About the following novella, the author recalls: "Travelling by
rail and road across America back in 1996, I made a detour to

Death Valley, prompted mostly by imaginary encounters with desert landscapes in countless films and books. It is one of the few places I've ever been which I would describe as truly 'other-worldly', evoking, as it does, an unsettling sense of isolation and mystery, combined with a fragmented geological weight and power.

"For a long time afterwards I tried repeatedly to write a story set in the valley, but could never come up with a narrative frame that would do justice to the landscape. When the opportunity came to write a ghost story for *The Dark*, I began toying with the idea of using Death Valley as a locale to explore the relationship between consciousness and landscape, originally intending to cast the valley itself in the role of ghost. Early drafts were written while listening to Hank Williams, and I guess that over the weeks, the story became more imbued with the desperate sense of lone-liness and longing that haunts so many of Hank's songs.

"By the time it was finished, it seemed that the restless Henry Woods had stumbled out of one of those songs and found a kind of home, if not peace, in this valley."

N OTHING IS INFINITE. IN a lifetime a man's heart will notch up somewhere in the region of 2,500 million beats, a woman's maybe 500 million more. These are big numbers but not infinite. There is an end in sight, no matter how far off it seems. People don't think about that. They talk instead about the sublime beauty of nature, about the insignificance of human life compared to the time it's taken to shape these rocks and moun-tains. Funny how time can weigh heavier on the soul than all these billions of tons of dolomite and dirt. A few years back a ranger found something squatting against the base of a mesquite tree at the mouth of Hanaupah Canyon. It was something dead, he saw, and the shape of it suggested a man. Curious, the ranger crouched down and touched it. The body, or whatever it was, had been so dessicated by heat and wind that it started to crumble and when the desert breeze caught it, the whole thing fell away to dust. No way to tell what it had really been, or if it was heat alone or time that caused its naturalization.

Fifty-year highs for July average 116 degrees. Anyone caught out here in that kind of heat without water has a couple of options. You can try to find shade, which, if you get lucky, will cut your rate of dehydration by about fifteen per cent. Or you can just rest instead of walking, which will save you something like forty per cent. But the ground temperature out here is half again higher than the air. Ideally, what you want is a shaded spot elevated above the ground. If you're lucky enough to find such a place, and if you're smart enough to keep your clothes on, which will cut your dehydration by another twenty per cent, then you might last two days at 120 degrees max without water. If you're out of luck, then just keeping still you'll sweat two pints in an hour. If you don't take in the equivalent amount of water, you'll begin to dehydrate. At five per cent loss of body weight you'll start to feel nauseous. Round about ten per cent, your arms and legs will begin tingling and you'll find it hard to breathe. The water loss will thicken your blood and your heart will struggle to pump it out to your extremities. Somewhere between fifteen and twenty per cent dehydration, you'll die.

Which goes to show that there is, after all, one thing that *is* infinite: the length of time you stay dead. There is no real correlation between what I'm thinking and the SUV that heads slowly south along the dirt road. Even when it pulls over and stops beside the dry lake running along the valley floor, I can't say for sure what will happen. I'm unwilling to speculate. Even when nothing happens I don't feel any kind of surprise.

I scan the oval playa with my binoculars. Indians are supposed to have raced horses across it, which is why it's called the Racetrack. There's an outcrop of rock at the north end which they call the Grandstand but I don't see any spectators up there. Never have. Below the ridge from where I watch, there are clumps of creosote bush and the odd Joshua tree. Further north, there are stands of beavertail and above them, on the high slopes of the Last Chance Range, are forests of juniper and pinyon pine. A glint of sunlight catches my eye and I glance towards the vehicle. But nothing has moved down there. I shift my gaze back out on to the playa, trying to pretend I don't feel the cold chill that settles on my bones. I look away at the last moment and wipe the sweat from my face. Thirst cracks my lips and dust coats the inside of my mouth. There's plenty of water in my Expedition, parked a half-mile further south along the road, but I make no move to return to

the vehicle. Whatever is happening here I have no choice but to
see how it plays out.

A shadow moves on the playa. When I search for it all I can see
are the rocks scattered across the honey-combed surface of the
dry lake. I scan them closely, looking for a lizard or rodent, even
though nothing lives out there. The air is still and quiet, no breeze
at all to rustle through the mesquites. Then something catches my
eyes and the hairs on the back of my neck stand up. A movement
so painfully slow I doubt it happened at all. Until it rolls forward
another inch. From this distance, I estimate its weight at eighty to
a hundred pounds. I glance at the rocks nearest to it but none of
them have moved. Only this one, its shadow seeming to melt in
the harsh sunlight as it heaves forward again. There's no wind,
nothing to explain its motion. All the stories I've heard about the
rocks have some rational explanation but there's no reason at all
to what I'm seeing here.

Except maybe that SUV and whatever's inside it. I look back to
where it was but it's not there. I scan the dirt road to north and
south and still don't see it. I search the playa in case the vehicle
drove out on the mud but there are only scattered rocks. The sun
is at its highest now, yet I'm not overheating. I don't feel nauseous
and my heart isn't struggling. Maybe it's because I'm barely
breathing. I stare along the dirt road for an age, looking for
something I might have missed. But there's no trail of dust, or
anything else to signal they were ever here.

The guy wore jeans and a loose-fit shirt, the woman had on
shorts, T-shirt and a baseball cap. He was leaning over beneath
the open hood of the Japanese SUV. A rusting stove lay on its
back beside the road and beyond it two lines of rubble were all
that marked a building which had long since gone.

The woman's face creased in a smile as I pulled up in front of
the Toyota Rav4. I got out of my vehicle. "You need a hand
here?"

"I think we've overheated," she said. I didn't recognize her
accent.

The guy stood up and wiped his face on his shirt. "Bloody air-
conditioning," he said. "I guess I was running it too hard. We're
not used to this kind of heat."

I nodded. "How long you been stuck here?"

Before the woman could answer, a young girl stuck her head out the back window. "Henry Woods," she said, reading my name tag. "Are you a policeman?"

"No, I'm a park ranger."

The woman leaned over and tousled the girl's hair. "Ranger Woods, meet Cath. I'm Sophie Delauney, this is my husband, Paul."

I shook hands with both of them and asked Delauney if there was anything they needed. He frowned, then laughed and said he doubted it. "I suppose you'll tell me I should have hired an American car."

"No. You just had bad luck, is all." I leaned in over the engine, saw there was nothing I could do. "Could happen to anyone."

"Yeah, well, it happened to us."

I got some bottles of water from the cooler in the Expedition and handed them around. Delauney went back to fiddling with the plugs and points, unwilling, I figured, to accept that all he could do was wait for the engine to cool.

"How'd you find us?" Sophie Delauney said.

"We have a plane that patrols the Valley. Must have seen you here and called it in. I was up at Zabriskie Point, twenty miles north of here."

"I didn't see it," she said, shielding her eyes as she looked up at the cloudless sky.

"I saw it," the girl said.

"Did you, baby? You never said."

"I did. You weren't listening.

"Where you folks from?" I asked.

"England," she said. "We live outside London."

The girl frowned and shook her head. "No, we don't – we live in Elstree."

"I know, dear, but Mr Woods might not have heard of Elstree."

"I always wanted to see England," I said. "Just never seem to find the time."

"You should."

Delauney finally saw that merely willing it wasn't going to get the engine to cool any faster and came to join us. "Where you headed?" I asked him.

"Not far, by the look of things. Can you recommend anywhere close by?"

"About an hour's drive will get you to the resort village at Stovepipe Wells." I don't know why I didn't mention the Inn at Furnace Creek, which was closer.

The girl piped up. "Do they have a swimming pool?"

I nodded. "Sure do."

Sophie drank some water. She wiped her hand across her mouth and said, "Do you ever get used to this heat?"

"Breathe lightly," I said. "It won't hurt so much."

After quarter of an hour, I told Delauney to try it again. The engine turned over and cut out. He tried again and this time it caught. "There you go," I said. "You should be okay now – just keep an eye on the temp gauge."

"Thanks for your help, Officer Woods," Sophie said. "It's much appreciated."

"It's what I'm here for."

They got in the vehicle. "Thanks again," Sophie said. I watched as they drove off, the girl hanging out the window, her mother too, staring back at me. Alone in the ruins of Greenwater, I tried to imagine what she saw, wondering if she had seen something in my eyes that I didn't know was there.

I paid rent to the government for the bungalow I occupied near Stovepipe Wells. It was small but even after six years I didn't seem to have accumulated enough belongings to fill the available space. Rae Hannafin said it looked unlived in, said if I hated it that much I should ask to be rehoused. She thought I was stuck in a rut, that I had been in the Valley too long and that I should apply for a transfer. But I didn't hate Death Valley or even the bungalow. Though I used to imagine that one day I would move on, over the years I've come to realize that I had reached the place I'd always been heading towards. It's not just the solitariness – it's the Valley itself that gets under your skin.

I sat in Arcan's Bar drinking Mexican beer. It was quiet, a dozen or so people, mostly couples, a few regulars shooting pool, half a dozen familiar faces perched on stools at the counter. Kenny Rogers, someone like that, on the jukebox. The young Hispanic behind the counter made small talk with a couple of girls. I caught his eye, he fetched another beer, set it down in front of me, gave me a scowl and went back to work his charm on the señoritas. Jaime had been working there nearly two years and still complained about the customers treating him like shit. Just because he was Mexican, he told me one time. No, I said, it's because you're an outsider.

"That 'sposed to make me feel better, man?" he asked.

"Yes," I said. "Because we're all outsiders here."

That was about the most I'd ever talked to him at one time. I'm not good at small talk. As a rule I only talk when I have something to say. This is probably a failing on my part. Hannafin says that talk is a social lubricant, that it's part of what makes us human, even when it doesn't mean anything. I'm not convinced. Everything we say means something, even if it's not what we intended. But I had to admit that it worked for her. She seemed to be able to get through to people, make them understand her meaning without spelling it out. Maybe that was what made her such a good ranger, why she would maybe one day make Assistant Chief.

I took a pull on my beer and stared in the mirror behind the counter, looking for something to take me out of myself. It was getting to be a habit. I'd watch other people and imagine their conversations or what they were feeling, see if that made me feel any more human. Sometimes I'd see other men just like me, that same soft hunger in their eyes as they searched for someone or something to help them discover meaning in their lives.

"Hey, ranger."

I came out of my reverie and stared at the guy who'd spoken.

"I was right." It was the guy whose SUV had overheated. "I said to Sophie it was you."

I saw her sitting at a table by the window with her daughter. The kid waved. "You're staying in the motel?"

"You recommended it," Delauney said. "Look, ah, let me buy you a drink."

I was about to decline when I looked at Sophie Delauney again and saw her smile. "Sure," I said. "I'll have another beer."

While he ordered drinks I walked over to the table. "Ranger Woods, what a surprise," Sophie said, and asked me to take a seat. "You live in the resort?"

"'Bout a mile away."

"Where's your hat?" the girl said.

"That's for keeping the sun off my head, not the stars."

"You look different but I knew it was you. Daddy thought you were someone else."

"You must have what we call the eagle eye."

"What is that?"

"It means you see too much," Sophie said, as she stroked the girl's hair. I wondered what she meant, what were the things the kid saw that she shouldn't have seen. "Since you're off duty, is it okay if we call you Henry?"

I told her it was fine. Delauney came over with two bottles of Dos Equis, a glass of red wine and a juice for the kid. I still felt a little awkward but something about Sophie made it easy to be in her company. She steered the conversation so that I didn't have to say too much, mostly listen as they talked about their own lives back in England. She taught history in high school, Delauney was an architect. They'd made their first trip to America nine years ago, when they got married and spent a week in New York. Now, with their daughter, they'd come to see the West. They'd flown to LA, spent four days down there, doing the "Disneyland thing" and the "Hollywood thing", which was the way Delauney put it, rolling his eyes. They'd driven up to Las Vegas, had two nights there, before rolling into the Valley this afternoon along highway 178. The Greenwater detour had seemed like a good idea at the time. Sophie's charm made me feel something like a normal human being. Sometimes I lost sight of that and I was grateful to her for reminding me who I was.

I got another round of drinks and when I returned Delauney asked me about the Valley. "What are the best places to see?"

"How much time you got?"

"A day."

"Don't try to squeeze in too much."

"He won't listen," Sophie said. "Paul has to turn everything into a major expedition."

He laughed. "Okay, tell me what I can't afford to miss."

I thought about it a while. "When you start to look closely," I said, "you'll notice all the things that aren't there." I wondered if Sophie understood, if she was capable of seeing what was missing.

She started to say something but Delauney talked across her. "I'll stick with what is here. Like Badwater, and maybe a ghost town."

I nodded. "Chloride City's an old silver-mining town about a half-hour north-east of here. Not a whole lot left up there but there's a cliff above the town that will give you some great views of the Valley."

The girl said, "Ask about the rocks."

"The rocks."

"Daddy said they move."

Delauney seemed a little embarrassed. "Guide book said that rocks get blown by high winds across the surface of a dry lake." He sounded sceptical but also willing to be persuaded. "Said they leave trails across the surface."

I took a sip of my beer. "I've heard that, too."

"Have you seen them move?" the girl asked.

"Never have."

"I still want to see them, anyway," she said.

"Maybe," Delauney said. "But tomorrow it's the ghost town, okay?"

"You won't be disappointed," I said.

Sophie was looking at me. She seemed unconscious of the intensity of her gaze or that I might be aware of it. I wondered what she saw in my face, whether there was something there that revealed more than I wanted her to see. There was a spray of freckles splashed beneath her eyes and across the bridge of her nose. She was beautiful. I wanted desperately to know what was inside her head at that moment, but Delauney leaned close and whispered something to her. Something I didn't catch. She laughed and her face flushed red and I didn't know what that meant. It was Cath's bedtime, she said. I smiled to let her know it was okay, but I could see she was troubled. She told Delauney to stay a while if he wanted. But I felt troubled suddenly too, angry that she was going. I wished he'd kept his mouth shut.

"I gotta go, too," I said, standing up. "Early start in the morning."

"No problem, Henry," Delauney said. "Thanks for all your help."

I turned to Sophie. "It was good to meet you," I said, shaking her hand, using formality just to feel the touch of her skin. There was no harm in it. "Enjoy your stay. You too, Cath – keep that eagle eye on your folks."

Sophie frowned, as if puzzled at something I'd said. I left the bar and set off out into the quiet darkness. It was less than a mile back to the empty bungalow but it seemed like the longest walk I ever took.

Before I came to Death Valley I lived out on the Coast. I was a deputy in the San Luis Obispo's Sheriff Department. I was good at the job and had ambitions to make Sheriff one day. There was a woman I'd been seeing and I'd begun to think maybe she was the one. But things didn't turn out the way I'd planned. Something happened I hadn't counted on, one of those situations nobody could foresee. There was no time to think and what I did I did instinctively. IAD ruled that it had been self-defence but I knew as well as anyone that the kid never had a gun. After the investigation things began to fall apart at work and my girlfriend began to cool on me. A week after she left I quit the department and spent eighteen months drifting round the Midwest, feeling sorry for myself and listening to songs about regret. Living in Death Valley cured me of that. Like Robert Frost said, whatever road you're on is the one you chose and the one you didn't take is no longer an option. I came here, worked as a volunteer, then, after six months, got a ranger's post and, in time, I saw there was no going back.

Some people find that hard to accept. This morning I got a call to check out a vehicle parked up at Quackenbush Mine. There was a dog in the back seat of the truck, a German Shepherd. Her tongue lolled out her open mouth and she managed a feeble wag of her tail against the seat when she saw me. The window was cracked open a half-inch but even so it must have been over 130 degrees inside. It took me twenty minutes to find the driver, coming down from Goldbelt Spring. He was a heavy-set guy, in shorts and vest, a 49ers cap hiding his close-cropped skull. Had a woman and two kids with him, a boy and a girl about ten or eleven.

"Is that your truck down there at the mine, sir?" I asked him.

"The Cherokee, yeah."

"Your dog is dying in there."

"Aw shit," he groaned, lurching down the slope. "I knew this would fucking happen."

They always say they knew what would happen. Which, instead of justifying what they did, only compounds the situation. He bleated on about how he didn't want to keep the dog on a leash and how his wife kept on about you had to because that was the rule and so, in truth, it wasn't his fault, he was just thinking about the dog. I led him back down to his vehicle, got him to open it up and lift the dog out onto the ground. Her eyes were glazed, her body still.

"She's still alive," the guy said. "I can feel her heart."

"Step back out of the way," I told him. I unholstered my gun, stuck the barrel against the dog's chest and squeezed the trigger.

The woman screamed.

"Jesus Christ," the guy said. "Jesus fucking Christ – you killed her!"

"No," I said. "You did that." I stood up and checked the vehicle over to see if there was anything else I could cite the son of a bitch for apart from animal cruelty. I gave him the ticket and drove off, leaving him to bury the dog in the dirt.

Heading south on the Saline Valley Road, I heard Rydell's voice crackling over the Motorola, requesting assistance at an incident in Hidden Valley. I responded and told him where I was.

"It's a vehicle come off the road, two people injured," he said. "Quick as you can, Henry. Hannafin's already on her way down from Grapevine."

I spun the Expedition around, throwing up a cloud of dust as I accelerated north along the dirt road. My heart was racing like it knew what I was going to find but the truth was I had no real idea what to expect up there.

When I saw the truck turned on its side ten yards off the road, the feeling of anticipation disappeared, leaving me vaguely disappointed. Five kids were seated in a semicircle a few yards away from the vehicle. One of them, a fair-haired kid about eighteen, got up and came over to me. "I think Shelley broke a leg," he said, nodding towards the others. "And Karl's maybe busted an arm."

"You the driver?"

He hesitated before nodding.

"You been drinking? Smoking some weed?"

"No way, man, nothing like that. Just took the bend too fast, I guess."

All of them were cut and bruised but only the two he'd named were badly injured. Shelley looked like she was in a lot of pain. I was splinting her leg when Hannafin arrived and went to work on the others. When we had them patched up, we put Karl and

Shelley in Hannafin's vehicle and two others in mine. The driver made to get in front beside me but I shook my head. "Take this," I said, handing him a two-litre bottle of water.

"What for?" He looked bewildered "Oh man, you saying I have to wait here?"

"There's a wrecker on its way from Furnace Creek. Should be here in three hours."

The journey to Grapevine took the best part of an hour. The two in the back remained silent for most of that time, either too dazed to talk or wary of saying something that would incriminate their buddy. Or maybe they sensed my own unease, a feeling of disquiet that had been bothering me all day. I'd been expecting some kind of revelation but all I had was the feeling that I'd been asking myself the wrong questions.

There was an ambulance waiting at Grapevine Station to take the two injured kids to the Emergency Room in Amargosa Valley. The other two said they'd wait at Grapevine for the tow truck to show up with their vehicle and driver. In the station office, Hannafin made fresh coffee while I stared out the window towards the mountains bordering Ubehebe Crater. She said something I didn't catch and I didn't ask her what it was.

"Is it any different today," she said, "from how it was last week?"

"They're the same," I said, though I knew she wasn't talking about the mountains.

She handed me a mug of steaming coffee. "You been keeping to yourself lately."

I felt weary and disinclined to have the conversation she wanted.

"What's bothering you, Henry?"

I sipped the coffee, trying put my thoughts in some kind of order.

"It's good to see you've lost none of your charm and conversational skills."

I forced a smile. "I'm sorry, Rae," I said. "Got things on my mind, is all."

"Anything I can help with?"

I liked Rae, liked her a lot, but that's all it was. I wasn't looking for any kind of relationship. I was never much good at explaining such things – feelings, or their absence. "Just some stuff I have to deal with," I said. "Nothing that matters too much."

"A problem shared is a problem halved."

"There is no problem."

"I forgot," she said. "You don't have problems, ever." She bit her lower lip, I guess to stop from saying anything else. I didn't know what she might have wanted to say and I didn't care. I felt empty inside, empty and lifeless as the salt flats.

I drained my coffee and set the mug down. "None I lose sleep over."

"I think you should talk to someone."

"I talk to people all the time."

"No, you don't, Henry. If you did you wouldn't be losing touch."

"I'll be seeing you, Rae," I said, leaving the office. Hannafin was my friend but that didn't mean she knew all there was to know about me. It was never that simple.

At first I saw nothing on the road. I drove past the Grandstand on my left and headed south another mile before pulling over, somewhat confused. I picked up the radio, intending to give HQ a piece of my mind. But before anyone could respond, I'd got out of the vehicle and was watching the small dust cloud that had appeared away to the south. I grabbed the binoculars from the dash. Between my position and the cloud a vehicle had stopped in the middle of the dirt road. The dust cloud seemed to be moving further south, as if marking the trail of some other vehicle, one I hadn't seen. Dry heat rippled across the exposed skin of my arms, sucked all the moisture from my mouth. As I stared at the dust cloud it was pulled apart by a wind I didn't feel.

Nothing moved around the SUV. I scrambled up the slope to my right, moving south-west towards a patch of creosote bush. From there I looked down at the road, first at my own vehicle, then at the other, half a mile, maybe less, from where I stood. I squatted down in the scrub, removed the Sig Sauer 9mm from my holster and laid it on the ground. The sun was falling slowly towards the mountain behind me, but its heat seemed to have intensified. A sudden movement caught my eye. I watched through the binoculars as a man got out of the SUV and walked to the edge of the dirt road. He just stood there gazing out at the playa like it was a picture of beauty rather than heat and desolation. Two other people joined him, standing either side. I tried to see what they were looking at but nothing moved out there, not even the goddam rocks. The mountain's shadow bruised the edge of the Racetrack.

A fourth person had arrived. I watched his lips moving as he pointed across the dry lake. Sound travels a fair distance in this stillness, but I didn't hear a word. There was something unsettling about the way he held himself, thumb looped into the belt at his waist, that made me feel numb and disconnected. After a few moments the first three set out walking, heading east across the playa. The last guy stood there a while, till they were two or three hundred yards out, then he followed them, taking his time, keeping his distance. A redtail circled above him and when he stopped to glance at it the bird flew off to the north. A line of thin ragged clouds chased each other away across the valley, as if anxious not to intrude. Beads of sweat dribbled from beneath the straw hat and down my face as I worked to fill the silence with the imagined sound of their footsteps crunching across the Racetrack.

Nothing made sense.

Long, thin shadows followed them, clawing the dry mud like the fingers of a man dying of thirst. The figures grew smaller as they receded into the distance. I clambered down the slope to the Expedition and drove south until I reached their vehicle. I thought about calling Rydell but wasn't sure what to tell him. All I'd seen was some folks setting out across the Racetrack on foot, same as countless visitors had done before them. But if there was no mystery, then why was my heart racing so fast? Why couldn't I shake off the feeling that this was all wrong?

I stood by the side of the road, no longer able to see any of them, accepting that I had no choice but to follow. Strange, disorienting sensations flowed through my body, setting flares off behind my eyes and thrumming in my ears. I began to walk. The ground was hard and bone dry but, even so, I found a trail of footprints. They were quite distinct but what disturbed me was that there was only one pair, not four. I tried to ignore this and figured how long it would take me to catch up with the group. After thirty minutes, I should have been able to see them but nothing moved out there. I quickened my pace. The mountains to the north and west punctured the sky, opening wounds that bled over the horizon and down onto the playa. Ten minutes later I stopped and listened. Nothing: no birds, no wind, no voices. I unholstered the 9mm again, held it up and fired two shots. And was appalled when I heard nothing. My hand shook as I stared at the pistol. I'd felt the recoil and the smell of cordite on the breezeless air contradicted the silence. I checked the magazine and saw that two rounds had been discharged. It was just the sound that had been lost, a realization that made my isolation more complete. If sound couldn't exist here, then what could? When I stared at the mountains enclosing both sides of the valley, I knew that even memories were not real in this place. I felt more alone than anyone had ever been, without even the company of the dead. With the light fading, I took a bearing on a western peak and set off towards Racetrack Road.

It took me the best part of an hour to find my vehicle and by then night had settled on the valley. I stared up, overwhelmed by the immense darkness. There was no moon, and the night seemed blacker than usual, as if half the stars were missing from the sky. It seemed the only way to account for the intensity of the night. I sat in the cab, radio in hand. I wanted to speak to someone, hear some familiar voice but I was stopped by a doubt that I couldn't explain. The feeling of wrongness persisted and had grown stronger in my head. It didn't make sense at first, not until I'd grabbed a bottle of water from the cooler, turned the key in the ignition and flicked on my headlights. The road in front of me was empty and I was alone with the fallen stars.

I sat in the Expedition in the parking lot, feeling a deep weariness in my bones, the sort that can hold you for hours on end. My hand was on the door but I couldn't move. I watched cars come and go, people walking by, like this was normal, like nothing at all had changed. I even saw Sophie Delauney walking across the parking lot, hand in hand with her daughter. She stopped halfway across the lot, turned, smiled and waved at me. She seemed unaware of the people around her and I felt my mind melting, my sense of being fading away in her presence. I thought that maybe there were things she wanted to say, words she'd left unspoken. I felt the wrongness of letting her go without talking to her again, at least one more time.

But before I could go to her, Delauney himself walked past,

though he appeared not to see me. He carried two large suitcases, which he stowed in the back of the Rav4. A vein began to throb in my temple. Drops of sweat stood out on my brow though the sun was low in the sky and the air-con was blowing. He got in the driver's seat and started the Toyota. Sophie stood by the passenger door and glanced my way again. She looked right at me but I knew she wasn't seeing me at all. Whatever look she had on her face, it didn't mean anything. By the time I got out of the Expedition, she'd climbed in beside Delauney and they were pulling out of the lot.

Later I sat in Arcan's, nursing a beer. Troubled by what I'd seen, I tried to cloak the strangeness in reason but I couldn't make it fit. The feeling that I was thinking about someone else had taken root in my brain. That I had no control of my own life nor any clear idea where I was heading. Maybe I'd spent too long in the Valley. Maybe it was time to leave. Only I wasn't sure I could.

Old Arcan himself came in the bar and made one of his regular attempts at playing the host. He claimed to be a direct descendant of one of the first men to cross Death Valley, but nobody believed it. His ex-wife told someone he'd been born plain Bill Judd. I watched him move from one guest to another, carefully selecting those on whom he wished to bestow his hospitality. Thankfully, I wasn't among them.

I found myself thinking about Sophie Delauney. They were the kind of thoughts I had no business thinking, that caused pleasure and pain in equal measure, but I thought them anyway. Some lives were full of certainties but mine seemed to be made up only of "what-ifs" and "maybes". It should have been no surprise that it had become less real to me.

I ordered another drink and stared into the mirror behind the counter. The people in there seemed to have purpose in their lives, to know what they were doing, where they were going. If I watched long enough, paid attention to the details, maybe I'd discover how to make my life more real. Arcan was holding forth to the group of Japs sitting round a table across the bar. Jaime was working his routine on a blonde girl at the end of the counter. She looked bored, and I guessed the only reason she was tolerating his bullshit was the lack of any other diversion. I wondered if the real Jaime was having any better luck than the one in the mirror. And here was Sophie Delauney, standing just a few feet behind me and watching my reflection watch her, or maybe it was her reflection watching us. Do mirrors take in sound the way they do light? I don't think so. I couldn't hear anything, no music, no talk, not even the clink of glasses. It was a long time before I remembered myself and thought to say hello. But a second before I did, she beat me to it. she climbed up onto the bar stool beside me and caught Jaime's eye.

He was there in a shot. She pointed to my half-empty bottle of Dos Equis, told him to bring one of those and a glass of Merlot. I said I hadn't expected to see her again. She shrugged and told me they'd had a long day. Drove down to Badwater where Delauney had decided to hike out on the salt flats. Went half a mile before the heat got to him and he returned to the car. Later, they went to Chloride City. She wasn't looking at me as she talked, but at the guy in the mirror, the fellow who looked just like me but whose thoughts were not the same as mine. The ache in her voice seemed to hint at some inner turmoil. I wanted to offer words of comfort and reassurance, tell her everything would be okay. But thinking the words was easier than saying them.

I asked if she'd seen any ghosts up there. She shook her head and smiled. No ghosts, just dust, heat and silence. I understood about the silence, but with all those ghosts up there she'd expected something more. Why hadn't the inhabitants from Chloride City's second boom period learned anything from the first? I told her there were more fools in the world than she might have imagined. Gold wasn't the only illusion that drew people to the Valley.

Did I mean that literally? I wasn't sure. I wondered if Delauney had seen anything out on the salt flats beyond Badwater, if his mind had been troubled by visions he couldn't explain. But I saw no sign of his existence in the mirror and didn't think to ask. Sophie wanted to know about my life and I told her some things that seemed important, others that kept a smile on her face. She told me Paul wanted her to have another child. She wasn't sure what to do. The dreams and ambitions she'd once had were largely unfulfilled, there were things she hadn't yet grasped. I understood her to mean that this was something she'd never told Delauney.

And then he was there, clapping me on the back and giving Sophie a proprietary kiss on the cheek. She fell quiet then, seemed to retreat into herself. I tried to maintain the connection to her but his voice kept intruding on my thoughts. There was nothing to distinguish his words from the other noises in the bar, a wavering chorus of sounds whose real purpose was little more than to fill the silence. A feeling of despair grew inside me as I watched Sophie close herself off. Her smile was gone and the lines around her eyes signalled the dreams she could no longer give voice to.

Delauney was asking me if it was possible to go to the Race-track and join route 190 heading west without coming back on himself. I told him it would add sixty or seventy miles to his journey, most of it on poor dirt roads. He nodded and said they might make the detour on their way out of the Valley tomorrow. I asked him what he hoped to see up there. Same as anyone, he said: he wanted to see the moving rocks for himself or, at the very least, the trails they left in their wake.

I told him he wouldn't, no one ever did. He believed me, he said, but seeing beat believing any day of the week.

I watch the shadows compose themselves. The way they move across mountains or desert dunes reveals how fluid identity really is. What we think of as solid has no more real substance than a whisper or a lie. It's just light and shadow which make the unknown recognizable, which sculpt unfamiliar surfaces into configurations we think we know. We stare a while at these faces or shapes, glad they mean something to us even if we can't name them, and then we blink and when we look again the face has changed to something we can't recognize. We try to retrieve the familiar face, needing to see it one more time to confirm that it was who we thought it was, but the new image persists, erasing the old. It's like trying to see the two leading faces of a line drawing of a transparent cube at the same time – it can't be done. One face is always behind the other. We close our eyes again and when we look one more time there isn't even a face to see, just a shadow moving over rock, sliding into all its dark places. It was the kind of illusion that made me feel less certain about my place in the world.

I woke up this morning no longer sure I am who I thought was. I showered, dressed and ate breakfast, feeling like an intruder in my own home. I sat in the Expedition, spoke to Rydell on the radio and drove up towards Hunter Mountain, feeling I was watching another man try out my life. I had hoped to find some certainties up there, something to which I could anchor myself but all I found was that everything flows. I didn't need to see it to know it was happening. Even the forests of pinyon pine and juniper were further down the mountain slopes than they were the day before.

In the spring, after heavy winter rainfalls, wild flowers turn certain parts of the Valley into a blaze of purple, red and orange. It wasn't possible to reconcile such beauty with that scorched and barren hell. If such a vastness could be transformed in what, in geological terms, was less than the blink of an eye, how could any of us hope to ever stay the same?

All those voices I heard on the radio – how could I be sure that they were speaking to me? If I couldn't be certain who I was, then how could they know I was the one they wanted to talk to? So when Rydell's voice came out of the radio, I had no way of knowing if it was really him. Short of driving down to Furnace Creek and standing right in front of him. And even then, there was no guarantee.

I heard Hannafin – or someone who sounded like her – asking where I was. I wanted to answer her but when I tried to talk I realized that I had nothing to say. I already knew where I was and where I was going. There was nothing Hannafin, or the voice that might have been hers, could do for me that I couldn't do for myself.

This person I had become had no more illusions. He was capable of seeing things as they really were. As he drove past the talc mines, across Ulida Flat and north into Hidden Valley, he was aware the land was watching him. He heard the creak of Joshua trees, the distant groans of the mountain ranges and the listless sigh of an unfelt breeze. And in those sounds he heard himself also, speaking in his usual voice, his tone neutral, the words precise, as he told them all they needed to know, the way he always did. Only it wasn't him talking.

The SUV is pulled off the dirt road onto the edge of the playa. The front passenger's door stands open. I glance up towards Ubehebe Peak, see no movement among the stands of mesquite. Approaching the vehicle, I move round the back and peer through the windscreen. There are two large suitcases behind the rear seat.

I continue on round the Toyota till I come back to the open door. I reach inside and grab the carry-all on the rear seat. Inside is a money belt with close to four hundred dollars in cash, plus a book of travellers' cheques. There's also a Nike fanny pack in there with three passports, a driver's licence and car-hire documentation. I look at the photographs, just for a moment, then put everything back in the holdall. On the floor by the front passenger's seat, there's a video camera. It's a Sony Hi-8 and the tape is about three-quarters of the way through. I sit on the running board, my feet resting on the ground, trying to decide what to do. The last thing I want to do right now is play the tape but I know that if I don't I'll never find the answers I need. Flipping open the viewfinder, I touch the play button and get nothing but blue. I press and hold the rewind, listening to the machine whirr as the world runs back to where it has already been. I watch shadows grow westwards from the Cottonwood Range and a strip of broken cloud which pulls itself together as it scrolls back across the sky. After a minute I release the button and the tape rolls forward.

Sophie Delauney and her daughter walk out of their apartment at Stovepipe Wells, holding hands. They stop halfway across the parking lot and Sophie turns, smiles and waves toward the camera before continuing on to the Rav4. The scene changes to a view of Ubehebe Crater from the north rim, stretching a half-mile across and five hundred feet deep. The girl skips into the shot from the right, Delauney from the left. Something blurs the picture for a second or two, but I can't tell what it is – a hand or part of a face in extreme close-up. Delauney talks about how the crater was formed, sounding vaguely authoritative. The kid complains about the heat. Next I see Sophie and the girl standing in front of the sign at Teakettle Junction. Delauney enters the frame from the left. The girl has a stick and she starts tapping out a rhythm on the kettles and pots hanging from the arms of the wooden cross. Sophie and Delauney start dancing round her, whooping like a couple of movie Indians. They look foolish but the girl laughs. No one seems to notice the single shadow that slips down the mountain behind them.

The scene changes abruptly, showing the three of them sitting in their vehicle, smiling and waving. After a second or two, I realize that there's no soundtrack. They get out of the Toyota and start walking directly towards the camera, their faces growing in the frame. The jump cut I'm expecting doesn't happen. Instead, as Delauney draws close, the scene shifts slightly to the left and catches his face in profile as he walks past the spot where the camera had been. It catches the other two as they walk by, then turns and tracks them to the side of the road. Their smiles have disappeared and they avoid looking at the camera until something prompts Sophie to glance up and say a single word which might have been "please". Moments later, she takes the girl by the hand and walks out onto the playa. After a second or two, Delauney wipes his face and follows them. The camera pans left and zooms in on the Grandstand to the north, holding the outcrop in the frame for what seems like an eternity. Nothing moves onscreen, even when I hold down the fast-forward button. When I release it, the camera moves upwards to capture a clear and cloudless sky. The tape has played almost to the end. The final shot is of Sophie, Delauney and the kid, three hundred yards out on the playa, growing smaller as they walk on without looking back. And then the screen turns blue.

My head has started aching and the heat is almost intolerable. I put the camera on the seat, understanding what I have to do. At my vehicle I grab the radio, press the call button and speak my name. Instead of voices all that comes out is feedback and white noise. I try once more but whatever I hear, it isn't human. I lack the will to do this, but there's no one else. I load half a dozen bottles of water into a backpack, grab my binoculars and head out onto the playa.

There are no tracks in the honeycombed surface. I walk five hundred yards due east, a little further than I had seen them go before the tape had stopped. I figure they must have been looking for the rocks, or at least for one of their trails. I look north to where the slanting sunlight blurs the edges of the Grandstand. Shielding my eyes, I turn my gaze southwards and pick out a few rocks of varying sizes scattered across the dry mud. There's little else to see out here, no signs of life. I head south and try not to think about the tape and the expressions on their faces as they had trudged past the camera. Almost twenty minutes pass before I am walking among the silent, unmoving rocks. Though I don't want to admit it, their watchful stillness bothers me. I don't want to think about what they've seen. Instinctively, I lay a hand on the

Sig Sauer at my hip, drawing some comfort from the touch of the gun. There's a picture forming in my head. It's the haunted look in Sophie's eyes as she stared at the camera for the last time, just before she took the child's hand in her own and started walking. I'd like to think that she looked back one last time but I really can't be sure.

I search among the lifeless rocks for an hour. The ground is flat and the rocks are neither plentiful nor large enough to provide cover for anything much bigger than a gecko. Finally, as the sun falls towards Ubehebe Peak, I sit down on a rock, feeling dizzy and nauseous. I drink about half a litre of tepid water and pour the rest over my head. I raise the binoculars and see the vehicles where I left them, two dusty sentinels watching over the playa. As I shift my gaze northwards I'm startled by a flash of light from the mountains above Racetrack Road. I turn back to the cars, then search the slopes above them, looking for something up there in the creosote. I lower the binoculars and feel a tightness across my chest. I breathe slowly, head hanging between my knees, and that's when I see it for the first time, the faint trail cut like a groove in the dried mud. It ends at the rock between my feet. It wasn't there when I sat down, I think, but I'm not certain. I'm spooked a little by it, even more when I notice more trails terminating at the other rocks lying nearby. I try to picture a rain-softened surface and a hundred-mile-an-hour wind pushing them along but it's all in vain.

The flesh crawls on my back and for some reason the air feels cooler. The silence is weird and when I hear the two shots ring out, I need no further prompting to leave the rocks behind. I pick up the backpack, unholster my pistol and set off at a slow trot north towards the sound of the gunfire. I don't think about what has happened, about the mess Delauney has got them into. Instead I concentrate on getting there, on locating their position even though there are no further sounds to guide me towards them.

I pass the vehicles on the road, a half-mile or so to my left, without having seen anything I don't recognize. But I keep on, another mile, until I realize I'm heading right towards the Grand-stand. I don't turn back. There's no point, even though I won't find anything there. Nothing alive. Yet I have to see.

There's nobody at the Grandstand. I drink another bottle of water to quiet my despair. Shadows stretch out across the playa towards the outcrop, painting the surface the colour of blood. For a while I stare at the rocks, losing track of time. There are a dozen or so, scattered in a wide circle round the outcrop. Had these shapes seen Sophie? I grind the dust and dirt from my faithless eyes and when I open them again I see that the rocks have drawn closer. The last rays of sunlight pick out their newly laid trails. My heart is racing and the band across my chest tightens even more. At first I think I'm having a heart attack, that I'm really dying, but after two minutes I realize that isn't possible. I focus on the nearest rock. It's eighteen inches high, a little more than that from back to front, weighing, I guess, about 300 pounds. The ground is bone dry, not even a whisper of wind. Even though I haven't seen it, I accept that the rock has moved. It's too late to matter a damn. I don't feel anything as I set off towards the road

The sky is almost dark by the time I reach the two vehicles. The Rav4 stands empty like a ruin. I sit in my own vehicle and try to call HQ to report the missing people. But once again I get no proper signal, no voices other than my own to trouble the darkness. I keep trying but nobody responds. After a while, I return to the Toyota. The camera is still on the seat where I left it, the tape stopped in exactly the same place. I press play and watch the blue screen, trying to see beyond it to what's on the other side. I let it run for a minute but it's a waste of time. Just as I'm about to stop it, the blue turns to white, which slowly reconfigures into a honeycombed pattern which moves back and forth across the frame. In quick succession three shots ring out on the tape, the first sounds since Teakettle Junction. I am calm, I don't feel any fear, not until another minute has passed and a fourth blast sounds out and the screen fades to black.

Outside, I peer into the dark and see the more intense darkness of the Grandstand looming up out of the Racetrack. It's no closer than it was before, I tell myself, though I no longer feel any inclination to trust my perceptions. An hour has passed when I climb back into the Expedition. Nobody has come. This time, when I call HQ, I do finally get something, a voice reporting an abandoned SUV out at the Racetrack. I shut the power off quickly, drink more water and try not to imagine the rocks gathering out on the playa. I think about the voice I heard and what it was saying. Speaking only to myself I respond, "You won't find anything out there."

And after a minute's silence I add, "They're gone."

Hearing something, I get out of the car. I walk to the side of the road, feeling the weight of the night as it falls on the Valley. I can't see anything but I look anyway, knowing that the rocks are edging their way up from the south. I tell myself someone must have heard them, that someone will come. These are the certainties that sustain me. I can't stop myself from listening so when they stop it comes as a shock. Then, before I can register it, they start moving again, heading west, towards the road. I have no strength left. I sit down in the dirt to wait for someone to arrive even though I already know that nobody is coming here, that no one else belongs. The truth is I have as much right to be here as the dark. It's reason that's out of place here, that doesn't belong. Reason can't explain the rocks that roll, the moans of night or the flakes of sky that drift quietly down to Earth, which, given time, I probably could.

SIMON CLARK
& TIM LEBBON

Exorcizing Angels

SIMON CLARK'S MOST RECENT books include *Vampyrrhic Rites*, *In This Skin*, *Stranger* and *The Night of the Triffids* (winner of the British Fantasy Award). His fiction has also been published in newspapers and broadcast on talk radio.

Tim Lebbon's books include the novels *Face*, *The Nature of Balance*, *Mesmer*, *Until She Sleeps*, *Dusk*, *Desolation* and *Into the Wild Green Yonder* (with Peter Crowther), plus the novellas *Naming of Parts*, *White*, *Changing of Faces* and *Dead Man's Hand*. His short fiction has been collected in *As the Sun Goes Down*, *White and Other Tales of Ruin* and *Fears Unnamed*. He has won two British Fantasy Awards and a Bram Stoker Award, and his work (including the novella that follows) has been optioned for the screen on both sides of the Atlantic.

While Clark readily acknowledges that war is a terrible thing, he reveals: "If the First World War hadn't happened I wouldn't be here, nor would the events have occurred that inspired this story. My grandmother was engaged to a young soldier who was killed in the trenches in France. About the time of that soldier's death the Welsh writer Arthur Machen wrote a story, 'The Bowmen', which sparked an astonishing episode of public hysteria rivalled only by Orson Welles's radio dramatization of *The War of the Worlds* a couple of decades later.

"I found the events surrounding Machen's story fascinating,

and when I was talking to Tim Lebbon I realized that I'd found a like mind and fellow Machen fan."

"I'm fascinated by the ever-shifting boundaries between truth and fiction," adds Lebbon, "and how they are often blurred, whether by events or by the perception of those viewing them. In the case of 'The Bowmen' a simple story was transformed into a great myth that enveloped a generation, and which still endures today."

"We both agreed that we must collaborate on a story that centred somehow on Machen and his tale that inspired the legend of 'The Angels of Mons'," continues Clark. "At last we did, and this is the result. A story about a story that just might have turned the tide of the Great War, which in turn shaped the world we live in today."

"Simon and I had been working on this story in various forms for a few years," Lebbon reveals, "and the invitation to collaborate on a book for Earthling Publications made it a reality. And being writers, perpetuating that ambiguous link between belief and disbelief, truth and fiction, was a natural part of our job."

This is the Blitz: the relentless aerial bombardment of London by German aircraft since July. Hundreds of tons of bombs, thousands of incendiaries and countless parachute mines have laid waste to whole tracts of the capital, destroyed factories, homes and our places of worship alike. So far, Hitler's war machine has killed more than twenty thousand men, women and children. Tonight, this December 17 1940, special services are to be held in churches across the whole of Great Britain. Our prayers will be in remembrance of those innocent victims of war and a plea to the Heavenly Father for divine protection against these Swastika'd angels of Death.
– The Bishop of London's open letter to the Nation
The Times, 17 December 1940

I

T HE CITY TOOK THE hammer blows with the fortitude only a 2,000-year-old city can. On the walk up here to the

London district of Highgate he'd heard a taxi driver call out to a policeman, "It's a bit lively out tonight." It was gallows humour, and he recognized it well.

The man chose to walk in the centre of the road. There was little traffic, and virtually no people were about. They were all snugged away in cellars and shelters on this September night, no doubt praying that the death raining down from hundreds of German bombers fell on someone else's street, someone else's house.

He pulled up the collar of his army greatcoat as the cold air caressed his skin like the chill fingers of a dead man. From here, the sound of the bombs came as strangely soft thuds that reminded him of books falling to a library floor. Through the midnight air he caught the scent of ancient roof timbers burning from the direction of Bloomsbury. Once, hot air belched against his face from a stray incendiary blazing in a nearby garden.

The street, like the rest of Britain, was subject to total blackout. In front of him was a fog of darkness through which he caught the glints of windows, shining like so many demon eyes, glaring at *him*, expecting a Nazi bomb to tear *him* to pieces at a moment's notice. But two decades ago he had walked through worse firestorms than these. And tonight he had the most important appointment of his life. Hitler and his henchmen would not deflect him.

He paused to look back. Here on Highgate Hill he could see down onto the burning capital of country and empire itself. Whole areas of the city blazed. It was as if he was looking down upon the face of an old friend that had erupted into fiery red sores. More bombs fell, ripping out the heart of offices and ancient houses. Anti-aircraft guns returned like for like, pouring out white-hot shells that ascended into the sky with a beauty that was as ethereal as it was deadly. And above the thud of bombs, so eerily deadened and softened by distance, he could make out the guttural drone of German Heinkel bombers as they passed overhead to deliver their lethal cargoes.

A line from a story he'd once read came to him: "*There was a glow in the sky as if great furnace doors were opened.*" Tonight those words were made real.

With a sigh he turned his back on the inferno and walked on. The time was just fifteen minutes to ten. A quarter of a mile to his right a bomb exploded in Highgate Cemetery, startling him into a crouch. Immediately his imagination flew to the site of the impact. How the hundred-kilogram ordnance would have penetrated the ground; male hardware entering female earth. How the steel shell would have shattered coffins, crunched through leathery skin and powdery bone. How the explosion would have torn a crater twenty feet across. How bones and rotten flesh would have come falling from the sky to be impaled on fence spikes. How arms and legs and heads would hang in the trees like the loathsome fruit of an orchard in hell.

"A night for resurrection," he murmured to himself. "A night when we raise the dead." His grim smile died immediately as the rising scream of another falling bomb slashed through the cold night air. The fear he felt wasn't for himself. No. What if the bomb struck the house he was walking toward now? He'd come a long way to meet the man whose letter he now gripped in his hand. If that man were to die . . . such cruel irony . . . he'd *never* know the truth.

Fifty yards away the road surface twitched, then bulged, as if some subterranean creature had briefly raised its head to see what was happening outside. The man walked toward the still-steaming mound. By the light of a burning church down the road in Archway he glimpsed the shining carcass of a bomb. The detonator might have failed. Then again, perhaps it was set on a delayed fuse, and the device was merely biding its time before it blasted the nearby houses into atoms.

The time was now five minutes to ten. He could not permit anything to delay him further. He walked a little faster up the hill to a row of houses that overlooked Highgate Cemetery. Built on the whim of an architect with obvious Gothic tastes, the tops of the walls were castellated and a tower stood at one end of the row, as evocative as any that had imprisoned a fairy-tale princess. He hurried to the house that bore a brass figure eight on the door. So here it was: Number 8 Sabulum Reach.

My God, my heart's beating hard. London's being bombed into the ground, yet I'm more unnerved about knocking on this door.

He even paused as he raised his gloved hand, ready to knock. A liquid sensation flooded his stomach. His pulse rate quickened. And even now a voice in the back of his head told him: *It's not too late. You can walk away. You don't have to meet him.*

But he knew he hadn't come so far to turn back now.

He rapped on the door, a firm rhythm that sent echoes announcing his arrival deep into the house. They seemed to recede into impossible distances, fading away beneath the foundations of the building.

Presently, the door opened. A white-haired man stood there with a tartan rug around his shoulders. In this light it resembled the cloak of some ancient wizard.

"Good evening . . ." But the sight of the old man robbed the next words from his lips. After all this time planning the visit, he wasn't sure what to say next.

The old man seemed to understand. With a benign smile he said, "Good evening. Lieutenant Daelamare Smith, isn't it?"

He nodded.

The old man continued, "It's rather a filthy night out. I half expected you wouldn't come."

"No." He almost shouted the response. "Nothing would have stopped me coming here tonight. *Nothing*."

"Well then, lieutenant, please come indoors. Something warming would be timely for us both, I believe. Ah, we haven't shaken hands . . ."

"Of course. Lieutenant Delamare Smith of the Monmouthshire Infantry Brigade."

"A Monmouthshire man, hmm? Honoured to meet you, sir." They shook hands. "And I, as you will have deduced, am Arthur Machen. Now, what is so important to have brought you all this way to see me?"

Smith closed his eyes before he passed across the threshold into Machen's house. In the distance, and all around, he could hear the impacts of bombs, the crackling of ack-ack, the grumble of collapsing buildings and the soft roar of firestorms in their infancy. London was taking a true pounding tonight, that was for sure, but his senses seemed to echo memories of a different war.

True, he thought, *it's all true*.

Drifting from the house before him was the pleasant warm tang of pipe smoke, but beneath it Smith could smell the rot of the trenches, corpses and muck and hopelessness mixing a rancid stew. He turned his face to the sky and rain pattered down onto his cheeks, but it could have been mud thrown up by the shelling, clouds of shrapnel and body parts pelting down like deathly snow. Water in his eyes . . . he hated that now. Back then, in the trenches, Hell had been water.

All true. I was there. There's no other way to explain this.

He opened his eyes and met the gaze of the old man before him. "I need you to tell me who I am."

II

There were ten thousand dead Germans laid out before them. Gunshots still rang out, but the offensive had halted. What they heard now were the individual reports of German officers shooting their men as they turned tail and fled, and perhaps the occasional sound of a suicide. They screamed and shouted, these officers, urging the attack onward even though the slaughter was already over, accusing their own men of treachery and cowardice. Blinded by terror at what they had seen, it was their Lugers that gave final judgement.

"Thousands of them!" Bill said. "There're thousands of them dead out there!"

Smith stood against the mud wall of the trench, rifle resting across the backs of two empty ammunition boxes. Its barrel was still hot. "Five thousand," he said. "Maybe even ten."

The nearest dead Hun lay only a stone's throw from their forward trench – seemingly untouched, Smith noticed, as if he had simply lain down and gone to sleep – and stretching back from this corpse was a sea of grey, a frozen-ocean tableau where the highest waves were made of piled corpses, and the troughs were where old craters held the dead in their watery embrace. There was little movement: an eddy here and there where a limb twitched, a head raised, a hand clasped at the air for help. A strange silence lay over the whole shattered landscape. The German artillery was mute and even the rain had ceased.

Smith hauled himself up the side of the trench and stood at its lip, walking forward a few paces, stepping over a rotten body from a battle of weeks before. He could not tell whether it was British or German.

"Delamare, back here, you bloody fool!" Bill hissed.

Smith took no notice. He was looking at the sea of dead, aware suddenly of what he could *not* see. There was mud and water and the pale faces of the dead, hair adrift in puddles and limbs askew and lost rifles smoking their last . . . but there was no blood.

No blood, anywhere.

He was used to the smell of it by now. The taste of blood misted the air after an artillery barrage, it had dried on his face and neck after one vicious hand-to-hand fight in a German trench just the week before, and with this many dead men before him he expected to be gagging. But the blood of these Germans remained just where it belonged: inside them. Stopped now, stagnant, already clotting and giving itself to rot.

Smith turned and looked back across his own lines. The pale faces of his mates started at him from their trench, and further back more trenches crissed and crossed, mud banks here and there like boils on the earth, a skeleton of trench supports pointing at the sky to his left where a shell had erupted within. He saw bodies – hundreds had died over the past couple of days, and there was never enough time or opportunity to bury them properly – but there was no hint of whatever had come to help them. No footprints, no disturbances in the smoke drifting slowly from left to right across the battlefield, no shadows disappearing back towards the rear. Only silence, and stench, and the mangled evidence of futility.

"There's no way I saw what I just saw," someone said from further along the trenches. It sounded like he was crying. "No bleedin' way at all."

"I saw nothing," another voice piped up, but its owner stared out at the sea of dead and repeated the other man's "No way," sounding as if he were arguing with himself.

"Angels," Bill said. "I saw angels."

Smith walked forward until he drew level with the first dead German. The young man looked barely old enough to bear arms. His helmet was lost somewhere in the mud, his rifle lay inches from his outstretched hand, and his eyes . . . they were wide, deep, amazed. Smith knelt down and touched the dead boy's neck, just in case. Nothing. He was still warm, but as dead as the million other men melting back into this hungry earth. His uniform was muddied and wet, but it showed no signs of damage, no point of impact. There was no blood. The boy's face . . . those eyes . . .

Smith heaved the corpse over. The muck relented unwillingly, and the sucking sound startled Smith so much that he stumbled over his own heels and fell into the mud. His hands sank down and touched old, hard things below the surface.

How old? he wondered. *Days, weeks or ancient? Too old to know of machine guns and gas, perhaps?*

"What's up, Delamare?" someone shouted from the trench behind him, but Smith did not answer, and the men had enough of their own disbelief and fear to contend with to pursue the matter.

He ran his hands over the dead German boy, lifting his leg, pulling apart the lapels of his greatcoat, tipping his head back so that he could see his neck. In the end, Smith stood and gazed out across the field of dead.

Only a few minutes earlier, he had seen the sky darken with cloud after cloud of singing arrows. He'd heard the hiss of longbow strings as the shafts were released. And now that the battle was over, and the dead could not come back to tell their story, there were no arrows to be seen.

None at all.

The only proof of what Smith had witnessed was ten thousand dead men.

III

"We are all someone different to ourselves," Machen said. "No one can ever really know us but us. So asking me to tell you who you are . . . that's foolishness." He puffed on his pipe and added to the dingy atmosphere of the room. A string of bombs fell in the distance, and glass buzzed in the blacked-out window frame. For some reason, the room felt incredibly safe.

"I've hinted at why I wanted to see you, I believe," Smith said. "In my letters to you, my desperation to meet you. Surely as a writer your interest must be piqued?"

Machen nodded, but said nothing. He never took his gaze from Smith's face. Smith felt scrutinized, his thoughts laid bare, as if this old man knew everything about him and could, given time, find things that he himself did not know.

"I mean to ask you about a story you wrote a long time ago," Smith said. "But first, I need to tell you of the angels that saved my life."

Machen relit his pipe. "Go on, Lieutenant Smith. You have my attention. Providing we have no surprise interruption . . ." He cocked his head toward the sound of falling bombs. "Then I should be pleased to hear your talk of angels."

"Sir, cast your mind back to the Great War." Smith leaned forward, his heart pumping hard. He longed to unburden himself of the secret that had weighed heavily for so long. Now he feared that the words would jam in his mouth and he would not be able to speak. A trickle of sweat rolled down his neck to his shirt collar. "Cast your mind back to the Great War," he repeated, willing his lips to form the words he'd ached to speak for twenty-five years. "I was with a company of a thousand men from my regiment, holding a salient in the fields of Mons. Though in reality, of course, there were no fields any more. Artillery had transformed the land into a morass of mud and shell craters, filled with stagnant water and the pulverized remains of thousands of men, from both the German and Allied armies. The German and British lines were separated by three hundred yards of ground at this point. We were close enough to hear the German troops singing their songs or calling to each other. That was a dreadful time for us. Everywhere, the Germans had been advancing. Our own troops were falling back in confusion. Mr Machen, I can still hear the terrified cries of our men as they threw away their rifles and ran for their lives. And I can still see the look of terror on the faces of infantrymen who just weeks before had been boys working in factories. Their eyes would be wide open, staring so hard you'd swear they were going to burst from their faces . . ."

Machen spoke gently. "Here, let me refill your glass."

"Thank you." Smith took a deep swallow of the whisky. He needed to feel that burning spirit in his mouth, but at that moment it had the potency of water. "My battalion – or the thousand that remained of it – had been ordered to hold the trench against a German assault. It was to allow our troops – all eighty thousand of them – to make good an orderly retreat to new, better-fortified trenches five miles behind our position. It was vital that my battalion held the line and prevented a German breakthrough. We knew only too well that if the Germans launched an attack and broke our line, they would flood through in their thousands to attack our retreating army. And believe me, Mr Machen, our men in that month of August were so exhausted and demoralized that they'd have either run like rabbits or surrendered." Once more he gulped at the whisky. If only it were stronger. The wretched liquor was tasteless.

"You and your men were courageous," Machen told him. "A thousand Welshmen pitted against an enemy of how many thousand strong?"

"Three hundred thousand." He shook his head. "And I don't know that we were courageous. I certainly didn't feel at all brave at the time. I simply knew it was my duty . . . my sacred duty. That we had to prevent a German breakout. If we failed, the Hun would overwhelm the British troops. Of that there would be little doubt. Then there would have been nothing between the enemy and the Channel ports. And if the Germans reached the coast, it wouldn't be long before the Kaiser's men would be marching into London."

"So you held fast."

"We did our best," Smith told him, as yet more squadrons of bombers throbbed their way through the night sky. The bitter smell of burning reached him, along with the distinctive scents of seared human flesh; the same aroma as pork roasting in an oven. But even the horrors of the Blitz weren't pungent enough to prevent the memories of more than two decades ago carrying him back to that Great War battlefield. "We vowed to stand and fight with our bare hands if our ammunition ran out. Then we waited. Many of my men crouched down in the trench to scribble a farewell note to parents and wives. And all the time I could sense the coming storm. There was an oppressive heat in the air. Thunder clouds rose on the horizon. The sun turned a bloody red. There was no birdsong. Even the rats fled the battlefield." Once more he tipped the whisky into his mouth. Good God, his taste was dead. The spirit was a bland liquid that did nothing to calm his nerves. "The German generals didn't dally. Their spotter planes must have reported the mass retreat, and that a mere thousand infantry had been left to hold the trench-line. Within moments the fiercest artillery barrage imaginable rained down on our heads. You know, it's not the big shells that are the most fearsome. No, they're slow and throw up a lot of mud, and mostly you could hear them coming. It was the little three-inch shells, what we called whizz-bangs, that terrified us. They were fast, with an almost flat trajectory, exploding in the air at head height. I've seen countless men dissolve into . . ." The words dried on his lips. He shrugged, hating the grim weight of the memory in his stomach. "It was the shrapnel. They just dissolved, that's all." He rubbed his face. "I do beg your pardon. I'm falling into the trap of the old soldier. Telling you old war stories."

"No, I'd disagree, lieutenant. This isn't just another war story, is it? This one is unique. Why?"

Smith looked into the old man's eyes. They were bright. Interested. Yet was there something else? A glitter of fear? As if he suspected he would hear truths expressed that he'd hoped would remain hidden.

"Lieutenant. You and your thousand men were subjected to an artillery bombardment. Then you were attacked by eighty thousand German soldiers. Tell me what happened next."

"We stepped up to the lip of the trench and fired as the Germans advanced. We kept firing until we ran out of ammunition, or the guns jammed. The barrels became so hot that they glowed red."

"And?"

"And the enemy kept advancing across the mud."

"What did you do?"

"That was the strangest thing. My men began to sing music-hall songs and make jokes about the Hun and the shells exploding all around them."

"Was that usual?"

"Before and after a battle, the men would sing and joke. But not during. You become focused on a tiny aspect of the conflict. You stop being aware of what is around you."

"They were singing and joking. Weren't your comrades suffering casualties?"

"Yes. Dreadfully. Within the hour our thousand-strong force was cut by half. Dead and dying men lay in the bottom of the trench."

"What made your men experience such a mood of elation?"

"I don't know, Mr Machen. It's strange. I was frightened. I knew I would be killed, it was inevitable . . . but my arms and legs *tingled*. It was as if my body was stimulated by some impending event . . . something extraordinary. And yet my mind could only realize the terrible aspect of what was to come."

"So it was as if mind and body had become somehow separate?"

"Yes . . . yes! That would be the best way of putting it, sir."

"What happened next?"

"The Hun advanced like a solid wall of grey. Then they stopped."

"Stopped?"

"*Were* stopped, would perhaps be more accurate."

"Your weapons?"

"No. We'd all but run out of ammunition. Our big guns were being pulled back so we had no covering artillery fire."

"And yet the enemy soldiers lay dead in no man's land." Machen inclined his grey head as he regarded Smith. "Dare I say the body count amounted to ten thousand?"

Smith nodded.

"And not a mark was found on the bodies? Not a single scratch?"

"That's correct. The enemy assault failed. Our men retreated to their new lines in good order. Even the enemy artillery was silenced, and we could walk into no man's land to collect their weapons. Our medical men eventually went out to examine the bodies. The doctors asked us how the enemy died and we told them—"

Machen harrumphed. "And you told them that they were slain by the ghostly archers of Agincourt?" His eyes burned with sudden anger.

"No, Mr Machen." Smith shook his head. "They were killed by angels."

Machen paused, but only for a few seconds. "Angels aren't noted for their blood-thirsty tendencies, lieutenant."

"So I was taught at Sunday School."

"Well?" Machen slowly shook his head. "How do you wish me to respond? With a 'Yes, lieutenant. Clearly they were avenging angels. Weren't we, the British, fortunate?' "

"No, Mr Machen. At Sunday School we are only taught a much-diluted version of Biblical events. The world of gods and spirits is far more complex than that."

"Ah, the spirit world . . ."

"Please don't mock me, sir."

"Why should I mock you? Whatever you and I believe to make this existence a more palatable one should not be open to mockery." The tremor of falling bombs jingled Machen's decanters in their tantalus. "We should be free to choose our gods."

"And to choose our angels?"

"If that is what is important to you, yes."

"Mr Machen. What is important to me is that I learn what happened to me on that day in August when I should have been killed. I was saved by something I cannot understand. Perhaps 'angels' is the wrong word, but how else can I describe them?"

"Lieutenant. If you believe angels were your saviours then continue to believe. Take strength from that."

"But I have to know what they were."

"No, you don't. And to dig deeper would be folly."

"No, I—"

"Be content; let it remain a mystery."

"That would be contemptible."

"Contemptible?" Colour rose in Machen's cheeks. "Contemptible? How can it be contemptible?"

"Listen, man. For Heaven's sake, listen!" Smith pointed toward the curtained window. "Out there hundreds of men, women and children are being slaughtered by the Germans. You hear the aircraft? You hear the bombs? There are *hundreds* of them, tearing the heart out of this city. Yet you calmly tell me to forget that when the British were last threatened with annihilation, some force of pure good – angels, whatever – looked down and saw the slaughter. And they chose to *stop* it." Smith sprang from the chair and swept the curtain open. Bursts of fire blossomed across the face of the city. The dome of St Paul's showed as a silhouette against the blood-red light. Smoke boiled into the sky. Searchlights stalked the clouds, while anti-aircraft guns hurled glittering tracer shells at enemy bombers.

"Don't forget," Machen said in even tones. "We have a blackout for a reason. Close the curtains, lieutenant."

"Help me uncover the truth about the angels."

"No."

"But think! Just for a moment! If we can summon the angels again, they may halt the bombing."

"Close the curtains. The pilots can see a lit match from 20,000 feet."

"Not until you agree to help me."

"Lieutenant, that is the worst kind of blackmail. And you don't mean it."

With a snarl Smith dragged the heavy blackout curtains shut. Machen was right. This was not the way. Taking a deep breath he said, "I'm sorry to have disturbed you. I'll bid you good night."

Machen sighed. "I don't blame you for trying to save London. Lord knows we need His help tonight. Sit down. Here . . . have a little more of this. You know . . ." He poured more whisky. "This is known as 'the water of life'. Not without good reason, hmm?"

Smith sagged into the chair, deflated. He'd become a man of straw; nothing but a suit full of fibres. He had suddenly lost the strength to continue with his quest . . . his quest . . . his quest for *what?* Angels? To learn about what had happened to him one day in August more than two decades ago? More importantly, to invoke those angels again, save his country from an evil enemy that was reducing it to ruin. And now what? The only man who could help him refused. Maybe it was time to simply walk away into the night.

There was a long pause, the only sound the continued thump of falling bombs.

At last Machen spoke. His voice's tone dropped into one that was as kind as it was mellifluous. "Lieutenant Smith. A while past you said you were going to ask me about a story I wrote a long time ago?"

"Yes." Defeat held him down like a stone weight. "What of it?"

A slow, sad smile spread across Machen's face. "Then why don't you ask me about it now?"

Smith took a drink and nodded. "After all these years, I still don't know what's happening to me when I read it," he said. "I grow cold, distanced, as if viewing myself from beyond my own body. My memory grows vague and much of what has happened between then and now vanishes, as if I've lived nothing. As if half of my life is *empty.* And at the same time I feel observed, as if someone a long way off is thinking of me, watching me, knowing my every move. It's as though I am reading about myself, and in the story I *know* that's the case. It's not a story, not really: it's a spell. A spell to invoke angels, Mr Machen, and you wrote it."

"Ha!" Machen said, standing and spitting sparks from his pipe. "You admit at least that the story is mine! Well, there's a good start, for sure. Many before now have denied me even that courtesy. The mad ones, mostly."

"It worked, sir. It can work again!" Smith grabbed the arms of his chair when he felt the familiar tremors coming on, starting from his feet and vibrating up through his bones and flesh, as if he were feeling a slow-motion explosion through the ground. The whisky glass he had set on the chair's arm shook and threatened to spill.

Machen watched him from beside the fireplace, calmly but not dispassionately. The old man's eyes were *filled* with passion, and a knowledge that humbled Smith.

"You wrote 'The Bowmen', Mr Machen, and the bliss in which you spun those words made them into much more than the sum of their parts. That is what I believe, and have *always* believed since returning from the front and first reading it. Even now, you knew part of the story I was telling. You knew the numbers of German dead and—"

"Of course I did, because I wrote the story!"

"Yes! There! That's it!"

"That isn't it at all!" Machen said. He shook his head angrily and turned to the fire, seeming to find comfort in the cheery flames even as the light of a burning London flickered at the edges of the blackout curtains, fiery fingers seeking entrance. He mumbled something and shook his head again, relighting his pipe and puffing clouds of fragrant smoke into the room.

"What did you say?" Smith asked, nervous now. He had come here to talk to this man, not anger him.

"I thought that story had stopped haunting me years ago," Machen said. He glanced back at Smith, and he had such a curious look in his eye—part fear, part fascination—that Smith's heart skipped a beat. "Are you real?" the old writer asked.

"I am," Smith said, unperturbed by the question. "Sometimes I wonder, but I know I am. I know what I did in the war, I know I've lived since then, and even though sometimes much of my life is a blank . . . of course I'm real. I'm as real as you."

"As real as me," Machen said. "Well, what more could I ask for?"

"The story," Smith persisted. "'The Bowmen'. Did you know what you were doing when you wrote it? Did you know what would happen?"

"That was an indifferent piece of work," Machen said. "There was neither power in the words, nor ecstasy to the writing. It was a trifling tale, nothing more. Whatever you saw, Mr Smith, you have my leave to believe. But it had nothing whatsoever to do with the story I wrote all those years ago."

"But—"

"When was the battle? When was the retreat, the slaughter of Mons? When was it you saw these Angels?"

"August, the hot August of 1914."

"There. My story appeared on 29 September of that same year. Not *before* the event, sir. After! There are those who say I stole the tale in some manner, and although that is certainly *not* the case, if it pleases you to believe so then please do. If that will detract you from this lunacy, then *please* do."

Another bomb fell outside, closer than any had fallen before, and the fire hissed in the grate as the heat-blast tried to suck it up and out of the chimney. Smith winced in his chair, but explosions held little fear for him. He could not see them. The blasts that tore his sleep to shreds were those he *had* seen, the ones full of mud and body parts, the explosions that lifted ten tons of mud and flung it down on top of a man, burying him alive, perhaps for ever. These detonations from outside were second-hand.

"You must have conceived of the tale before, though," Smith persisted.

"No."

"I know what I saw, Mr Machen—"

"*No!*"

"I know what I saw and I know what I read. And I know for sure that they were one and the same. I saw unearthly visions – angels, ghosts, apparitions, whatever – that we need to save us from destruction right now, and I read of them, and you wrote what I read."

"Please just stop," Machen said, looking suddenly tired, so old and tired.

"Whether they were Agincourt bowmen or true mercenaries from Heaven, you wrote those words. I really don't see any way out of that."

"Then you, sir, are a fool. Old soldier or not – and it shames me to say it – you are still a fool."

"But—"

"Did you suffer from a blast-shock in the war? Were you shipped from the trenches on a stretcher, raving?"

"Well . . ." Smith thought back to that time at Mons, how silent the battlefield had become for a brief few minutes while he walked from corpse to corpse . . .

. . . Checking their pulses, suddenly certain that he would find them all alive. They were feigning, it was part of some diabolical Hun ploy, an hallucinogenic gas, and any minute now they would leap up and complete the slaughter that they had begun.

But no, they were all dead.

"Delamare!" The captain called from the trenches. "Get back here, you bloody fool! That's not all of them, you know. There'll be more on their way soon!"

"I think not," Smith said to himself, looking down into the disbelieving eyes of a dead enemy soldier. He saw himself reflected there, and he realized that the two of them looked very similar. The dead man even had a shaving cut under his jaw, just as Smith had given himself only the day before. He reached up and scratched his own cut, pleased that it could bleed.

He walked further in, and it was like wading through frozen waves at the seaside. Grasping hands dropped back down as he brushed by, legs fell to the side, heads lolled on necks, and every one of them was dead. Smith turned one body over, lifted the arms on another, looking for the wounds that had killed them. Still, he could find none. His feet squelched in the mud that would be these men's eternal resting place.

From his own trenches Smith could hear the amazed muttering of his comrades in arms. One of them was crying, a few were praying, and many more seemed to be talking to themselves, trying to find some sort of truth in whatever words they could utter. *Miracle*, he heard, and *Angels*, and *Saved us, saved us* . . .

Out here he needed to find truth, a revelation that would prove him sane, and yet there was only more madness in the faces of these dead Huns.

And then he heard a sound. It was something he recognized and knew that he could not escape. However far he ran, however fast, he could just as easily have been running into its path. What set the sound of this shell aside was that it was on its own, cutting a single whistling line through the August sky, fired in anger, haste or sad defiance.

He turned and looked back at the trenches, and the only man

he saw was Bill. Everyone else had ducked down to find whatever cover they could.

Their stares met, and Smith knew: *My time is now*.

The shell landed and exploded twenty feet to his left. He was aware of the eruption, the slap of the shock wave as it tore his skin and flipped him sideways onto the ground, the heat singeing his hair and setting his clothes smouldering. And then from above came a flock of shadows blotting out the sun: the dead enemy raining down in broken pieces to bury him.

The noise was nightmarish. The sounds of a house dying around him, wood splitting and plaster powdering, floors ruptured, water hosing across the walls as plumbing was ripped to shreds by the force of the explosion.

Smith found himself on the floor. Whisky had spilled from his tumbled glass and now he wished he had drunk some more, ineffectual though it had seemed. In his memories a cold hand slapped his face, as the rest of its dead owner showered down upon him.

Here, and now, he heard a shout from the old writer as a ball of flame and smoke rushed in through the shattered window, setting the curtains instantly ablaze and dripping fire across the carpet.

"Smith!" Machen shouted.

Smith tried to lift himself up, but something held him down. Another explosion rocked the floor beneath his body, and he heard a house grumbling its last as it collapsed further along the street.

The first explosion seemed to be continuing. Its initial blast had shattered beams and walls, and now the house was slowly crumbling in on itself with a terrible clamour, the noise just as loud and shocking as the initial blast. Smith was buried, as he had been buried before, but this time he was conscious. He looked up and saw stars, winking in and out of existence as if time itself had increased to an incredible speed . . . or perhaps they were angels, come to take him . . . and then he realized that he was watching tiny explosions high in the air, anti-aircraft fire seeking out dark shapes caught in converging searchlights.

"Smith!" Machen shouted again, and a shadow blotted out the violent light. A hand closed around Smith's wrist, Machen grunted and cursed as he heaved, and seconds later the two men were sprawled in the road outside the house, witnessing its final collapse.

As if the destruction of this house had been the culmination of their aims, the German bombers drifted away for the night. The sudden reduction in noise was shocking – there were still explosions, fires roaring in the distance and setting the horizon aflame, shouting, the sounds of fire tenders racing through the streets – but the bombing had stopped, and to Smith it felt like morning. Another night of nightmare ended.

"Are you hurt?" Machen asked. "Are you all right?" Smith ran his hand over his body, feeling for broken bones but finding only old wounds. There was the knot in his hip where a dead German's head had landed with such force that it had smashed the bone. Scar tissue across his neck from shrapnel wounds. And other places, traumas he could not touch because they were inside him, scorched on his mind.

"I think so," Smith said, his answer ambiguous even to himself. *Was he all right? Had he* ever *been all right*?

Machen was looking around at the wreck of the house, shaking his head. "My friend will be upset," he said. "I was merely lodging here. Pity – lovely house. Charming fireplace, and a wine cellar I shall mourn for the rest of my days."

Smith stood on shaking legs, still searching for new injuries. It appeared that he had escaped relatively unharmed. He would have called it a miracle, had he not already been witness to one.

"You seem unconcerned at our near miss," he said.

Machen looked at him and smiled. Somehow he had rescued his pipe, and now he put it to his mouth and puffed until fresh smoke began to issue forth. "I am an old man now. If the Lord chooses my time, then he does. Though I must admit, the thought that maybe *this* was my time was still worrying."

"So now do you see why we need their help?"

"Oh, your angels."

"Yes!"

Machen puffed at his pipe, frowning. He seemed to be deep in thought, and Smith sensed that now was not the time to interrupt. Finally, the old man spoke.

"I admit that you have me intrigued," he said, "but for reasons all my own. There is certainly further investigation we can carry out into your claims. This is a matter I have long wished to put behind me – it makes me sick to the core, to tell the truth – but your insistence is pressing." He regarded Smith with a look that only the aged can really muster. "You seem a polite young man, although perhaps not possessing all your senses. You appear certain of what you saw. And for that, I believe that *you* believe it is the truth."

"I don't *believe*, I *know*!"

"Truth and certainty are not good bedfellows, Lieutenant Smith. Come! We have somewhere to go!"

IV

They walked in silence through the suburbs before Lieutenant Smith realized he hadn't asked the logical question. "Mr Machen, you said we have somewhere to go?"

"Indeed I did, sir."

"Where?"

"I believe we require a little hard evidence. Something tactile to grasp in our hands."

"Oh?"

"You feel well enough? The explosion at the house . . ."

"I feel perfectly fine. Perhaps even better than I ought in the circumstances. That bomb scored a direct hit."

"We were fortunate. Or maybe there are forces at work requiring us to seek a resolution to our mystery."

Smith saw Machen's grim smile by the light of burning buildings.

"So where are we going?"

"To the archive of the London *Evening News* in Bloomsbury."

"I don't see that—"

"Ah, lieutenant. Remember the ancient Oriental proverb: 'The longest journey begins with a single step.' A trip to the newspaper's document depository will furnish us with that first step." The man nodded in the direction of central London, a city ringing with fire-engine bells, glowing with a thousand incendiary fires. "That is if the building hasn't been reduced to ashes. Ah, careful where you step, my dear fellow. I dare say the authorities will collect these with due respect."

Human remains, especially blood spilled on a flat, hard surface, are astonishingly slippery. Smith recalled a young corporal slipping on human entrails on a cobbled yard, falling with such force that it detonated the rifle grenade in his backpack. Even as Smith walked through this present-day apocalypse, he sensed the tug of the past drawing him back to the trenches of the Great War. That was a haunted time; and, dear God, he refused to be haunted by it just at that moment.

To prevent himself from slipping back into malignant reverie he said, "Mr Machen . . . won't you tell me something of yourself and what led to you write 'The Bowmen'?"

"Why not? It's a filthy night in so many respects. A little storytelling now might do us some good."

The old writer began to speak in his deep, resonant voice about the beginning of his own life. Smith found himself drifting into a state that was nearer trance than wakefulness. Here he was, walking through London in the dead of night, body parts littering an otherwise empty street, the surviving occupants still taking refuge in their shelters. The sky above London burned a bloody red. And from all quarters of the ancient city sirens rose in a single note to signify the "all clear", although it could equally have been the trumpets of angels calling newly released souls to heaven. Trying not to let the air of unreality settle too deeply into his bones, Smith concentrated on Machen's words.

"'. . . I shall always esteem it as the greatest piece of fortune that has fallen on me, that I was born in that noble, fallen Caerleon-on-Usk, in the heart of Gwent.' If you will excuse an author's conceit, those words I've just recited are from my autobiography. And I still stand by them. On 3 March 1863 I was born into what seemed a magical borderland between this reality and others too fabulous for mortals to describe with any accuracy. I'm still far from adept at capturing the quiddity of the land I grew up in. A land of hills, deep lanes and dark woods aplenty. Of rivers that foamed red after rain. And peopled by men and women who spoke an ancient language that no Englishman could fathom. My father was rector there, and I grew up an only child, often with only my imagination as a companion. I roamed what, for me, is a faery land of ineffable mystery. It was littered with the romantic ruins of the Roman occupation. It was saturated to the very roots with Celtic myth. No wonder, then, that I grew into a young man with one burning ambition: *to write!* As soon as I could I left my native Wales for London. And there, as many a young man has done before me, I wrote beautifully incomprehensible literature in an attic room. I sustained my body on green tea, dry bread and tobacco. And all the time my mind blazed with stories – such incredible stories! Tales of mystery, gods and spirit worlds that would astonish the world of letters. Of course, publishers rejected them as the awfully conceited trumpery of an eager but inexperienced scribbler, such as I was in those days. And like so many young men who'd followed their star to Grub Street, I starved. Well . . . I managed to avoid the workhouse and death by malnutrition . . . by a whisker, I should add. I earned a meagre wage as by turns a teacher, cataloguer, publisher's assistant. And step by step, inch by inch I began to earn my daily bread as a writer. And so I saw my strange compositions begin to appear in print, only to puzzle the great British public, I dare say. *The Great God Pan, The Inmost Light, The Three Impostors* . . . and many short stories and essays. If you disregard the piffling sums I received for my work you could almost describe it as a successful literary life. I found a home. I married, only to lose my wife, Amy, within twelve years to cancer. No angel was at hand then at her deathbed, you'll note. At least none that I saw. In order to try and cope with bereavement I changed careers. At the age of thirty-seven, in 1900, I became an actor with the Benson company. Marvellous times. Forget what they say about schooldays – those were the happiest of my life, treading the boards. Did you know I even starred in a silent picture? Good grief, *me*! Can you believe such a thing? Ah . . . then by the end of the decade I'd retired, gracefully I hope, from a life of acting, to earn my daily bread with the pen once more. I'd also rather fortuitously acquired a second wife along the way. She's at home at Amersham at the moment. Safe, I hope, bearing in mind this little outbreak of hellfire tonight." Machen indicated bombed buildings with his unlit pipe. Flames still licked at exposed timbers. At the end of the street men directed water hoses onto a burning post office. "Now where was I? Uhm . . . ah, yes, back to the quarry face of literature. From the heaven of greasepaint and make-believe to my own personal hell – becoming a reporter on the London *Evening News*. Lieutenant, I'd dreamt of weaving tales of magic and awe only to find myself sitting at my desk in the journalists' cattle shed of an office, writing interminable copy concerning the rich and famous of London society. My given quests? To learn whether the Duke of Richmond favoured flannels over tweed that particular season, or whether it was fashionable for the daughters of admirals to devour their pâté on toast or wafer, or to discover the name of Lady Such-and-such's favorite poodle. It was deadly dull work; my family straddled the line between being merely hard-up and actually poverty-stricken. There you have it, the needs of providing for my family – poor though it was – made a prisoner of me in a newspaper office. A job, you will have surmised, that I hated with absolute passion."

"You still wrote fiction?"

"Yes, there were still short stories and literary sketches for magazines."

"Then the war. The Great War."

"Yes, lieutenant. The Great War. My age required me to view the battles in Europe from afar. And I was still a slave of the press galley. However, I saw that for the first time my talent, what there was of it, might have a greater purpose than I first supposed. Those first months of the war were bad ones for Britain. Food ran short, tens of thousands of our soldiers were killed, towns and villages alike grieved for the loss of their young men, we were in constant retreat as the Germans scored victory after victory. People from the lowest classes to the aristocracy were considering the awful possibility that we might lose the war, and that the Kaiser would claim the British Empire for himself. It seemed to me that although I could never fire a rifle in anger, I might help alleviate this pervading air of despondency. With my editor's blessing I began to write short articles in praise of the British way of life, in studies of how ordinary men and women went about their work. I strove to illuminate the working folks' innate sense of honesty and goodness. As well as the factual articles I contributed short squibs of fiction to the newspaper, intended to warm the patriot's heart and perhaps raise the spirits of the reader, at least for a few moments."

"Then came 'The Bowmen'?"

"Yes, sir, then along came 'The Bowmen'." Despite his age, the old man moved effortlessly through the darkened streets. Stepping over rubble, or sidestepping a bloodied human limb, did not interrupt his faultless discourse. "My story 'The Bowmen' wasn't a great work of literature that had been maturing inside me. Far from it! The tale suggested itself to me on the last Sunday of

August, 1914. Before going to church I – like my countrymen – had been reading press reports of terrible calamity on the battle-fields of Europe. Our army was in retreat. The Germans were close to breaking through our lines before racing to capture the Channel ports. In short, it looked as if the British nation was doomed. During the singing of the Gospel by the deacon in church I, unbidden, found myself imagining the British Army embroiled in a furnace of torment, agony and death. In the midst of this our brave fighting men were consumed by the flame, yet aureoled in it; they were scattered like ashes and yet triumphant; they were martyred yet forever glorious. I saw our men with a *shining* about them. And this vision, I suppose you could call it, formed the basis of the story 'The Soldier's Rest', which is a far better work than 'The Bowmen'. Incidentally, I did write 'The Bowmen', despite rumours you might have heard to the contrary that I had secret knowledge of an actual event, or that the manuscript of the completed story was delivered to me by 'a lady-in-waiting' and that I simply added my name beneath the title in an act of literary piracy! No, I penned a tale that, although mediocre in execution, I hoped would at least moderate the misery of a small percentage of our people who were living in such unhappiness and fear. And so the story appeared in the *Evening News* of 29 September 1914. I apologize for making its genesis appear such a profound event. It wasn't; it was merely a short tale about British soldiers being saved by the ghostly archers of Agincourt. As it appeared in an evening newspaper, I believed it would be forgotten by the time the following morning's paper arrived on the public's doormat. However, a month or two later, I received requests from the editors of a number of parish maga-zines to reprint the tale. As I did not own the copyright of 'The Bowmen', my editor agreed. I wasn't unhappy. If readers' hearts were lifted by my work then all well and good. However, when letters began to arrive at the office with requests to reprint the story as a pamphlet – together with a plea that I write an introduction, citing the source of my material, giving dates and names of witnesses of the miraculous event – I found myself in very peculiar territory indeed. In short, within the space of a few months, rational men and women the length of Britain – perhaps even the Empire – believed that 'The Bowmen' was not a work of fiction at all, but a newspaper report containing nothing but hard fact. In retrospect, I understand that my story delivered a power-ful morale boost to the nation. But at the time it turned my life into a nightmare. When I replied to countless hopeful letters that my story was 'made up', I was greeted with disbelief. People had read the story in a newspaper so it must be true; that's how the logic ran. And when I insisted 'The Bowmen' was fiction, that it contained not a shred of fact, that was when men and women turned on me as viciously as starving dogs. I was spat upon in the street, threatened with a beating in bars. My wife was pushed to the ground in our own garden when a priest, who'd called to remonstrate with me, didn't believe that I was not at home. And then another miracle occurred: the miracle of mass self-delusion. When it seemed that I had the upper hand – when at last I began to build an argument that 'The Bowmen' was a piece of fiction – some very senior churchmen launched a counter-argument. They conceded that while 'The Bowmen' was intended as fiction, I had, in fact, experienced a God-given vision of a genuine miracle: the rescue of our troops on the battlefield by some immortal agency. Moreover, the churchmen claimed I was so conceited, so con-sumed by greed that I'd passed this wonderful vision off as my own work, whereby I could benefit from the fame it would bring me and become monstrously rich! The public accepted the churchmen's argument. I was seen as something lower than a swindler and blackmailer."

Smith glanced at the shadowed face of the writer. "But the money you earned must have helped compensate you for the social discomfort."

"Money? What money? I didn't earn a penny from the story. I wrote it as part of my salaried duties for the newspaper. The newspaper owner collected all the royalties and reprint fees, and kept them for himself without so much as a thank-you flung in my direction. There was no money, lieutenant. Not for me. Merely national contempt."

"So you discount that the churchmen might have been right? That there's no supernatural element entering into the equation?"

"As I wrote a little while later: 'Here indeed we have the maggot writhing in the midst of corrupted offal denying the existence of the sun.' I'm not saying that there was never a supernormal intervention during that war, or this one. Only that I have no evidence one way or the other. And 'The Bowmen' is certainly not evidence of such divine intervention. It is a story, a story, a *story*. Fiction and nothing more."

The old man awarded the younger one that searching glance again. "But you, Lieutenant Smith, would take the contrary point of view. After all, you say you believe you saw the events of my story take place in reality."

"I believe so, yes."

"Then let us prove to ourselves that 'The Bowmen' story exists in the real world. Ah! At least the archive hasn't been blasted to smithereens. If you step through that gateway to your right . . ."

Smith passed through a gate set in a brick wall. Just along the road he could make out the imposing bulk of the British Museum. Searchlights still probed the clouds' underbelly. A smell of burning persisted in the air, but here at least the city had fallen silent.

Machen said, "Take care. It's very dark in this yard. Do you think it would be safe for me to smoke my pipe now . . . ahm, best not. The rules against naked lights at night are very strict. Now . . . where is it?"

"Can I help?"

"I'm trying to find the bell push. Good Lord, it's so dark I can't see my hand in front of my face . . . ah, this is it. No, no . . ." He chuckled. "I'm trying to push my finger into a satyr's eye. I should add, a carved one. If you could see this old door frame you'd see how intricately carved it is. Ah, this is it."

Smith heard a bell sound faintly inside the building, and after a long pause a muffled, disgruntled voice came through the carved door hidden in the darkness.

"The archive is closed. Opening hours are nine till five. Goodnight."

"Benjamin, it's me. Machen."

"Arthur? Why didn't you say?"

"I just did, Benjamin." Machen's tone was good-natured. "Aren't you going to let us enter your fortress?"

"Of course, of course." There came the sound of bolts being drawn, a key turned, and the darkness changed shade. "Careful how you go, Arthur. I can't switch on the light until I've closed the door behind you. Blackout regulations, you know."

"Of course, Benjamin. Ah, I have a friend along, too. We're on something of a quest."

"Splendid! In you come, then. Ah, terrible tonight. I heard there were two hundred bombers in the formation."

"Terrible indeed, Benjamin. They won't rest until they have us living in the sewers."

Smith walked into an echoing hallway and the door clunked shut behind him. There was another *click* and a dazzling light lit up the surroundings. Standing close by was an elderly man, stooped and disturbingly frail. Smith noted that he wore an exotic cricket blazer, trimmed with pale blue at the cuffs and collar, a team badge adorning the breast pocket.

"Now, what can I do you for, Arthur?" Despite his frailty the old man sounded cheerful. Evidently he was delighted to see Machen. "You've not been this way in a long while."

"No, I'm stranded out at the end of the line in Amersham. I haven't been up to town for months. However, I've come now to raid your archive, if I may?"

"Of course, of course. How's the family?"

"Purefoy relentlessly knits socks for sailors, while Janet is training to become a nurse . . . she's my daughter, you know?"

"Yes, I remember. And your son?"

"Hilary. He was captured by the Italians. They've had him picking grapes in Tuscany."

"Too bad. I'm sorry, Arthur."

"At least he's out of harm's way, but I dare say he wishes he was back in the thick of it again. We've had letters so we know he's in good health."

"I'm glad to hear it. Well, you know the way. I'll scuttle back to the office. I'm ordered to remain by the phone in case anyone in editorial needs back issues from way back when. They never do, of course. So I sit, drink tea, wait."

After the old man had wandered off into the labyrinth, Machen led Smith to a long room filled with filing cabinets.

"This is the manuscript room," Machen told him. "We should find what we're looking for here." He consulted a leather-bound ledger filled with page after page of entries. "I've known Benjamin since 1910 . . . or was it 1909?"

"A rather colourful garb for a caretaker."

"Ah, the cricket blazer. Benjamin was once a first-class county player for Kent. After he retired from the game he became the staff sports writer, rising to sports editor by the time of the Great

War. But Lord Alfred Douglas – he's the owner of the newspaper group – despises cricket. With the outbreak of hostilities Douglas demoted Benjamin to sweep the floors here and run errands for editorial staff. Something, you'll agree, of a bitter insult to the man?"

Smith didn't have a chance to reply as Machen declaimed, "Hah! Here we are. Number 23 dash 406. 23 refers to the filing-cabinet number . . . let's see that will be . . . uhm, there to your left, lieutenant. Continue to the end of the row."

Smith followed Machen along the line of green metal cabinets. His whole night was becoming increasingly surreal.

Is Machen leading me on a wild goose chase? I went to his house to find the truth about what happened to me on that day in 1914. Now we're haring round London looking for scraps of paper. Is he humouring me? Perhaps hoping I tire of this and simply go?

Machen heaved open a drawer that had not been opened in years. The wheels screeched on their steel runners. "Now 406 . . . 406 . . . ah, 403, 405. 406! Well, I must say I'd forgotten what a slender envelope it was. All that fuss, thunder and lightning over this little thing. Move across to the light where we can see it better. Here we are: 'The Bowmen'. You know, I'm almost afraid to open the envelope just in case the manuscript isn't there. Or perhaps the pages are blank? Or maybe I'll find the story written in a hand other than my own." He smiled grimly. "Imagine what a shock *that* would be."

Smith saw the old man's hand tremble as he opened the brown quarto envelope and withdrew half a dozen sheets of paper, neatly folded in half and covered with handwriting.

Machen unfolded the manuscript and laid it flat on the table beneath the light.

Smith heard the note of relief in the man's voice. "Yes, of course this is mine. Written in pencil under my own name. Look, there are the editor's initials approving its publication. And here's the sub-editor's signature along with his rather heavy-handed editorial marks. But then he was notorious for his dislike of adjectives and a poetic turn of phrase. A few years later he drowned in Stratford-upon-Avon. Rather poetic justice, I always thought. Nevertheless, lieutenant, here is the manuscript. Hold it if you wish."

"And these blue pencil marks?"

"In those days – just as in this war – a Ministry censor was assigned to the editorial office to read everything we wrote before publication. He amended or deleted anything he judged to be injurious to the war effort. There's his official stamp and initials. And he's made a few deletions, too. There is—"

"No! Don't show me them!"

"I beg your pardon?"

"Don't show me."

"What on earth—"

Smith took a deep breath. His heart thudded in his chest. "Listen, Mr Machen. It's just possible there's something in the manuscript that will help prove to you that I'm not mistaken. That I really did witness a miraculous intervention on the battlefield."

"And what might that *something* be?"

Smith frowned, closed his eyes, trying to clear his mind. "Let me get this straight, sir. You wrote the manuscript in your own hand?"

"Indeed, I did."

"So the only people to see the finished story before it was typeset would be the editor, sub-editor . . ."

"And the censor, yes. So?"

"Did the censor delete any references to place names?"

"As a matter of fact, he did blue pencil the name of a Belgian village, even though I was most strenuous to point out that it was fictitious. A romantic concoction of my own and nothing more. It was—"

"No, don't tell me." Lieutenant Smith moved back from the manuscript on the table, holding his hands toward it to make clear to Machen that he couldn't see any of the text. "Near where I saw the angels there lay the remains of a village that formed a section of our lines." He watched Machen's face for any reaction when he spoke the name. "The village was called Sierville-en-Caux." Machen raised his eyebrows, and Smith continued. "The village church had been reduced to its foundations by shellfire, but rising from the rubble in its centre was—"

"A statue of St Jude, the patron saint of lost causes," Machen whispered. "Good Lord . . . oh my good Lord . . ."

"And the statue was unmarked, despite the destruction surrounding it."

Machen turned over two pages of the manuscript. "There's . . . it's difficult to see. The censor worked hard with that blue pencil of his. But you can just make out my handwriting: *Sierville-en-Caux*. And the description of a church with not a stone intact, yet with the unmarked statue of St Jude remaining upright and glorious." Machen looked suddenly tired. Some of the fire had gone from his eyes. "You do realize, lieutenant, that I am now a man standing upon the thinnest of ice above the most lethal of rapids. The border between fact and fiction has become fluid. I don't know what to believe . . . I don't . . ." He shrugged and sighed.

"I don't know what to feel." Smith took a deep breath, shaking, cold and yet sweating. "For the first time since it happened I've found real evidence. Perhaps now people will stop regarding me as a lunatic when I tell them that I witnessed a miracle."

"You're still some way from proving any celestial intervention, lieutenant. Many will dismiss the place name in my manuscript as coincidence, or even accuse you of breaking in here and reading the excised text." Machen slipped the manuscript back into its envelope. "In truth, I believed what I termed as the first step in our investigation would be the only step. That sight of 'The Bowmen' script would dissuade you from looking further."

Smith touched Machen's shoulder. "And now?"

"Everything has changed . . . everything." The old writer weighed the envelope in his hand, and then seemed to reach a decision. "My instincts now are for us to hold a council of war and decide where we go next. But first, I need to reread my tale. It's been many years, and my memory is rusty to say the least."

"Do you think there may be more in there? More proof, more evidence?"

"I truly don't know, lieutenant. Truly. Now, why don't you go and find Benjamin, have a chat to him while I peruse this again? I'd welcome the solitude. It helps me think. Right now my brain is in danger of overload, I feel, and yet I wonder if something eludes us still."

Smith nodded, went to clasp the old writer's hand – contact with this man would have felt good, comforting – but Machen had already turned away. Given his leave, Smith left the room. The corridors beyond were dark and musty, lit faintly here and there by candles which Benjamin must have left burning for their navigation back to the outside door. There were many doors, huddled in shadow as if trying hard to hide, and Smith stopped outside one or two. He put his ear to the wood and listened, but there was only a thick, oppressive silence. Spider webs hung heavy with dust from the corridor ceiling. Yet he saw no spiders. It was as if this whole place was waiting for something to happen.

Smith found himself back in the vestibule where they had entered. He had no real wish to chat with the old caretaker, so he leaned against a wall, hearing nothing but the rushing of his own blood and the thump of his heart. He coughed lightly to kill the silence.

They would be walking home soon. He did not have his watch with him so he decided to look outside and see whether dawn had arrived. The glaring light was still on so he flicked the switch off, shifted the blackout curtain, and glanced through the dust-smeared window.

It was raining. It was dark. And yet for a few seconds as he glanced out, the rain was illuminated into silvery spears cast earthward, darting streaks caught in the glow from something nearby or far away. The light soon faded, however, plunging the alley back into a darkness rattled by the impacts of raindrops.

Smith pulled back from the door and let the curtain drop into place. An explosion high in the air, he guessed, or a searchlight reflected from the low cloud ceiling.

"Tea?"

Smith jumped and spun around. The old caretaker stood behind him, holding a lighted candle in one hand. "You startled me!" Smith said.

Benjamin smiled and raised his eyebrows. "Sorry. I've even startled myself in here a few times! Weird sound qualities, all these corridors have. I've coughed and heard myself coughing back on many occasions. And once . . ."

"Yes?"

Benjamin frowned and looked away. "No matter. Tea? I make very good tea. And perhaps you'd like to hear a little about Mr Machen?"

That decided Smith. He followed Benjamin through a couple of corridors, left turn, right turn, thinking how the old man seemed to be winding down with time. *How old was he when I was fighting in the trenches?* Smith wondered. *Would he believe me?*

Or would he, a friend of the writer, display Machen's own angry doubt?

Doubt, yes. But Machen had been shaken over the matter of the village name. That was surely no coincidence, and no man of his intelligence would claim it as such.

"I have cheap tea, I'm afraid, but I make up for it by a lengthy brew while still boiling. Makes for an interesting taste, I'm sure you'll agree."

They reached Benjamin's room: small, comfortable, obviously a place where the old man spent a lot of time. "That sounds fine," Smith said.

"Did Arthur say how long he'd be?"

Smith shook his head.

"Ah! Well, I'll make him a cup, anyway." Benjamin went about brewing his tea, everything he did measured and smooth from long practice. He was certainly a man of habit.

"How long have you known Mr Machen?" Smith asked.

Benjamin laughed. "Longer than I care to remember! Longer than you *could*."

"I've read all his work," Smith said. "Everything. The books, the stories. Everything."

"Oh, I doubt that, sir." Benjamin poured boiling water and stirred the tea, returning it to the boil to get the most out of the insipid tea leaves.

"Then is there more? Hidden work that perhaps I could peruse?"

The old man looked at Smith, fleetingly suspicious. "You don't know the man, do you? I could tell that by the way he introduced you. But even though you don't know him, you've got him flustered and disturbed. I could sense that, too. And I'm not sure it's something I feel wholly comfortable with, to be honest, sir."

Smith shook his head, but he could think of nothing to say, no defence for what he had brought into Machen this night.

Benjamin continued. "However . . . I'm not one to jump to conclusions. And I know Arthur would have never brought you here if he didn't have good reason."

"He's a great man," Smith said, wondering where that had come from. He had often thought of the writer as a genius, a true wordsmith and perhaps, at times, capable of magic. But 'great' was a heavy word, one with consequences.

"He is that," Benjamin said, handing Smith a steaming cup. "He's a good man, a great man. Some would say a prophet."

Prophet! thought Smith. *Yes, a prophet!*

"Who would say that?"

Benjamin shrugged and took a sip of his hot tea, gasping and blowing softly to salve his burned lips. "Some," he said. "Indeed, I heard of one American scholar who described Mr Machen as The Apostle of Wonder."

Machen came into the room at that moment, seemingly having taken the few minutes to compose himself. "There you are, lieutenant! Oh dear, you're not drinking Benjamin's tea, are you? That dreadful brew is our first line of defence should Hitler invade."

"We were just talking about you," Benjamin said.

Machen shook his head. "Oh dear, oh dear, and I thought my night could not get any worse. Come, lieutenant! One more place to visit tonight, and then perhaps it's time to let our brains rest for a while." He turned back to Benjamin and shook the old man's hand warmly. "Splendid to see you again, Benjamin. I only hope it's not too long before the next time."

"Me too, Arthur."

The men smiled, and Smith saw an old friendship in their eyes.

Outside, dawn was creeping into the eastern sky. The rain dampened down the smoke rising over the city, but the air still stank of burning, and of war. Sirens sang across the capital, ferrying firemen to fires or the injured away from them, and although the danger was barely passed, there were people in the streets. Milkmen, making their deliveries; men and women going to work; policemen, bearing sad news. Smith strode after Machen, wanting to question him again but honouring the older man's silence.

Finally, rounding corner after corner, they reached a small park. It was in a square between large houses, an overgrown refuge of plant and tree and squirrel, and upon entering Smith already felt further away from the war. The flowers were bright, the ground dark and clean from the recent downpour, and even the smells of burning seemed lessened.

"Here," Machen said. "This will do."

"What are we here for?" Smith said, looking around. He was tired – he had not realized how tired until now, trudging once again through the London streets – and Machen himself seemed exhausted. The old writer eased himself onto a bench with a sigh, servicing his pipe and lighting it before answering.

"We're here to talk," Machen said. "Only briefly, for I am truly exhausted, and Purefoy will doubtless be getting worried already. I told her I would be home at sunup, at the latest." He puffed contentedly on his pipe and looked around at the trees. "Do you like nature, lieutenant?"

Smith looked around, nodding. "Yes. It's very . . . peaceful."

Machen scoffed. "Pah! Peaceful is one thing it is not! Basic, elemental, relaxing, wondrous, revealing and secretive. But nature is *alive*, Smith, an evolving thing, always on the move. Never peaceful. And it *allows* us. This park, here, is our own pretence at nature."

"How do you mean?"

Machen pointed with the stem of his pipe. "See how the trees are spaced? See how regular the shrub borders are? All very ordered and fake, a sham of reality, and we made it for our own pleasure. Real nature has an order all its own."

Smith looked around, frowning, wishing that the old man would make his point but not wanting to push him.

"Yet most people come here and are fooled," Machen said. "They view this place and see what the designers and gardeners intended, yet at the same time the truth is far different. Just as I do with my writing, they dream in fire and work in clay. Their ultimate aims are effectively unachievable, because the perfection of nature cannot be manufactured. They are deceived. They are . . ." He trailed off, seemingly confused for a few seconds, puffing his pipe to gather his thoughts. "They think they see something that is not really there. They believe that they view one thing, while in reality it's something quite different. Do you understand my meaning?"

"You mean," Smith said, "that my story and yours are not alike. That even through all the similarities, I am deluding myself. That's what you mean."

"In a way, yes."

"But that is not what I believe."

Machen stood and extended his hand. "I have to go home, Lieutenant Smith. It has been a night I shall not forget in a hurry! You have opened my eyes a little, and for that I am thankful."

"But that's not all!" Smith said, becoming agitated. This had not gone the way he had intended, nowhere near, and now that there was an end in sight his frustration came to the fore.

"No, it is not. Please be my guest this evening, lieutenant, at a little church on Banwick Road. A church I often frequent."

"The church where . . .?"

"Indeed," Machen said. "The church where my muse first presented me with this tale. Perhaps there, in that divine place, the truth may be more readily visible. Now, sir, I must bid you farewell."

Machen walked from the park, and within seconds he had disappeared behind a row of trees.

Smith sat on the bench and looked around, trying to analyse what Machen had said about this little park. Did he mean that it was not as it should be, and therefore that Smith's story was unbelievable? Or was he trying to get across that many people came here and thought they were in the depths of nature . . . whereas, in fact, they were deceived?

Was Smith deceiving himself? Were his memories as trustworthy as he believed?

He closed his eyes and smelled the mud, the stench of rotting dead friends, saw earth blossoming skywards in slow-motion explosions, felt the slick coolness of trench foot, heard the report of a rifle and the scream of a fallen man, on one side or the other, dying in pain whichever country he fought for.

No, he was not deceived. Now more than ever he believed that what he had seen in those trenches, what he and hundreds of others had witnessed, had been provoked by this one old writer. A man whose words had far more power than he was ready to admit.

A man who could conjure angels.

V

Smith was staying in a hotel not far from where he and Machen parted company. He walked slowly through the streets, musing upon what the night had brought, and wondering whether anything had really been resolved.

The sun was edging above the horizon but it was a cloudy morning, and although it had stopped raining the light was still weak. He took a back street as a short cut, keen to reach his bed and sleep for a few precious hours, and that was when he realised he was being followed.

There was no sound to give away his pursuer, no fleeting figure glimpsed from the corner of his eye; he simply knew that he was not alone in that street. He stopped and turned around, scanned the way he had come. No one hid in doorways, no one hunkered down behind a parked car, no one turned and fled. Yet that sense was there, an undeniable crawling down his spine, a certainty that he was being watched.

"Hello!" Smith called, brave now that night was sinking back into shadows. Perhaps Mr Machen had followed to ask him something else, or simply to prove to himself that Smith was no madman? But nobody answered his call. Pigeons fluttered on window ledges, a dog trotted across the street and a cat watched him from inside a house, tail twitching as it regarded him coolly.

He hurried to the end of the street and turned left . . . and then stopped, pressing himself against a wall, listening out for footsteps or the panting of a running man. He heard neither. A car passed him from left to right, its driver giving him a wary glance, and Smith tried to smile. But the expression no longer fitted his face. He was tried and confused. He needed a sleep without dreams, a long rest, and then tonight perhaps he and Machen would experience some epiphany, the truth made plain to their refreshed minds. His own conviction had been diluted by Machen's scepticism.

He took one last quick glance around the corner, and saw light fade away.

It might have been a blur on his eye, a piece of dust floating on the air. Or perhaps it was a trick of the sun, someone opening a window and casting a fleeting reflection. But the sun was hidden by thick clouds. And though he wiped his eyes, still he saw the silvery light crawling across an expanse of red brick. No shadow was cast there. The brick sucked in the light and stood as silent testament to its existence.

Smith closed his eyes, opened them again, thought of the illuminated downpour of rain outside the Bloomsbury archive building. *Searchlight*, he had thought at the time, but now that seemed unlikely. Now, he had to wonder just who or what was following him.

He hurried away, comforted by the appearance of several

people in the street. He glanced back often, pleased that daylight had now taken a firm hold, and yet somewhat disappointed as well.

He had not felt threatened, fearful or in danger.

In fact, he wished the light would appear again. It reminded him . . .

Smith reached his room, drank a glass of water to wash away the dust of the previous night, stripped off his clothes – torn and made tatty by his virtual burial in the collapsed house – and within a minute of lying down, he slept.

Perhaps he dreamed.

When he woke he shouted out loud, rolling from the bed and huddling beneath the sheets, hiding himself, making it safe. The room was brightly lit, a shimmering illumination that seemed to be peering in from outside, assaulting his senses in concert with the squeal of brakes (*the scream of a falling shell*), the shout of a newspaper seller (*the cry of a dying man calling for his mother*), the sound of rain hitting the window (*water in the trenches, squelching underfoot, trying to suck him down into the mud where so many of his friends lay rotting . . . for ever*). Smith shivered and groaned, perceiving the shifting light even through the thickness of the blanket. He tried to link his fears with what had happened all those years ago, but that time felt vague as a dream, fading like dreams do into a feeling, a sensation, a memory with no definable detail.

Smith remembered where he was and why. He held in a breath, threw aside the blanket, and the room was lit by sunlight. It slanted in through dusty window-panes, catching a million specks of dust dancing before his eyes. It was still raining – a summer shower, fresh and invigorating – and perhaps that accounted for the strange quality of light. Constantly shifting. Refracted through raindrops, diluted and silvered by the water.

Or perhaps he dreamed.

The church was small, innocuous, subsumed by other large, contemporary buildings. Whereas its history and standing should have made the surrounding structures look out of place, the opposite was true. The church, here for hundreds of years, had lost its identity to its new companions. Its façade was blackened from the effects of exhaust fumes, its once-proud oaken door a darker entrance now than had ever been intended. Even the openings of its bell tower had been bricked in.

Smith stood on the opposite side of the road for a while, staring at the church. He was trying to make a connection, feel something pertinent to his reason for being here. It was in this place that Machen had conceived the story, after all. Perhaps that very thought had held more power than any normal prayer. But Smith could feel nothing, no sense of revelation, and by the time he saw Machen approaching slowly along the street he was depressed and gloomy.

Dusk was falling. The bombers would be here again soon. People were rushing home, to the safety of their shelters or the Tube stations. Cars, buses and other vehicles hurried through the streets, a few of them turning on their covered headlights but most defying the coming dark.

"Lieutenant Smith!" Machen called from across the street, waving his walking cane.

Smith waved back. *Perhaps tonight*, he thought. *Perhaps tonight the truth will out.*

He crossed the road and shook Machen's hand.

"Did you sleep well?" Machen asked.

"I had a nightmare."

"Sorry to hear that." Machen avoided Smith's gaze, looking down at the pavement, up at the church. "I had an odd dream, too. But then I am an old man, and my mind often wanders of its own accord. Shall we?" He indicated the church doorway, inviting Smith to enter first.

"After you," Smith said. And as they walked through into the lobby and then the cool church interior, he knew that they would see a light in there, a luminescence shimmering above the pews, hanging beneath the ceiling like a great bat examining them soundlessly.

But there was nothing. The stained-glass windows on the left shone with the pink of the setting sun, yielding a little light to see by. The church was empty but for the two of them.

"I thought a church would be busy in these times," Smith said.

"It is, during the day," Machen smiled. "But when it comes to night-time and bombings, people would rather worship from the safety of an air-raid shelter. Did you hear about St Paul's? Lost one of its clock towers, I hear. Terrible shame. Lovely building. I was in the Whispering Gallery once, alone, and someone whispered to me."

They sat together in a pew halfway down the nave, silent and companionable. Agitated though he was, Smith felt an immediate sense of tranquillity. His beliefs and faith were a mixed stew, but how could one not come to such a serene place, a place where so many found comfort and peace, and not find peace oneself?

"This is approximately where I was sitting," Machen said. "The church was full then, brimming with people desperate to understand. To come to terms with what was happening over the Channel. Fear permeated the atmosphere. Tales of the barbaric Hun were rife in the press – the crucified soldier, the spearing of babies, how German soldiers cut off the hands and feet of nurses – and there was true terror in the idea that the Kaiser's armies would cross to our fair isle. So we prayed. We prayed for the victory of Good over Evil, because in those days the definitions were clear-cut."

"I saw thousands of dead Germans," Smith said. "They all looked like me. They had parents and siblings and lovers who mourned them. We were all equally as scared out there."

"And yet the demonization of Germany exists today as much as it did twenty-five years ago," Machen continued. "It is neither right, nor wrong. It is simply how the public has to deal with these things. We – you and I – are useless in this current fight. We have to lend moral support, and for that we have to believe ourselves morally right."

They sat in silence again for a while, but Smith sensed that Machen was uncomfortable. The old writer kept glancing at him, as if to confirm to himself that this lieutenant was the same man with whom he'd had such an adventure last night.

"Tell me," Machen said at last. "Tell me of the time in the trenches, when your angels came and saved you and your men. What did they look like? Describe them to me."

"But you know what they looked like, you wrote of them."

"I wrote *some* of what I imagined. But the translation between imagination and paper is imprecise at best. Please, humour me."

"Are you starting to believe?" Smith asked, suddenly excited. "Do you see some truth in what I say?"

"I see inconsistencies which I must explore. And I feel . . . obliged to pursue our inquiry. Please, Delamare . . . tell me."

Smith closed his eyes for a few moments, gathering his thoughts, sending himself back to that time in the trenches. The guns roared, explosions flared along the front, and a tide of grey-clad men headed their way across the plains of Hell.

And then . . .

And then the muttering began, and the laughing, and the muttering again in a language that Smith did not recognize. One of his mates in the trench had gone mad, and in amongst the snippets of music-hall song and encouraging shouts, his voice was quiet and yet loud, loudest of all.

And then something passed over their heads, singing through the air, going the wrong way because all their own artillery had been pulled back.

The first line of Germans fell, struck down by spears of light.

Smith turned around, his gun hot in his hands, slipping down the wall of the trench as he saw what approached.

At first he thought it was a cloud of gas, but it was drifting sideways against the breeze, its trajectory exact and defined. And as it came closer and let loose another cloud of whistling shapes – they passed straight over the trenches, slashing through the air as fast as bullets – he saw figures beginning to manifest from the cloud. The outlines of men, archers, their longbows constantly drawn and letting fly, drawn again. The arrows ripped across the ruined land and buried themselves in the lines of advancing Germans. A new hail was fired every second, even as the shining, glowing shapes approached nearer, nearer . . . and then passed over the British trenches, advancing onward.

The rattle of German gunfire cut smoky holes in the nebulous shapes, but their forms flowed to fill the spaces slashed through reality, and their bows let loose once more.

At their head, astride a shining horse, a man in armour. He waved his sword and encouraged a charge, charging himself, sword hacking at the air and cutting down ten grey men. The arrows passed through him and rather than damaging his glowing inconsistency it seemed to empower their shafts even more. A dozen men fell from each arrow, its path hacked back through the hordes.

Smith watched the horse rear, its rider shouting silent exhortations heard only in the minds of those British warriors watching and not believing . . . and he blinked back a sudden blast of recognition.

That way, true madness lay.

"It must have been from books," Smith said. "I'd seen his image before, and it was stored in my mind. He was known to me."

Machen sat silent, ashen-faced in the pew beside Smith. His eyes were closed. Smith hoped that he was praying.

"And now?" Smith asked quietly. "And now, what do you think?"

"I will assume nothing," Machen said, "and neither should you. But your account is as I imagined it, similar in every detail. When I reread my tale last night, hidden in the depths of the archive, I realized how ambiguous my descriptions were. Given the restrictions of length that I had to obey – it was for a newspaper article, after all – I intimated rather than described. But your account . . . it is as if you were me, sitting here all those years ago and conceiving the tale. Your words are my thoughts. I . . . I do not understand."

Smith smiled and sank back into the pew, certain that truth was finding its own way. What that truth was, and how its complexities worked, did not concern him for the moment.

"And now," Machen said, "perhaps you would be so good as to view the third west-facing window. It was there that my gaze rested twenty-five years ago when the bones of the tale came to me. And it is there that now lies an enigma stranger than I can bear. I was not sure, I doubted my recollection, but now . . ."

Smith stood and walked to the window, squinting at the sunset beaming in, enlivening the rich colours. "What?" he said. "What do you believe? Do you . . ."

He trailed off, feeling language leave him, understanding fleeing with every step he took. Reality twisted around him, and he was at once alone and accompanied by multitudes in this church. The spirits of a thousand worshippers looked over his shoulder as he stared at the window, and they were as amazed as he.

Set in an intricate web of lead and stained glass, St George stood tall and proud in a suit of golden armour; protector and saint, warrior and king.

And as the sunset turned red as blood, Smith saw that St George's face was his own.

VI

Smith turned to Machen and breathed the words, "Mr Machen, when you look at the stained glass window, what do you see?"

Machen looked from the face of St. George in painted glass, with the light of the dying sun shining through, to Smith. "I . . ."

Smith turned suddenly, tilting his head to one side, listening.

Machen began again, clearly puzzled by the man's reaction. "I see the face I imagined all those years—"

Smith held his finger to his lips. "Just a moment," he whispered. "I don't think we're alone." He moved to the centre of the aisle and looked back toward the entrance doors. Beneath the archway that supported the tower above it was a void of deep shadow. *I did hear something*, he told himself. Or was it a sound? Perhaps it was more a sixth sense, warning him that someone had slipped into the church. He recalled the same feeling earlier when he'd sensed that he was not alone in the street; almost a primitive residual instinct, signalling that – what? He was being watched? Followed?

"Wait here a moment," he told Machen, then moved quietly between the bench pews. He saw no one, but he thought he heard footsteps as light as feathers brushing the flagstone floor to his right. By now the daylight was almost gone. With blackout regulations in force there was no artificial lighting. The only illumination was the afterglow of the sun throwing ghostly projections from stained-glass windows onto pews, stone columns and white-painted walls. Smith turned and retraced his steps toward the altar, and multicoloured images of saints, unicorns, lambs and cherubs flowed across him, dappling him in greens, golds, reds and heavenly blues.

Maybe it's this place, he thought. *It's working on my imagination, especially as this was the birthplace of Machen's story. Then there's the stained-glass depiction of St George, and his face . . . It's like a firestorm in my mind. Truth and make-believe are stirring themselves together.*

He glanced toward Machen, standing there with the light

shining around him, looking every inch a saint conjured from the distant past, his silver hair changing colour as the remaining daylight seeped through the church windows. Machen watched him approach.

"Anyone, lieutenant?"

"No. My imagination's getting a little jumpy of late."

"No small wonder." Machen turned to the stained glass of St George. "Now, this image. It dates back to the sixteen-hundreds. I should very much like it if you were to stand beside it so that I can . . ."

Machen continued speaking as Smith's attention was drawn to a statue carved in dark wood. It stood so close to the lectern that Smith thought it formed the central column. The statue was in deep shadow and he could make out barely any detail, but for some reason he could not tear his gaze away from it, from the hard, rounded head to the over-large eyes that glinted eerily in the depths of that shadow. Machen was still talking about comparing the image of St George with Smith. Of collecting a camera. Of bringing respected individuals who could verify the uncanny similarity. Only Smith was no longer listening. The statue . . . there was something wrong . . . the silhouette was man-sized. And it did not obey any sculptor's convention. Not the prime attribute of the statue which was: *a statue shall not of its own volition move* . . .

A rush of ice plunged down Smith's backbone. The statue glided smoothly forward. Machen had still not noticed, and he continued talking, enthralled by the similarity between the painted representation and the flesh-and-blood figure of the lieutenant standing beside to him. "Remarkable, quite remarkable. Of course, there are some that will dismiss it as coincidence . . . pure coincidence. But if I'm not—."

"Mr Machen, stand back."

"Pardon?"

"Back . . . get out of my way." Smith unbuckled the holster flap and drew out his revolver.

"Lieutenant . . . Delamare, what on earth's wrong?"

"Keep back." Smith moved forward, pushing the old man to one side as the dark figure glided out of the shadows. It passed through the blood-red projection of Christ on the Cross. Dolorous. Martyred. The magnified eyes were momentarily superimposed on the large eyes of the man now approaching. A crown of thorns slid over the glossily dark head.

Then Smith realized why the eyes were so large and unblinking. As the man emerged from the dappling of refracted light Smith saw his goggles, the leather flying helmet sheathing his head, the pilot's tunic and leather-gauntleted hands.

"Dear Lord," Machen breathed. "That uniform is Luftwaffe!"

Smith cocked the revolver with his thumb and aimed. "Stay where you are. You are now a prisoner of war. Do you understand? Stay back."

The man merely grinned. The goggles flashed red, green, yellow as he moved forward.

"*Nein*," Smith barked. "*Nein*! Halt!"

But the German pilot did not stop, and neither did his smile falter. He moved forward faster, breaking into a run, heading straight for Smith.

Smith fired two shots point-blank into the man's chest. The German charged into him, pushing him back. Smith tried to resist but his feet slid on the floor – his attacker's muscular strength was formidable. Effortlessly the pilot shoved him back and back, until he slammed into a stone pillar with enough force to wind him.

And then the pilot's hands found Smith's throat to crush with agonizing ferocity. Instantly the air locked in Smith's lungs; he could not breathe, could barely move. He could only look into the smiling face of the pilot, the eyes masked by the tinted goggles. As Smith's vision blurred he saw Machen stride up behind the pilot, grab him by the tunic and try to haul him back. Despite his age, Machen possessed the powerful build of his countrymen, with long muscular arms that succeeded in breaking the pilot's grip from Smith's throat. However, the pilot repositioned his hands to force Smith backward again, as if trying to crush him into the stone walls of the church.

Smith grunted a breath into his lungs. Then, realizing that he still held the revolver, he jabbed the muzzle into the man's side just above his right hip and fired a .38 calibre round through his body. It must have torn through kidney and intestine alike.

Even though the German twitched as the bullet passed through him, it did not shift his expression. The smile remained fixed – immobile, as if carved on that grey face. With his free hand the pilot struck back at Machen, knocking the old man to the church floor where he lay stunned by the uncanny force of the blow.

Then, with the speed of a striking cobra, those black gauntlets sliced through the air to seize Smith by the throat, once more squeezing his windpipe shut. Blood thundered in his ears. His vision blurred. Behind his attacker he saw Machen try to stand, but fail. Instead the writer sat supported by one hand, unable to act to save Smith, but still able to watch his imminent demise. Even though the lieutenant struggled with every shred of his strength, he could not break the steely grip on his throat. In front of him the German's face distorted and rippled as Smith's senses began to fade away.

And then the pilot moved that ballooning, shapeshifting head closer to Smith's. The dark lips parted and a voice hissed: "*Alea jacta est.*"

For a second the man reverted to statue-like stillness. Then the pressure vanished from Smith's throat, and the pilot crumpled to the floor with the limpness of an empty sack. Smith gasped a few frantic breaths. Air had never tasted so sweet or cool. He tried to cock the revolver in case the man renewed his attack, but his hands were still weak. Instead, he steadied himself against the pillar with his free hand while breathing deeply. The pilot lay flat on his back without moving. Maybe those pistol shots had hit their mark after all.

"It's all right, Arthur," he said at length. "He's out for the count." Smith walked unsteadily to the old man and helped him stand. "How do you feel?"

"I might be old, lieutenant, but I'm tougher than I look." In the deep twilight Machen glanced down at the fallen pilot, then back at Smith. "Moreover, I don't believe the man poses much of a threat now, considering the holes you've stitched in his chest."

Smith nodded. "He must have bailed out from one of the bombers last night and has been hiding in the church. What he hoped to achieve with his bare hands, heaven alone knows; the fool should have given himself up."

Machen regarded the pilot. "Just before he collapsed, lieutenant, he spoke to you?"

"That he did, but apart from a few words I don't speak German."

"Our friend didn't use any German words. It was Latin."

"Latin?"

"He spoke the phrase: *Alea jacta est*."

Smith gave a grim smile. "My Latin is as good as my German, I'm afraid."

"*Alea jacta est*, Lieutenant. It means 'the dice are cast.'"

"The man must have lost his mind."

"Or he was delivering a message to you." Machen rubbed his jaw. "'The dice are cast'. Meaning, I venture, a sequence of events has been triggered which will have a decisive result. Though one which no one can predict."

"But who sent him? How did he know we'd be here in this church tonight? His commanding officer couldn't have ordered him here when even we didn't know we'd be in the place until a few hours ago."

"Lieutenant Smith, you've missed the point."

"What point?"

"The man's commanding officer ordered him to bomb London, not deliver a warning in Latin to you."

"Then who did?"

"I don't know. But I dare say there was no mortal hand in this."

"I disagree. There was."

Machen looked at him levelly. "Whose mortal hand?"

"His. The pilot's."

Smith watched Machen kneel down with some difficulty beside the man.

"Don't get too close, Arthur."

"He won't move again. Not of his own volition, anyway."

"Then I'm a better shot than I thought."

The writer pulled back the tunic collar and touched the pilot's bare neck. "He is dead. And he's been dead for hours."

"Impossible."

Machen tugged up the flying goggles to reveal two raw sockets devoid of eyes. The writer drew a breath of distaste. "This man died in his aircraft. The shock wave from an anti-aircraft shell destroyed his eyes, no doubt at the same moment that it disintegrated his plane. See how the arms and legs bend? Every bone in his body was shattered when he struck the ground. The neck is dislocated, allowing extreme—"

"Stop it . . . please don't tell me any more."

"So, you'll realize why two bullets in the man's chest didn't stop him. You can't kill a dead man."

Smith shook his head, feeling reality flee with the daylight. "Tell me, Arthur. What forces are at work here?"

"I don't know. But I believe some course of action is expected of you." He looked up at Smith. "I'm beginning to wonder if *you* were the individual responsible in the Great War for summoning divine intervention on the battlefield."

"No. I merely witnessed it. I wasn't the instigator."

"No?"

"No. How can I have been? I did nothing."

"Maybe you didn't have to perform a conscious act or ritual. Or even utter an incantation. Perhaps you acted as a passive catalyst—"

"No."

"Or a conduit for a greater power."

This was not what Smith had anticipated. He'd come seeking this man – looking for answers, not more complex questions. "Please, Arthur. I'd rather leave here now." He could not look away from the face that had no eyes.

"Very well. It's probably for the best."

"We should inform the police about—"

"Don't worry, he'll be found soon enough. Come."

Smith followed the writer as he hurried along the aisle. When they reached the door Smith glanced back.

The dead man sat bolt upright. The empty eye sockets fixed on him as if the corpse looked deep into his soul. "*Alea jacta est*," the voice cracked the silence. "*Alea jacta est.*"

The dice are cast.

Saying nothing, *believing* nothing, Smith followed Machen out into the night.

VII

For the first mile of their walk through the night-time streets Smith repeatedly glanced back, expecting to see the dead pilot loping after them. What he could do then to protect Machen and himself, he had no idea. The corpse had been immune to bullets, it was no respecter of sacred ground, and Smith was no match for its phenomenal strength.

However, by the second mile he was confident that the corpse was not following. For the time being, they were safe.

Smith glanced at Machen as they walked side by side. "You believe that somehow I invoked the miracle that I witnessed – the same one you wrote about in 'The Bowmen'?"

"I'm reaching that conclusion. As I'm reaching the conclusion that we find ourselves on this quest to learn more about the matter, because somehow it will become relevant shortly. The dice are cast. I feel that we are somehow suspended between disaster and salvation."

"And am I the key to this?"

"Yes, lieutenant, I believe you are. Your time is come again. You must act to save your nation."

Smith scoffed, shook his head, desperate to deny this madness. "How? And save the country against what?"

"We are at war."

"That I do know. But I can't win a war single-handed. Am I to arrive in Berlin with a pistol in my hand and assassinate Hitler?"

"If only you could . . ." Machen tilted his head, his hair glinting silver in the near-dark. "All I do know is that you will be required to act . . . and act soon."

"But I don't know . . ."

"I don't think I should be with you right now," Machen said.

"What? What do you mean?"

"I'm an old man, and I've had more than my share of frights these past days. Much as I've sought wonders all my life, I simply feel right now that I should go home to my wife. She'll be waiting for me. I'm very old, lieutenant. Very old. Soon the time will come when I know the truth of things for sure, but right now . . . right now, I believe it's time for you to be alone. It's time for me to leave things to happen." He turned to walk away, and then glanced back at Smith, a smile askew on his face. "Who knows . . . maybe one day I'll write a story about this."

Machen left Smith on the darkened street. Within seconds the old man had disappeared into the shadows, lost to the night. Smith stared after him open-mouthed, feeling lost and loss.

A siren sang out in the distance, warning of yet another night of bombing and destruction, chaos and death. Smith's confusion was supplanted by an increasing desperation, the idea that he had failed totally to carry out the task he had set himself. Though he had learned much since meeting Machen and escaping the bombed house, he had not discovered enough, nowhere *near* enough to effect any change. The bombers were still drifting in from the east, the slaughter would continue, and all the mysteries piled up behind him – the window, the living-dead German airman, his knowledge of what only Machen should truly know – they were nothing compared to the horror about to come once again to London.

Smith spun around, wondering what to do and where to go, when he saw the glow growing from the mouth of an alley along the street. To begin with he thought someone had forgotten to close their blackout curtains, but the glow was growing. Perhaps they were opening a door, ignorant of the light they were spilling, the target they were creating for enemy bombers? Smith tried to shout but his voice stuck in his throat. He ran instead, but soon slowed as the luminescence expanded, grew stronger . . . and it was a silvery light, a shine growing from the impenetrable dark, not spreading from one single source.

Smith came to a standstill, about to turn and run the other way, to follow Machen, find his home, track him down and extract the final truth.

The light expanded some more, its edges straining as if contained within a filled balloon. He even heard the creaking, wrenching sound of something beginning to split . . . the air-raid siren fading . . . the darkness becoming strangely deeper, the further the light pushed out . . .

And then it broke.

The silvery light erupted from the alley like a slow-motion explosion. Before Smith could react it was upon him, warm and slick across his skin, penetrating his ears and eyes and mind, showing him . . . showing him the truth that even Machen been unable to truly comprehend . . .

As realization struck Smith down and picked him up in its impossible arms, the first bombs of the night fell on his beloved city.

VIII

"How is your wife?" Smith asked.

"She's well," Machen said. "Scared. Worried that I've been out so much of late. But well. And I've told her . . . I've told her that this is my last meeting with you."

Smith nodded. "I knew you'd want to see me again. And I guessed this was the best place to find you."

They stood at the entrance to Highgate Cemetery, a ten-minute walk from the house in which they had first met. A group of men worked deep in the cemetery, gathering body parts from a huge crater carved out by a land mine the previous night.

"At least the dead cannot be killed," Machen said.

Smith laughed. It was the first time he had laughed in a long time.

The two men stood silently for a few minutes: Machen, an old man, forever questing for the truth of things, the reality behind the façade; and Delamare Smith, a veteran of the Great War trenches, a man confused by what he had seen, now confused no more.

Now he *knew* the truth. He had glimpsed beyond the veil. And he knew that the old writer was waiting as patiently as he could to be told.

"There was a bomber carrying pneumonic plague," he said at last. Machen stared at him aghast, but Smith went on. "It was hidden away deep within the largest formation of the night. Those flying around it were not told of the cargo – this was a plot of the Nazis, not the common German soldiery – but they were instructed to keep it safe, sacrifice themselves should the need arise. Many did.

"They were going to drop to three thousand feet and release it into the atmosphere, minute droplets that would carry on the breeze, disperse all across London, settling down on our capital just as the all-clear sounded and our women and children came up from the shelters, the Tube stations, the other holes in the ground we've been forced to hide in."

"Like rats," Machen said.

"Like rats. And like rats, they were going to slaughter us."

"It will be . . . catastrophic!" Machen stared into the grave-yard, as if looking for room for a million more graves.

"It would have been, had I not destroyed that bomber."

Machen could only stare.

Smith smiled at the old man. "You'll hear stories," he said. "They'll be told in newspapers and perhaps books over the coming days and weeks. Stories of an explosion in the night sky, bright as the sun, but a cool silver, not the angry yellow of fire. Stories of a German squadron blasted out of the sky, though there were no fighters nearby at the time." Smith leaned on the wall, staring up at the sun as if enjoying the heat on his face for the very first time. "And I'm sure – I'm positive – that in the fullness of time, fighter pilots will begin claiming that they saw it all happen as well. The countless German aircraft, far too many for them to shoot down, strafed by spears of silver light. Brought down by angels."

"I don't . . ." Machen was speechless.

"Divine intervention, Mr Machen," Smith said. He held out his hand. "It was an honour to meet you, sir. I don't think I ever did tell you just how much I enjoy your work. How *inspirational* you've been to me. Your tales of wonders beneath and beyond what we accept . . . they have helped me. Without your writing . . ." He shook his head. "Well, it's time for me to leave."

Machen's dazed wonder had been replaced by a calm acceptance. His eyes, still confused, were smiling once again. "It has been an honour for me, too, lieutenant. And now, I suspect . . .?" He nodded along the street, towards where his friend's house lay in ruins.

Smith smiled and nodded. "You suspect right, sir. In the ruins, you will find something that may help you to understand."

Without another word, Smith stepped past the old writer and walked down the street. He stepped across rubble blown into the road, shattered crockery crunching underfoot, but the further he went the fainter grew the sound of his footsteps, the smell of burning faded slowly away, and London opened her arms to receive him for ever.

Arthur Machen stood looking at the ruins of the house. How he and Smith had ever crawled out of there alive . . .

Eventually, gathering his courage about him, tapping the ground before him with his cane, he advanced on the wreckage. He had to climb a little mound of rubble and splintered floor-boarding before he could pass under the overhanging roof. It was stupidly dangerous, he was aware of that, but he had to know.

He *had* to.

It seemed that he had spent his whole life working towards this moment of epiphany.

He saw something protruding from beneath one of the blown-out doors. It was a boot-clad foot, the boot being First World War army issue. Next to the boot, shattered on the floor, the remains of a whisky glass caught the rays of the early-morning sun.

Breathing hard, grabbing the door's brass handle, Machen stood and pulled. And he opened the portal to the ecstasy of truth.

STEPHEN JONES & KIM NEWMAN

Necrology: 2003

WITH EACH PASSING YEAR, we are marking the deaths of more and more writers, artists, performers and technicians who, during their lives, made significant contributions to the horror, science fiction and fantasy genres (or left their imprint on popular culture and music in other, often fascinating, ways). It is depressing to note that this is by far our longest column to date . . .

AUTHORS/ARTISTS/COMPOSERS

Daphne Oram, a pioneer of electronic music who, in 1957, persuaded the BBC to launch its Radiophonic Workshop (remembered for the *Doctor Who* theme music), died on 5th January, aged 77.

British film composer **Ron Goodwin**, best known for his classic war-film scores, died on January 8th, aged 77. He had suffered from asthma for many years. Goodwin's many scores include *Village of the Damned*, *Children of the Damned*, *Day of the Triffids*, *Jules Verne's Rocket to the Moon* (a.k.a. *Those Fantastic Flying Fools*), Alfred Hitchcock's *Frenzy*, *Gawain and the Green Knight*, the TV movie of *Beauty and the Beast* (1976) and Disney's *One of Our Dinosaurs is Missing* and *Unidentified Flying Oddball* (a.k.a. *The Spaceman and King Arthur*). He won the Ivor Novello Award in 1994 for Lifetime Achievement in Music.

British satirical writer **Peter Tinniswood** died of oral cancer on January 9th, aged 66. Best known for his novels, stage plays and radio dramas, he also contributed three ghost stories to anthologies edited by James Hale.

American literary agent, author and SF anthologist [Mildred] **Virginia Kidd** died in her sleep after prolonged health problems on January 11th, aged 81. Her second husband was SF writer James Blish (from 1947–62). Kidd's novelette "Kangaroo Court" appeared in Damon Knight's *Orbit 1* (1966) and she edited several SF anthologies, including *Saving Worlds* (with Roger Elwood), *Millennial Women* (a.k.a. *The Eye of the Heron and Other Stories*) and *Interfaces* and *Edges* (both with Ursula K. Le Guin). She established the Virginia Kidd Literary Agency in 1965.

British-born multi-millionaire songwriter and musician **Maurice Gibb** CBE, who founded the Bee Gees with his brothers Barry, twin Robin and Andy (who died in 1988), died of complications from a twisted bowel the same day, aged 53. He had suffered a heart attack three days earlier and was operated on for an intestinal blockage in a Miami hospital. From 1969–73 he was married to singer Lulu. The Bee Gees sold more than 100 million records, and their songs include "Massachusetts", "Jive Talkin'", "Stayin' Alive", "How Deep is Your Love" and "Night Fever". Maurice Gibb composed the music and had an uncredited cameo in *The Supernaturals* (1985).

Emmy Award-winning screenwriter and producer **Paul Monash** died of pancreatic cancer on January 14th, aged 85. Creator of the TV series *Peyton Place* (1964–69), his other credits include *Touch of Evil*, *Slaughterhouse-Five*, *Big Trouble in Little China*, *Carrie*, *The Rage: Carrie 2* and TV's *Salem's Lot* (1979) and *V.* His draft scripts for *The Dead Zone* (1979), another Stephen King adaptation, were not used.

Virginia ("Ginny") [Gerstenfeld] **Heinlein**, the widow of SF author Robert A. Heinlein, died in her sleep on January 18th, aged 86. After her husband's death in 1988, she oversaw publication of several posthumous works, including his selected letters as *Grumbles from the Grave*, his travel memoir *Tramp Royale*, the political handbook *Take Back Your Government* and restored editions of such SF novels as *Red Planet*, *The Puppet Masters* and *Stranger in a Strange Land*. Her ashes were scattered in the Pacific Ocean, joining those of her husband.

American caricaturist **Al** (Albert) **Hirschfeld** died in his sleep on January 20th, aged 99. Best known for his spot-on caricatures of Broadway and Hollywood celebrities over seven decades for the *New York Times*, he was a former art director and poster designer at Selznick Pictures and Warner Bros. His books include *The World of Hirschfeld* and *The American Theatre as Seen by Hirschfeld*, and in 1993 he designed a series of stamps for the US Postal Service honouring silent film stars, including Lon Chaney, Sr. as The Hunchback of Notre Dame.

Senior principal show set designer at Walt Disney Imagineering, 46-year-old **David Kent Mumford**, died the same day of non-Hodgkin's lymphoma and paraneoplastic pemphigus. Co-author of *Disneyland: The Nickel Tour*, his book about Disney matte artist Peter Ellenshaw, *Ellenshaw Under Glass*, was published posthumously.

Bestselling British thriller writer **Gavin** [Tudor] **Lyall** also died of cancer on January 20th, aged 70. His thirteen novels include *The Most Dangerous Game* and *Shooting Script* and often incorporated fantastic elements. One of his stories formed the basis of Hammer Films's *Moon Zero Two*.

Award-winning advertising art director **Ed Harridsleff**, who designed hundreds of movie posters, including *King Kong* (1976) and *The Terminator*, died in Los Angeles on January 21st, aged 68.

Two-time Pulitzer Prize-winning cartoonist **Bill Mauldin**, who created GIs Willie and Joe for *Stars & Stripes* during World War II, died of Alzheimer's complications and pneumonia on January 22nd, aged 81.

African-American SF author **John M.** (Matthew) **Faucette** was found dead of an apparent heart attack in front of his computer in late January, aged 59. His books include *Age of Ruin*, *Crown of Infinity*, *The Warriors of Terra*, *Siege of Earth* and the self-published collection *Black Science Fiction*.

Controversial mainstream critic **Leslie A.** (Aron) **Fiedler**, whose books include the 1975 "historical-critical" SF anthology *In Dreams Awake* and the 1982 biography *Olaf Stapledon: A Man Divided*, died after battles with Parkinson's disease and prostate cancer on January 29th, aged 85. His one SF novel was *The Messengers Will Come No More* (1974).

Oscar-winning screenwriter and novelist **William Kelley** died of cancer on February 3rd, aged 73. His credits include the 1983 TV movie *The Demon Murder Case*.

Reclusive American SF fan, publisher and historian **Harry** [Backer] **Warner, Jr.**, died on February 17th, aged 80. A fanzine publisher since 1938 with *Spaceways* (which included contributions from H.P. Lovecraft, Jack Williamson, Forrest J Ackerman and others), his histories of fandom in the 1940s and 1950s were published as *All Our Yesterdays* (1969) and *A Wealth of Fable* (1976). A 1992 revision of the latter volume won him a nonfiction Hugo Award, and he also received the 1969 and 1972 Hugos for Best Fan Writer. He was a Guest of Honour at the 1971 Boston World SF Convention.

Russian-born artist [Yura] **"George" Solonevich**, whose illustrations appeared in *Analog* during the 1960s, died following a series of strokes in a Virginia nursing home on February 21st, aged 87.

Oscar-winning screenwriter **Daniel Taradash**, who wrote *From Here to Eternity*, died of pancreatic cancer on February 22nd, aged 90. His other scripts include Fritz Lang's *Rancho Notorious*, *Bell Book and Candle* and *Castle Keep*.

American composer, arranger and music director **Walter Scharf** died of heart failure on February 24th, aged 92. His more than 250 film and TV credits include *The Masked Marvel*, *Haunted Harbor*, *Zorro's Black Whip*, *The Adventures of Sherlock Holmes*, *The Lady and the Monster*, *Captain America*, *King of the Rocket Men*, *Invisible Monster*, *Francis*, *Abbott and Costello Meet the Invisible Man*, *Missile Monsters*, *Cinderfella*, *The Nutty Professor* (1963), *Willy Wonka and the Chocolate Factory*, *Journey Back to Oz*, *The Man from U.N.C.L.E.*, *Mission: Impossible* and *The Wild Wild West*. He was nominated for ten Academy Awards and won the 1972 Golden Globe for the title song for *Ben*, sung by Michael Jackson.

American writer **Jane** [Dixon] **Rice** (a.k.a. "Allison Rice") who contributed ten stories to the pulp magazine *Unknown* between 1940 and 1943, died after a brief illness on March 2nd, aged 89. Her best-known tales include "The Crest of the Wave", "The Idol of the Flies" and the much-anthologized "The Refugee". She later contributed to slick magazines like *Charm*, *Collier's* and other women's periodicals, eventually returning to the genre with a number of stories in *The Magazine of Fantasy & Science Fiction* and *Alfred Hitchcock's Mystery Magazine*. *The Sixth Dog* was a chapbook collection published by Necronomicon Press in 1996 (from which the title story was reprinted in *Best New Horror Volume Seven*), and in 2003 Midnight House published *The Idol of the Flies*, a retrospective collection of all her macabre tales.

Australian-born composer and Master of the Queen's Music since 1975, **Malcolm Williamson** died the same day after a long illness. He was 71. Williamson composed the music for Hammer's *Brides of Dracula*, *Crescendo* and *The Horror of Frankenstein*, as well as *Nothing But the Night*, *Watership Down*, *The Masks of Death* and the Tyburn TV documentary *Peter Cushing: One-Way Ticket to Hollywood*.

British-born children's author **Monica Hughes** (Monica Ince) died of a stroke in Canada on March 7th, aged 77. The winner of a number of literary awards, her novels include the Phoenix Award-winning "Isis" trilogy: *The Keeper of the Isis Light*, *The Guardian of Isis* and *The Isis Pedlar* (1980–82). Amongst her other books are *Devil on My Back* and its sequel *The Dream Catcher*. In 1998 she edited *What If?*, an anthology of SF and fantasy stories by Canadian authors.

Blacklisted American novelist **Howard** [Melvin] **Fast** (a.k.a. "E.V. Cunningham"), died on March 12th, aged 88. His more than eighty books include the self-published *Spartacus* (1951), which was the source for Stanley Kubrick's film and the recent TV remake. Fast's first story appeared in a 1932 edition of *Amazing* when he was seventeen, and many of his SF and fantasy tales were published in *The Magazine of Fantasy & Science Fiction* and were collected in *The Edge of Tomorrow*, *The General Zapped an Angel* and *A Touch of Infinity*. When he refused to name names before the House of Un-American Activities Committee, he was imprisoned for three months in 1950 on charges of contempt.

British TV scriptwriter **Lewis Greifer** died of complications from a stroke on March 18th, aged 87. His numerous credits include the six-part SF series *The Voodoo Factor* (1959) and episodes of *The Prisoner* and *Doctor Who*.

Prolific screenwriter and producer **Philip Yordan** died of pancreatic cancer on March 24th, aged 88. Best known as a producer of Westerns and action films in the 1950s and 1960s, he is credited for scripting more than sixty movies, including the Oscar-nominated *Dillinger* (1945), *Conquest of Space*, *King of*

Kings (with Christ's final monologue and Orson Welles's narration written by an uncredited Ray Bradbury), *The Fiend That Walked West*, *The Day of the Triffids* (with Bernard Gordon), *Night Train to Terror* (a.k.a. *Cataclysm* and *Death Wish Club*) and *The Unholy*. He also produced *Crack in the World*. Yordan defied the Hollywood blacklist by hiring banned writers and sometimes controversially fronting for them himself. As a result, in 1996 a panel of the Writers Guild of America reduced or cut his credit from eighty-two films.

Pulitzer Prize-winning playwright and screenwriter **Paul Zindel** died of lung cancer on March 27th, aged 66. During the 1980s he scripted the TV movies *Alice in Wonderland*, *Babes in Toyland* and *A Connecticut Yankee in King Arthur's Court*. More recently, he wrote a number of young-adult horror novels, including *Loch*, *The Doom Stone*, *Reef of Death*, *Raptor*, *Rats*, *Bats* and *Night of the Bat*.

American TV writer **Rudolph Borchert** died on March 29th, aged 75. In 1974 he worked with David Chase as a story editor on the ABC-TV series *Kolchak: The Night Stalker*.

Prolific British author **Anthony Masters**, author of the non-fiction book *The Natural History of the Vampire* (1972) and editor of the horror anthology *Cries of Terror* (1976), died on April 4th, aged 62. He wrote a number of books in the young-adult "Weird World", "Dark Diary" and "Ghosthunters" series. As "Richard Tate", he wrote the Dracula-themed mystery paperback *The Dead Travel Fast* (1972).

Cecile de Brunhoff, who created the character later developed by her husband Jean (who died in 1937) as Babar the Elephant, died in France of complications following a stroke on April 5th, aged 99.

Academic editor **Willis E.** (Everett) **McNelly**, who compiled the Hugo-nominated *The Dune Encyclopedia* (1984), died of cancer on April 7th, aged 82. McNelly also edited the anthologies *Mars, We Love You* (with Jane Hipolito), *Above the Human Landscape: A Social Science Fiction Anthology* (with Leon Stover) and *Science Fiction Novellas* (with Harry Harrison).

Blacklisted Hollywood screenwriter **Maurice Rapf**, the son of Metro-Goldwyn-Mayer co-founder Harry Rapf, died on April 15th, aged 89. He was a member of the American Communist party when he co-scripted Walt Disney's *Song of the South*

(1946), and he later worked uncredited on the studio's *Cinderella* (1950). A co-founder of the Screen Writers' Guild, Rapf was excused from testifying before the House of Un-American Activities Committee because he had mumps.

French SF editor and translator **Jacques Chambon** died of a heart attack on April 16th, aged 60. An editor for twelve years at Editions Denoël (where he created the "Presence du Fantastique" horror line), and since 1998 at Editions Flammarion, he also wrote criticism for *Fiction*, the French edition of *The Magazine of Fantasy & Science Fiction*.

Felice Bryant (Matilda Genevieve Scaduto), who co-wrote the Everly Brothers' songs "Wake Up, Little Susie" and "Bye Bye Love", died of cancer the same day, aged 77. With her husband Boudleaux Bryant (who died in 1987) she wrote the words to an estimated 800 songs while he wrote the music. The couple were inducted into the Country Music Hall of Fame in 1991.

Comics publisher **Helen Honig Meyer**, one of the first women to head a major publishing company, died on April 21st, aged 95. She joined Dell Publishing when she was sixteen years old and in 1940 acquired the Disney, Warner Bros. and Walter Lantz cartoon characters for Western/Dell comics (later Gold Key), adding Hanna-Barbera in the 1950s. The line also included titles featuring Flash Gordon, Tarzan, Buck Rogers and John Carter of Mars. Meyer left the company as chief executive in 1976 when it was sold to Doubleday & Co.

Film and TV composer **Johnny Douglas** died of pancreatic cancer on April 23rd, aged 82. His credits include *The Day of the Triffids* (1963), *Crack in the World*, *Circus of Fear* and the animated TV adventures of *The Incredible Hulk* and *The Amazing Spider-Man*.

Film publicist **Robert Suhosky** died of pancreatic cancer on April 24th, aged 74. He scripted the 1982 film *The House Where Evil Dwells*.

The first person to win an Oscar, Emmy and Tony Award, American screenwriter and playwright **Peter Stone** died of pulmonary fibrosis on April 26th, aged 73. His film scripts include the glossy thrillers *Charade*, *Mirage* and *Arabesque*. He co-wrote *The Truth About Charlie* (2002) under the pseudonym "Peter Joshua", the name of Cary Grant's character in the film of which it was a remake, *Charade*. At the time of his death, Stone was working with Maury Yeston on a stage musical of *Death Takes a Holiday*.

Elaine Anderson Steinbeck, the widow of Nobel Prize-winning author John Steinbeck (who died in 1968), died after a long illness in New York City on April 27th, aged 88. She was one of the first women to work as a Broadway stage manager in the 1940s, and her first husband was Hollywood actor Zachary Scott.

Composer and arranger **George Wyle** (Bernard Weissman), who wrote more than 400 songs, died of leukaemia on May 2nd, aged 87. He is best remembered for Andy Williams's Christmas song "The Most Wonderful Time of the Year" and the catchy theme for the CBS-TV series *Gilligan's Island* (1964–67).

Disney screenwriter **Lowell S. Hawley**, whose credits include *The Swiss Family Robinson*, *The Sign of Zorro*, *Babes in Toyland* (1961) and *In Search of the Castaways*, died on May 6th, aged 94. He was also story editor on the *Zorro* TV series and wrote many of the episodes.

Old-time American SF fan, collector and 1966 Worldcon Chairman **Ben Jason** (Benedict P. Jablonski), who created the Hugo Award in its current form, died on May 15th, aged 86.

Best-known for his Vietnam novel (and 1988 film script) *Bat*21*, author **William C.** (Charles) **Anderson** died of heart failure on May 16th, aged 83. His more than twenty books include the SF novels *Penelope*, *Adam M-1*, *Pandemonium on the Potomac* and *Penelope: The Damp Detective*.

British fan artist **Dave Mooring** died of pancreatic cancer on May 21st, aged 42. A four-time winner of the Nova Award for fanzine art (1989–93), he married his fiancée of twenty years the morning he died.

78-year-old American fan [Le]**Roy Tackett**, affectionately known as "HORT – Horrible Old Roy Tackett", died of heart failure on May 23rd following a series of strokes and heart attacks. He produced more than 100 issues of his fanzine *Dynatron* since 1960, and was the Trans-Atlantic Fan Fund delegate to the 1976 British Eastercon.

George O'Nale and **Jan** [Landau] **O'Nale**, publishers of quality small-press fantasy and SF imprint Cheap Street Press, committed double suicide from asphyxiation on May 27th by pumping helium into plastic bags they put over their heads. Both were aged 56 and claimed to acquaintances that their health was failing. Cheap Street was launched at the 1980 World Fantasy Convention in Baltimore and published such authors as Ursula K. Le Guin, Charles de Lint, Fritz Leiber, Gene Wolfe, Thomas M. Disch and Howard Waldrop.

81-year-old comics artist **Al Hartley** died the same day after undergoing open-heart surgery earlier in the month. Best known for his work on *Archie* comics (1966–93), he also contributed to Marvel's comics from the 1940s.

American scriptwriter **Ernie Wallengren**, whose credits include episodes of TV's *Touched by an Angel* and *Knight Rider*, died of Lou Gehrig's disease on May 27th, aged 51.

Comedy writer **Henry Garson**, who scripted such films as the Jerry Lewis vehicle *Visit to a Small Planet* (1960) and *G.I. Blues* for Elvis, died on May 29th, aged 91.

American author and radio journalist **Ken[neth] Grimwood** died of a heart attack on June 6th, aged 59. Grimwood's cult time-travel novel *Replay* won the World Fantasy Award in 1988, and his other books include *Breakthrough*, *Elise* and *Into the Deep*. He was working on a sequel to *Replay* at the time of his death.

British poet and novelist **Peter Redgrove** died on June 16th, aged 71. His magical novels include *The Sleep of the Great Hypnotist*, *The Beekeepers* and its sequel *The Facilitators*. The stories in Redgrove's 1980 collection *The One Who Set Out to Study Fear* were based on the original tales by the Brothers Grimm.

American-born Hawaiian ghost-story writer and historian **Glen Grant** died after a year-long battle with cancer on June 19th, aged 56. Published over thirty years, his collections of *obake*, or ghost, stories included *Obake: Ghost Stories in Hawaii*, *McDougal's Honolulu Mysteries: Case Studies in the Life of a Honolulu Detective* and the "Chicken Skin" (i.e. "goose-bumps") series of supernatural tales. In 1995, Grant was honoured by the Honolulu City Council as one of Hawaii's Treasures of Multi-culturalism.

American TV writer **Michael Morris** died of Alzheimer's disease on June 20th, aged 84. He wrote for such series as *Bewitched*, *It's About Time* and *Nanny and the Professor*.

American stage- and screenwriter **George Axelrod**, whose movies include *The Manchurian Candidate*, *Paris – When it*

Sizzles and *Lord Love a Duck* (which he also directed), died on June 21st, aged 81. His daughter is actress Nina Axelrod.

Veteran American SF fan "**Russ**" (Louis Russell) **Chauvenet** died on June 24th, aged 83. In the 1940s he published *Detours* and *Sardonyx*, and he is credited in the *Oxford English Dictionary* for coining the words "fanzine" and "prozine" in October 1940. Deaf since the age of ten, he was Fan Guest of Honour at the 1989 Boston Worldcon.

Oscar-nominated screenwriter **David Newman**, whose film credits include the first three *Superman* films (1978–83), *Sheena* (1984), *Santa Claus* (1985) and Michael Jackson's *Moonwalker*, died of a stroke on June 27th, aged 66. With fellow *Esquire* editor and regular collaborator Robert Benton, Newman wrote the short-lived Broadway musical *It's a Bird, It's a Plane, It's a Superman*.

Screenwriter and mystery novelist **George** [Leonard] **Baxt** died on June 28th in New York from complications following heart surgery. He was 80. The cult movies he scripted include *Circus of Horrors*, *The Shadow of the Cat*, *City of the Dead* (a.k.a. *Horror Hotel*), *Strangler's Web* and *Night of the Eagle* (a.k.a. *Burn, Witch, Burn!*). Baxt was reputedly paid £1,000 just for coming up with the title for Hammer's *Vampire Circus*, and he also wrote the original story for *Tower of Evil* (a.k.a. *Horror on Snape Island*). Baxt's debut novel *A Queer Kind of Death* (1966) introduced black and openly gay investigator Pharoah Love as the lead character. It was followed by the sequels *Swing Low, Sweet Harriet* and *Topsy and Evil*. His other novels include *The Alfred Hitchcock Murder Case* and *The Fred Astaire and Ginger Rogers Murder Case*.

American young-adult writer **Joan Lowery Nixon**, winner of four Edgar Allan Poe Awards, died on July 5th, aged 76. Her more than 100 books include *The Gift*, *The Ghosts of Now*, *Haunted Island*, *Whispers from the Dead* and *The Haunting*.

Non-fiction writer, editor and antiquarian book and pulp collector **Sheldon R.** (Ronald) **Jaffery** died of a stroke related to complications from lung cancer at midnight on July 10th. He was 69. A former workers' compensation lawyer, his books include *Horrors and Unpleasantries: A Bibliographical History & Collector's Price Guide to Arkham House* (updated as *The Arkham House Companion*), *The Collector's Index to Weird*

Tales (with Fred Cook), *Future and Fantastic Worlds: A Bibliographical Retrospective of DAW Books* and *Double Trouble: A Bibliographic Chronicle of Ace Mystery Doubles*. Jaffery also edited *Sensuous Science Fiction from the Weird and Spicy Pulps*, *Selected Tales of Grim and Grue from the Horror Pulps*, *The Weirds: A Facsimile Selection of Fiction from the Era of the Shudder Pulps*, *House of Three Horrors and Other Spicy Tales*, *To the Stars and Beyond*, *Monsters of Voodoo Island and Other Strange Tales of the Jungle* and the 1988 Hugh B. Cave collection *The Corpse Maker*.

The same day saw the death of 93-year-old **Winston Graham**, best-selling author of the *Poldark* historical series. Several of his short horror stories were reprinted in Denys Val Baker's anthologies from William Kimber. His *Marnie* (1961) was filmed by Alfred Hitchcock.

Comedy scriptwriter **Eliot Wald**, who paired movie critics Gene Siskel and Roger Ebert for Chicago PBS affiliate WTTW in 1975, died of liver cancer in Los Angeles on July 12th, aged 57.

Controversial and opinionated film critic **Alexander Walker**, whose reviews appeared in London's *Evening Standard* newspaper for forty-three years, died at a clinic while undergoing tests for cancer on July 15th, aged 73. He was the author of more than twenty books, mostly biographies of Hollywood's leading ladies. Despite seeing James Whale's *Frankenstein* when he was only seven, he rarely had anything positive to say about genre cinema.

Gordon Creighton, British diplomat, civil servant and editor of *Flying Saucer Review* since 1982, died on July 16th, aged 95. He claimed to have seen his first UFO in 1941.

Comics writer **Bill** (William) **Woolfork** died of congestive heart failure on July 20th, aged 86. During the 1940s he scripted *Superman* and *Batman* for DC and created the character of Plastic Man. He also claimed to have coined Captain Marvel's ejaculation "Holey Moley!" He later became a novelist and TV scriptwriter.

Comics illustrator and art editor **Warren Kremer**, who helped create *Hot Stuff* and *Richie Rich* with publisher Alfred Harvey and editor Sid Jacobson for New York's Harvey Comics in the 1950s, died on July 24th, aged 82. Originally a pulp magazine illustrator, Kremer also developed *Casper the Friendly Ghost*, as well as producing some of the most gratuitous covers and stories for Harvey's pre-Code horror comics *Black Cat* and *Tomb of Terror*. In 1982 he moved to Marvel's new children's imprint, Star Comics, where he adapted *Star Wars' Ewoks* and Hanna-Barbera's *The Flintstone Kids*. Kremer's final comic title was based on Cosgrove Hall's *Count Duckula* before a stroke ended his drawing career.

70-year-old Italian erotic cartoonist **Guido Crepax**, whose sado-masochistic strip *Valentina* (1965–95) was the basis for the 1973 movie *Baba Yaga* and a 1988 television adaptation, died of multiple sclerosis on July 31st.

New Zealand-born artist **Mike Hinge**, who lived in America from the late 1950s and worked for such publications as *Amazing Stories*, *Fantastic*, *Analog*, *Algol*, *Heavy Metal* and *Time* magazine, died in his Pennsylvania apartment on or around August 7th, aged 72. The Hugo-nominated Hinge did design work for *2001: A Space Odyssey* and a selection of his work appeared in the 1973 volume *The Mike Hinge Experience*.

Film journalist and TV commercials director **Bill Kelley** died in Florida of apparent heart failure on August 11th, aged 54. He suffered from a number of serious medical problems for many years. Kelley worked for such magazines as *American Film*, *Cinefantastique* and *Video Watchdog*, and contributed the nationally syndicated "Primal Screen" column to the *New York Times* group. As well as making public service TV commercials in Miami, he was a story-writer for DC Comics (*House of Mystery*, *Tales of the Unexpected*, etc.) and Warren Publications (*Creepy*, *Eerie*), and was associate producer on the 1994 documentary *Flesh and Blood: The Hammer Heritage of Horror*.

James Hale, the British editor and literary agent who "discovered" Iain Banks's *The Wasp Factory* (1984) on the Macmillan slush pile, died of pancreatic cancer on August 14th, aged 57. In the late 1970s he edited the final volumes of the long-running *Ghost Book* anthology series (*The Thirteenth Ghost Book*, *The Midnight Ghost Book* and *The After Midnight Ghost Book*) as well as *The Twilight Book* (1981).

American psychoanalyst (Dr) **Ernest H.** (Henry) **Taves** (a.k.a. "Ernest Keith Taves"), who co-authored *The UFO Enigma* (1977) with Dr Donald H. Menzel, died on August 16th, aged 87. His SF stories were published in *Galaxy* and *If* between 1969 and 1976.

Horror author and children's writer **Gene-Michael Higney** died in mid-August. His story "Build a Wall Against the Night" appeared in *The Asylum 3: The Quiet Ward*.

41-year-old special-effects artist and animator **Kevin Oakley** drowned at sea while attempting to rescue his son from a stream in Hawaii on August 18th. His credits include *The Swan Princess*, *Space Jam*, *The Mighty Kong*, *Quest for Camelot*, *The Iron Giant*, *Mission to Mars*, *Osmosis Jones*, and *Sinbad: Legend of the Seven Seas*.

Literary agent **Marilyn E. Marlow**, who became executive VP at Curtis Brown, died of cancer on August 25th, aged 75. Her clients included Jane Yolen and Robert Cormier.

Russian SF author and screenwriter **Kir Bulychev** (Igor Vsevolodovisch Mojeiko) died of complications from hypertension and diabetes on September 5th, aged 69. His best-known works are the young-adult books about Alice Selezneva, a little girl from the future, collected in English as *Alice: The Girl From Earth*. Bulychev's other books include the collections *Half a Life*, *Gusliar Wonders* and *Earth and Elsewhere*. Among the writer's film credits are *The Secret of the Third Planet*, *Humanoid Woman* and *The Witches' Cave*.

Novelist and film publicist **Marc Olden**, author of the novel *Poe Must Die*, died of peritonitis the same day, aged 69.

Animation writer/artist **Jay Morton**, who started working at the Fleischer Studios in Miami in 1937, died in North Carolina of a brain aneurysm on September 6th, aged 92. A former *Our Gang* child actor (he played "Stinky"), Morton worked on such cartoon series as *Felix the Cat*, *Betty Boop* and *Popeye*. He also scripted around twenty-five *Superman* cartoon shorts in the early 1940s. As part of that job he is credited with creating the memorable narration: "Faster than a speeding bullet, more powerful than a locomotive, able to leap tall buildings in a single bound." After leaving Fleischer, Morton became a newspaper publisher and inventor, and co-created two board games with his wife.

Hungarian-born animator **Jules Engel** died after a short illness the same day, aged around 94. He contributed to the Chinese and Russian dance sequences of Walt Disney's *Fantasia* and worked on *Bambi*. Following the Second World War he became a founding member of UPA (United Productions of America) where, with Robert "Bobe" Cannon, he developed such characters as Mr Magoo and Gerald McBoing-Boing. He made the Oscar-nominated short *Icarus Montgolfier Wright* (1963), based on a story by Ray Bradbury, produced an animated TV series of *The Lone Ranger* (1966–67) and was the production designer on the 1971 animated feature *Shinbone Alley*.

Film and TV writer **Jameson Brewer**, who worked on *Fantasia* in the story department, died on September 11th, aged 87. His career spanned more than five decades, encompassing radio, commercials, theatre, sitcoms and such TV shows as *The Alfred Hitchcock Hour, Mod Squad* and *The Addams Family*. In the late 1970s and 1980s, he adapted Japanese *anime* series such as *Voltron* and *Battle of the Planets* for American TV viewers. His feature credits include *The Incredible Mr Limpet, Terror in the Wax Museum, Arnold* and *Alice Through the Looking Glass* (1991).

Polish-born Surrealist painter **Joseph Natanson** died in Rome on September 15th, aged 94. From the late 1940s he worked as a designer and special-effects artist in films, including *The Red Shoes, Colossus and the Amazon Queen* and *Spirits of the Dead*.

Seventy-six-year-old American author **George Plympton** died in his sleep on September 25th. Co-founder of the *The Paris Review* literary journal in 1953, he appeared in a number of films, documentaries and TV shows, including voicing a cartoon version of himself on an episode of *The Simpsons*.

Henry Hardy Heins, author of *A Golden Anniversary Bibliography of Edgar Rice Burroughs* (1964), died on October 1st, aged 79.

Disney animator **Dale Oliver** died of an aneurysm on October 2nd, aged 84. He worked on *Sleeping Beauty, Peter Pan, One Hundred & One Dalmatians, Winnie the Pooh, The Rescuers Down Under, Robin Hood* and *The Fox and the Hound*.

American cartoonist and children's novelist **William Steig**, best known for his 1990 picture book *Shrek!* (filmed in 2001), died in Boston on October 3rd, aged 95. Over a career that spanned seven decades, he produced more than 1,600 drawings and 117 covers for *The New Yorker*. Steig began writing children's books when he was 60, and his more than thirty titles include the Caldecott Medal-winning *Sylvester and the Magic Pebble, Roland the Minstrel Pig, Amos and Boris, The Amazing Bone, Caleb and Kate* and *When Everybody Wore a Hat*.

British children's writer **Vivien Alcock** died on October 11th, aged 79. She married author Leon Garfield in 1948, but her own literary career didn't begin until more than thirty years later. Alcock's novels include *The Haunting of Cassie Palmer*, *The Stonewalkers*, *Travellers by Night*, *The Thing in the Woods*, *The Red-Eared Ghosts* and *The Boy Who Swallowed a Ghost*. *Ghostly Companions* is a collection of her supernatural stories.

American scriptwriter and former actor **Mark Hanna**, whose credits include the cult classics *Not of This Earth* and *Attack of the 50-Foot Woman*, died of complications from a stroke on October 16th, aged 86. His other writing credits include *The Undead*, *The Amazing Colossal Man* and episodes of the Boris Karloff TV series *Thriller*.

Leonard Shannon, former Disney film publicist and author of the 1993 history *Disneyland: Dreams, Traditions and Transitions*, died of heart failure the same day, aged 88.

Sixty-two-year-old **Patricia Mullen**, who contributed a number of stories to Marvin Kaye's anthologies and wrote the fantasy novel *The Stone Movers* (1995), also died on October 16th after falling from her nineteenth-floor apartment in Greenwich Village. Mullen had been diagnosed with terminal cancer and her partner had been recently killed in a car accident.

Polish-born film and theatrical producer **Jack Temchin** died of a heart attack in New York City on October 26th, aged 57. He produced Brian DePalma's 1979 film *Home Movies* and scripted for such TV series as *Tales from the Crypt* and *Freddy's Nightmares*.

Catalan writer and lawyer **Joan Perucho**, who was awarded Spain's National Literature Prize in 2002 for his life's work, died in Barcelona on October 28th, aged 82. His 1960 Gothic novel *Les Histoires Naturals* (*Natural History*) was about a nineteenth-century vampire.

American "hard" science fiction writer **Hal Clement** (Harry Clement Stubbs, a.k.a. "George Richard") died in his sleep on October 29th, aged 81. A former high-school teacher, his first story "Proof" appeared in *Astounding* in 1942, and his books include *Mission of Gravity* (1954), *Iceworld*, *The Nitrogen Fix*, *Half Life* and *Noise* (2003). Clement won a 1996 Retro Hugo for his 1945 story "Uncommon Sense", he was both Fan and Professional Guest of Honour respectively at the 1989 and

1991 World Science Fiction Conventions, and the SFWA chose him as its Grand Master in 1999.

American writer, publisher and fan **Lloyd Arthur Eshbach** died the same day, aged 93. After publishing fiction in *Weird Tales*, *Strange Stories*, *Amazing*, *Wonder Stories* and other pulps in the 1930s and early 1940s Eshbach founded the influential Fantasy Press imprint in 1946, publishing forty-four books over the next decade. He edited the first contemporary study of SF: *Of Worlds Beyond: The Science of Science Fiction Writing* (1947), while several later novels include the four-book "Gates of Lucifer" sequence, beginning with *The Land Beyond the Gate* (1984). Eshbach's 1983 memoir, *Over My Shoulder: Reflections on a Science Fiction Era*, looked at the history of small-press publishing from the 1930s to the 1950s. He was Guest of Honour at the 1949 World Science Fiction Convention and the 1995 World Fantasy Convention.

British journalist and biographer **Derek Hudson** died on Hallowe'en, aged 92. His subjects include Arthur Rackham, Sir Joshua Reynolds, Lewis Carroll and Charles Keene.

American TV writer **Margaret Armen**, who scripted several episodes of both the original *Star Trek* series ("The Cloud Minders", "The Gamesters of Triskelion" and "The Paradise Syndrome") and the animated show, died of a heart attack on November 10th, aged 82. One of the first women to write for television in the late 1950s, she also scripted episodes of *Land of the Lost*, *Fantasy Island*, *The Six Million Dollar Man*, *The Bionic Woman* and *Wonder Woman*.

American writer **Mark Siegel** died on November 12th, aged 54. He published critical studies on James Tiptree Jr. and Hugo Gernsback, and his first novel, *Echo and Narcissus*, appeared in 2003.

Sixty-three-year-old Scottish author and literary agent **Giles [Alexander Esmé] Gordon** died in Edinburgh on November 14th, after falling down the front stairs at his home on Hallowe'en night and suffering head injuries. The author of six novels, he contributed a number of stories to various editions of *The Ghost Book* series and published stories in *New Worlds* from 1967 to 1975. Gordon also edited the anthologies *Prevailing Spirits* (a.k.a. *Scottish Ghost Stories*), *A Book of Contemporary Nightmares* and *Selected Ghost Stories*.

Oscar-nominated American composer and conductor **Michael Kamen** died of a heart attack in London on November 18th, aged 55. He had been diagnosed with multiple sclerosis in 1996. The eclectic Kamen's credits include all four *Lethal Weapon* films, the three *Die Hard* movies, plus *S*H*E*, *Venom*, *The Dead Zone*, the Grammy-winning *Robin Hood Prince of Thieves* (including the #1 hit "[Everything I Do] I Do It for You"), *Brazil*, *Highlander*, *The Adventures of Baron Munchausen*, *Last Action Hero*, *101 Dalmatians*, *Event Horizon*, *What Dreams May Come*, *The Iron Giant*, *Frequency*, *X-Men*, the James Bond film *Licence to Kill*, and such TV series as *Edge of Darkness*, *Amazing Stories* and *Tales From the Crypt*.

David J. Stern, author of the 1940s *Francis the Talking Mule* books, which were filmed by Universal in the 1950s, died on November 22nd, aged 94. He also wrote the scripts for *Swamp Women* and *Francis Goes to the Races*.

Margaret Winch, who co-edited the Australian SF anthologies *Alien Shores* and *Forever Shores* with Peter McNamara, died the same day. She had been diagnosed with advanced cancer just six weeks earlier.

Australian-born TV scriptwriter and novelist **Bill** (William) **Strutton** died of a heart attack in Catalonia on November 23rd, aged 80. In 1965 he created the giant ant-like Zarbi for the *Doctor Who* episode "The Web Planet" and he novelized his story the same year in *Doctor Who and the Zarbi*. Strutton also wrote for such early British TV series as *The Avengers*, *The Saint* and *Strange Report*. He retired in the mid-1970s.

Marguerite "Maggie" Bradbury (Marguerite Susan McClure) who was married to Ray Bradbury since 1947, died in Los Angeles on November 24th, aged 81. She typed the manuscript for *The Martian Chronicles*, which is dedicated to her.

American film composer **Michael Small** died of prostate cancer on November 25th, aged 64. His more than fifty film credits include *Child's Play*, *The Parallax View*, *The Stepford Wives*, *Audrey Rose*, *Rollover*, *Dream Lover*, *Jaws: The Revenge* and the 1980 TV movie of *The Lathe of Heaven*.

French dental surgeon **Pierre Pairault**, who published science fiction under the name "Stefan Wul", died of cardiac arrest while undergoing treatment for throat cancer on November 26th, aged 81. His 1957 book *Oms en Serie* was filmed as the animated

Fantastic Planet (*La Planète Sauvage*) in 1973, and the 1958 *L'Orphelina de Perdide* inspired *Les Maitres du Temps* in 1982, both directed by Rene Laloux. *Le Temple du Passé* (1957) was his only novel translated into English (in 1973, as *The Temple of the Past*), and his final book, *Noo*, appeared in 1977.

American film and TV scriptwriter **Edmund L. Hartmann** died on November 28th, aged 92. Although best known for his zany comedies featuring Bob Hope, Dean Martin and Jerry Lewis, and the Three Stooges, he also worked (sometimes uncredited) on the scripts for *Black Friday* (with Karloff and Lugosi), *Sherlock Holmes and the Secret Weapon*, *Ali Baba and the Forty Thieves*, *The Scarlet Claw*, *Ghost Catchers* (which he also produced), *The Face of Marble* (with John Carradine), *Here Come the Girls* and *The Sword of Ali Baba*. *Bound and Gagged in Hollywood* was a recent biography of Hartmann by Donald McCaffrey.

British author **Mollie Hardwick** (Mary Greenhalgh) died on December 13th, aged 88. With her husband Michael (who died in 1991), she collaborated on books about Charles Dickens, Conan Doyle and Sherlock Holmes (including the novelization of Billy Wilder's *The Private Life of Sherlock Holmes*).

American linguist and speculative "non-fiction" author **Charles Berlitz** died on December 16th, aged 90. His bestsellers include *The Bermuda Triangle* and *The Philadelphia Experiment* (with William I. Moore), both of which were filmed.

Sixty-nine-year-old former BBC scriptwriter **Ted Rhodes**, whose credits include *Doctor Who*, died on the same date, two days after being attacked by a cyclist in a London street.

Pierre Charles, editor of the long-running French fanzine *Cine-Zine-Zone*, died on Christmas Day, aged 52.

British comics artist **Don Lawrence** died of pneumonia and emphysema on December 29th, aged 75. He illustrated such strips as the *Marvelman*, *Thunderbirds Are Go!* and Mike Butterworth's superb *The Trigon Empire* (1965–82). His second major series, *Storm*, achieved huge sales in the Netherlands, earning him a Dutch knighthood.

American novelist, journalist and screenwriter **John Gregory Dunne** died of a heart attack on December 30th, aged 71. *Dharma Blue*, his UFO script for Jerry Bruckheimer and Don Simpson, remains unfilmed. Dunne's books *The Studio* (1969) and *Monster: Living Off the Big Screen* (1997) are critical insights into the Hollywood studio system and should be required reading for anyone interested in making movies.

PERFORMERS

Thirty-year-old adult-film actress **Holly Landers** (Veronica Browning) was killed in an automobile accident on January 1st while celebrating New Year's Eve in Costa Rica. She made around thirty hardcore films, including *The Blowjob Adventures of Dr Fellatio*, *Fountain of Youth*, *Extreme Teen 2*, *75 Nurse Orgy* and *Busty Pom-Pom Girls*.

British character actor **Cyril Shaps**, best known as the voice of the "Mr Kipling" TV commercials, died after a short illness the same day, aged 79. He made his acting debut in the 1955 BBC-TV production of *Quatermass II* and appeared in more than eighty films, including Hammer's *Terror of the Tongs* and *Rasputin The Mad Monk*, the James Bond film *The Spy Who Loved Me*, Disney's *Unidentified Flying Oddball* (a.k.a. *The Spaceman and King Arthur*), *Erik the Viking*, *Sherlock Holmes and the Leading Lady*, *Gulliver's Travels* (1996), *Simon Magus*, *Murder Rooms: The Kingdom of Bones* and *Jack and the Beanstalk: The Real Story*. Shaps was also the voice of Professor Rudolph Popkiss in the 1961 TV series *Supercar*.

Sixty-four-year-old American actor and stand-up comedian **Royce Applegate** was found dead in a Hollywood Hills mansion fire, also on January 1st. He portrayed Chief Manilow Crocker on the TV series *SeaQuest DSV*, and his film credits include *The Mad Bomber*, *Brenda Starr*, *Alligator*, Disney's *Splash* and the remake of *Doctor Doolittle*.

Italian leading man **Massimo Girotti** died of cardiac arrest on January 5th, aged 84. His career spanned eight decades, and included the 1939 fairy tale *La Carona Di Ferro*, *The Giants of Thessaly*, *The Witches* (1966), *Baron Blood*, *Cagliostro*, *Mr Klein* and Roberto Benigni's serial-killer comedy *Il Monstro* (1994).

Billy Van, who portrayed vampiric mad scientist Count Frightenstein (and six other roles) in the Candian TV series *The Hilarious House of Frightenstein* (1970–72), hosted by Vincent Price, died of cancer on January 8th, aged 69.

The Sheik (Edward Farhat), who wrestled professionally in

Detroit from 1952 until 1998, died of a heart attack the same day, aged 78.

American actor **Richard "Dick" Simmons**, who starred in the CBS-TV series *Sergeant Preston of the Yukon* (1955–58), died after a long illness at a California rest home on January 11th, aged 89. His film credits include *Angels in the Outfield* (1951), Alfred Hitchcock's *Rear Window*, *Brigadoon* and *The Resurrection of Zachary Wheeler*.

Fifty-five-year-old **Mickey Finn**, bongo player with the 1970s glam-rock group T. Rex, died of kidney and liver failure the same day. Although T.Rex sold thirty-nine million albums, Finn died penniless after years of alcohol and heroin addiction. Three other members of the band died in tragic accidents between 1979–81.

Dependable Hollywood leading man **Richard Crenna** died of pancreatic cancer on January 17th, aged 76. His various film and TV credits include *It Grows on Trees*, *Wait Until Dark*, *Marooned*, *Devil Dog The Hound of Hell*, *A Fire in the Sky*, *The Evil*, *Death Ship*, *Doubletake* (and six sequels as NYC Det. Lt. Frank Janek), *Leviathan*, *Intruders*, *20,000 Leagues Under the Sea* (1996) and all three *Rambo* movies as Colonel Sam Trautman.

Actress **Mary Todd Andrews**, the widow of Dana Andrews (who died in 1992), died of complications from Alzheimer's disease the same day, aged 86. During the 1970s she toured with her husband in a stage production of *Gaslight*.

Character actress **Nedra Volz** died of complications from Alzheimer's disease on January 20th, aged 94. Best known as a regular on such TV series as *Diff'rent Strokes* and *The Dukes of Hazzard*, her film credits include *Earth Girls Are Easy*, *Mortuary Academy* and *The Silence of the Hams*.

British comedy actor **David Battley** died of a heart attack the same day, aged 67. Best known for his role as Mr Turkentine in *Willy Wonka & the Chocolate Factory* (1971), his other film credits include *Krull* and the 1966 TV version of *Alice in Wonderland*.

Radio pioneer and NBC announcer **Don Stanley** died of complications from cancer, also on January 20th, aged 85. He could be heard on numerous radio shows, including *The Saint* and *Nero Wolfe*.

American character actor **Cliff Norton**, who played The Boss in the 1966 prehistoric comedy series *It's About Time*, died of lung cancer on January 25th, aged 84. A prolific TV actor and voice artist (*The Jetsons*, etc.), his other credits include the films *It's a Mad Mad Mad Mad World*, *The Ghost and Mr Chicken*, *Munster Go Home!* and *The Phantom Tollbooth*.

Character actor **Robert Rockwell**, who portrayed the Man of Steel's father Jor-El on the first episode of *The Adventures of Superman* (1952) died of cancer the same day, aged 82. He also appeared (uncredited) in the 1953 version of *War of the Worlds*.

Italian actor and screenwriter **Leopoldo Trieste**, whose credits include Mario Bava's *Bay of Blood*, *Caligula*, *Don't Look Now*, *The Name of the Rose* and *Momo*, died of a heart attack, also on January 25th, aged 85.

Egyptian-born Hollywood actress **Jeanne Sorel**, the mother of actress Louise Sorel, died on January 27th, aged 89. Although she gave up her film career in the 1930s after marrying producer Albert J. Cohen, she made occasional appearances in such movies as *Prehistoric Women* (1950) and on TV in episodes of *Bewitched*, *The Monkees* and *Logan's Run*.

American leading man **Anthony Eisley** (Frederick Glendinning Eisley, a.k.a. "Fred Eisley"), best known for his co-starring role as Tracy Steele in the TV series *Hawaiian Eye* (1959–63), died of heart failure on January 29th, aged 78. His film roles include *The Wasp Woman*, *The Navy vs. the Night Monsters*, *Journey to the Center of Time*, *The Mighty Gorga*, *The Witchmaker*, Al Adamson's *Dracula vs. Frankenstein*, *Monster*, *The Mummy and the Curse of the Jackal*, *The Doll Squad*, *Deep Space*, *UFO Syndrome* and *Evil Spirits*. He later became a stunt driver.

American-born opera singer **Mary Ellis** (Mary Elsas), who inspired Ivor Novello to write three musicals for her, died in London on January 30th, aged 105. Married to British actor Basil Sydney during the 1930s, her film credits include the Ray Harryhausen production *The 3 Worlds of Gulliver* and in later years she appeared in two TV movies featuring Jeremy Brett as Sherlock Holmes. Her autobiography was published in 1982.

Forty-year-old topless actress **Lana Clarkson**, who starred in such Roger Corman direct-to-video productions as *Deathstalker*, *Barbarian Queen*, *Barbarian Queen II: The Empress Strikes Back*, *Wizard of the Lost Kingdom II* and *The Haunting of Morella*, was found shot to death on February 3rd in the foyer of the Los Angeles mansion owned by reclusive 62-year-old multi-millionaire music producer Phil Spector. The six-foot-tall Clarkson also appeared in the movie *Amazon Women on the Moon* and more than fifty TV shows, including *Knight Rider*, *Amazing Stories* and *Black Scorpion*. Spector, who had only met the actress hours earlier while she was working as a VIP hostess at a Hollywood blues club, was arrested on suspicion of first-degree murder and released on $1 million bail. He subsequently claimed that Clarkson had accidentally shot herself after putting the gun in her mouth.

Vera Hruba Ralston (Vera Helena Hruba), the Czechoslovakian ice-skating champion who became a star at Republic Pictures after marrying its studio chief, died of cancer on February 9th, aged 79. Born in Prague, she participated in the 1936 Berlin Olympics before she was spotted by head of Republic, Herbert J. Yates, who featured her in the musical *Ice Capades of 1940*. In 1943, she signed a long-term contract with Republic, where she became Yates's protégée and, in 1952, his wife. Her first non-skating role was in the horror film *The Lady and the Monster*, (1944, a.k.a. *The Lady and the Doctor/Tiger Man*), and co-star Helen Vinson recalled that "The only horror was Vera's inability to act." Even John Wayne refused to appear with her again after they had made two films together. She retired from the screen in 1958 when her husband, who was more than twice her age, was voted off the board of Republic. When he died in 1966 she inherited half his estimated $10 million estate.

Forty-four-year-old professional wrestler **Curt "Mr Perfect" Lennig** was found dead in a hotel room on February 10th.

American actor **Stacy Keach, Sr.**, the father of actor Stacy Keach, died of congestive heart failure on February 13th, aged 88. After starting his career as a dialogue director at Universal on such films as *Ali Baba and the 40 Thieves* and *The Scarlet Claw*, he went on to appear in *It Happened at Lakewood Manor*, *The Clone Master*, *Saturday the 14th* and *Road Games*. As a voice artist, Keach, Sr. worked on a number of TV cartoon series, including *Thundarr the Barbarian* and *Ultraman*.

Character actor **Peter Schrum** died of a heart attack on February 8th, aged 68. He appeared in *Trancers*, *Eliminators*, *Terminator 2: Judgment Day* (as the Dennis Etchison lookalike biker), *Galaxina*, *Flicks* and *Demonic Toys*.

Bassist **Howie Epstein**, who after twenty years was kicked out of Tom Petty & the Heartbreakers in 2002 following a drug conviction, died of a heroin overdose in Sante Fé on February 23rd, aged 47. His common-law wife was Carlene Carter, Johnny Cash's stepdaughter.

Alberto Sordi, the Italian voice of Oliver Hardy on screen, died of a heart attack on February 24th, aged 82. His body was displayed inside the Rome town hall. Sordi also appeared in such films as *The Flying Saucer*, *The Witches* (1966) and *Fellini's Roma*.

1940s Hollywood actress and dancer **Jean Sullivan**, who returned to the screen in *Squirm* (1976), died of cardiac arrest on February 27th, aged 79. She was married to actor Tom Poston from 1955 to 1968.

American children's TV host **Fred Rogers** died of stomach cancer the same day, aged 74. *Mister Rogers' Neighborhood*, which always included a magical trolley ride into the Neighborhood of Make-Believe, ran on PBS affiliates from 1968 to 2001 and continues in re-runs. Rogers also appeared in the movies *Casper* and *Honey I Blew Up the Kid*.

Character actor **Johnny Carpenter**, who appeared in numerous "B" Westerns, died of cancer on February 27th, aged 88. His film credits include *Dante's Inferno* (1935), Edward D. Wood's *Night of the Ghouls* and *Hellborn*.

American singer-songwriter **Hank Ballard** (John H. Kendricks), whose 1959 hit "The Twist" ushered in the 1960s dance craze (when covered by Chubby Checker), died of throat cancer on March 2nd. His age was given as anywhere between 66 and 76.

Once considered "the German James Dean", **Horst Buchholz** died of pneumonia in Berlin on March 3rd, aged 69. After breaking his thigh bone in a fall, he had been released from hospital in February but never completely recovered from his injuries. Best remembered for his role as Chico, one of *The Magnificent Seven*, his numerous film and TV roles also included *The Savage Bees*, *Dead of Night* (1976), *The Amazing Captain Nemo*, *Return to Fantasy Island* and voicing The Emperor in the German-language version of Disney's *Mulan*.

1960s British pop star turned actor and producer **Adam Faith** (Terence Nelhams), who made and lost a £32 million fortune during his career, died of a heart attack on March 8th, aged 62.

He was with his 22-year-old mistress in a hotel room at the time. Faith had sixteen Top Twenty hit records between 1959 and 1964, including the UK #1s, "What Do You Want (If You Don't Want Money)?" and "Poor Me". He starred in *What a Whopper* (1961) and had an uncredited cameo the same year in *What a Carve Up!* (a.k.a. *No Place Like Homicide*). He also toured on stage in Keith Waterhouse and Willis Hall's *Billy Liar*, and appeared with Dame Sybil Thorndyke in Emlyn Williams's play *Night Must Fall*. Faith published two autobiographies (in 1961 and 1996).

1930s Hollywood star **Karen Morley** (Mildred Linton), who appeared in Howard Hawks's *Scarface* and *The Mask of Fu Manchu* (both featuring Boris Karloff), died of pneumonia the same day, aged 93. She also appeared in *Phantom of Crestwood*, *Mata Hari*, *Arsene Lupin*, *Gabriel Over the White House*, *The Girl from Scotland Yard*, *The Unknown* (1946), *The 13th Hour* and the 1951 remake of *M*. In 1947, her refusal to answer questions before the House of Un-American Activities Committee resulted in her being cut from *Samson and Delilah* and ultimately ended her career. She was married to Hungarian-American director Charles Vidor and stage actor Lloyd Gough.

Tony Award-winning stage and screen actress **Lynne Thigpen** died of a heart attack on March 12th, aged 54. Her film credits include *Godspell*, *Streets of Fire*, *The Warriors*, *Hello Again*, *Blankman* and *Bicentennial Man*.

Italian leading man **Ivan Rassimov** (Ivan Djrassimovic, a.k.a. "Sean Todd") died following a brief illness on March 13th, aged 64. His films include Mario Bava's *Planet of the Vampires*, *The Witch in Love*, *Blade of the Ripper*, *Deep River Savages*, *They're Coming to Get You!*, *Spirits of Death*, *Spasmo*, *The Sexorcist*, *Ilsa, Harem Keeper of the Oil Sheikhs*, *Shock* (a.k.a. *Beyond the Door II*), *The Humanoid*, *Eaten Alive*, *The Atlantis Interceptors* and *Body Count*. He subsequently retired from acting and became a comics publisher.

Ninety-one-year-old British North Country character actress and comedienne Dame **Thora Hird** died on March 15th, a week after suffering a stroke. Best known for her TV work, she was discovered by George Formby and put under contract by Ealing Studios. Hird appeared in such films as *The Black Sheep of Whitehall* (with Will Hay), *Went the Day Well?*, *Corridor of*

Mirrors (with Christopher Lee), Hammer's *The Quatermass Experiment* (a.k.a. *The Creeping Unknown*) and *The Nightcomers* (the prequel to Henry James's *Turn of the Screw*, with Marlon Brando). The mother of actress Janette Scott, her autobiography *Scene and Hird* was published in 1976.

Canadian-born musician and actress **Marguerite Campbell**, who began her musical career as a child in The Hollywood Baby Orchestra and appeared in numerous films during the 1930s and 1940s, died of heart disease on March 19th, aged 75. She joined Kay Kyser's band in 1945, and her final two film credits were *My Science Project* and *The Golden Child* in the 1980s.

Japanese character actor **Eisei Amamoto** died of acute pneumonia on March 23rd, aged 77. His numerous credits include *Goarth*, *Attack of the Mushroom People*, *The Lost World of Sinbad* (as a female witch), *Atragon*, *Dagora The Space Monster*, *Ghidrah The Three-Headed Monster*, *Godzilla vs. The Sea Monster*, *King Kong Escapes* (as the villain, Dr Who), *Son of Godzilla*, *Godzilla's Revenge*, *Message from Space* and *Godzilla, Mothra and King Ghidorah: Giant Monsters All-Out Attack* (2001).

Former child actor **Dwight David Frye**, the son of classic horror film star Dwight Frye (who died in 1943), died in New York City on March 27th, aged 72. He appeared with his father in the 1936 film *The Man Who Found Himself*. A frequent guest at conventions, Frye collaborated with Greg Mank and Jim Coughlin on the 1997 biography *Dwight Frye's Last Laugh*.

Actor and stuntman **Richard Schuyler** died of renal cell carcinoma on March 29th, aged 76. He appeared in *The Human Duplicators* and *The Resurrection of Zachary Wheeler*, and doubled Ronald Reagan.

The body of HIV-positive character actor **Michael Jeter** was found at his Hollywood home on March 30th. He was 50. Jeter appeared in such films as *Zelig*, *The Fisher King*, *Waterworld*, *Mouse Hunt*, *The Green Mile*, *The Gift*, *Jurassic Park III* and *The Polar Express*. Since 2000 he was a regular on TV's *Sesame Street* as the bumbling Mr Noodle, and one of his final roles was in the last episode of Steven Spielberg's TV miniseries *Taken* (2002).

84-year-old **Anne Gwynne** (Marguerite Gwynne Trice) the blonde starlet of several 1940s Universal horror films, died of complications from a stroke following surgery on March 31st. Moving to Los Angeles from Waco, Texas, she became a Catalina swimsuit model before being put under contract by Universal without a screen test. She appeared in the serials *Flash Gordon Conquers the Universe* and *The Green Hornet*, and her other credits include *Black Friday* (with Karloff and Lugosi), *The Black Cat* (1941), *The Strange Case of Dr Rx*, *Weird Woman* (based on a story by Fritz Leiber), *Murder in the Blue Room*, *House of Frankenstein*, *The Ghost Goes Wild*, *Dick Tracy Meets Gruesome* (as Tess Truheart), *Phantom of the Jungle* and *Teenage Monster*.

Openly gay Hong Kong actor and singer **Leslie Cheung** [Kwokwing] (Cheung Fat-chung) committed suicide by jumping to his death from the twenty-fourth floor of a hotel on April 1st. He was 46 and had reportedly been suffering from depression for many years, leading to an earlier suicide attempt. A Canton-pop star since 1982, Cheung appeared in around sixty movies, including *A Chinese Ghost Story*, *A Chinese Ghost Story Part II*, *Rouge*, *The Bride with White Hair* and its sequel, *Ashes of Time*, *The Phantom Lover* (which he also produced) and *Inner Senses*. Cheung's father was a tailor to Alfred Hitchcock.

American actor, singer and Motown Records music producer **Booker Bradshaw** died of a heart attack the same day. He appeared in the role of Dr M'Benga in the 1960s *Star Trek* episodes, "A Private Little War" and "That Which Survives". His other credits include the film *Skullduggery* and episodes of such TV shows as *Tarzan* and *Planet of the Apes*.

British adult-film actor and scriptwriter **John M. East** died the same day, aged 70. He appeared in *The Playbirds*, *Emmanuelle in Soho*, *Confessions from the David Galaxy Affair*, *Mary Millington's Striptease Extravaganza* and *Hellcat Mud Wrestlers*. East also wrote a biography of comedian Max Miller.

Sixty-one-year-old American soul singer **Edwin Starr** (Charles Edwin Hatcher), best remembered for his 1970 Motown hit "War (What is it Good For)", died of an apparent heart attack at his home in England on April 2nd. His other hits include "Agent Double O-Soul" and "Stop Her on Sight (S.O.S.)". In 1995, Starr was featured on *Mousercise*, a Walt Disney children's workout album.

Mexican comedy actor **Adalberto Martinez "Resortes"**, died of heart and respiratory failure on April 4th, aged 87. A former dancer, he appeared in more than 100 film and TV productions including *El Nieto del Zorror* (1948), *Yo Dormi Con un Fan-*

tasma, Los Fantasmas Burlones, Santo and the Blue Demon vs. The Monsters and *El Teatro del Horror.*

Hollywood character actor **Anthony Caruso** died after a long illness the same day, aged 86. Best known for his villainous roles, he appeared in such movies as *Isle of Missing Men, The Ghost and the Guest, The Phantom* (1943), *Whistling in Brooklyn, Tarzan and the Leopard Woman, The Catman of Paris, My Favorite Brunette, Tarzan and the Slave Girl, Phantom of the Rue Morgue, The Most Dangerous Man Alive* and *Claws.*

Mexican wrestler-actor **Ray Mendoza** died on April 7th, aged 73. He appeared in *Santo contra Los Mujires Vampiros, Las Lobas del Ring, Blue Demon contra el Poder Satanico, Santo contra los Villanos del Ring* and *Santo y Blue Demon contra el Dr Frankenstein.*

Prolific American character actor **Bing Russell** died of cancer on April 8th, aged 77. He appeared (usually uncredited) in *Kiss Me Deadly, Tarantula, The Deadly Mantis, The Land Unknown, Billy the Kid vs. Dracula,* plus Disney's *Blackbeard's Ghost, The Computer Wore Tennis Shoes* and *The Love Bug.*

Sixty-three-year-old actress **Kathie Browne McGavin**, the wife of Darren McGavin, with whom she appeared in TV's *Kolchak: The Night Stalker*, died the same day. Her other credits include the films *The Brass Bottle, Cinderfella, The Underwater City* and *Happy Mother's Day Love George.*

R&B singer **Little Eva** (Eva Narcissus Boyd), best known for her #1 dance hit "The Loco-Motion", died of cancer on April 9th, aged 59.

Chicago-born character actor **Sydney Lassick**, the poor man's Peter Lorre, died on April 12th, aged 80. For the past several years he had suffered from diabetes and related health problems. His more than 100 film credits include *Sinderella and the Golden Bra, Carrie* (1976), *Alligator, The Unseen, Pandemonium, Silent Madness, Ratboy, Lady in White, Curse II The Bite, Future Shock, An American Vampire Story* and *Freeway.*

New Orleans R&B singer and songwriter **Earl King** (Earl Silas Johnson IV) died on April 17th, aged 69. He had been suffering from diabetes for many years. His hits include "Those Lonely Lonely Nights" and "Come On (Let the Good Times Roll)". Unlike many of his contemporaries, he retained the publishing rights to his compositions.

American-born jazz and blues singer **Nina Simone** (Eunice Kathleen Waymon), "The High Priestess of Soul", died in her sleep after a long illness at her home in southern France on April 21st. She was 70. Her best-known songs include "My Baby Just Cares for Me", "Don't Let Me Be Misunderstood" and her cover of the Bee Gees's "To Love Somebody". Her biography, *I Put a Spell on You*, appeared in 1991.

French-born Hollywood actress **Andrea King** (Georgette André Barry, a.k.a. "Georgette McKee") died on April 22nd, aged 84. Best known for her role in *The Beast With Five Fingers*, opposite Peter Lorre, her many other credits include *Mr Peabody and the Mermaid*, *Red Planet Mars*, *Daddy's Gone A-Hunting*, *House of the Black Death* (with Lon Chaney, Jr. and John Carradine) and *Blackenstein*. She was reportedly sacked from her contract at Warner Bros. in the late 1940s as a result of her rivalry with Bette Davis.

Italian comedian **Ciccio Ingrassia**, one half of the comedy team of "Franco and Ciccio" with Franco Franchi, died on April 28th, aged 79. He appeared in *Maciste Against Hercules in the Valley of Woe*, *002 Operazione Luna*, Mario Bava's *Dr Goldfoot and the Girl Bombs* with Vincent Price, *How We Stole the Atomic Bomb*, *Pinocchio* (1972), *Il Cav. Costane Nicosia Demoniaco Ovvero: Dracula in Brianza*, *Amarcord*, *Kaos* and *Fatal Frames*.

Texas fashion model and actress **Suzy Parker** (Cecilia Anne Renee Parker) died on May 3rd, aged 69. Christian Dior described her as "The most beautiful woman in the world." Her few film appearances include *Chamber of Horrors* (1966), and she appeared on TV in episodes of *Twilight Zone* ("Number Twelve Looks Just Like You"), *Tarzan* and *Night Gallery*. Parker's third husband was actor Bradford Dillman.

Brazilian actor **Wilson Vianna** died of a heart attack the same day, aged 75. Best known as superhero Captain Aza in the Brazilian children's series *TV Tupi* (1966–79), he also appeared in *Curucu Beast of the Amazon*, *Love Slaves of the Amazon*, *The Super He-Man* and *The Wizard of Oroz* (1984).

Prolific British character actor and comedian **Bernard Spear** died on May 9th, aged 83. His film credits include *Daleks' Invasion Earth 2150 AD*, *Bedazzled* (1967), *Chitty Chitty Bang Bang*, *Wombling Free* and *Gulliver's Travels* (1977), and he appeared on TV in such series as *Ghost Squad* and the 1958 *Quatermass and the Pit*.

Fifty-seven-year-old [David] **Noel Redding**, songwriter and bass player for The Jimi Hendrix Experience from 1966–69, was found dead at his home in southern Ireland on May 12th. Redding had also formed his own bands, Fat Mattress and The Noel Redding Band.

Hollywood leading man **Robert Stack** (Robert Langford Modini) died of a heart attack on May 14th, aged 84. Best remembered for his Emmy Award-winning role as Eliot Ness in the TV series *The Untouchables* (1959–62), his many credits include the 3-D *B'wana Devil, Transformers: The Movie, Joe versus the Volcano*, and the TV movies *Strange and Deadly Occurence* and the Stephen King-inspired *Perry Mason: The Case of the Sinister Spirit*. From 1987–2003 he also hosted the syndicated TV show *Unsolved Mysteries*. In 1980 he published his autobiography, *Straight Shooting*.

British stage and Oscar-winning screen actress Dame **Wendy Hiller** (Wendy Margaret Watkin) died the same day, aged 90. One of George Bernard Shaw's favourite actresses, she appeared in such films as *The Cat and the Canary* (1977), *The Elephant Man* and on TV in *The Curse of King Tut's Tomb* and *Miss Morison's Ghosts* (1983).

Seventy-three-year-old American singer-songwriter **June Carter** [Cash], the wife of Johnny Cash, died on May 15th, eight days after surgery to replace a heart valve. She toured with Elvis and married Cash in 1968. They co-wrote "Ring of Fire", one of the country singer's biggest hits.

French character actor, writer, director and lyricist **Jean Yanne** (Jean Gouyé) died of a heart attack on May 19th, aged 69. His many film appearances include *Le Boucher* (*The Butcher*), *Weekend* and *Le Pacte des Loups* (*Brotherhood of the Wolf*), and he worked on the production of Robert Bresson's *Lancelot du Lac*.

British stage and screen actress **Rachel Kempson**, the widow of actor Michael Redgrave, mother of Vanessa, Lynn and Corin, and grandmother of Natasha Richardson, died of a stroke on May 24th, aged 92. Her credits include *The Case of the Frightened Lady* (1938), *Curse of the Fly, Jane Eyre* (1970) and the Boris Karloff TV series *Colonel March of Scotland Yard*.

Oscar-nominated American actress **Martha** [Ellen] **Scott**, who appeared in both the stage and screen versions of *Our Town* as a returning spirit, died on May 28th, aged 90. Her other films include *The Ten Commandments*, *Charlotte's Web*, *Airport 1975* and *Doin' Time on Planet Earth*, plus *The Devil's Daughter* and *The Word* on TV. She had a recurring role as Helen Elgin, Steve Austin's mother and Jaime Sommers's foster mother, in both *The Six Million Dollar Man* and *The Bionic Woman*.

Jennifer Elliot, the 37-year-old daughter of actor Denholm Elliott, hanged herself at the end of May in the garden of the lbiza villa where her father died of AIDS-related tuberculosis in 1992. A former heroin addict, she had apparently been suffering from depression.

Legendary British record producer **Mickie Most** (Michael Peter Hayes) died of the rare lung cancer mesothelioma on May 30th, aged 64. He had been suffering from the disease for more than a year, which he probably contracted from long hours in recording studios where he was exposed to asbestos fibres in soundproofing tiles. After a career as a major pop star in South Africa, Most is credited with producing more #1 hits worldwide than anybody else, including "House of the Rising Sun" by The Animals, "I'm Into Something Good" by Herman's Hermits and "To Sir With Love" by Lulu. He had an estimated fortune of £50 million.

Sixty-two-year-old **Dave Rowberry**, a former keyboards player with British group The Animals (1965–66), was found dead on June 6th at his home in London. He had reportedly been suffering from heart problems. Rowberry played on such hits as "It's My Life" and "Don't Bring Me Down", and he can be seen in the 1967 film *It's a Bikini World*.

1930s British actress **Belle Chrystall**, who appeared in *The Frightened Lady* (1933) and *Scotland Yard Mystery* (a.k.a. *The Living Dead*), died on June 7th, aged 93. She became a model in 1940 and was briefly the face of Lux toilet soap, before retiring in 1946.

Thirty-eight-year-old Australian-born actor **Trevor Goddard**, best known for his recurring role (1998–2001) as Lt. Cmdr. Michael "Mic" Brumby in the TV series *JAG*, was found dead from a probable suicide overdose at his North Hollywood home on June 8th. Goddard's film credits include *Mortal Kombat*, *Deep Rising*, *Hollywood Vampyr* and *Pirates of the Caribbean: The Curse of the Black Pearl*.

78-year-old African-American character actor **William Marshall**, best known for his title role in the 1970s "blaxploitation" films *Blacula* and *Scream Blacula Scream*, died on June 11th in a Los Angeles rest home after a long struggle with Alzheimer's disease and diabetes. His other credits include *Sabu and the Magic Ring* (as a Genie), *To Trap a Spy*, *The Boston Strangler*, *Tarzan's Jungle Rebellion*, *Skullduggery*, *Abby*, *Twilight's Last Gleaming*, *Curtains*, *Amazon Women on the Moon*, *The Fisher King*, *Sorceress*, *Dinosaur Valley Girls* and TV's *Star Trek*, *Wild Wild West* and *Pee-wee's Playhouse* (as The King of Cartoons).

Oscar-winning Hollywood star [Eldred] **Gregory Peck** died in his sleep on June 12th, aged 87. His more than sixty films include Alfred Hitchcock's *Spellbound*, Ray Bradbury's 1956 adaptation of *Moby Dick* (and the 1998 TV remake, which was his last film), *On the Beach* (1959), *The Stalking Moon*, *The Chairman* (a.k.a. *The Most Dangerous Man in the World*), *Marooned*, *The Omen*, *The Boys from Brazil*, *Old Gringo* (as writer Ambrose Bierce) and both versions of *Cape Fear* (1962 and 1991).

Canadian-born writer, director and stage and screen actor **Hume Cronyn** (Hume Blake) died of prostate cancer on June 15th, aged 91. With his second wife of fifty-two years, Jessica Tandy (who died in 1994), he was half of one of the theatre's most memorable pairings. Descended from one of London's oldest families, he made his Broadway debut in 1934, and entered movies in 1943 with Alfred Hitchcock's *Shadow of a Doubt*. He contributed to the scripts for the director's films *Under Capricorn* and *Rope*, and his other film and TV appearances include *Phantom of the Opera* (1943), *Hamlet* (1964), *The Parallax View*, *Rollover*, *Impulse*, *Yesterday's Children*, *The World According to Garp*, **Batteries Not included*, *Cocoon* and *Cocoon: The Return* (the latter four titles also featuring Tandy). On stage, the couple co-starred in the 1987 play *Foxfire*, about a widow dealing with the ghost of her husband. It was adapted by Cronyn and YA author Susan Cooper from a series of books. Tandy won an Emmy for her performance in the 1987 TV adaptation, and in June 1994 the couple were presented with the first Tony Lifetime Achievement Award. Following Tandy's death, Cronyn married Cooper in 1996.

British character actor **Philip Stone** (Philip Stones) died the same day, aged 79. His credits include Stanley Kubrick's *A Clockwork Orange* and *The Shining*, plus *The Unearthly Stranger*, *Thunderball*, *Fragment of Fear*, *O Lucky Man*, *Lord of the Rings* (1978), *The Medusa Touch*, *Flash Gordon* (1980), *The*

Phantom of the Opera (1983), *Indiana Jones and the Temple of Doom, Shadowlands* and the 1999 TV movie *Doomwatch: Winter Angel* (as Dr Quist).

Mexican-born character actor **Carlos Rivas** died of prostate cancer on June 16th, aged 78. He appeared in *The Beast of Hollow Mountain, The Black Scorpion, They Saved Hitler's Brain, Tarzan and the Valley of Gold* and *Doc Savage The Man of Bronze*.

Japanese actor **Ren Yamamoto** died of cerebral apoplexy on June 17th, aged 73. His numerous credits include *Yurei Otoko* (*Ghost Story*), *Gojira, Godzilla Raids Again, Rodan, Secret of the Telegian, The Human Vapor, Mothra, King Kong vs. Godzilla, Godzilla vs. The Thing, Frankenstein Conquers the World* and *War of the Gargantuas*.

Hollywood star **Katharine Hepburn** died on June 29th, aged 96. She had suffered from Parkinson's disease for many years. The winner of a record four Best Actress Oscars after famously being declared "box-office poison", her films include the classic 1930s screwball comedy *Bringing Up Baby* and Tennessee Williams's *Suddenly Last Summer* (1960). She had a love affair with actor Spencer Tracy for twenty-seven years, until his death from alcoholism in 1967. Hepburn's 1991 autobiography was entitled *Me*.

Seventy-eight-year-old American comedian **Buddy Hackett** (Leonard Hacker) was found dead on June 30th at his Malibu home. Best known for his *risqué* Las Vegas nightclub act, his contrasting film career included such titles as the 1947 *Slave Girl* (his screen debut, as the voice of a talking camel), George Pal's *The Wonderful World of the Brothers Grimm, It's a Mad Mad Mad Mad World, Muscle Beach Party, Scrooged* (as Scrooge), and Disney's *The Love Bug* (1969) and *The Little Mermaid*. Hackett often cited Lou Costello as one of his idols, and he portrayed the rotund comic in the 1978 TV movie, *Bud and Lou*.

Irish actress **Constance Smith** died in London in June, aged 75. She appeared in *Jassy, The Perfect Woman* and two Jack the Ripper-inspired movies, *Room to Let* and *Man in the Attic*.

South African Bushman **N!xau** (Gcao Coma) was found dead in the bush outside Tsumkwe in northern Namibia on July 2nd. The star of the 1980 film *The Gods Must be Crazy*, who was believed to be around 59 years old, had tuberculosis and had failed to return from a search for wood. Paid just $300 for his appearance in the original film (which grossed nearly $100 million worldwide), he reprised his role in a 1989 sequel and three Hong Kong action comedies, including *Crazy Safari*, which included a battle between a vampire and zombie.

Hollywood actress **Barbara Weeks** died the same day, aged 90. The promising Goldwyn starlet disappeared from the screen in 1938. Fifty years later, despite *Variety* having listed her death in 1954, she was discovered living as a landlady in Las Vegas.

Seventy-three-year-old American jazz flautist **Herbie Mann** (Herbert Jay Soloman) who helped create the Bossa Nova craze of the 1960s, died after a long battle with prostate cancer in early July.

The twenty-six-stone "Walrus of Love", soul singer **Barry White**, (a.k.a. "Barry Lee") died on July 4th, aged 58. He had suffered from seriously high blood pressure and associated kidney problems for many years. While undergoing dialysis treatment in May, he suffered a stroke that impaired his speech and left him partially paralysed. A former record producer (Bob and Earl's "Harlem Shuffle") and engineer (Bobby Fuller's "I Fought the Law"), White sold more than 100 million record albums world-wide and his best-known hits include "You're the First, the Last, My Everything" and "Can't Get Enough of Your Love, Babe". He also wrote songs for TV's *The Banana Splits*.

American actor **Skip Ward** died after a long illness the same day, aged 69. His film credits include *Voyage to the Bottom of the Sea*, *The Nutty Professor* (1963), *The Mad Room*, *Myra Breckenridge* and *Kitten with a Whip*, and he guest-starred in numerous TV shows.

Actor and song-and-dance man **Buddy Ebsen** (Christian Rudolph Ebsen, Jr.) died on July 6th, aged around 95 (he was born in either 1904 or 1908). Best known for his starring roles in the CBS-TV series *The Beverly Hillbillies* (1962–71) and *Barnaby Jones* (1972–80), illness caused by the aluminium dust in the make-up forced him to give up the role of the Tin Man after two weeks to Jack Haley in *The Wizard of Oz* (1939), although his singing can reportedly still be heard on the soundtrack. When the former vaudevillian turned down a $2,000-per-week, seven-year contract from Louis B. Mayer, Ebsen was unofficially blacklisted from the movies for many years until television revived his career with Disney's *The Adventures of Davy Crockett* (1955). He was Ron Howard's first choice to star in *Cocoon*, but lost out to Don

Ameche when he couldn't get out of his TV contract for *Matt Houston* (1985). His other credits include episodes of *Twilight Zone* and *Night Gallery*, and the TV movie *The Horror at 37,000 Feet*.

Brazilian actor **Ayres Campos**, who starred as the eponymous SF hero in the 1954 children's TV series *Capitao 7*, died on July 6th, aged 80. His film credits include *Curucu Beast of the Amazon* and *Love Slaves of the Amazon*.

British-based American singer **Elisabeth Welch** died at an actors' retirement home on July 15th, aged 99. Her occasional film appearances included Ealing Studio's *Dead of Night* (1945), *Arabian Adventure* and Derek Jarman's *The Tempest*.

Argentine-born British actress **Renée Gadd** died at a nursing home on July 20th, aged 97. Her film credits include the *doppelgänger* fantasy *The Man in the Mirror* and also Ealing's *Dead of Night*.

American stage actress and writer **Carol Matthau** (a.k.a. "Carol Grace"), the widow of actor Walter Matthau (who died in 2000), died the same day, aged 78. Her first two marriages were both to Pulitzer Prize-winning author William Saroyan, and she was the inspiration for Holly Golightly in Truman Capote's *Breakfast at Tiffany's*.

Veteran British-born comedian **Bob Hope** (Leslie Townes Hope) died in his sleep of pneumonia on July 27th in his Toluca Lake home, two months after celebrating his 100th birthday. In a career that encompassed vaudeville, Broadway, radio, film, TV and personal appearances, he starred in more than fifty movies, including *The Cat and the Canary* (1939), *The Ghost Breakers*, *My Favorite Blonde* (with Gale Sondergaard and George Zucco), *My Favorite Brunette* (with Peter Lorre and Lon Chaney, Jr.), *Here Come the Girls*, *Casanova's Big Night* (with Basil Rathbone, Vincent Price and Chaney, Jr. again), *The Muppet Movie*, *Spies Like Us* and seven *Road* movies with Bing Crosby and Dorothy Lamour. He won five special Academy Awards and was appointed an honorary CBE in 1976, was made the first "honorary veteran" by US Congress in 1997 and received an honorary KBE (Knight Commander of the Most Excellent Order of the British Empire) in 1998 for his services to British troops during World War II. One of the wealthiest men in the entertainment business, his obituary in London's *Evening Standard* newspaper was written by film critic Alexander Walker, who died two weeks before him, and the one in the *New York Times* was written by journalist Vincent Canby, who died in 2000. Hope also published several volumes of memoirs.

Forty-one-year-old French actress **Marie Trintignant**, the daughter of actor Jean-Louis Trintignant, died of head injuries on August 1st after being attacked five days earlier in a Lithuanian hotel by her boyfriend, Bertrand Cantat, multi-millionaire lead singer with the popular French rock band Noir Desir. Despite claiming in court that her death was an accident, the 40-year-old Cantat was sentenced to eight years in jail for manslaughter.

Tony Award-winning tap dancer and actor **Gregory** [Oliver] **Hines** died of cancer on August 9th, aged 57. His films include *Wolfen*, *The Muppets Take Manhattan*, *Eve of Destruction* and *The Preacher's Wife*, and he appeared on TV in episodes of *Amazing Stories* and *Faerie Tale Theatre*. Broadway dimmed its lights in his honour.

British character actress **Ann Tirard** died on August 12th, aged 86. She appeared in *The Frozen Dead*, *Witchfinder General*, *Memoirs of a Survivor*, *The Witches* (1994) and the 1979 TV production of J. Sheridan Le Fanu's *Schalken the Painter*.

Margaret "Margie" Raia who, as a 10-year-old girl, played one of 124 Munchkins in *The Wizard of Oz* (1939), died of a brain seizure on August 17th, aged 75. Her late brother, Matthew Raia, appeared as a Munchkinland official who welcomed Dorothy to the city.

Tony Jackson, founding bass player and vocalist for the Merseybeat combo The Searchers, died of liver disease on August 18th, aged 63. After performing on such hits as "Sweets for My Sweet" and "Sugar and Spice", Jackson left the group in 1964.

Former British child star **Andrew Ray** (Andrew Olden) the younger son of comedian Ted Ray, died of a heart attack on August 20th, aged 64. His credits include several episodes of *Tales of the Unexpected* and a 1975 TV movie of *Great Expectations*.

Diminutive French comedian **Pieral** died in Paris on August 22nd, aged 79. His many film credits include *The Hunchback of Notre Dame* (1956) and *Spermula*.

British stage and screen actress **Zena Walker** died on August

24th, aged 69. She appeared in episodes of TV's *The Prisoner* and *Journey to the Unknown*, and the first of her three husbands was actor Robert Urquhart.

British TV sports commentator **Kent Walton** died on August 24th, aged 86. Born in Egypt, where his father served in the colonial government, Walton also hosted several music shows on TV during the 1960s. He was a partner in Pyramid Films, which produced *Virgin Witch* and *Keep it Up Downstairs*.

American tough-guy actor **Charles Bronson** (Charles Buchinski) died of pneumonia on August 30th. Although his official age was given as 81, he was reportedly eight years older and had been suffering from Alzheimer's disease. Best known for his five *Death Wish* films, his other movies include *House of Wax* and *Master of the World* (both with Vincent Price), *Someone Behind the Door*, *The White Buffalo*, *Telefon* and *10 to Midnight*. In the early 1960s he also appeared in episodes of TV's *One Step Beyond* and *The Twilight Zone*. The second of Bronson's three wives was actress Jill Ireland (who died in 1990).

British character actor **Reg Thomason** died in his sleep the same day, aged 84. He appeared in many films and was Kenneth Williams's stunt double in numerous entries in the *Carry On* series.

Mexican comedy actor **Eulalio Gonzalez** [Ramirez] **"Piporro"** died of a heart attack on September 1st, aged 82. His numerous films include *La Nave de los Monstruos*, *Los Hijos del Diablo* and *El Diablo, el Santo y el Tonto*.

Hollywood actor **Rand Brooks** died on his horse ranch the same day, aged 84. Best known for his role as Scarlett O'Hara's bland husband Charles Hamilton in *Gone With the Wind* (1939), he also played Hopalong Cassidy's sidekick Lucky Jenkins in a number of "B" Westerns and was Corporal Boone on the TV series *The Adventures of Rin Tin Tin* (1954–59). His other credits include *In Like Flint* and the TV shows *Rocky Jones Space Ranger* and *The Munsters*.

British character actor **Ben** (Benjamin) [Patrick] **Aris** died on September 4th, aged 66. Best known for his stage and TV roles (including *Doctor Who*), he also appeared in such films as Hammer's *Plague of the Zombies*, *Tommy*, *If . . .*, *O Lucky Man*, *Digby the Biggest Dog in the World* and *UFO: The Movie*.

Satirical singer/songwriter **Warren Zevon** died in West Holly-wood of mesothelioma, a rare form of untreatable lung cancer usually associated with asbestos, on September 7th, aged 56. When told by doctors more than a year before that he had less than two months to live, he said, "I'm okay with it, but it'll be a drag if I don't make it 'til the next James Bond movie comes out." A former alcoholic who quit a lifelong smoking habit nine years before his death, Zevon is best known for his cult 1978 hit "Werewolves of London". A child prodigy, he learned piano from Igor Stravinsky, was inspired by Bob Dylan, and over a thirty-year career recorded with Jackson Browne, Bruce Spring-steen, REM and the Everly Brothers, as well as writing the music for such TV series as *Tales from the Crypt* and *TekWar*.

Emmy Award-winning actor **John** (Jonathan) [Southworth] **Ritter** was taken ill on set and died – in the hospital where he had been born – from a previously undetected flaw in his heart's aorta on September 11th, less than a week before his 55th birthday. The son of singing cowboy and actor Tex Ritter, he was best known for his appearances on such sitcoms as ABC-TV's *Three's Company* (1977–84) and *Eight Simple Rules for Dating My Teenage Daughter* (2002-). Ritter's other credits include the films *The Barefoot Executive, The Other, The Night That Pan-icked America, Hero at Large, The Flight of Dragons, Wholly Moses!, The Dreamer of Oz* (as L. Frank Baum), Stephen King's *It, Stay Tuned, North, The Colony, It Came from the Sky* and *Bride of Chucky*. He also provided the voice for the PBS animated series *Clifford the Big Red Dog* and played a psychotic cyborg on a 1997 episode of TV's *Buffy the Vampire Slayer* ("Ted"). Ritter's second wife was actress Amy Yasbeck.

"The Man in Black", American country music legend **Johnny** (John R.) **Cash**, died in Nashville of complications from diabetes that resulted in respiratory failure on September 12th, aged 71. The Grammy-winning singer/songwriter ("A Boy Named Sue", "I Walk the Line", etc.) had recently battled autonomic neuropathy, a disease of the nervous system. His second wife, June Carter Cash, died in May. Cash was jailed seven times for drugs and alcohol-related problems and published two autobiographies. He also acted in *Door-to-Door Maniac* (1961) and a number of Westerns and TV shows.

Russian stage and screen actress **Nelli Myshkova,** who starred as the Princess of Lake Ilmen in the 1953 film *Sadko* (a.k.a. *The Magic Voyage of Sinbad*), died on September 13th, aged 77. She also appeared in the 1956 fantasy *Ilya Muromets* (a.k.a. *The Sword and the Dragon*).

Actor and country singer **Sheb** (Shelby) **Wooley** (a.k.a. "Ben Colder") died of leukaemia on September 16th, aged 82. Although his humorous 1958 pop hit "Purple People Eater" sold three million copies and reached 1 in the charts, an attempt at a follow-up hit, "Santa Meets The Purple People Eater", was not a success. Wooley appeared in more than sixty movies (mostly Westerns) and wrote the theme song for TV's *Hee Haw*. One of his last credits was the 1988 SF comedy of *Purple People Eater* starring Ned Beatty and Shelley Winters.

American bodybuilder turned actor **Gordon Mitchell** (Charles Allen Pendleton) died of a heart attack on September 20th, aged 80. After being discovered in the 1950s by Mae West on California's Muscle Beach, he was in *The Ten Commandments* and *Around the World in Eighty Days* before appearing in mostly Italian sword-and-sandal epics and horror films such as *Maciste in the Land of the Cyclops* (as Maciste), *The Giant of Metropolis*, *Hercules and the Princess of Troy*, *La Vendetta di Lady Morgan*, *2+5 Mission Hydra*, *Fenomenal and the Treasure of Tutankamen*, *Frankenstein '80*, *Frankenstein's Castle of Freaks*, *Dr Jekyll Like 'em Hot*, *Endgame*, *She* (1983), *Goliath and the Cheerleaders*, *Evil Spawn* and *The Cross of the Seven Jewels*. More recent credits include *Blood Delirium*, *The Alien Within*, *Bikini Drive-In* and *An Enraged New World*.

Fifty-four-year-old former child actor **Stanley Fafara**, best known for his role as "Whitey Whitney" on the popular sitcom *Leave it to Beaver* (1957–63), died on the same day of kidney and liver failure due to complications from surgery on a constricted intestine. After the show was cancelled, a teenaged Fafara battled with drug and alcohol problems, and in the 1980s he was sentenced to a year in jail for stealing from pharmacies. He contracted hepatitis C while using drugs.

Seventy-seven-year-old American character actor **Gordon Jump**, best known as Mr Carlson, the radio station owner on TV's *WKRP in Cincinnati*, and as the Maytag commercials repairman (replacing the late Jesse White since 1989), died from complications of pulmonary fibrosis on September 22nd. His film credits include *Conquest of the Planet of the Apes*, *The Fury* and TV's *Midnight Offerings*.

Veteran American character actor **Lyle Bettger** died on September 24th, aged 88. He mostly appeared in 1950s and 1960s Westerns as the villain, plus episodes of TV's *Voyage to the Bottom of the Sea* and *The Time Tunnel*.

Thirty-six-year-old wrestler **Pitbull** (Anthony Durante) was found dead of a drug overdose with his girlfriend, Dianna Hulsey, on September 25th. In the mid-1990s he competed in the ECW Tag Team championship with his wrestling partner Gary Smith.

Dapper British singer-songwriter **Robert Palmer** (Alan Palmer) died of an apparent heart attack during a two-day break in Paris on September 26th, aged 54. His hits include "Addicted to Love" with its classic video in 1985, "Some Guys Have All the Luck", "I Didn't Mean to Turn You On" and "Simply Irresistible".

Singer, dancer and actor turned TV director **Donald O'Connor** (Donald David Dixon Ronald O'Connor) died of heart failure after a long illness on September 27th, aged 78. From 1949–55 he starred with a talking mule in Universal's first six *Francis* movies, based on the novel by David Stern (who died in November). His other film credits include *The Wonders of Aladdin*, *Pandemonium* and *Alice in Wonderland* (1985), plus episodes of TV's *The Bionic Woman*, *Fantasy Island*, *Highway to Heaven* and *Tales from the Crypt*. Although he never won an Oscar, he reportedly quipped on his deathbed: "I'd like to thank the Academy for my lifetime achievement award that I will eventually get."

Hollywood actress **Fay Helm** died the same day, aged 94. Best remembered for her role as the luckless Jenny in Universal's *The Wolf Man*, her other credits include *Blondie Has Servant Trouble*, *Night Monster* (with Bela Lugosi and Lionel Atwill), *Captive Wild Woman* (with John Carradine), *Calling Dr Death* (with her *Wolf Man* co-star Lon Chaney, Jr.) and *One Body Too Many* (again with Lugosi). She retired from the screen in 1946.

Diminutive actor **Cork Hubbert** died of complications from diabetes on September 28th. Best known for his recurring role as Luther on the fantasy-comedy TV series *The Charmings* (1987), he also appeared in *Caveman*, *Legend*, *Under the Rainbow*, *Sinbad of the Seven Seas* and the TV films *Lifepod*, *The Santa Trap* and *Knee-High PI*.

American film and TV actress **Julie Parrish** (Ruby Joyce Wilbar) died of causes that were likely related to a history of ovarian cancer on October 1st, aged 62. Her credits include *The Nutty Professor* (1963), *Paradise Hawaiian Style* (with Elvis), *The Devil and Max Devlin*, the TV movie *The Time Machine* (1978) and the *Star Trek* pilot "The Menagerie".

Character actress **Florence Stanley** died of complications from a stroke on October 3rd, aged 79. She was the voice of Sobbing Josette in the *Dark Shadows* series, Grandma Ethyl in the puppet TV series *Dinosaurs* (1991) and Wilhelmina Bertha Packard in Disney's *Atlantis: The Lost Empire*. Stanley also appeared in *The Day of the Dolphin*.

British stage and screen actor **Denis Quilley** OBE died of cancer on October 5th, aged 75. In 1980 the actor won the Society of West End Theatres Award for playing the title role in *Sweeney Todd*, opposite Sheila Hancock, at the Theatre Royal, Drury Lane. Quilley returned to the Stephen Sondheim musical during the 1990s. In 1978, he starred in the London stage premiere of Ira Levin's *Deathtrap* and on TV he portrayed the mysterious Commander Charles Traynor in the children's SF series *Timeslip* (1970).

Conservative American talk show host **Wally George** (George Walter Pearch) died of pneumonia the same day, aged 71. The controversial TV host made cameo appearances in *A Nightmare on Elm Street 5: The Dream Child* and *Repossessed*, and was the biological father of actress Rebecca De Mornay.

American character actor and scriptwriter **Matt Roe**, who played Mayor Artie Worth in the 1995 cable TV movie *Black Scorpion* and the subsequent series, died of multiple myeloma on October 9th, aged 51. He also appeared in *Puppet Master*, *Child's Play 2*, *The Unborn* and the TV movie *The Big One: The Great Los Angeles Earthquake*.

American character actress **Victoria Horne** [Oakie] died on October 10th, aged 91. Her many film credits include *The Scarlet Claw, Murder in the Blue Room, The Unseen, That's the Spirit, Secret Agent X-9* (1945), *Pillow of Death, The Ghost and Mrs Muir, Abbott and Costello Meet the Killer Boris Karloff* and the classic *Harvey* (1950). She married actor Jack Oakie in 1950 and retired from the screen several years later.

Lieutenant Commander **Patrick Dalzel-Job**, the World War II hero whose exploits reputedly provided the inspiration for Ian

Fleming's character James Bond, died in Scotland on October 12th, aged 90. Dalzel-Job admitted that Fleming told him that he was the model for Bond, but he was not impressed: "I have never read a Bond book or seen a Bond movie," he said. "They are not my style."

American stage and screen actress turned psychoanalyst **Janice Rule** died of a brain haemorrhage on October 17th, aged 72. The former showgirl and nightclub singer made her film debut in 1951, and her credits include *Bell, Book and Candle*, *The Ambushers*, *Three Women* and the TV movie *The Devil and Miss Sarah*. From 1961 to 1979 she was married to her third husband, actor Ben Gazzara.

Dependable British character actor **David Lodge**, best known for his comedy roles alongside Peter Sellers and others, died of cancer on October 18th, aged 82. His many credits include *Bobbikins*, Hammer's *The Ugly Duckling*, *Captain Clegg* (a.k.a. *Night Creatures*) and *The Pirates of Blood River*, *The Hellfire Club*, *Catch Us if You Can*, *Casino Royale*, *Corruption*, *The Magic Christian*, *Scream and Scream Again*, *Incense for the Damned* (a.k.a. *Bloodsuckers*), *Mr Horatio Knibbles*, *The Fiend* (a.k.a. *Beware the Brethren*), *Go For a Take*, *The Amazing Mr Blunden*, *Bloodbath at the House of Death* and *Edge of Sanity*.

Cadaverous British character actor **Guy Rolfe** (Edwin Arthur Rolfe) died on October 19th, aged 91. Best known for his eponymous role in William Castle's *Mr Sardonicus*, the former racing driver and boxer's many other films include *Uncle Silas* (a.k.a. *The Inheritance*, based on the story by J. Sheridan Le Fanu), Hammer's *The Stranglers of Bombay*, *Snow White and The Three Stooges*, —*And Now the Screaming Starts!* (based on a story by David Case), *The Bride* and Stuart Gordon's *Dolls*. More recently, he appeared as crazed creator Andre Toulon in four of the *Puppet Master* sequels. His TV work includes classic episodes of *Thriller* ("Terror in Teakwood") and *The Avengers* ("Fog").

Wall-eyed American character actor **Jack Elam** died of emphysema at his home in Oregon on October 20th, aged 84. Official biographies put his age at two years older. Best known for playing villains in numerous Westerns, the former bookkeeper and auditor (who lost the sight in his left eye after a childhood accident) appeared in more than 130 films, including

Bird of Paradise, Fritz Lang's *Moonfleet*, *Kiss Me Deadly*, *Tarzan's Hidden Jungle*, *A Knife for the Ladies*, *The Creature from Black Lake*, *The Aurora Encounter*, *The Girl, the Gold Watch and Dynamite*, *Uninvited*, *Shadow Force*, *The Giant of Thunder Mountain* and *Suburban Commando*. He portrayed the Frankenstein Monster in the short-lived TV sitcom *Struck by Lightning* (1979).

African-American actor and dancer **Fred "Rerun" Berry**, who starred in the 1970s sitcom *What's Happening!!* and its 1985 successor *What's Happening Now!*, died on October 21st, aged 52. A millionaire by the age of 29, he lost all his money due to drug addiction, depression and an expensive lifestyle. In 1985 he became a Baptist minister and was married six times to four women (remarrying his first two wives twice).

Academy Award-nominated indie singer-songwriter **Elliott Smith** (Steven Paul Smith) committed suicide in Los Angeles the same day. After reportedly arguing with his girlfriend, he stabbed himself in the chest with a knife. The 34-year-old had reportedly battled drink and drug addiction problems.

TV writer, producer and director **Joanna Lee** died of bone cancer on October 24th, aged 72. She began her career as an actress, playing the alien Tanna in Ed Wood's legendary *Plan 9 from Outer Space*. After appearing in *The Brain Eaters* and following a serious car crash, she began writing for television with *The Flintstones* and *Bewitched*, eventually winning an Emmy in 1974 for a Thanksgiving episode of *The Waltons*. Her autobiography, *A Difficult Woman in Hollywood*, appeared in 1999.

Former Texas disc jockey and announcer **Rod Roddy** (Robert Ray Roddy) died of colon, prostate and breast cancer on October 27th, aged 66. Best known for telling audience members to "Come on down!" for nearly twenty years on the CBS-TV game show *The Price is Right*, he also narrated the surreal sitcom *Soap* (1977–81).

Dorothy Fay Ritter (Dorothy Fay Southworth, a.k.a. "Dorothy Fay"), the wife of singing cowboy Tex Ritter, died after a long illness on November 5th, aged 88. During the 1930s and 1940s, she appeared in a number of Western films and the serial *The Green Archer*. Her son, actor John Ritter, died two months earlier.

Mexican film and *telenova* star **Eduardo Palomo** died of a heart attack in a Los Angeles restaurant on November 6th, aged 41. He provided the voice of Tarzan in the Spanish-language version of the Disney cartoon movie.

Tenor **Bobby Hatfield** who, with baritone Bill Medley, formed one half of The Righteous Brothers, was found dead in a hotel room the same day, aged 63. The singing duo are best known for their 1960s hit "You've Lost That Loving Feeling", produced by Phil Spector, and their "Unchained Melody" was used in *Ghost*.

Prolific British session singer and musician **Michael John** died on November 7th, aged 76. During the 1950s and early 1960s he was the voice of string-puppet piglet Perky in the BBC children's TV series *Pinky and Perky*. Charles Young voiced the identical twin puppet pig, and together they recorded a number of high-pitched hit singles – well before Alvin and the Chipmunks did the same act in America.

Academy Award-winning American comedy actor **Art** (Arthur) [William Matthew] **Carney**, best remembered for his role as bumptious neighbour and *Captain Video* fan Ed Norton in the classic CBS-TV series *The Honeymooners* (1955–56), died after a long illness on November 9th, aged 85. He had also appeared in *Alfred Hitchcock Presents*, *The Twilight Zone*, *Batman* (as The Archer) and *The Snoop Sisters*, and his film credits include *The Muppets Take Manhattan*, Stephen King's *Firestarter* (1984), *Ravagers*, *Last Action Hero* and the TV movies *The Star Wars Holiday Special* (1978, as Saundan), *Death Scream* and *The Night They Saved Christmas* (as Santa Claus).

Scottish actor **Robert Brown**, who played James Bond's boss in four films, died on November 11th, aged 85. He appeared as Admiral Hargreaves in the 1977 Bond film *The Spy Who Loved Me*, and returned to the series as "M" in *Octopussy*, *A View to a Kill*, *The Living Daylights* and *Licence to Kill*. His other credits include Hammer's *The Abominable Snowman* and *Demons of the Mind*, Roger Corman's *Masque of the Red Death*, *Merlin of the Crystal Cave* and *Warlords of Atlantis*.

Twenty-seven-year-old American actor **Jonathan Brandis**, who starred as teenage genius Lucas Wolenczek in the TV series *SeaQuest DSV* and *SeaQuest 2032* (1993–95), committed suicide by hanging himself in a Los Angeles hospital on November 12th.

He had also appeared in *Stepfather II*, *The Neverending Story 2: The Next Chapter* and Stephen King's *It*.

American actress **Penny Singleton** (Dorothy McNulty), who from 1938 to 1950 starred as the eponymous *Blondie* in twenty-eight movies based on Chic Young's comic strip, died of complications from a stroke the same day, aged 96. The series included the old-dark-house entry *Blondie Has Servant Trouble* (1940). Singleton also played Blondie Bumstead on radio (1939–50), and in 1962 she became the voice of wife Jane in the TV cartoon series *The Jetsons*. She reprised the role in *The Jetsons Christmas Carol*, *The Jetsons Meet the Flintstones* and *Jetsons: The Movie*.

Veteran character actor **Kay E. Kuter** died of pulmonary complications, also on November 12th, aged 78. His numerous film credits include *The Mole People*, *The Last Starfighter*, *Zombie High*, *Frankenstein General Hospital*, *Warlock* and Disney's *The Little Mermaid II: Return to the Sea*.

American TV actress **Kellie** [Suzanne] **Waymire**, who portrayed Ensign Elizabeth Cutler on *Enterprise* and also appeared in *Star Trek: Voyager*, died of a previously undetected medical condition on November 13th, aged 36. Waymire was one of the leads on the short-lived supernatural sitcom *The Pitts* (2003) on Fox, guested in such shows as *The X Files* and *Six Feet Under* and starred in the serial-killer romantic comedy *Maniacts*.

American actor **Gene Anthony Ray**, best known for his role as Leroy Johnson in the movie *Fame* and the spin-off TV series, died of complications from a stroke and HIV the same day, aged 41.

Stand-up comedian and actress **Margaret Trigg** died on November 15th, aged 39. She starred as Cookie Brody in the 1996 TV series *Aliens in the Family*.

American character actor **Jim Siedow**, who played the Old Man in *The Texas Chain Saw Massacre* and the Cook in its 1986 sequel, died of emphysema after a long illness on November 20th, aged 83.

British actor **Robert Addie**, best known for his role as Sir Guy of Gisburne in the 1980s TV series *Robin of Sherwood*, died of lung cancer the same day, aged 43. He also starred as Mordred in John Boorman's *Excalibur*.

Sixty-four-year-old Scottish actor [James] **Gordon Reid**, who appeared in the *Doctor Who* episode "Invasion of the Dinosaurs" and the Nicole Kidman film *The Others*, died of a massive heart attack on November 26th, after collapsing during the second act of *Waiting for Godot* on stage in London. Reid also voiced the megalomaniac computer Angel Two in BBC Radio 4's *Earthsearch*.

American actor **Norman Burton** (a.k.a. "Normann Burton"), best remembered for his role as Joe Atkinson on the CBS-TV series *The New Adventures of Wonder Woman* (1977–79), was killed in a traffic accident in Mexico on November 29th, aged 79. His many film credits include *Hand of Death*, *Planet of the Apes* (1967), *Simon, King of the Witches*, the James Bond adventure *Diamonds Are Forever* (as Felix Leiter), *Escape from the Planet of the Apes*, *The Terminal Man*, *The Reincarnation of Peter Proud*, *Fade to Black*, *Mausoleum*, *Deep Space* and *Bloodsport*.

American character actress **Frances Morris** died on December 2nd, aged 98. She appeared as Ma Kent in the ABC-TV series *The Adventures of Superman* (1952–58), and her film credits include *Professor Beware*, *Sky Raiders*, *Dick Tracy vs. Crime Inc.*, *The Bermuda Mystery*, *The Ghost Goes Wild*, *The Secret Life of Walter Mitty* (with Boris Karloff), *Alias Nick Beal* and *The Night Has a Thousand Eyes*.

Sixty-two-year-old British actor and director **David** [Leslie Edward] **Hemmings**, who exemplified "Swinging London" during the 1960s, died of a heart attack on December 3rd after filming his final scene for the supernatural drama *Blessed* (a.k.a. *Samantha's Child*) in Romania. Best remembered for his starring role in Michelangelo Antonioni's *Blowup* (1966), he also appeared in *The Eye of the Devil* (a.k.a. *13*), *Barbarella*, *Camelot* (as Mordred), *Unman, Wittering and Zigo*, *Fragment of Fear* and *Voices* (the latter two with Gayle Hunnicutt, his wife from 1968 to 1974), Dario Argento's *Deep Red* (a.k.a. *Profundo Rosso*), *Murder by Decree*, *Thirst*, *Harlequin* (which he also directed), *Equilibrium* and *The League of Extraordinary Gentlemen*. With John Daly he formed the production and distribution company Hemdale in 1967, executive producing such films as *Dead Kids* (a.k.a. *Strange Behaviour*) and *Escape 2000* (a.k.a. *Turkey Shoot*). Hemmings portrayed *Dr Jekyll and Mr Hyde* for the BBC in 1980 and appeared in *Out of this World*, *Airwolf* (as recurring villain Dr Charles Henry Moffett), *Tales from the Crypt*, the pilot for *The Vanishing Man*, a mummy episode of

Father Dowling Mysteries and *Nightmare Classics: The Turn of the Screw* (as an eleven-year-old he had played the original Miles in Benjamin Britten's 1954 opera). His credits as a director also include an adaptation of James Herbert's *The Survivor* and episodes of such TV series as *Werewolf* and *Quantum Leap*.

Hollywood leading lady **Ellen Drew** (Esther Loretta Ray, a.k.a. "Terry Ray" and "Erin Drew") died of a liver ailment the same day, aged 89. Discovered working as a waitress in an ice-cream parlour, she appeared in *Night of Mystery*, *The Mad Doctor* (with Basil Rathbone), *The Remarkable Andrew*, *The Monster and the Girl* (with George Zucco), *Isle of the Dead* (with Boris Karloff), *Crime Doctor's Man Hunt* and *The Baron of Arizona* (with Vincent Price). During the 1950s she starred in two episodes of TV's *Science Fiction Theatre* before finally retiring in 1961.

American actress **Claire Hagen**, the wife of actor Ross Hagen, died of cancer, also on December 3rd. She appeared in *Wonder Women*, *Angels Wild Women*, *Bikini Drive-In*, *Star Hunter*, *Attack of the 50-Foot Centerfold* and *Invisible Dad*. She also produced *B.O.R.N.* starring her husband, and the 1985 video compilation *Reel Horror*.

Brazilian-born **Francine Weisweiller** (Francine Worms), who was the patron of French film-maker, writer and artist Jean Cocteau for the final thirteen years of his life, died on December 8th, aged 87. She appeared as "the ghost who got the century wrong" in Cocteau's film *The Testament of Orpheus* and arranged the reconciliation between Cocteau and Pablo Picasso at her Riviera villa.

Keiko, the killer-whale star of the three *Free Willy* films, died on December 12th. Rescued from captivity in Mexico by conservationists, he was eventually relocated to Norway but reportedly missed human companionship. "He's free now and in the wild," said one of the caretakers at the funeral, without a trace of irony.

French-born Canadian actor **Alexis Kanner**, best remembered for his two appearances in TV's *The Prisoner*, died of a heart attack on December 13th, aged 61. He wrote, directed and co-starred with Patrick McGoohan in the film *Kings and Desperate Men*, and also appeared in *Goodbye Gemini* and an episode of Gerry Anderson's *U.F.O.* ("The Cat With Ten Lives").

Oscar-nominated Hollywood leading lady **Jeanne Crain** died of a heart attack on December 14th, aged 78. Late in her career she co-starred with Vincent Price in the Italian *Queen of the Nile* and appeared in the psycho-thriller *The Night God Screamed*.

Thirty-one-year-old **Patrick Presley**, Elvis Presley's first cousin once removed, was found hanged in a Mississippi prison cell where he was serving life for causing the death of a woman during a car crash while high on drugs.

American character actress **Madlyn Rhue** (Madeleine Roche) died of pneumonia and heart failure on December 16th, aged 68. Diagnosed with multiple sclerosis in 1977, in later years she acted from a wheelchair. Her credits include the TV movies *Poor Devil* and *Fantasies* plus episodes of *Alfred Hitchcock Hour*, *The Man from U.N.C.L.E.*, the original *Star Trek*, *Wild Wild West*, *Land of the Giants*, *Ghost Story*, *Kolchak: The Night Stalker* and *Fantasy Island*.

Character actor **Alan Tilvern** died on December 17th, aged 84. His numerous film credits include *The Malpas Mystery*, Hammer's *Rasputin the Mad Monk*, *The Frozen Dead*, *Percy's Progress*, the animated *Lord of the Rings*, *Superman*, *Firefox*, *Little Shop of Horrors* and *Who Framed Roger Rabbit?*

Australian actor **Ed Devereaux**, best known for his role in the children's TV series *Skippy* (1966–68), died in his sleep of renal failure the same day, aged 78. He also appeared in the 1974 comedy *Barry McKenzie Holds His Own . . .*, Hammer's *To the Devil a Daughter* and *I Bought a Vampire Motorcycle*.

American model turned actress **Hope** [Elise Ross] **Lange** died of complications from acute colitis on December 19th, aged 72. Best remembered for her double Emmy Award-winning role as Carolyn Muir in TV's *The Ghost and Mrs Muir* (1968–70), her other credits include *Nightmare on Elm Street Part Two: Freddy's Revenge*, *Blue Velvet*, *Dead Before Dawn* and the TV movies *Crowhaven Farm* (with John Carradine) and *Fer-De-Lance*. The first two of her three marriages were to actor Don Murray and director Alan J. Pakula.

Veteran character actor **Les Tremayne** died of heart failure in Santa Monica the same day, aged 90. His numerous film credits include *Francis Goes to West Point*, *It Grows on Trees*, *War of the Worlds* (as General Mann), *Forbidden Planet* (as the narrator), *The Monolith Monsters*, *The Monster of Piedras Blancas*, *Angry Red Planet*, *King Kong vs. Godzilla* (again as narrator), *The Slime People*, *Creature of Destruction*, *The Phantom Toll-*

booth, *Fangs* (1978), *Starchaser: The Legend of Orin* and *Attack of the B-Movie Monster*. In later years the British-born Tremayne became a prolific voice actor on TV cartoons.

Canton-pop star and actress **Anita Mui** [Mui Yim-fong] died of cervical cancer in Hong Kong on December 23rd, aged 40. She won the Golden Horse Award for Best Actress in 1987 for her role as a ghost in *Rouge* and portrayed masked crime-fighter Wonder Woman in *The Heroic Trio* and its sequel. Her other films include *Scared Stiff*, *Black Heart Ghost*, *Moon Warriors* and *House of Flying Daggers*.

Distinguished British stage and screen actor Sir **Alan** [Arthur] **Bates** CBE died of cancer on December 27th, aged 69. His many film credits include *The Shout*, *Britannia Hospital*, *Dr M*, *Hamlet* (1990), *Mister Frost*, *The Grotesque*, *Arabian Nights* (1999), *The Mothman Prophecies*, *Salem Witch Trials* and *The Sum of All Fears*.

British comedy actor and TV personality **Bob** (Robert) [Alan] **Monkhouse** OBE, died on December 29th, aged 75. He had been diagnosed with incurable prostate cancer more than two years earlier. A major collector of comic strips and cartoons, he began his career as a gag writer (in partnership with Denis Goodwin) for other comedians, including Bob Hope. His eclectic film credits include providing the voice for one of the puppet characters in the Gerry Anderson film *Thunderbirds Are Go!* For more than thirty years film buff Monkhouse was president of London's Gothique Film Society and regularly contributed illustrations to the annual programme notes as well as being an occasional visitor to screenings. His autobiographies *Crying With Laughter* and *Over the Limit* were published in 1993 and 1999 respectively.

British stage and screen actor **Dinsdale** [James] **Landen** died of cancer the same day, aged 71. His many credits include Hammer's *Rasputin the Mad Monk* (with Christopher Lee), *Every Home Should Have One*, *Digby – The Biggest Dog in the World*, *Morons from Outer Space* and TV's *Doctor Who* and *The Avengers*.

British leading lady of the 1940s **Patricia Roc** (Felicia Miriam Ursula Herold, aka "Felicia Reif") died in Switzerland of kidney failure on December 30th, aged 88. Once described by studio head J. Arthur Rank as "The Goddess of the Odeons", her films include *The Gaunt Stranger*, *Madonna of the Seven Moons*, *Jassy*, *The Perfect Woman* (as a robot), *The Hypnotist* (1955),

The House in the Woods (with Michael Gough) and *Bluebeard's Ten Honeymoons*. Roc was fined £25.00 in 1975 for shoplifting in London's Oxford Street. She was married three times and reportedly had affairs with actors Ronald Reagan and Anthony Steel.

American leading lady **Paula Raymond** (Paula Ramona Wright, a.k.a. "Rae Patterson" and "Paula Rae Wright") died on December 31st, aged 79. Best remembered as the heroine of *The Beast from 20,000 Fathoms* (1953), based on a story by Ray Bradbury, she also appeared in *The Flight That Disappeared*, *Hand of Death*, *The Man From U.N.C.L.E.* feature *The Spy With My Face*, *Blood of Dracula's Castle* (with John Carradine as the Count), *Five Bloody Graves* and *Mind Twister* (1993). She dubbed the singing voice of Hedy Lamarr in Jacques Tourneur's *Experiment Perilous* (1944). A 1962 automobile accident almost ended her career when she was initially pronounced dead at the hospital and subsequently required extensive face reconstruction.

PRODUCERS/DIRECTORS/TECHNICIANS

Sound and music editor **Robert Hathaway** died on January 1st, aged 67. His many credits include *Terror from the Year 5000*, *Sisters*, *Alien*, *Tron*, *Something Wicked This Way Comes*, *Superman II*, *III* and *IV*, *Mickey's Christmas Carol*, *Frankenweenie*, *Splash*, *Lifeforce*, *The Neverending Story*, *Baby: Secret of the Lost Legend*, *Labyrinth* and *Frankenstein Unbound*.

Two-time Oscar-winning cinematographer **Conrad L. Hall** died of complications from bladder cancer in California on January 4th, aged 76. Born in Tahiti, he was the son of *Mutiny on the Bounty* author James Norman Hall and was married to actress Katharine Ross from 1969–75. Hall's credits include the original *Outer Limits* TV series and such movies as the Esperanto *Incubus*, *In Cold Blood*, *The Day of the Locust*, *Black Widow*, *Jennifer Eight* and Tim Burton's *Sleepy Hollow*. He won a posthumous Oscar in 2003 for his work on *Road to Perdition*.

British film producer and writer **Sir Anthony** [James Allan] **Havelock-Allan** died of heart failure on January 11th, aged 98. His credits include such classics as *Blithe Spirit* (1945) and *Great Expectations* (1946), both directed by David Lean. From 1939–52 he was married to actress Valerie Hobson.

Japanese director [Kantoyuku] **Kinji Fukasaku** died of prostate cancer on January 12th, aged 72. Along with many violent gangster dramas, his films include *The Green Slime*, *Message from Space*, *Virus*, *Ghost of Yotsuya* and the international hit *Battle Royale*. When he became too ill, he handed over the direction of *Battle Royale II* to his son, Kenta Fukasaku.

Hollywood writer, producer and director **Norman Panama**, best known for his creative partnership with Melvin Frank (who died in 1988), died of Parkinson's disease on January 13th, aged 88. His many credits include the Oscar-nominated Bob Hope–Bing Crosby comedy *Road to Utopia*, both the Broadway and film versions of *Li'l Abner*, *The Court Jester*, *Road to Hong Kong* and *The Maltese Bippy*.

Animator **Zack Schwartz** died in Israel the same day. In 1940 he served as art director on "The Sorcerer's Apprentice" sequence in Disney's *Fantasia*, and he later co-founded UPA.

Canadian-born television writer and executive producer **John [Truman] Mantley**, the second cousin of silent film star Mary Pickford, died of heart failure and complications from Alzheimer's disease on January 14th, aged 83. Mantley executive produced more than 500 hours of prime-time television, including *The Wild Wild West*, *Buck Rogers in the 25th Century* and *MacGyver*. He also adapted his own SF novel *The 27th Day* for Columbia in 1957 and scripted *My Blood Runs Cold* starring Troy Donahue.

American production designer **Mel Bourne** died of heart failure the same day, aged 79. He collaborated on seven films with Woody Allen, including *A Midsummer Night's Sex Comedy* and *Zelig*, and also worked on *Still of the Night*, *FX Murder by Illusion*, *Manhunter* and *Fatal Attraction*. He received a third Academy Award nomination for his work on *The Fisher King*.

American scriptwriter, producer and *bon vivant* **Sheldon Reynolds** died after a long battle with emphysema on January 25th, aged 79. After creating the syndicated TV series *Foreign Intrigue* (1951–55), he produced the 1954 series *Sherlock Holmes* (starring Ronald Howard) in Paris, France. In 1982, he developed another Holmes series, *Sherlock Holmes and Dr Watson* (starring Geoffrey Whitehead), shot entirely in Poland.

Visual effects supervisor **Peter Donen**, the son of director Stanley Donen, died of a heart attack on January 31st, aged

50. He worked in various capacities on such films as *Superman*, *Clan of the Cave Bear*, *Altered States*, *Runaway*, *Ladyhawke*, *Gremlins*, *Twilight Zone*, *Spaceballs* and *Flatliners*. His stepfather was actor Robert Wagner.

Producer and agent **Peter Shaw**, the husband of actress Angela Lansbury, died of congestive heart failure the same day, aged 84. As an actor, he played the miniature Devil in *The Bride of Frankenstein*.

Belgium-born exploitation-film director, producer and writer **Charles L. Nizet** was murdered in Flores da Cunha, Brazil, on February 4th. He was 71. Nizet's low-budget films, usually shot in or around Las Vegas, include the legendary *Voodoo Heartbeat*, *Help Me . . . I'm Possessed* and *Slaves of Love*.

French writer and director **Jean Kerchbron** died on February 3rd, aged 78. His credits include *The Golem* (1967), *L'Atalantide* (1972) and *President Faust*.

Mexican film director, producer and writer **Rene Cardona, Jr.** died of cancer on February 5th, aged 63. The son of veteran director Rene Cardona (who died in 1988), the former child actor began directing in the early 1960s and his numerous credits include *El Asesino Invisible*, *Night of the Bloody Apes*, *Capulina contra los Vampiros*, *Night of a Thousand Cats*, *Invasion de los Muertos*, *Capulina contra los Vampiros*, *Tintorera*, *Devil's Triangle*, *Guyana: Cult of the Damned*, *Treasure of the Amazon*, *Beaks* and *Santa Sangre* (as executive producer).

Eighty-five-year-old American TV writer-producer **Joe Connelly** died on February 13th at a California nursing home after suffering a stroke. In the early 1970s he had suffered a near-fatal aneurysm. With writing partner Bob Mosher (who died in 1972) he wrote the *Amos 'n' Andy* radio show and created and developed such hit TV shows as *The Munsters* and *Leave It to Beaver*. Connelly also produced the 1966 movie *Munster Go Home!* and *A Change of Habit* starring Elvis.

Emmy-winning make-up artist **Rod B. Wilson** died on February 22nd, aged 68. His credits include *Planet of the Apes* (1967), *Waterworld* and TV's *Batman* and *Airwolf*.

Legendary American television producer and writer **Fred Freiberger** (a.k.a. "Charles Woodgrove") died on March 2nd, aged 88. His many credits include the 1968–69 season of *Star Trek*, *The Wild Wild West*, *The Six Million Dollar Man*, *Superboy*,

Beyond Westworld and the revamped second season of *Space: 1999*. He also produced such movies as *The Beast from 20,000 Fathoms* and *The Beginning of the End*. Freiberger spent three years at Hanna-Barbera, where he wrote for several animated series including *Scooby-Doo Where Are You!* and *Super Friends*. He also created the live-action series *Korg, 70,000BC*.

Special-effects designer **Bert Luxford**, who worked on Hammer's *Countess Dracula* and *Twins of Evil*, *Hawk the Slayer*, and *Highlander*, died on February 4th, aged 91. He also contributed many uncredited gadgets to the Bond films.

Canadian-born British TV producer **Lloyd George Shirley** died of cancer after a long illness in London on March 5th, aged 72. A founder of Euston Films, his numerous credits include the series *The Rivals of Sherlock Holmes* and the 1988 miniseries *Jack the Ripper*.

Sir **Hardy Amies**, Queen Elizabeth II's official dressmaker for nearly fifty years, died of a heart attack the same day, aged 93. In 1967 he was the wardrobe designer on *2001: A Space Odyssey*.

Bernard Schwab, the last survivor of four brothers who founded Hollywood's famous Schwab's Pharmacy on Sunset Boulevard, also died on March 5th, aged 94. A hang-out for stars, studio executives and wannabes (legend has it that Lana Turner was famously discovered there while drinking soda), the drugstore was forced to close in 1983 and the building was eventually demolished.

American scriptwriter-producer **Ben Brady** died on March 20th, aged 94. A former lawyer, he scripted such radio shows as *The Thin Man* and *Inner Sanctum* before moving into TV in the 1950s. He developed the format for *Perry Mason* (1957–60) with Erle Stanley Gardner and later produced and wrote for the second series of *The Outer Limits* (1964). Vice-president in charge of programming for ABC-TV from 1962–65, he also co-founded the Producers Guild of America.

American film producer **Michael** [Anthony Morrison] **Wayne**, the eldest son of late actor John Wayne (who died in 1979), died of heart failure on April 2nd following surgery. He was 68 and had been suffering from Lupus.

French-born cinematographer **Jean-Yves Escoffier** died of a heart attack in Los Angles on April 4th, aged 52. After moving to America in the early 1990s, his credits include *2046*, *Witch Hunt*,

Dream Lover, *The Crow: City of Angels*, *Possession* and *The Cradle Will Rock*. He also shot commercials and music videos for such directors as David Lynch, Luc Besson and Jean Pierre Jeunet, and took the pictures in *One-Hour Photo*.

British-born film and TV director **David Greene** died of pancreatic cancer at his home in California on April 7th, aged 82. A former stage and film actor, he worked in TV on such series as *Shirley Temple's Storybook*, *Twilight Zone* and *The Saint* before turning to films with the 1966 adaptation of the H.P. Lovercraft-August Derleth story *The Shuttered Room*. His other credits include *I Start Counting*, *Godspell* and the TV movies *Madame Sin*, *World War III*, *Prototype*, *Night of the Hunter* (1991) and *Whatever Happened to Baby Jane?* (1991).

Mexican-born inventor-sound engineer **Charles** [Rolland] **Douglass** died on April 8th, aged 93. While working as a broadcast engineer for CBS-TV he created the "Laff Box" in 1953 to enhance live-audience reaction with "canned laughter". Probably the invention's most unlikely use was on the 1960s cartoon series *The Flintstones*, which could not possibly have had a studio audience. Douglass received a Lifetime Achievement Emmy Award in 1992.

33-year-old special-effects technician and production designer **Trevor Murray** was found dead on location in Bangkok on April 14th. Amongst the films he worked on are *Space Truckers*, *Virus* and *The Forsaken*.

American-born billionaire philanthropist Sir **John Paul Getty II**, son of the richest man in the world, died on April 17th, aged 70. A former hippie and heroin addict, he had been admitted to a London clinic with a chest infection a few days earlier. He became a British citizen in 1997 and gave away around £120 million to a variety of causes, including £20 million to the British Film Institute.

Mowtown choreographer **Cholly Atkins**, who worked with such acts as the Supremes, Smokey Robinson and the Miracles, Aretha Franklin and Marvin Gaye, died of pancreatic cancer the same day. He was 89.

Emmy Award-winning TV production designer **Jan Scott** also died on April 17th, aged 88. Her credits include *Trilogy of Terror* and the 1973 remake of *Miracle on 34th Street*.

American film and TV editor **Fred Berger** died on May 23rd, aged 94. His numerous credits include *Back from the Dead*, *The Unknown Terror* and *The Resurrection of Zachary Wheeler*.

Special-effects director **Arthur Brewster** died of cancer on May 24th, aged 57. His credits include *Swamp Thing*, *The Hitcher*, *Masters of the Universe*, *Cherry 2000* and *Chopper Chicks in Zombietown*.

Film and TV producer **Jules Levy** died the same day after a long illness, aged 80. In a career that began in the early 1940s, he produced such films as *Hellzapoppin'*, *The Hairy Ape*, *The Monster That Challenged the World*, *The Vampire* (1957), *The Return of Dracula* and *The Flame Barrier*.

Lee Katz, who was an assistant director on such films as *Mystery of the Wax Museum* and *Casablanca*, died of heart failure on May 29th, aged 89. He also worked on the scripts for *The Return of Doctor X* (with Humphrey Bogart) and *British Intelligence* (with Boris Karloff).

Cinematographer **Haskell "Buzz" Boggs**, whose credits include the cult classic *I Married a Monster from Outer Space*, died of heart disease on May 30th, aged 94.

British-born film producer **Alex Gordon** died of cancer on June 24th in Los Angeles after a long illness. He was 80. After serving in World War II, he worked at independent distributor Renown Pictures as head of advertising and publicity. Emigrating to America in 1947, he was employed by singing cowboy Gene Autry before joining the fledgling American International Pictures, where he produced eighteen movies including Roger Corman's *The Day the World Ended*, *The She Creature* and *Voodoo Woman*. Gordon also worked on the scripts for two Edward D. Wood, Jr. pictures, *Jail Bait* and the infamous *Bride of the Monster* starring Bela Lugosi, whose British stage tour he arranged in the early 1950s. After leaving AIP in 1957, he produced such independent films as *The Atomic Submarine* and *The Underwater City*. Gordon went to 20th Century-Fox in 1968, where he instituted a film-restoration project, rediscovering more than thirty of Fox's "lost" silents and early talkies. He is survived by his younger brother Richard, also a producer, with whom he worked on *Old Mother Riley Meets the Vampire* (a.k.a. *My Son the Vampire*), also starring Lugosi.

Film and TV director **Fielder Cook** died of a stroke on June 29th, aged 80. He specialized in remaking movies for the small screen, including *Harvey* (1972), *Miracle on 34th Street* (1973) and *Beauty and the Beast* (1976).

Writer, producer and director **Rod Amateau** died of a cerebral haemorrhage the same day, aged 79. He produced the series *My Mother the Car* (1965–66), directed episodes of *Mr Ed* and *Gilligan's Island* (including the pilot), and his film credits include *Supertrain*, *Hitler's Son* and *The Garbage-Pail Kids Movie*.

Special-effects pioneer **Milton Altman**, credited with inventing the "blue screen", died on July 6th, aged 83.

Oscar-nominated film editor **Marjorie Fowler**, the daughter of producer-director Nunnally Johnson and widow of editor Gene Fowler, Jr (who died in 1998), died on July 8th, aged 83. Her credits include *Mr Peabody and the Mermaid*, *Man in the Attic*, *Doctor Dolittle* (1967) and *Conquest of the Planet of the Apes*.

Film and TV art director **Walter "Matt" Jeffries**, best known for designing the USS *Enterprise* with its "Jeffries Tube" crawl spaces for the original *Star Trek* series, died of congestive heart failure on July 21st, aged 81.

Polish-born film producer **Serge Silberman** died on July 22nd, aged 86. He worked with such directors as Akira Kurosawa (*Ran*), Nagisa Oshima (*Max Mon Amour*), David Lean (the unproduced *Nostromo*) and, most famously, Spanish surrealist film-maker Luis Buñuel (*The Discreet Charm of the Bourgeoisie*, *The Phantom of Liberty*, *That Obscure Object of Desire*, etc).

British-born former actor and magician turned film director **John [Richard] Schlesinger** CBE died on July 25th, aged 77. He was taken off a life-support machine in Palm Springs and had been in fragile health since suffering a debilitating stroke in 2001. Schlesinger's *Midnight Cowboy* is the only X-rated film to win an Oscar for Best Picture. The gay director's other films include *Billy Liar*, *The Day of the Locust* (featuring William Castle and Angelo Rossito), *Marathon Man*, *The Believers*, *Pacific Heights* and the cable TV movie *The Tale of Sweeney Todd*.

American TV producer **Philip L. Parslow**, whose network series include *Prey* and *Brimstone*, died of a heart attack on July 29th, aged 65.

Sun Records producer **Sam Phillips**, the man credited with having discovered Elvis Presley, died of respiratory problems on July 30th, aged 80. Former DJ Phillips was also instrumental in launching the careers of Johnny Cash, Jerry Lee Lewis, Carl Perkins, Roy Orbison, Charlie Rich and lke Turner.

Film editor **Thomas J. McCarthy** died of respiratory failure and complications from Alzheimer's and Parkinson's disease on August 1st, aged 76. Among the films he edited were George Pal's *The Power* and *Doc Savage: The Man of Bronze*.

Former sound recordist and film archivist **John Huntley** died of cancer on August 7th, aged 82. Among the films he worked on were *A Matter of Life and Death*, *The Red Shoes* and *Hamlet* (1948). He also selected the incidental music for the BBC-TV version of *Quatermass II*.

Pioneering female cinematographer **Brianne "Bri" Murphy** died of a brain tumour and lung cancer in Mexico on August 20th, aged 70. Born in London to an American family, Murphy was paid $50.00 by exploitation producer Jerry Warren to do odd jobs on *Man Beast* (1955). This led directly to a career in cinematography, and the couple were subsequently married. Murphy also worked in various capacities on Warren's *Teenage Zombies*, *Incredible Petrified World* and *Bloodlust, House of the Black Death* and *Agent for H.A.R.M.* The first woman to join the American Society of Cinematographers, her other credits include *Secrets of the Bermuda Triangle* and TV's *Wonder Woman*. She was nominated for an Emmy Award in 1985 for her work on the series *Highway to Heaven*.

81-year-old film editor, associate producer and post-production supervisor **George E. Swink** died on August 22nd of heart failure following surgery. He worked closely with Irwin Allen on many film and TV projects, including *The Story of Mankind*, *The Swarm*, *Aliens from Another Planet*, *City Beneath the Sea*, *Alice in Wonderland*, *Voyage to the Bottom of the Sea* and *Land of the Giants*.

Czech film director **Jindrich Polak** died after a long illness the same day, aged 78. His films include *Rocket to Nowhere* and *Voyage to the End of the Universe*.

American film and TV director **Jack Smight** died of cancer on September 1st, aged 78. His credits include Ray Bradbury's *The Illustrated Man* and *The Screaming Woman*, *No Way to Treat a Lady*, *The Travelling Executioner*, *Frankenstein: The True Story*, *Airport 1975* and Roger Zelazny's *Damnation Alley*, as well as episodes of *The Twilight Zone* and *Alfred Hitchcock Hour*.

Controversial German director and photographer **Leni Riefen-stahl** (Berta Helene Amalie Riefenstahl), whose cinematic depictions of Adolf Hitler's Nazi regime forever tainted her career, died in Berlin on September 8th, aged 101. Her highly influential and technically innovative documentary/propaganda films *Triumph of the Will* (about the 1934 Nuremberg rallies) and *Olympia* (a four-hour look at the 1936 Berlin Olympic Games) were accused of being paeans to the Third Reich and were an acknowledged influence on George Lucas's *Star Wars*, Paul Verhoeven's *Starship Troopers* and even Disney's *The Lion King*. Riefenstahl always denied a romance with the Führer.

Special-effects artist **Louis Lichtenfield** died of cancer on September 12th, aged 84. He entered films in the 1950s and worked as a matte artist on the remakes of *King Kong* and *Flash Gordon*.

Television assistant director **Jerry** (Gerald R.) **Fleck** died on September 14th, aged 55. As a first or second AD he worked on *Beetle Juice*, *Running Delilah*, *Halloween 4: The Return of Michael Myers*, *Edward Scissorhands*, *Star Trek: First Contact*, *Star Trek: Insurrection* and the TV series *Star Trek: The Next Generation*, *Star Trek: Voyager* and *Enterprise*.

Revolutionary Turkish-American stage and screen director **Elia Kazan** (Elia Kazanjoglous) died on September 28th, aged 94. A founder of the Actors' Studio, after naming a number of colleagues before the House of Un-American Activities Committee in 1952, he was controversially awarded an Honorary Lifetime Achievement Award at the 1999 Academy Awards ceremony.

Emmy-winning British TV scriptwriter and producer **John** [Stanley] **Hawkesworth** died on September 30th, aged 82. An art student who studied under Picasso in Paris, he began his career as a set designer for Alexander and Vincent Korda's London Films in the late 1940s (including *The Third Man* and *Pandora and the Flying Dutchman*). For nearly a decade he was the consultant on more than forty episodes of the 1980s Granada/WGBH TV series *The Return of Sherlock Holmes*, scripting eight of the shows himself.

Film-maker **Joy N. Houck, Jr.** died of heart failure on October 1st, aged 61. He wrote, produced and directed the 1969 horror film *Night of Bloody Horror* starring Gerald McRaney, and went on to direct *Night of the Strangler* (featuring Mickey Dolenz), *Creature from Black Lake* and *The Brain Machine* (1977). He also produced *The Barbaric Beast of Boggy Creek Part II* and was an actor in *Creature from Black Lake* and *The Shadow of Chikara*.

Disney animator **Dale Oliver** died of an aneurysm on October 2nd, aged 84. He worked on *Peter Pan*, *Sleeping Beauty*, *One Hundred & One Dalmatians*, *Winnie the Pooh and Tigger Too*, *The Fox and the Hound* and *The Rescuers Down Under*.

Film and music editor **Eve Newman** died of complications from lung cancer on October 10th, aged 88. After beginning her career in the late 1930s as an animator on Disney's *Snow White and the Seven Dwarfs*, she worked as a music editor on such films as *Flight to Mars*, *The Maze*, *Invasion of the Body Snatchers* (1956), *Spook Chasers*, *I Bury the Living*, *The Fall of the House of Usher* (1960), *Master of the World*, *Pit and the Pendulum*, *Tales of Terror*, *The Raven*, *X – The Man With X-Ray Eyes*, *Black Sabbath* and *The Comedy of Terrors*. She became a film editor at AIP, cutting such features as *Muscle Beach Party*, *Pajama Party*, *How to Stuff a Wild Bikini*, *Dr Goldfoot and the Bikini Machine*, *The Ghost in the Invisible Bikini*, *Three in the Attic* and *Wild in the Streets* (for which she was nominated for an Academy Award).

British stage and screen designer **Julia Trevelyan Oman** (Lady Strong) died of cancer the same day, aged 73. In 1966 she designed Jonathan Miller's experimental adaptation of *Alice in Wonderland* for the BBC.

American film and television producer **Bernard Schwartz** died of complications from a stroke on October 17th, aged 85. He oversaw production of the TV series *One Step Beyond* and also produced the movies *Journey to the Center of the Earth* (1959), *The Shuttered Room*, *Eye of the Cat*, *Roadgames* and *Psycho 2*.

Manager and producer **Roy Silver** died from the effects of a brain tumour in Los Angeles on October 18th, aged 71. He managed such acts as Bill Cosby, Tiny Tim and Jackson Browne, and produced the films *Johnny Got His Gun* by Dalton Trumbo and *Picasso Summer*, based on a story by Ray Bradbury.

Low budget American director **Donald G. Jackson** (a.k.a. "Maximo T. Bird"), whose *Roller Blade* (1984) was funded on his own $20,000 credit-card budget and grossed $1 million for New World, died of leukaemia on October 20th, aged 60. His first film was *Demon Lover* (1976) and as well as producing a

string of roller-skating movies, he also wrote, produced and directed *Hell Comes to Frogtown*, starring wrestler "Rowdy" Roddy Piper, which was followed by the sequels *Frogtown II*, *Toad Warrior* and *Max Hell Comes to Frogtown*. As a script-writer, his credits include *Vampire Child* and *Ghost Taxi*.

Documentary film-maker **Robert Guenette**, whose credits include the 1981 feature *The Man Who Saw Tomorrow* (in which host Orson Welles repeats Nostradamus's prediction of a cataclysmic attack on Manhattan by Muslims around the end of the 20th century), died of brain cancer on Hallowe'en, aged 68. Amongst Guenett's other films are *Bigfoot the Mysterious Monster*, *The Amazing World of Psychic Phenomena*, *Monsters! Mysteries or Myths?* and the TV specials *The Making of Star Wars*, *SPFX: The Empire Strikes Back* and *Great Movie Stunts: Raiders of the Lost Ark*.

Canadian-born film and TV production designer **Raymond G. Storey** died of cancer in Glendale, California, on November 2nd, aged 75. A graduate of USC Film School, his credits include *The Time Travelers* (1964), *Spider Baby* (with Lon Chaney, Jr.), *Blue Sunshine*, *Baby . . . Secret of the Lost Legend*, *Return of the Living Dead*, *The Stranger Within* and *Splash Too*. Storey also produced the 1974 horror movie *The House on Skull Mountain* and appeared (uncredited) in *It Came from Beneath the Sea*.

Dino Alexander De Laurentiis, Italian-born grandson of veteran film producer Dino, died of melanoma on November 3rd, aged 31. His varied career in production included post-production supervisor and unit photographer on *Dragonheart: A New Beginning*.

Oscar-nominated sound-effects editor **Fred J. Brown** died in Los Angeles of multiple organ failure on November 9th, aged 68. His many credits include *The Exorcist*, *Grizzly*, *Day of the Animals*, *The Deep*, *Ruby*, *The Manitou*, *The Last Starfighter*, *Conan the Barbarian*, *Red Dawn*, *DeepStar Six*, *Highlander III: The Sorcerer* and TV's *Bewitched*.

British stage, radio and television director and writer **Don (Donald) Taylor** died of brain cancer on November 11th, aged 67. Although he turned down launching *Doctor Who* with some contempt, his prolific list of credits includes an episode of Nigel Kneale's *Beasts*, the 1972 ghost story *The Exorcism* (later rewritten as a stage play, at which actress Mary Ure died on the opening night), and the BBC drama *The Roses of Eyam*, about a 17th-century village infected with the Plague.

Sixty-five-year-old Italian film-maker **Stefano Rolla** was killed in a car-bomb attack on an Italian military base in Iraq on November 12th. From the early 1960s he worked as an assistant director on such films as *Spy in Your Eye*, *Deep Red*, *The Last Survivor* and *Battle Force*.

New Line Cinema executive **Janis Chaskin** died of cancer on November 13th, aged 53. She worked on such films as *Frequency*, *Blink*, *Se7en* and *The Island of Dr Moreau* (1996).

American special-effects supervisor **Frank H. Isaacs** died of cancer on November 14th. His numerous credits include *Galaxina*, *Metalstorm: The Destruction of Jared-Syn*, *Evil Spawn*, *Lady in White*, *Get Smart Again!*, *Skeeter*, *Alien Intruder*, *Cyber Tracker*, *Cyber Tracker 2*, *The Power Within*, *Hologram Man* and the SciFi Channel's miniseries of Frank Herbert's *Dune* and *Children of Dune*.

Japanese-born art director **Albert Nozaki** died of complications of pneumonia in Los Angeles on November 16th, aged 91. His career at Paramount was interrupted when he and his wife were sent to a Californian internment camp shortly after the attack on Pearl Harbor. He was allowed to leave a year later after signing a loyalty pledge, and he became a US citizen in 1954. Nozaki worked on *When Worlds Collide* and received an Academy Award nomination for his work on *The Ten Commandments*. However, he considered *War of the Worlds* (1953), for which he built a miniature downtown Los Angeles, his "masterpiece". He storyboarded the entire movie and designed the Martian war machines and their three-eyed inhabitants. Despite being stricken with retinitis pigmentosa in 1963 and going blind a decade later, Paramount appointed him supervising art director for features, a job he held until his retirement in 1969.

Film producer and writer **Jack Pollexfen** died of pneumonia and complications from diabetes after a long illness on November 22nd, aged 95. After beginning his career as a newspaper reporter, he became involved in films in the early 1940s. His many credits include *The Man from Planet X*, *The Son of Dr Jekyll*, *Captive Women*, *Port Sinister*, *The Neanderthal Man*, *Son of Sinbad*, *The Indestructible Man* (which he also directed), *Daughter of Dr Jekyll* and *Monstrosity* (a.k.a. *The Atomic Brain*).

Francis Creighton, who wrote, directed and starred in *The Malibu Beach Vampires* (1991), died on November 24th, aged 48.

Mexican cinematographer Jorge Stahl, Jr. died of a respiratory disease the same day, aged 82. The son of a Mexican film pioneer, the younger Stahl worked on nearly 200 movies including *The Beast of Hollow Mountain*, *Witch's Mirror*, *Santo vs. the Martian Invasion*, *Zachariah* and *The Sexorcist*.

TV executive Ethel Winant died of complications from a heart attack and stroke on November 29th, aged 81. At CBS she cast such shows as *The Twilight Zone* and *Lost in Space*, eventually working her way up to Senior Vice-President of talent, casting and special projects.

Prolific American film and TV director Earl Bellamy died of a heart attack on November 30th, aged 86. After beginning his career in the 1940s as an assistant director on such films as *The Return of the Vampire*, he went on to direct *Munster Go Home*! and numerous episodes of TV's *Jungle Jim*, *The Munsters*, *Tarzan*, *The Sixth Sense*, *The Six Million Dollar Man*, *Isis*, *Future Cop*, *Fantasy Island*, *Blue Thunder* and *V*.

Swiss-born Carl Schenkel, who directed the 1979 German comedy *Dracula Blows His Cool* under the name "Carlo Ombra", died of heart failure in Los Angeles on December 1st, aged 55. His other credits include the claustrophobic chiller *Out of Order*, *Bay Coven*, *Knight Moves*, *Tarzan and the Lost City* and episodes of HBO's *The Hitchhiker*.

American stage and film producer Lewis M. Allen died of pancreatic cancer on December 8th, aged 81. Best known for the Tony Award-winning Broadway hit *Annie*, his movie credits include *Lord of the Flies* and Francois Truffaut's version of Ray Bradbury's *Fahrenheit 451*.

Academy Award-winning animator Wah [Ming] Chang died of complications from polio on December 22nd, aged 86. Born in Honolulu, Chang joined Walt Disney's Effects and Model Department in 1939, where he created wooden models of Pinocchio and Bambi so that animators could study the characters's body movements. His later film credits include the George Pal productions *Tom Thumb*, *The Time Machine*, *The Wonderful World of the Brothers Grimm*, *The 7 Faces of Dr Lao* and *The Power*. Chang also helped create the masks for *Planet of the Apes* (1967) and worked on *Cat-Women of the Moon*, *The Monster from Green Hell*, *Journey to the Seventh Planet*, *Dinosaurus!*, *Master of the World*, *Voyage to the Planet of Prehistoric Women* and such classic TV series as *The Outer Limits* and the original *Star Trek*.

American-born literary agent and film producer **Dick Brand** died of a heart attack in England the same day, aged 72. He packaged several movies with Walter Seltzer, including *The Omega Man* and *Soylent Green*.

British special visual effects supervisor **Guy Hudson** died of a brain haemorrhage on December 24th, aged 45. His film credits include *Alien*, *The Empire Strikes Back*, *Jurassic Park*, *Enemy Mine*, *Star Wars* (the "Special Edition"), *Naked Lunch*, *The Neverending Story*, *Dragonslayer* and the TV miniseries *Dinotopia*. At the time of his death he was working on *Harry Potter and the Prisoner of Azkaban*.

USEFUL ADDRESSES

THE FOLLOWING LISTING OF organizations, publications, dealers and individuals is designed to present readers and authors with further avenues to explore. Although I can personally recommend most of those listed on the following pages, neither the publisher nor myself can take any responsibility for the services they offer. Please also note that the information below is only a guide and is subject to change without notice.

ORGANIZATIONS

The British Fantasy Society <www.britishfantasysociety.org.uk> was founded in 1971 and publishes the bi-monthly newsletter *Prism* and a tri-annual magazine featuring articles, reviews, interviews and fiction, along with occasional special booklets. The BFS also enjoys a lively on-line community – there is an e-mail news-feed, a discussion board with numerous links, and a CyberStore selling various publications. FantasyCon is one of the UK's friendliest conventions and there are social gatherings and meet-the-author events organized around Britain. Yearly membership is £25.00 (UK), £30.00 (Europe) and £45.00 (USA and the rest of the world) made payable in sterling to "The British Fantasy Society" and sent to The BFS Secretary, c/o 201 Reddish Road, South Reddish, Stockport SK5 7HR, UK. You can also join on-line through the CyberStore.

The Ghost Story Society <www.ash-tree.bc.ca/GSS.html> is organized by Barbara and Christopher Roden. They publish the superb *All Hallows* three times a year, and annual membership is £20.00 (UK), $30.00 (USA) and Cdn$38.00 (Canada) made payable to "The Ghost Story Society" and sent to PO Box

1360, Ashcroft, British Columbia, Canada VOK 1A0. E-mail: <nebuly@telus.net>. You can join their discussion group at <html://groups.yahoo.com/group/All_Hallows>.

The Horror Writers Association <www.horror.org> is a world-wide organization of writers and publishing professionals dedicated to promoting the interests of writers of Horror and Dark Fantasy. It was formed in the early 1980s. Interested individuals may apply for Active, Affiliate or Associate membership. Active membership is limited to professional writers. HWA publishes a monthly Newsletter, and organizes an annual conference and the Bram Stoker Awards ceremony. Apply online or write to HWA Membership, PO Box 50577, Palo Alto, CA 94303, USA. For information in the UK contact: <www.horror.org/UK/>.

The London Vampyre Group <www.revamped.co.uk> is an organization aimed at fans of the undead from all over the world. A one-year membership includes four issues of the glossy digest magazine *The Chronicles*, a supplement, membership card and the quarterly newsletter *The London Vampyre* (which contains lists of events etc.). Membership is £15.00 (UK) per single person, £20.00 (UK) per household, £22.00 (overseas membership) and should be sent to: The London Vampyre Group, PO Box 487, London WC2H 9WA, UK.

World Fantasy Convention <www.worldfantasy.org> is an annual convention held in a different (usually American) city each year, oriented particularly towards serious readers and genre professionals.

World Horror Convention <www.worldhorrorsociety.org> is a smaller, more relaxed, event. It is aimed specifically at horror fans and professionals, and is held in a different city each year, so far only in North America.

SELECTED SMALL-PRESS PUBLISHERS

Agog! Press <www.catsparks.net>, PO Box U302, University of Wollongong, NSW 2522, Australia. E-mail: <cat@catsparks.net>.

The Alchemy Press <www.alchemypress.co.uk>, 46 Oxford Road, Acocks Green, Birmingham B27 6DT, UK. E-mail: <info @alchemypress.demon.co.uk>.

Babbage Press <www.babbagepress.com>, 8740 Penfield

Avenue, Northridge, CA 91324, USA. E-mail: <books @babbagepress.com>

Borderlands Press <www.borderlandspress.com>, PO Box 1529 Grantham, NH 03753, USA.

Chico Kidd <www.chico.nildram.co.uk>, 113 Clyfford Road, Ruislip Gardens, Middx HA4 6PX, UK. E-mail: <chico @chico.nildram.co.uk>.

Earthling Publications <www.earthlingpub.com>, 12 Pheasant Hill Drive, Shrewsbury, MA 01545, USA. E-mail: <earthlingpub @yahoo.com>.

Fedogan & Bremer, P.O. Box 6508, Minneapolis, MN 55406, USA.

IFD Publishing <www.ifdpublishing.com> PO Box 40776, Eugene, OR 97404, USA. E-mail: <respond@ifdpublishing.com>.

Ministry of Whimsy Press <www.ministryofwhimsy.com>, 1718 Weber Drive, Madison, WI 53713, USA. E-mail: <ministryofwhimsy@yahoo.com>.

Midnight House <www.darksidepress>, 7713 Sunnyside Avenue North, Seattle, WA 98013, USA.

Mythos Books LLC <www.mythosbooks.com>, 351 Lake Ridge Road, Poplar Bluff, MO 63901–2177, USA. E-mail: <dwynn@LDD.net>.

Nemonymous <www.nemonymous.com>.

Night Shade Books <www.nightshadebooks.com>, 3623 SW Baird St, Portland, OR 97219, USA. E-mail: <night@night shadebooks.com>.

Prime Books, <www.primebooks.net> PO Box 36503, Canton, OH 44735, USA. E-mail: <saw@neo.rr.com>

PS Publishing <www.pspublishing.co.uk>, Hamilton House, 4 Park Avenue, Harrogate HG2 9BQ, UK. E-mail: <crowth 1@attglobal.net>.

Sandglass Enterprises <www.sandglass.com.au>, 44 Bellotti Avenue, Winston Hills, NSW 2153, Australia. E-mail: <mark @sandglass.com.au>.

Sarob Press <www.home.freeuk.net/sarobpress>, "Ty Newydd", Four Roads, Kidwelly, Carmarthenshire SA17 4SF, Wales, UK. E-mail: <sarobpress@freeuk.com>.

Savoy Books <www.savoy.abel.co.uk>, 446 Wilmslow Road, Withington, Manchester M20 3BW, UK. E-mail: <office @savoy.abel.co.uk>.

Small Beer Press <www.smallbeerpress.com>, 176 Prospect Avenue, Northampton, MA 01060, USA. E-mail: <info@small beerpress.com>.

Subterranean Press <www.subterraneanpress.com>, PO Box 190106, Burton, MI 48519, USA. E-mail: <subpress@earthlink. net>.

Telos Publishing <www.telos.co.uk>, 61 Elgar Avenue, Tolworth, Surrey KT5 9JP, UK. E-mail: <david@telos.co.uk>.

Tartarus Press <www.tartaruspress.com>, Coverley House, Carlton-in-Coverdale, Leyburn, North Yorkshire DL8 4AY, UK. E-mail: <tartarus@pavilion.co.uk>.

Wheatland Press <www.wheatlandpress.com>, P.O. Box 1818, Wilsonville, OR 97070, USA.

Wildside Press <www.wildsidepress.com>, P.O. Box 301, Holicong, PA 18928–0301, USA.

DVD DISTRIBUTORS

El Independent Cinema <www.SeductionCinema.com> produces low-budget horror (Shock-O-Rama Cinema) and erotic genre movies (SeductionCinema). 10 Park Place, Bldg. 6A, 2nd Floor, Butler, NJ 07405, USA. E-mail: <eicinema@aol.com>.

Mondo Macabro <www.mondomacabrodvd.com> distributor of obscure European and other foreign horror and exploitation movies. Boum Productions Ltd., PO Box 3336, Brighton BN2 3GW, UK. E-mail: <video@boumproductions.com>.

SELECTED MAGAZINES

Black Gate: Adventures in Fantasy Literature <www.blackgate. com> is a nicely designed magazine devoted to the best in epic fantasy. Sample issues are $10.00 (US) and $15.00 (Canada) and a 4-issue subscription is $29.95 (US) and $49.00 (Canada). For international shipping rates check their website. New Epoch Press, 815 Oak Street, St. Charles, IL 60174, USA. E-mail: <john@blackgate.com>.

The Bulletin of the Science Fiction and Fantasy Writers of America <www.sfwa.org> is published quarterly by the Science Fiction and Fantasy Writers of America, Inc. You do not need to be a SFWA member to subscribe, and the magazine features many

interesting and important articles aimed at professional genre authors and would-be writers, including market reports. Single copies are $4.99 and a Full Year subscription (four issues) is $18.00. Send cheque or money order (payable in US dollars) to "SFWA Bulletin", PO Box 10126, Rochester, NY 14610, USA. Overseas subscriptions add $17.00 for the rest of the world. You can sample articles or purchase back issues and subscriptions on the magazine's website <www.sfwa.org/bulletin/>. E-mail: <bulletin@sfwa.org>.

Cemetery Dance Magazine <www.cemeterydance.com> is edited by Richard Chizmar and Robert Morrish and includes fiction up to 5,000 words, interviews, articles and columns by many of the biggest names in horror. Cover price is $5.00 and a one-year subscription (six issues) is $27.00 payable by cheque or credit card to "Cemetery Dance Publications", 132-B Industry Lane, Unit 7, Forest Hill, MD 21050, USA. E-mail: <info@cemetery dance.com>.

Interzone <www.ttapress.com> Britain's leading magazine of science fiction and fantasy is now bi-monthly and has a new editor and a new publisher. Cover price is £4.00/$7.00, and a 6-issue subscription is £21.00 (UK), £24.00 or €36.00 (Europe), $36.00 (USA) or £27.00 (rest of the world) to "TTA Press", 5 Martins Lane, Witcham, Ely, Cambs CB6 2LB, UK. Subscriptions by credit card via the secure on-line website < www. ttapress.com/onlinestore1.html>. E-mail: <ttapress@aol.com>.

Locus <www.locusmag.com> is the monthly newspaper of the SF/fantasy/horror field. $5.95 a copy, a 12-issue subscription is $52.00 (USA periodical mail), $55.00 (Canada/Mexico periodical mail), international rates: $55.00 (surface mail), $88.00 (airmail) to "Locus Publications", PO Box 13305, Oakland, CA 94661, USA. Subscription information with other rates and order forms are also available on the website. Sterling-equivalent cheques can be sent to Fantast (Medway) Ltd, PO Box 23, Upwell Wisbech, Cambs PE14 9BU, UK. E-mail: <locus@locusmag.com>.

The Magazine of Fantasy & Science Fiction <www.fsfmag. com> has been publishing some of the best imaginative fiction for more than fifty years and is now edited by Gordon Van Gelder. Single copies are $3.99 (USA) or $5.99 (Canada) and an annual subscription (which includes the double October/November anniversary issue) is $32.97 (USA) and $42.97 (rest of the world).

US cheques or credit card information to "Fantasy & Science Fiction", PO Box 3447, Hoboken, NJ 07030, USA., or subscribe online.

Rue Morgue <www.rue-morgue.com>, is a glossy bi-monthly magazine edited by Rod Gudino and subtitled "Horror in Culture & Entertainment". Packed with full-colour features and reviews of new films, books, comics, music and game releases, single copies are $7.95 (USA/Canada). A 6-issue subscription is $39.95 (USA/Canada) or $55.00 (rest of the world, US funds) by cheque or international money order to: Marris Media, Inc., 700 Queen Street, East Toronto, Ontario M4M 1G9, Canada, or you can subscribe by credit card on the website. E-mail: <info@ ruemorgue.com>.

SF Site <www.sfsite.com> has been posted twice each month since 1997. Presently, it publishes around thirty to fifty reviews of SF, fantasy and horror from mass-market publishers and some small presses. They also maintain link pages for Author and Fan Tribute Sites and other facets including pages for Interviews, Fiction, Science Fact, Bookstores, Small Press, Publishers, E-zines and Magazines, Artists, Audio, Art Galleries, Newsgroups and Writers's Resources. Periodically, they add features such as author and publisher reading lists. Past examples include Jonathan Carroll, Charles de Lint, Philip K. Dick, Paul McAuley, Ian McDonald, Kim Stanley Robinson, Dan Simmons and Michelle West.

Space and Time <www.cith.org/space&time>, the magazine of fantasy, horror and science fiction is published twice a year by editor-in-chief Gordon Linzner. Single issues are $5.00 plus $1.50 shipping (USA). Subscriptions are two issues for $10.00 and four issues for $20.00 (USA), or two issues for $12.00 and four issues for $24.00 outside the USA. Please use US postal money order or cheque payable against any US bank. Space and Time, 138 West 70th Street (4B), New York, NY 10023–4468, USA. In the UK order from BBR Distributing, PO Box 625, Sheffield S1 3GY, UK for £3.50 per copy or four issues for £12.00.

Supernatural Tales <www.chico.nildram.co.uk/Supernatural Tales.html> is a small-press magazine of stories and non-fiction edited by David Longhorn. Individual copies are £3.50 (including p&p) and a two-year (four issue) subscription is just £12.00 in the UK. Overseas subscriptions in sterling cheques, Euros or US dollars cash are $8.00/€8.00 per copy or $25.00/€25.00 per four-issue subscription. Make cheques payable to "D. Longhorn" and send to Supernatural Tales, 291 Eastbourne Avenue, Gateshead NE8 4NN, UK. E-mail: <davidlonghorn@hotmail.com>.

Talebones <www.talebones.com> is an attractive digest magazine of science fiction and dark fantasy edited and published by Patrick and Honna Swenson. Cover price is $6.00 (USA)/ $7.50 (Canada), and subscriptions are $20.00 (USA) for four issues and $38.00 (USA) for eight issues. Canadian subscribers add $1.50 per issue and all other foreign subscribers add $4.50 per issue, US funds only. Credit cards accepted. Send to: 5203 Quincy Avenue S.E., Auburn, WA 98092, USA. E-mail: <info@ talebones.com>.

The 3rd Alternative <www.ttapress.com> is a quarterly magazine of new horror fiction, interviews, artwork, articles and reviews edited by Andy Cox. Cover price is £4.50/$8.00, and a 6-issue subscription is £21.00 (UK), £24.00 or €36.00 (Europe), $36.00 (USA) or £27.00 (rest of the world) to "TTA Press", 5 Martins Lane, Witcham, Ely, Cambs CB6 2LB, UK. Subscriptions by credit card via the secure on-line website < www.ttapress.com/onlinestore 1 .html>. E-mail: <ttapress@aol.com>. You can also visit the TTA Press message boards at: <www.ttapress.com/discus>.

Video Watchdog <www.videowatchdog.com> is a full-colour monthly review of horror, fantasy and cult cinema on tape and disc, published by Tim and Donna Lucas. Now in its 15th year, the award-winning digest-sized magazine is $7.95 a copy, an annual 12-issue subscription is $60.00 bulk/$82.00 first class (USA), $75.00 surface/$100.00 airmail (overseas). US funds only or VISA/MasterCard to "Video Watchdog", PO Box 5283, Cincinnati, OH 45205–0283, USA. E-mail: <orders @videowatchdog.com>.

Weird Tales <www.dnapublications.com> is the latest large-size incarnation of "The Unique Magazine", edited by George H. Scithers and Darrell Schweitzer, and is published six times a year by DNA Publications, Inc. and Wildside Press, in association with Terminus Publishing Co., Inc. Single copies are $5.95 (USA), $7.00 (Canada) and $10.00 (elsewhere) in US funds. A 6-issue subscription is $24.00 (USA), $33.00 (Canada) and $60.00 (elsewhere) in US funds and should be sent to "DNA Publications", PO Box 2988, Radford, VA 24143–2988, USA. Submissions should be addressed to Weird Tales, 123 Crooked Lane,

King of Prussia, PA 19406–2570, USA. An e-mail version of the magazine's writers's guidelines (no electronic submissions) is available from <weirdtales@comcast.net>. You can also visit the message board at <www.wildsidepress.com>.

BOOK DEALERS

Borderlands Books <www.borderlands-books.com> is a nicely designed store with friendly staff and an impressive stock of new and used books from both sides of the Atlantic. 866 Valencia Street (at 19th), San Francisco, CA 94110, USA. Tel: (415) 824–8203 or (888) 893–4008 (toll free in the US). Credit cards accepted. Worldwide shipping. E-mail: <office@borderlands-books.com>.

Cold Tonnage Books <www.coldtonnage.com> offers excellent mail-order new and used SF/fantasy/horror, art, reference, limited editions, etc. Write to Andy & Angela Richards, Cold Tonnage Books, 22 Kings Lane, Windlesham, Surrey GU20 6JQ, UK. Credit cards accepted. Tel: +44 (0)1276–475388. E-mail: <andy@coldtonnage.com>.

Ken Cowley offers mostly used SF/fantasy/horror/crime/supernatural, collectibles, pulps, videos etc. by mail order at very reasonable prices. Write to Trinity Cottage, 153 Old Church Road, Clevedon, North Somerset, BS21 7TU, UK. Tel: +44 (0) 1275–872247. E-mail: <kencowley@blueyonder.co.uk>.

Dark Delicacies <www.darkdel.com> is a friendly Burbank, California, store specializing in horror books, toys, vampire merchandise and signings. They also do mail order and run money-saving book-club and membership discount deals. 4213 West Burbank Blvd., Burbank, CA 91505, USA. Tel: (818) 556–6660. Credit cards accepted. E-mail: <darkdel@darkdel.com>.

DreamHaven Books & Comics <www.dreamhavenbooks. com> store and mail order offers new and used SF/fantasy/ horror/art and illustrated etc. with regular catalogues (both print and e-mail). Write to 912 West Lake Street, Minneapolis, MN 55408, USA. Credit cards accepted. Tel: (612) 823–6070. E-mail: <dream@dreamhavenbooks.com>.

Fantastic Literature <www.fantasticliterature.com> mail order offers the UK's biggest online out-of-print SF/fantasy/horror genre bookshop. Fanzines, pulps and vintage paperbacks as well. 17,500+ titles with regular catalogues. Write to Simon and Laraine

Gosden, Fantastic Literature, 35 The Ramparts, Rayleigh, Essex SS6 8PY, UK. Credit cards and Pay Pal accepted. Tel/Fax: +44 (0)1268–747564. E-mail: <sgosden@netcomuk.co.uk>.

Fantasy Centre <www.fantasycentre.biz> shop (open 10:00 a.m.– 6:00 p.m., Monday to Saturday) and mail order has used SF/fantasy/ horror, art, reference, pulps, etc. at reasonable prices with regular bi-monthly catalogues. They also stock a wide range of new books from small, specialist publishers. Write to 157 Holloway Road, London N7 8LX, UK. Credit cards accepted. Tel/Fax: +44 (0)20– 7607 9433. E-mail: <books@fantasycentre.biz>.

Ghost Stories run by Richard Dalby issues semi-regular mail-order lists of used ghost and supernatural volumes at very reasonable prices. Write to 4 Westbourne Park, Scarborough, North Yorkshire YO12 4AT, UK. Tel: +44 (0)1723 377049.

Robert A. Madle issues a huge annual list of used hardcovers, paperbacks and rare pulps for the serious collector. Write to 4406 Bestor Drive, Rockville, MD 20853, USA. Visa/Mastercard accepted. Tel: (301) 460–4712 (10:00 a.m.–10:00 p.m. Eastern time).

David Wynn's Mythos Books LLC <www.mythosbooks.com> is a mail-order company presenting books and curiosities on Lovecraftiana, Cthulhu Mythos, horror and weird fiction releases with regular e-mail and website updates. Write to 351 Lake Ridge Road, Poplar Bluff, MO 63901–2177, USA. Major credit cards accepted. Tel/Fax: (573) 785–7710. E-mail: <dwynn@LDD.net>.

Porcupine Books offers regular catalogues and extensive mail order lists of used fantasy/horror/SF titles via e-mail <brian @porcupine.demon.co.uk> or write to 37 Coventry Road, Ilford, Essex IG1 4QR, UK. Tel: +44 (0)20 8554–3799.

Kirk Ruebotham <www.abebooks.com/home/kirk61/> is a mail-order-only dealer, who sells out-of-print and used horror/ SF/fantasy/crime and related non-fiction at very good prices, with regular catalogues. Write to 16 Beaconsfield Road, Runcorn, Cheshire WA7 4BX, UK. Tel: +44 (0) 1928–560540 (10:00 a.m.– 8:00 p.m.). E-mail: <kirk.ruebotham@ntlworld.com>.

Bob and Julie Wardzinski's The Talking Dead offers reasonably priced paperbacks, rare pulps and hardcovers, with catalogues issued regularly. They accept wants lists and are also the exclusive supplier of back issues of Interzone. Credit cards accepted. Contact them at 12 Rosamund Avenue, Merley, Wimborne, Dorset BH21 1TE, UK. Tel: +44 (0)1202–849212 (9:00 a.m.–9:00 p.m.). E-mail: <books@thetalkingdead.fsnet.co.uk>.

MARKET INFORMATION AND NEWS

Although the weekly **DarkEcho** <www.darkecho.com> newsletter for horror writers and others ceased publication a few years ago, editor Paula Guran still sends out periodic, personal e-mails whenever time and whim allows. They don't cover horror news comprehensively or list market news, but it's still worth subscribing for free by e-mailing: <subscribe@darkecho.com>.

The Fix <www.ttapress.com> features in-depth reviews of all SF/fantasy/horror magazines publishing short fiction; interviews with editors, publishers and writers; stories; news and comment columns; artwork and much more. 6-issue subscriptions are £15.00 (UK), €29.00 (Europe), $29.00 (USA) and £21.00 (rest of the world). Payable to "TTA Press", 5 Martins Lane, Witcham, Ely, Cambs CB6 2LB, UK. Subscriptions by credit card via the secure online website <www.ttapress.com/onlinestore 1.html>. E-mail: <ttapress@aol.com>.

The Gila Queen's Guide to Markets is an e-mail newsletter detailing markets for SF/fantasy/horror plus other genres, along with publishing news, contests, dead markets, anthologies, updates, etc. The newsletter comes out every three weeks. A sample copy is $3.00, while a 20-issue subscription costs $25.00. Make cheques or money orders out to "Kathryn Ptacek", US funds only, and send to Kathryn Ptacek, PO Box 97, Newton, NJ 07860–0097, USA. Subscriptions can also be paid via PayPal (and credit card) as well; the PayPal and e-mail address is <GilaQueen@worldnet.att.net>.

Hellnotes <www.hellnotes.com> is described as "The Insider's Edge to Horror!". This weekly Newsletter offers reviews, interviews, news, and commentaries, and is available in an e-mail edition for $23.00 per year or hard-copy subscriptions are available for $60.00 per year (USA delivery only). Subscriptions available through PayPal (in US Funds to <JRohrig@aol.com>) or by mail (send US cheques or money order to: "Hellnotes", 4212 Derby Lane, Evansville, IN 47715–1568, USA. E-mail: <info @hellnotes.com>.